ATLAS OF AMERICAN HISTORY

100K 51[00]
COST

ATLAS OF
AMERICAN HISTORY

ATLAS OF AMERICAN HISTORY

Revised Edition

KENNETH T. JACKSON

EDITOR

JAMES TRUSLOW ADAMS

EDITOR IN CHIEF, ORIGINAL EDITION

CHARLES SCRIBNER'S SONS / NEW YORK

THIS BOOK PUBLISHED SIMULTANEOUSLY IN
THE UNITED STATES OF AMERICA AND IN CANADA—
COPYRIGHT UNDER THE BERNE CONVENTION

5 7 9 11 13 15 17 19 V/C 20 18 16 14 12 10 8 6 4

PRINTED IN THE UNITED STATES OF AMERICA

Library of Congress Catalog Card Number 77-76851

ISBN 0-684-15052-2

CONTENTS

CONTENTS

INTRODUCTION TO THE REVISED EDITION

James Truslow Adams died in 1949, just six years after the *Atlas of American History* first appeared. Although he was noted for many books which achieved both critical and commercial success, Adams took special pride in this volume because of the great care with which it was produced. Coordinating the efforts of many talented individuals, Adams operated on the premise that a map should be easily understandable and should not require a half hour of concentration in order for the information to come across. To this end, he chose a narrow focus for most of the maps and adopted the uncluttered format with which users of this volume have become familiar. Adams' second passion was accuracy, and he was adamant in his insistence that the user see the area exactly as it was during the period under consideration. Thus, no locations appear that were not there at the time.

Because of *Atlas of American History* has earned a well-deserved reputation for scholarship and usefulness, we have retained every map that originally appeared in the first edition. We have, however, added fifty-one maps to the 147 which made up the 1943 volume. The heavy emphasis of that edition was on the frontier—broadly considered. The Atlas was particularly strong on boundary disputes during the colonial period, on battles of the American Revolution and the Civil War, on early routes to the West, and on the American Indian. Only occasionally have we seen fit to add to these distinguished series. For example, we have added maps on Indian Tribal Groups, Indian Wars Before 1690, and Indian reservations, none of which appeared in the first edition. In addition, we have added maps on Commercially Navigable Waterways, Railroad Passenger Lines, and the Interstate Highway System to the earlier coverage of transportation.

Most of the new maps deal with twentieth-century developments or with other subjects that were considered only slightly or not at all by Adams and his co-workers. Under the broad category of human rights, we have added maps on Major Utopian Experiments Before 1860, Universal Male Suffrage, Woman's Suffrage, the Abolition of Slavery, and Major Race Riots. For general economic developments, we have added maps showing Major Industrial Centers Before 1860, Leading Industrial States in 1850 and 1973, Labor Strife, and the contemporary economic development of some of the significant growth states of modern America—Texas, Florida, California, Hawaii, and Alaska. A third of the new maps are essentially demographic in nature; they show sources of immigration, percentage of foreign born by state at various times, black migration to cities, population density in 1970, changes in farm population, the country's largest cities at different periods, and the change in the nation's center of population. We have also introduced a series of maps depicting areas of settlement in 1700, 1800, 1850, and 1890. Finally, whereas none of the maps in the first edition dealt with areas outside the continental United States, we have added maps showing America as a world power and tracing overseas conflicts from the Spanish-American War to the Vietnam War. Less dramatic interventions, as in the case of various Pacific territories, the Panama Canal Zone, and the Caribbean, are also depicted in special maps, as are the locations of contemporary American military installations, both domestic and foreign.

The essentially chronological organization of the maps adopted in the first edition has been retained. We have added a Table of Contents, that was missing from the earlier work, and have revised and expanded the Index.

The cartographic work for the revised edition was done with care and resourcefulness by David Lunn. In addition, I wish to thank Aaron Berman, Amy Helaine Mittleman, and Mark L. Kenchelian, all of Columbia University, for their assistance with research, documentation, and proof-reading. At Charles Scribner's Sons, Hope Hockenberry and Christiane Deschamps became valued co-workers on the enterprise. Finally, Norman Kotker, the editor of Pictorial Books at Scribners, gave himself to this project with great generosity. I am grateful to him for the initial conception of the book, for his precise and imaginative probing of historical materials, for his assistance in solving more than a dozen problems, and for the drive and inspiration which he provided for the *Atlas of American History*.

I accept full responsibility for any errors.

KENNETH T. JACKSON
Columbia University
November, 1977

FOREWORD

DISCOVERY, exploration, frontier posts, settlement, territorial organization, extension of communication—this, repeated time after time, has, to a large degree, been the history of the United States.

Thus, much of our history is concerned with places; and to understand *what* happened, we must also know *where* it happened.

Yet, to locate many places commonly mentioned in our factual histories has heretofore called for reference to scores of widely separated books, atlases or original maps, often difficult of access and seldom at hand when needed, clumsy to handle—and generally not available in the average library.

The preparation and publication of the *Dictionary of American History* pointed the need for a concise, easy to use, carefully thought out, authoritative atlas of American history. The editors and scholars associated with the production of the earlier work accordingly set themselves the task of making an atlas which would present our geographical history as completely and as readily as the *Dictionary of American History* presents our written history.

The plan and scope of the work received long and careful editorial consideration. It was the judgment of the editors that the need was for maps that would interpret our history through the location of places as they actually existed and exactly where they existed at a given time. Graphs, diagrams and other nonexact pictorial interpretations were, in general, to be avoided as having no place in this Atlas.

That the maps should proceed chronologically was obvious. That the areas and periods dealt with in each map should be entities was desirable. That each map should gear in with the preceding and succeeding maps was important. The intent was to so arrange the maps that, as the pages turned, the development of the country would become more clear and take on a new meaning and significance.

The decision as to what places to show on each map was arrived at by a number of approaches. The standard histories and source materials were indexed. Contemporary maps were examined. Partly on the basis of frequency of reference to a place, and partly on the basis of whether a place was sufficiently important historically to be shown, the locations were made on rough drafts—subject to criticism and revisions.

Then the supervision of each map was assigned to an historian or group of historians familiar with the period and area involved. The supervisor added or eliminated or criticized, and thus the map progressed. But no map was finished until it had been considered in connection with the related maps—to the end that each should supplement the other. From the rough drafts—often worn to tatters by revision—the finished drawings were made.

Every map in this work has been drawn in our editorial offices, under the direct supervision of the editors for factual presentation, and of Mr. Appleton for cartographic presentation—and in every case subject to the final approval of the supervisors.

In general the maps are based upon the best and latest government surveys, but with adjustments to earlier maps in case physical changes have occurred, such as rivers cutting new channels or reefs forming where formerly no reefs existed.

Sixty-four historians actively supervised the drawing of the 147 plates which appear in this Atlas. Many others advised and assisted. Thus, the exact location of Fort Ross was directed by Prof. E. O. Essig of the University of California. Stella Drumm, of the Missouri Historical Society, advised regarding locations on the Missouri River. Prof. R. L. Meriwether, of the University of South Carolina, aided in locations relating to Kings Mountain. Painstaking research, sometimes on the ground, went into the location of many places.

To enable the user of the Atlas to find, easily and quickly, the place which he is looking for, a place index has been made a part of the volume. Where was Kaskaskia? Logstown? Fallen Timbers? South Pass? or any one of the hundreds of other historically important places now lost from our maps or buried under a mass of other names? The index carries the reader instantly to the map or maps where these places are shown. There he sees not only the location of the place, but its relation to other historically important places of the same time.

For those who wish to trace a particular subject from period to period and from area to area, the chronological arrangement of the maps, together with the index, will prove helpful. For example, suppose the reader is interested in following the advance of the frontier: Through the Index, and from map to map, he will see the falling back of the Indians, the establishment of trading posts, the growth of settlements, the formation of territories and the organization of states.

An illustration of the importance of geographical knowledge in our history may be found in so well known a story as that of Boone's blazing the trail to Kentucky. Every schoolchild thinks he knows it. But does he know it? Boone started from the Sycamore Shoals of the Watauga. (Only the local historians now know the spot, yet, there, in 1775, was held a great treaty by which the Cherokee Indians ceded to the Transylvania Company the vast territories of Kentucky and part of Tennessee.) Boone went across the Long Island of Holston. (That location is not readily found on present-day maps, yet it was a landmark in the history of the early southwest.) He passed through Moccasin Gap. (This appears only on the most detailed maps.) He went over Clinch River and Powell Mountain to Cumberland Gap and on into Kentucky. Some of these places are shown on several maps in the Atlas, and all are shown with the route indicated on Plate 62. To see not only the route, but its relation to other routes (shown on other maps) coming down from Virginia and up from Carolina enables one to understand the importance of what Boone did, and why he did it when he did it.

The organization and admittance of states is treated as a part of our western development, yet every territory is brought into being in its proper area and proper period and every new state is admitted, with the dates given in each case, and with the changes in area of each territory or state clearly shown.

In the making of this Atlas, as in the making of all works of this sort, the question of where to stop has been a problem. Many more maps could have been made—and there was often the wish to make them. Many places could have been shown which are not shown, and there was often the inclination to show them. The editors can only hope that they have shown, and have shown in their proper relationship, those places having importance in our history in so far as that history had significance in our national development. Strictly local history, if one can say what is local history as differentiated from national history, had to be passed by. That a question may be raised as to why one place is shown and another not, the editors recognize full well and can only say that they have made the best decisions they could.

Throughout, the intent has been to provide a sufficient number of maps to avoid overcrowding any area. Where a relatively congested area has appeared in an otherwise general map, that area has been treated in broad outline on the general map and then given a separate map in which the details are shown without crowding. The test which the editors themselves applied was whether every location could readily be found without resort to guides on the margins of the maps. Accordingly, it is the belief of the editors that the grid (cross-section) method of indexing has properly been omitted.

As our task nears completion, we wish to express our appreciation of the contribution made by the members of the Advisory Council, who have given most generously of their time and knowledge in helping to plan the work as a whole.

To the Supervisors we are deeply indebted not only for advice and criticism in connection with the drawing of their particular maps, but also for their patience and understanding as the work progressed and each map had to be revised time after time in order to bring it into proper relationship with other maps dealing in part with related periods and areas.

We also desire to express special appreciation of the service of LeRoy H. Appleton, the Chief Cartographer, for his skillful and beautiful presentation of the subject matter of each map, either as drawn by his own pen or as a result of his direction of others. The drawing of maps is an art, to an extent not often realized. It is our belief that Mr. Appleton has set a new standard for maps as drawn in America —in their clarity, their balance of letter and line, and their artistic quality.

Back of each map and back of the work as a whole, lies an immense amount of careful, patient work. To those who, through the two years in which the Atlas was being prepared, faithfully worked out the details, we wish to extend our thanks: To Thomas Robson Hay, Associate Editor, for his constant oversight and particularly for his help on the Civil War maps; to Arthur S. Bryant, Assistant Cartographer, whose sure and experienced hand appears in almost every map; to E. Graham Platt, who was associated with the work throughout; to Marion G. Barnes, whose careful checking, from the making of the rough drafts of the maps to the completion of the Index, has saved us from many a possible error.

Finally, as Editor in Chief, I wish to express my personal and deep indebtedness to R. V. Coleman, Managing Editor. Not only has he supervised the entire work and seen that threads did not become tangled in what became an increasingly complex task, but he did much more. His knowledge of American history, not merely in its broad outlines but in its local details in all sections, has been of immense help in enabling us so to plan the maps and their relations to one another that instead of a series of disjointed plates they form an articulated whole which, in its unity, tells the story of the growth of the nation.

It is the earnest hope, as it has been the

constant effort, of all those who have shared in the preparation of this work, that it may prove to be a genuinely useful aid to the better understanding and more correct interpretation of our national story. In scope and plan we have endeavored not only to provide the professional scholar with a new and accurate tool for his research, but also to help the students and readers in high schools, colleges and the home to gain access to that geographical material relating to our history, which is so essential but which hitherto has been difficult or impossible for them to obtain. We can only trust that we have in part, at least, succeeded in accomplishing the task to which we set ourselves.

Feb. 8, 1943

JAMES TRUSLOW ADAMS

ADVISORY COUNCIL

Randolph G. Adams
Director, William L. Clements Library of American History, University of Michigan

Paul M. Angle
Librarian, Illinois State Historical Library

Julian P. Boyd
Librarian, Princeton University

Lloyd Arnold Brown
Librarian, Peabody Institute Library

Solon J. Buck
Director of Publications, The National Archives

Dan E. Clark
Head, Department of History, University of Oregon

E. Merton Coulter
Professor of History, University of Georgia

Douglas Southall Freeman
Editor, The Richmond News Leader; President, Southern Historical Society

LeRoy R. Hafen
Historian and Curator, Colorado State Historical Society

Louise Phelps Kellogg
Research Associate, Wisconsin State Historical Society

Lawrence Martin
Chief, Division of Maps, Library of Congress

Walter Prichard
Head, Department of History, Louisiana State University

Milo M. Quaife
Secretary-Editor, The Burton Historical Collection of the Detroit Public Library

Charles W. Ramsdell
Professor of American History, University of Texas

John K. Wright
Director, American Geographical Society

LeRoy H. Appleton
Cartographer

I AMERICA AT THE TIME OF DISCOVERY

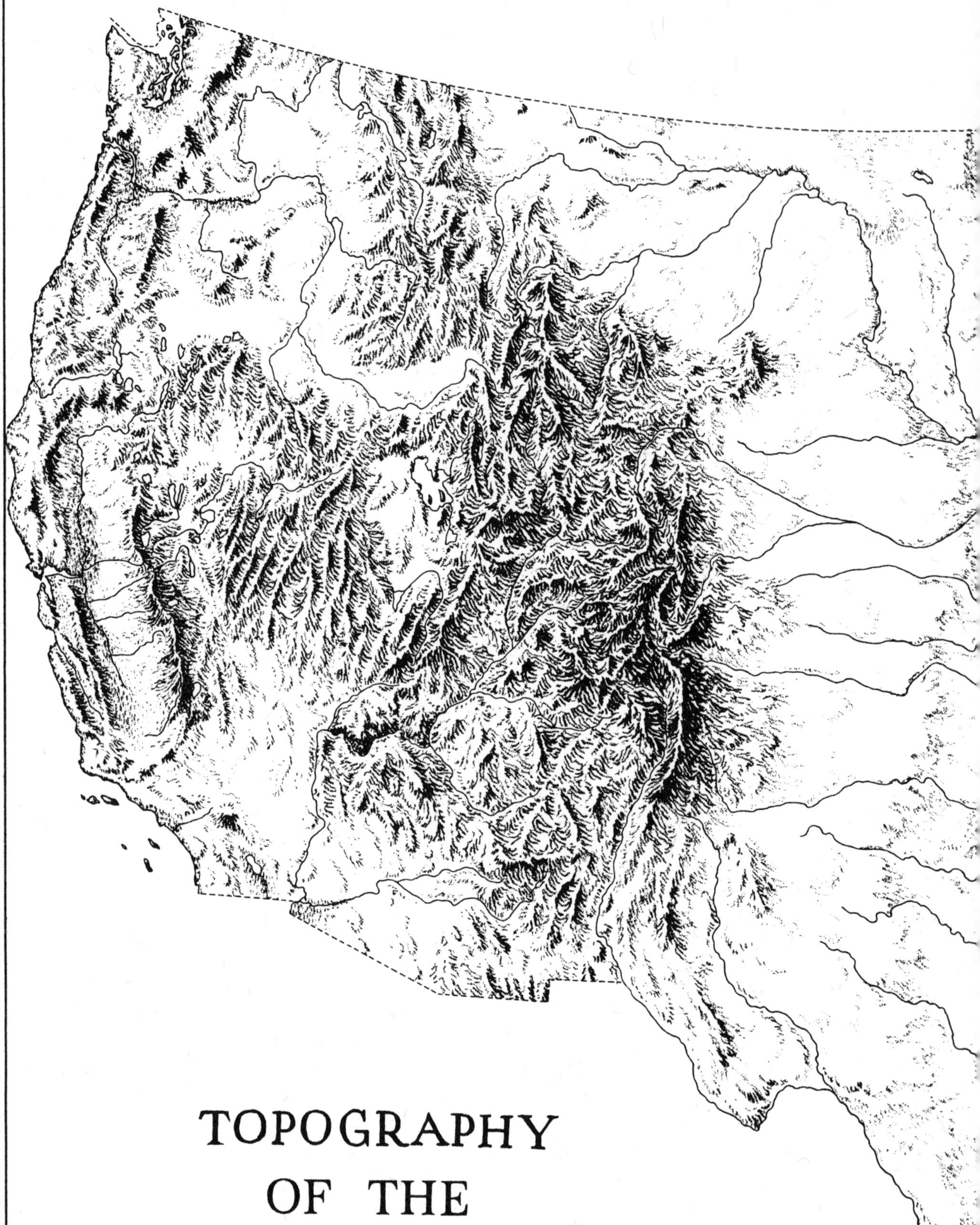

TOPOGRAPHY OF THE UNITED STATES

Drawn under the supervision of LLOYD A. BROWN

4

FORESTS OF THE

UNITED STATES

Drawn under the supervision of LLOYD A. BROWN

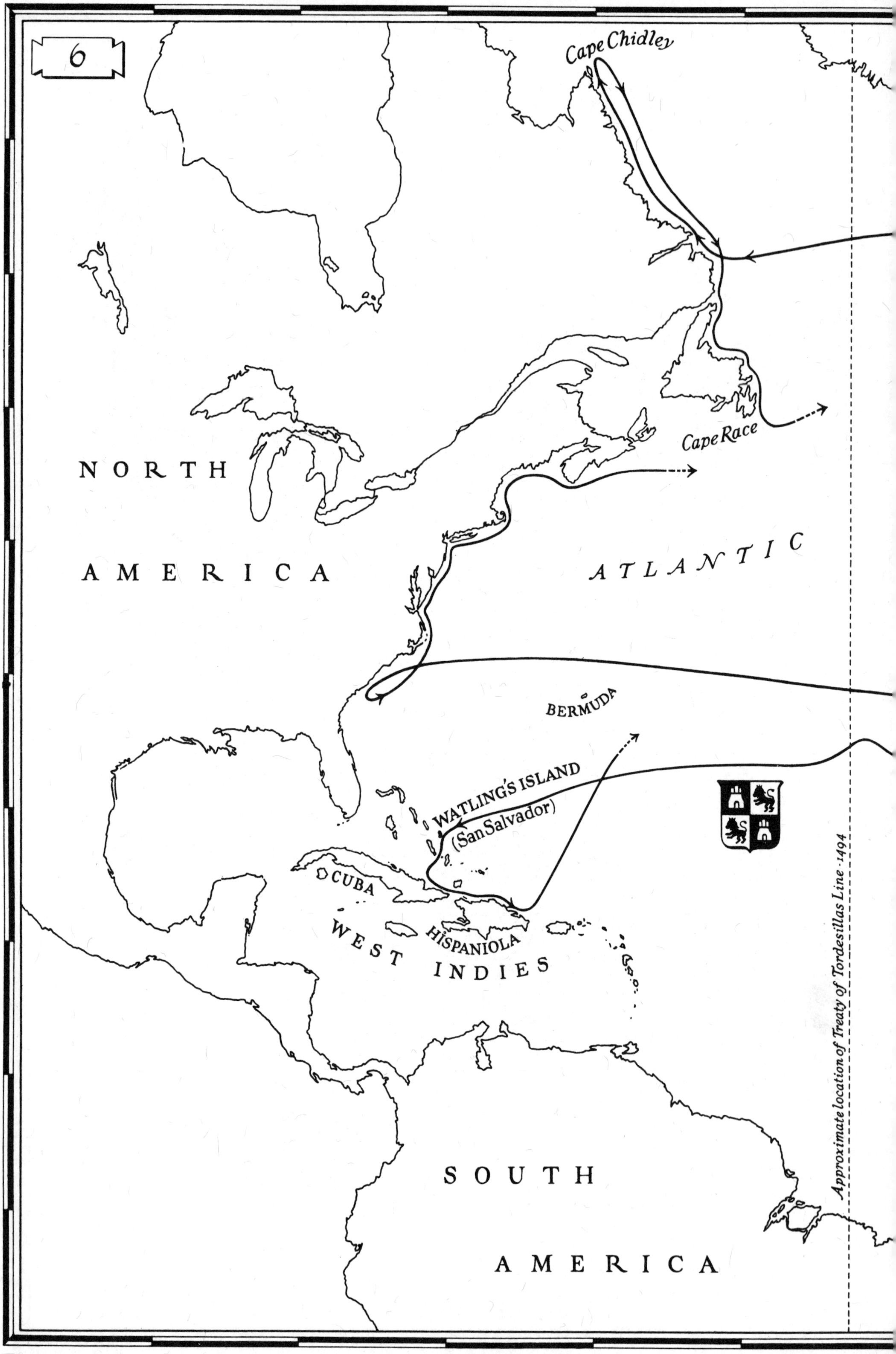
6
Cape Chidley
Cape Race
NORTH
AMERICA
ATLANTIC
BERMUDA
WATLING'S ISLAND
(San Salvador)
CUBA
HISPANIOLA
WEST
INDIES
SOUTH
AMERICA
Approximate location of Treaty of Tordesillas Line: 1494

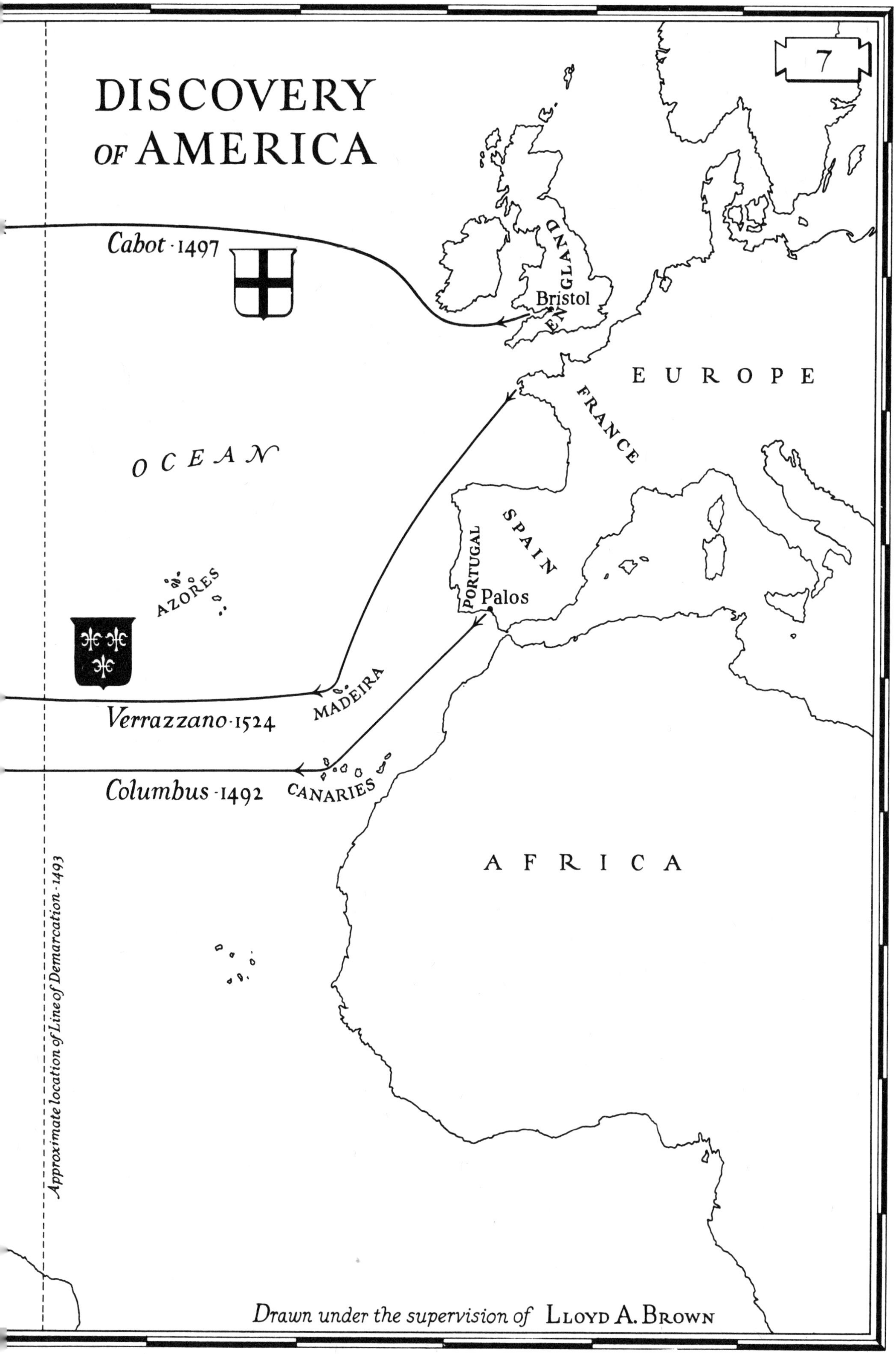
7
DISCOVERY
OF AMERICA
Cabot · 1497
ENGLAND
Bristol
EUROPE
FRANCE
OCEAN
SPAIN
PORTUGAL
Palos
AZORES
MADEIRA
Verrazzano · 1524
Columbus · 1492
CANARIES
AFRICA
Approximate location of Line of Demarcation · 1493
Drawn under the supervision of LLOYD A. BROWN

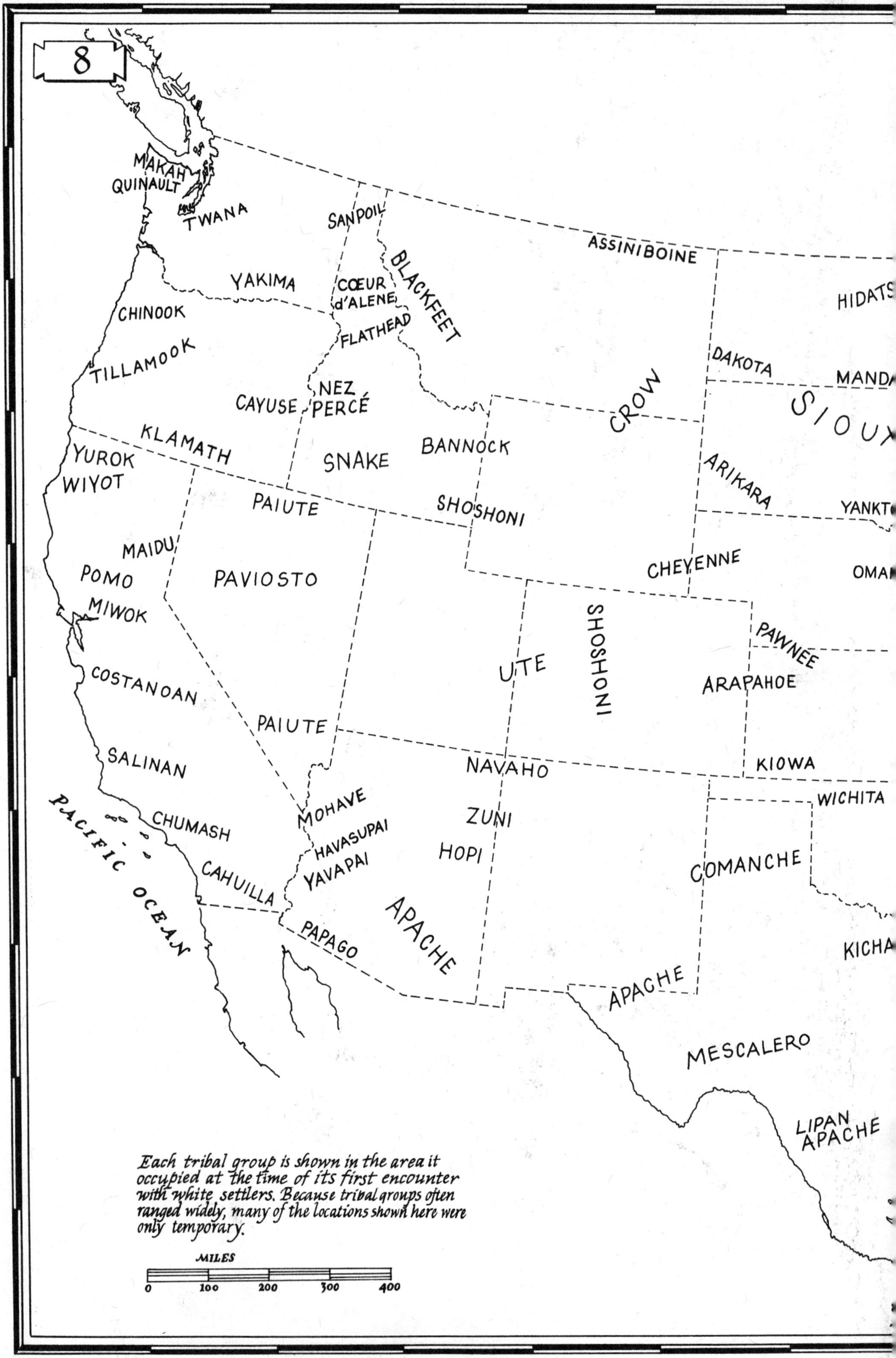

Each tribal group is shown in the area it occupied at the time of its first encounter with white settlers. Because tribal groups often ranged widely, many of the locations shown here were only temporary.

9

INDIAN TRIBAL GROUPS

II FRENCH AND SPANISH EXPLORATION AND SETTLEMENT

12

SIXTEENTH CENTURY

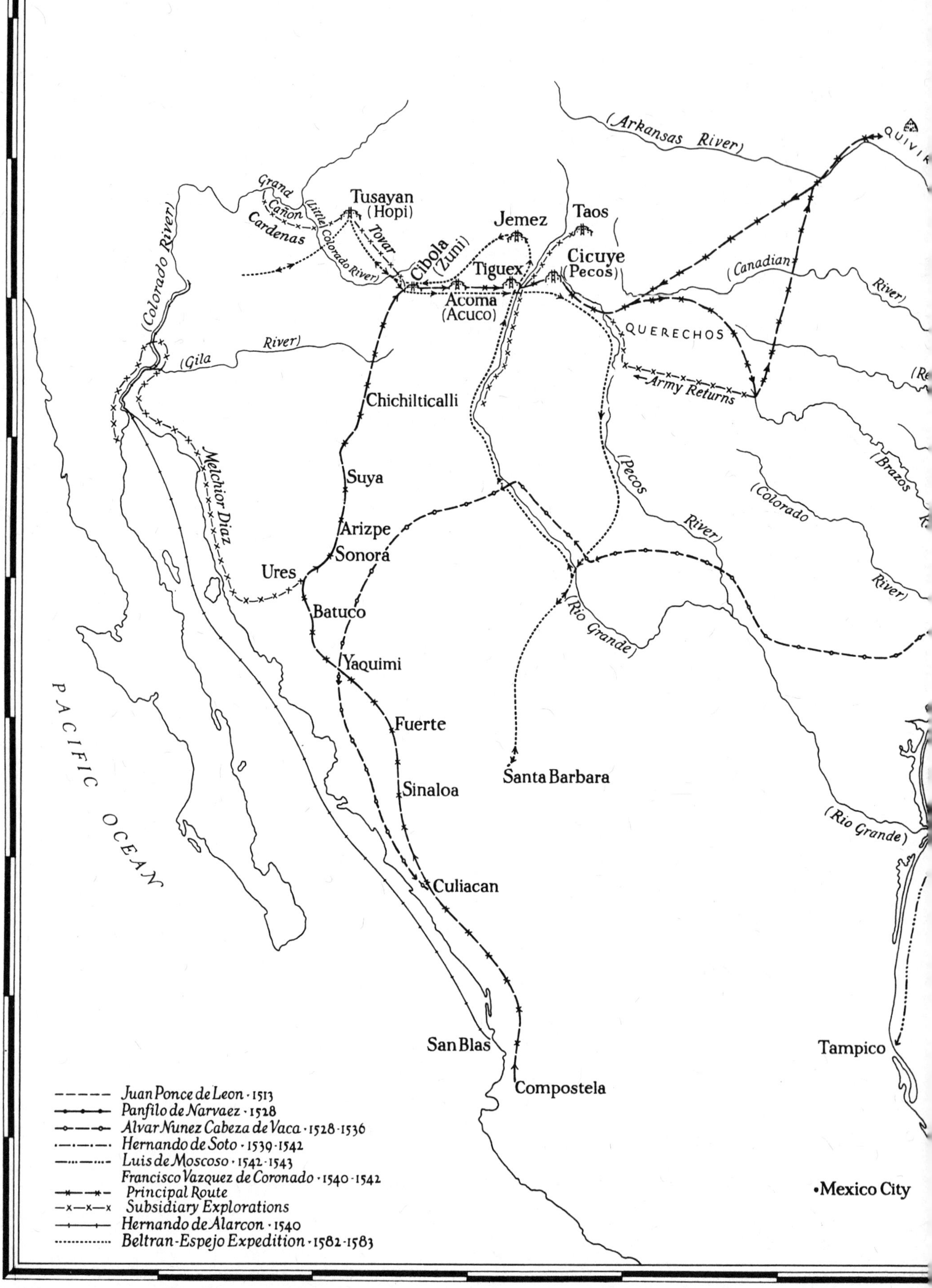

SPANISH EXPLORATIONS

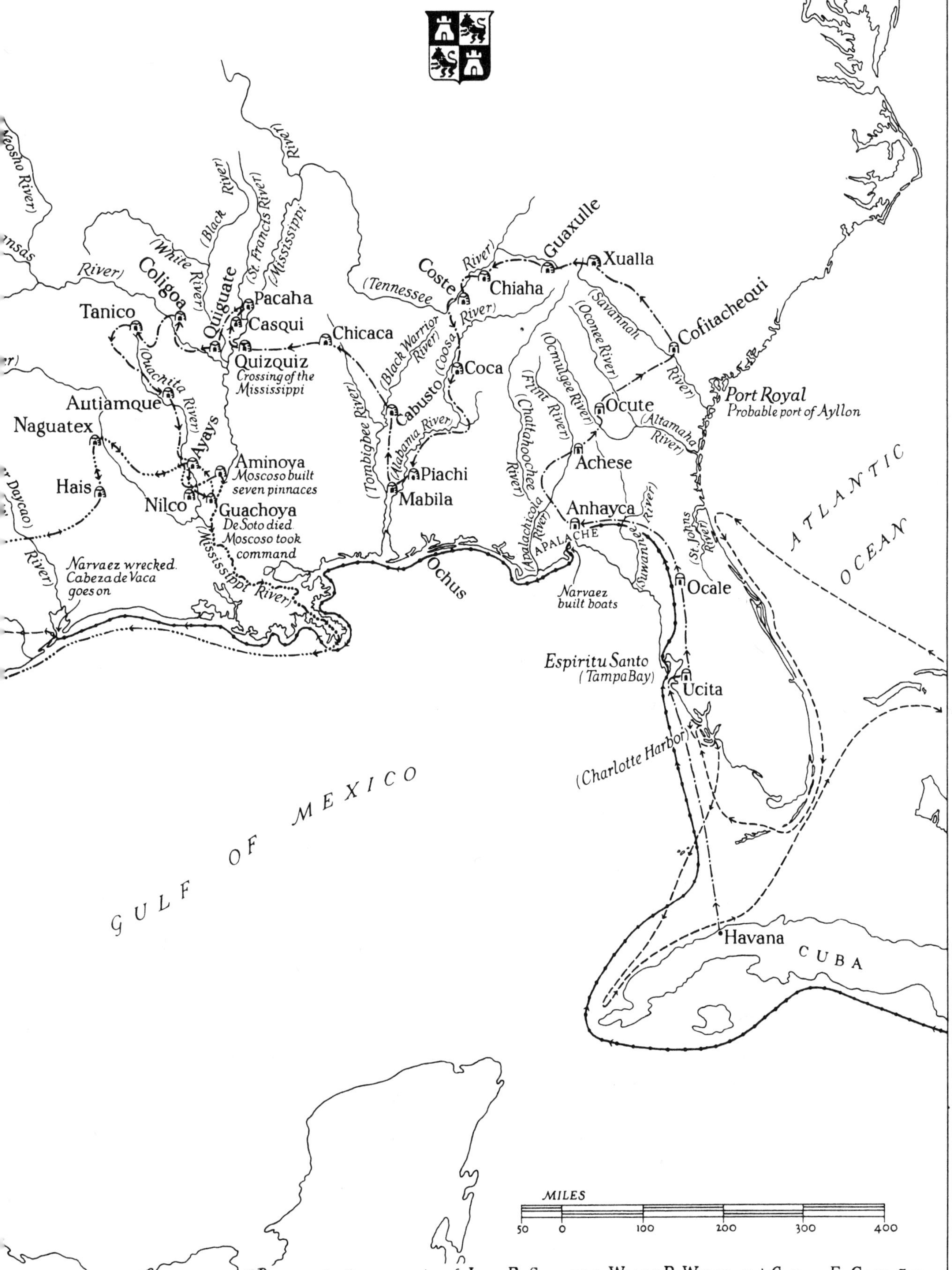

Drawn under the supervision of JOHN R. SWANTON, WALDO R. WEDEL and CARLOS E. CASTAÑEDA

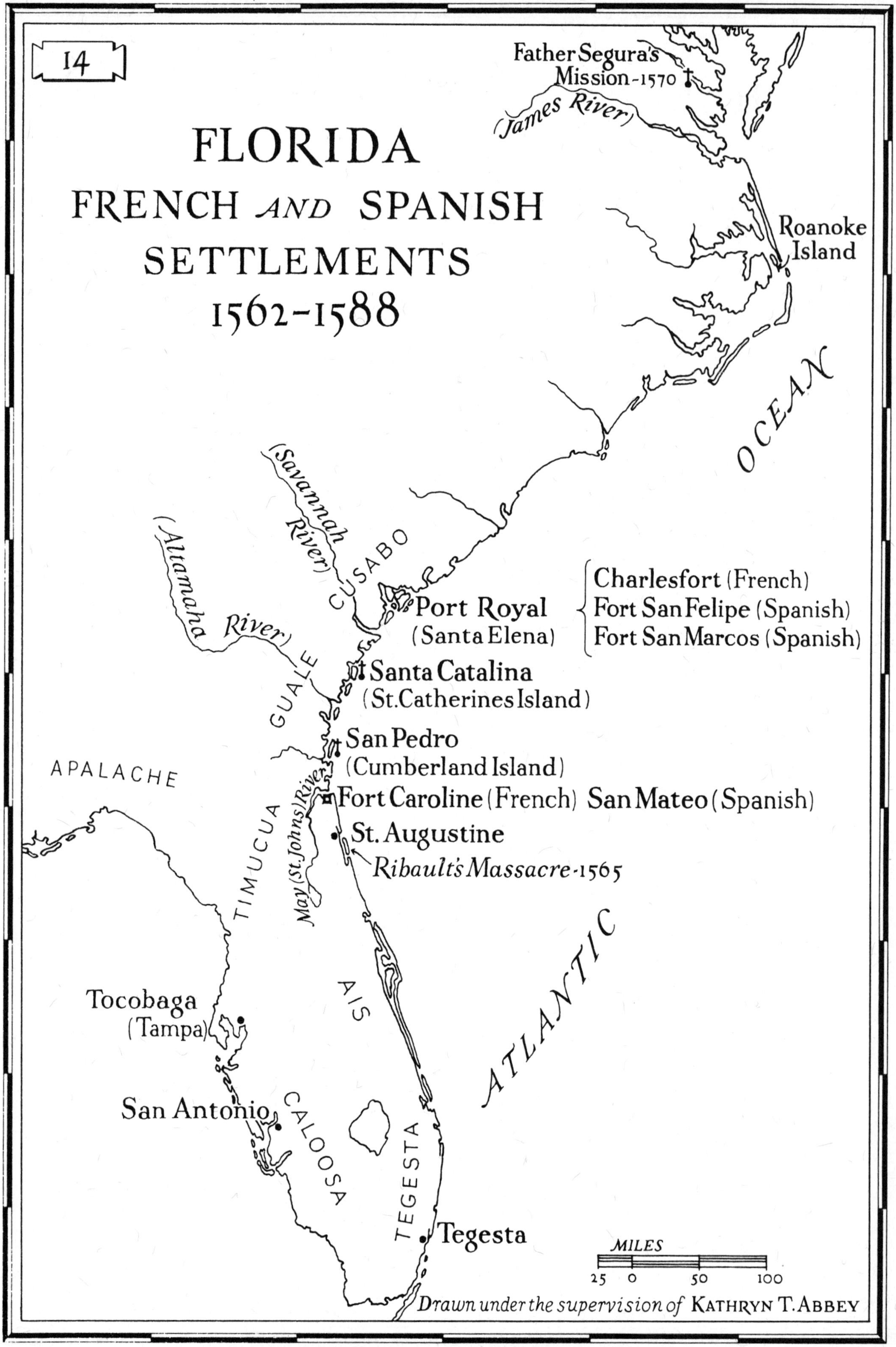
14
FLORIDA
FRENCH AND SPANISH
SETTLEMENTS
1562-1588
Father Segura's
Mission-1570
(James River)
Roanoke
Island
OCEAN
(Savannah
River)
(Altamaha
River)
CUSABO
Port Royal
(Santa Elena)
Charlesfort (French)
Fort San Felipe (Spanish)
Fort San Marcos (Spanish)
GUALE
Santa Catalina
(St. Catherines Island)
San Pedro
(Cumberland Island)
APALACHE
May (St. Johns) River
Fort Caroline (French) San Mateo (Spanish)
St. Augustine
Ribault's Massacre-1565
TIMUCUA
AIS
ATLANTIC
Tocobaga
(Tampa)
San Antonio
CALOOSA
TEGESTA
Tegesta
MILES
25 0 50 100
Drawn under the supervision of KATHRYN T. ABBEY

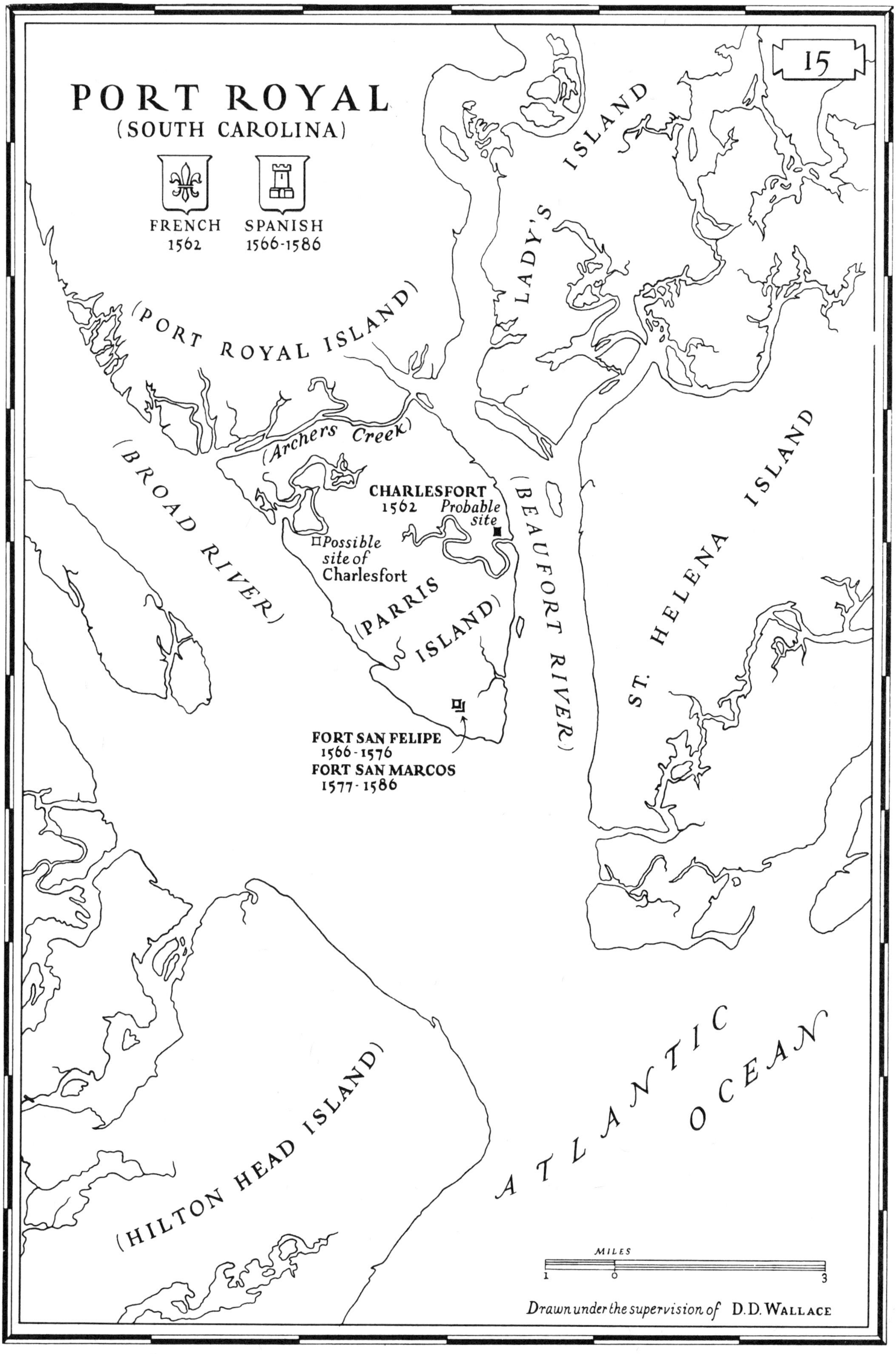
15
PORT ROYAL
(SOUTH CAROLINA)
FRENCH
1562
SPANISH
1566-1586
(PORT ROYAL ISLAND)
LADY'S ISLAND
Archers Creek
(BROAD RIVER)
CHARLESFORT
1562
Probable site
Possible site of Charlesfort
(PARRIS ISLAND)
(BEAUFORT RIVER)
ST. HELENA ISLAND
FORT SAN FELIPE
1566-1576
FORT SAN MARCOS
1577-1586
(HILTON HEAD ISLAND)
ATLANTIC OCEAN
MILES
1 0 3
Drawn under the supervision of D.D. WALLACE

DISCOVERY OF THE MISSISSIPPI

JOLLIET and MARQUETTE

1673

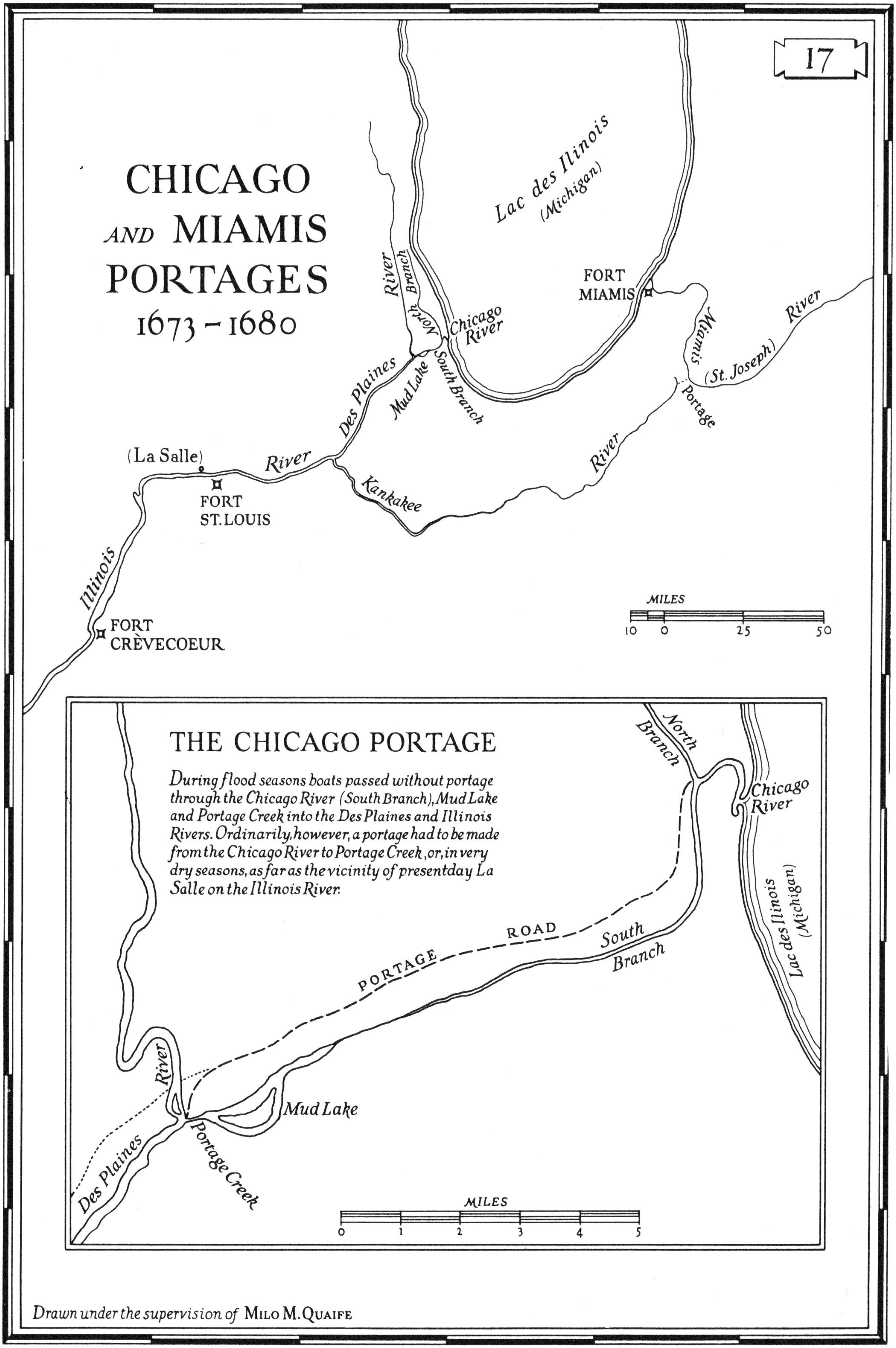

Drawn under the supervision of MILO M. QUAIFE

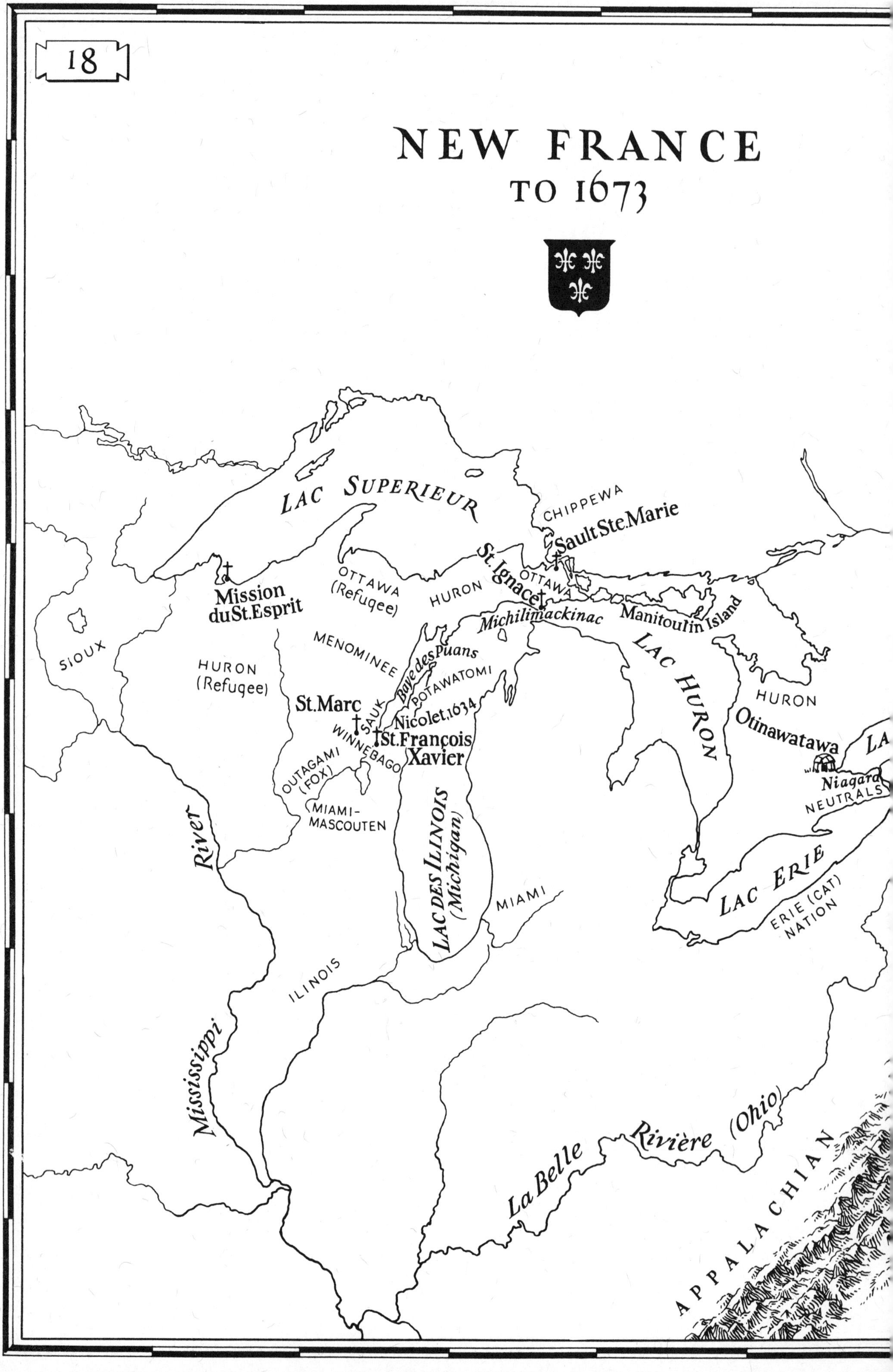
18
NEW FRANCE
TO 1673
LAC SUPERIEUR
CHIPPEWA
Sault Ste.Marie
St.Ignace
OTTAWA
Mission du St.Esprit
OTTAWA (Refugee)
HURON
Michilimackinac
Manitoulin Island
SIOUX
MENOMINEE
HURON (Refugee)
Baye des Puans
POTAWATOMI
LAC HURON
HURON
St.Marc
SAUK
Nicolet.1634
St.François Xavier
WINNEBAGO
Otinawatawa
OUTAGAMI (FOX)
Niagara
NEUTRALS
MIAMI-MASCOUTEN
River
LAC DES ILINOIS (Michigan)
LAC ERIE
MIAMI
ERIE (CAT) NATION
ILINOIS
Mississippi
La Belle Rivière (Ohio)
APPALACHIAN

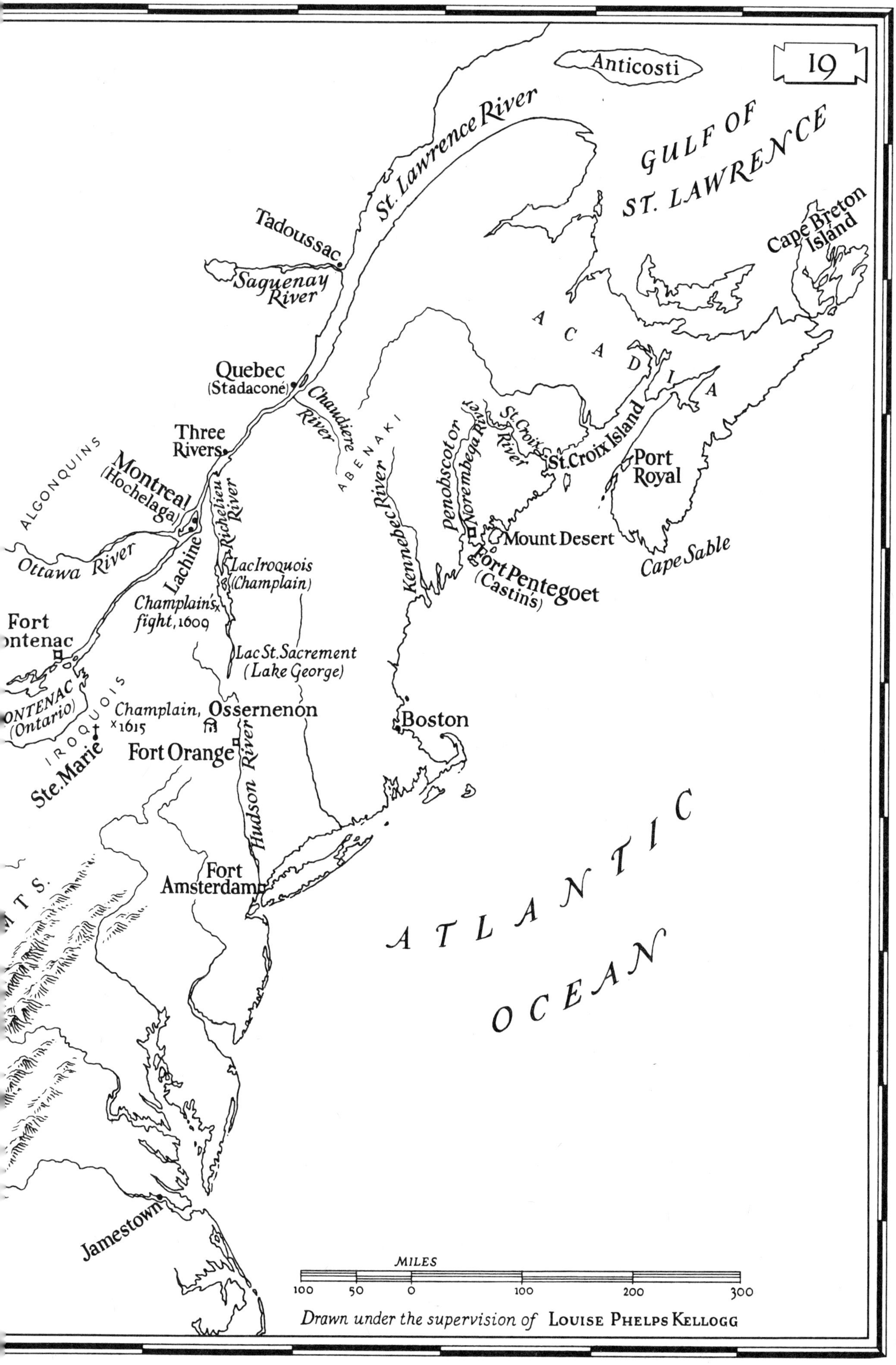
19
Anticosti
St. Lawrence River
GULF OF
ST. LAWRENCE
Cape Breton Island
Tadoussac
Saguenay River
ACADIA
Quebec
(Stadaconé)
Chaudière River
ABENAKI
Penobscot or Norembega River
St. Croix River
St. Croix Island
Port Royal
Three Rivers
ALGONQUINS
Montreal
(Hochelaga)
Richelieu River
Kennebec River
Mount Desert
Cape Sable
Ottawa River
Lachine
Lac Iroquois
(Champlain)
Fort Pentegoet
(Castin's)
Champlain's fight, 1609
Lac St. Sacrement
(Lake George)
IROQUOIS
Champlain, 1615
Ossernenon
Boston
Fort Orange
Ste. Marie
Hudson River
ATLANTIC
OCEAN
Fort Amsterdam
Jamestown
MILES
100
50
0
100
200
300
Drawn under the supervision of LOUISE PHELPS KELLOGG

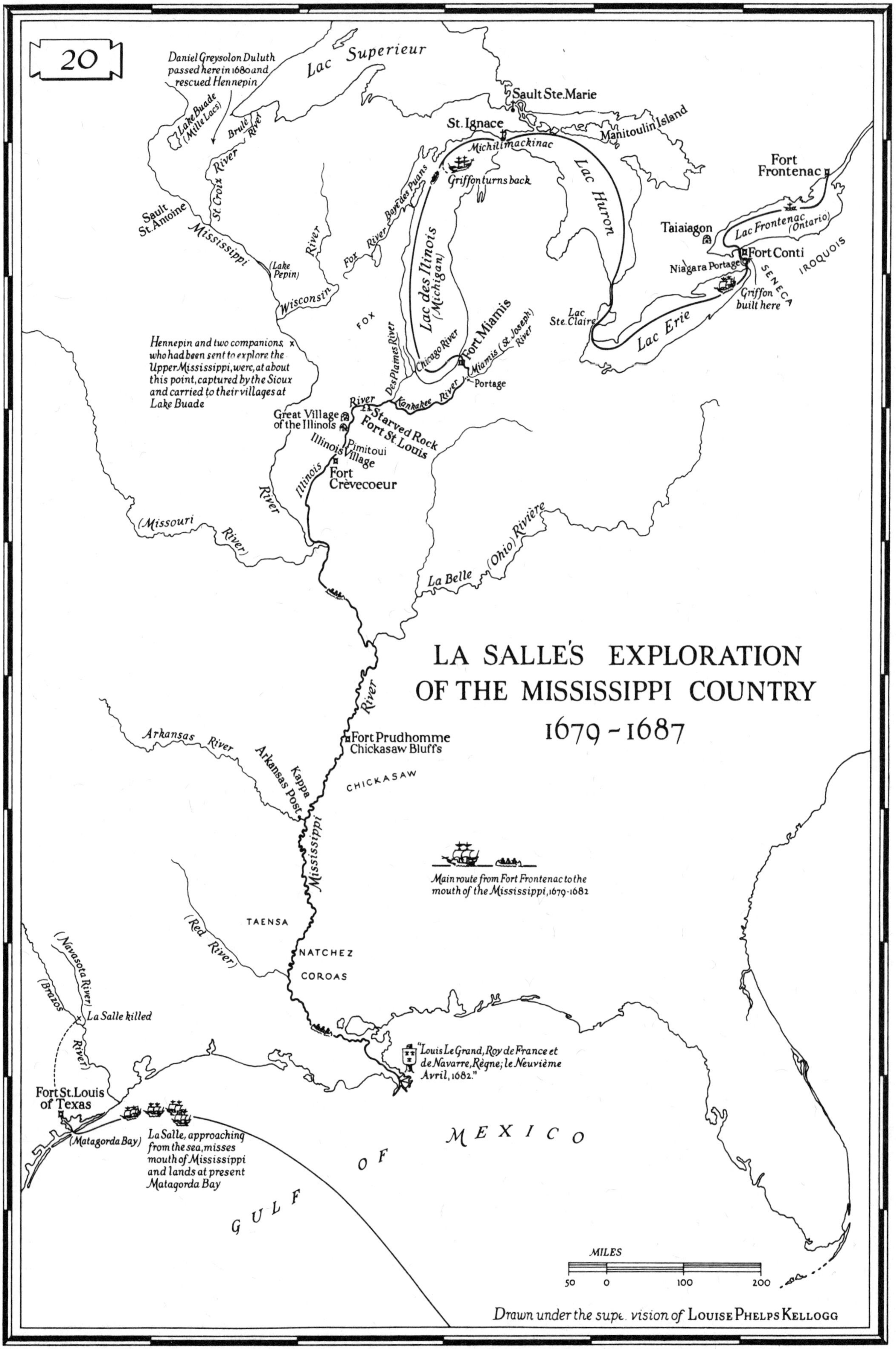
20
LA SALLE'S EXPLORATION OF THE MISSISSIPPI COUNTRY 1679 - 1687
Daniel Greysolon Duluth passed here in 1680 and rescued Hennepin
Lac Superieur
Lake Buade (Mille Lacs)
Brulé River
St. Croix River
Sault St. Antoine
Mississippi
(Lake Pepin)
Wisconsin
River
Fox River
Baye des Puans
Sault Ste. Marie
St. Ignace
Michilimackinac
Manitoulin Island
Griffon turns back
Lac Huron
Lac des Ilinois (Michigan)
Fort Frontenac
Taiaiagon
Lac Frontenac (Ontario)
Fort Conti
Niagara Portage
IROQUOIS
SENECA
Griffon built here
Lac Ste. Claire
Lac Erie
FOX
Hennepin and two companions, who had been sent to explore the Upper Mississippi, were, at about this point, captured by the Sioux and carried to their villages at Lake Buade
Des Plaines River
Chicago River
Fort Miamis
Miamis (St. Joseph) River
Portage
Kankakee River
Great Village of the Illinois
Starved Rock
Fort St. Louis
Pimitoui
Illinois Village
Illinois
Fort Crèvecoeur
River
(Missouri River)
La Belle (Ohio) Rivière
River
Fort Prudhomme
Chickasaw Bluffs
Arkansas River
Kappa
Arkansas Post
CHICKASAW
Mississippi
Main route from Fort Frontenac to the mouth of the Mississippi, 1679-1682
TAENSA
(Red River)
NATCHEZ
COROAS
(Navasota River)
(Brazos
River
La Salle killed
"Louis Le Grand, Roy de France et de Navarre, Règne; le Neuvième Avril, 1682."
Fort St. Louis of Texas
(Matagorda Bay)
La Salle, approaching from the sea, misses mouth of Mississippi and lands at present Matagorda Bay
GULF OF MEXICO
MILES
50 0 100 200
Drawn under the supervision of Louise Phelps Kellogg

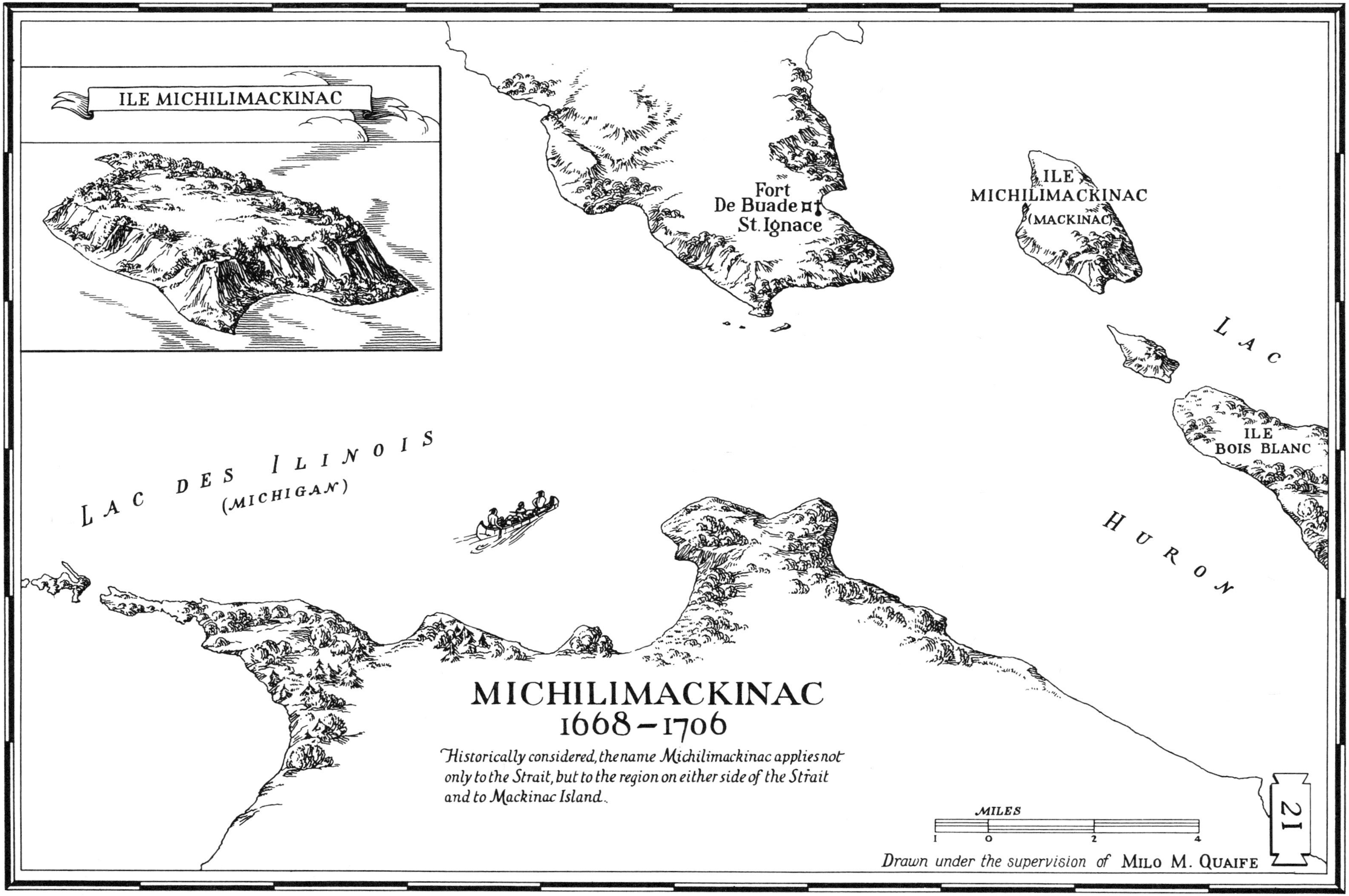
ILE MICHILIMACKINAC
Fort
De Buade
St. Ignace
ILE
MICHILIMACKINAC
(MACKINAC)
LAC HURON
ILE
BOIS BLANC
LAC DES ILINOIS
(MICHIGAN)
MICHILIMACKINAC
1668–1706
Historically considered, the name Michilimackinac applies not only to the Strait, but to the region on either side of the Strait and to Mackinac Island.
MILES
1 0 2 4
Drawn under the supervision of MILO M. QUAIFE
21

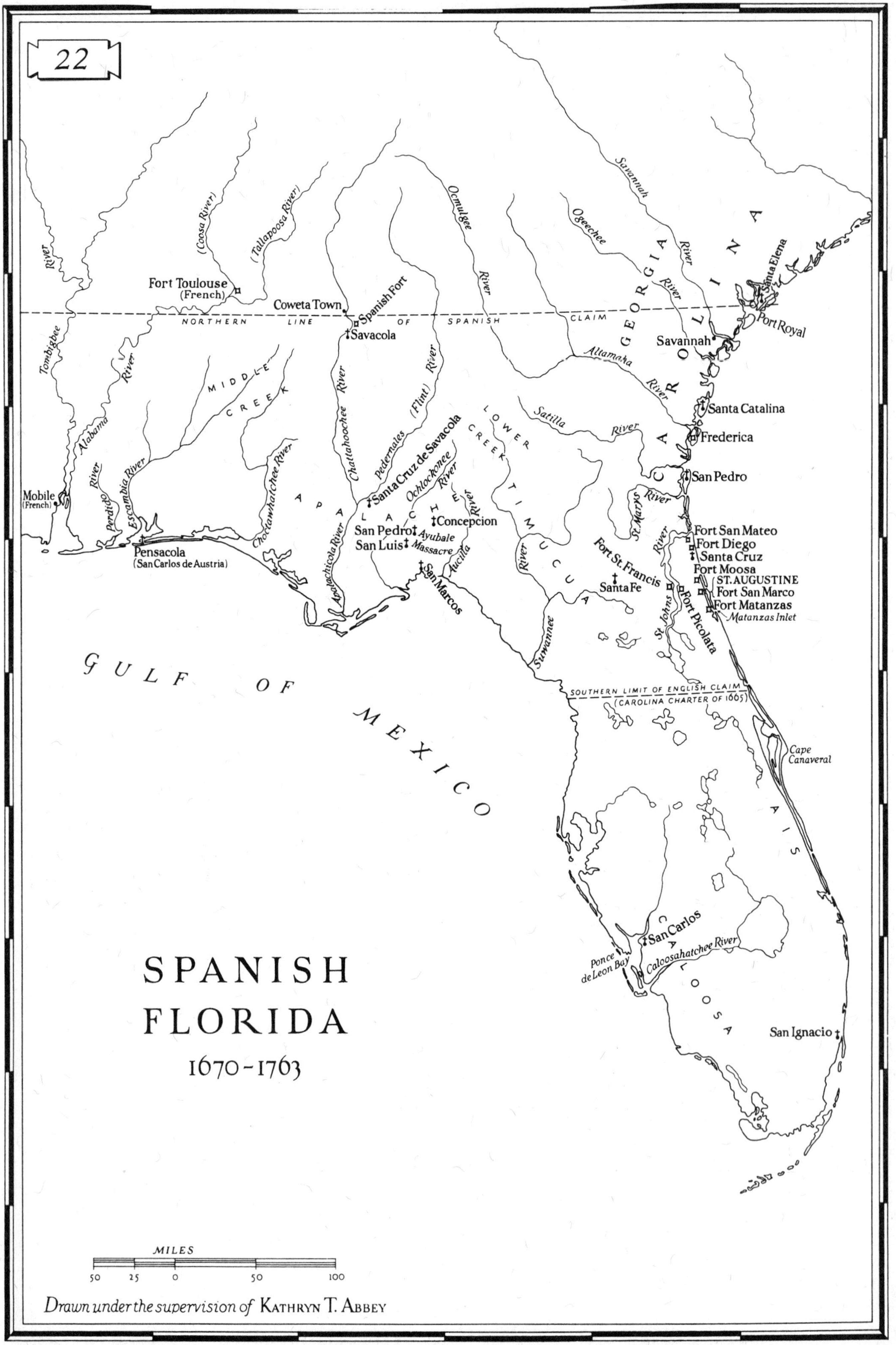
22
SPANISH FLORIDA
1670-1763
Drawn under the supervision of Kathryn T. Abbey
MILES
50
25
0
50
100
GULF OF MEXICO
NORTHERN LINE OF SPANISH CLAIM
SOUTHERN LIMIT OF ENGLISH CLAIM
(CAROLINA CHARTER OF 1665)
CAROLINA
GEORGIA
MIDDLE CREEK
LOWER CREEK
APALACHE
TIMUCUA
AIS
CALOOSA
Fort Toulouse
(French)
Coweta Town
Spanish Fort
Savacola
Mobile
(French)
Pensacola
(San Carlos de Austria)
Santa Cruz de Savacola
San Pedro
San Luis
Ayubale
Massacre
Concepcion
San Marcos
Santa Fe
Fort St. Francis
Fort Picolata
Savannah
Port Royal
Santa Elena
Santa Catalina
Frederica
San Pedro
Fort San Mateo
Fort Diego
Santa Cruz
Fort Moosa
ST. AUGUSTINE
Fort San Marco
Fort Matanzas
Matanzas Inlet
Cape Canaveral
San Carlos
Ponce de Leon Bay
Caloosahatchee River
San Ignacio
River
(Coosa River)
(Tallapoosa River)
Tombigbee
River
Alabama
Perdido River
Escambia River
Choctawhatchee River
Chattahoochee River
Apalachicola River
Pedernales
(Flint) River
Ochlockonee River
Aucilla River
Ocmulgee River
Ogeechee
Savannah River
River
Altamaha River
Satilla River
St. Marys River
St. Johns River
River
Suwannee

TRANS-MISSISSIPPI - FRENCH & SPANISH
1600 – 1750

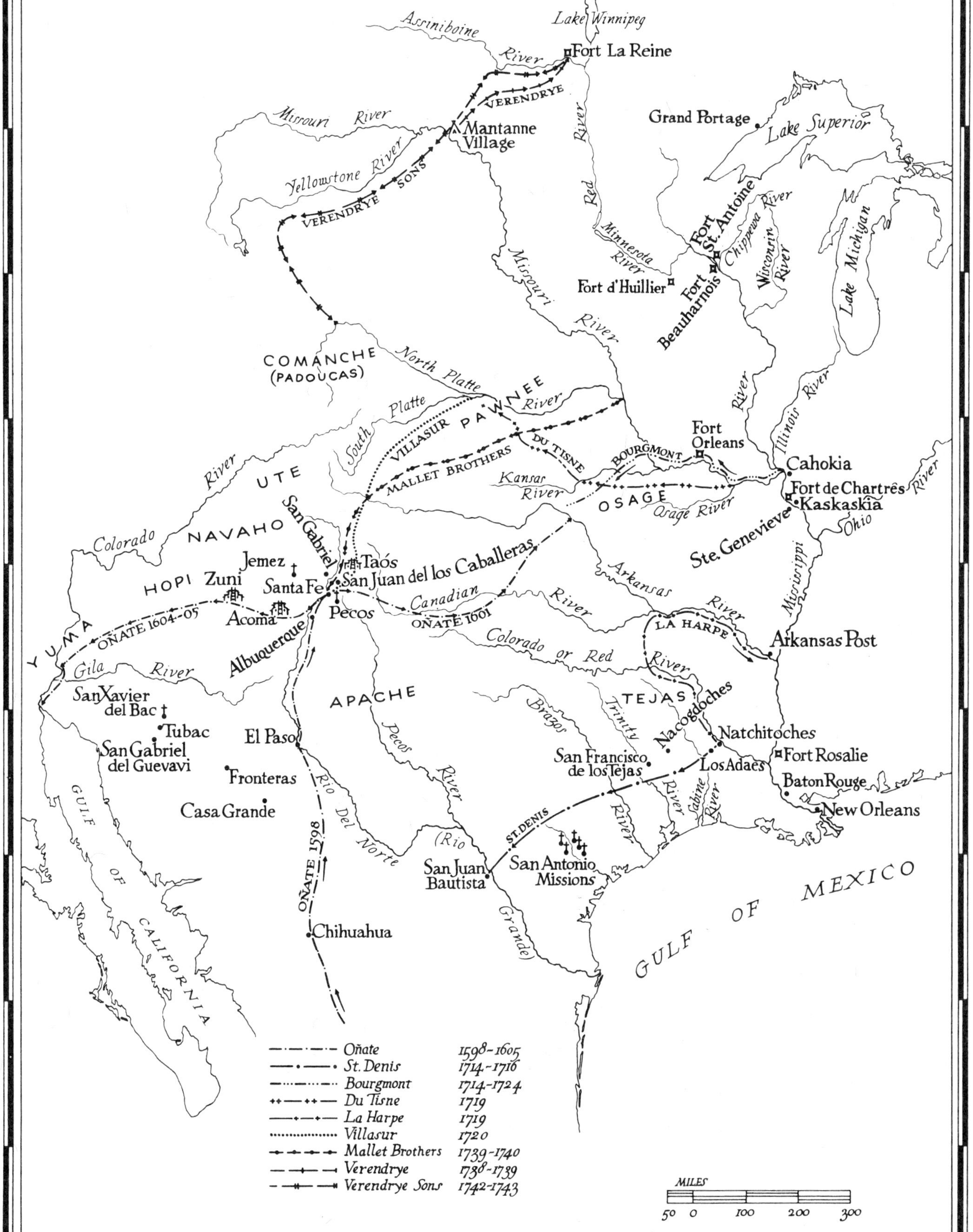

Drawn under the supervision of WALTER PRICHARD & CARLOS E. CASTAÑEDA
The Verendrye routes drawn under the supervision of O. G. LIBBY

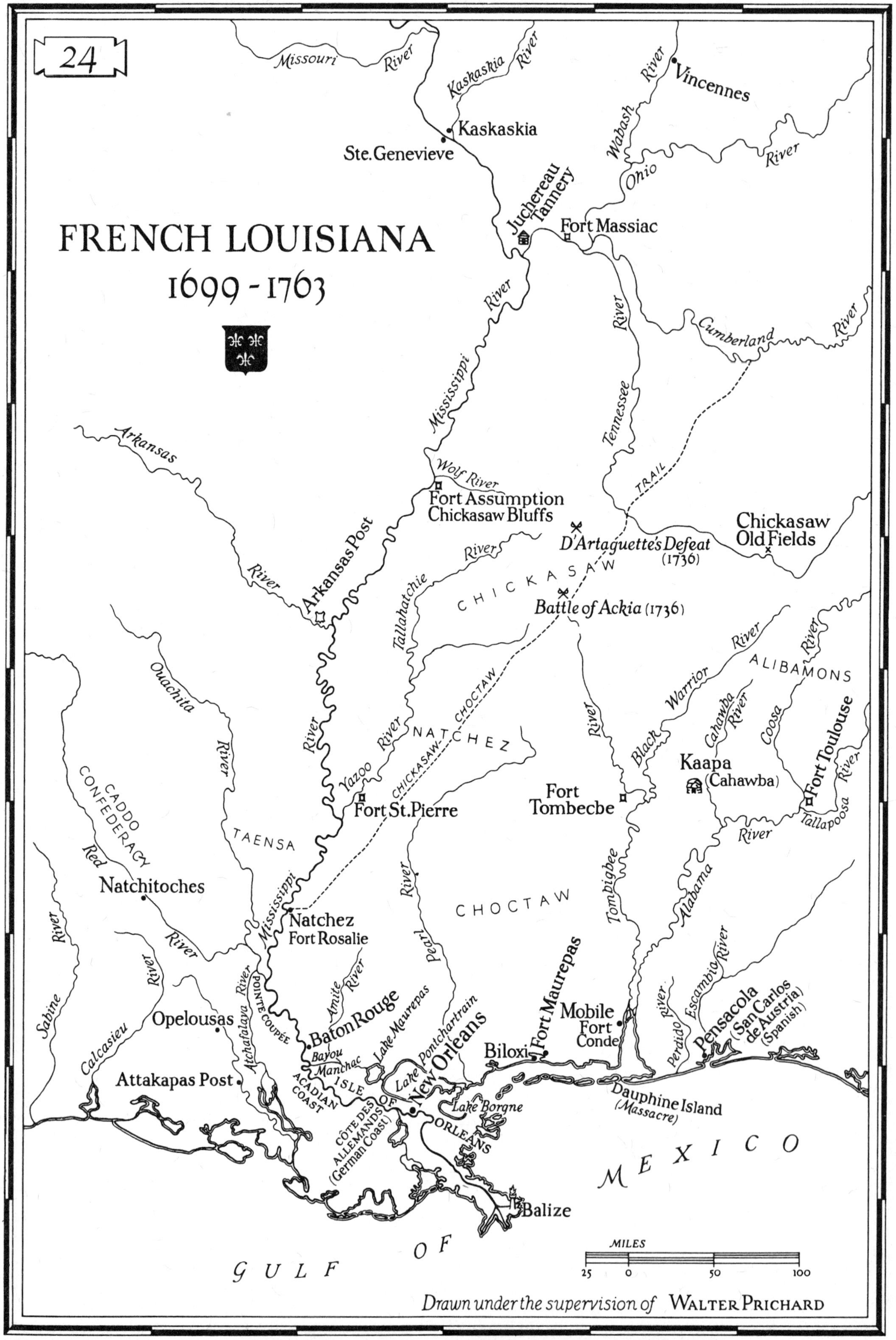
24
FRENCH LOUISIANA
1699 - 1763
Missouri River
Kaskaskia River
Kaskaskia
Ste. Genevieve
Wabash River
Vincennes
Ohio River
Juchereau Tannery
Fort Massiac
Mississippi River
Tennessee River
Cumberland River
TRAIL
Arkansas River
Wolf River
Fort Assumption
Chickasaw Bluffs
Arkansas Post
Tallahatchie River
CHICKASAW
D'Artaguette's Defeat (1736)
Battle of Ackia (1736)
Chickasaw Old Fields
Ouachita River
Yazoo River
NATCHEZ
CHICKASAW-CHOCTAW
River
Black Warrior River
ALIBAMONS
Cahawba River
Coosa River
Fort Toulouse
Kaapa (Cahawba)
Tallapoosa River
Fort Tombecbe
Fort St. Pierre
CADDO CONFEDERACY
TAENSA
Red River
Natchitoches
Mississippi
Natchez
Fort Rosalie
Pearl River
CHOCTAW
Tombigbee
Alabama River
Escambia River
Sabine River
Calcasieu River
Atchafalaya River
POINTE COUPÉE
Amite River
Baton Rouge
Lake Maurepas
Lake Pontchartrain
New Orleans
Biloxi
Fort Maurepas
Mobile
Fort Conde
Perdido River
Pensacola (San Carlos de Austria) (Spanish)
Opelousas
Attakapas Post
Bayou Manchac
ACADIAN COAST
ISLE OF ORLEANS
CÔTE DES ALLEMANDS (German Coast)
Lake Borgne
Dauphine Island (Massacre)
Balize
GULF OF MEXICO
MILES
25 0 50 100
Drawn under the supervision of WALTER PRICHARD

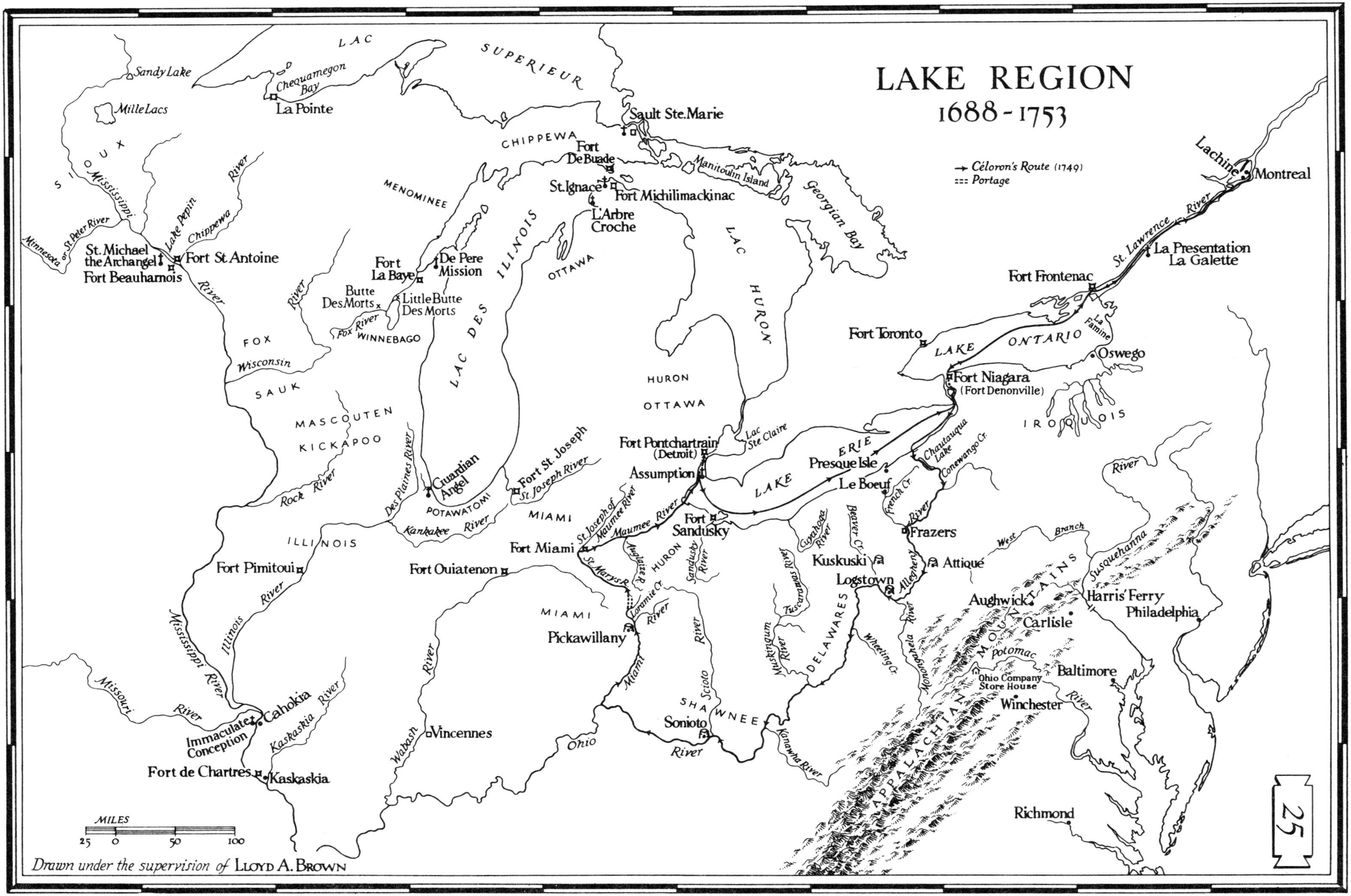
LAKE REGION
1688-1753
Céloron's Route (1749)
Portage
25
LAC SUPERIEUR
Sandy Lake
Mille Lacs
SIOUX
Mississippi
La Pointe
Chequamegon Bay
Sault Ste. Marie
CHIPPEWA
Fort De Buade
St. Ignace
Fort Michilimackinac
L'Arbre Croche
Manitoulin Island
Georgian Bay
LAC HURON
MENOMINEE
Minnesota or St. Peter River
Lake Pepin
Chippewa
River
St. Michael the Archangel
Fort St. Antoine
Fort Beauharnois
Fort La Baye
De Pere Mission
Butte Des Morts
Little Butte Des Morts
Fox River
WINNEBAGO
ILLINOIS
OTTAWA
LAC DES ILLINOIS
FOX
Wisconsin
SAUK
MASCOUTEN
KICKAPOO
Rock River
Des Plaines River
Guardian Angel
POTAWATOMI
Kankakee River
Fort St. Joseph
St. Joseph River
MIAMI
HURON
OTTAWA
Fort Pontchartrain (Detroit)
Lac Ste. Claire
Assumption
St. Joseph of Maumee River
Maumee River
Fort Miami
St. Marys R.
Auglaize R.
Loramie Cr.
Fort Sandusky
Sandusky River
Fort Ouiatenon
ILLINOIS
Fort Pimitoui
Illinois River
Mississippi River
Missouri River
Cahokia
Immaculate Conception
Kaskaskia River
Fort de Chartres
Kaskaskia
Wabash River
Vincennes
Ohio River
Pickawillany
Miami River
Scioto River
SHAWNEE
Sonioto
Kanawha River
LAKE ERIE
Presque Isle
Le Boeuf
French Cr.
Chautauqua Lake
Conewango Cr.
Cuyahoga River
Beaver Cr.
Kuskuski
Tuscarawas River
Muskingum River
DELAWARES
Logstown
Allegheny River
Frazers
Attiqué
Wheeling Cr.
Monongahela River
Fort Toronto
LAKE ONTARIO
Fort Frontenac
La Famine
Oswego
Fort Niagara (Fort Denonville)
IROQUOIS
St. Lawrence River
La Presentation La Galette
Lachine
Montreal
West Branch
Susquehanna
Harris' Ferry
Philadelphia
Aughwick
Carlisle
APPALACHIAN MOUNTAINS
Potomac River
Ohio Company Store House
Winchester
Baltimore
Richmond
MILES
25 0 50 100
Drawn under the supervision of LLOYD A. BROWN

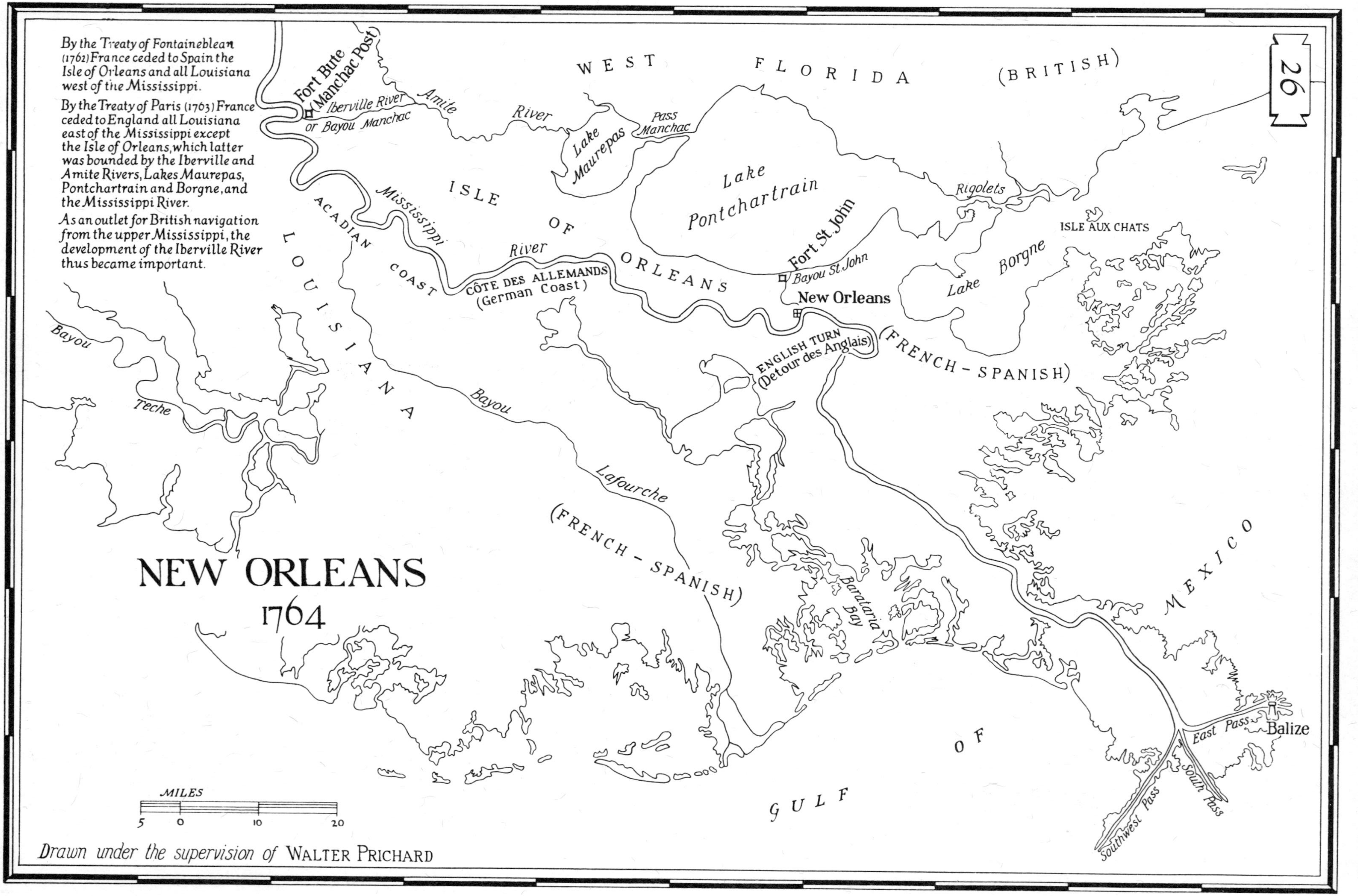
26
NEW ORLEANS
1764
By the Treaty of Fontaineblean (1762) France ceded to Spain the Isle of Orleans and all Louisiana west of the Mississippi.
By the Treaty of Paris (1763) France ceded to England all Louisiana east of the Mississippi except the Isle of Orleans, which latter was bounded by the Iberville and Amite Rivers, Lakes Maurepas, Pontchartrain and Borgne, and the Mississippi River.
As an outlet for British navigation from the upper Mississippi, the development of the Iberville River thus became important.
WEST FLORIDA (BRITISH)
ISLE OF ORLEANS
LOUISIANA
(FRENCH - SPANISH)
(FRENCH - SPANISH)
GULF OF MEXICO
Fort Bute (Manchac Post)
Iberville River or Bayou Manchac
Amite River
Lake Maurepas
Pass Manchac
Lake Pontchartrain
Rigolets
Lake Borgne
ISLE AUX CHATS
Fort St. John
Bayou St. John
New Orleans
ENGLISH TURN (Detour des Anglais)
Mississippi River
ACADIAN COAST
CÔTE DES ALLEMANDS (German Coast)
Bayou Lafourche
Bayou Teche
Barataria Bay
East Pass
South Pass
Southwest Pass
Balize
MILES
5
0
10
20
Drawn under the supervision of WALTER PRICHARD

27
ILLINOIS COUNTRY
1700 - 1763
Lake Michigan
Guardian Angel
Chicago Portage
Des Plaines River
Rock River
Starved Rock
Kankakee River
Illinois River
Fort Pimitoui
Mississippi
Cahokia Mounds
Cahokia
Missouri River
Des Peres
Kaskaskia River
Wabash River
Vincennes
St. Philippe
Michigamea
Fort de Chartres
Prairie du Rocher
Kaskaskia
Ste. Genevieve
River
Juchereau Tannery
Ohio River
Fort Massiac
MILES
25
0
50
Drawn under the supervision of PAUL M ANGLE

28

ST. AUGUSTINE 1700-1764

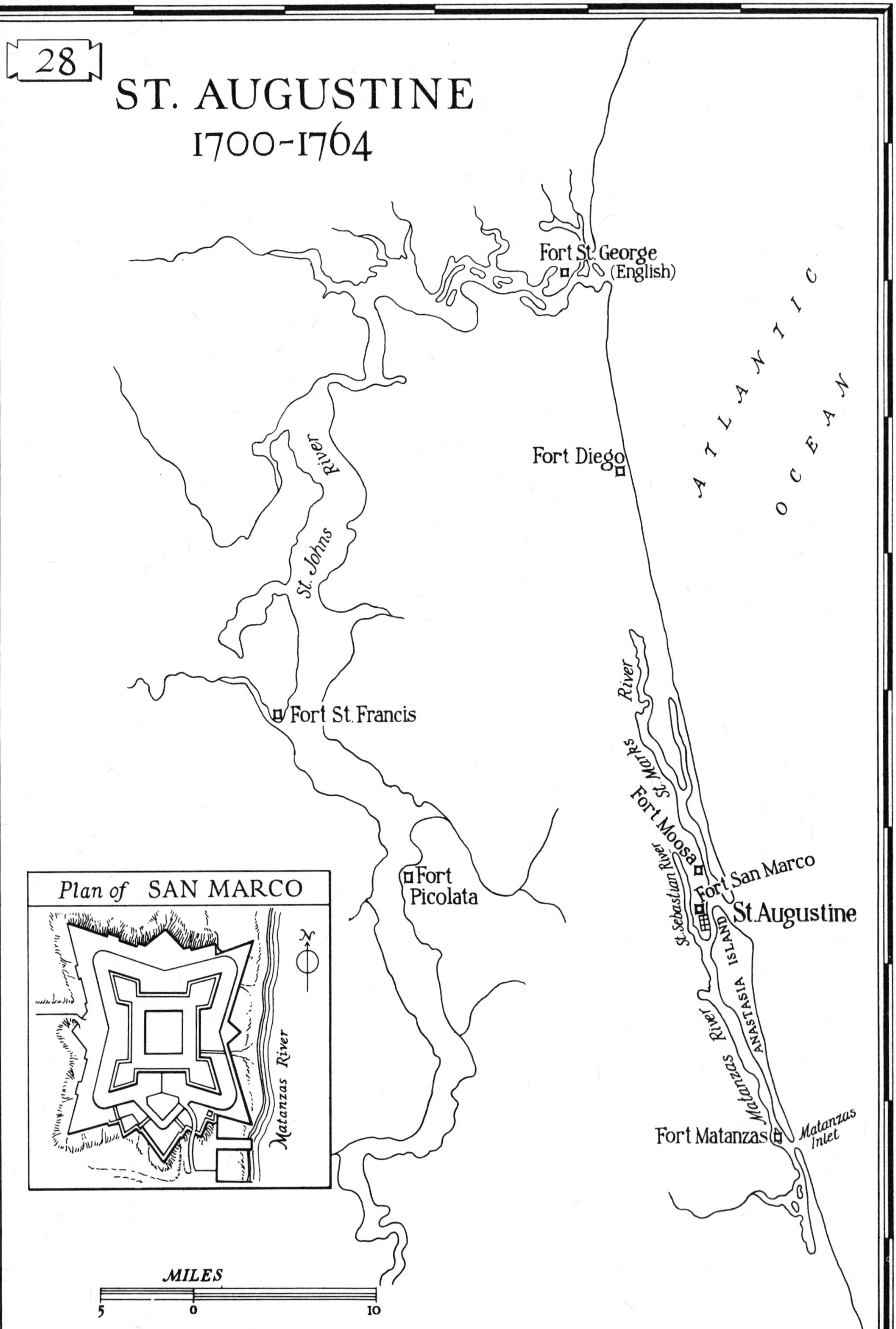

Drawn under the supervision of KATHRYN T. ABBEY

III LAND GRANTS AND SETTLEMENT OF THE THIRTEEN COLONIES

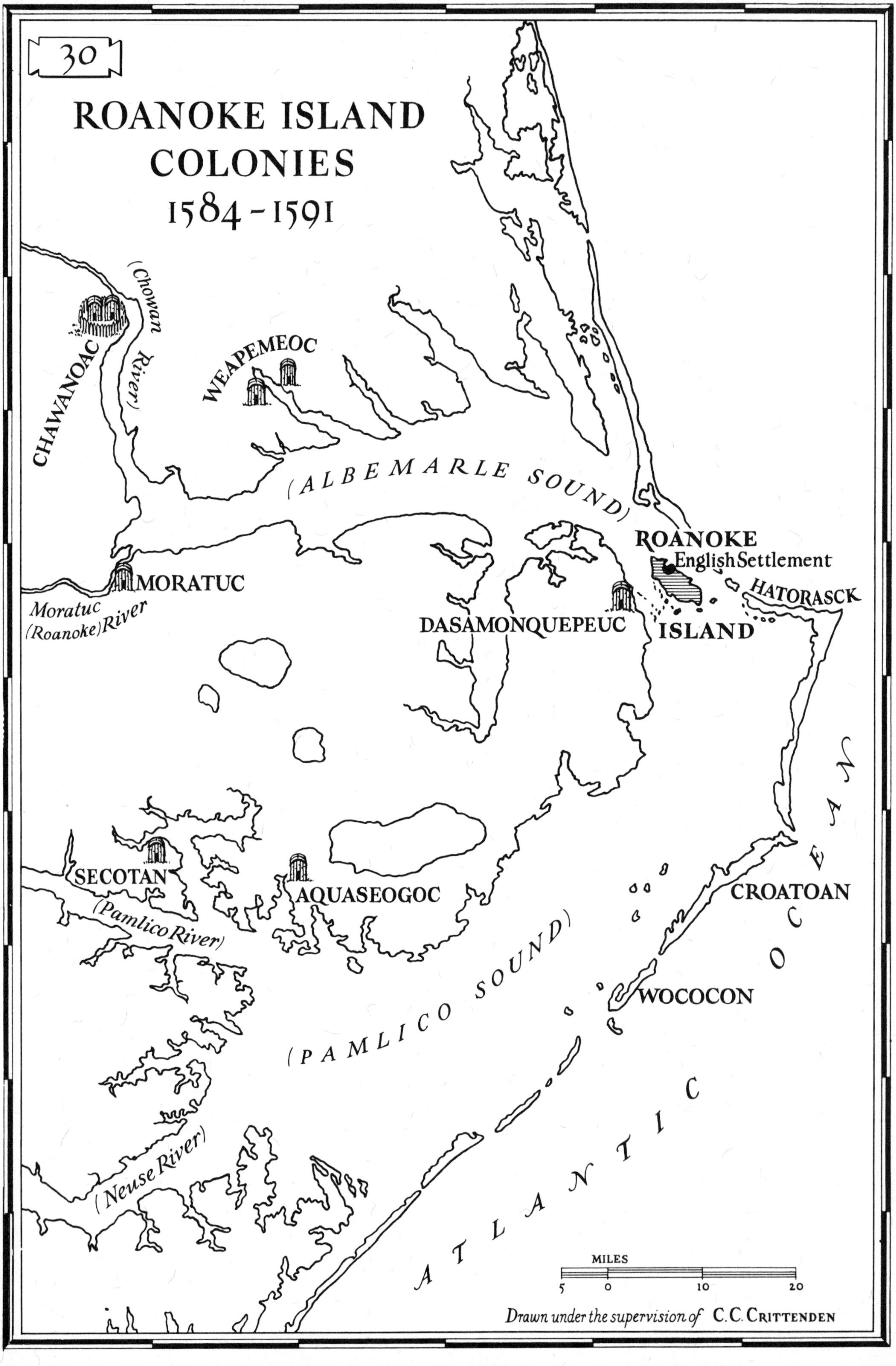
30
ROANOKE ISLAND COLONIES 1584-1591
(Chowan River)
CHAWANOAC
WEAPEMEOC
(ALBEMARLE SOUND)
ROANOKE
English Settlement
HATORASCK
ISLAND
MORATUC
Moratuc (Roanoke) River
DASAMONQUEPEUC
SECOTAN
AQUASEOGOC
(Pamlico River)
CROATOAN
(PAMLICO SOUND)
WOCOCON
(Neuse River)
ATLANTIC OCEAN
MILES
5
0
10
20
Drawn under the supervision of C. C. Crittenden

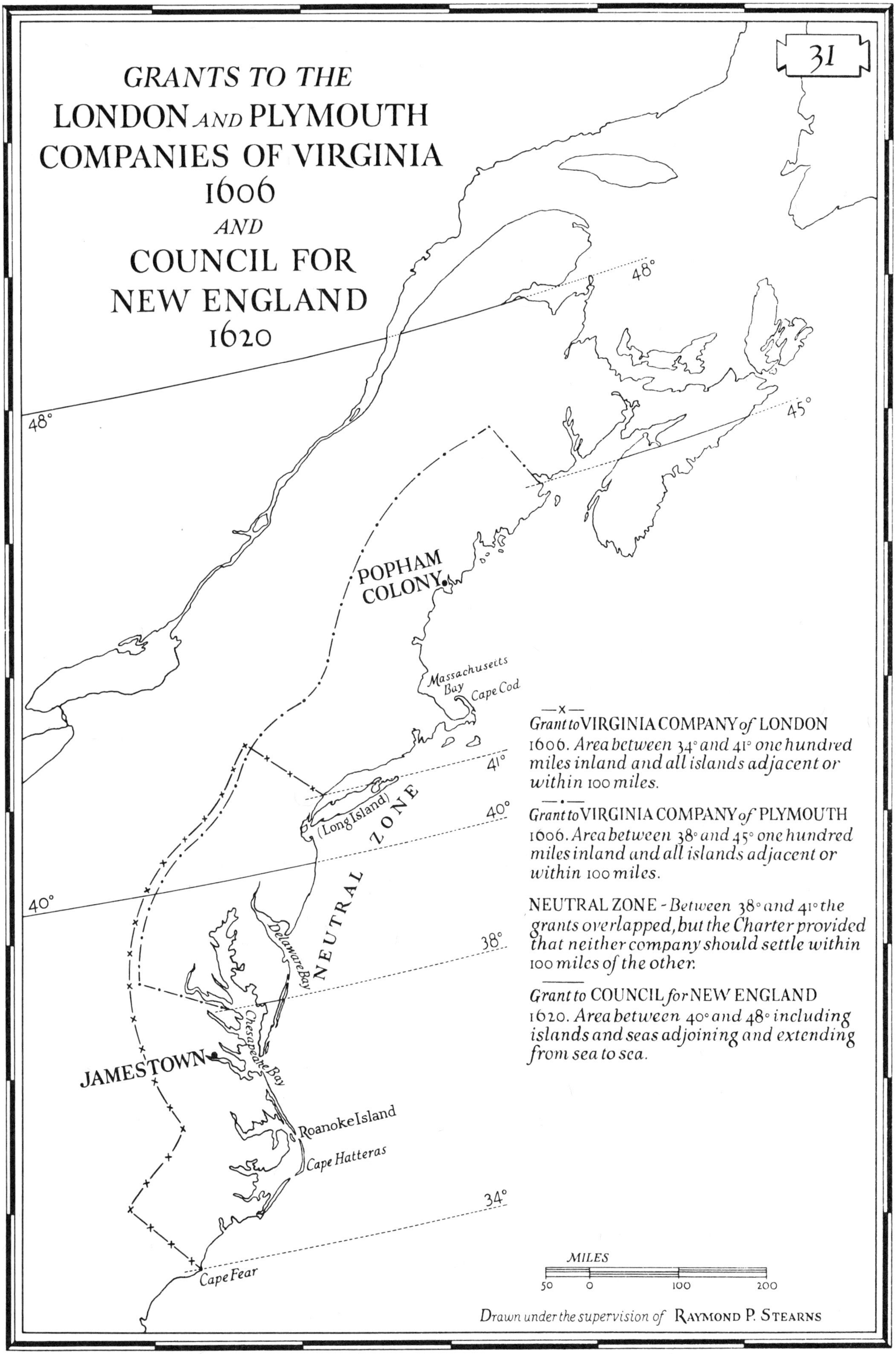
31
GRANTS TO THE
LONDON AND PLYMOUTH
COMPANIES OF VIRGINIA
1606
AND
COUNCIL FOR
NEW ENGLAND
1620
48°
48°
45°
POPHAM COLONY
Massachusetts Bay
Cape Cod
41°
40°
40°
(Long Island)
NEUTRAL ZONE
Delaware Bay
38°
Chesapeake Bay
JAMESTOWN
Roanoke Island
Cape Hatteras
34°
Cape Fear
—x— Grant to VIRGINIA COMPANY of LONDON 1606. Area between 34° and 41° one hundred miles inland and all islands adjacent or within 100 miles.
—·— Grant to VIRGINIA COMPANY of PLYMOUTH 1606. Area between 38° and 45° one hundred miles inland and all islands adjacent or within 100 miles.
NEUTRAL ZONE - Between 38° and 41° the grants overlapped, but the Charter provided that neither company should settle within 100 miles of the other.
—— Grant to COUNCIL for NEW ENGLAND 1620. Area between 40° and 48° including islands and seas adjoining and extending from sea to sea.
MILES
50 0 100 200
Drawn under the supervision of Raymond P. Stearns

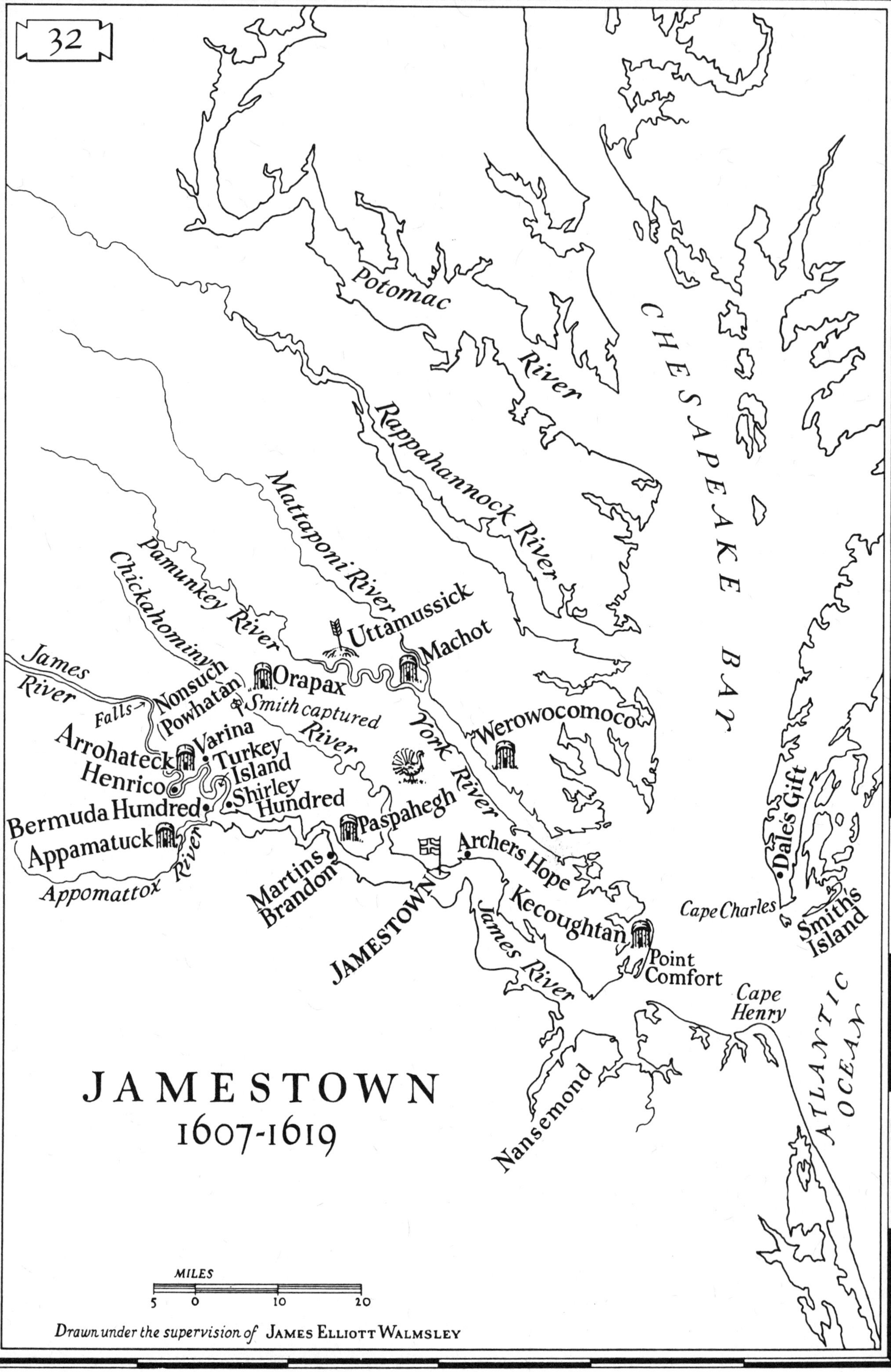

JAMESTOWN
1607-1619

Drawn under the supervision of James Elliott Walmsley

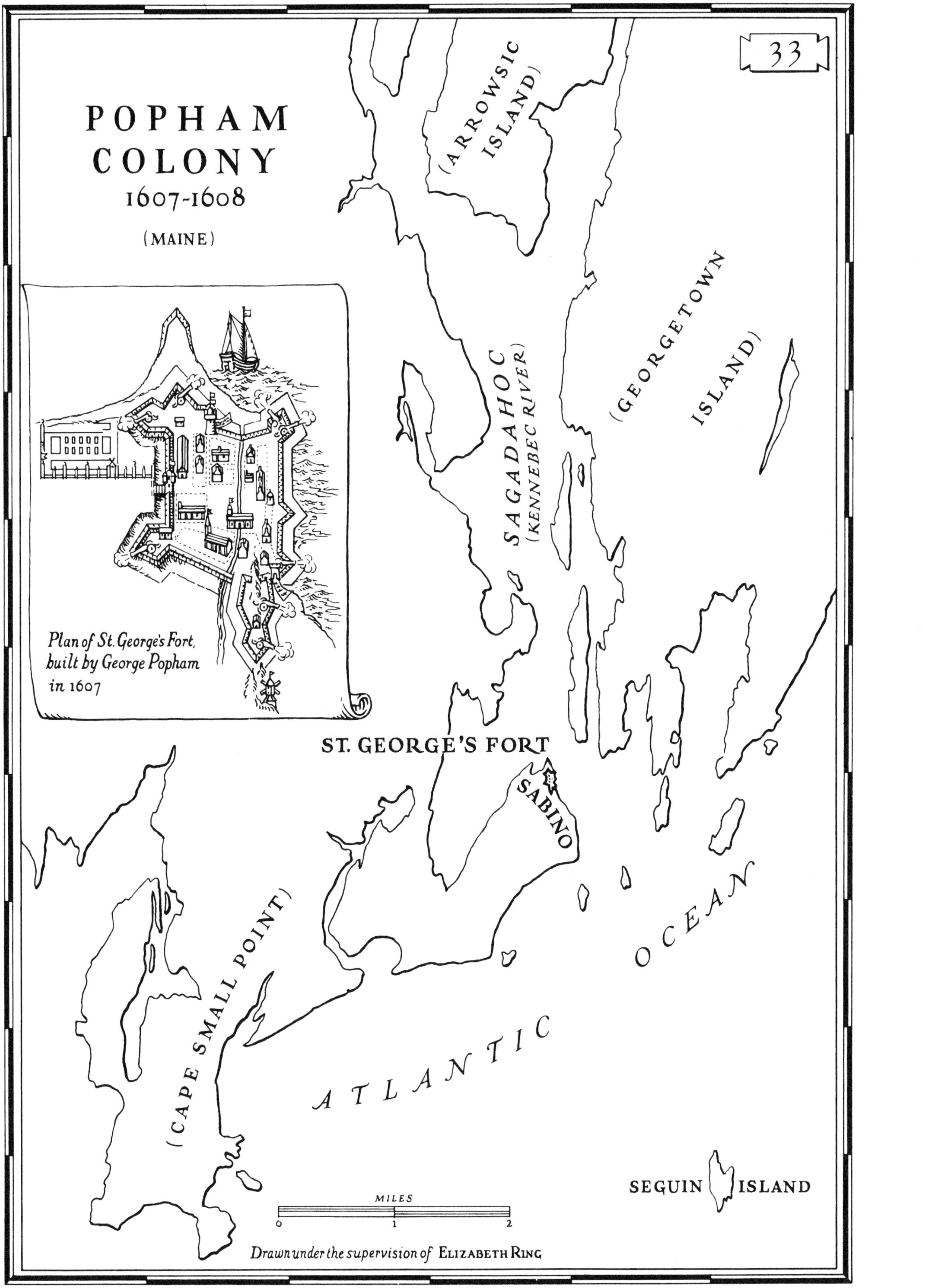
33
POPHAM
COLONY
1607-1608
(MAINE)
Plan of St. George's Fort, built by George Popham in 1607
(ARROWSIC ISLAND)
(GEORGETOWN ISLAND)
SAGADAHOC
(KENNEBEC RIVER)
ST. GEORGE'S FORT
SABINO
(CAPE SMALL POINT)
ATLANTIC OCEAN
SEGUIN ISLAND
MILES
0
1
2
Drawn under the supervision of ELIZABETH RING

PLYMOUTH PLANTATION
1620 – 1630
Cape Ann
Naumkeag (Salem)
MASSACHUSETTS BAY
Cohasset
Northern boundary claimed by Plymouth Plantation
Mount Wollaston
site of Merry Mount where Morton had his Maypole
Wessagusset
Weston's Settlement (1623)
Clark's Island
PLYMOUTH
The exploring party landed at Plymouth Harbor, Dec. 11, 1620 Mayflower came up, Dec. 16, Pilgrims landed, Dec. 18
Provincetown
First landfall of Mayflower, Nov. 11, 1620
Pamet River, (Truro Village) Expeditions by land, Nov. 15-17 by water, Nov. 27-30
CAPE COD BAY
(Eastham)
First encounter with Indians Dec. 8
Route of shallop and exploring party Third expedition, Dec. 6
Namassakett
Wampanoag Village
Manonscussett
Manomet
CAPE COD
Manamoiak
Nauset Indian Village
(BUZZARD'S BAY)
NANTUCKET SOUND
Cuttyhunk
CAPAWACK
(Martha's Vineyard)
NANTUCKET
Dates as indicated on this map are Old Style. Ten days must be added to bring the dates into conformity with the New Style, or present-day, dating
MILES
5
0
10
20
Drawn under the supervision of Raymond P. Stearns

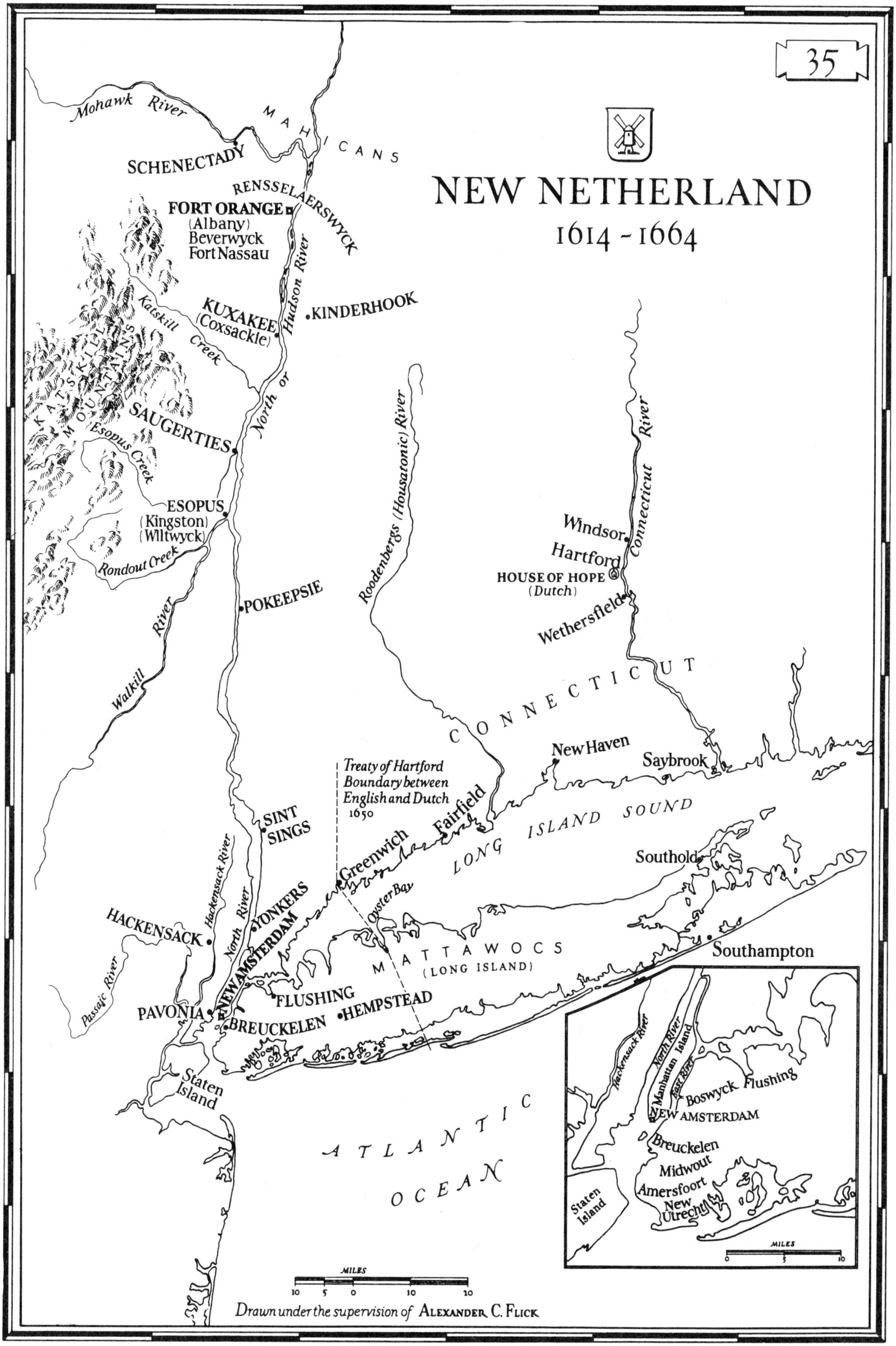
35
NEW NETHERLAND
1614-1664
Mohawk River
MAHICANS
SCHENECTADY
RENSSELAERSWYCK
FORT ORANGE
(Albany)
Beverwyck
Fort Nassau
Hudson River
KINDERHOOK
KUXAKEE
(Coxsackie)
Katskill Creek
KATSKILL MOUNTAINS
North or
SAUGERTIES
Esopus Creek
ESOPUS
(Kingston)
(Wiltwyck)
Rondout Creek
POKEEPSIE
Walkill River
Roodenbergs (Housatonic) River
Connecticut River
Windsor
Hartford
HOUSE OF HOPE
(Dutch)
Wethersfield
CONNECTICUT
New Haven
Saybrook
Treaty of Hartford
Boundary between
English and Dutch
1650
Fairfield
SINT
SINGS
LONG ISLAND SOUND
Greenwich
Southold
Oyster Bay
Hackensack River
HACKENSACK
North River
YONKERS
NEW AMSTERDAM
MATTAWOCS
(LONG ISLAND)
Southampton
Passaic River
PAVONIA
FLUSHING
HEMPSTEAD
BREUCKELEN
Staten
Island
ATLANTIC
OCEAN
MILES
10 5 0 10 20
Hackensack River
North River
Manhattan Island
East River
Boswyck
Flushing
NEW AMSTERDAM
Breuckelen
Midwout
Amersfoort
New
Utrecht
Staten
Island
MILES
0 5 10
Drawn under the supervision of ALEXANDER C. FLICK

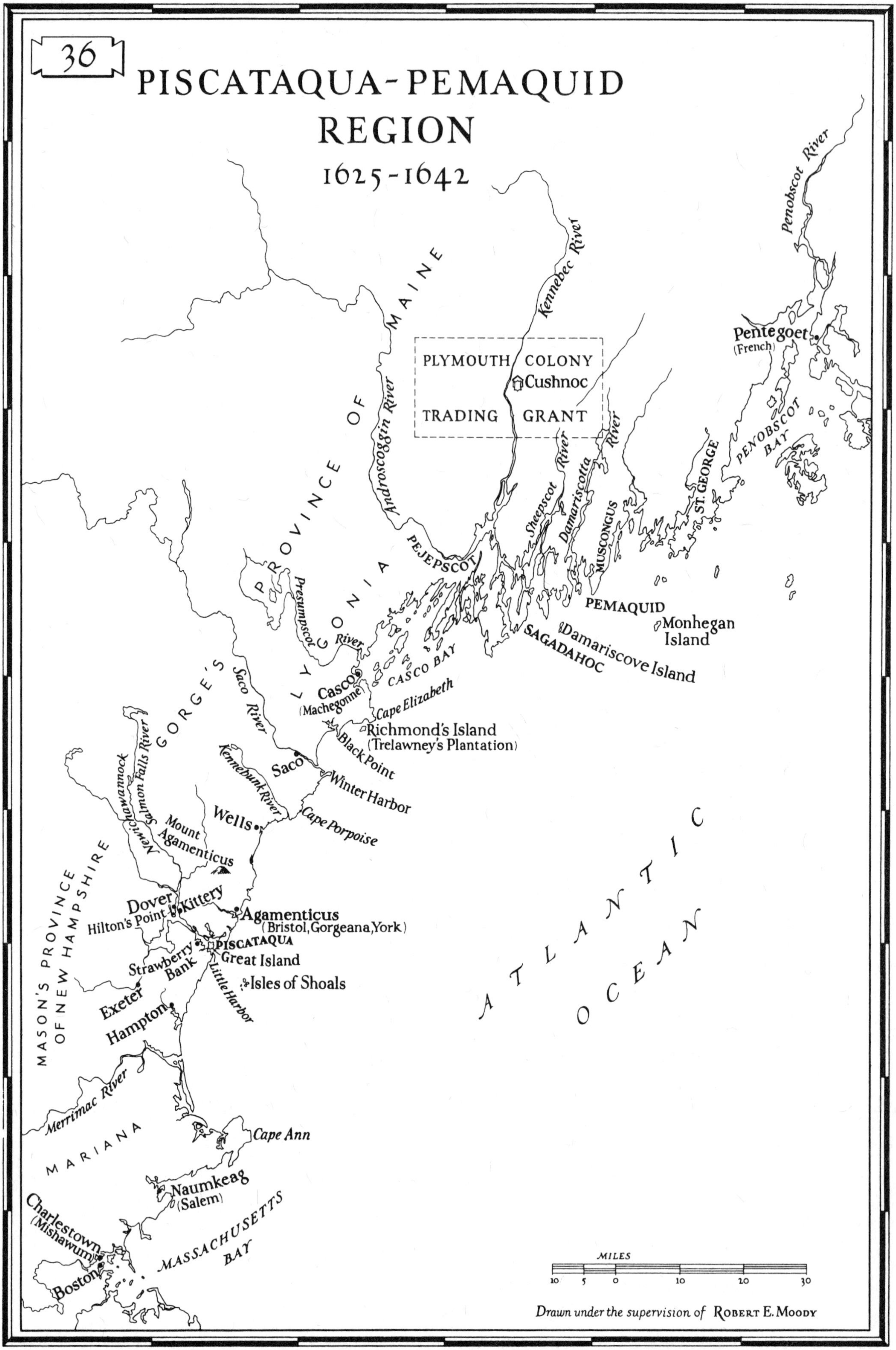
36
PISCATAQUA-PEMAQUID REGION
1625-1642
PROVINCE OF MAINE
Penobscot River
Kennebec River
Pentegoet
(French)
PLYMOUTH COLONY
Cushnoc
TRADING GRANT
Androscoggin River
PENOBSCOT BAY
ST. GEORGE
MUSCONGUS
River
Sheepscot River
Damariscotta River
PEJEPSCOT
PEMAQUID
Monhegan Island
Damariscove Island
SAGADAHOC
LYGONIA
Presumpscot River
CASCO BAY
Casco
(Machegonne)
Cape Elizabeth
Richmond's Island
(Trelawney's Plantation)
Black Point
GORGE'S
Saco River
Saco
Winter Harbor
Kennebunk River
Wells
Cape Porpoise
Newichawannock
Salmon Falls River
Mount Agamenticus
Dover
Hilton's Point
Kittery
Agamenticus
(Bristol, Gorgeana, York)
PISCATAQUA
Strawberry Bank
Great Island
Little Harbor
Isles of Shoals
Exeter
Hampton
MASON'S PROVINCE OF NEW HAMPSHIRE
ATLANTIC OCEAN
Merrimac River
MARIANA
Cape Ann
Naumkeag
(Salem)
Charlestown
(Mishawum)
Boston
MASSACHUSETTS BAY
MILES
10 5 0 10 20 30
Drawn under the supervision of Robert E. Moody

MASSACHUSETTS BAY 1630-1642

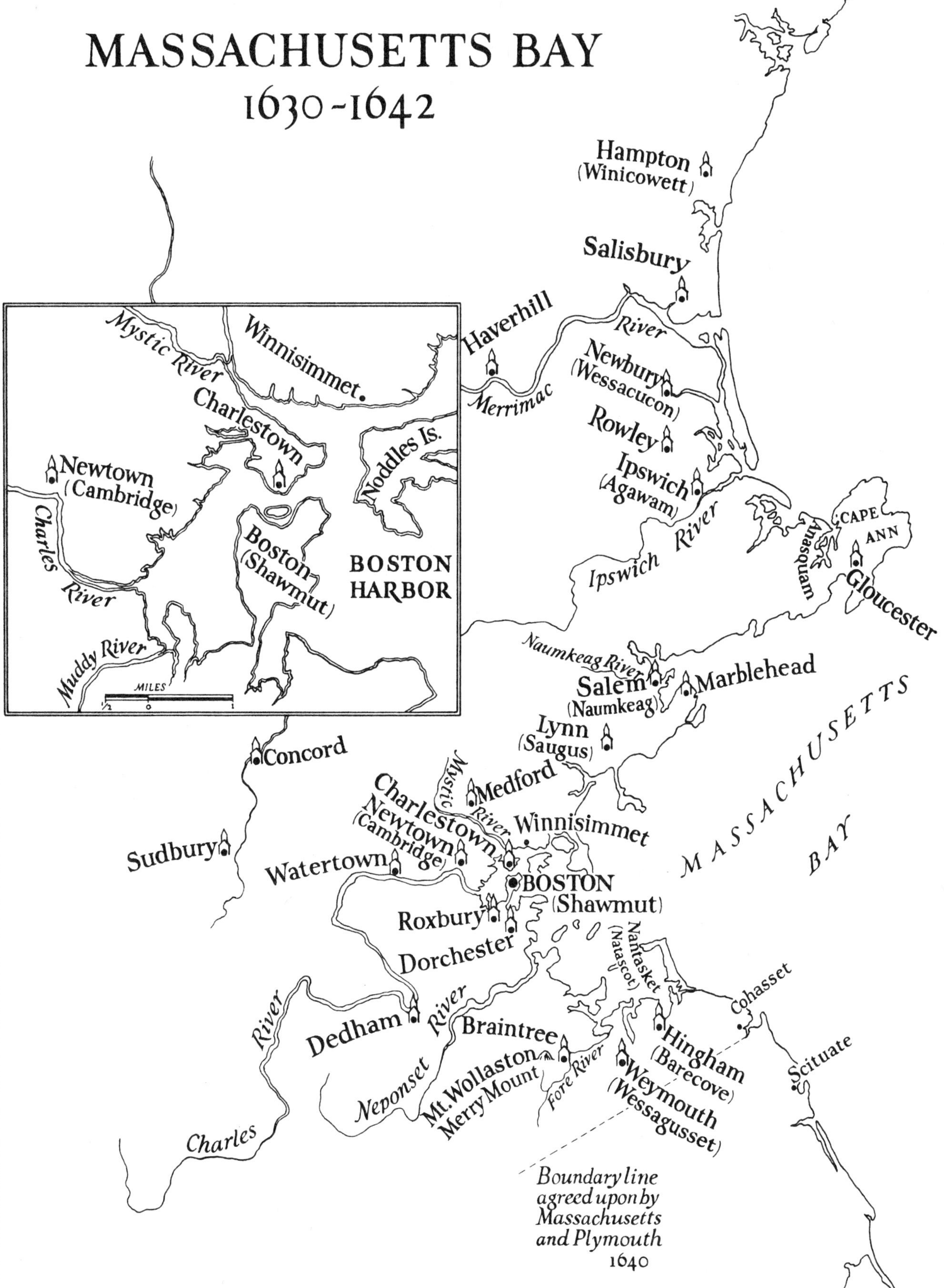

Drawn under the supervision of ROBERT E. MOODY

38

CONNECTICUT AND NEW HAVEN COLONIES
1635–1660

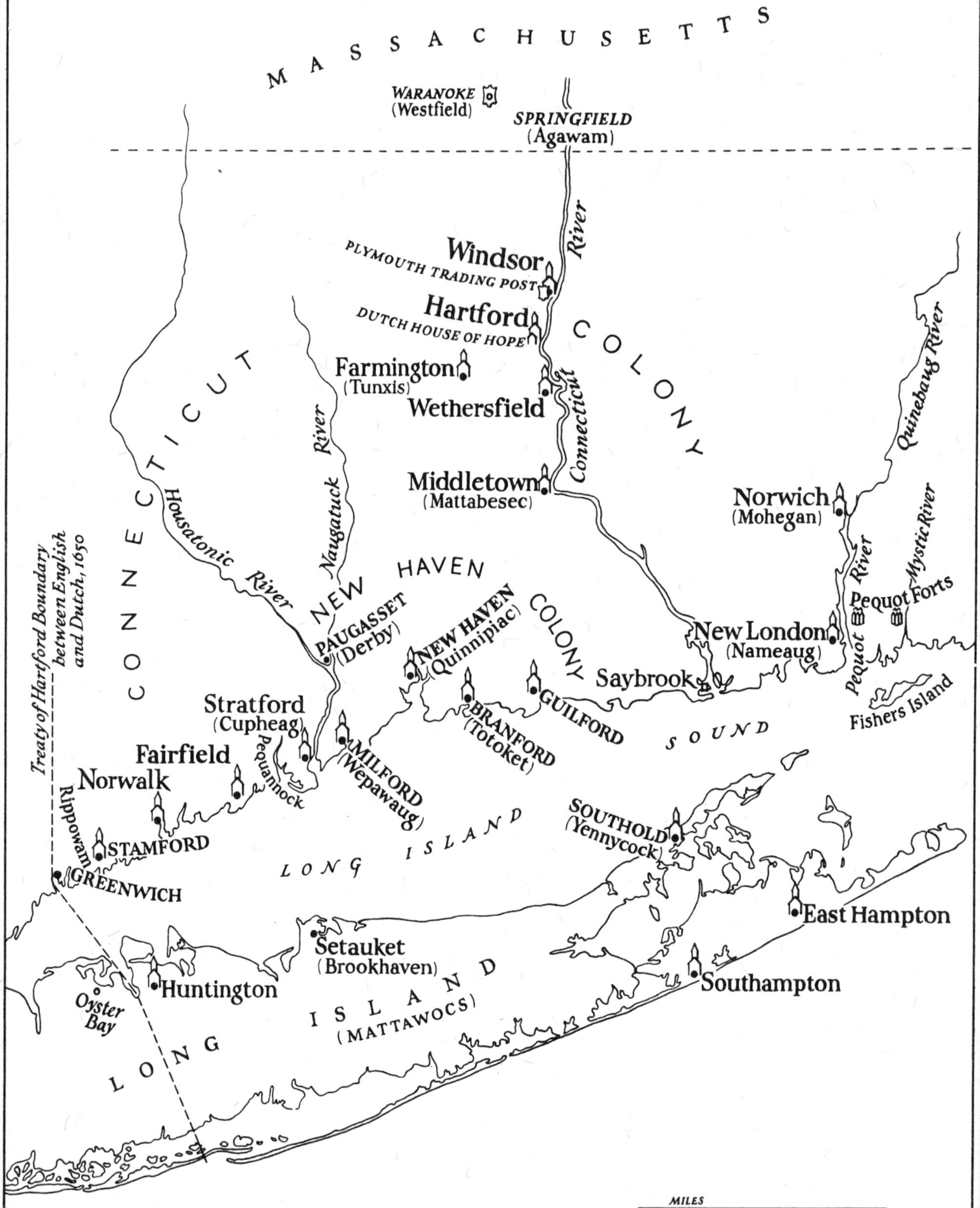

Connecticut Colony Towns thus - Windsor
New Haven Colony Towns thus - MILFORD

Drawn under the supervision of MARJORIE E. CASE

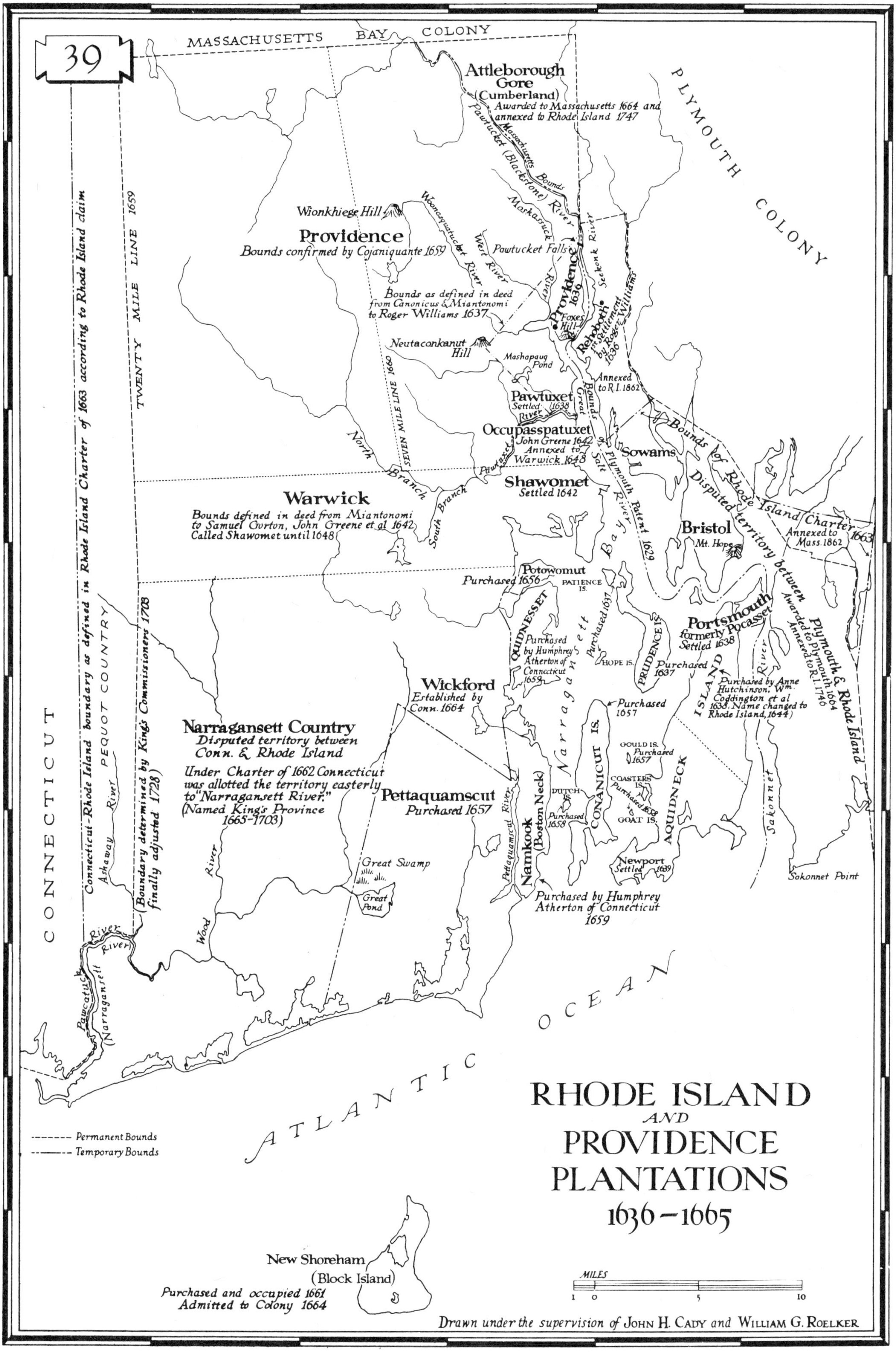
39
MASSACHUSETTS BAY COLONY
PLYMOUTH COLONY
CONNECTICUT
Attleborough Gore (Cumberland)
Awarded to Massachusetts 1664 and annexed to Rhode Island 1747
Pawtucket (Blackstone) River
Massachusetts Bounds
Moshassuck River
Wionkhiege Hill
Providence
Bounds confirmed by Cojaniquante 1659
Woonasquatucket River
West River
Pawtucket Falls
Seekonk River
Providence 1636
Bounds as defined in deed from Canonicus & Miantonomi to Roger Williams 1637
Foxes Hill
Rehoboth
1st Settlement by Roger Williams 1636
Neutaconkanut Hill
Mashapaug Pond
Annexed to R.I. 1862
Pawtuxet
Settled 1638
River
Great Bounds
Occupasspatuxet
John Greene 1642
Annexed to Warwick 1648
Sowams
Bounds of Rhode Island Charter 1663
Disputed territory between Plymouth & Rhode Island
Awarded to Plymouth 1664
Annexed to R.I. 1746
North Branch
SEVEN MILE LINE 1660
TWENTY MILE LINE 1659
Pawtuxet
Shawomet
Settled 1642
Warwick
Bounds defined in deed from Miantonomi to Samuel Gorton, John Greene et al 1642
Called Shawomet until 1648
South Branch
Salt River
Plymouth Patent 1629
Bristol
Mt. Hope
Annexed to Mass. 1862
Potowomut
Purchased 1656
PATIENCE IS.
Purchased 1637
QUIDNESSET
Purchased by Humphrey Atherton of Connecticut 1659
Narragansett Bay
HOPE IS.
PRUDENCE IS.
Purchased 1637
Portsmouth
formerly Pocasset
Settled 1638
RHODE ISLAND
Purchased by Anne Hutchinson, Wm. Coddington et al 1638. Name changed to Rhode Island, 1644
River
Connecticut-Rhode Island boundary as defined in Rhode Island Charter of 1663 according to Rhode Island claim
PEQUOT COUNTRY
Boundary determined by King's Commissioners 1703 finally adjusted 1728
Wickford
Established by Conn. 1664
Purchased 1657
Narragansett Country
Disputed territory between Conn. & Rhode Island
Under Charter of 1662 Connecticut was allotted the territory easterly to "Narragansett River."
(Named King's Province 1665-1703)
Pettaquamscut
Purchased 1657
Pettaquamscut River
CONANICUT IS.
GOULD IS.
Purchased 1657
COASTERS IS.
Purchased 1658
GOAT IS.
DUTCH IS.
Purchased 1658
AQUIDNECK
Sakonnet
Sakonnet Point
Namkook (Boston Neck)
Newport
Settled 1639
Purchased by Humphrey Atherton of Connecticut 1659
Ashaway River
Wood River
Great Swamp
Great Pond
Wood
River
River
Pawcatuck
(Narragansett River)
ATLANTIC OCEAN
Permanent Bounds
Temporary Bounds
RHODE ISLAND AND PROVIDENCE PLANTATIONS 1636–1665
New Shoreham (Block Island)
Purchased and occupied 1661
Admitted to Colony 1664
MILES
1 0 5 10
Drawn under the supervision of JOHN H. CADY and WILLIAM G. ROELKER

40

MARYLAND AND THE CHESAPEAKE REGION 1634–1660

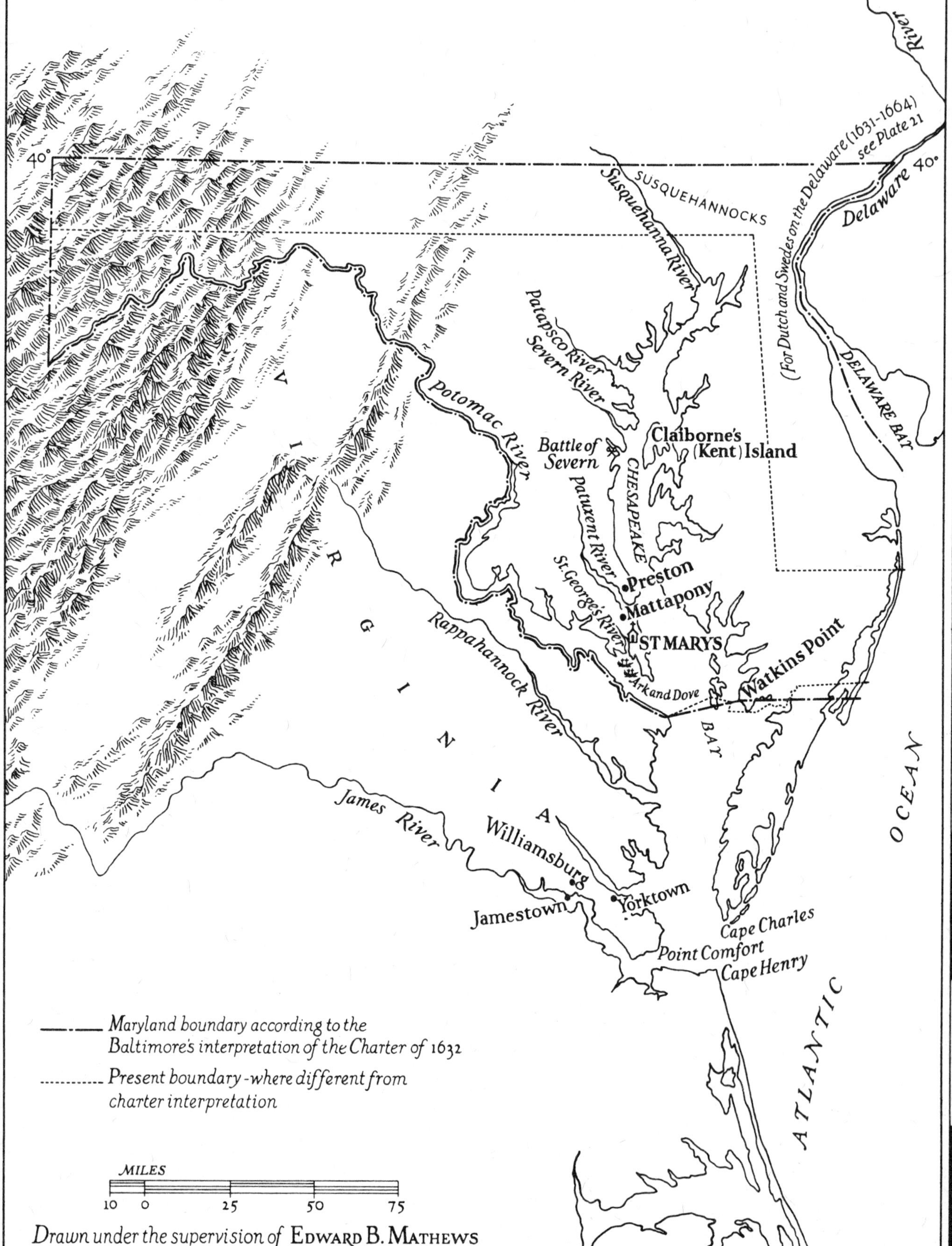

Drawn under the supervision of EDWARD B. MATHEWS

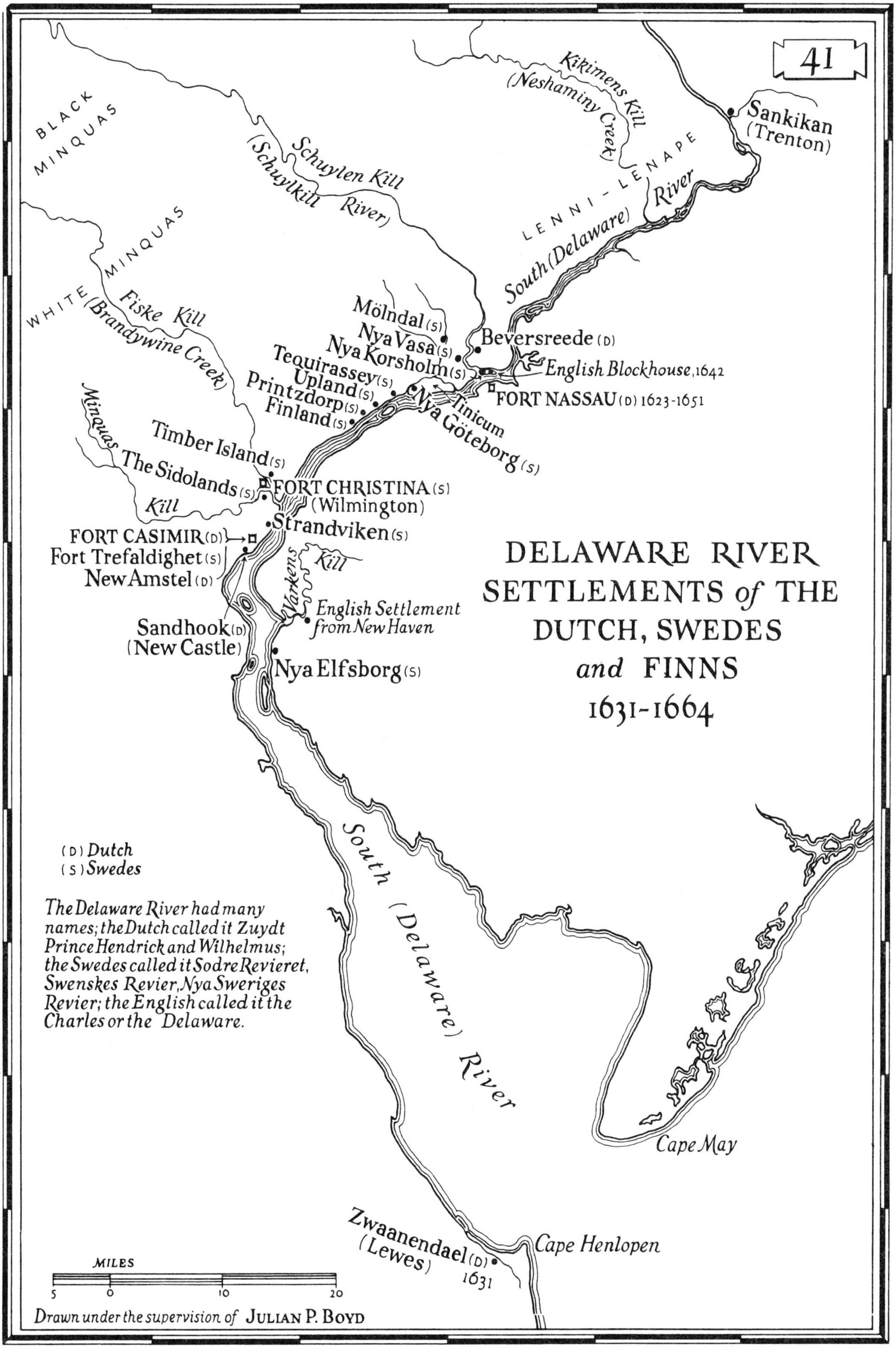
41
DELAWARE RIVER SETTLEMENTS of THE DUTCH, SWEDES and FINNS 1631-1664
BLACK MINQUAS
WHITE MINQUAS
LENNI-LENAPE
Schuylen Kill
(Schuylkill River)
Kikimens Kill
(Neshaminy Creek)
Sankikan
(Trenton)
South (Delaware) River
Fiske Kill
(Brandywine Creek)
Minquas Kill
Mölndal (S)
Nya Vasa (S)
Nya Korsholm (S)
Tequirassey (S)
Upland (S)
Printzdorp (S)
Finland (S)
Beversreede (D)
English Blockhouse, 1642
FORT NASSAU (D) 1623-1651
Tinicum
Nya Göteborg (S)
Timber Island (S)
The Sidolands (S)
FORT CHRISTINA (S)
(Wilmington)
Strandviken (S)
FORT CASIMIR (D)
Fort Trefaldighet (S)
New Amstel (D)
Varkens Kill
English Settlement from New Haven
Sandhook (D)
(New Castle)
Nya Elfsborg (S)
South (Delaware) River
(D) Dutch
(S) Swedes
The Delaware River had many names; the Dutch called it Zuydt Prince Hendrick and Wilhelmus; the Swedes called it Sodre Revieret, Swenskes Revier, Nya Sweriges Revier; the English called it the Charles or the Delaware.
Cape May
Cape Henlopen
Zwaanendael (D)
(Lewes)
1631
MILES
5 0 10 20
Drawn under the supervision of JULIAN P. BOYD

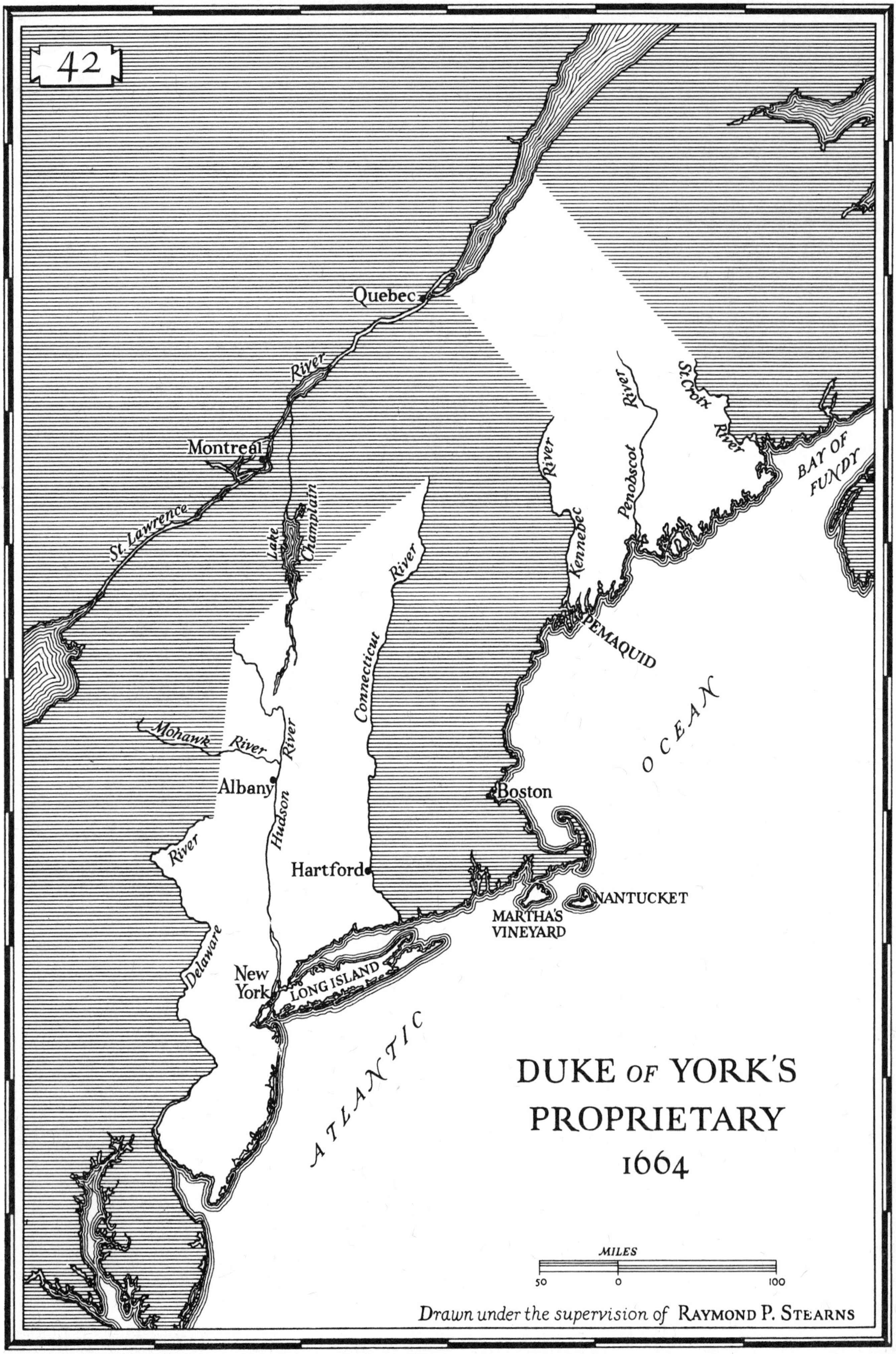
42
Quebec
St. Lawrence
River
Montreal
Lake
Champlain
Mohawk
River
Albany
Hudson
River
Connecticut
River
Hartford
River
Delaware
New
York
LONG ISLAND
River
Kennebec
River
Penobscot
St. Croix
River
BAY OF
FUNDY
PEMAQUID
Boston
MARTHA'S
VINEYARD
NANTUCKET
ATLANTIC
OCEAN
DUKE OF YORK'S
PROPRIETARY
1664
MILES
50
0
100
Drawn under the supervision of RAYMOND P. STEARNS

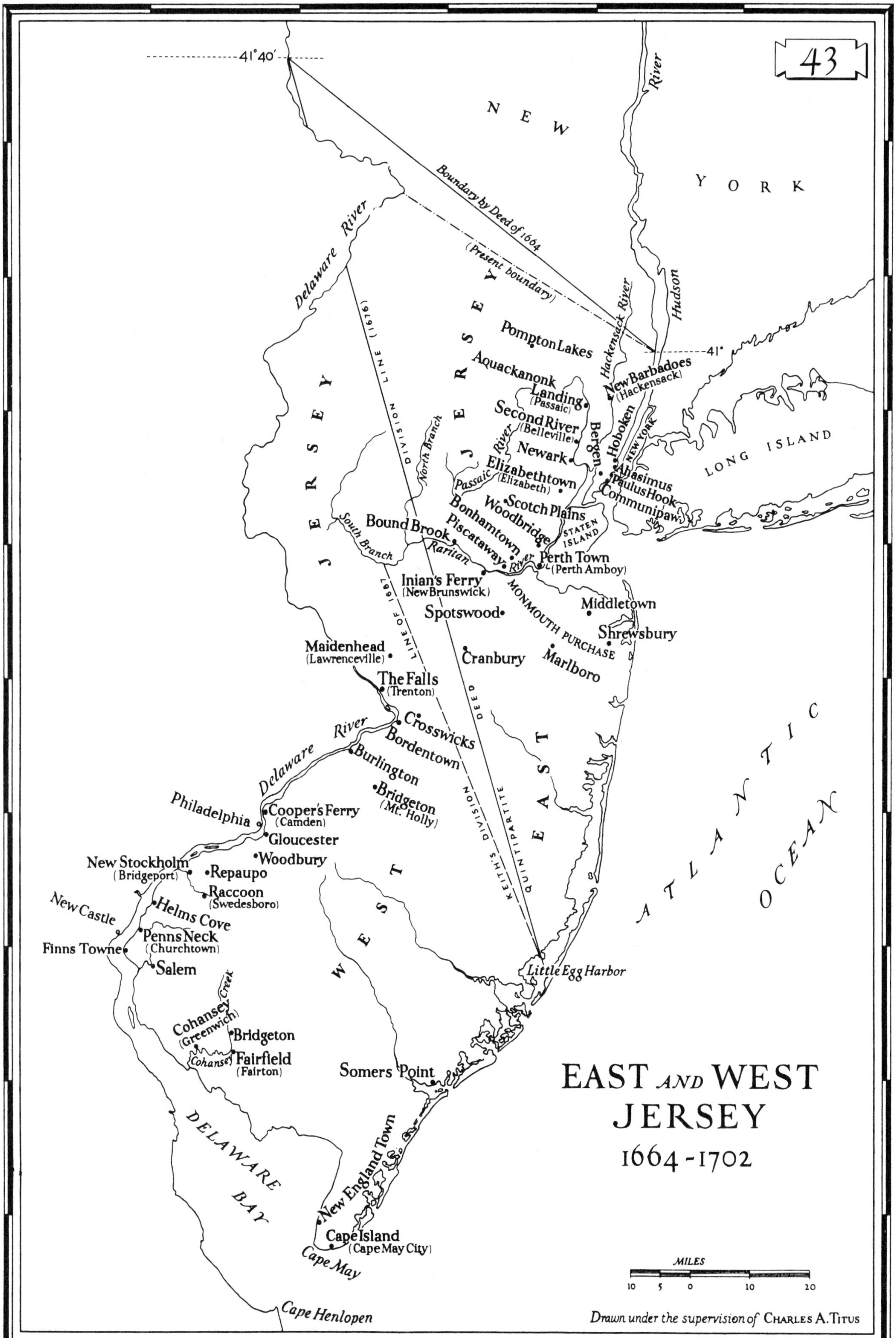

EAST AND WEST JERSEY 1664-1702

44
CAROLINAS
AND VIRGINIA
1663-1729
WEST JERSEY
Cape May
LOWER COUNTIES OF DELAWARE
MARYLAND
Potomac River
FAIRFAX PROPRIETARY (Northern Neck)
Western boundary of the Fairfax Proprietary
Germanna
Rappahannock River
Route of Spotswood's Expedition
Shenandoah
WILLIAMSBURG
James River
Fort Henry
Yorktown
Norfolk
Northern Boundary of Carolina under Charter of 1665
36° 30'
Currituck
Northern Boundary of Carolina under Charter of 1663
36°
VIRGINIA
Roanoke River
Chowan River
ALBEMARLE
Edenton
35° 34'
(GRANVILLE GRANT)
NORTH CAROLINA
Neuse River
Fort Nohoroco
Pamlico Sound
New Berne
TUSCARORA
Cape Fear River
CLARENDON
Brunswick
Cape Fear
CHEROKEE
CATAWBA
Broad River
Wateree River
Saluda River
Peedee River
SOUTH CAROLINA
Santee River
Jamestown
ST. JOHN'S BERKELEY
Cooper R.
The Orange Quarter
Ashley R.
Edisto River
CHARLESTON
Savannah River
YAMASEE
Ogeechee River
Beaufort
Stuart's Town
Port Royal
CREEK
Oconee River
Ocmulgee River
Altamaha River
Coweta Town
Savacola (Spanish)
Chattahoochee River
Flint River
Fort King George
Southern Boundary of Carolina under Charter of 1663
31°
St. Marys River
Santa Cruz de Savacola (Spanish)
AYUBALE
San Luis (Spanish)
Apalachicola River
Ochlockonee River
APALACHE
St. Johns River
St. Augustine (Spanish)
Southern Boundary of Carolina under Charter of 1665
29°
MILES
25 0 50 100
Drawn under the supervision of E. Merton Coulter

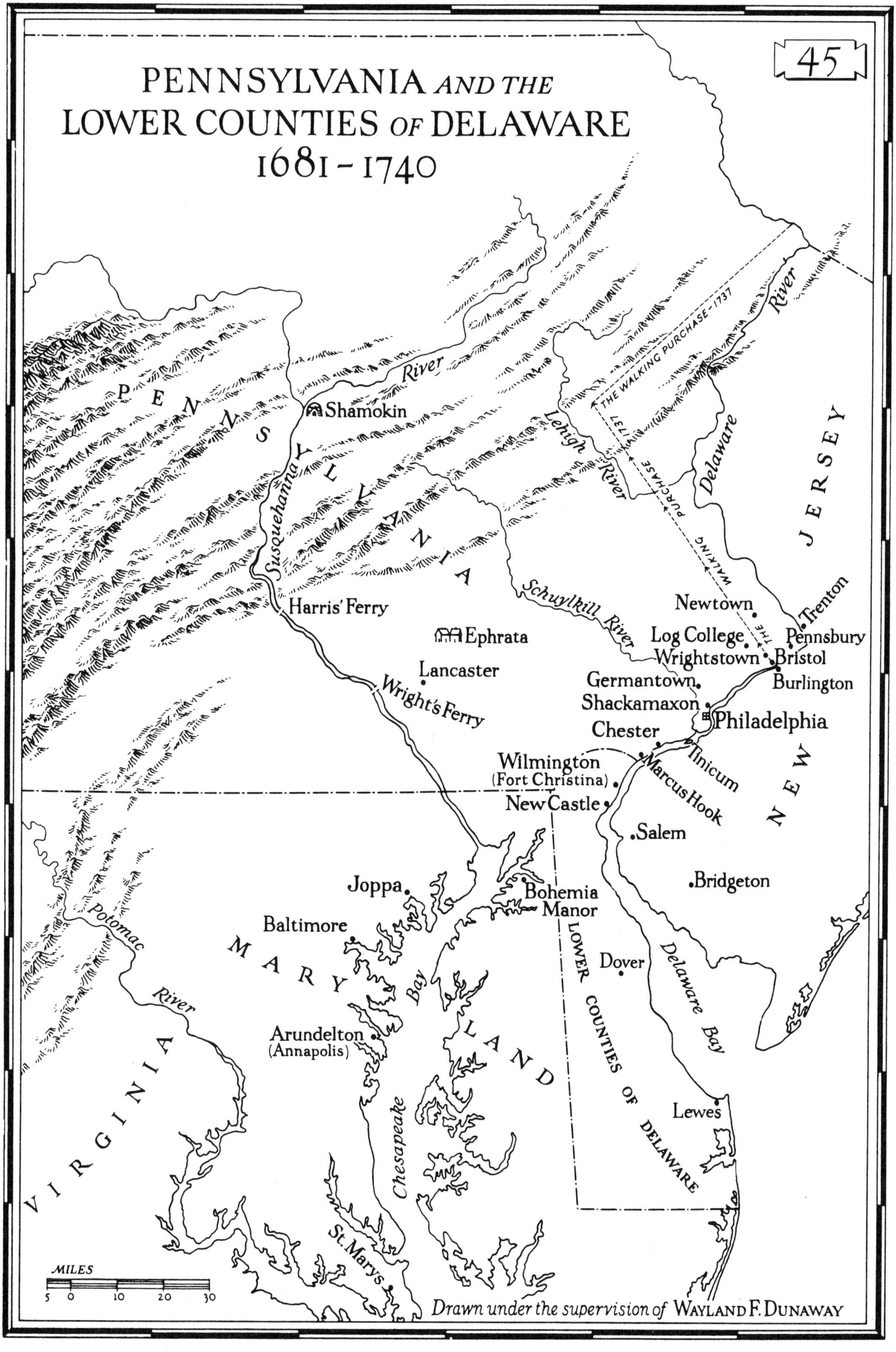
45
PENNSYLVANIA AND THE LOWER COUNTIES OF DELAWARE 1681 - 1740
PENNSYLVANIA
River
Shamokin
Susquehanna
Lehigh
River
THE WALKING PURCHASE - 1737
THE WALKING PURCHASE 1737
Delaware
River
NEW JERSEY
Schuylkill River
Harris' Ferry
Ephrata
Lancaster
Wright's Ferry
Newtown
Log College
Wrightstown
Trenton
Pennsbury
Bristol
Burlington
Germantown
Shackamaxon
Philadelphia
Chester
Tinicum
Wilmington
(Fort Christina)
Marcus Hook
New Castle
Salem
Bridgeton
Joppa
Bohemia
Manor
Baltimore
MARYLAND
Bay
Potomac
River
Dover
LOWER COUNTIES OF DELAWARE
Delaware Bay
Arundelton
(Annapolis)
Chesapeake
Lewes
VIRGINIA
St. Marys
MILES
5 0 10 20 30
Drawn under the supervision of WAYLAND F. DUNAWAY

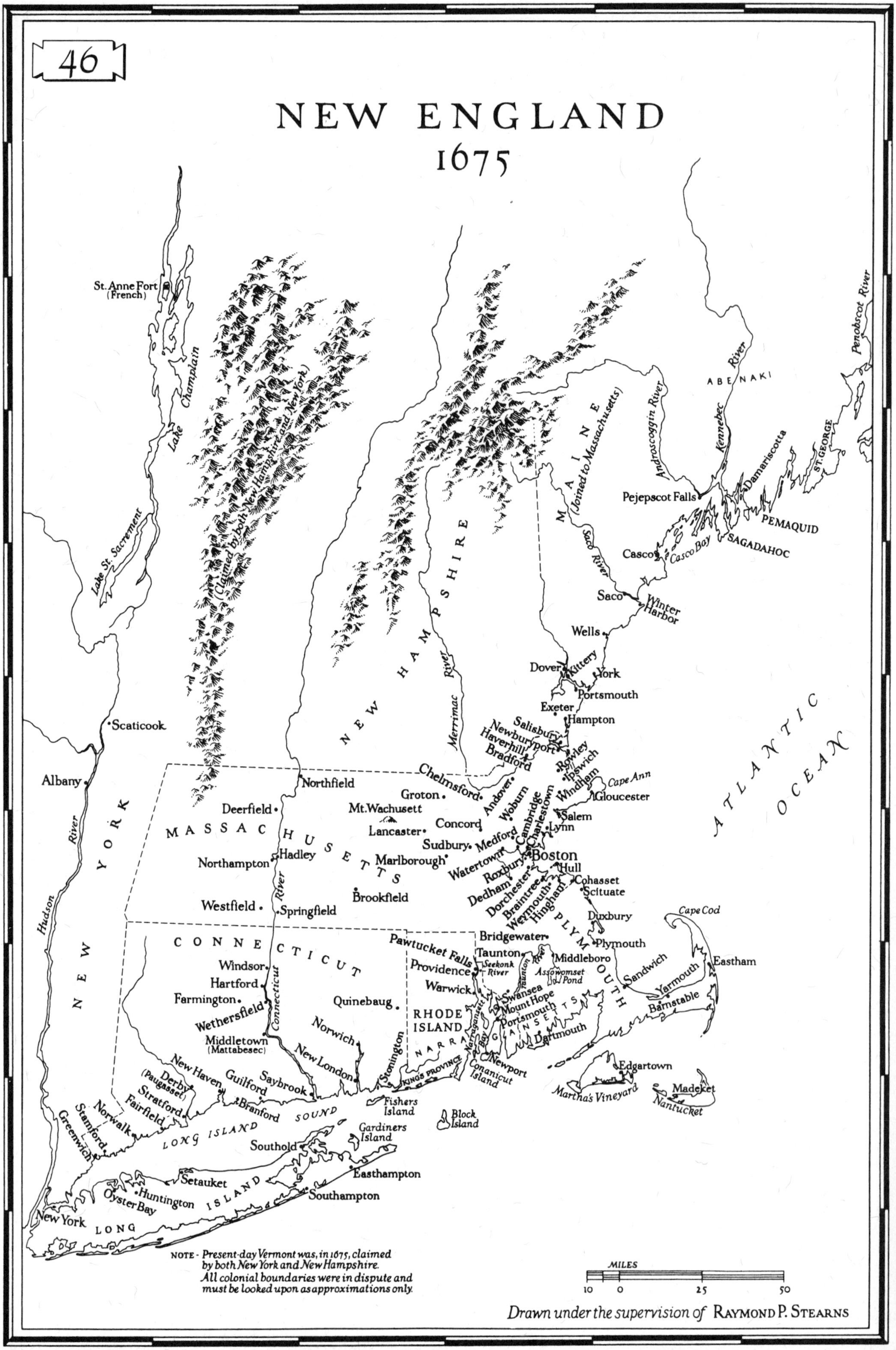
46
NEW ENGLAND
1675
St. Anne Fort (French)
Lake Champlain
Lake St. Sacrement
(Claimed by both New Hampshire and New York)
Scaticook
Albany
Hudson River
NEW YORK
MASSACHUSETTS
CONNECTICUT
RHODE ISLAND
NEW HAMPSHIRE
MAINE (Joined to Massachusetts)
PLYMOUTH
NARRAGANSETTS
KINGS PROVINCE
ABENAKI
PEMAQUID
SAGADAHOC
ATLANTIC OCEAN
Penobscot River
ST. GEORGE
Damariscotta
Kennebec River
Androscoggin River
Pejepscot Falls
Casco
Casco Bay
Saco River
Saco
Winter Harbor
Wells
Dover
Kittery
York
Portsmouth
Exeter
Hampton
Merrimac River
Salisbury
Newburyport
Haverhill
Bradford
Rowley
Ipswich
Wenham
Cape Ann
Gloucester
Salem
Lynn
Chelmsford
Andover
Woburn
Cambridge
Charlestown
Medford
Groton
Concord
Mt. Wachusett
Lancaster
Sudbury
Watertown
Marlborough
Roxbury
Boston
Hull
Dedham
Dorchester
Braintree
Weymouth
Hingham
Cohasset
Scituate
Duxbury
Northfield
Deerfield
Hadley
Northampton
Westfield
Springfield
Brookfield
Connecticut River
Bridgewater
Plymouth
Cape Cod
Eastham
Pawtucket Falls
Taunton
Middleboro
Providence
Seekonk River
Taunton River
Assowomset Pond
Warwick
Swansea
Mount Hope
Portsmouth
Sandwich
Yarmouth
Barnstable
Narragansett Bay
Dartmouth
Newport
Conanicut Island
Edgartown
Martha's Vineyard
Madeket
Nantucket
Windsor
Hartford
Farmington
Wethersfield
Quinebaug
Middletown (Mattabesec)
Norwich
New London
Stonington
Saybrook
Guilford
New Haven
Derby (Paugasset)
Branford
Stratford
Fairfield
Norwalk
Stamford
Greenwich
Fishers Island
Block Island
Gardiners Island
LONG ISLAND SOUND
Southold
Easthampton
Southampton
Setauket
Huntington
Oyster Bay
New York
LONG ISLAND
NOTE - Present-day Vermont was, in 1675, claimed by both New York and New Hampshire. All colonial boundaries were in dispute and must be looked upon as approximations only.
MILES
10 0 25 50
Drawn under the supervision of RAYMOND P. STEARNS

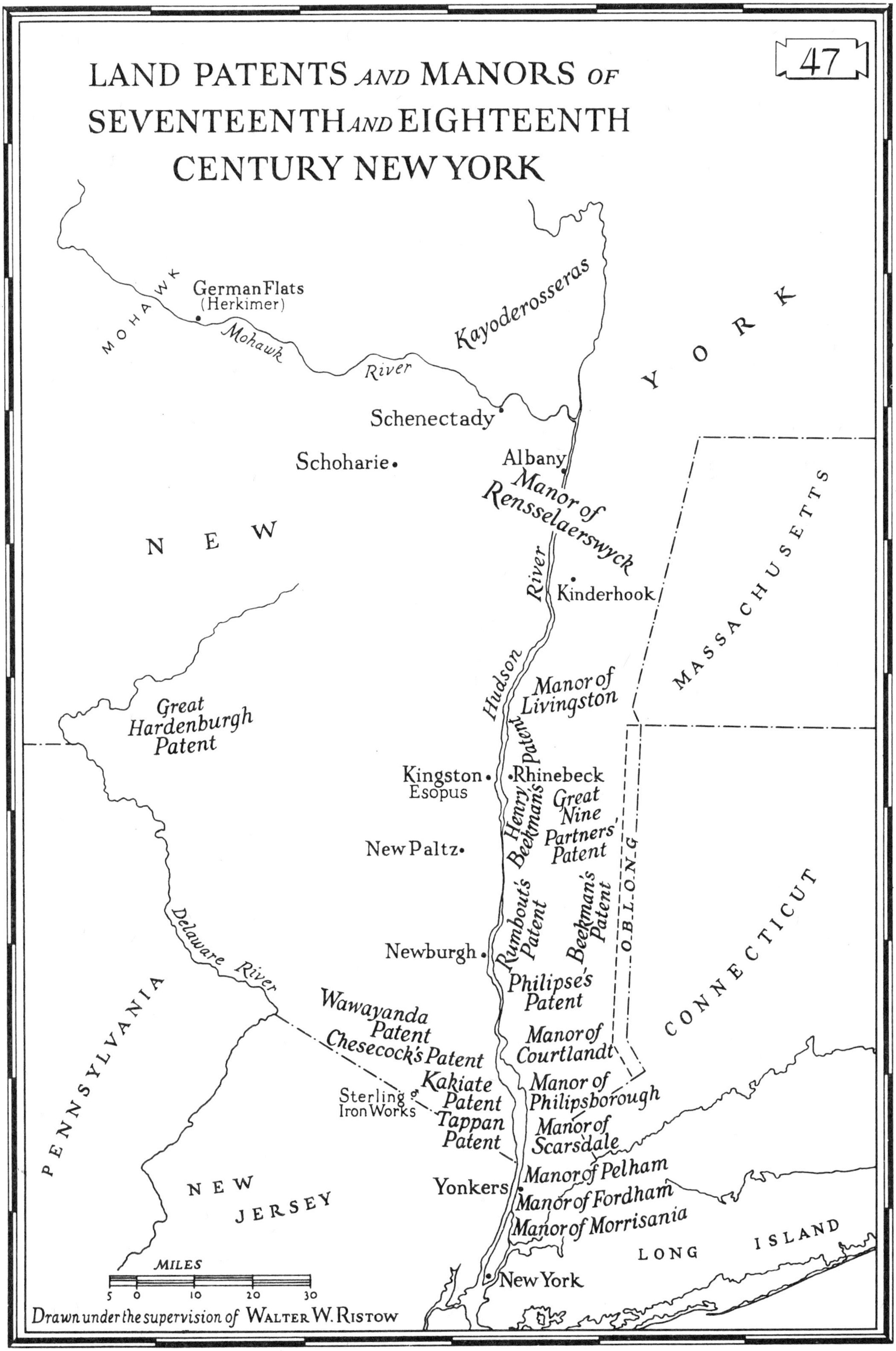

47
LAND PATENTS AND MANORS OF SEVENTEENTH AND EIGHTEENTH CENTURY NEW YORK
German Flats
(Herkimer)
MOHAWK
Mohawk River
Kayoderosseras
NEW YORK
Schenectady
Schoharie
Albany
Manor of Rensselaerswyck
Hudson River
Kinderhook
MASSACHUSETTS
Manor of Livingston
Great Hardenburgh Patent
Kingston
Esopus
Rhinebeck
Henry Beekman's Patent
Great Nine Partners' Patent
New Paltz
OBLONG
Rumbout's Patent
Beekman's Patent
CONNECTICUT
Newburgh
Philipse's Patent
Delaware River
PENNSYLVANIA
Wawayanda Patent
Chesecock's Patent
Manor of Courtlandt
Kakiate Patent
Sterling Iron Works
Manor of Philipsborough
Tappan Patent
Manor of Scarsdale
Manor of Pelham
Yonkers
Manor of Fordham
Manor of Morrisania
NEW JERSEY
LONG ISLAND
New York
MILES
5 0 10 20 30
Drawn under the supervision of WALTER W. RISTOW

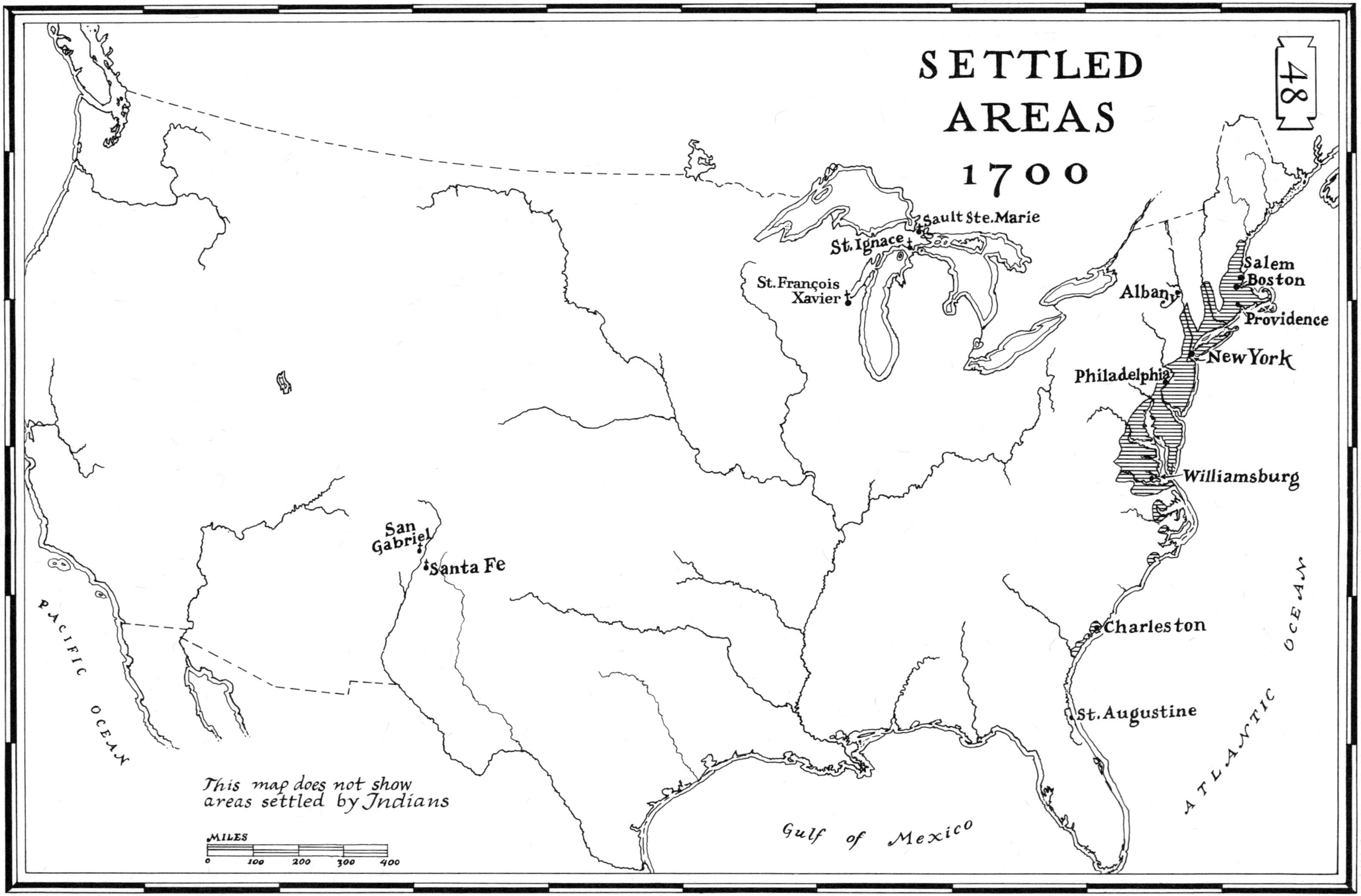
48
SETTLED
AREAS
1700
Sault Ste. Marie
St. Ignace
St. François
Xavier
Albany
Salem
Boston
Providence
New York
Philadelphia
Williamsburg
Charleston
St. Augustine
San
Gabriel
Santa Fe
PACIFIC OCEAN
ATLANTIC OCEAN
Gulf of Mexico
This map does not show
areas settled by Indians
MILES
0
100
200
300
400

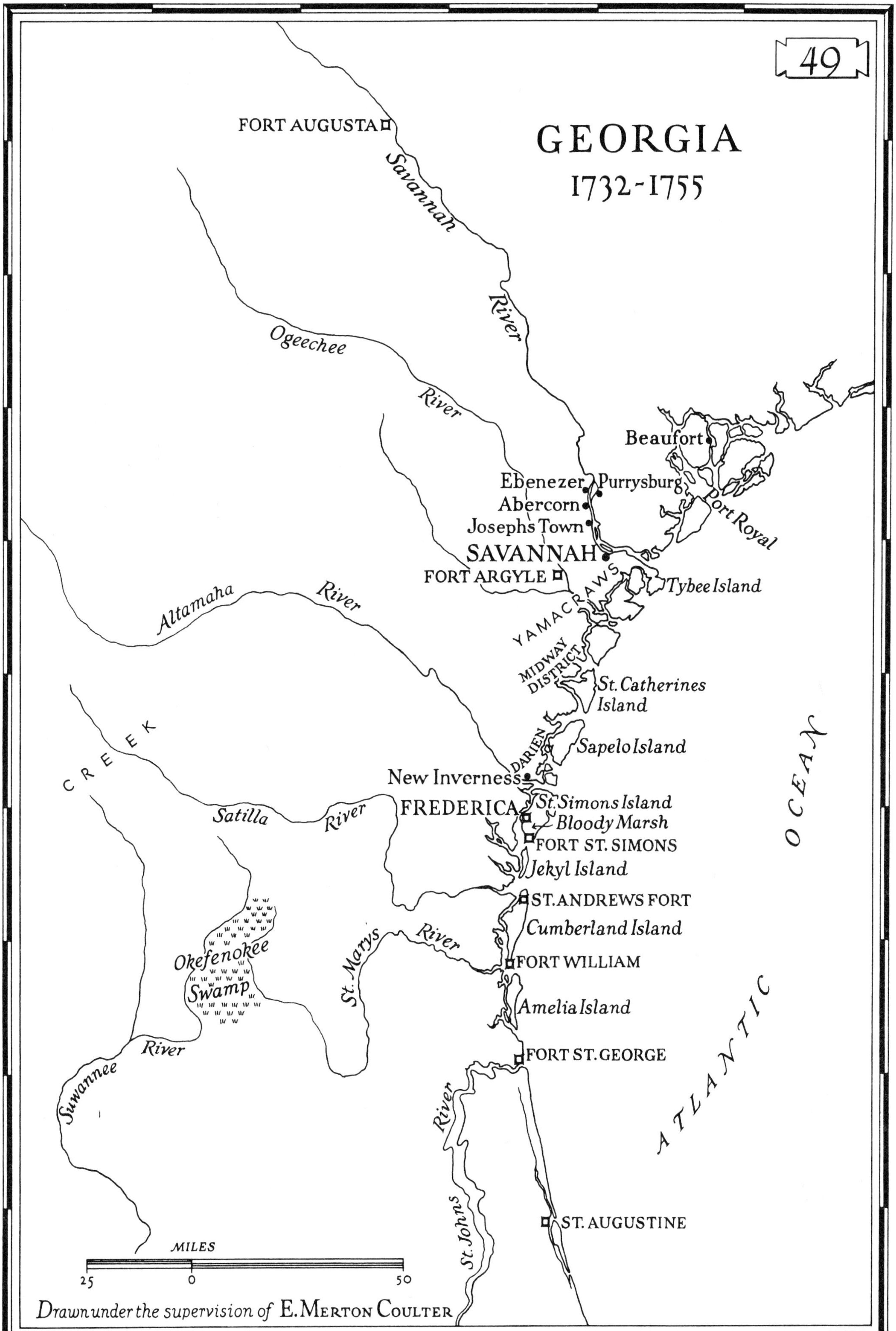
49
GEORGIA
1732-1755
FORT AUGUSTA
Savannah River
Ogeechee River
Beaufort
Ebenezer
Purrysburg
Abercorn
Josephs Town
Port Royal
SAVANNAH
FORT ARGYLE
Tybee Island
Altamaha River
YAMACRAWS
MIDWAY DISTRICT
St. Catherines Island
CREEK
DARIEN
Sapelo Island
New Inverness
FREDERICA
St. Simons Island
Bloody Marsh
FORT ST. SIMONS
Satilla River
Jekyl Island
ST. ANDREWS FORT
Cumberland Island
St. Marys River
FORT WILLIAM
Okefenokee Swamp
Amelia Island
FORT ST. GEORGE
Suwannee River
St. Johns River
ATLANTIC OCEAN
ST. AUGUSTINE
MILES
25
0
50
Drawn under the supervision of E. Merton Coulter

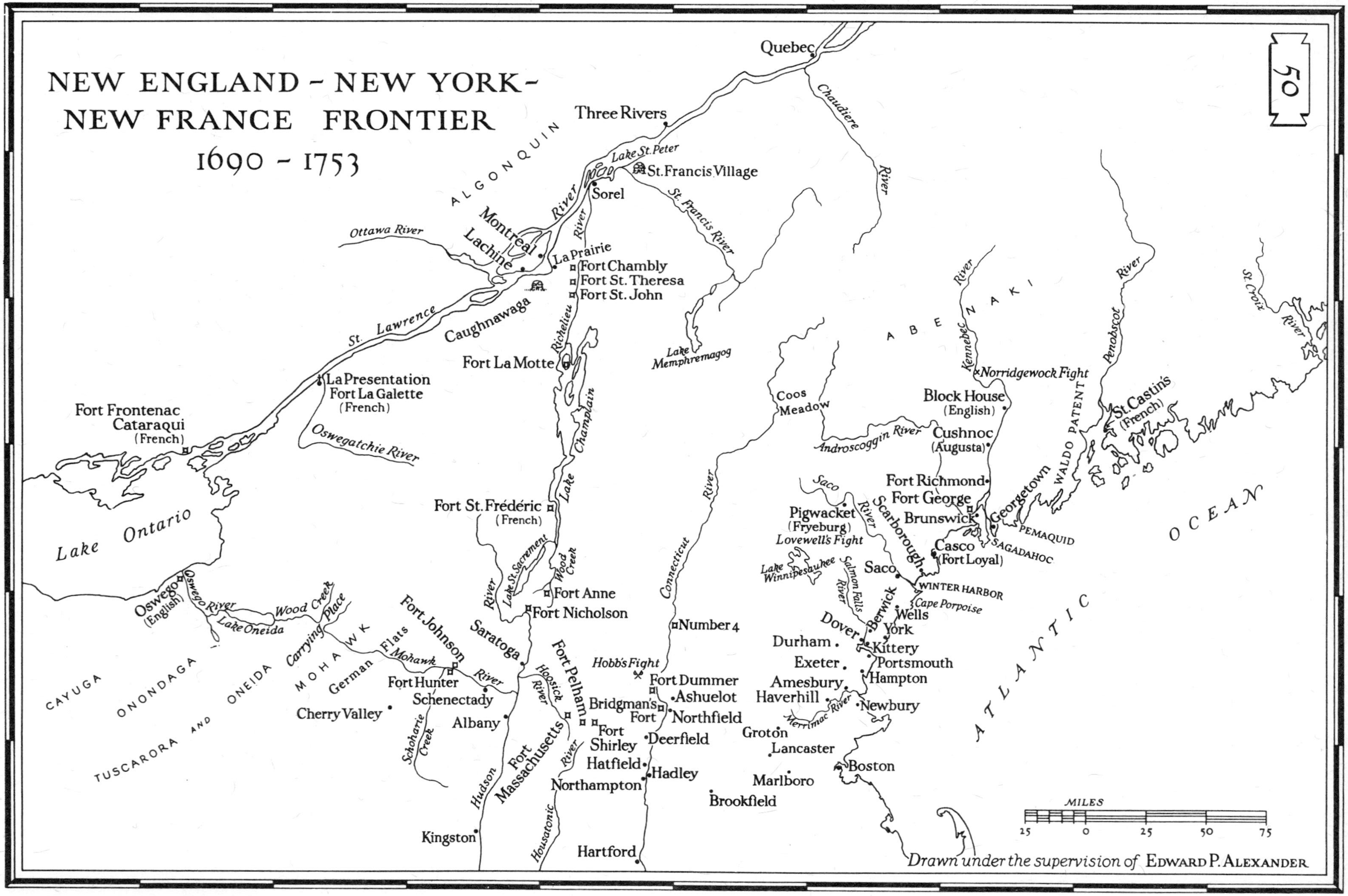
50
NEW ENGLAND - NEW YORK -
NEW FRANCE FRONTIER
1690 - 1753
Quebec
Chaudiere River
Three Rivers
ALGONQUIN
Lake St. Peter
St. Francis Village
Sorel
St. Francis River
Montreal
Lachine
River
Ottawa River
La Prairie
Fort Chambly
Fort St. Theresa
Fort St. John
Caughnawaga
St. Lawrence
Richelieu
Fort La Motte
Lake Memphremagog
La Presentation
Fort La Galette
(French)
Fort Frontenac
Cataraqui
(French)
Oswegatchie River
Lake Champlain
Fort St. Frédéric
(French)
Lake Ontario
Lake St. Sacrement
Wood Creek
Fort Anne
Fort Nicholson
Oswego
(English)
Oswego River
Lake Oneida
Wood Creek
Carrying Place
MOHAWK
Mohawk Flats
Fort Johnson
Saratoga
German
Fort Hunter
Schenectady
Cherry Valley
Albany
Schoharie Creek
CAYUGA
ONONDAGA
TUSCARORA AND ONEIDA
Hoosick River
Fort Pelham
Fort Massachusetts
Hudson
Housatonic
Kingston
Northampton
Hartford
Coos Meadow
Connecticut River
Number 4
Hobb's Fight
Fort Dummer
Ashuelot
Bridgman's Fort
Northfield
Fort Shirley
Deerfield
Hatfield
Hadley
Brookfield
Marlboro
Lancaster
Groton
Boston
Merrimac River
Newbury
Haverhill
Amesbury
Hampton
Exeter
Portsmouth
Durham
Kittery
Dover
York
Wells
Berwick
Salmon Falls River
Lake Winnipesaukee
Lovewell's Fight
Pigwacket
(Fryeburg)
Saco River
Saco
Scarborough
Cape Porpoise
WINTER HARBOR
Casco
(Fort Loyal)
SAGADAHOC
PEMAQUID
Brunswick
Fort George
Fort Richmond
Georgetown
WALDO PATENT
Androscoggin River
Cushnoc
(Augusta)
Block House
(English)
Norridgewock Fight
Kennebec River
ABENAKI
Penobscot River
St. Castin's
(French)
St. Croix River
ATLANTIC OCEAN
MILES
25 0 25 50 75
Drawn under the supervision of EDWARD P. ALEXANDER

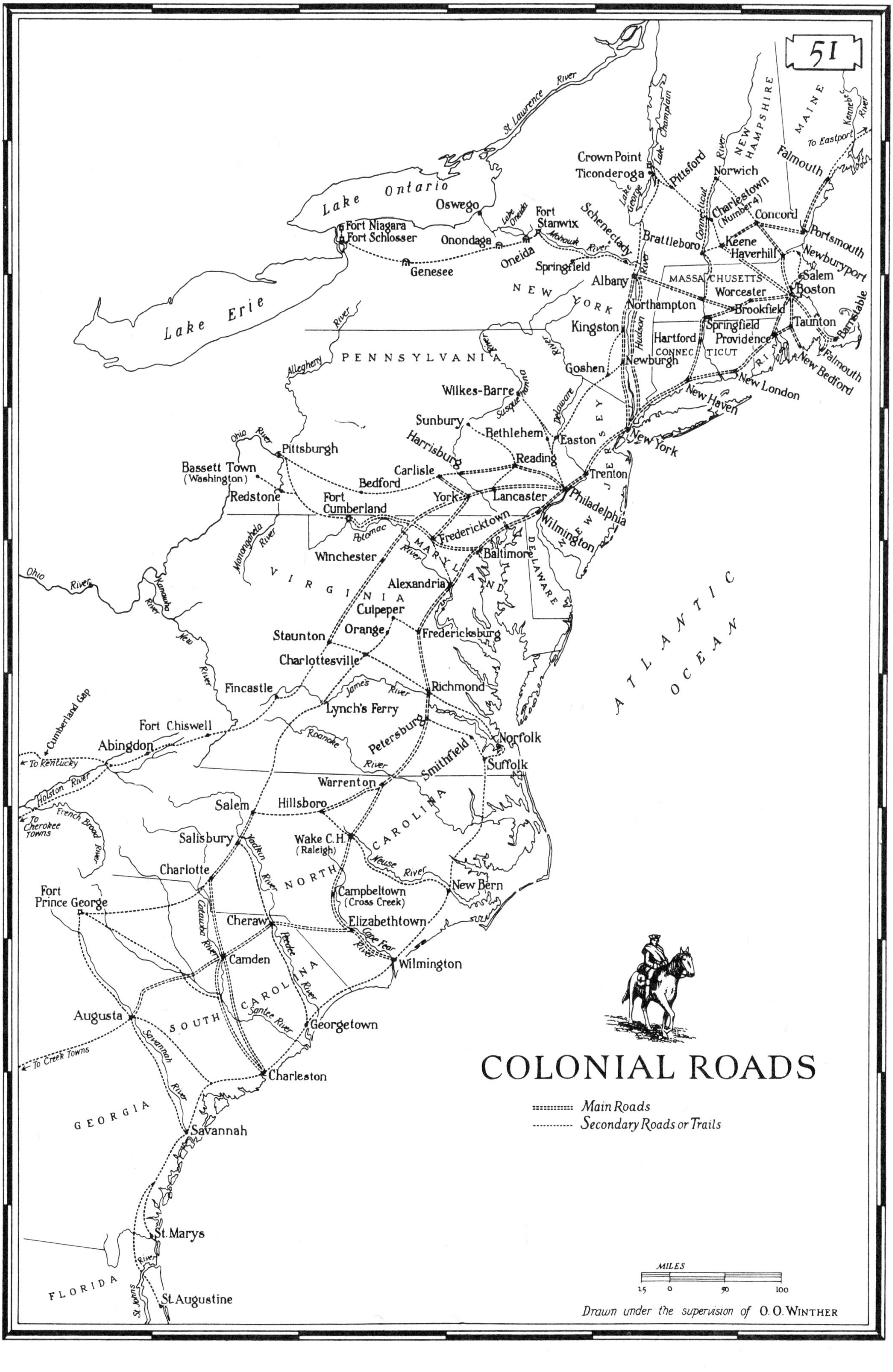
51
COLONIAL ROADS
Main Roads
Secondary Roads or Trails
MILES
25
0
50
100
Drawn under the supervision of O. O. WINTHER
Lake Ontario
Lake Erie
St. Lawrence River
Lake Champlain
ATLANTIC OCEAN
NEW HAMPSHIRE
MAINE
MASSACHUSETTS
CONNECTICUT
R.I.
NEW YORK
PENNSYLVANIA
NEW JERSEY
MARYLAND
DELAWARE
VIRGINIA
NORTH CAROLINA
SOUTH CAROLINA
GEORGIA
FLORIDA
To Eastport
Kennebec River
Falmouth
Portsmouth
Concord
Norwich
Charlestown (Number 4)
Keene
Haverhill
Newburyport
Salem
Boston
Worcester
Brookfield
Springfield
Providence
Taunton
Barnstable
Falmouth
New Bedford
New London
New Haven
Hartford
Northampton
Brattleboro
Pittsford
Crown Point
Ticonderoga
Lake George
Connecticut River
Albany
Schenectady
Springfield
Fort Stanwix
Mohawk River
Lake Oneida
Oneida
Onondaga
Oswego
Fort Niagara
Fort Schlosser
Genesee
Kingston
Hudson River
Newburgh
Goshen
New York
Wilkes-Barre
Susquehanna River
Delaware River
Sunbury
Bethlehem
Easton
Reading
Harrisburg
Carlisle
Bedford
Trenton
Philadelphia
Lancaster
York
Allegheny River
Ohio River
Pittsburgh
Bassett Town (Washington)
Redstone
Fort Cumberland
Monongahela River
Potomac River
Fredericktown
Baltimore
Wilmington
Winchester
Alexandria
Culpeper
Orange
Fredericksburg
Staunton
Charlottesville
Richmond
James's River
Lynch's Ferry
Fincastle
Kanawha River
New River
Ohio River
Cumberland Gap
To Kentucky
Fort Chiswell
Abingdon
Holston River
Petersburg
Roanoke River
Smithfield
Norfolk
Suffolk
Warrenton
Hillsboro
Salem
To Cherokee Towns
French Broad River
Salisbury
Yadkin River
Wake C.H. (Raleigh)
Neuse River
New Bern
Charlotte
Campbeltown (Cross Creek)
Elizabethtown
Cape Fear River
Wilmington
Fort Prince George
Cheraw
Catawba River
Pedee River
Camden
Santee River
Georgetown
Augusta
To Creek Towns
Savannah River
Charleston
Savannah
St. Marys
St. Johns River
St. Augustine

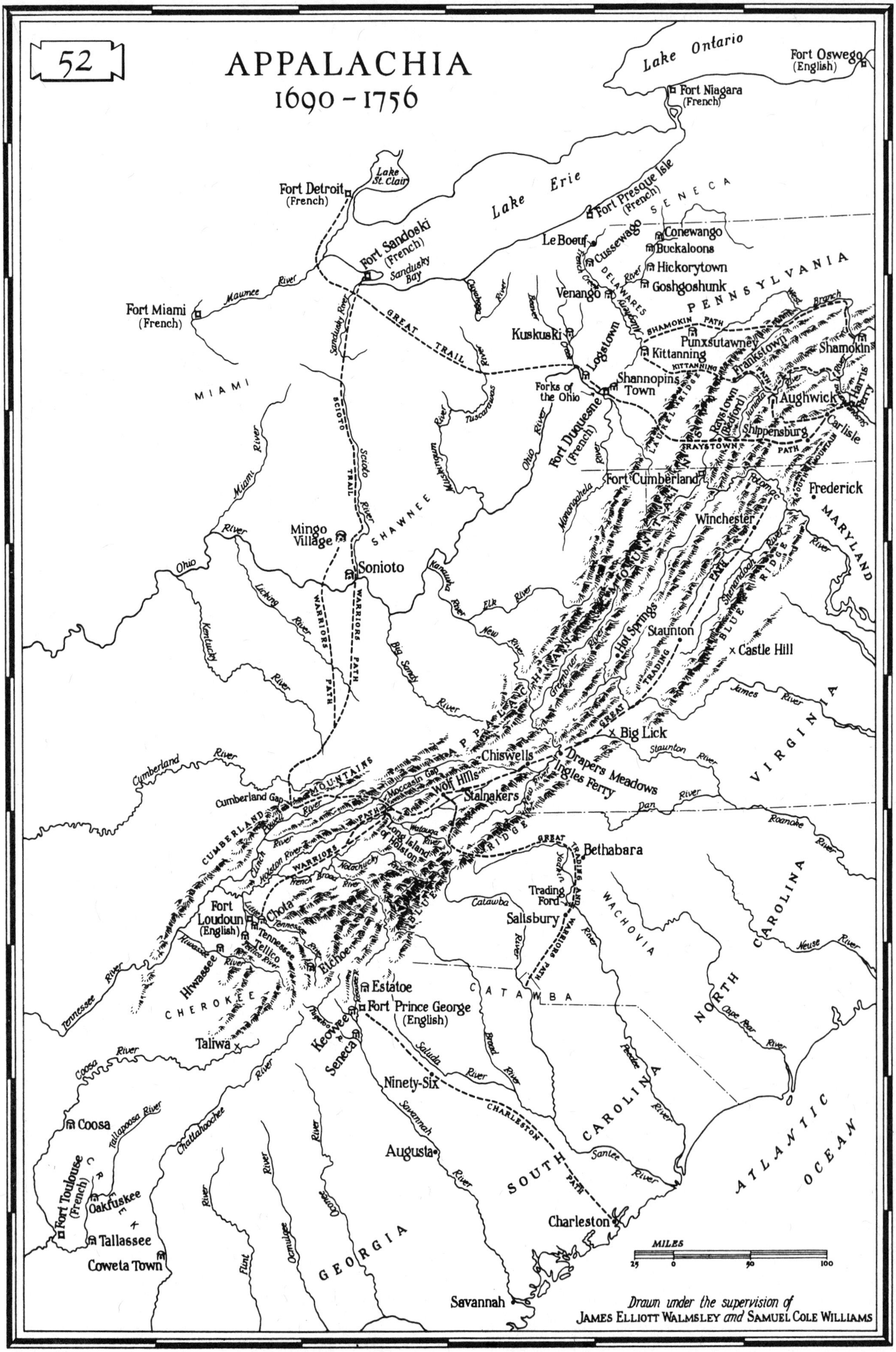
52
APPALACHIA
1690 – 1756
Lake Ontario
Fort Oswego
(English)
Fort Niagara
(French)
Lake St. Clair
Fort Detroit
(French)
Lake Erie
Fort Presque Isle
(French)
SENECA
Le Boeuf
Cussewago
Conewango
Buckaloons
Hickorytown
Goshgoshunk
DELAWARES
Venango
PENNSYLVANIA
Fort Sandoski
(French)
Sandusky Bay
Maumee River
Fort Miami
(French)
GREAT TRAIL
Sandusky River
Cuyahoga River
Beaver Creek
Kuskuski
Logstown
SHAMOKIN PATH
Punxsutawney
Kittanning
KITTANNING PATH
Frankstown
Shamokin
Harris Ferry
West Branch
Juniata River
Aughwick
Carlisle
Shippensburg
Raystown (Bedford)
RAYSTOWN PATH
LAUREL RIDGE
Forks of the Ohio
Shannopins Town
Fort Duquesne
(French)
MIAMI
SCIOTO TRAIL
Scioto River
Tuscarawas
Muskingum River
Ohio River
Monongahela
Fort Cumberland
Frederick
Potomac
SOUTH MOUNTAIN
MARYLAND
Winchester
Miami River
Mingo Village
SHAWNEE
Sonioto
Ohio River
Kanawha River
Elk River
New River
Licking River
WARRIORS PATH
Kentucky River
Big Sandy River
Greenbrier River
Hot Springs
Staunton
Shenandoah River
BLUE RIDGE
GREAT TRADING PATH
Castle Hill
James River
VIRGINIA
APPALACHIAN MOUNTAINS
Big Lick
Staunton River
Chiswells
Drapers Meadows
Ingles Ferry
Wolf Hills
Stalnakers
Moccasin Gap
Cumberland River
Cumberland Gap
CUMBERLAND
Clinch River
Holston River
Long Island of Holston
Watauga River
Nolachucky River
French Broad River
Dan River
Roanoke River
GREAT TRADING AND WARRIORS PATH
Bethabara
Yadkin
Trading Ford
Salisbury
Catawba River
WACHOVIA
NORTH CAROLINA
Neuse River
Fort Loudoun
(English)
Chota
Tennessee River
Tellico
Hiwassee
Echoe
Estatoe
Fort Prince George
(English)
CHEROKEE
CATAWBA
Tennessee River
Taliwa
Keowee
Seneca
Saluda River
Broad River
Ninety-Six
Cape Fear River
Pee Dee River
SOUTH CAROLINA
CHARLESTON PATH
Coosa River
Coosa
Tallapoosa River
Chattahoochee
Savannah River
Augusta
Santee River
ATLANTIC OCEAN
CREEK
Fort Toulouse
(French)
Oakfuskee
Tallassee
Coweta Town
Flint
Ocmulgee
Oconee
GEORGIA
Charleston
Savannah
MILES
25 0 50 100
Drawn under the supervision of
JAMES ELLIOTT WALMSLEY and SAMUEL COLE WILLIAMS

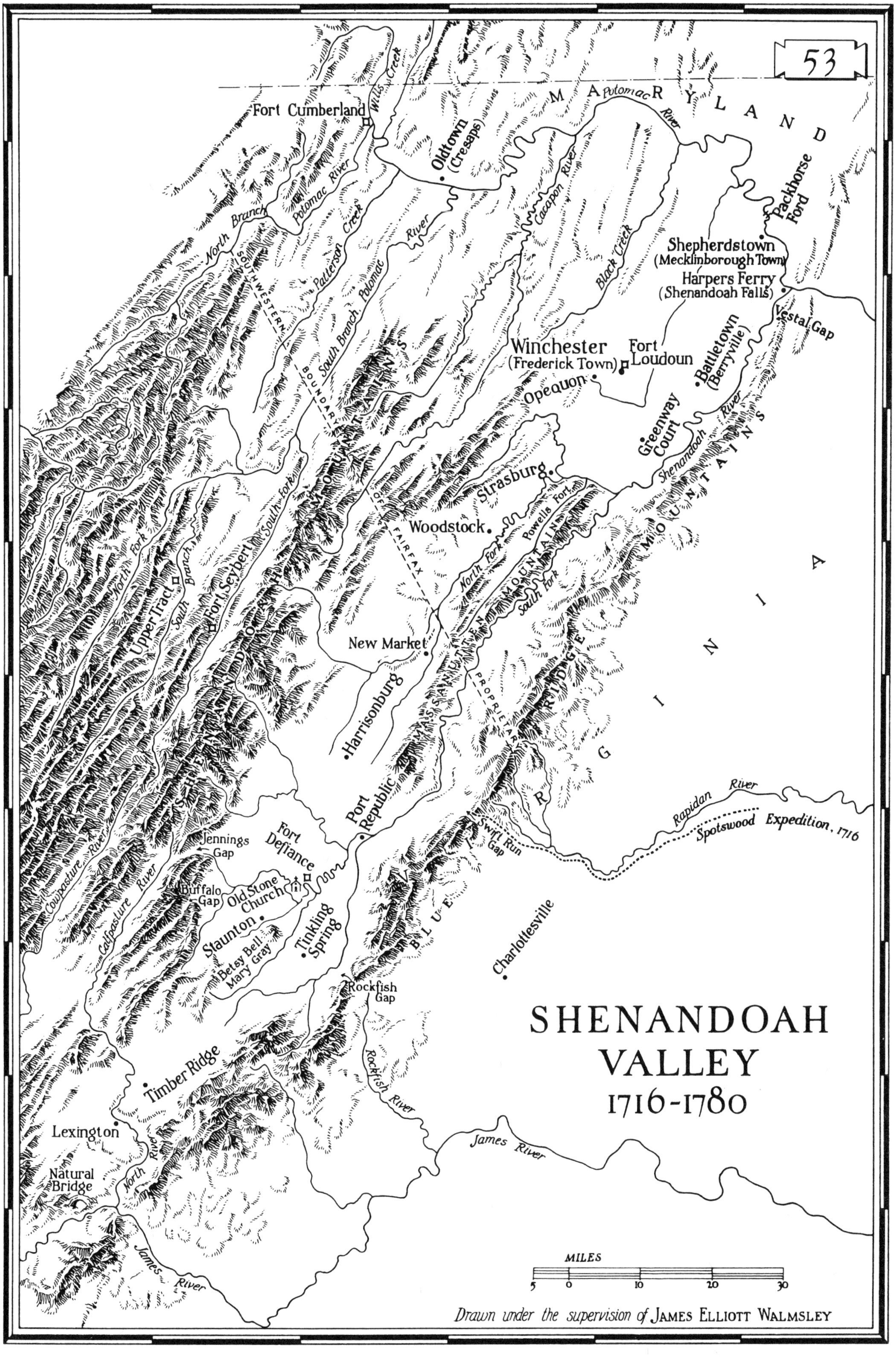

SHENANDOAH VALLEY 1716-1780

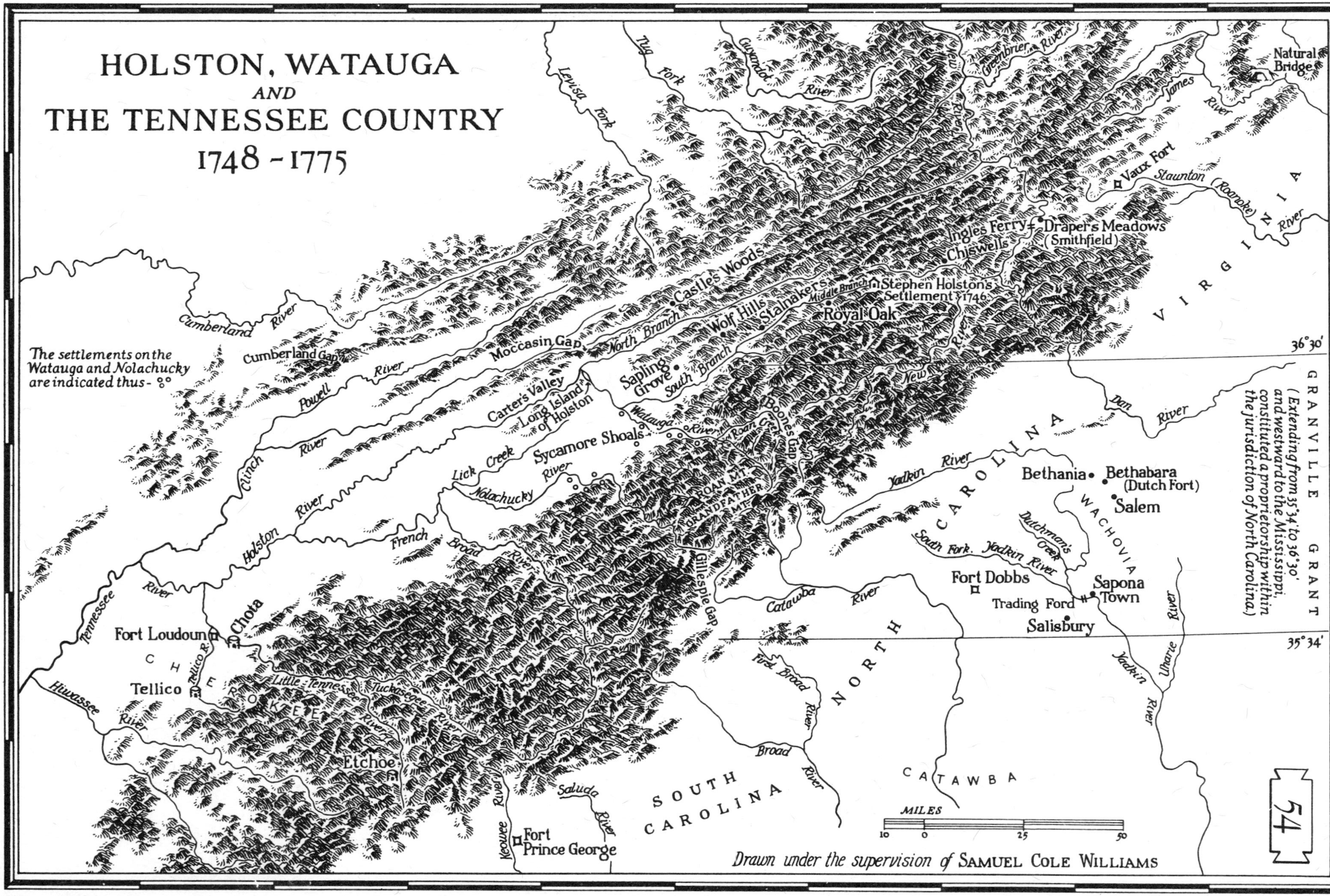

HOLSTON, WATAUGA
AND
THE TENNESSEE COUNTRY
1748 - 1775
The settlements on the Watauga and Nolachucky are indicated thus - °°
Natural Bridge
Greenbrier River
James River
Guyandot River
Tug Fork
Levisa Fork
Vaux Fort
Staunton (Roanoke) River
VIRGINIA
Ingles Ferry
Draper's Meadows (Smithfield)
Chiswells
Castle's Woods
Stephen Holston's Settlement 1746
Middle Branch
Stalnakers
Royal Oak
Wolf Hills
North Branch
Moccasin Gap
Cumberland River
Cumberland Gap
Powell River
Sapling Grove
South Branch
New River
36°30'
Carter's Valley
Long Island of Holston
Watauga River
Roan Creek
Boones Gap
Sycamore Shoals
Lick Creek
Nolachucky River
Clinch River
Holston River
French Broad River
ROAN MT.
GRANDFATHER MT.
Gillespie Gap
Dan River
GRANVILLE GRANT
(Extending from 35°34' to 36°30' and westward to the Mississippi, constituted a proprietorship within the jurisdiction of North Carolina.)
Yadkin River
Bethania
Bethabara (Dutch Fort)
Salem
WACHOVIA
Dutchman's Creek
South Fork. Yadkin River
Fort Dobbs
Sapona Town
Trading Ford
Salisbury
Catawba River
NORTH CAROLINA
35°34'
Uharie River
Yadkin River
Tennessee River
Fort Loudoun
Chota
Tellico R.
Tellico
CHEROKEE
Hiwassee River
Little Tennessee
Tuckasegee River
Etchoe
First Broad River
Broad River
CATAWBA
SOUTH CAROLINA
Keowee River
Saluda River
Fort Prince George
MILES
10 0 25 50
Drawn under the supervision of SAMUEL COLE WILLIAMS
54

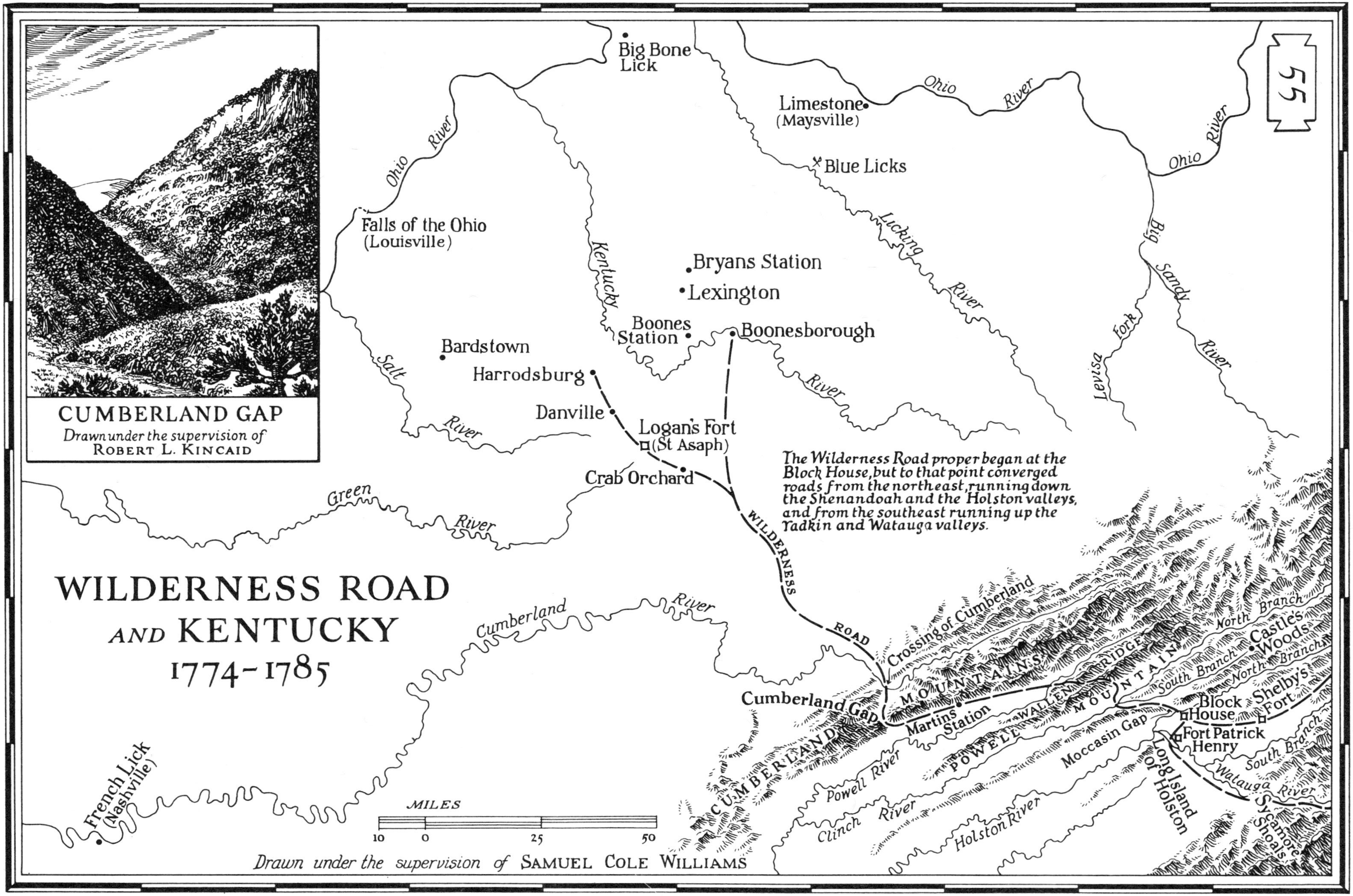
55
WILDERNESS ROAD AND KENTUCKY 1774-1785
CUMBERLAND GAP
Drawn under the supervision of ROBERT L. KINCAID
Big Bone Lick
Limestone (Maysville)
Ohio River
Blue Licks
Falls of the Ohio (Louisville)
Kentucky
Licking River
Big Sandy River
Levisa Fork
Bryans Station
Lexington
Boones Station
Boonesborough
River
Bardstown
Harrodsburg
Salt River
Danville
Logan's Fort (St Asaph)
Crab Orchard
Green River
The Wilderness Road proper began at the Block House, but to that point converged roads from the northeast, running down the Shenandoah and the Holston valleys, and from the southeast running up the Yadkin and Watauga valleys.
WILDERNESS ROAD
Cumberland River
Crossing of Cumberland
Cumberland Gap
CUMBERLAND MOUNTAINS
Martins Station
POWELL
WALLENS RIDGE
MOUNTAIN
North Branch
Castle's Woods
South Branch
North Branch
Shelby's Fort
Block House
Fort Patrick Henry
Moccasin Gap
Long Island of Holston
South Branch
Watauga River
Sycamore Shoals
Powell River
Clinch River
Holston River
French Lick (Nashville)
MILES
10 0 25 50
Drawn under the supervision of SAMUEL COLE WILLIAMS

IV COLONIAL WARS OF THE INDIANS, FRENCH AND BRITISH

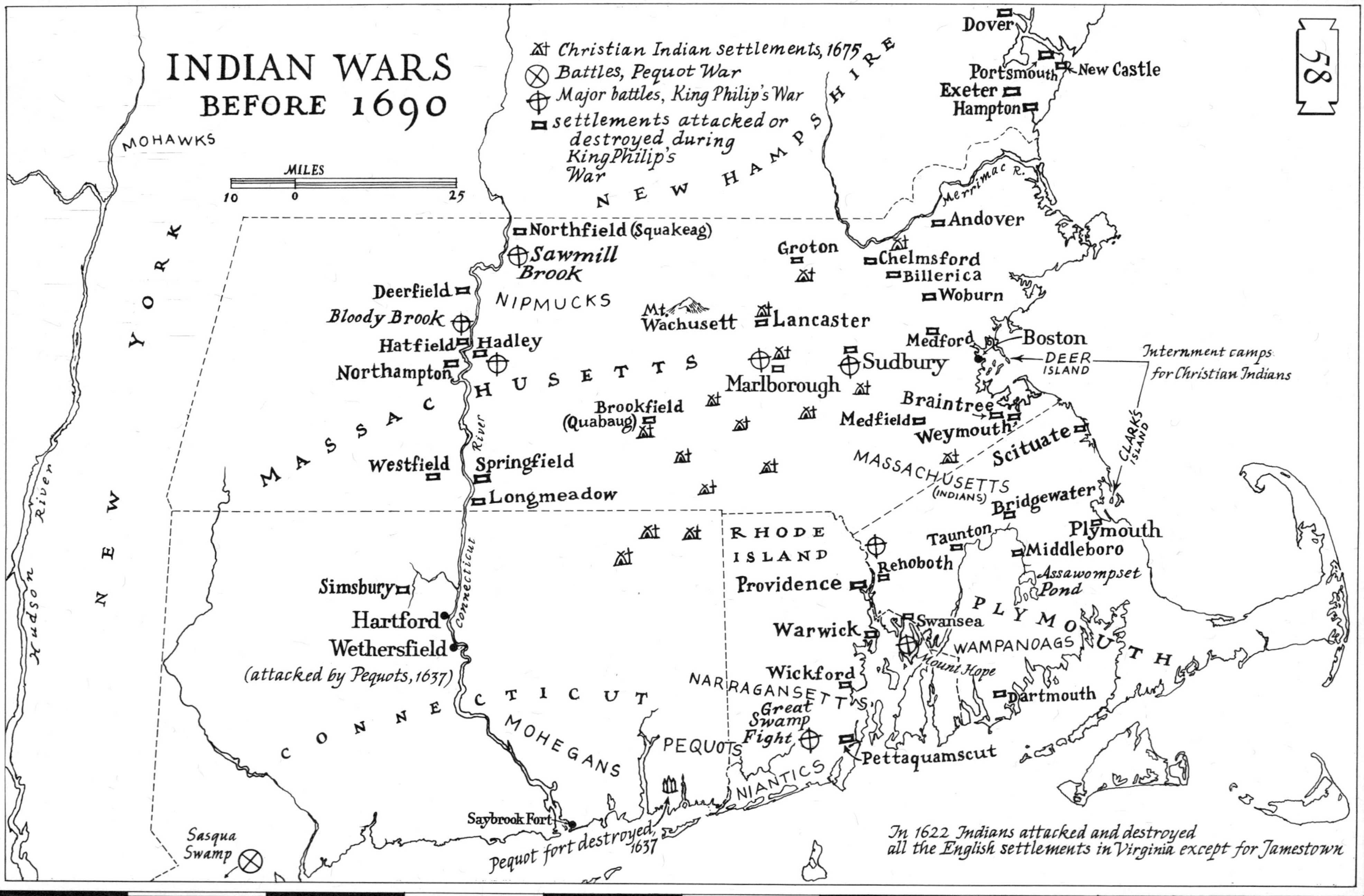
INDIAN WARS BEFORE 1690
Christian Indian settlements, 1675
Battles, Pequot War
Major battles, King Philip's War
settlements attacked or destroyed during King Philip's War
MILES
10
0
25
MOHAWKS
NEW YORK
NEW HAMPSHIRE
MASSACHUSETTS
CONNECTICUT
RHODE ISLAND
PLYMOUTH
Hudson River
Connecticut River
Merrimac R.
Dover
Portsmouth
New Castle
Exeter
Hampton
Andover
Northfield (Squakeag)
Sawmill Brook
Groton
Chelmsford
Billerica
Woburn
Deerfield
NIPMUCKS
Mt. Wachusett
Lancaster
Bloody Brook
Hatfield
Hadley
Medford
Boston
Northampton
Sudbury
DEER ISLAND
Internment camps for Christian Indians
Marlborough
Braintree
Brookfield (Quabaug)
Medfield
Weymouth
Westfield
Springfield
Scituate
CLARK'S ISLAND
MASSACHUSETTS (INDIANS)
Longmeadow
Bridgewater
Plymouth
Taunton
Middleboro
Rehoboth
Assawompset Pond
Simsbury
Providence
Hartford
Swansea
Warwick
WAMPANOAGS
Wethersfield (attacked by Pequots, 1637)
Mount Hope
Wickford
NARRAGANSETTS
Dartmouth
Great Swamp Fight
MOHEGANS
PEQUOTS
Pettaquamscut
NIANTICS
Saybrook Fort
Sasqua Swamp
Pequot fort destroyed, 1637
In 1622 Indians attacked and destroyed all the English settlements in Virginia except for Jamestown

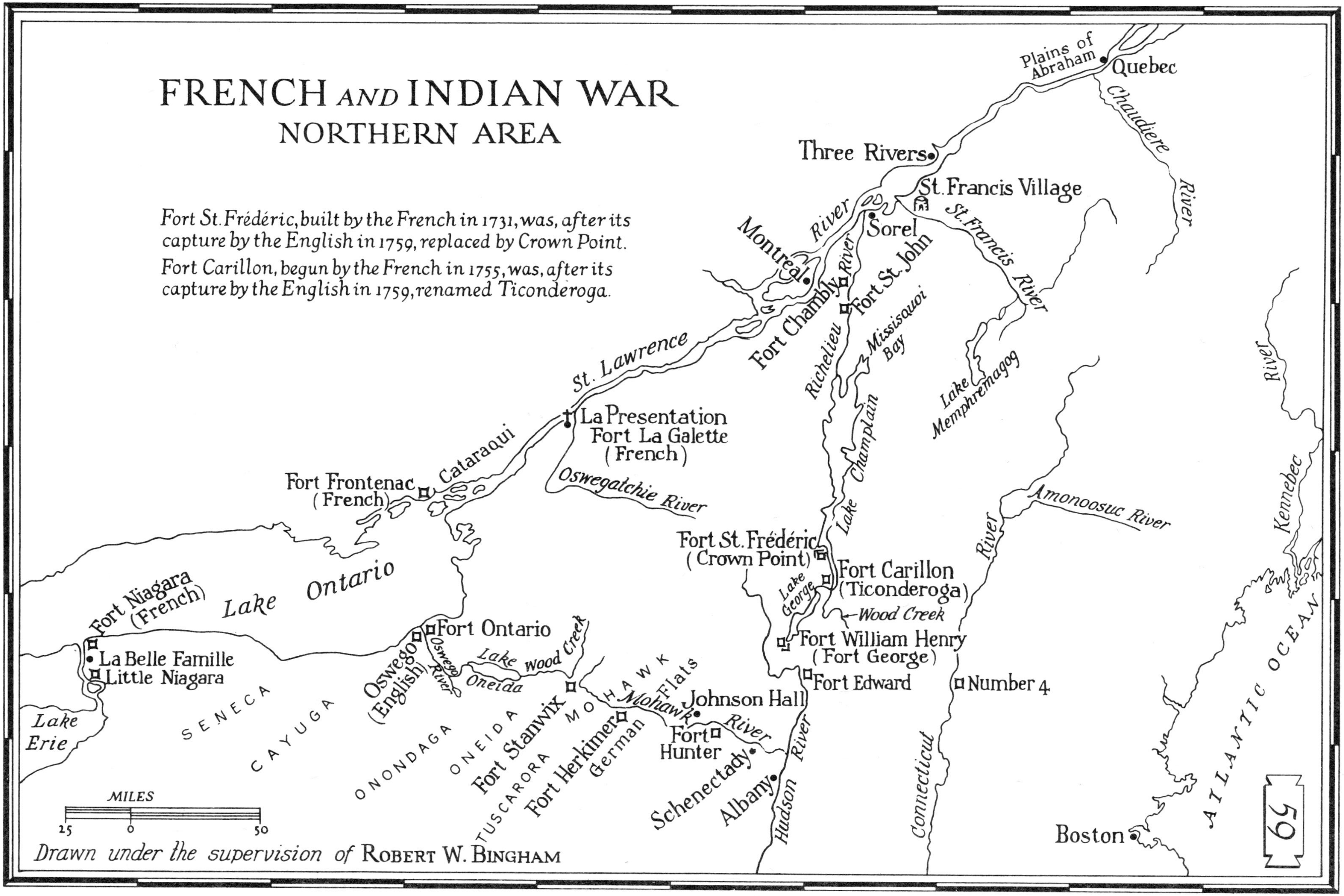
FRENCH AND INDIAN WAR
NORTHERN AREA
Fort St. Frédéric, built by the French in 1731, was, after its capture by the English in 1759, replaced by Crown Point.
Fort Carillon, begun by the French in 1755, was, after its capture by the English in 1759, renamed Ticonderoga.
Plains of Abraham
Quebec
Chaudiere River
Three Rivers
St. Francis Village
St. Francis River
Sorel
Montreal
River
Fort St. John
Fort Chambly
Richelieu River
Missisquoi Bay
Lake Memphremagog
Lake Champlain
St. Lawrence
La Presentation
Fort La Galette
(French)
Oswegatchie River
Cataraqui
Fort Frontenac
(French)
Lake Ontario
Fort Niagara
(French)
La Belle Famille
Little Niagara
Lake Erie
Fort Ontario
Oswego
(English)
Oswego River
Lake Oneida
Wood Creek
Fort St. Frédéric
(Crown Point)
Fort Carillon
(Ticonderoga)
Lake George
Wood Creek
Fort William Henry
(Fort George)
Fort Edward
Number 4
Amonoosuc River
Connecticut River
River
Kennebec River
ATLANTIC OCEAN
Boston
SENECA
CAYUGA
ONONDAGA
ONEIDA
TUSCARORA
MOHAWK Flats
Mohawk River
Fort Stanwix
Fort Herkimer
German
Johnson Hall
Fort Hunter
Schenectady
Albany
Hudson River
MILES
25
0
50
Drawn under the supervision of ROBERT W. BINGHAM
59

ACADIA AND LOUISBURG
1740 - 1755

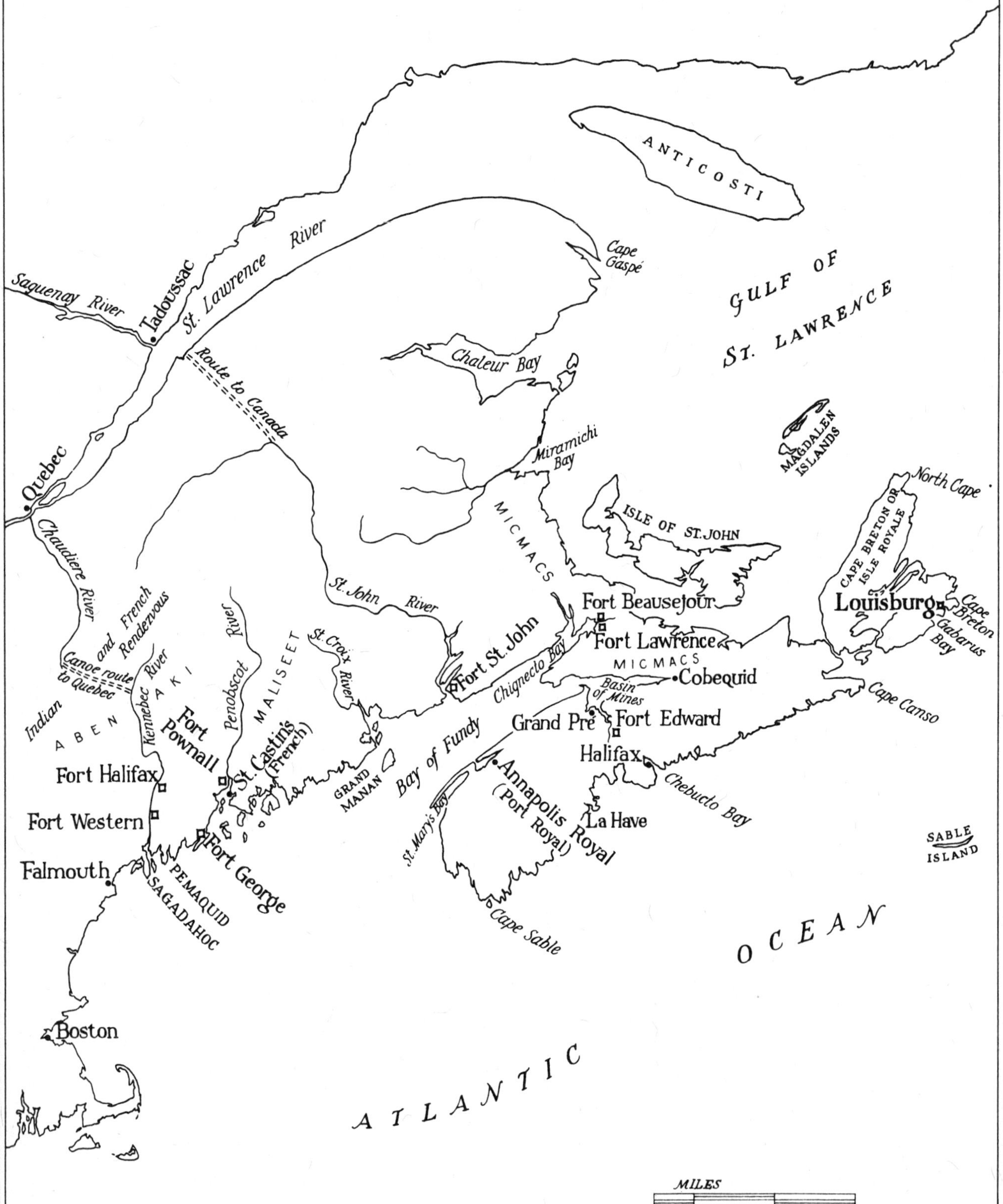

Drawn under the supervision of LAWRENCE J. BURPEE

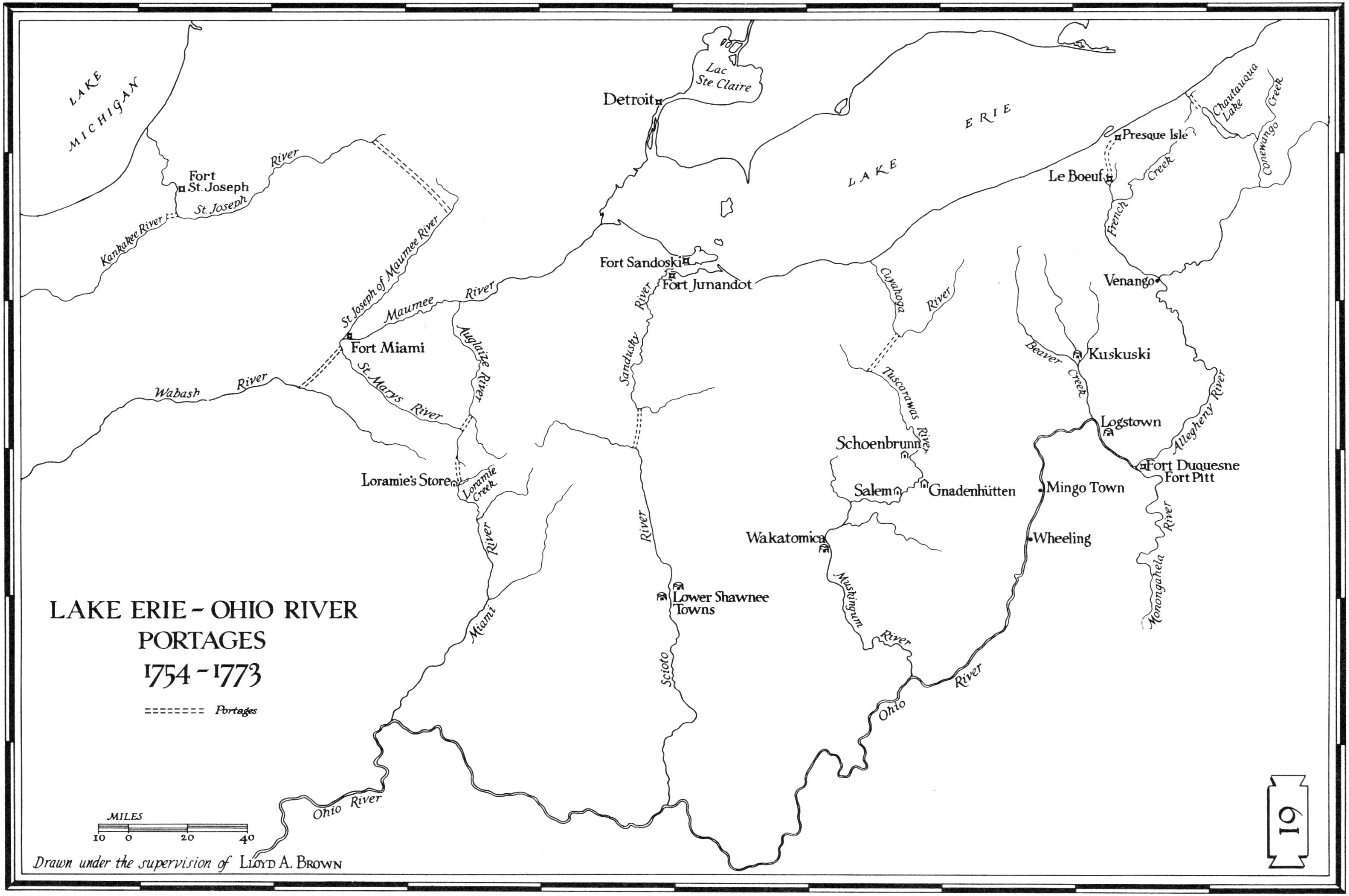
LAKE ERIE - OHIO RIVER
PORTAGES
1754 - 1773
Portages
MILES
10 0 20 40
Drawn under the supervision of Lloyd A. Brown
19
LAKE MICHIGAN
LAKE ERIE
Lac Ste. Claire
Detroit
Fort St. Joseph
St. Joseph River
Kankakee River
St. Joseph of Maumee River
Maumee River
Fort Miami
St. Marys River
Wabash River
Auglaize River
Loramie's Store
Loramie Creek
Miami River
Fort Sandoski
Fort Junandot
Sandusky River
Scioto River
Lower Shawnee Towns
Cuyahoga River
Tuscarawas River
Schoenbrunn
Salem
Gnadenhütten
Wakatomica
Muskingum River
Ohio River
Presque Isle
Le Boeuf
French Creek
Chautauqua Lake
Conewango Creek
Venango
Kuskuski
Beaver Creek
Logstown
Allegheny River
Fort Duquesne
Fort Pitt
Monongahela River
Mingo Town
Wheeling

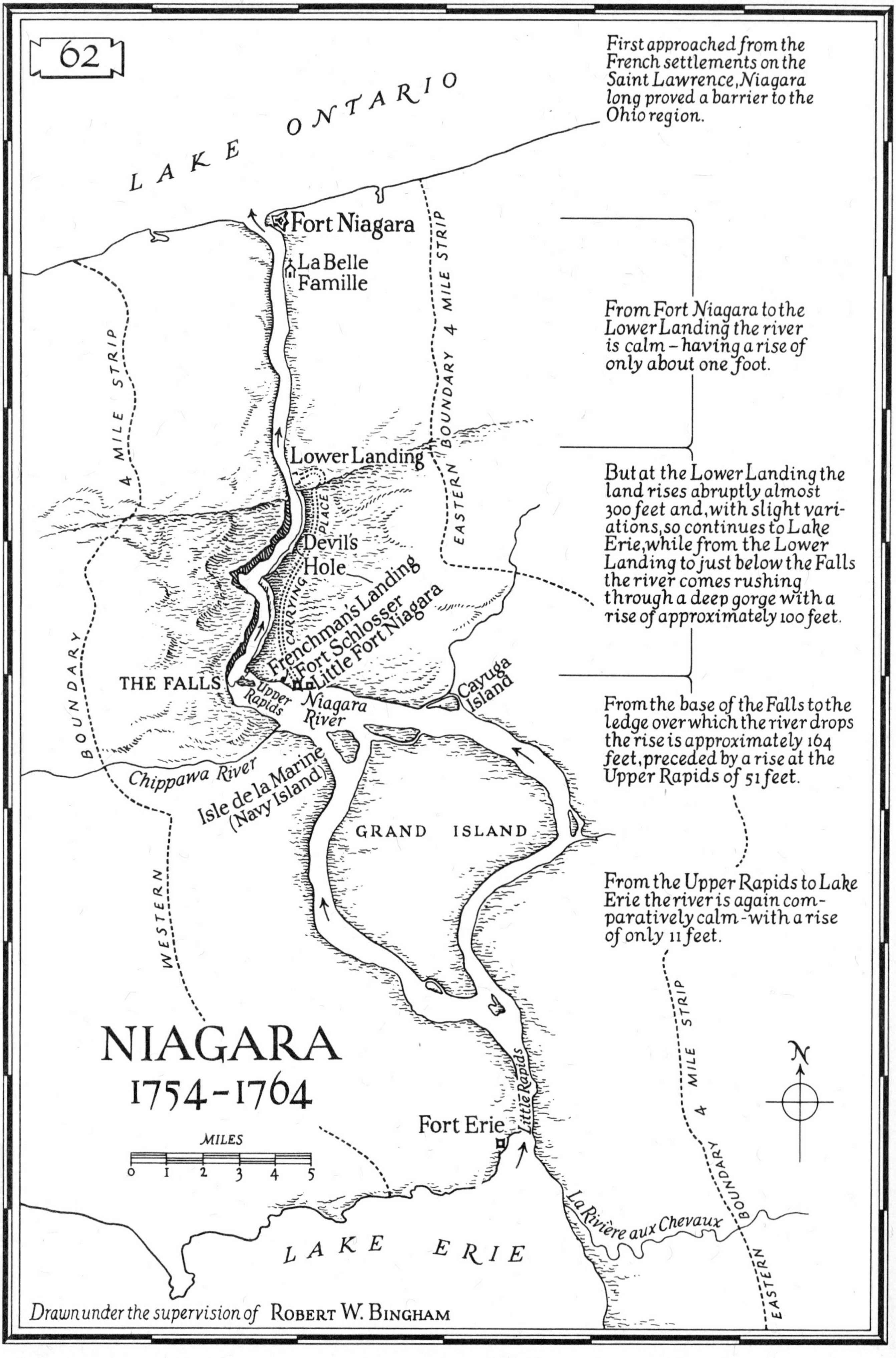
62
LAKE ONTARIO
First approached from the French settlements on the Saint Lawrence, Niagara long proved a barrier to the Ohio region.
Fort Niagara
La Belle Famille
From Fort Niagara to the Lower Landing the river is calm – having a rise of only about one foot.
But at the Lower Landing the land rises abruptly almost 300 feet and, with slight variations, so continues to Lake Erie, while from the Lower Landing to just below the Falls the river comes rushing through a deep gorge with a rise of approximately 100 feet.
From the base of the Falls to the ledge over which the river drops the rise is approximately 164 feet, preceded by a rise at the Upper Rapids of 51 feet.
From the Upper Rapids to Lake Erie the river is again comparatively calm – with a rise of only 11 feet.
WESTERN BOUNDARY 4 MILE STRIP
EASTERN BOUNDARY 4 MILE STRIP
Lower Landing
CARRYING PLACE
Devil's Hole
Frenchman's Landing
Fort Schlosser
Little Fort Niagara
THE FALLS
Upper Rapids
Niagara River
Cayuga Island
Chippawa River
Isle de la Marine (Navy Island)
GRAND ISLAND
NIAGARA
1754-1764
MILES
0 1 2 3 4 5
Fort Erie
Little Rapids
N
La Rivière aux Chevaux
LAKE ERIE
Drawn under the supervision of ROBERT W. BINGHAM

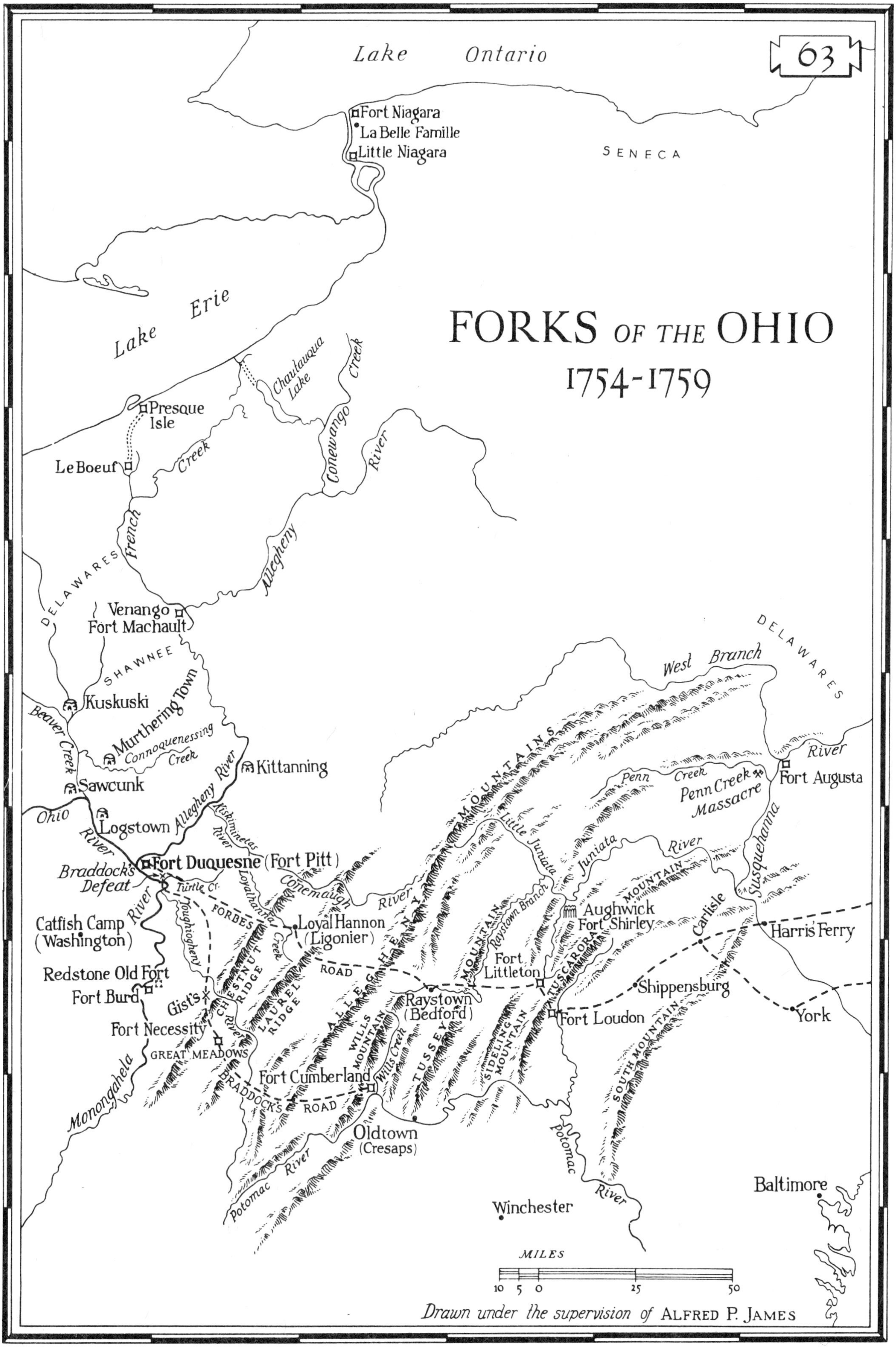
63
FORKS OF THE OHIO
1754-1759
Lake Ontario
Fort Niagara
La Belle Famille
Little Niagara
SENECA
Lake Erie
Chautauqua Lake
Presque Isle
Le Boeuf
Creek
French
Conewango Creek
River
Allegheny
DELAWARES
Venango
Fort Machault
SHAWNEE
Kuskuski
Murthering Town
Beaver Creek
Connoquenessing Creek
Kittanning
Sawcunk
Ohio River
Logstown
Allegheny River
Kiskiminetas River
Fort Duquesne (Fort Pitt)
Braddock's Defeat
Turtle Cr.
Conemaugh River
Loyalhanna Creek
FORBES ROAD
Catfish Camp (Washington)
Loyal Hannon (Ligonier)
Youghiogheny River
Redstone Old Fort
Fort Burd
Gist's
CHESTNUT RIDGE
LAUREL RIDGE
Fort Necessity
GREAT MEADOWS
Monongahela River
BRADDOCK'S ROAD
Fort Cumberland
WILLS MOUNTAIN
Wills Creek
ALLEGHENY MOUNTAINS
Raystown (Bedford)
TUSSEY
Oldtown (Cresaps)
Potomac River
MOUNTAIN
Raystown Branch
Little Juniata
Fort Littleton
TUSCARORA
SIDELING MOUNTAIN
Aughwick
Fort Shirley
Juniata River
MOUNTAIN
West Branch
DELAWARES
Penn Creek
Penn Creek Massacre
Fort Augusta
River
Susquehanna
Carlisle
Harris' Ferry
Shippensburg
Fort Loudon
York
SOUTH MOUNTAIN
Potomac River
Winchester
Baltimore
MILES
10 5 0 25 50
Drawn under the supervision of ALFRED P. JAMES

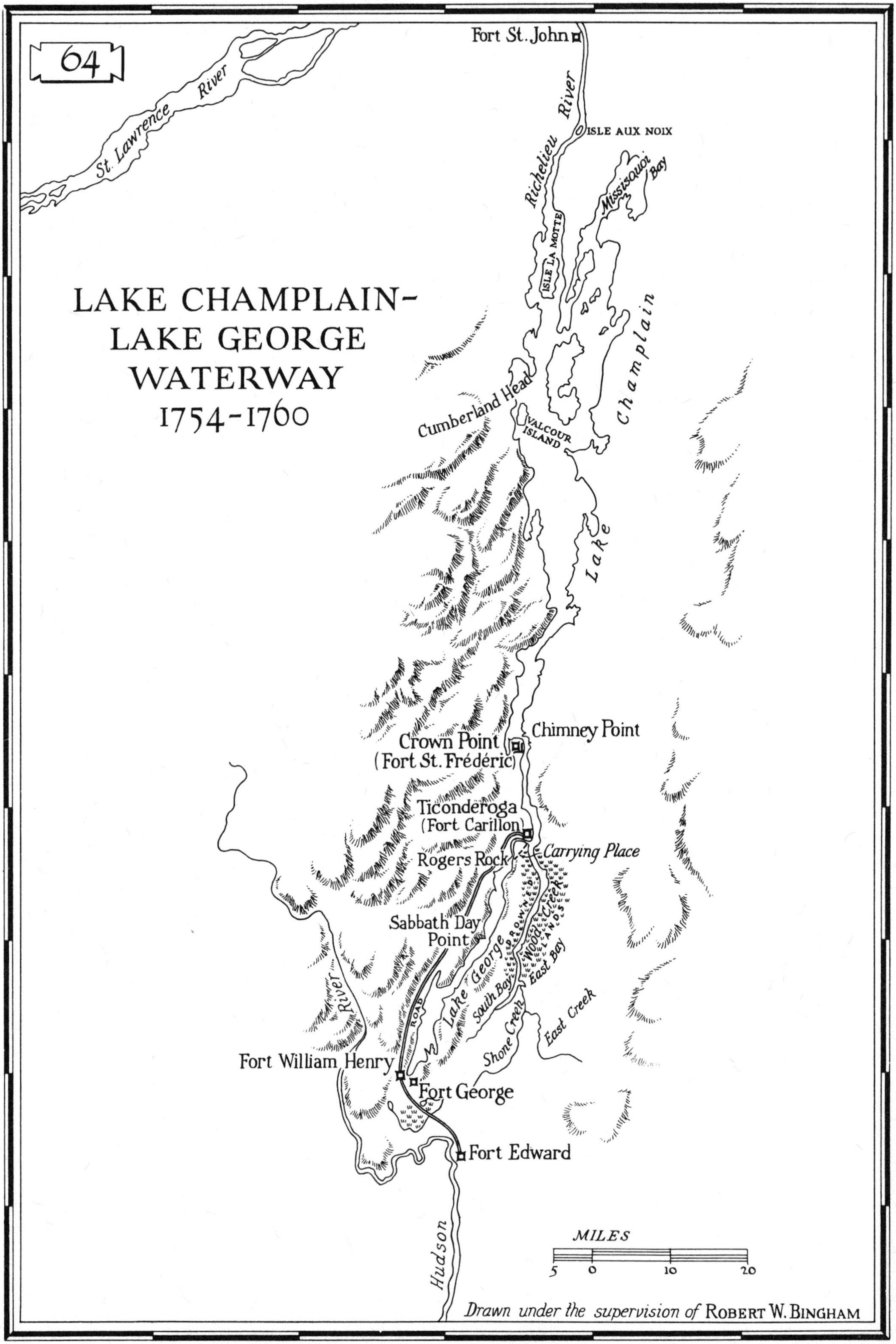
64
LAKE CHAMPLAIN-
LAKE GEORGE
WATERWAY
1754-1760
St. Lawrence River
Fort St. John
Richelieu River
ISLE AUX NOIX
Missisquoi Bay
ISLE LA MOTTE
Lake Champlain
Cumberland Head
VALCOUR ISLAND
Chimney Point
Crown Point
(Fort St. Frédéric)
Ticonderoga
(Fort Carillon)
Carrying Place
Rogers Rock
Sabbath Day Point
Lake George
ROAD
DROWNED LANDS
Wood Creek
South Bay
East Bay
Shone Creek
East Creek
River
Fort William Henry
Fort George
Fort Edward
Hudson
MILES
5 0 10 20
Drawn under the supervision of ROBERT W. BINGHAM

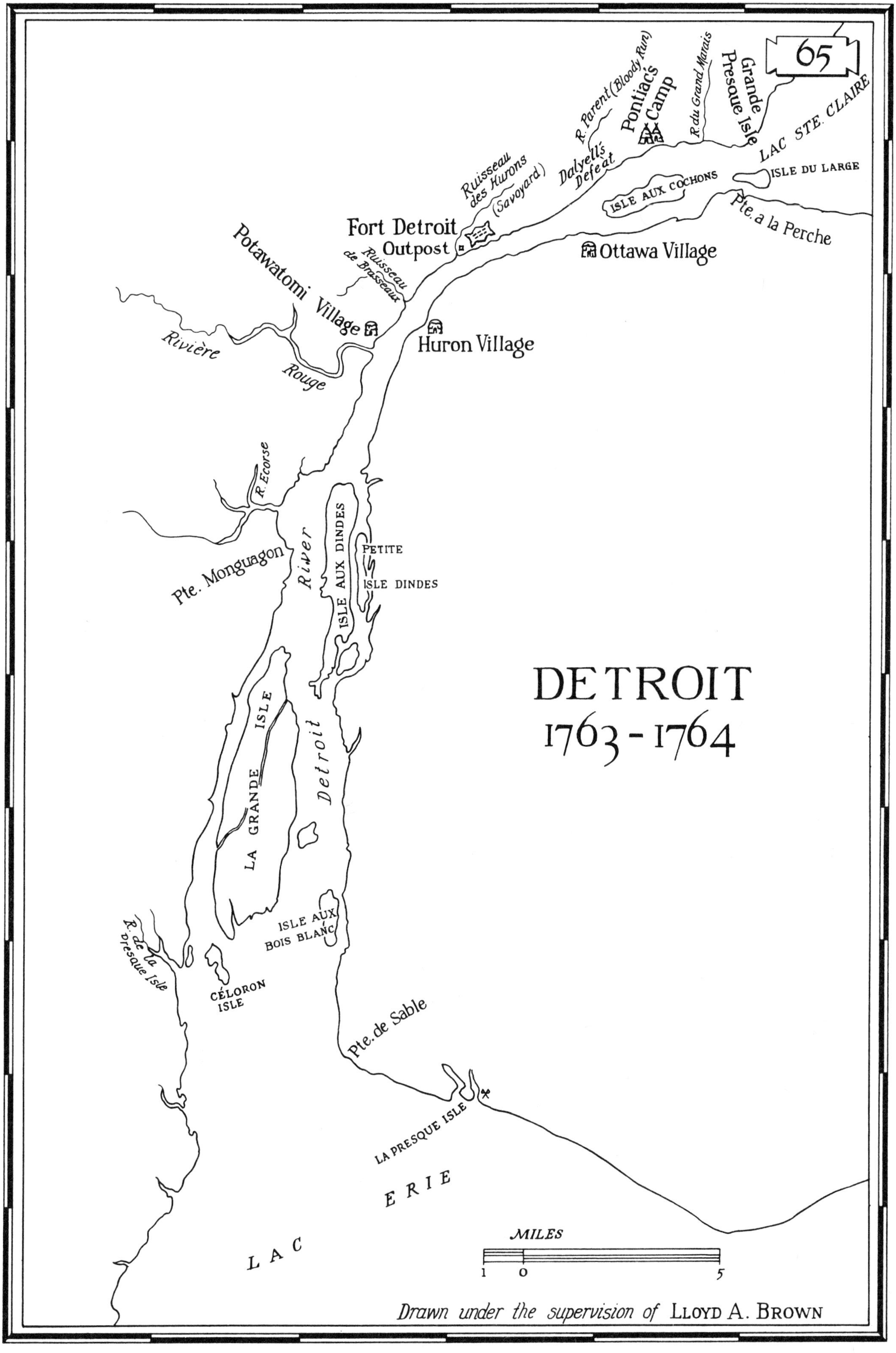
65
DETROIT
1763-1764
Grande Presque Isle
R. du Grand Marais
Pontiac's Camp
R. Parent (Bloody Run)
Dalyell's Defeat
Ruisseau des Hurons (Savoyard)
LAC STE. CLAIRE
ISLE DU LARGE
ISLE AUX COCHONS
Pte. a la Perche
Fort Detroit
Outpost
Ottawa Village
Potawatomi Village
Ruisseau de Brasseaux
Huron Village
Rivière Rouge
R. Ecorse
Pte. Monguagon
River
ISLE AUX DINDES
PETITE ISLE DINDES
LA GRANDE ISLE
Detroit
ISLE AUX BOIS BLANC
R. de la Presque Isle
CÉLORON ISLE
Pte. de Sable
LA PRESQUE ISLE
LAC ERIE
MILES
1 0 5
Drawn under the supervision of LLOYD A. BROWN

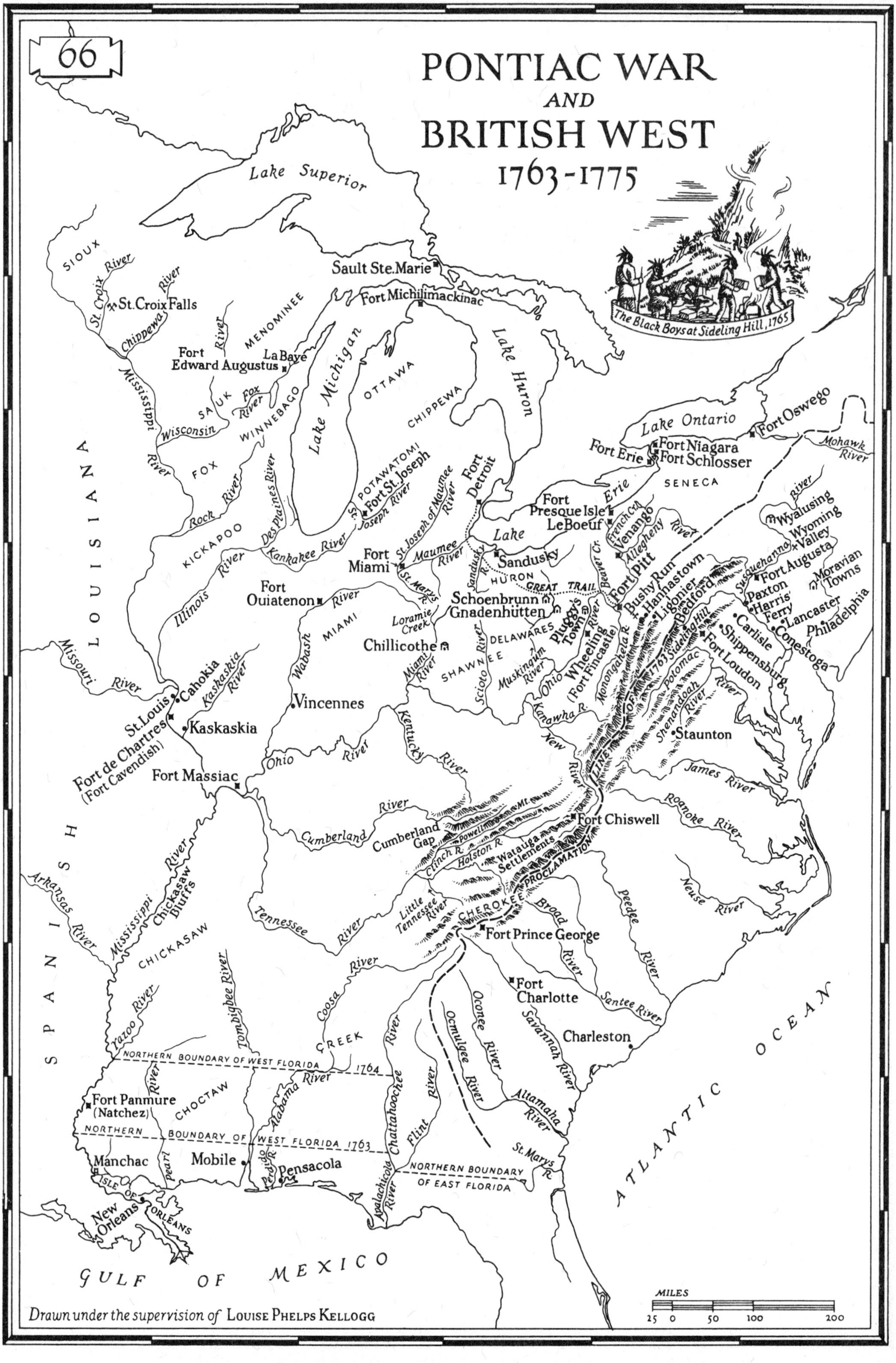
66
PONTIAC WAR
AND
BRITISH WEST
1763-1775
The Black Boys at Sideling Hill, 1765
Lake Superior
Lake Michigan
Lake Huron
Lake Ontario
Lake Erie
SIOUX
St. Croix River
St. Croix Falls
Chippewa River
MENOMINEE
Sault Ste. Marie
Fort Michilimackinac
Fort Edward Augustus
La Baye
SAUK
Fox River
WINNEBAGO
OTTAWA
CHIPPEWA
Wisconsin
Mississippi River
FOX
Rock River
POTAWATOMI
Fort St. Joseph
St. Joseph River
Des Plaines River
KICKAPOO
Kankakee River
Illinois River
Fort Detroit
Fort Miami
St. Joseph of Maumee River
Maumee River
St. Marys R.
Sandusky R.
Sandusky
HURON
GREAT TRAIL
Fort Ouiatenon
Wabash River
MIAMI
Loramie Creek
Chillicothe
Schoenbrunn
Gnadenhütten
DELAWARES
SHAWNEE
Scioto River
Muskingum River
Pluggy's Town
Miami River
LOUISIANA
Missouri River
Cahokia
Kaskaskia River
St. Louis
Fort de Chartres
(Fort Cavendish)
Kaskaskia
Vincennes
Ohio River
Fort Massiac
Kentucky River
Fort Erie
Fort Niagara
Fort Schlosser
Fort Oswego
Mohawk River
SENECA
Fort Presque Isle
LeBoeuf
French Cr.
Venango
Allegheny River
Beaver Cr.
Fort Pitt
Bushy Run
Hannastown
Ligonier
Bedford
Sideling Hill
Monongahela R.
Wheeling
(Fort Fincastle)
Ohio River
Kanawha R.
New River
Wyalusing
Wyoming Valley
Susquehanna
Fort Augusta
Moravian Towns
Paxton
Harris' Ferry
Lancaster
Philadelphia
Carlisle
Conestoga
Shippensburg
Fort Loudon
Potomac
Shenandoah River
Staunton
James River
Roanoke River
Fort Chiswell
PROCLAMATION LINE OF 1763
Cumberland River
Cumberland Gap
Powell Mt.
Clinch R.
Holston R.
Watauga Settlements
Little Tennessee River
CHEROKEE
Fort Prince George
Broad River
Peedee River
Neuse River
Tennessee River
Arkansas River
Mississippi River
Chickasaw Bluffs
CHICKASAW
Tombigbee River
Coosa River
Yazoo River
CREEK
SPANISH
Fort Charlotte
Santee River
Charleston
Oconee River
Ocmulgee River
Savannah River
Altamaha River
Flint River
Chattahoochee River
NORTHERN BOUNDARY OF WEST FLORIDA 1764
CHOCTAW
Alabama River
Fort Panmure
(Natchez)
NORTHERN BOUNDARY OF WEST FLORIDA 1763
Manchac
Pearl
Mobile
Perdido R.
Pensacola
NORTHERN BOUNDARY OF EAST FLORIDA
Apalachicola River
St. Marys R.
ISLE OF ORLEANS
New Orleans
ATLANTIC OCEAN
GULF OF MEXICO
MILES
25 0 50 100 200
Drawn under the supervision of LOUISE PHELPS KELLOGG

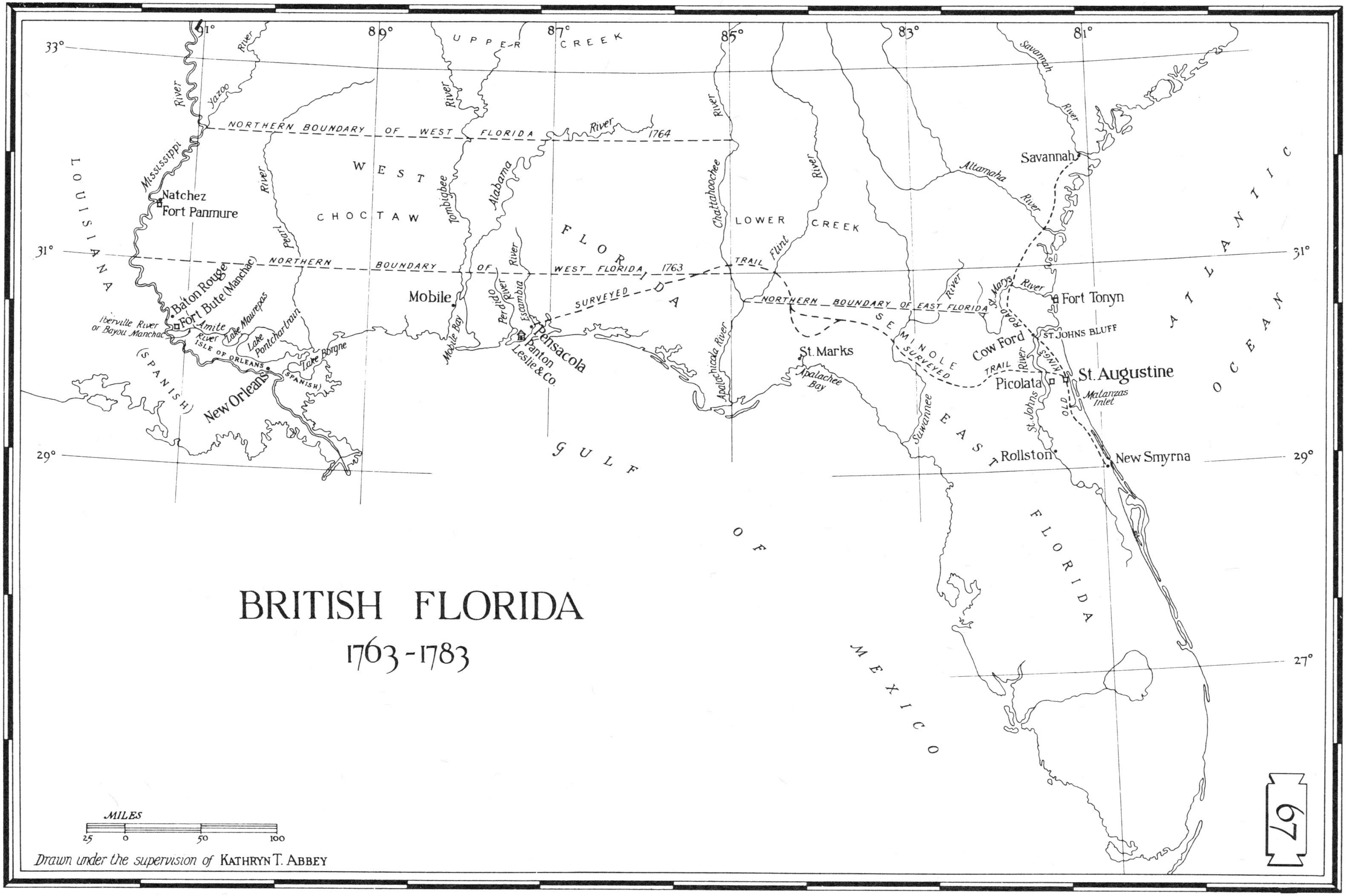
67
BRITISH FLORIDA
1763-1783
Drawn under the supervision of KATHRYN T. ABBEY
MILES
25
0
50
100
33°
31°
29°
27°
91°
89°
87°
85°
83°
81°
ATLANTIC OCEAN
GULF OF MEXICO
LOUISIANA
(SPANISH)
WEST FLORIDA
EAST FLORIDA
UPPER CREEK
LOWER CREEK
CHOCTAW
SEMINOLE
NORTHERN BOUNDARY OF WEST FLORIDA 1764
NORTHERN BOUNDARY OF WEST FLORIDA 1763
NORTHERN BOUNDARY OF EAST FLORIDA
SURVEYED
TRAIL
KINGS ROAD
OLD
Natchez
Fort Panmure
Baton Rouge
Fort Bute (Manchac)
Iberville River or Bayou Manchac
Amite River
Lake Maurepas
Lake Pontchartrain
Lake Borgne
ISLE OF ORLEANS
New Orleans
Mobile
Mobile Bay
Pensacola
Panton Leslie & Co.
St. Marks
Apalachee Bay
Savannah
Fort Tonyn
ST. JOHNS BLUFF
Cow Ford
Picolata
St. Augustine
Matanzas Inlet
Rollston
New Smyrna
Mississippi River
Yazoo River
Pearl River
Tombigbee River
Alabama River
Escambia River
Perdido River
Chattahoochee River
Flint River
Apalachicola River
Suwannee
St. Marys River
St. Johns River
Altamaha River
Savannah River

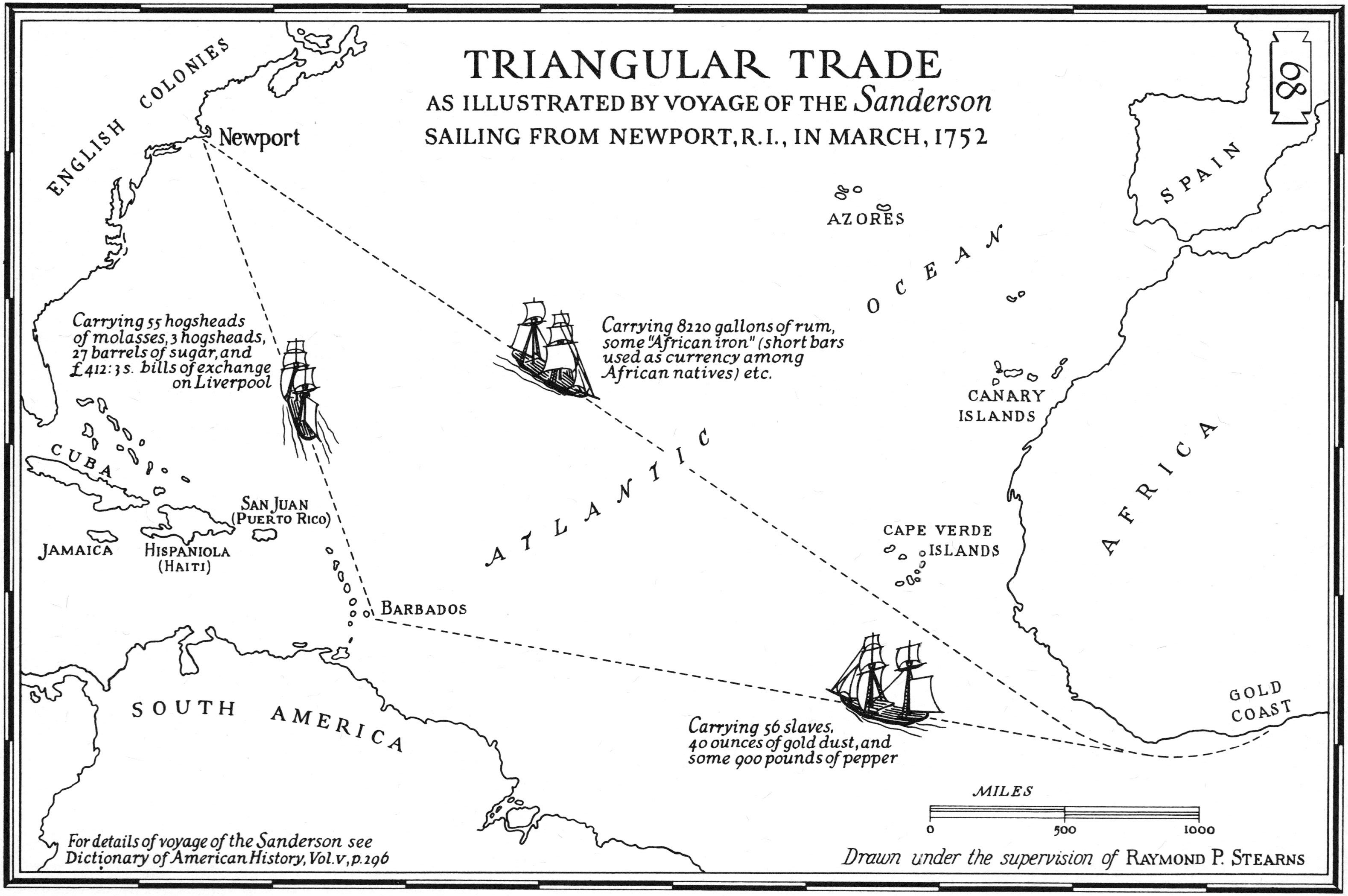
TRIANGULAR TRADE
AS ILLUSTRATED BY VOYAGE OF THE Sanderson
SAILING FROM NEWPORT, R.I., IN MARCH, 1752
68
ENGLISH COLONIES
Newport
SPAIN
AZORES
OCEAN
ATLANTIC
AFRICA
CANARY ISLANDS
CAPE VERDE ISLANDS
GOLD COAST
Carrying 55 hogsheads of molasses, 3 hogsheads, 27 barrels of sugar, and £412:3s. bills of exchange on Liverpool
Carrying 8220 gallons of rum, some "African iron" (short bars used as currency among African natives) etc.
Carrying 56 slaves, 40 ounces of gold dust, and some 900 pounds of pepper
CUBA
JAMAICA
HISPANIOLA (HAITI)
SAN JUAN (PUERTO RICO)
BARBADOS
SOUTH AMERICA
MILES
0
500
1000
For details of voyage of the Sanderson see Dictionary of American History, Vol. v, p. 296
Drawn under the supervision of RAYMOND P. STEARNS

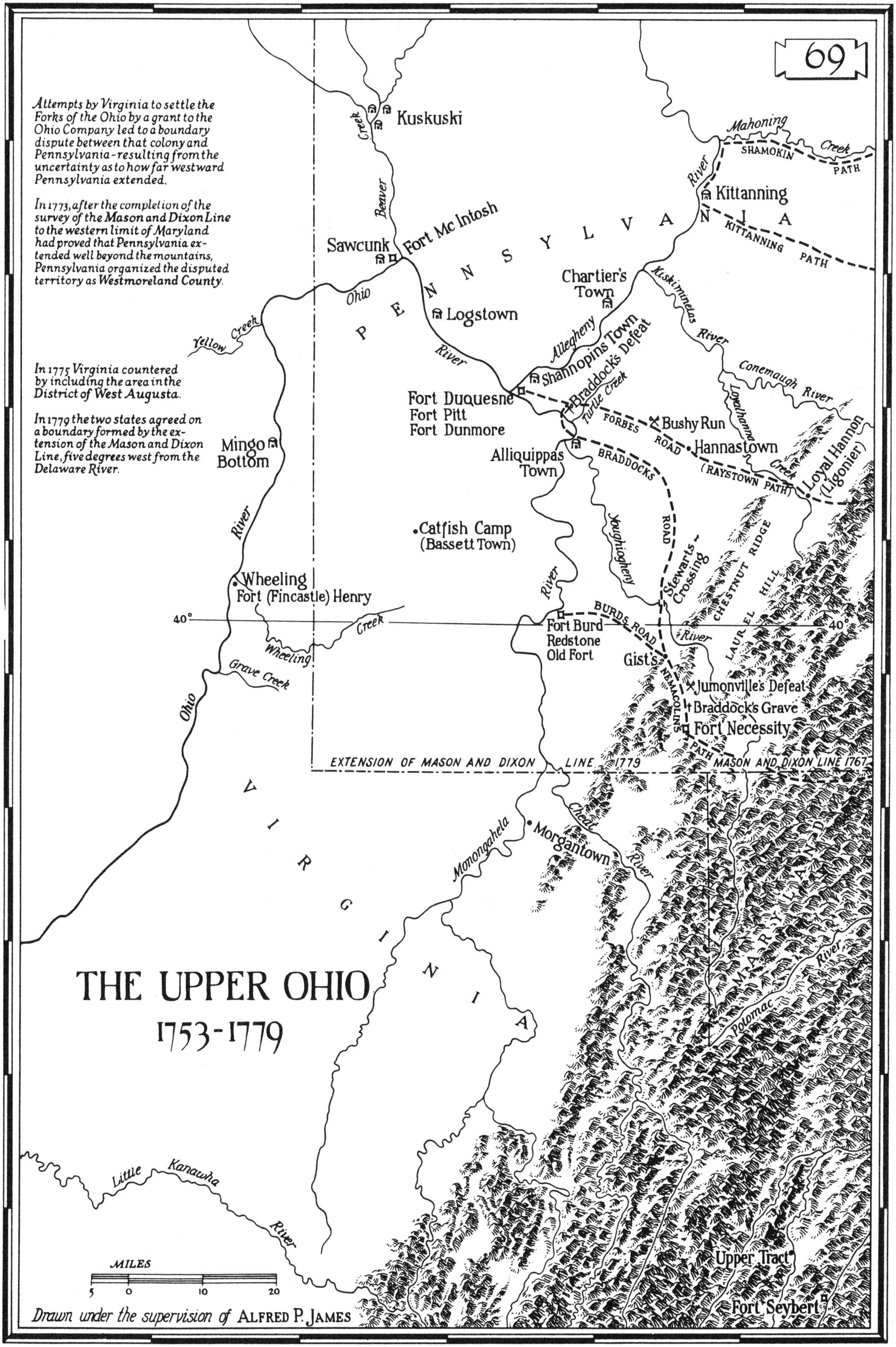
69
THE UPPER OHIO
1753-1779
Attempts by Virginia to settle the Forks of the Ohio by a grant to the Ohio Company led to a boundary dispute between that colony and Pennsylvania - resulting from the uncertainty as to how far westward Pennsylvania extended.
In 1773, after the completion of the survey of the Mason and Dixon Line to the western limit of Maryland had proved that Pennsylvania extended well beyond the mountains, Pennsylvania organized the disputed territory as Westmoreland County.
In 1775 Virginia countered by including the area in the District of West Augusta.
In 1779 the two states agreed on a boundary formed by the extension of the Mason and Dixon Line, five degrees west from the Delaware River.
PENNSYLVANIA
VIRGINIA
MARYLAND
Kuskuski
Beaver Creek
Sawcunk
Fort Mc Intosh
Mahoning Creek
SHAMOKIN PATH
Kittanning
KITTANNING PATH
Chartier's Town
Logstown
Ohio River
Yellow Creek
Allegheny River
Kiskiminetas River
Shannopins Town
Braddock's Defeat
Turtle Creek
Conemaugh River
Fort Duquesne
Fort Pitt
Fort Dunmore
FORBES ROAD
Bushy Run
Hannastown
(RAYSTOWN PATH)
Loyalhanna Creek
Loyal Hannon (Ligonier)
Mingo Bottom
Alliquippas Town
BRADDOCKS ROAD
Catfish Camp (Bassett Town)
Youghiogheny River
Stewarts Crossing
CHESTNUT RIDGE
LAUREL HILL
Wheeling
Fort (Fincastle) Henry
40°
Wheeling Creek
BURDS ROAD
Fort Burd
Redstone Old Fort
Gist's
Grave Creek
NEMACOLINS PATH
Jumonville's Defeat
Braddock's Grave
Fort Necessity
EXTENSION OF MASON AND DIXON LINE 1779
MASON AND DIXON LINE 1767
Monongahela
Morgantown
Cheat River
Potomac River
Little Kanawha River
Upper Tract
Fort Seybert
MILES
5 0 10 20
Drawn under the supervision of ALFRED P. JAMES

PROCLAMATION LINE *of* 1763 INDIAN CESSIONS *and* THE LAND COMPANIES

— — — The Proclamation of 1763 forbade the purchase or settlement of Indian lands westerly of a line running through the heads of the rivers which fell into the Atlantic from the west or northwest.

—x—x— Tryon's Line, 1767, (by agreement with the Cherokee) directed that no white settlement should be made westerly of a line running from a point where Reedy River was intersected by the then North Carolina-South Carolina boundary, to Tryon's Mountain and thence to Fort Chiswell.

—+—+—+ The Treaty of Fort Stanwix, 1768, (with the Iroquois) extinguished Iroquois claims to the lands southeasterly of a line running from Fort Stanwix to Fort Pitt, and thence along the southern bank of the Ohio to the mouth of the Tennessee (Cherokee) River.

—o—o— —x—x— The Treaty of Hard Labor, 1768, (with the Cherokee) confirmed Tryon's Line of 1767 and extended it from Fort Chiswell to the mouth of the Kanawha River.

—•—•— The Treaty of Lochaber, 1770, (with the Cherokee) moved the northern part of the line established at the Treaty of Hard Labor westerly to run from six miles east of Long Island of Holston directly to the mouth of the Kanawha River. Lochaber was the name of the plantation of Alexander Cameron, Assistant Commissioner of Indian Affairs for the Southern Provinces.

—••—••— Donelson's Line. When Col. Donelson acting for Virginia, and Chief Attakullakulla and Alex. Cameron, acting for the Cherokee, came to run the Lochaber Line, some agreement was entered into by which it was turned westward and made to run with the Kentucky (Louisa) River.

The Treaty of Sycamore Shoals, 1775, negotiated between the Transylvania Company and the Cherokee, consumated the sale, by the Cherokee, of TRANSYLVANIA, comprising the land lying between the Kentucky River and the south watershed of the Cumberland River plus a path from the white settlements to the newly acquired lands.

•••••••••• VANDALIA originated in the grant, by the Iroquois at the Treaty of Fort Stanwix, of a tract, between Pennsylvania and the Little Kanawha, known as "Indiana."

Settlements on the Watauga and Nolachucky are indicated thus - ∘∘

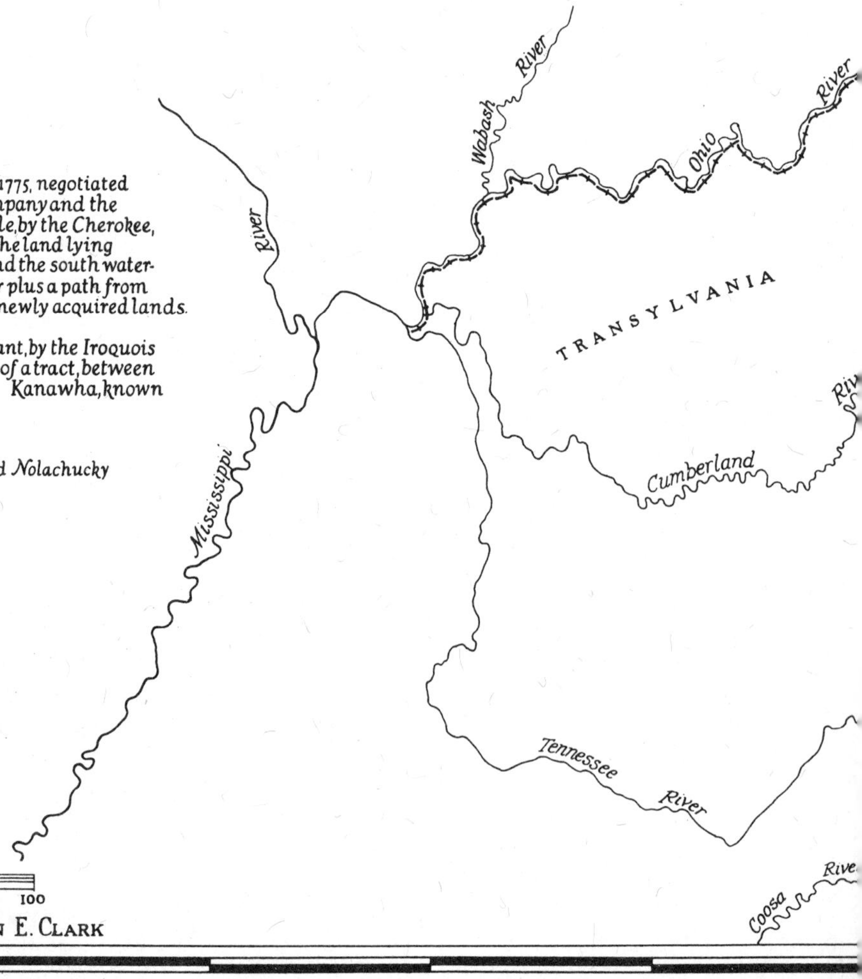

MILES
25 0 50 100

Drawn under the supervision of DAN E. CLARK

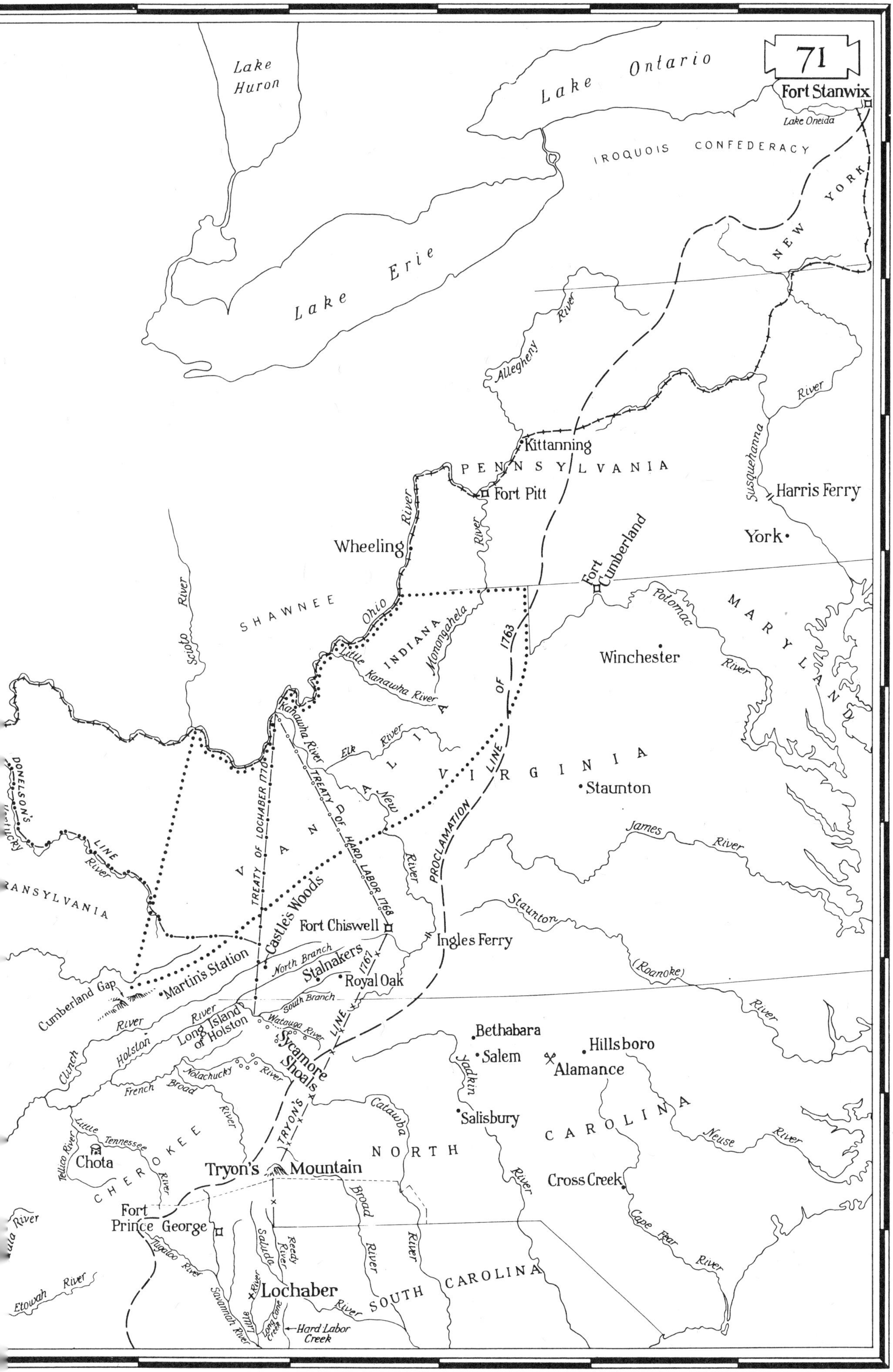
71
Fort Stanwix
Lake Oneida
Lake Ontario
Lake Huron
Lake Erie
IROQUOIS CONFEDERACY
NEW YORK
Allegheny River
River
Susquehanna
Kittanning
PENNSYLVANIA
Fort Pitt
Harris Ferry
York
Wheeling
Ohio River
River
Fort Cumberland
Potomac River
MARYLAND
Winchester
SHAWNEE
Scioto River
INDIANA
Monongahela
Little Kanawha River
PROCLAMATION LINE OF 1763
VANDALIA
Kanawha River
Elk River
New River
VIRGINIA
Staunton
James River
TREATY OF LOCHABER 1770
TREATY OF HARD LABOR 1768
DONELSON'S LINE
Kentucky River
TRANSYLVANIA
Fort Chiswell
Castle's Woods
Ingles Ferry
Staunton River
(Roanoke)
River
North Branch
Stalnakers
Royal Oak
Martin's Station
Cumberland Gap
1767
South Branch
LINE
Clinch River
Holston River
Long Island of Holston
Watauga River
Sycamore Shoals
Bethabara
Salem
Hillsboro
Alamance
Yadkin
Nolachucky River
French Broad River
Salisbury
Catawba
NORTH CAROLINA
Neuse River
Little Tennessee
Tellico River
Chota
CHEROKEE
River
TRYON'S LINE
Tryon's Mountain
Cross Creek
Broad River
River
Fort Prince George
Tugaloo River
Saluda
Reedy River
River
Cape Fear River
SOUTH CAROLINA
Etowah River
Savannah River
Little River
Lochaber
Long Cane Creek
Hard Labor Creek
River

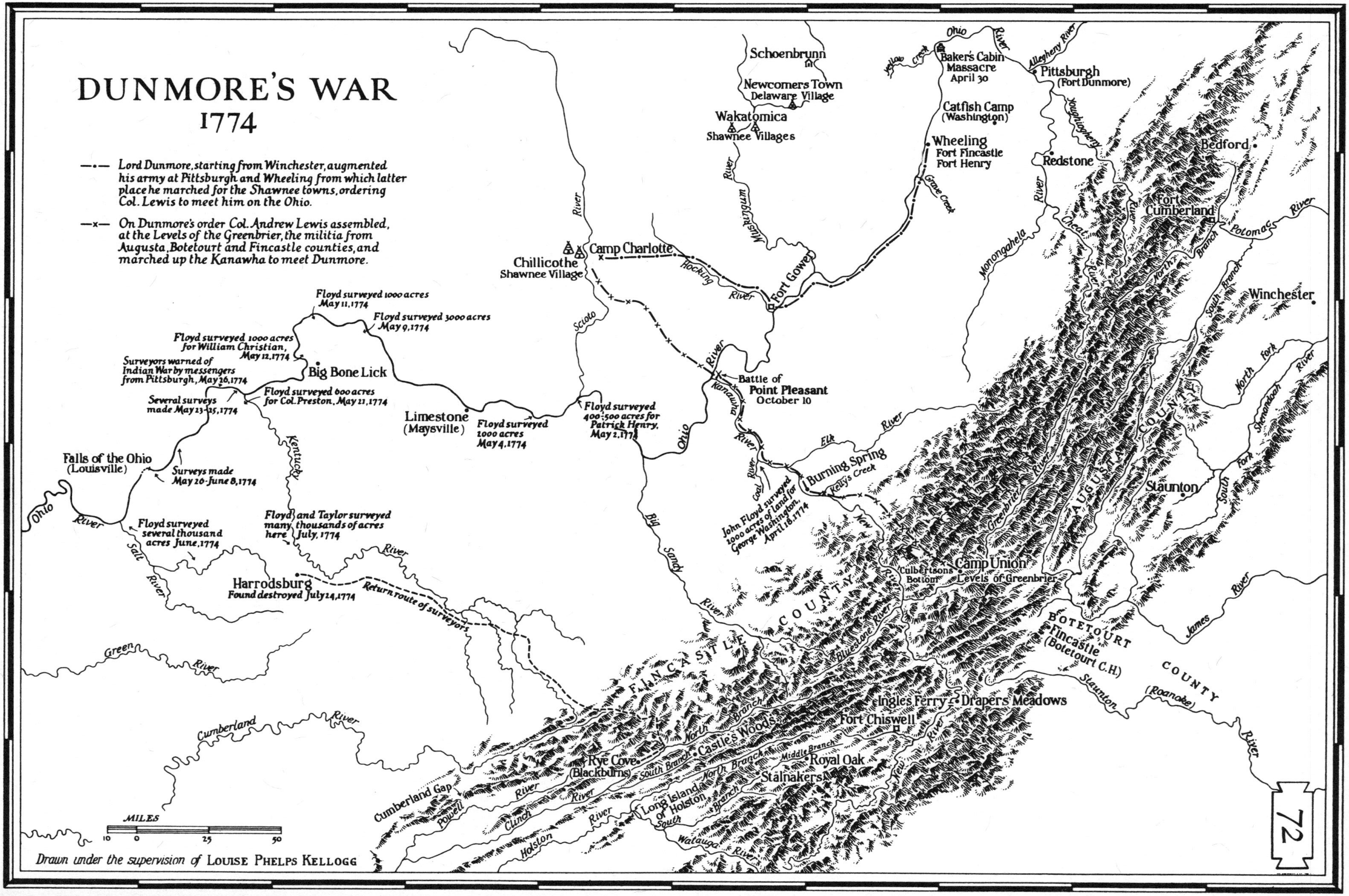
DUNMORE'S WAR
1774
Lord Dunmore, starting from Winchester, augmented his army at Pittsburgh and Wheeling from which latter place he marched for the Shawnee towns, ordering Col. Lewis to meet him on the Ohio.
On Dunmore's order Col. Andrew Lewis assembled, at the Levels of the Greenbrier, the militia from Augusta, Botetourt and Fincastle counties, and marched up the Kanawha to meet Dunmore.
72
Schoenbrunn
Newcomers Town
Delaware Village
Wakatomica
Shawnee Villages
Bakers Cabin
Massacre
April 30
Pittsburgh
(Fort Dunmore)
Catfish Camp
(Washington)
Wheeling
Fort Fincastle
Fort Henry
Redstone
Bedford
Fort Cumberland
Winchester
Staunton
Chillicothe
Shawnee Village
Camp Charlotte
Fort Gower
Battle of
Point Pleasant
October 10
Burning Spring
Kellys Creek
John Floyd surveyed 2000 acres of land for George Washington, April 18, 1774
Camp Union
Levels of Greenbrier
Culbertsons Bottom
BOTETOURT COUNTY
Fincastle
(Botetourt C.H.)
AUGUSTA COUNTY
FINCASTLE COUNTY
Ingles Ferry
Drapers Meadows
Fort Chiswell
Royal Oak
Stalnakers
Castle's Woods
Rye Cove
(Blackburns)
Long Island of Holston
Cumberland Gap
Floyd surveyed 1000 acres May 11, 1774
Floyd surveyed 3000 acres May 9, 1774
Floyd surveyed 1000 acres for William Christian, May 12, 1774
Surveyors warned of Indian War by messengers from Pittsburgh, May 26, 1774
Big Bone Lick
Floyd surveyed 600 acres for Col. Preston, May 21, 1774
Several surveys made May 23-25, 1774
Limestone
(Maysville)
Floyd surveyed 2000 acres May 4, 1774
Floyd surveyed 400-500 acres for Patrick Henry, May 2, 1774
Falls of the Ohio
(Louisville)
Surveys made May 26-June 8, 1774
Floyd and Taylor surveyed many thousands of acres here July, 1774
Floyd surveyed several thousand acres June, 1774
Harrodsburg
Found destroyed July 24, 1774
Return route of surveyors
Ohio River
Allegheny River
Yellow Creek
Youghiogheny
Monongahela
Cheat River
Potomac River
North Branch
South Branch
North Fork
South Fork
Shenandoah River
James River
Roanoke
Staunton
Muskingum River
Hocking River
Scioto
Kanawha River
Coal River
Elk River
Grave Creek
New River
Greenbrier River
Bluestone River
Big Sandy River
Kentucky
Salt River
Green River
Cumberland River
Powell River
Clinch River
Holston River
Middle Branch
Watauga River
MILES
10 0 25 50
Drawn under the supervision of Louise Phelps Kellogg

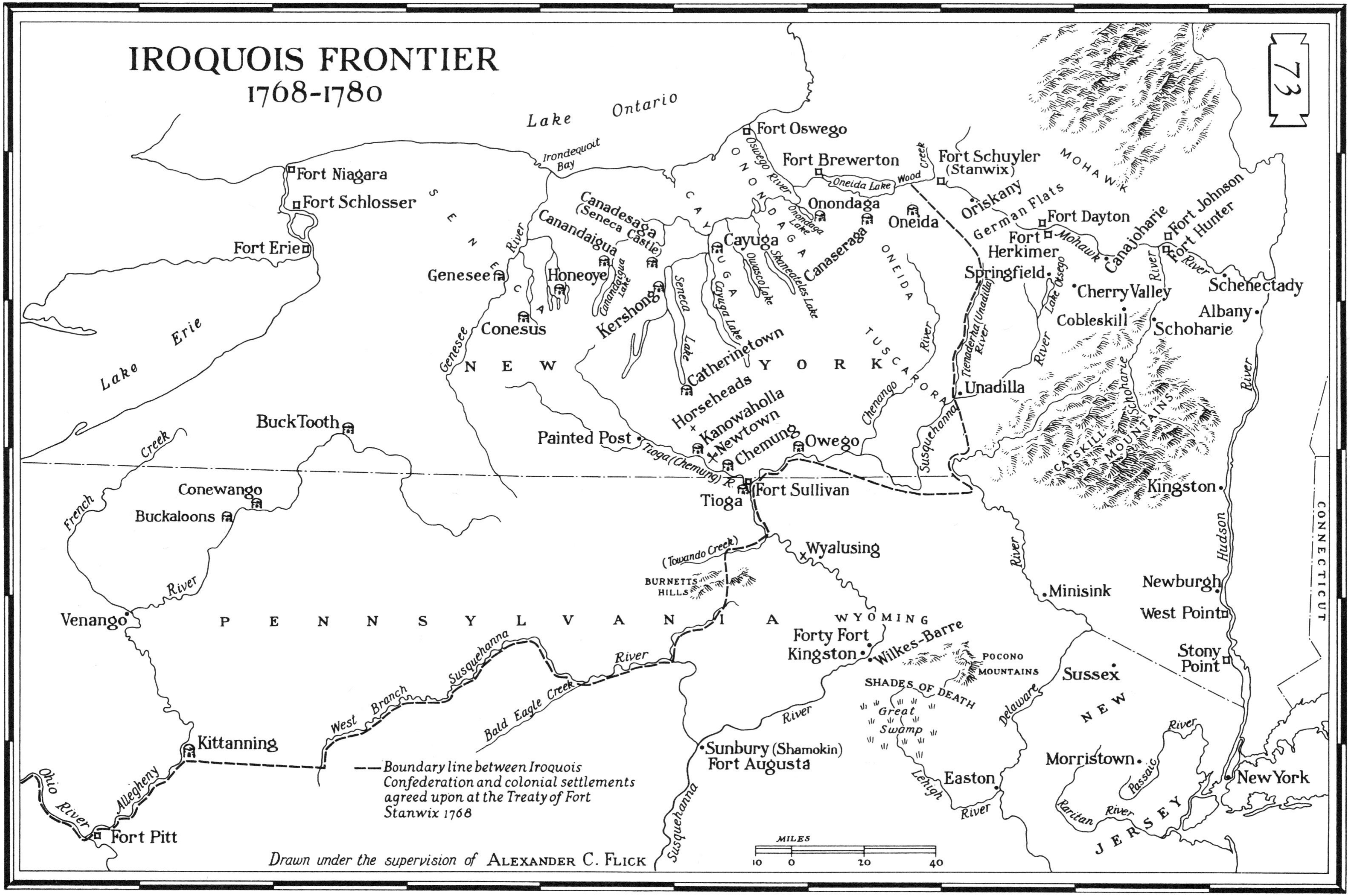
73
IROQUOIS FRONTIER
1768-1780
Lake Ontario
Irondequoit Bay
Fort Oswego
Fort Brewerton
Fort Schuyler (Stanwix)
MOHAWK
Fort Niagara
Fort Schlosser
Fort Erie
SENECA
CAYUGA
ONONDAGA
ONEIDA
TUSCARORA
Oswego River
Oneida Lake
Wood Creek
Onondaga
Onondaga Lake
Oneida
Oriskany
German Flats
Fort Dayton
Fort Herkimer
Mohawk
Canajoharie
Fort Johnson
Fort Hunter
River
Canadesaga (Seneca Castle)
Canandaigua
Canandaigua Lake
Genesee
Honeoye
Cayuga
Owasco Lake
Skaneateles Lake
Canaseraga
Springfield
Lake Otsego
Cherry Valley
Schenectady
Albany
Cobleskill
Schoharie
Conesus
Kershong
Seneca Lake
Cayuga Lake
Genesee River
NEW YORK
Catherinetown
Tienaderha (Unadilla) River
Unadilla
Chenango
Susquehanna
CATSKILL MOUNTAINS
Horseheads
Kanowaholla
Newtown
Chemung
Owego
Painted Post
Tioga (Chemung) R.
Tioga
Fort Sullivan
Kingston
Hudson River
Buck Tooth
French Creek
Conewango
Buckaloons
Lake Erie
Venango
PENNSYLVANIA
(Towando Creek)
BURNETTS HILLS
Wyalusing
WYOMING
Forty Fort
Kingston
Wilkes-Barre
POCONO MOUNTAINS
SHADES OF DEATH
Great Swamp
Minisink
Delaware River
Newburgh
West Point
Stony Point
CONNECTICUT
Sussex
NEW JERSEY
Morristown
Passaic River
Raritan River
New York
West Branch Susquehanna River
Bald Eagle Creek
Kittanning
Allegheny
Ohio River
Fort Pitt
Sunbury (Shamokin)
Fort Augusta
Lehigh River
Easton
Boundary line between Iroquois Confederation and colonial settlements agreed upon at the Treaty of Fort Stanwix 1768
MILES
10 0 20 40
Drawn under the supervision of ALEXANDER C. FLICK

V THE AMERICAN REVOLUTION

THE THIRTEEN COLONIES

NEW HAMPSHIRE · MASSACHUSETTS · CONNECTICUT
RHODE ISLAND · NEW YORK · NEW JERSEY · PENNSYLVANIA
DELAWARE · MARYLAND · VIRGINIA · NORTH CAROLINA
SOUTH CAROLINA · GEORGIA

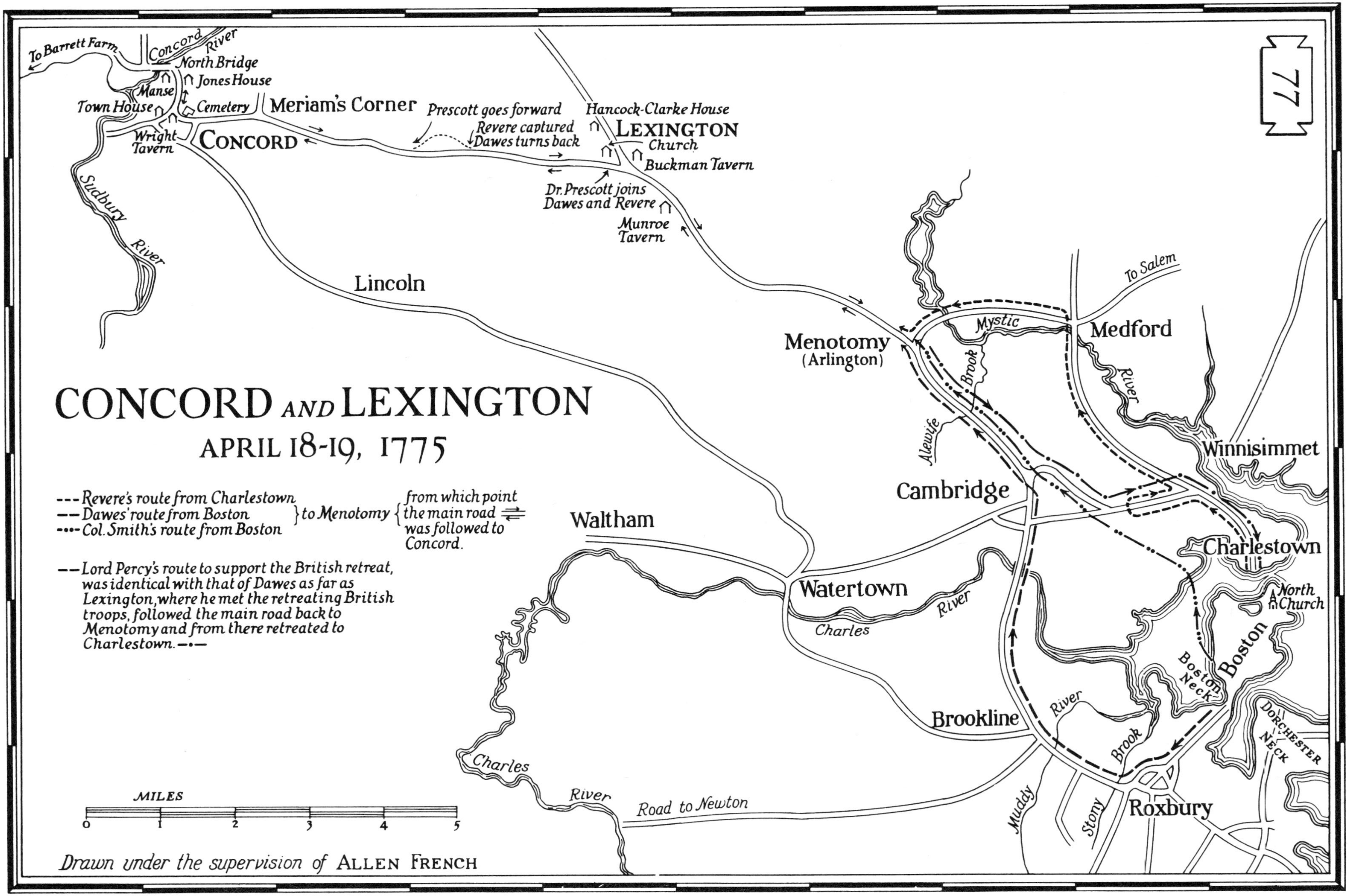
77
CONCORD AND LEXINGTON
APRIL 18-19, 1775
---Revere's route from Charlestown
——Dawes' route from Boston
-•••-Col. Smith's route from Boston
} to Menotomy { from which point the main road ⇄ was followed to Concord.
——Lord Percy's route to support the British retreat, was identical with that of Dawes as far as Lexington, where he met the retreating British troops, followed the main road back to Menotomy and from there retreated to Charlestown. —•—
MILES
0 1 2 3 4 5
Drawn under the supervision of ALLEN FRENCH
To Barrett Farm
Concord River
North Bridge
Jones House
Manse
Town House
Cemetery
Wright Tavern
CONCORD
Meriam's Corner
Prescott goes forward
Revere captured
Dawes turns back
Hancock-Clarke House
LEXINGTON
Church
Buckman Tavern
Dr. Prescott joins Dawes and Revere
Munroe Tavern
Sudbury River
Lincoln
Menotomy
(Arlington)
Mystic
Brook
Alewife
To Salem
Medford
River
Winnisimmet
Cambridge
Waltham
Watertown
Charles
River
Charlestown
North Church
Boston
Boston Neck
Brookline
River
Brook
Dorchester Neck
Charles
River
Road to Newton
Muddy
Stony
Roxbury

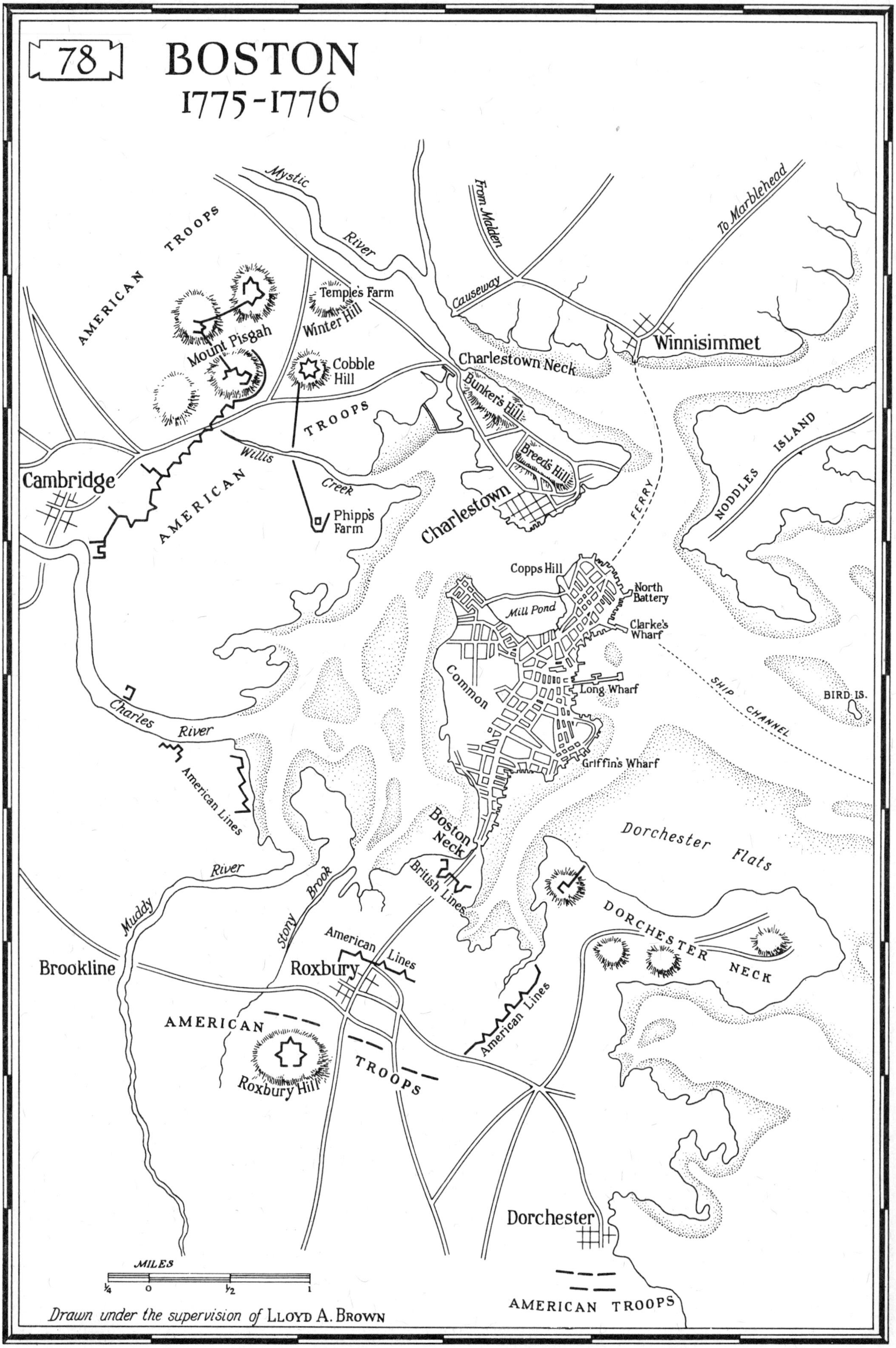
78
BOSTON
1775-1776
Mystic River
From Malden
To Marblehead
AMERICAN TROOPS
Temple's Farm
Winter Hill
Mount Pisgah
Cobble Hill
Causeway
Winnisimmet
Charlestown Neck
Bunker's Hill
Breed's Hill
Charlestown
TROOPS
AMERICAN
Willis Creek
Cambridge
Phipp's Farm
NODDLES ISLAND
FERRY
Copps Hill
North Battery
Mill Pond
Clarke's Wharf
Common
Long Wharf
SHIP CHANNEL
BIRD IS.
Charles River
Griffin's Wharf
American Lines
Boston Neck
Dorchester Flats
British Lines
Muddy River
Stony Brook
American Lines
DORCHESTER NECK
Brookline
Roxbury
American Lines
AMERICAN TROOPS
Roxbury Hill
Dorchester
MILES
1/4 0 1/2 1
AMERICAN TROOPS
Drawn under the supervision of Lloyd A. Brown

INVASION OF CANADA 1775–1776

79

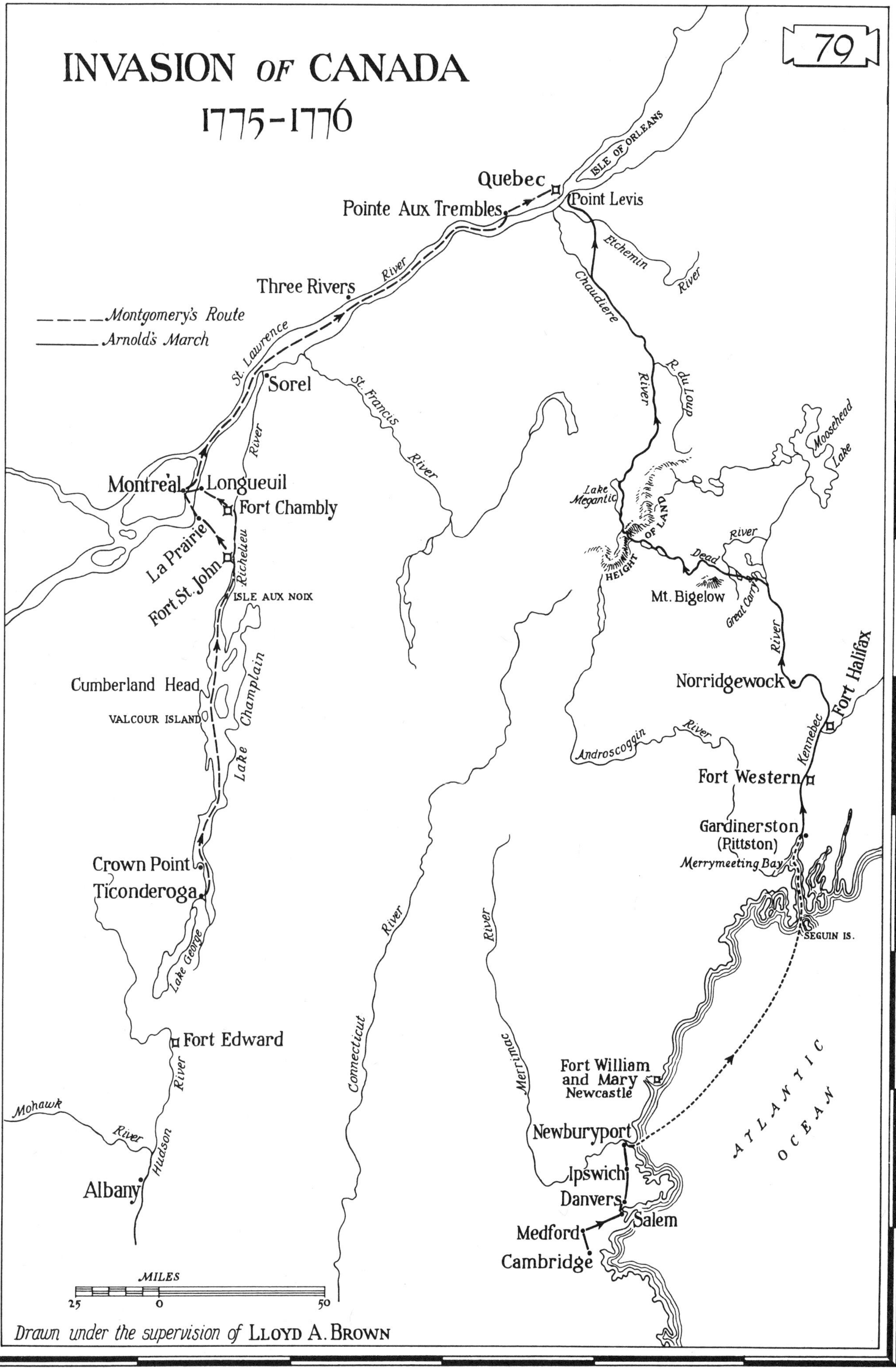

Drawn under the supervision of LLOYD A. BROWN

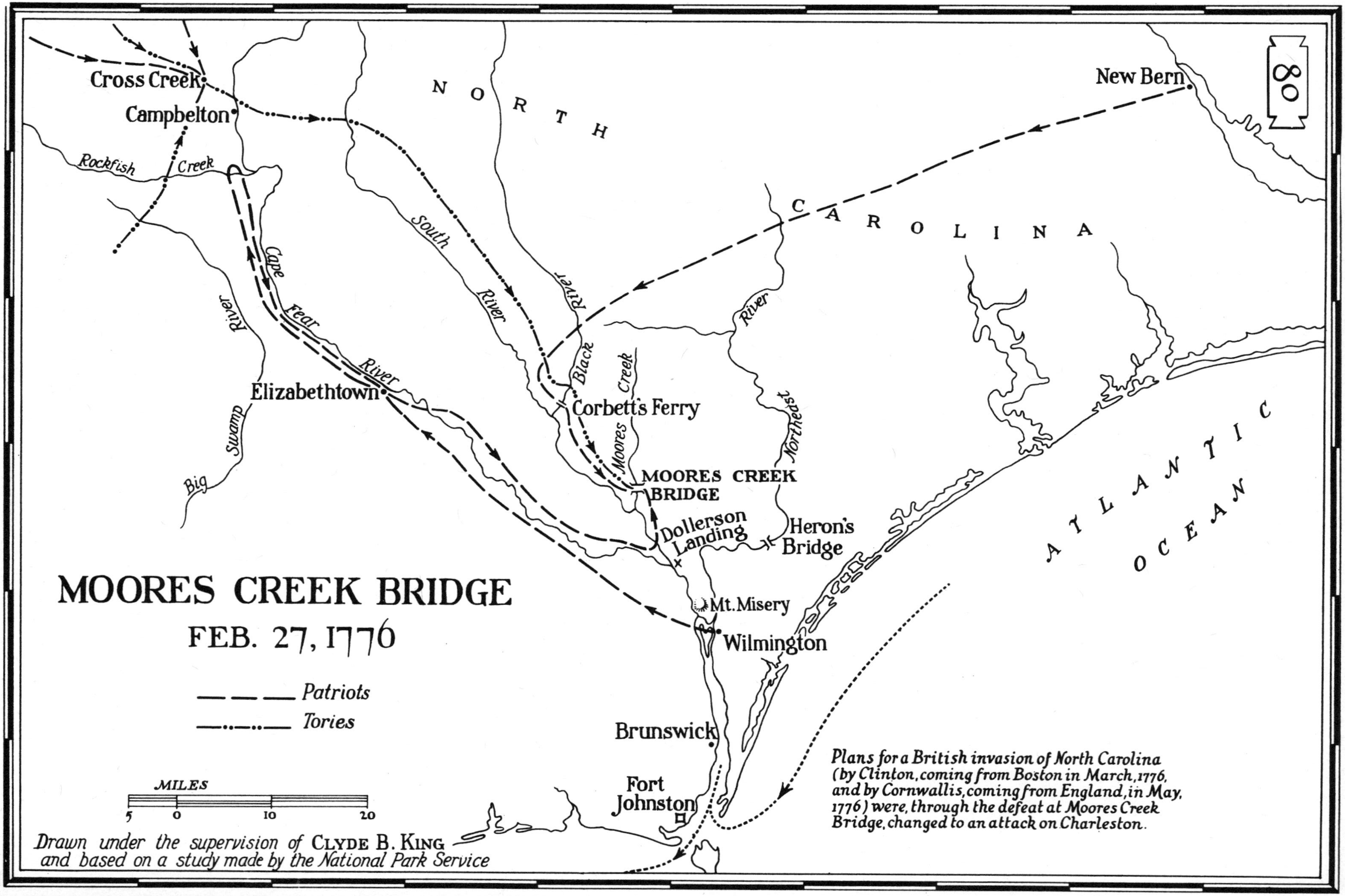
80
MOORES CREEK BRIDGE
FEB. 27, 1776
Patriots
Tories
MILES
5
0
10
20
Drawn under the supervision of CLYDE B. KING and based on a study made by the National Park Service
Plans for a British invasion of North Carolina (by Clinton, coming from Boston in March, 1776, and by Cornwallis, coming from England, in May, 1776) were, through the defeat at Moores Creek Bridge, changed to an attack on Charleston.
NORTH CAROLINA
ATLANTIC OCEAN
Cross Creek
Campbelton
Rockfish Creek
Cape Fear River
Big Swamp River
Elizabethtown
South River
Black River
Moores Creek
Corbett's Ferry
MOORES CREEK BRIDGE
Dollerson Landing
Northeast River
Heron's Bridge
Mt. Misery
Wilmington
Brunswick
Fort Johnston
New Bern

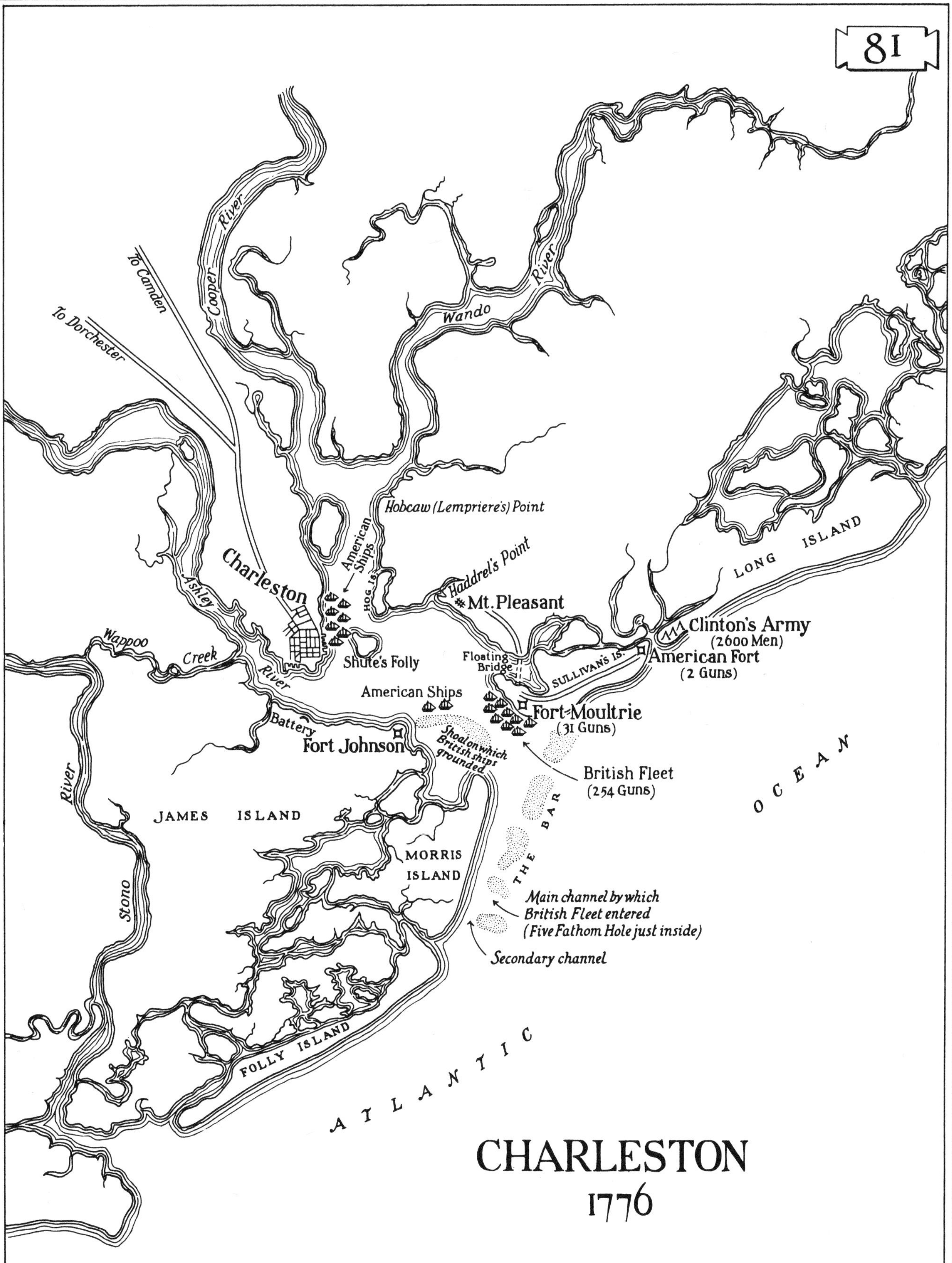

CHARLESTON
1776

Drawn under the supervision of D. D. WALLACE

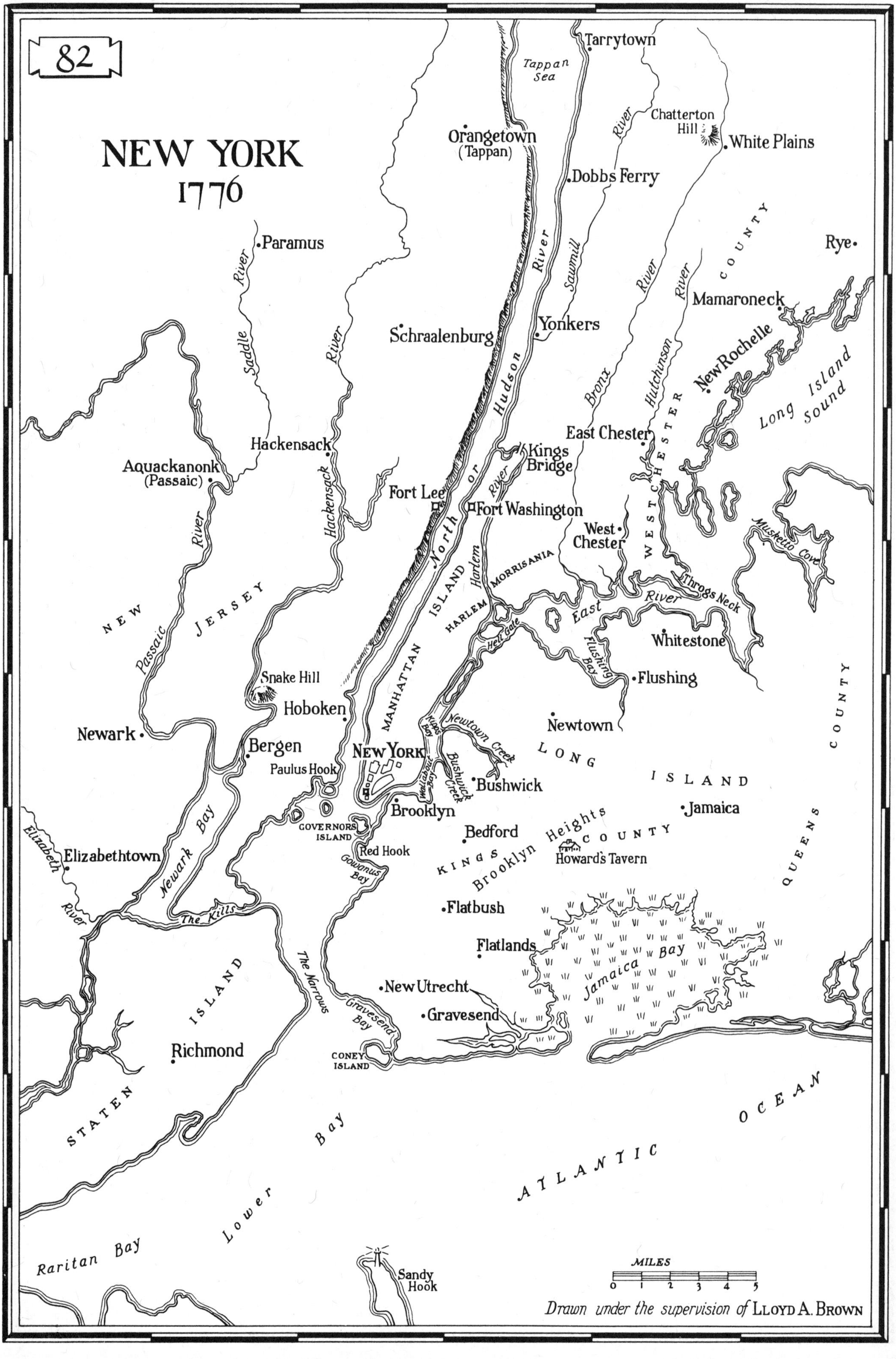
82
NEW YORK
1776
Tarrytown
Tappan Sea
Orangetown
(Tappan)
Chatterton Hill
White Plains
Dobbs Ferry
Paramus
Saddle River
Saw mill River
Bronx River
Hutchinson River
WESTCHESTER COUNTY
Rye
Mamaroneck
Yonkers
Schraalenburg
Hackensack River
Hudson or North River
New Rochelle
Long Island Sound
East Chester
Kings Bridge
Hackensack
Aquackanonk
(Passaic)
Fort Lee
Fort Washington
West Chester
Musketo Cove
Harlem River
MORRISANIA
HARLEM
Throgs Neck
East River
Whitestone
NEW JERSEY
Passaic River
Hell Gate
Flushing Bay
Flushing
Snake Hill
Hoboken
MANHATTAN ISLAND
Kips Bay
Newtown Creek
Newtown
Newark
Bergen
NEW YORK
Paulus Hook
Wallabout Bay
Bushwick Creek
Bushwick
LONG ISLAND
Jamaica
Brooklyn
Newark Bay
Elizabeth River
Elizabethtown
GOVERNORS ISLAND
Red Hook
Gowanus Bay
Bedford
Brooklyn Heights
Howard's Tavern
KINGS COUNTY
QUEENS COUNTY
The Kills
Flatbush
Flatlands
Jamaica Bay
STATEN ISLAND
The Narrows
New Utrecht
Gravesend
Gravesend Bay
Richmond
CONEY ISLAND
ATLANTIC OCEAN
Lower Bay
Raritan Bay
Sandy Hook
MILES
0 1 2 3 4 5
Drawn under the supervision of LLOYD A. BROWN

83
NEW JERSEY AND PHILADELPHIA CAMPAIGNS 1776-1778
PENNSYLVANIA
NEW JERSEY
DELAWARE
MARYLAND
ATLANTIC OCEAN
DELAWARE BAY
Tarrytown
Dobbs Ferry
Paramus
Hackensack
Aquackanonk (Passaic)
Fort Lee
Morristown
Newark
Springfield
Basking Ridge
Elizabethtown
New York
Scotch Plains
Watchung Mts.
Rahway
Bound Brook
Piscataway
Metuchen
Staten Island
Middle Brook
Brunswick
Perth Amboy
Raritan Bay
Sandy Hook
Spotswood
Middletown
Princeton
Shrewsbury
Pennington
Englishtown
Freehold (Monmouth C.H.)
Trenton
Allentown
Crosswicks
Bordentown
Burlington
Mt. Holly
Coryell's Ferry
McConkey's Ferry
Nazareth
Easton
Bethlehem
Reading
Valley Forge
Barren Hill
Swede's Ford
Whitemarsh
Chestnut Hill
Germantown
Paoli
Jeffries Ford
Trimble's Ford
Chad's Ford
Kennett Square
Wilmington
Christiana
Cooch's Bridge
New Castle
PHILADELPHIA
Cooper's Ferry
Gloucester
Haddonfield
Fort Mifflin
Fort Mercer
Chester
Woodbury
Billingsport
Salem
Little Egg Harbor
Absecon Inlet
Great Egg Harbor
Cape May
Cape Henlopen
Lewes
Delaware River
Hudson River
Hackensack River
Passaic River
Raritan River
Schuylkill River
Perkiomen Creek
Wissahickon Creek
Neshaminy Creek
Assanpink Creek
Navesink River
Toms River
Brandywine Creek
Christiana Creek
Elk River
Chesapeake Bay
Maurice River
Great Egg Harbor River
MILES
5 0 10 20 30
Drawn under the supervision of LLOYD A. BROWN

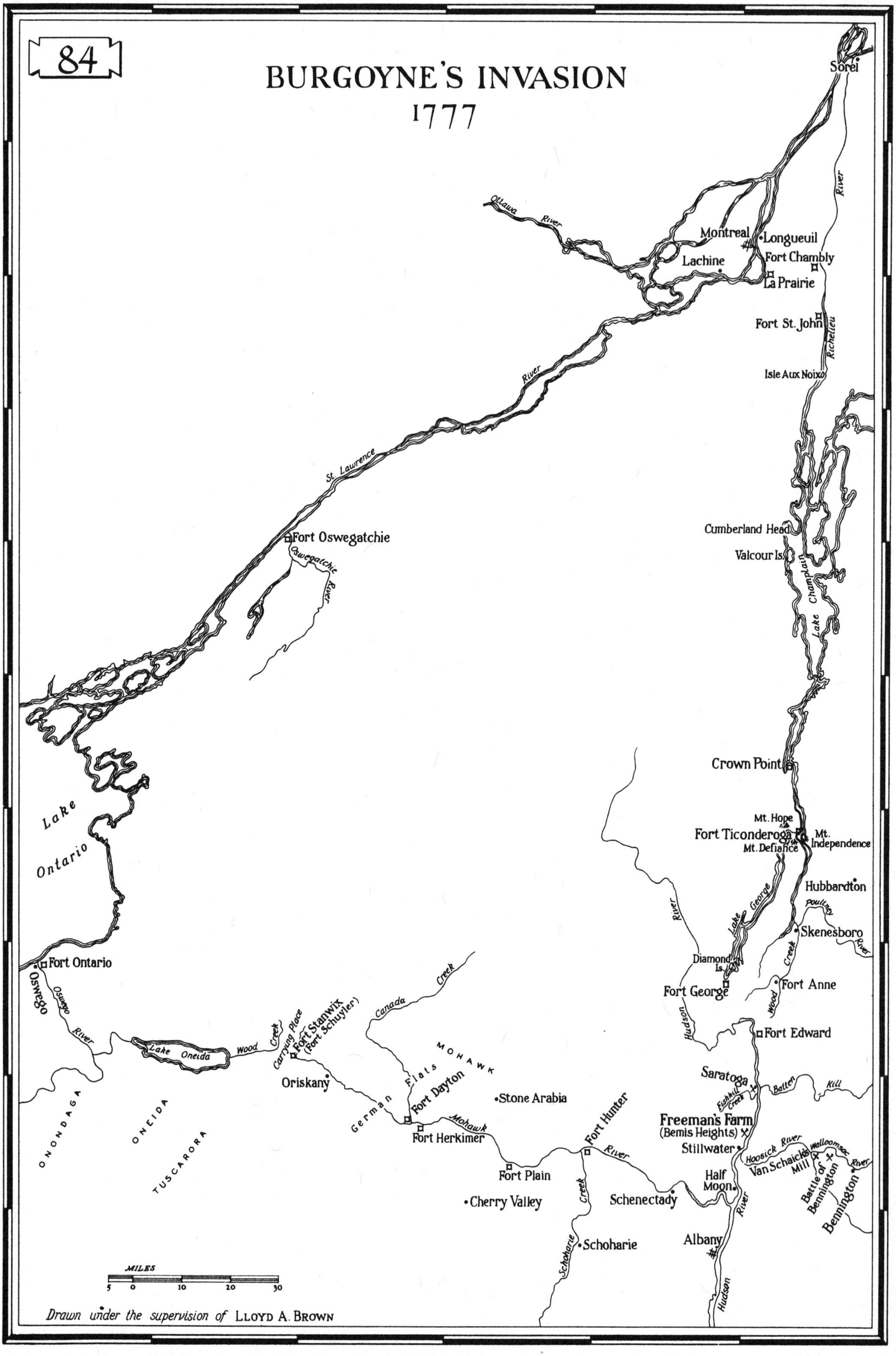
84
BURGOYNE'S INVASION
1777
Sorel
Ottawa River
Montreal
Longueuil
Lachine
Fort Chambly
La Prairie
Fort St. John
Richelieu River
Isle Aux Noix
St. Lawrence River
Fort Oswegatchie
Oswegatchie River
Cumberland Head
Valcour Is.
Lake Champlain
Lake Ontario
Crown Point
Mt. Hope
Fort Ticonderoga
Mt. Defiance
Mt. Independence
Hubbardton
Lake George
Poultney River
Skenesboro
Diamond Is.
Fort George
Wood Creek
Fort Anne
Hudson River
Fort Edward
Fort Ontario
Oswego River
Lake Oneida
Wood Creek
Carrying Place
Fort Stanwix (Fort Schuyler)
Canada Creek
MOHAWK
Oriskany
German Flats
Fort Dayton
Stone Arabia
Mohawk River
Fort Herkimer
Fort Hunter
Saratoga
Batten Kill
Fishkill Creek
Freeman's Farm (Bemis Heights)
Stillwater
Hoosick River
Walloomsac River
Van Schaicks Mill
Battle of Bennington
Bennington
ONONDAGA
ONEIDA
TUSCARORA
Fort Plain
Half Moon
Schenectady
Cherry Valley
Schoharie Creek
Schoharie
Albany
MILES
5 0 10 20 30
Drawn under the supervision of LLOYD A. BROWN

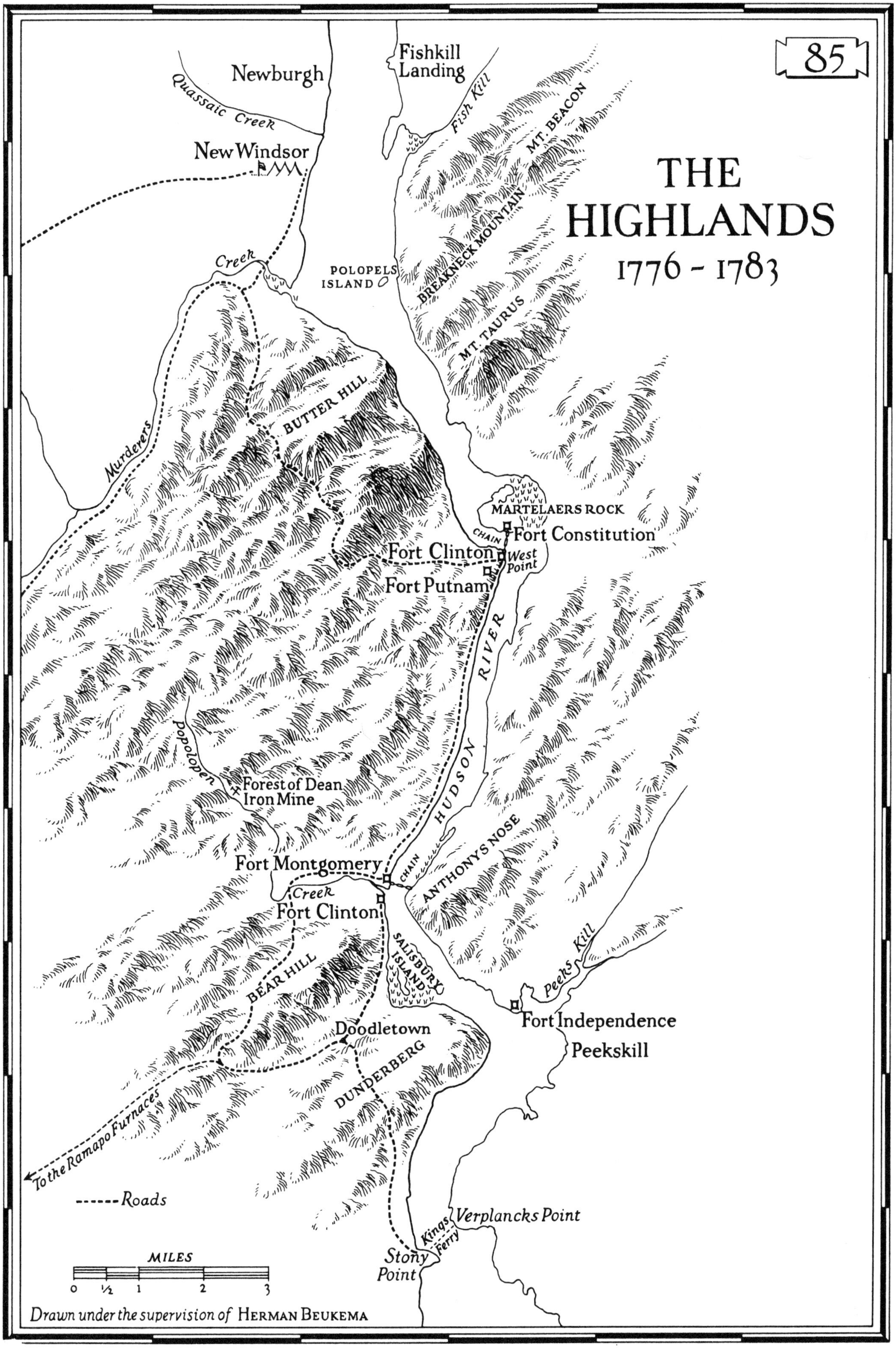
THE HIGHLANDS
1776 - 1783
Newburgh
Fishkill Landing
Quassaic Creek
Fish Kill
New Windsor
MT. BEACON
BREAKNECK MOUNTAIN
Creek
POLOPELS ISLAND
MT. TAURUS
BUTTER HILL
Murderers
MARTELAERS ROCK
CHAIN
Fort Constitution
Fort Clinton
West Point
Fort Putnam
HUDSON RIVER
Popolopen
Forest of Dean Iron Mine
ANTHONYS NOSE
Fort Montgomery
CHAIN
Creek
Fort Clinton
SALISBURY ISLAND
BEAR HILL
Peeks Kill
Fort Independence
Peekskill
Doodletown
DUNDERBERG
To the Ramapo Furnaces
Roads
Verplancks Point
Kings Ferry
Stony Point
MILES
0 ½ 1 2 3
Drawn under the supervision of HERMAN BEUKEMA

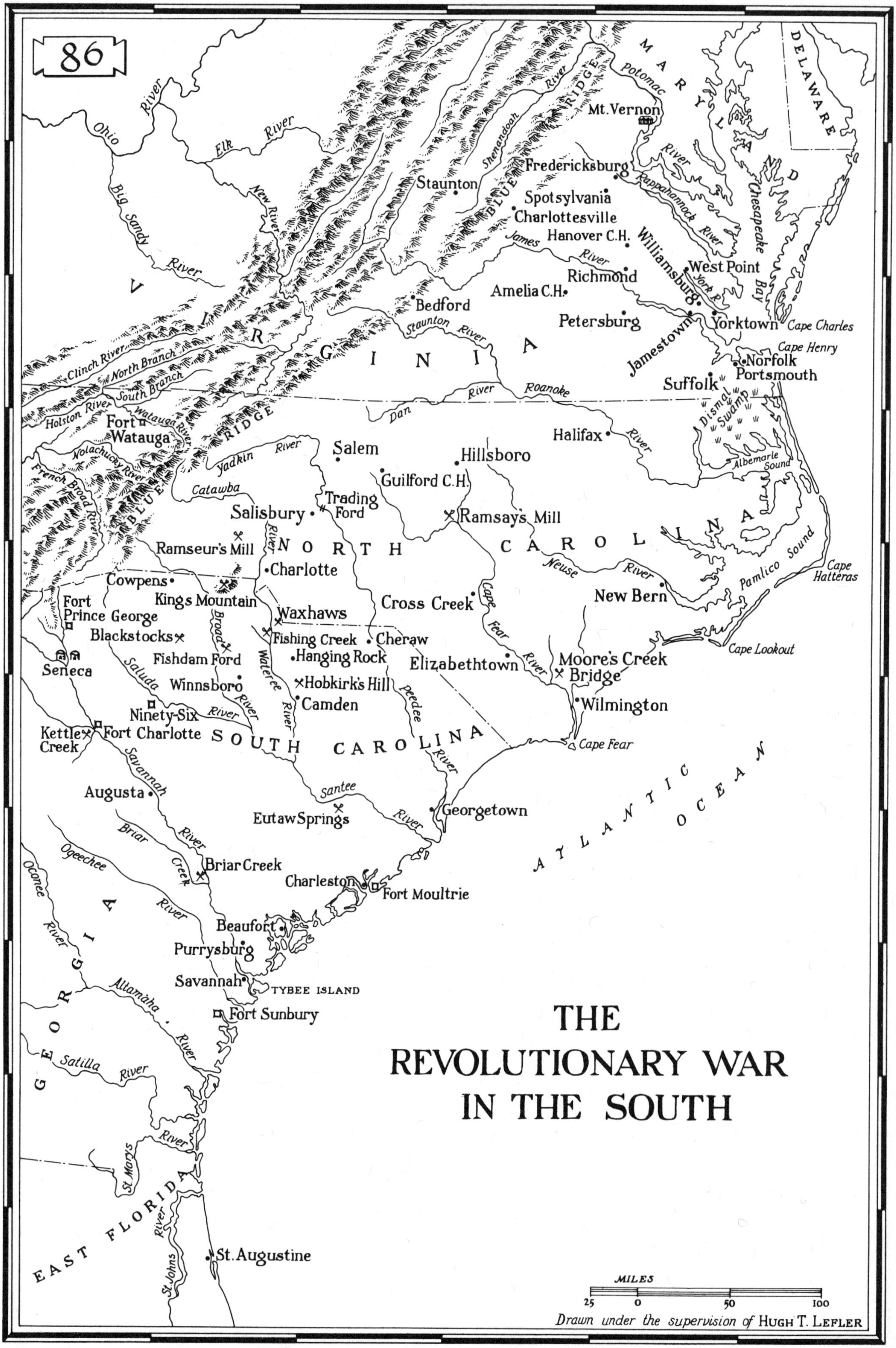

THE REVOLUTIONARY WAR IN THE SOUTH

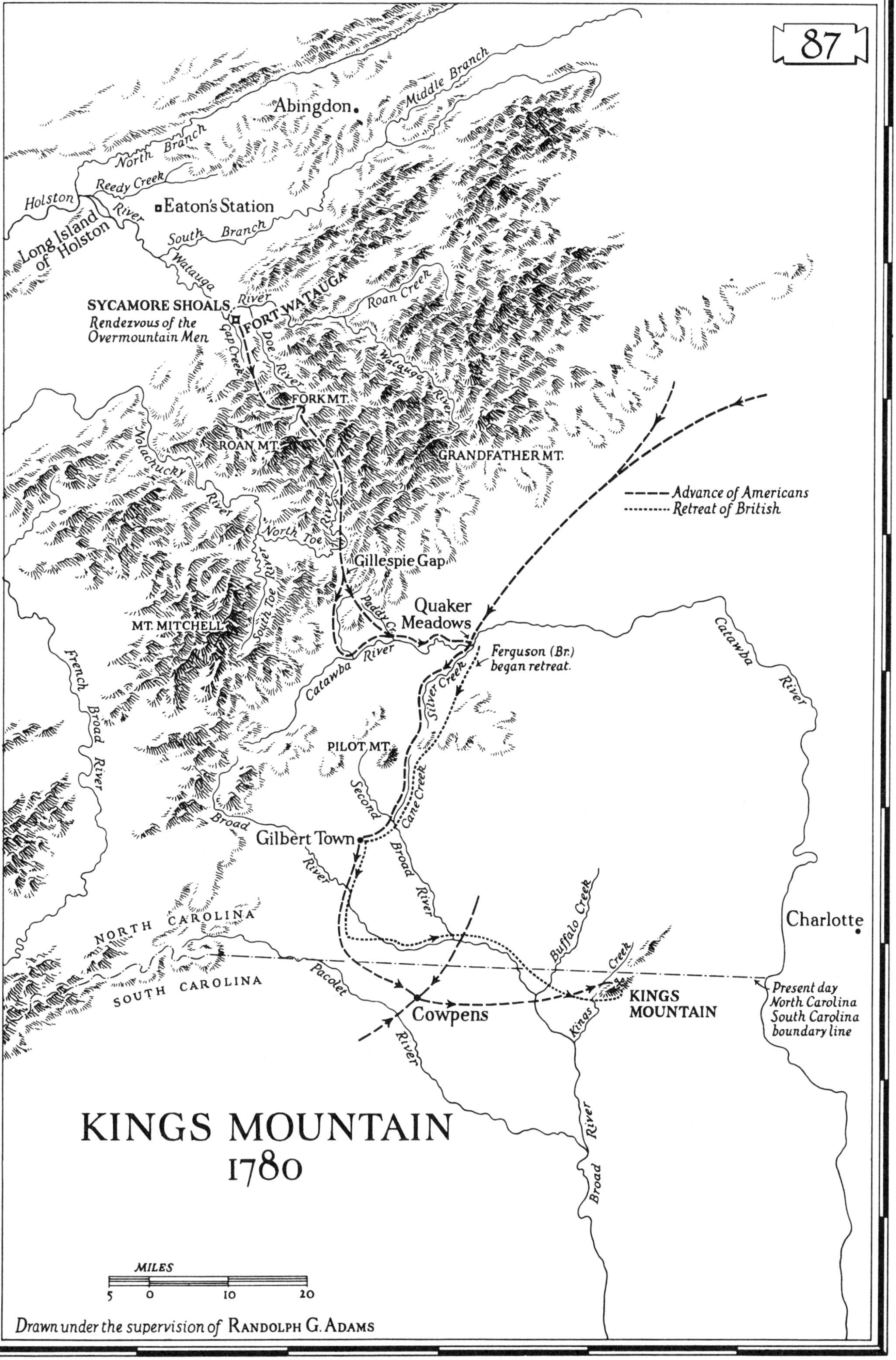

KINGS MOUNTAIN
1780

Drawn under the supervision of RANDOLPH G. ADAMS

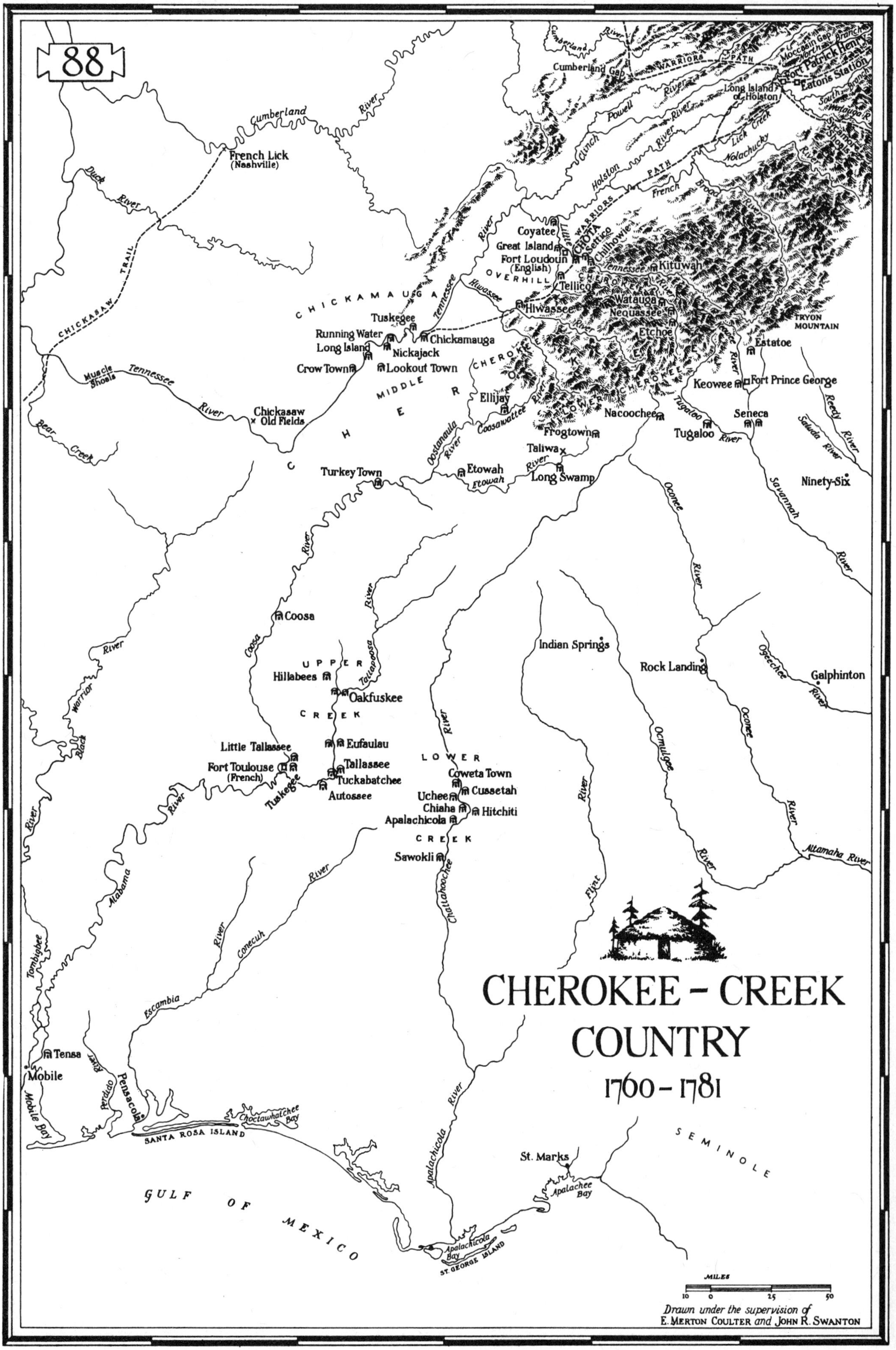
88
CHEROKEE – CREEK COUNTRY
1760 – 1781
Cumberland River
Cumberland Gap
WARRIORS PATH
Moccasin Gap
North Branch
Fort Patrick Henry
Eaton's Station
Long Island of Holston
South Branch
Watauga R.
Sycamore Shoals
Powell River
Clinch River
Holston River
Lick Creek
Nolachucky
French Broad River
French Lick
(Nashville)
Duck River
CHICKASAW TRAIL
Coyatee
Great Island
Fort Loudoun
(English)
Little
CHOTA
Settico
Chilhowie
Tennessee
Kituwah
OVERHILL
Tellico
CHEROKEE
Hiwassee
Hiwassee
Watauga
Nequassee
Etchoe
TRYON MOUNTAIN
Estatoe
CHICKAMAUGA
Tuskegee
Running Water
Long Island
Nickajack
Chickamauga
Crow Town
Lookout Town
MIDDLE CHEROKEE
Muscle Shoals
Tennessee River
Chickasaw Old Fields
Bear Creek
Ellijay
Coosawattee River
Oostanaula River
LOWER CHEROKEE
Nacoochee
Keowee
Fort Prince George
Seneca
Tugaloo
Tugaloo River
Frogtown
Taliwa
Long Swamp
Etowah
Etowah River
Turkey Town
Reedy River
Saluda River
Ninety-Six
Savannah River
Oconee River
Coosa River
Coosa
Tallapoosa River
UPPER CREEK
Hillabees
Oakfuskee
Eufaulau
Little Tallassee
Fort Toulouse
(French)
Tallassee
Tuckabatchee
Autossee
Tuskegee
Warrior River
Black River
Alabama River
Tombigbee River
LOWER CREEK
Coweta Town
Cussetah
Uchee
Chiaha
Hitchiti
Apalachicola
Sawokli
Chattahoochee River
Indian Springs
Rock Landing
Ogeechee River
Galphinton
Ocmulgee River
Oconee River
Altamaha River
Flint River
Conecuh River
Escambia River
Tensa
Mobile
Mobile Bay
Perdido River
Pensacola
SANTA ROSA ISLAND
Choctawhatchee Bay
GULF OF MEXICO
Apalachicola River
Apalachicola Bay
ST. GEORGE ISLAND
St. Marks
Apalachee Bay
SEMINOLE
MILES
10 0 25 50
Drawn under the supervision of
E. Merton Coulter and John R. Swanton

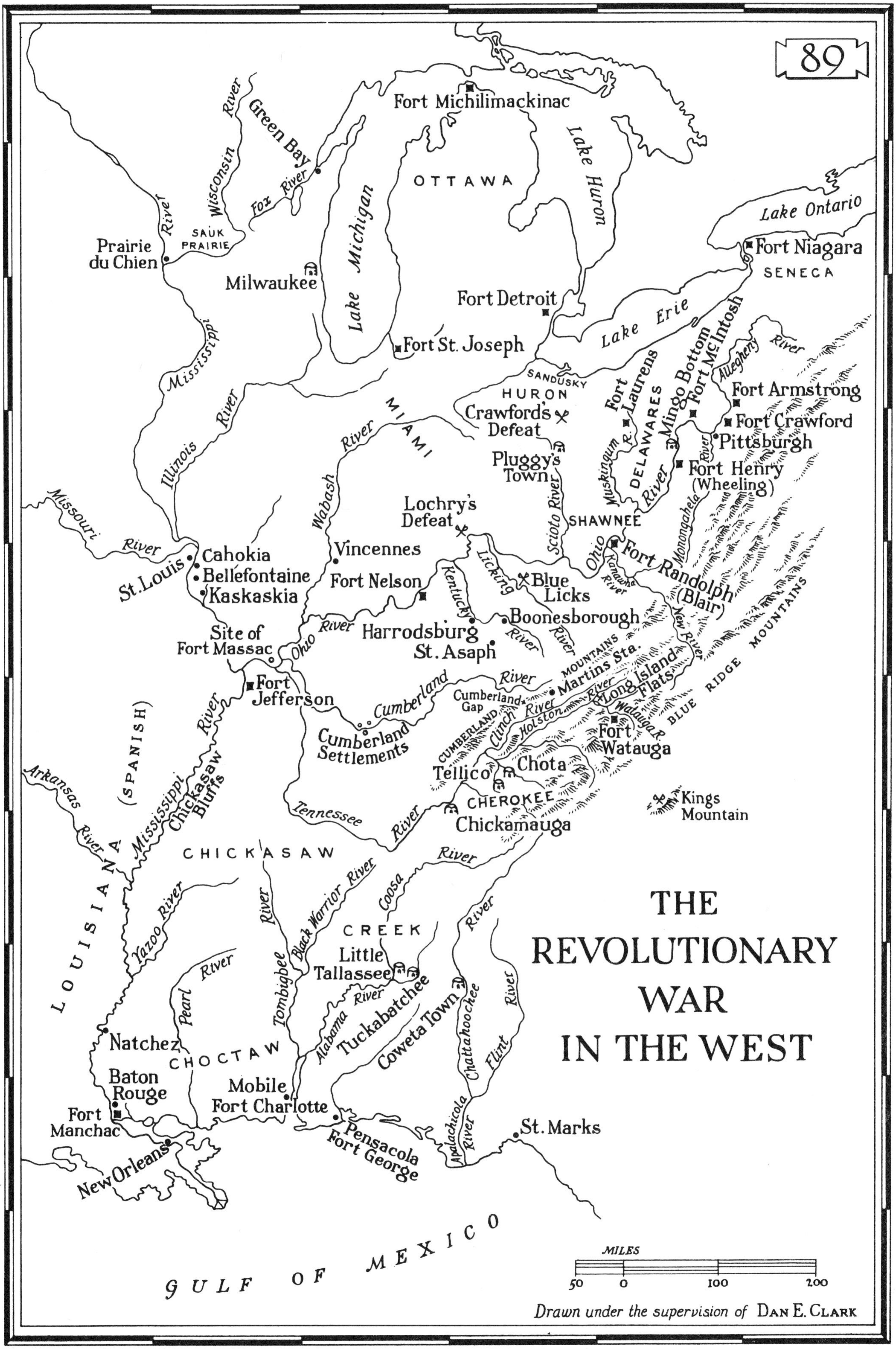
89
THE REVOLUTIONARY WAR IN THE WEST
Fort Michilimackinac
Green Bay
Wisconsin River
Fox River
OTTAWA
Lake Huron
Lake Michigan
Lake Ontario
Fort Niagara
SENECA
Prairie du Chien
SAUK PRAIRIE
Milwaukee
Fort Detroit
Lake Erie
Fort St. Joseph
Mississippi River
Illinois River
SANDUSKY
HURON
Crawford's Defeat
Fort Laurens
Mingo Bottom
Fort McIntosh
Allegheny River
Fort Armstrong
Fort Crawford
Pittsburgh
Fort Henry (Wheeling)
DELAWARES
Muskingum R.
MIAMI
Wabash River
Pluggy's Town
Lochry's Defeat
Scioto River
SHAWNEE
Monongahela
Missouri River
Cahokia
Bellefontaine
Kaskaskia
St. Louis
Vincennes
Fort Nelson
Kentucky
Licking
Blue Licks
Fort Randolph (Blair)
Kanawha River
Ohio
Boonesborough
Harrodsburg
St. Asaph
Site of Fort Massac
Ohio River
New River
Fort Jefferson
Cumberland River
Cumberland Gap
Martins Sta.
Long Island Flats
Clinch River
Holston River
Watauga R.
Fort Watauga
CUMBERLAND MOUNTAINS
BLUE RIDGE MOUNTAINS
Cumberland Settlements
Tellico
Chota
CHEROKEE
Chickamauga
Kings Mountain
(SPANISH)
Chickasaw Bluffs
Arkansas River
Tennessee River
CHICKASAW
LOUISIANA
Yazoo River
Black Warrior River
Coosa River
CREEK
Little Tallassee
Tombigbee River
Pearl River
Alabama River
Tuckabatchee
Coweta Town
Chattahoochee
Flint River
Natchez
CHOCTAW
Baton Rouge
Fort Manchac
Mobile
Fort Charlotte
Pensacola
Fort George
New Orleans
Apalachicola River
St. Marks
GULF OF MEXICO
MILES
50 0 100 200
Drawn under the supervision of DAN E. CLARK

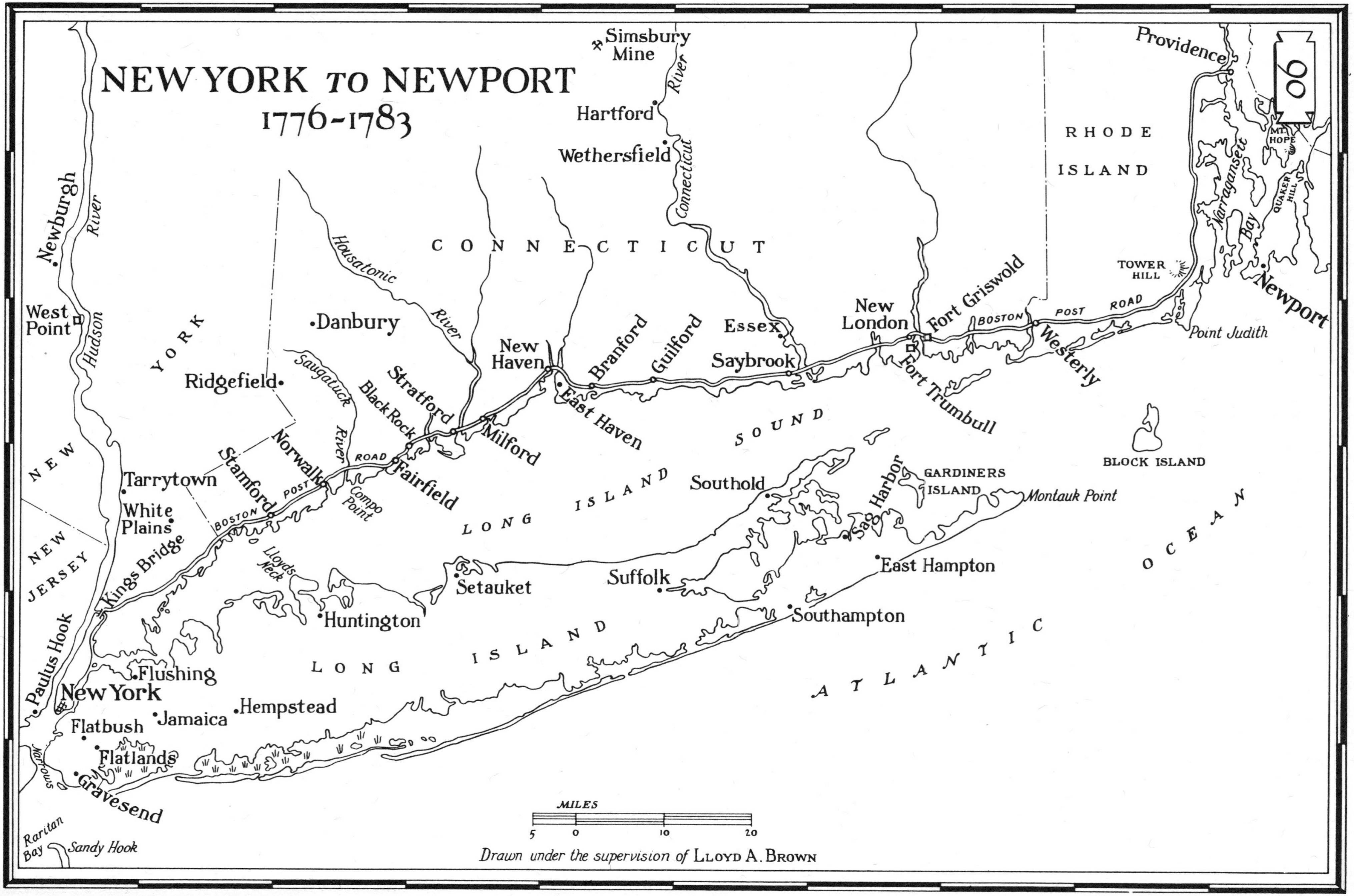

Drawn under the supervision of Lloyd A. Brown

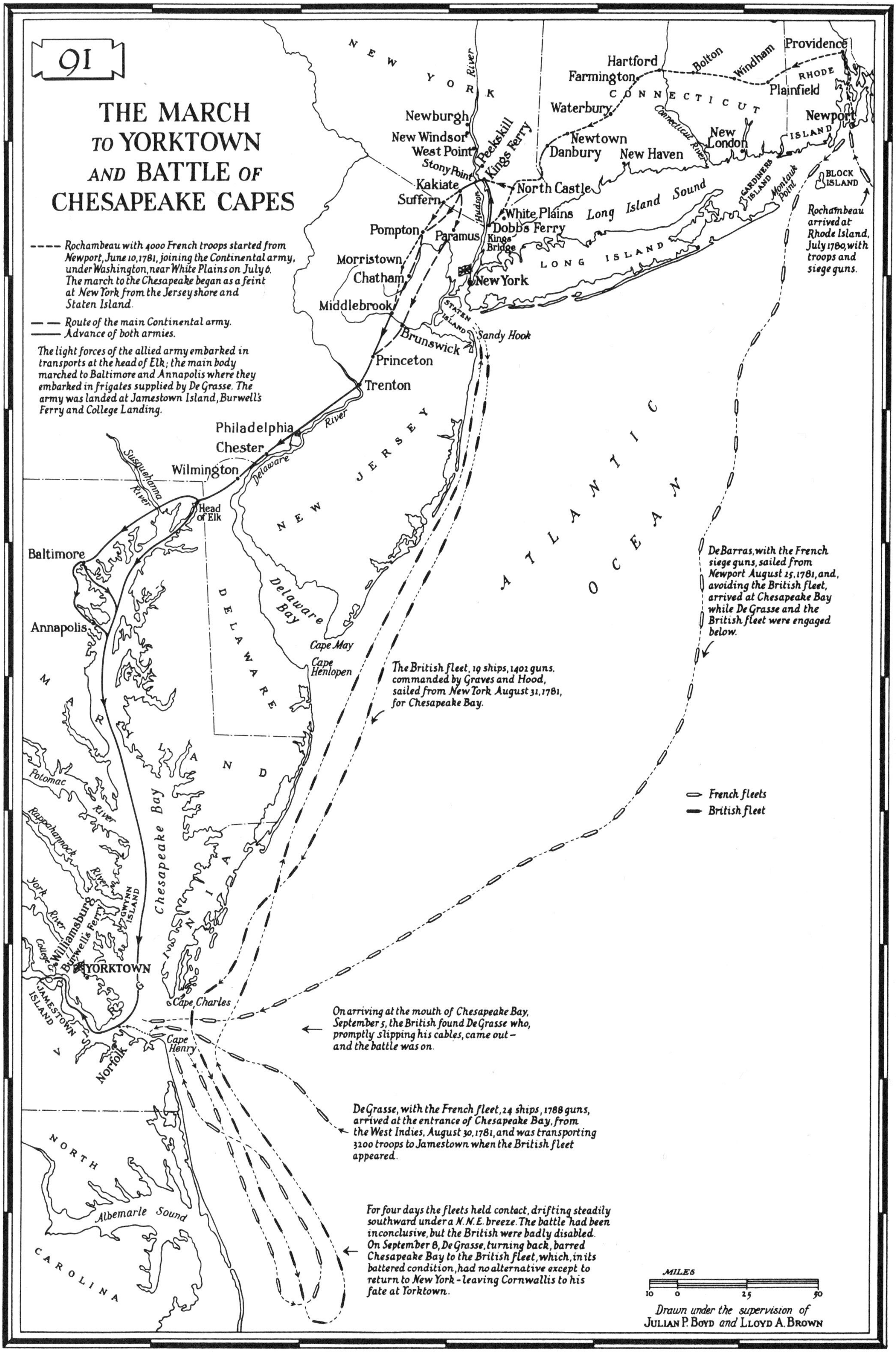
91
THE MARCH TO YORKTOWN AND BATTLE OF CHESAPEAKE CAPES
Rochambeau with 4000 French troops started from Newport, June 10, 1781, joining the Continental army, under Washington, near White Plains on July 6. The march to the Chesapeake began as a feint at New York from the Jersey shore and Staten Island.
Route of the main Continental army.
Advance of both armies.
The light forces of the allied army embarked in transports at the head of Elk; the main body marched to Baltimore and Annapolis where they embarked in frigates supplied by De Grasse. The army was landed at Jamestown Island, Burwell's Ferry and College Landing.
NEW YORK
CONNECTICUT
RHODE ISLAND
Providence
Hartford
Bolton
Windham
Farmington
Plainfield
Waterbury
Newport
Newtown
New London
Danbury
New Haven
Connecticut River
Newburgh
New Windsor
West Point
Stony Point
Peekskill
Kings Ferry
Hudson River
Kakiate
Suffern
North Castle
White Plains
Dobbs Ferry
Kings Bridge
Pompton
Paramus
Morristown
Chatham
New York
Middlebrook
Brunswick
Princeton
Trenton
Philadelphia
Chester
Wilmington
Delaware River
Susquehanna River
Head of Elk
Baltimore
Annapolis
Long Island Sound
LONG ISLAND
GARDINERS ISLAND
Montauk Point
BLOCK ISLAND
Rochambeau arrived at Rhode Island, July 1780, with troops and siege guns.
STATEN ISLAND
Sandy Hook
NEW JERSEY
ATLANTIC OCEAN
Delaware Bay
Cape May
Cape Henlopen
DELAWARE
MARYLAND
VIRGINIA
Potomac River
Rappahannock River
York River
Chesapeake Bay
GWYNN ISLAND
Williamsburg
Burwell's Ferry
College
YORKTOWN
JAMESTOWN ISLAND
Norfolk
Cape Charles
Cape Henry
DeBarras, with the French siege guns, sailed from Newport August 25, 1781, and, avoiding the British fleet, arrived at Chesapeake Bay while De Grasse and the British fleet were engaged below.
The British fleet, 19 ships, 1402 guns, commanded by Graves and Hood, sailed from New York August 31, 1781, for Chesapeake Bay.
French fleets
British fleet
On arriving at the mouth of Chesapeake Bay, September 5, the British found De Grasse who, promptly slipping his cables, came out – and the battle was on.
De Grasse, with the French fleet, 24 ships, 1788 guns, arrived at the entrance of Chesapeake Bay, from the West Indies, August 30, 1781, and was transporting 3200 troops to Jamestown when the British fleet appeared.
For four days the fleets held contact, drifting steadily southward under a N.N.E. breeze. The battle had been inconclusive, but the British were badly disabled. On September 8, De Grasse, turning back, barred Chesapeake Bay to the British fleet, which, in its battered condition, had no alternative except to return to New York – leaving Cornwallis to his fate at Yorktown.
NORTH CAROLINA
Albemarle Sound
MILES
10 0 25 50
Drawn under the supervision of JULIAN P. BOYD and LLOYD A. BROWN

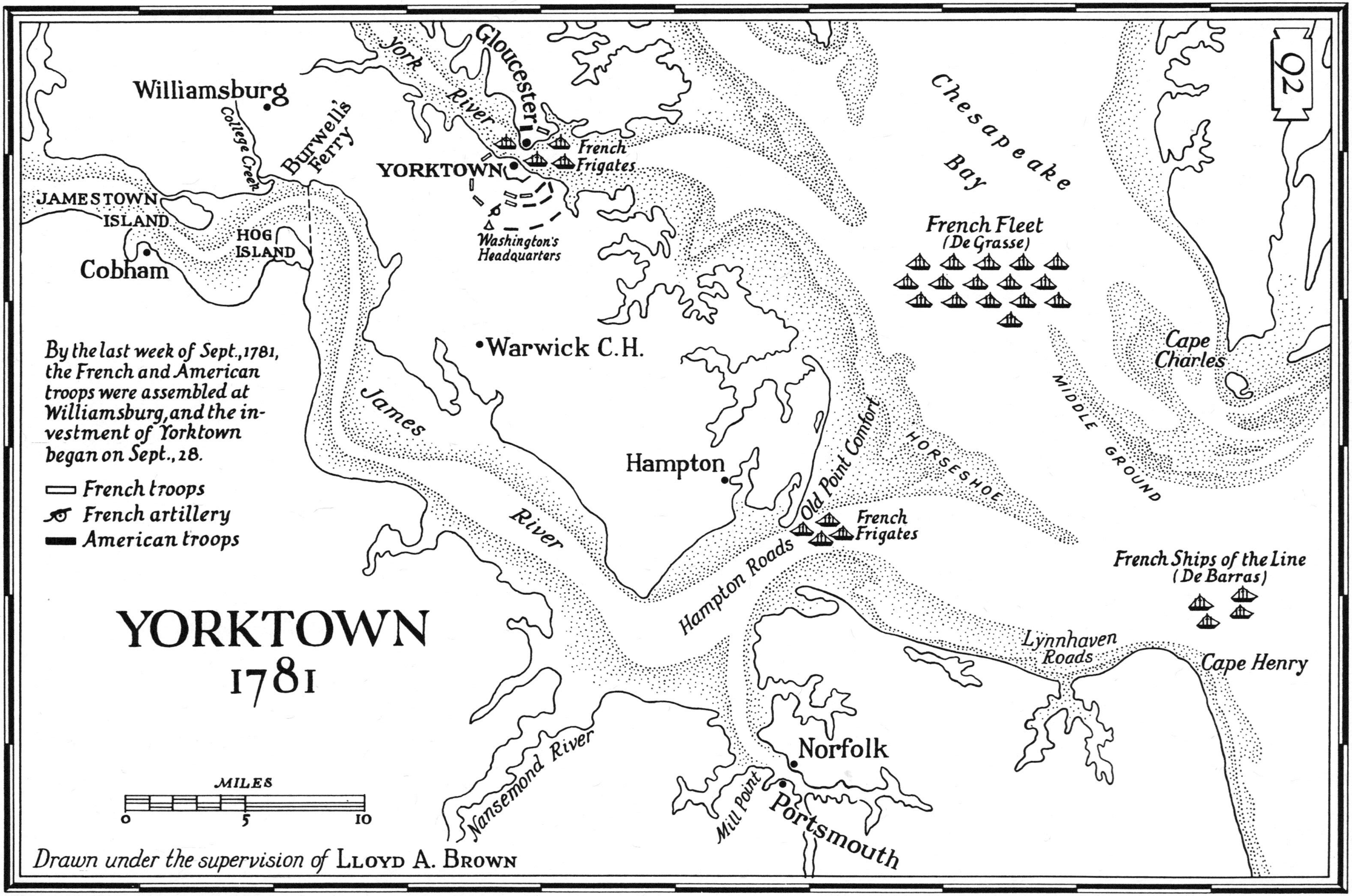

92
Williamsburg
College Creek
Burwell's Ferry
JAMESTOWN ISLAND
HOG ISLAND
Cobham
York River
Gloucester
YORKTOWN
French Frigates
Washington's Headquarters
Chesapeake Bay
French Fleet (De Grasse)
Cape Charles
MIDDLE GROUND
HORSESHOE
Warwick C.H.
James River
Hampton
Old Point Comfort
French Frigates
Hampton Roads
French Ships of the Line (De Barras)
Lynnhaven Roads
Cape Henry
Norfolk
Portsmouth
Mill Point
Nansemond River
By the last week of Sept., 1781, the French and American troops were assembled at Williamsburg, and the investment of Yorktown began on Sept., 28.
French troops
French artillery
American troops
YORKTOWN
1781
MILES
0
5
10
Drawn under the supervision of Lloyd A. Brown

VI THE NEW NATION

THE UNITED STATES, 1783-1802

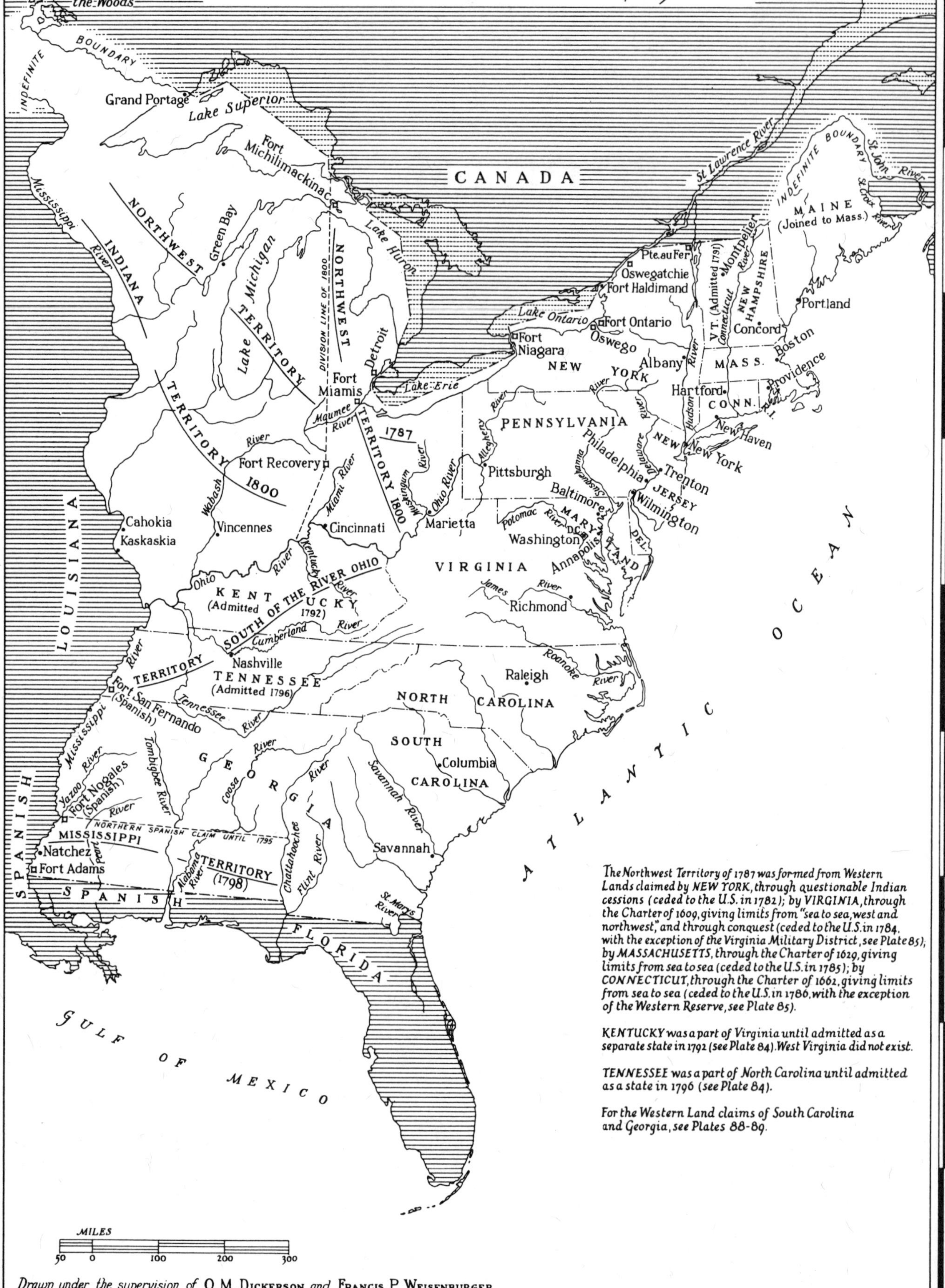

The Northwest Territory of 1787 was formed from Western Lands claimed by NEW YORK, through questionable Indian cessions (ceded to the U.S. in 1782); by VIRGINIA, through the Charter of 1609, giving limits from "sea to sea, west and northwest," and through conquest (ceded to the U.S. in 1784, with the exception of the Virginia Military District, see Plate 85); by MASSACHUSETTS, through the Charter of 1629, giving limits from sea to sea (ceded to the U.S. in 1785); by CONNECTICUT, through the Charter of 1662, giving limits from sea to sea (ceded to the U.S. in 1786, with the exception of the Western Reserve, see Plate 85).

KENTUCKY was a part of Virginia until admitted as a separate state in 1792 (see Plate 84). West Virginia did not exist.

TENNESSEE was a part of North Carolina until admitted as a state in 1796 (see Plate 84).

For the Western Land claims of South Carolina and Georgia, see Plates 88-89.

Drawn under the supervision of O. M. DICKERSON *and* FRANCIS P. WEISENBURGER

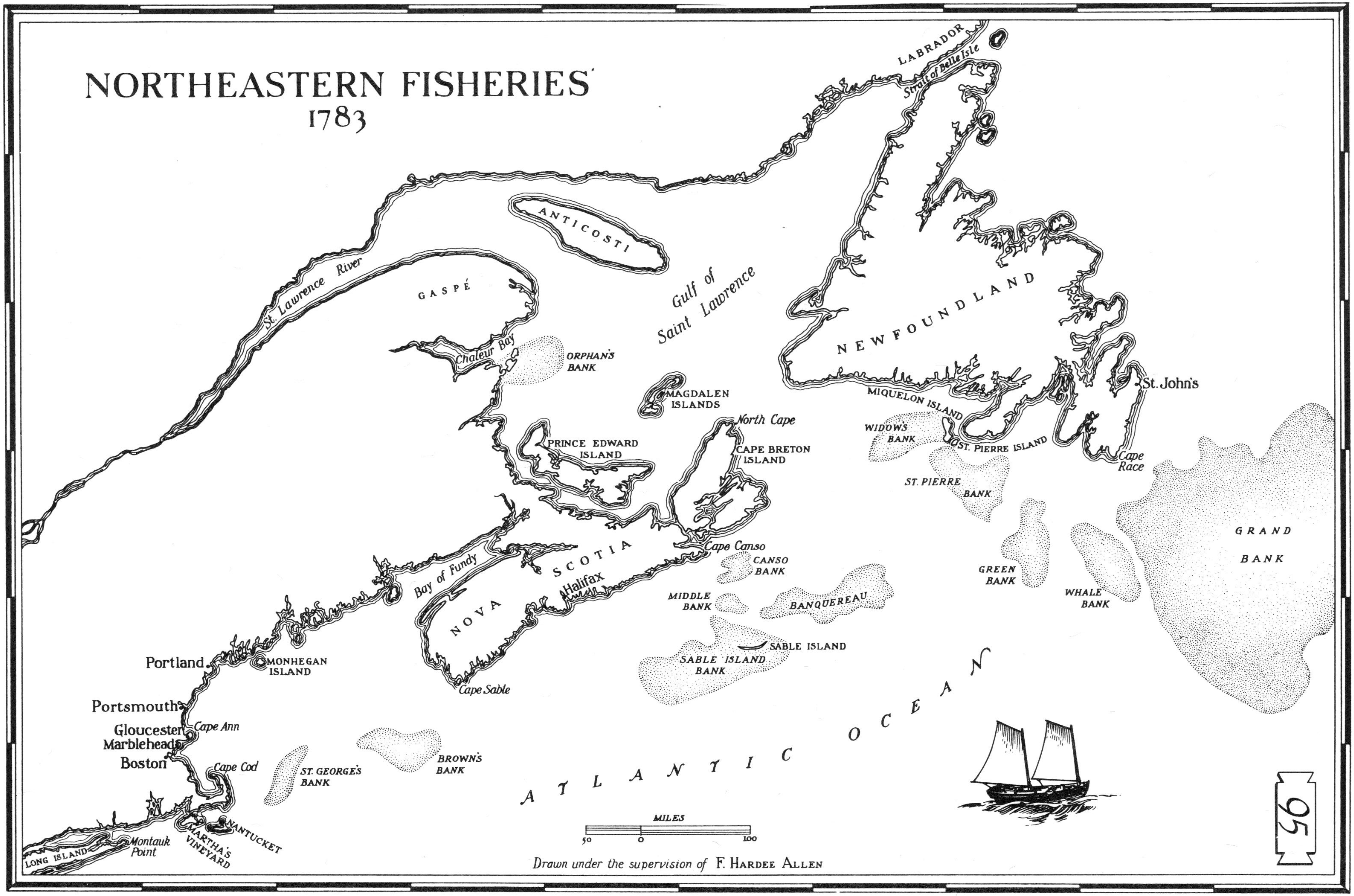

Drawn under the supervision of F. Hardee Allen

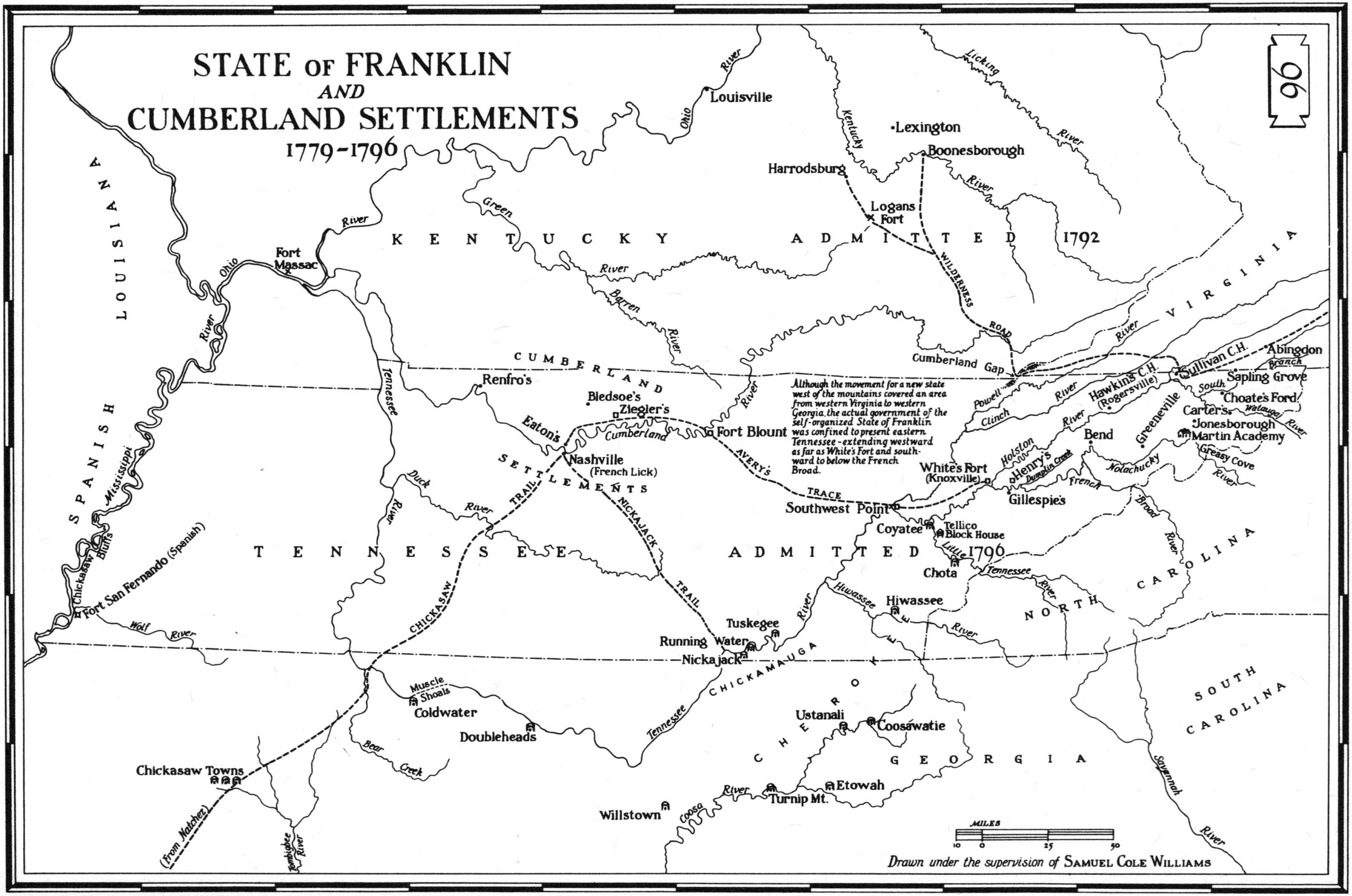
96
STATE OF FRANKLIN
AND
CUMBERLAND SETTLEMENTS
1779-1796
KENTUCKY ADMITTED 1792
TENNESSEE ADMITTED 1796
VIRGINIA
NORTH CAROLINA
SOUTH CAROLINA
GEORGIA
SPANISH LOUISIANA
CHEROKEE
CHICKAMAUGA
CUMBERLAND SETTLEMENTS
Although the movement for a new state west of the mountains covered an area from western Virginia to western Georgia, the actual government of the self-organized State of Franklin was confined to present eastern Tennessee - extending westward as far as White's Fort and southward to below the French Broad.
Louisville
Lexington
Boonesborough
Harrodsburg
Logans Fort
Fort Massac
WILDERNESS ROAD
Cumberland Gap
Abingdon
Sullivan C.H.
Sapling Grove
Choate's Ford
Carter's
Jonesborough
Martin Academy
Greasy Cove
Hawkins C.H. (Rogersville)
Greeneville
Bend
Henry's
Gillespie's
White's Fort (Knoxville)
Southwest Point
AVERY'S TRACE
Fort Blount
Renfro's
Bledsoe's
Ziegler's
Eaton's
Nashville (French Lick)
NICKAJACK TRAIL
CHICKASAW TRAIL
Coyatee
Tellico Block House
Chota
Hiwassee
Tuskegee
Running Water
Nickajack
Muscle Shoals
Coldwater
Doubleheads
Ustanali
Coosawatie
Etowah
Turnip Mt.
Willstown
Chickasaw Towns
(From Natchez)
Chickasaw Bluffs
Fort San Fernando (Spanish)
Ohio River
Licking River
Kentucky River
Green River
Barren River
Cumberland River
Tennessee River
Duck River
Clinch River
Powell River
Holston River
South Branch
Watauga River
Nolachucky River
French Broad River
Dumplin Creek
Little Tennessee River
Hiwassee River
Coosa River
Savannah River
Mississippi River
Wolf River
Bear Creek
Tombigbee River
MILES
10 0 25 50
Drawn under the supervision of SAMUEL COLE WILLIAMS

THE TWELVE LARGEST CITIES AND TOWNS 1790

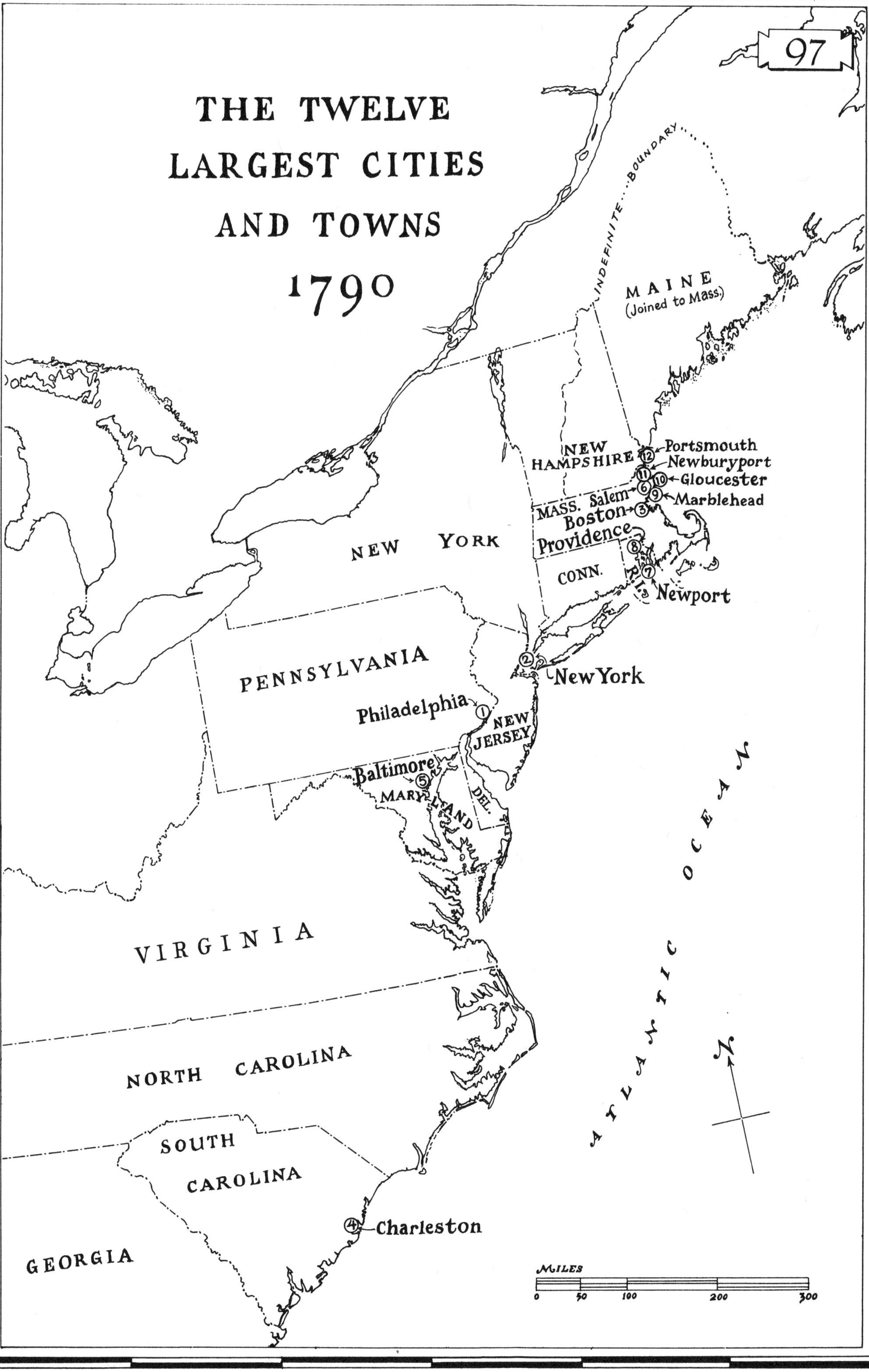

CALIFORNIA, NEW MEXICO TEXAS AND LOUISIANA 1763-1802

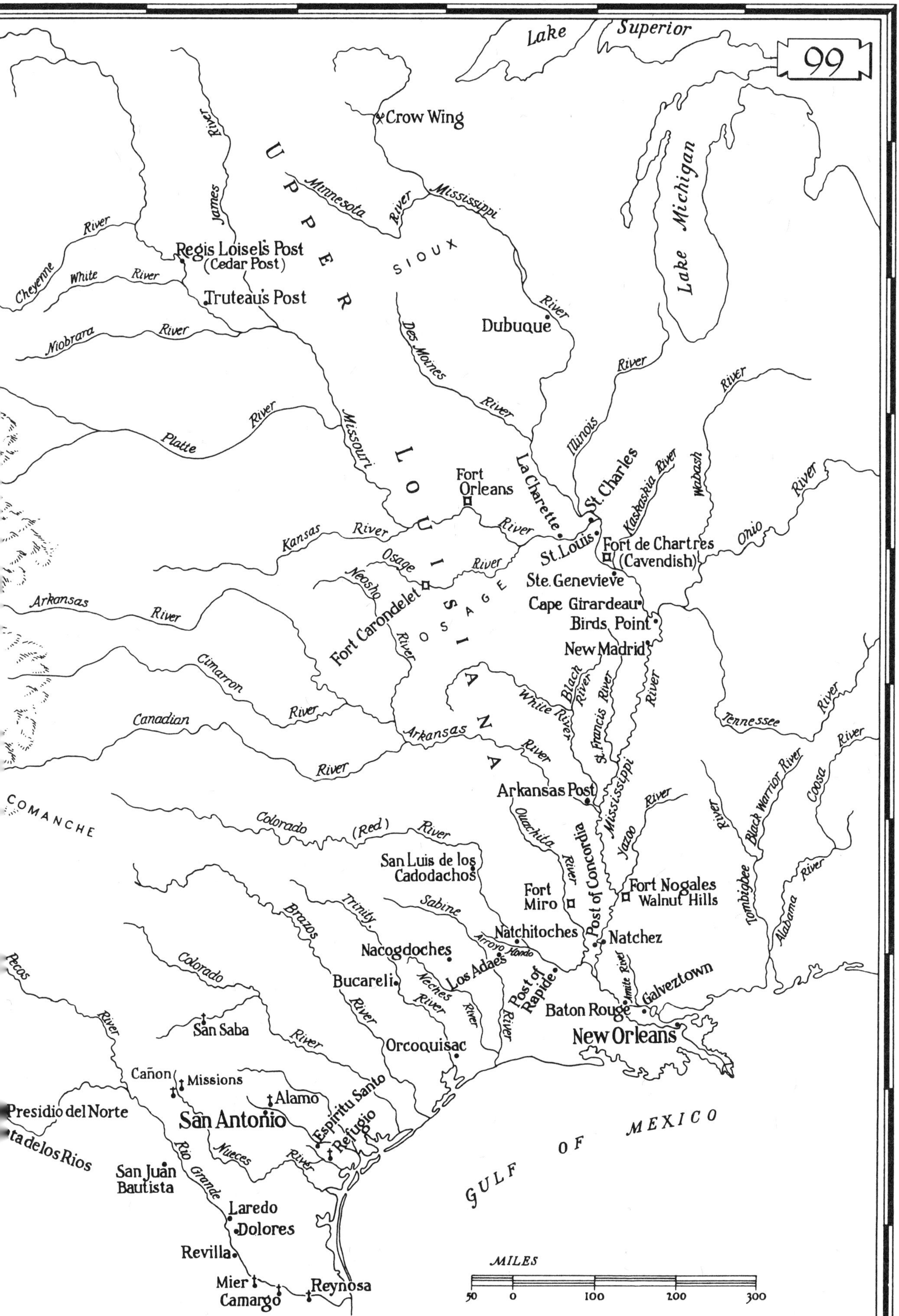

Drawn under the supervision of WALTER PRICHARD *and* CARLOS E. CASTANEDA

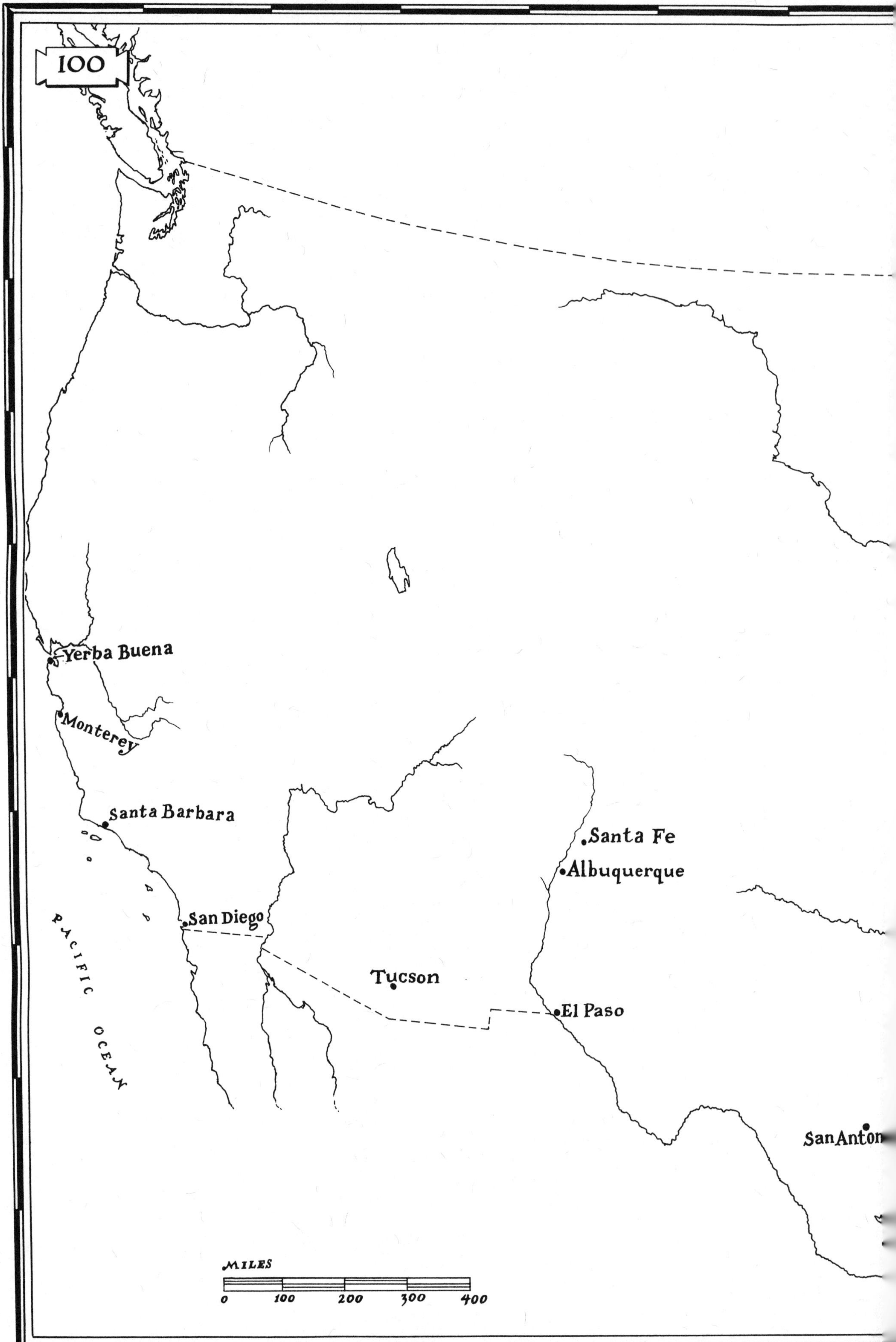
100
Yerba Buena
Monterey
Santa Barbara
San Diego
Tucson
Santa Fe
Albuquerque
El Paso
San Anton
PACIFIC OCEAN
MILES
0
100
200
300
400

SETTLED AREAS 1800

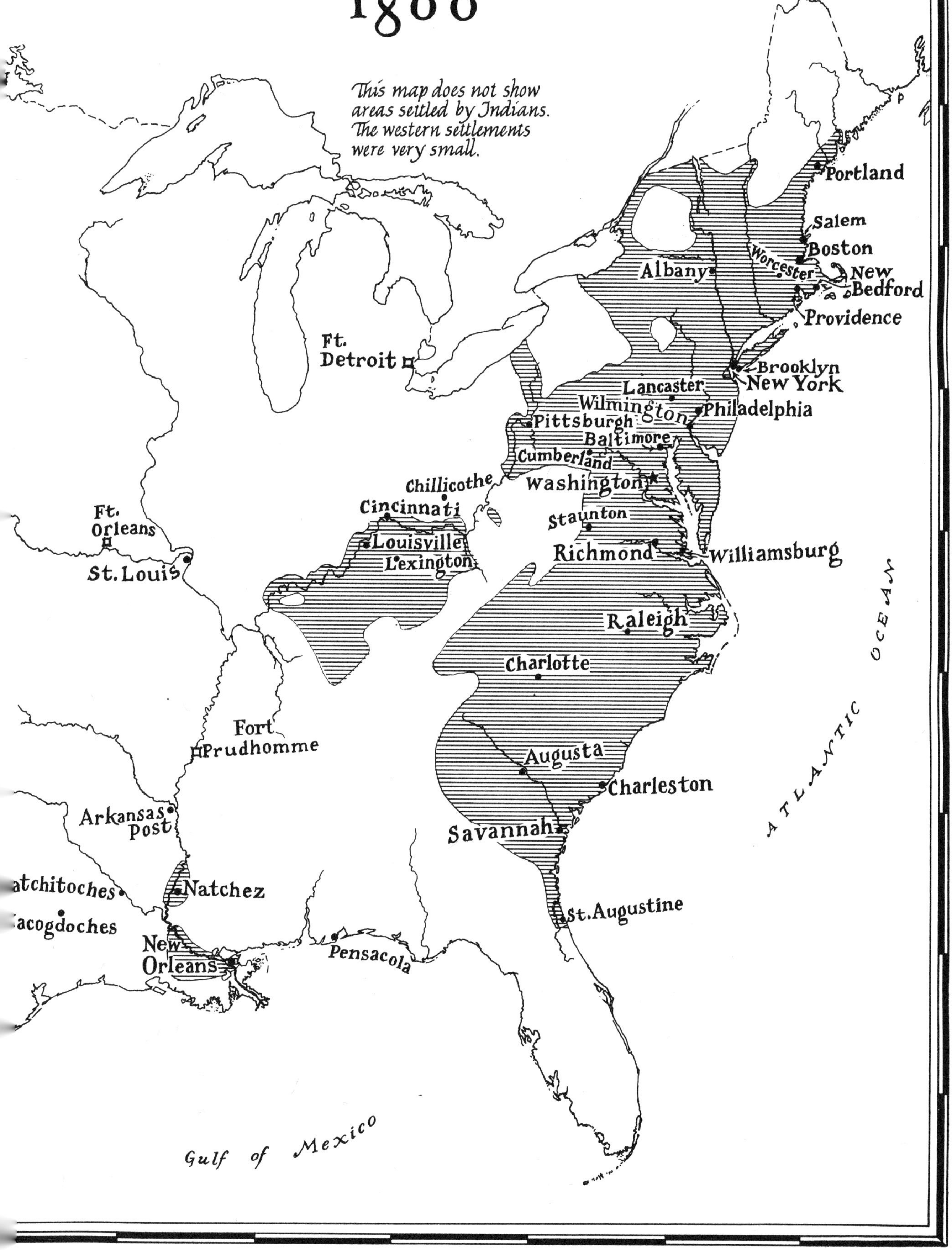

MAJOR INSURRECTIONS AND SLAVE REVOLTS 1676–1859

OHIO COUNTRY 1787-1803

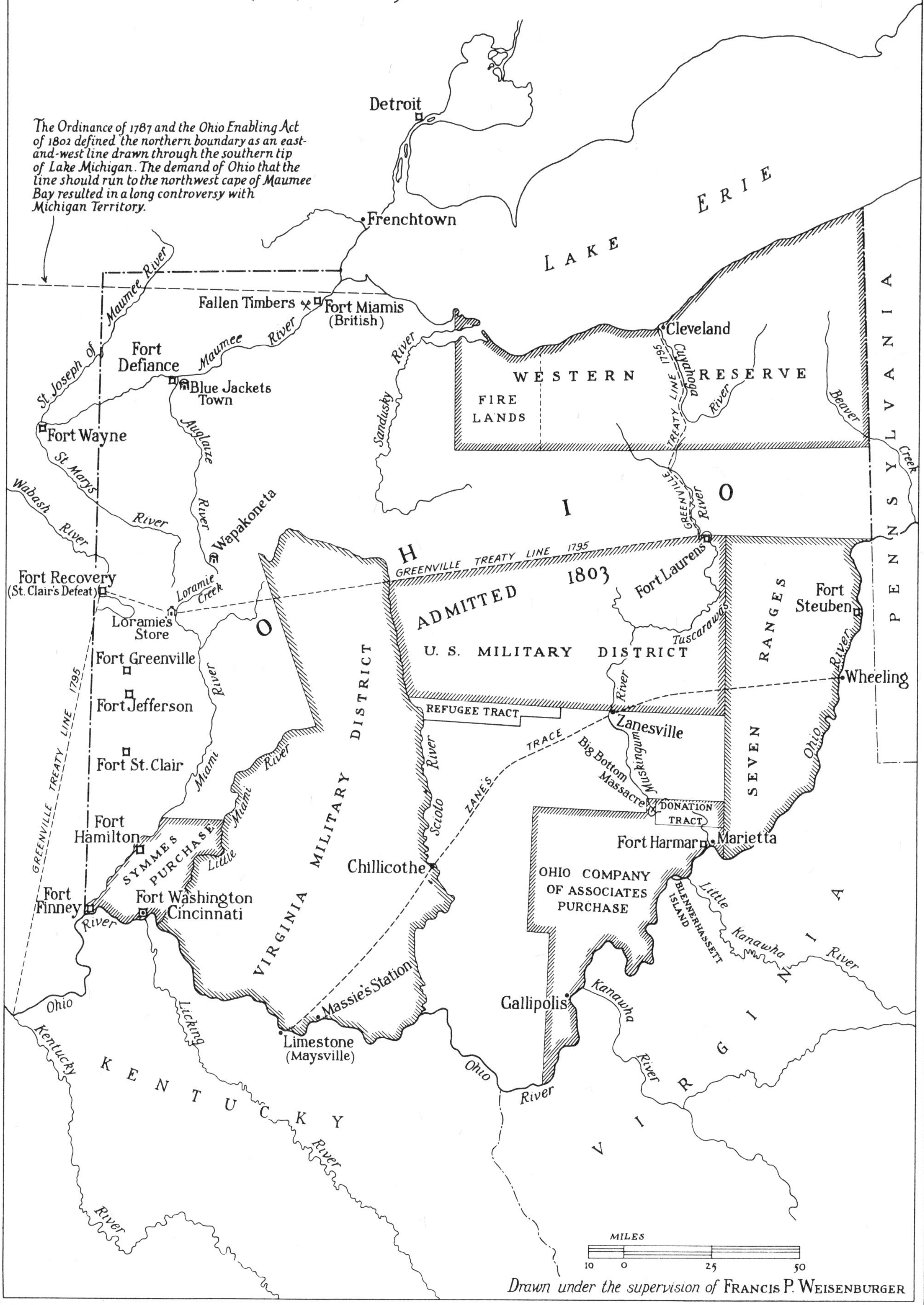

Drawn under the supervision of FRANCIS P. WEISENBURGER

GEOGRAPHER'S LINE *AND* THE SEVEN RANGES

Based on survey begun in 1785 by Thomas Hutchins, Geographer to the United States. Physical features follow presentday surveys.

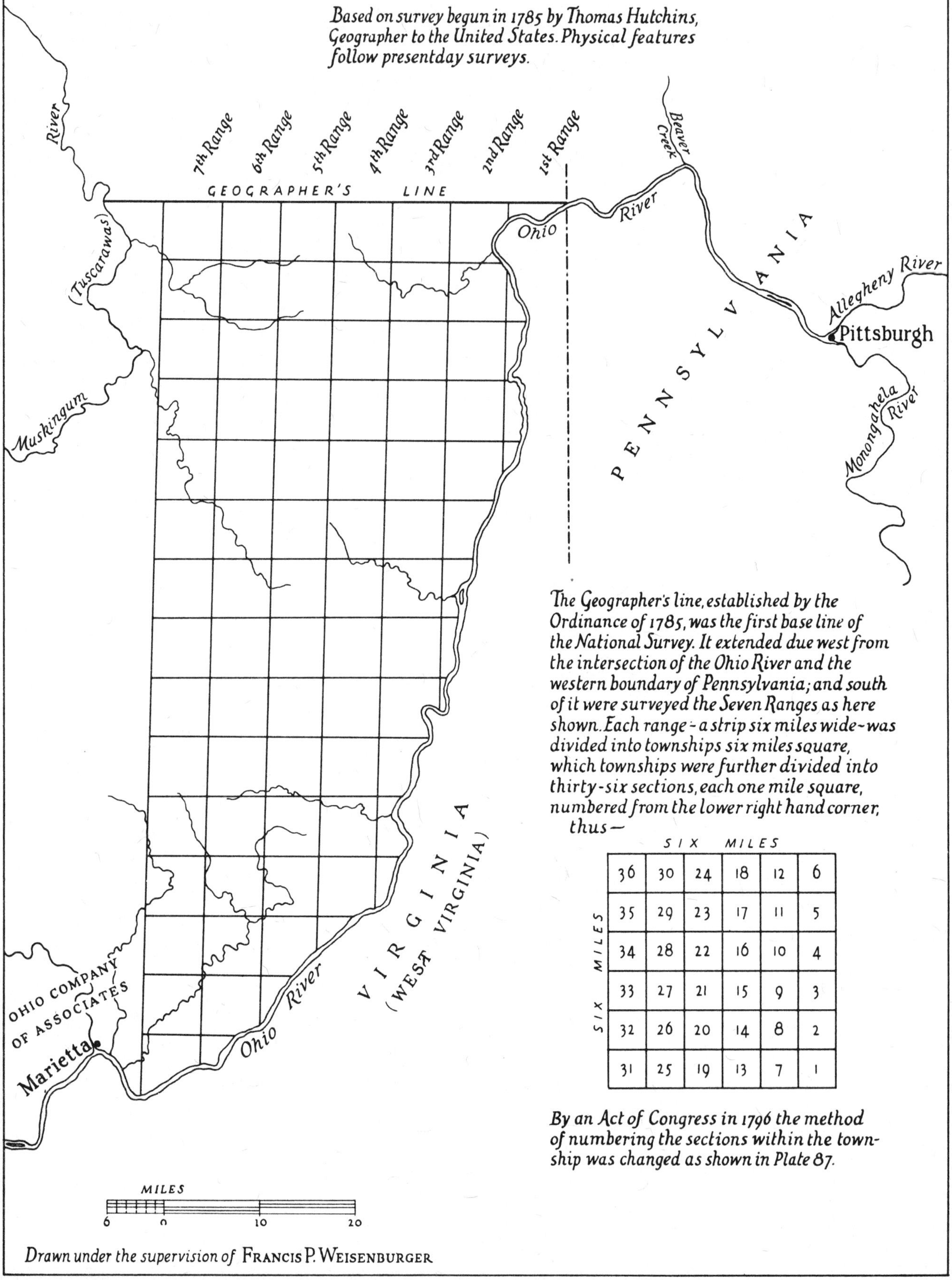

The Geographer's line, established by the Ordinance of 1785, was the first base line of the National Survey. It extended due west from the intersection of the Ohio River and the western boundary of Pennsylvania; and south of it were surveyed the Seven Ranges as here shown. Each range - a strip six miles wide - was divided into townships six miles square, which townships were further divided into thirty-six sections, each one mile square, numbered from the lower right hand corner, thus—

SIX MILES (across); SIX MILES (down)

36	30	24	18	12	6
35	29	23	17	11	5
34	28	22	16	10	4
33	27	21	15	9	3
32	26	20	14	8	2
31	25	19	13	7	1

By an Act of Congress in 1796 the method of numbering the sections within the township was changed as shown in Plate 87.

Drawn under the supervision of FRANCIS P. WEISENBURGER

THE SURVEY *of the* PUBLIC DOMAIN

is based upon the Ordinance of 1785. Beginning with the Seven Ranges (see Plate 86), this survey was continued across the country, although there still remains, in the mountainous sections of the Far West, over one hundred million acres of unsurveyed land. However, with a few local exceptions, the survey applies in every state in the Union, except in the Thirteen Colonies and in Maine, Vermont, Kentucky, Tennessee, West Virginia, and Texas. From arbitrarily selected east-and-west Base Lines and north-and-south Meridians, the land is surveyed into Ranges of Townships, lying north and south of the Base Lines, and east and west of the Meridians. The Ranges are numbered east and west from the Meridians: The Townships, each six miles square, are numbered north and south from the Base Lines. The diagrams below illustrate the actual survey east of the Sixth Principal Meridian and south of a Base Line located on 40° north latitude.

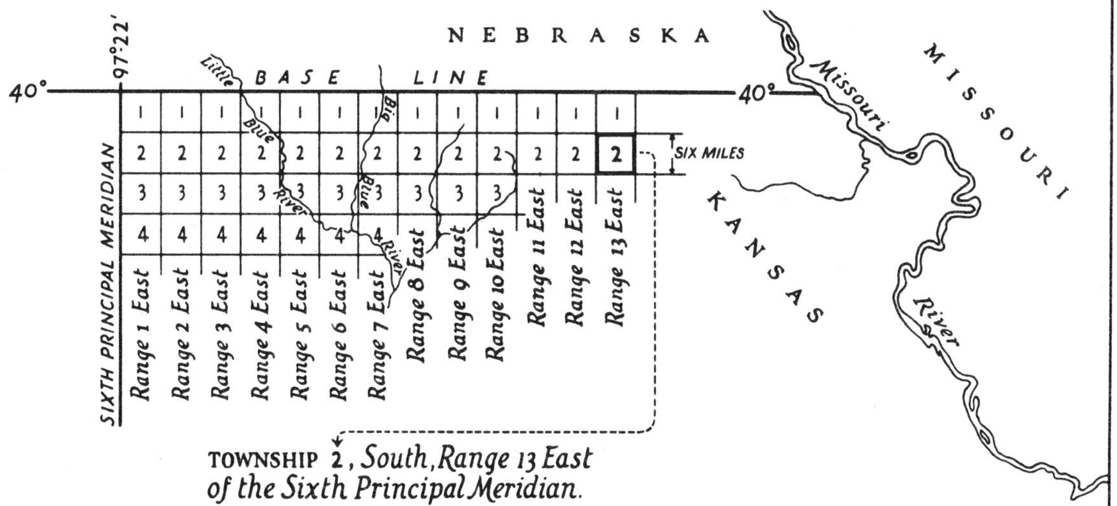

TOWNSHIP 2, *South, Range 13 East of the Sixth Principal Meridian.*

6	5	4	3	2	1
7	8	9	10	11	12
18	17	16	15	14	13
19	20	21	22	23	24
30	29	28	27	26	**25**
31	32	33	34	35	36

SIX MILES × SIX MILES

In 1796 Congress directed that the method of numbering the sections should be as here shown, thus discarding the method followed in the Seven Ranges, (see Plate 86). This method of numbering has prevailed in all surveys subsequent to that date.

SECTION 25, *Township 2, South, Range 13 East of the Sixth Principal Meridian.*

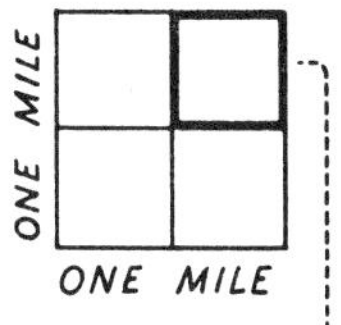

A Section contains 640 acres

NORTHEAST ONE-FOURTH *of Section 25, Township 2, South, Range 13 East of the Sixth Principal Meridian,*

A Quarter Section contains 160 acres

which, by this description, can be instantly located as lying in an exact place in northeastern Kansas.

Drawn under the supervision of
PAUL WALLACE GATES

106

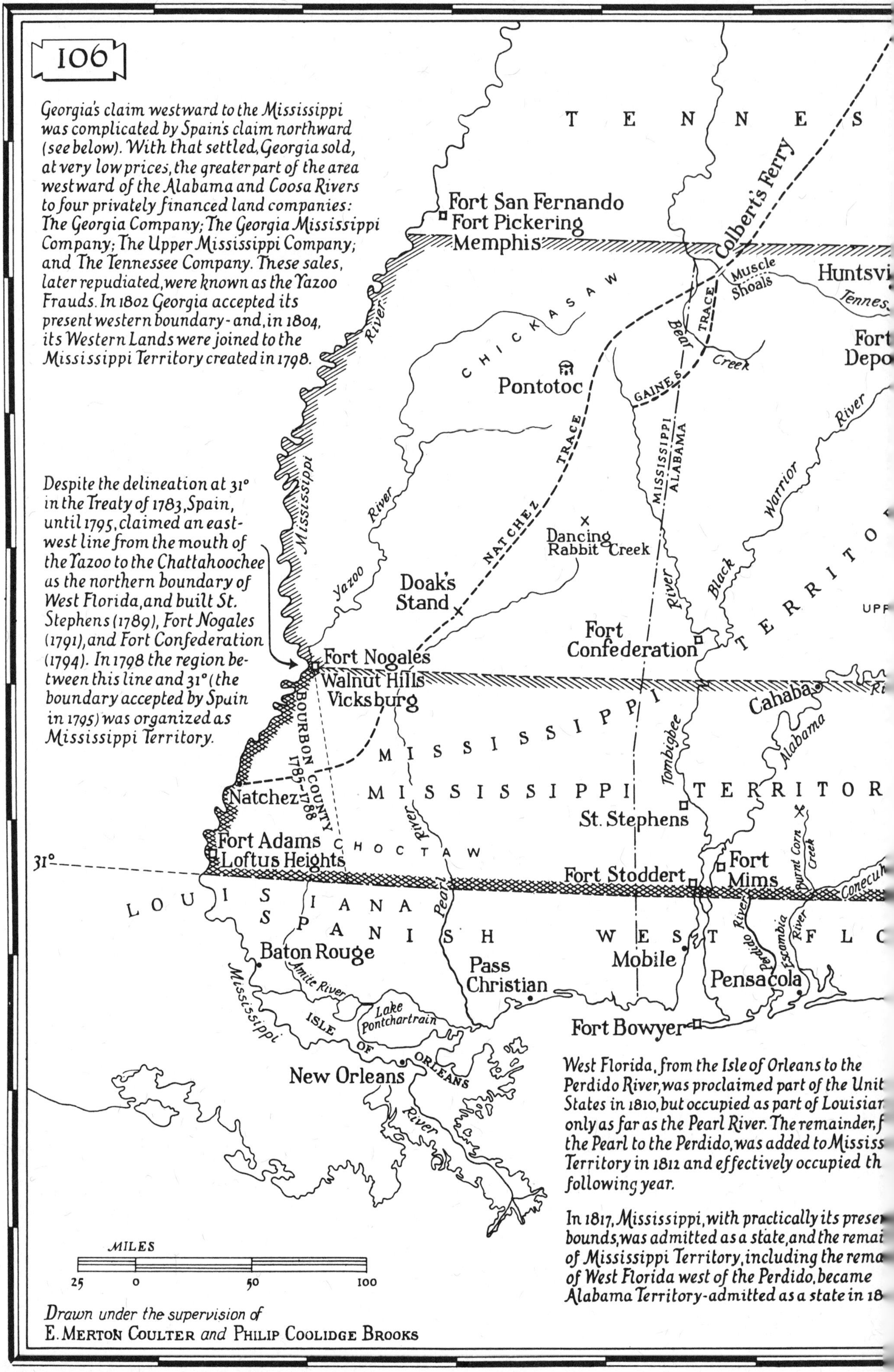

Georgia's claim westward to the Mississippi was complicated by Spain's claim northward (see below). With that settled, Georgia sold, at very low prices, the greater part of the area westward of the Alabama and Coosa Rivers to four privately financed land companies: The Georgia Company; The Georgia Mississippi Company; The Upper Mississippi Company; and The Tennessee Company. These sales, later repudiated, were known as the Yazoo Frauds. In 1802 Georgia accepted its present western boundary - and, in 1804, its Western Lands were joined to the Mississippi Territory created in 1798.

Despite the delineation at 31° in the Treaty of 1783, Spain, until 1795, claimed an east-west line from the mouth of the Yazoo to the Chattahoochee as the northern boundary of West Florida, and built St. Stephens (1789), Fort Nogales (1791), and Fort Confederation (1794). In 1798 the region between this line and 31° (the boundary accepted by Spain in 1795) was organized as Mississippi Territory.

West Florida, from the Isle of Orleans to the Perdido River, was proclaimed part of the Unit States in 1810, but occupied as part of Louisiar only as far as the Pearl River. The remainder, f the Pearl to the Perdido, was added to Mississ Territory in 1812 and effectively occupied th following year.

In 1817, Mississippi, with practically its prese bounds, was admitted as a state, and the remai of Mississippi Territory, including the rema of West Florida west of the Perdido, became Alabama Territory - admitted as a state in 18

Drawn under the supervision of
E. MERTON COULTER *and* PHILIP COOLIDGE BROOKS

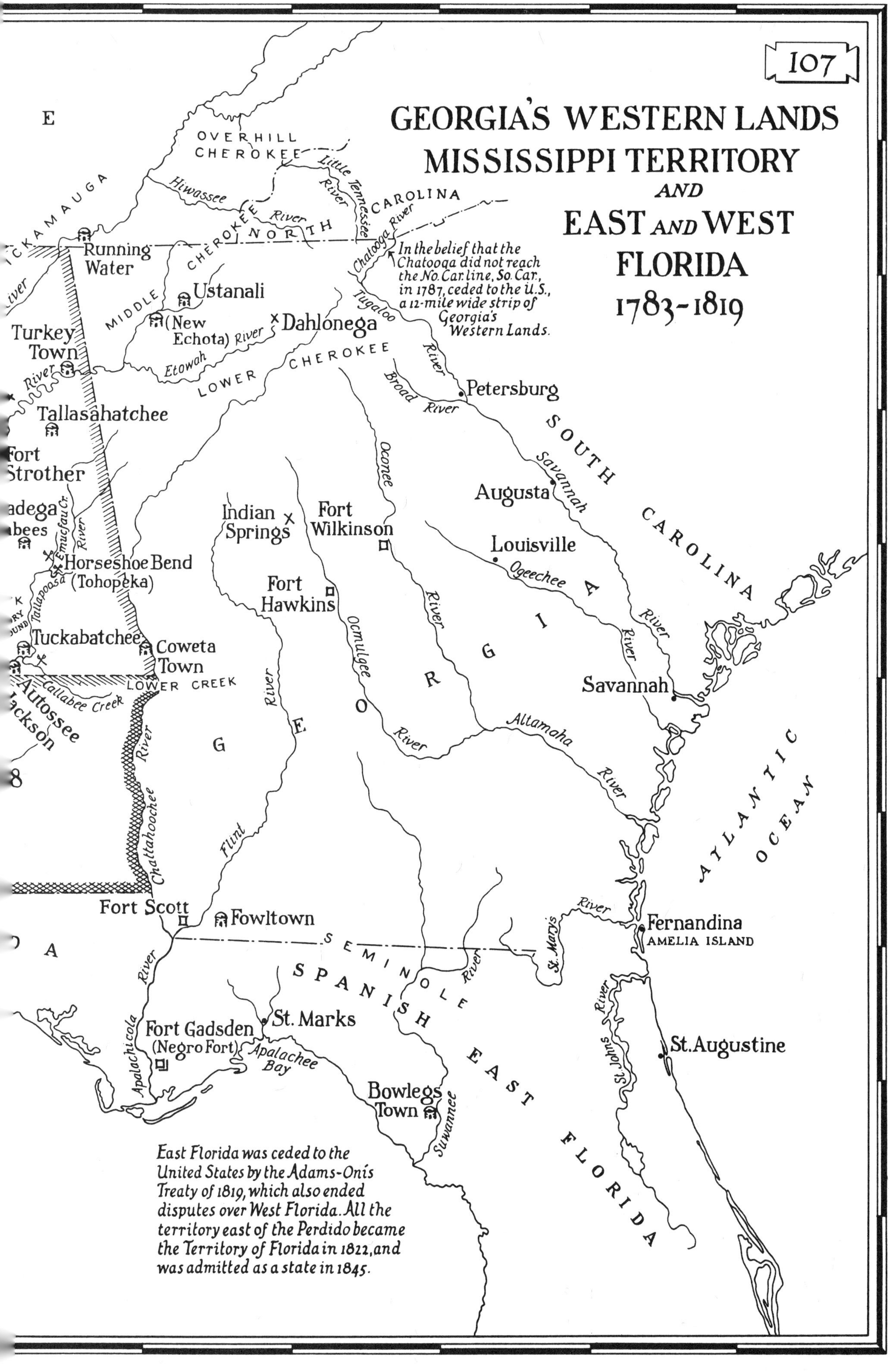
GEORGIA'S WESTERN LANDS
MISSISSIPPI TERRITORY
AND
EAST AND WEST
FLORIDA
1783-1819
In the belief that the Chatooga did not reach the No. Car. line, So. Car., in 1787, ceded to the U.S., a 12-mile wide strip of Georgia's Western Lands.
East Florida was ceded to the United States by the Adams-Onís Treaty of 1819, which also ended disputes over West Florida. All the territory east of the Perdido became the Territory of Florida in 1822, and was admitted as a state in 1845.
OVERHILL CHEROKEE
Little Tennessee River
Hiwassee River
NORTH CAROLINA
Chatooga River
Running Water
MIDDLE CHEROKEE
Ustanali
(New Echota)
Etowah River
Dahlonega
LOWER CHEROKEE
Tugaloo River
Turkey Town
Tallasahatchee
Fort Strother
Broad River
Petersburg
SOUTH CAROLINA
Savannah River
Augusta
Oconee
Indian Springs
Fort Wilkinson
Louisville
Ogeechee River
Horseshoe Bend (Tohopeka)
Emucfau Cr.
Tallapoosa
Fort Hawkins
Ocmulgee River
Tuckabatchee
Coweta Town
LOWER CREEK
Callabee Creek
Autossee
GEORGIA
Savannah
Altamaha River
Flint River
Chattahoochee River
ATLANTIC OCEAN
Fort Scott
Fowltown
SEMINOLE
St. Marys River
Fernandina
AMELIA ISLAND
SPANISH EAST FLORIDA
Apalachicola River
Fort Gadsden (Negro Fort)
St. Marks
Apalachee Bay
Bowlegs Town
Suwannee
St. Johns River
St. Augustine

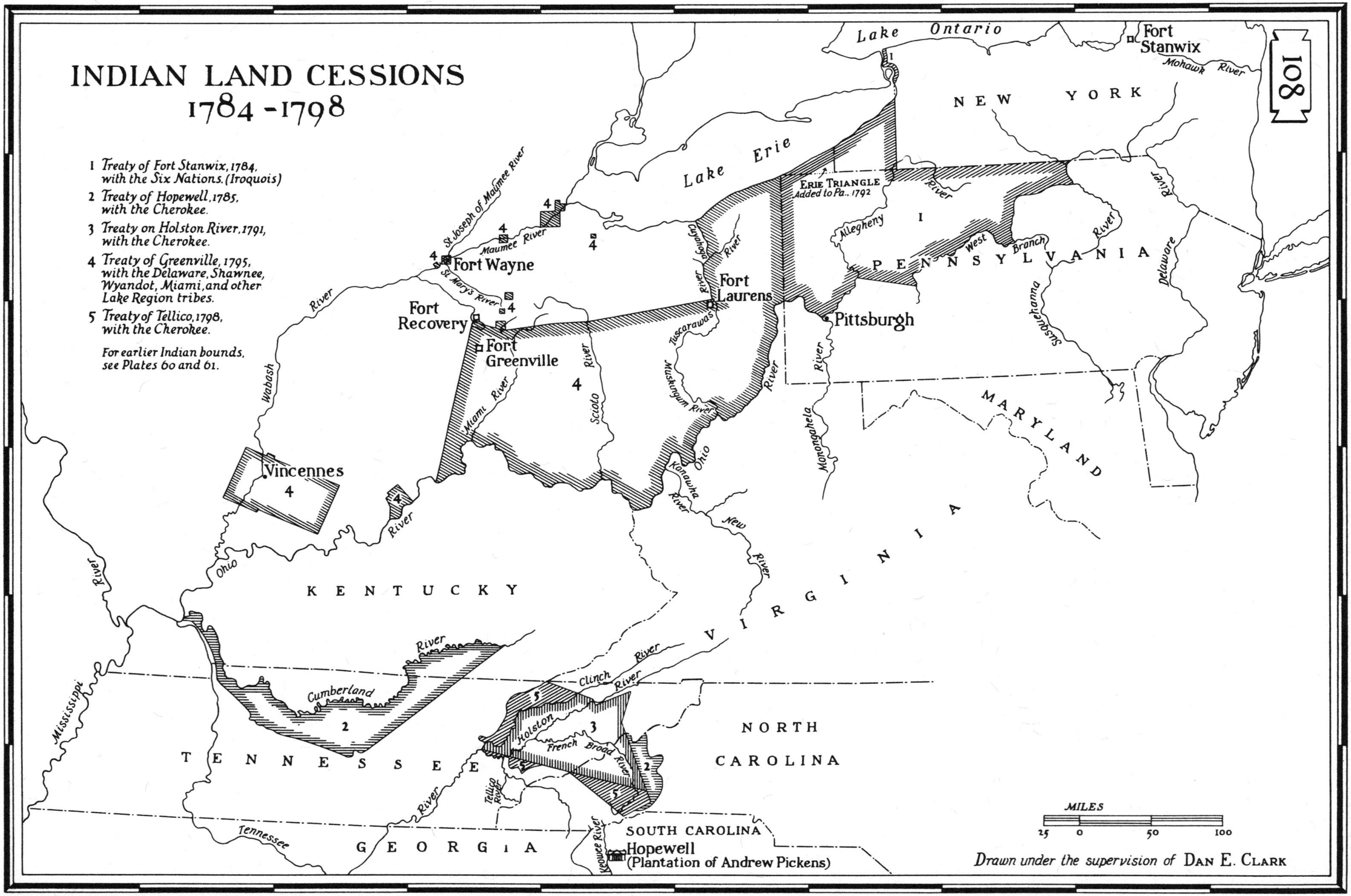
INDIAN LAND CESSIONS
1784-1798
1 Treaty of Fort Stanwix, 1784, with the Six Nations. (Iroquois)
2 Treaty of Hopewell, 1785, with the Cherokee.
3 Treaty on Holston River, 1791, with the Cherokee.
4 Treaty of Greenville, 1795, with the Delaware, Shawnee, Wyandot, Miami, and other Lake Region tribes.
5 Treaty of Tellico, 1798, with the Cherokee.
For earlier Indian bounds, see Plates 60 and 61.
Lake Ontario
Fort Stanwix
Mohawk River
NEW YORK
Lake Erie
ERIE TRIANGLE Added to Pa., 1792
Allegheny River
West Branch
PENNSYLVANIA
Susquehanna River
Delaware River
Pittsburgh
Monongahela River
MARYLAND
VIRGINIA
Fort Laurens
Cuyahoga River
Tuscarawas River
Muskingum River
Ohio River
Kanawha River
New River
Scioto River
Miami River
Fort Greenville
Fort Recovery
Fort Wayne
Maumee River
St. Joseph of Maumee River
St. Mary's River
Wabash River
Vincennes
KENTUCKY
Cumberland River
TENNESSEE
Mississippi River
Clinch River
Holston
French Broad River
Tellico River
NORTH CAROLINA
SOUTH CAROLINA
Keowee River
Hopewell (Plantation of Andrew Pickens)
GEORGIA
Tennessee
MILES
25 0 50 100
Drawn under the supervision of DAN E. CLARK

NEW YORK LAND PURCHASES, 1786-1793

By virtue of the Charter of 1629, Massachusetts claimed territorial rights to the land between the Mohawk River settlements of New York (see Plate 78) and the Western Lands ceded to the Federal Government (see Plate 82).

In 1786 New York and Massachusetts reached an agreement by which, in Boston Ten Townships and in the area west of a north-south line 82 miles west of the intersection of the New York-Pennsylvania boundary by the Delaware River (the Pre-emption Line), the jurisdictional rights were vested in New York and the right of ownership (purchase or sale) was vested in Massachusetts.

In both cases the pre-emption rights were promptly sold by Massachusetts, the area west of the Pre-emption Line being first acquired by Phelps and Gorham.

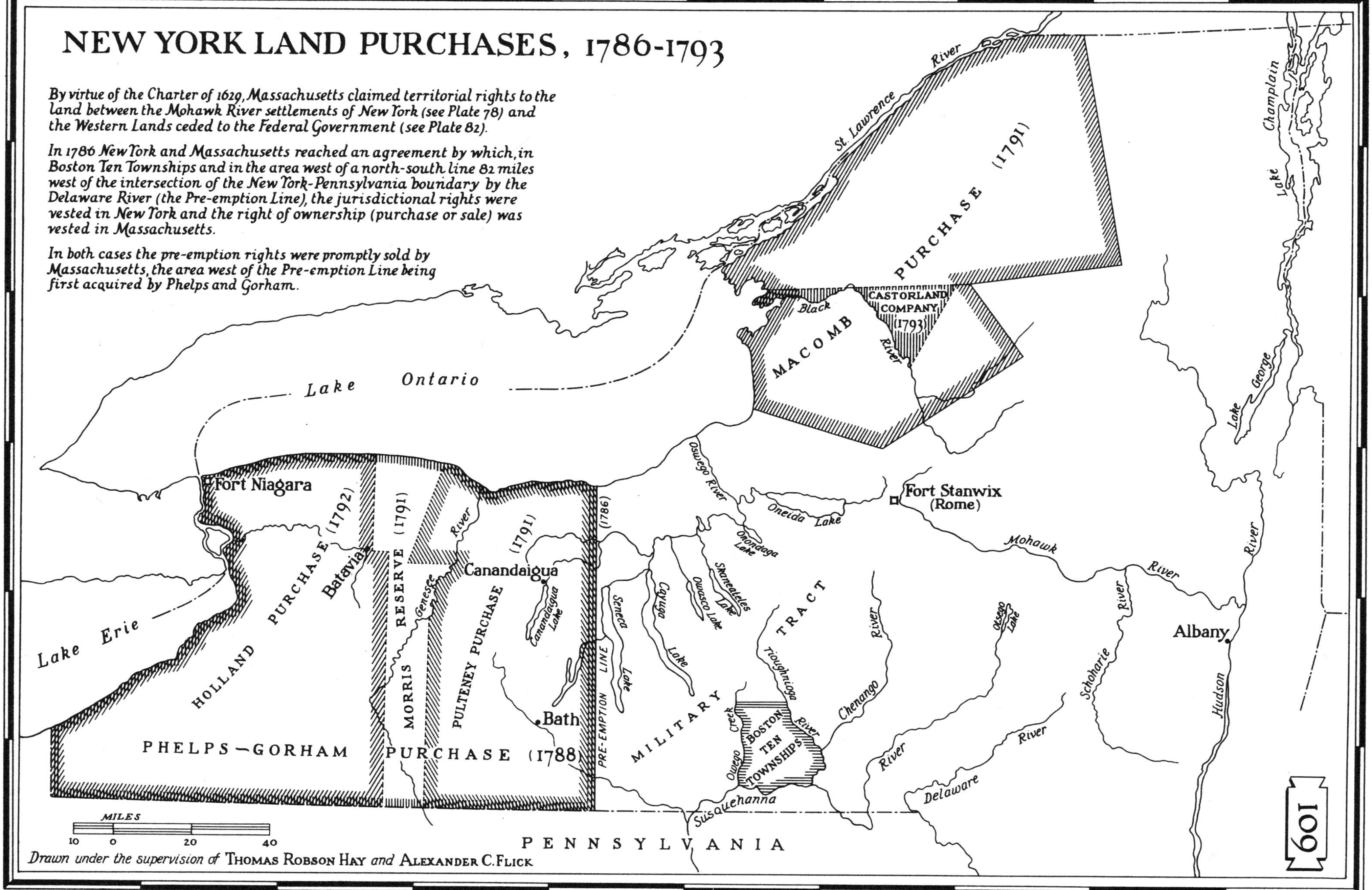

Drawn under the supervision of THOMAS ROBSON HAY *and* ALEXANDER C. FLICK

110 INDIANA AND ILLINOIS TERRITORIES 1800–1818

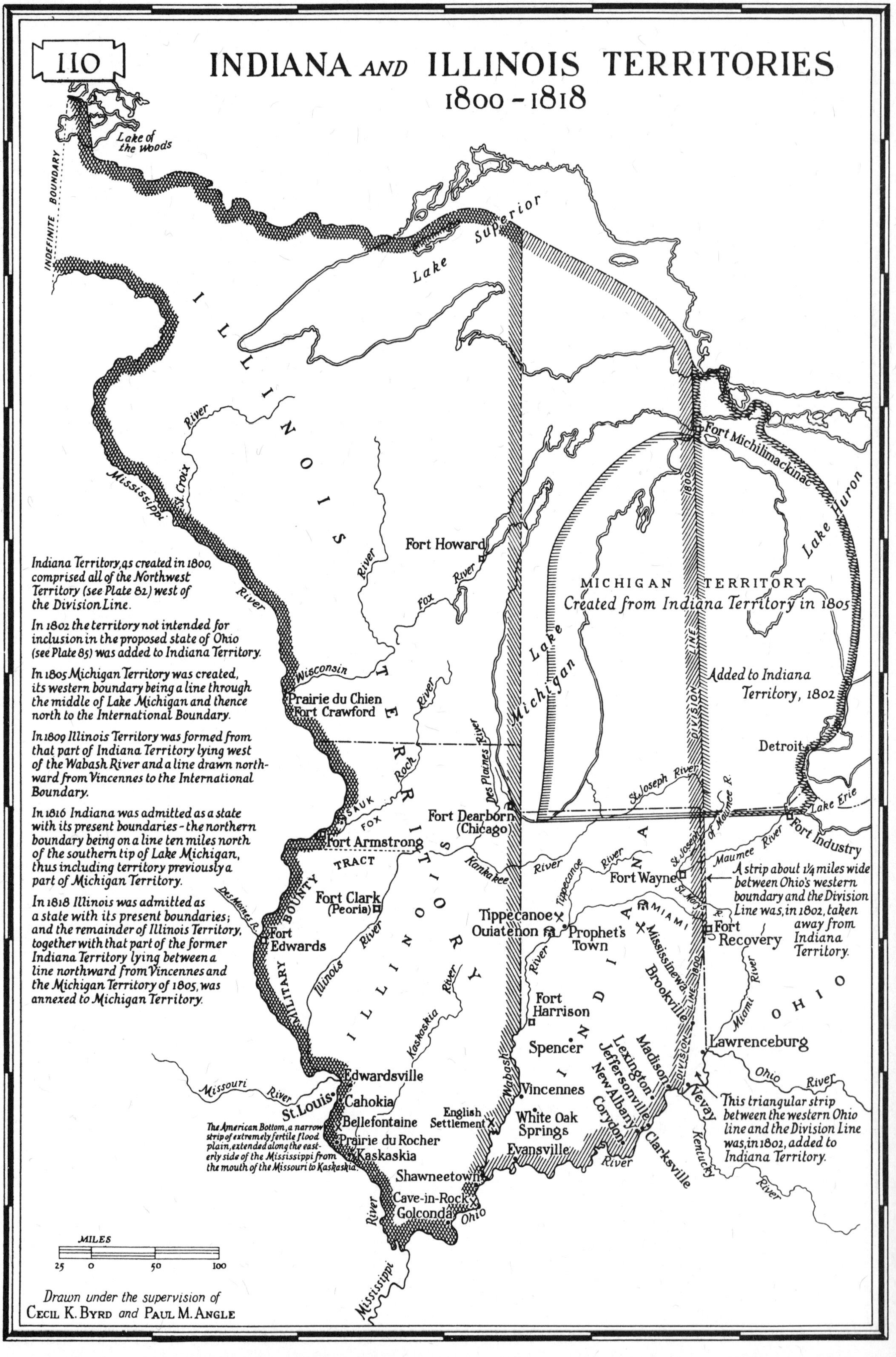

Lake of the Woods
INDEFINITE BOUNDARY
Lake Superior
ILLINOIS TERRITORY
Mississippi River
St. Croix River
River
Fort Howard
Fox River
Wisconsin
Prairie du Chien
Fort Crawford
Rock River
Des Plaines River
SAUK FOX
Fort Armstrong
MILITARY BOUNTY TRACT
Fort Dearborn (Chicago)
Kankakee
Fort Clark (Peoria)
Des Moines R.
Fort Edwards
Illinois River
ILLINOIS
Kaskaskia River
Missouri River
St. Louis
Edwardsville
Cahokia
Bellefontaine
Prairie du Rocher
Kaskaskia
The American Bottom, a narrow strip of extremely fertile flood plain, extended along the easterly side of the Mississippi from the mouth of the Missouri to Kaskaskia.
English Settlement
Shawneetown
Cave-in-Rock
Golconda
Ohio
Mississippi
MICHIGAN TERRITORY
Created from Indiana Territory in 1805
Lake Michigan
Lake Huron
Fort Michilimackinac
1800 DIVISION LINE
Added to Indiana Territory, 1802
Detroit
St. Joseph River
Maumee R.
Lake Erie
Fort Industry
Maumee River
St. Joseph
St. Marys R.
A strip about 1¼ miles wide between Ohio's western boundary and the Division Line was, in 1802, taken away from Indiana Territory.
Fort Wayne
Tippecanoe River
River
MIAMI
Tippecanoe
Ouiatenon
Prophet's Town
Mississinewa
Fort Recovery
INDIANA
Fort Harrison
Brookville
Miami River
OHIO
Spencer
Lawrenceburg
Wabash
Vincennes
White Oak Springs
Evansville
River
Lexington
Jeffersonville
New Albany
Corydon
Madison
Clarksville
Vevay
Ohio River
Kentucky River
This triangular strip between the western Ohio line and the Division Line was, in 1802, added to Indiana Territory.
Indiana Territory, as created in 1800, comprised all of the Northwest Territory (see Plate 82) west of the Division Line.
In 1802 the territory not intended for inclusion in the proposed state of Ohio (see Plate 85) was added to Indiana Territory.
In 1805 Michigan Territory was created, its western boundary being a line through the middle of Lake Michigan and thence north to the International Boundary.
In 1809 Illinois Territory was formed from that part of Indiana Territory lying west of the Wabash River and a line drawn northward from Vincennes to the International Boundary.
In 1816 Indiana was admitted as a state with its present boundaries – the northern boundary being on a line ten miles north of the southern tip of Lake Michigan, thus including territory previously a part of Michigan Territory.
In 1818 Illinois was admitted as a state with its present boundaries; and the remainder of Illinois Territory, together with that part of the former Indiana Territory lying between a line northward from Vincennes and the Michigan Territory of 1805, was annexed to Michigan Territory.
MILES
25 0 50 100
Drawn under the supervision of
CECIL K. BYRD and PAUL M. ANGLE

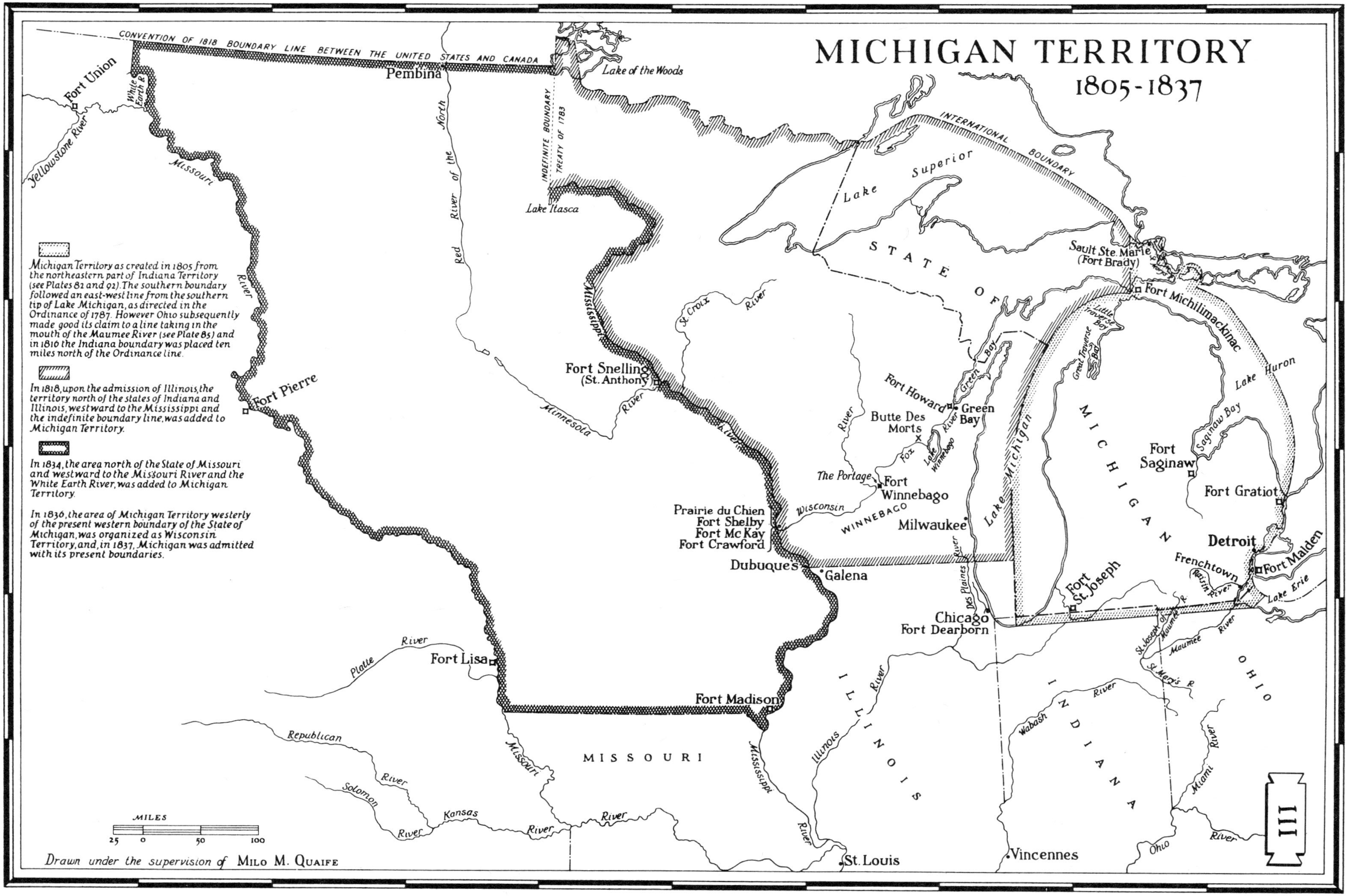
MICHIGAN TERRITORY
1805-1837
III
Michigan Territory as created in 1805 from the northeastern part of Indiana Territory (see Plates 82 and 92). The southern boundary followed an east-west line from the southern tip of Lake Michigan, as directed in the Ordinance of 1787. However Ohio subsequently made good its claim to a line taking in the mouth of the Maumee River (see Plate 85) and in 1816 the Indiana boundary was placed ten miles north of the Ordinance line.
In 1818, upon the admission of Illinois, the territory north of the states of Indiana and Illinois, westward to the Mississippi and the indefinite boundary line, was added to Michigan Territory.
In 1834, the area north of the State of Missouri and westward to the Missouri River and the White Earth River, was added to Michigan Territory.
In 1836, the area of Michigan Territory westerly of the present western boundary of the State of Michigan, was organized as Wisconsin Territory, and, in 1837, Michigan was admitted with its present boundaries.
MILES
25 0 50 100
Drawn under the supervision of Milo M. Quaife
CONVENTION OF 1818 BOUNDARY LINE BETWEEN THE UNITED STATES AND CANADA
INTERNATIONAL BOUNDARY
INDEFINITE BOUNDARY TREATY OF 1783
Fort Union
White Earth R.
Yellowstone River
Missouri River
Fort Pierre
Pembina
Red River of the North
Lake of the Woods
Lake Itasca
Minnesota River
Fort Snelling (St. Anthony)
Mississippi River
St. Croix River
Lake Superior
STATE OF MICHIGAN
Sault Ste. Marie (Fort Brady)
Fort Michilimackinac
Little Traverse Bay
Great Traverse Bay
Lake Huron
Saginaw Bay
Fort Saginaw
Fort Gratiot
Detroit
Fort Malden
Frenchtown
Raisin River
Lake Erie
Fort St. Joseph
Lake Michigan
Green Bay
Fort Howard
Green Bay
Butte Des Morts
Fox River
Lake Winnebago
The Portage
Fort Winnebago
WINNEBAGO
Wisconsin
Milwaukee
Prairie du Chien
Fort Shelby
Fort Mc Kay
Fort Crawford
Dubuque's
Galena
Des Plaines River
Chicago
Fort Dearborn
Platte River
Fort Lisa
Fort Madison
Republican River
Solomon River
Kansas River
Missouri
MISSOURI
Mississippi River
St. Louis
Illinois River
ILLINOIS
INDIANA
Wabash River
Vincennes
OHIO
Maumee River
St. Joseph R.
St. Mary's R.
Miami River
Ohio River

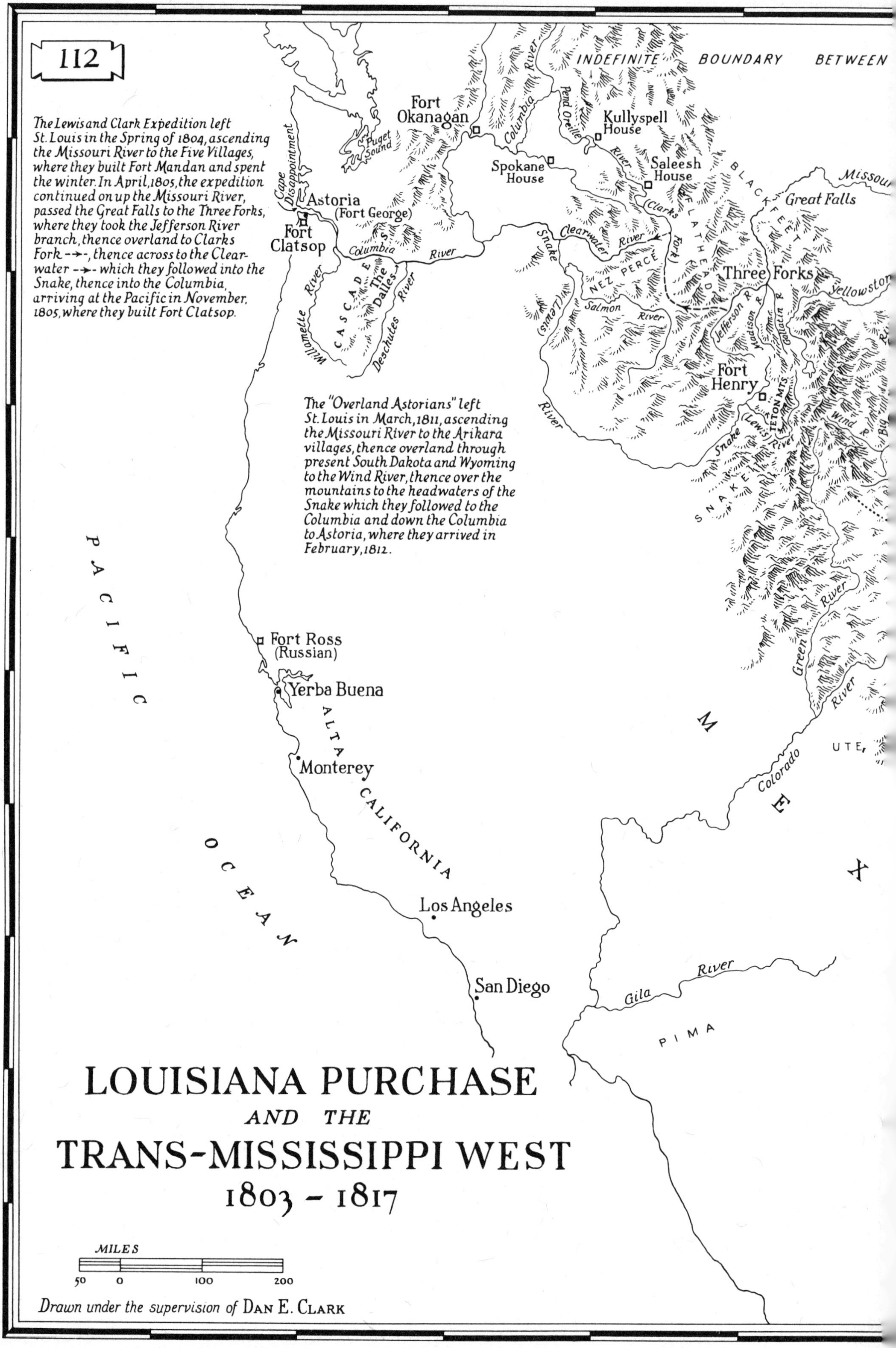
112
The Lewis and Clark Expedition left St. Louis in the Spring of 1804, ascending the Missouri River to the Five Villages, where they built Fort Mandan and spent the winter. In April, 1805, the expedition continued on up the Missouri River, passed the Great Falls to the Three Forks, where they took the Jefferson River branch, thence overland to Clarks Fork -→-, thence across to the Clearwater -→- which they followed into the Snake, thence into the Columbia, arriving at the Pacific in November, 1805, where they built Fort Clatsop.
The "Overland Astorians" left St. Louis in March, 1811, ascending the Missouri River to the Arikara villages, thence overland through present South Dakota and Wyoming to the Wind River, thence over the mountains to the headwaters of the Snake which they followed to the Columbia and down the Columbia to Astoria, where they arrived in February, 1812.
INDEFINITE BOUNDARY BETWEEN
Fort Okanagan
Kullyspell House
Spokane House
Saleesh House
Puget Sound
Cape Disappointment
Astoria (Fort George)
Fort Clatsop
Columbia River
Pend Oreille River
Clarks Fork
BLACKFEET
FLATHEAD
Missouri
Great Falls
Snake
Clearwater River
NEZ PERCE
Three Forks
Yellowstone
CASCADES
The Dalles
Deschutes River
Willamette River
Salmon River
(Lewis)
Jefferson R.
Madison R.
Gallatin R.
Fort Henry
TETON MTS.
Snake (Lewis) River
Wind R.
SNAKE
PACIFIC
OCEAN
Fort Ross (Russian)
Yerba Buena
ALTA CALIFORNIA
Monterey
Los Angeles
San Diego
Green River
UTE
Colorado
MEX
Gila River
PIMA
LOUISIANA PURCHASE AND THE TRANS-MISSISSIPPI WEST 1803 - 1817
MILES
50 0 100 200
Drawn under the supervision of DAN E. CLARK

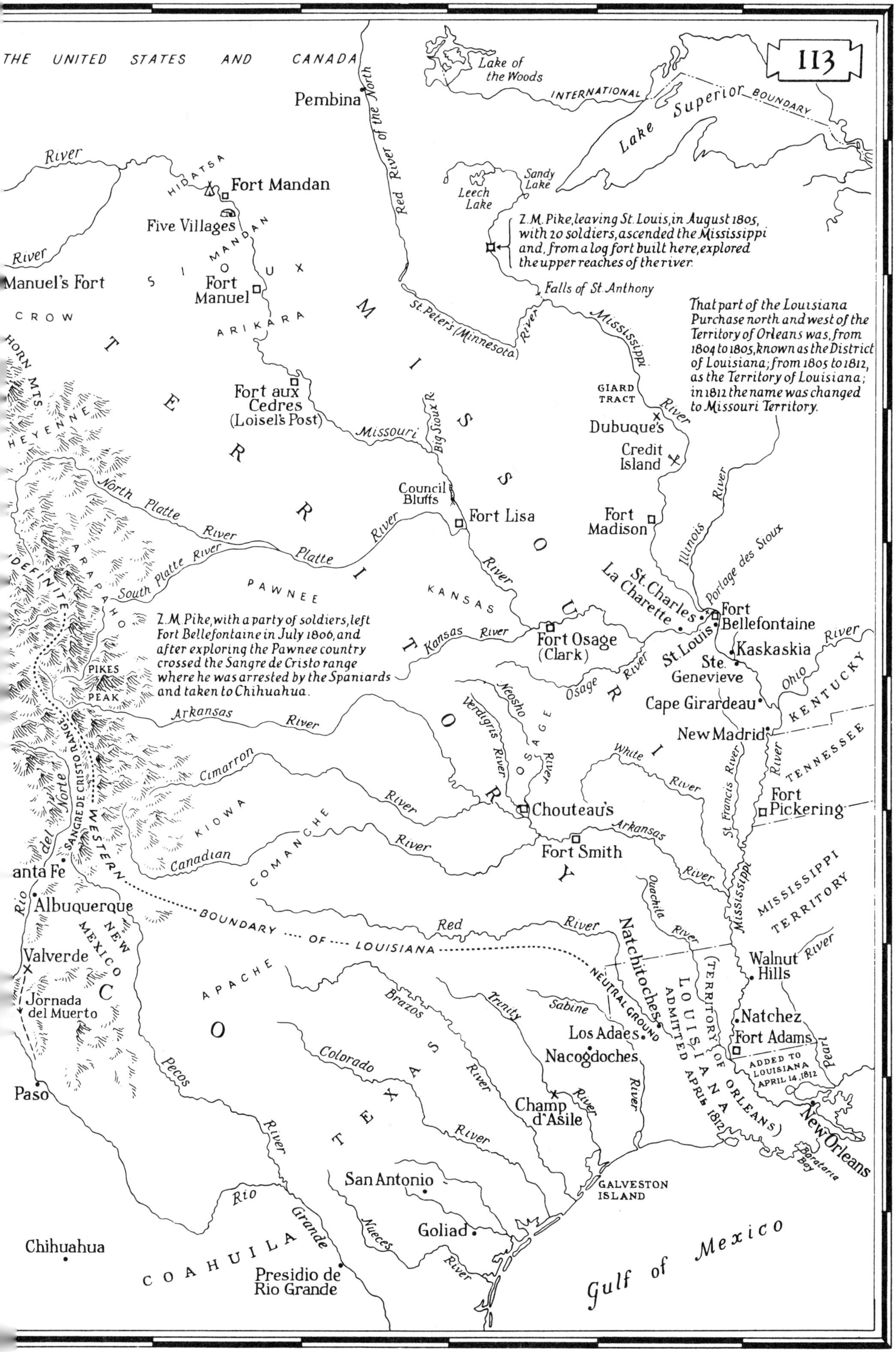
THE UNITED STATES AND CANADA
Lake of the Woods
INTERNATIONAL
Lake Superior
BOUNDARY
Pembina
Red River of the North
River
HIDATSA
Fort Mandan
Five Villages
MANDAN
SIOUX
River
Manuel's Fort
Fort Manuel
CROW
ARIKARA
Sandy Lake
Leech Lake
Z.M. Pike, leaving St. Louis, in August 1805, with 20 soldiers, ascended the Mississippi and, from a log fort built here, explored the upper reaches of the river.
Falls of St. Anthony
St. Peter's (Minnesota) River
Mississippi River
MISSOURI TERRITORY
That part of the Louisiana Purchase north and west of the Territory of Orleans was, from 1804 to 1805, known as the District of Louisiana; from 1805 to 1812, as the Territory of Louisiana; in 1812 the name was changed to Missouri Territory.
HORN MTS.
CHEYENNE
Fort aux Cedres (Loisel's Post)
Missouri
Big Sioux R.
GIARD TRACT
Dubuque's
Credit Island
Council Bluffs
Fort Lisa
Fort Madison
River
Illinois
North Platte River
Platte River
South Platte River
ARAPAHO
PAWNEE
KANSAS
River
Portage des Sioux
St. Charles
La Charette
Fort Bellefontaine
Z.M. Pike, with a party of soldiers, left Fort Bellefontaine in July 1806, and after exploring the Pawnee country crossed the Sangre de Cristo range where he was arrested by the Spaniards and taken to Chihuahua.
Kansas River
Fort Osage (Clark)
St. Louis
Kaskaskia
Ste. Genevieve
Ohio River
KENTUCKY
PIKES PEAK
Osage River
Cape Girardeau
Arkansas River
Neosho
Verdigris River
OSAGE
New Madrid
TENNESSEE
White River
Cimarron River
St. Francis River
River
Fort Pickering
Chouteau's
Arkansas
Fort Smith
KIOWA
COMANCHE
Canadian River
SANGRE DE CRISTO RANGE
WESTERN
Rio del Norte
anta Fe
Albuquerque
NEW MEXICO
River
Ouachita River
Mississippi
MISSISSIPPI TERRITORY
BOUNDARY OF LOUISIANA
Red River
Natchitoches
Valverde
Walnut Hills
River
APACHE
NEUTRAL GROUND
LOUISIANA ADMITTED APRIL 1812
(TERRITORY OF ORLEANS)
Jornada del Muerto
Brazos
Trinity
Sabine
Natchez
Los Adaes
Fort Adams
Pearl
ADDED TO LOUISIANA APRIL 14, 1812
Nacogdoches
Colorado
TEXAS
River
Pecos River
Champ d'Asile
River
River
New Orleans
Paso
Barataria Bay
GALVESTON ISLAND
San Antonio
Rio Grande
Goliad
Nueces River
Gulf of Mexico
Chihuahua
COAHUILA
Presidio de Rio Grande

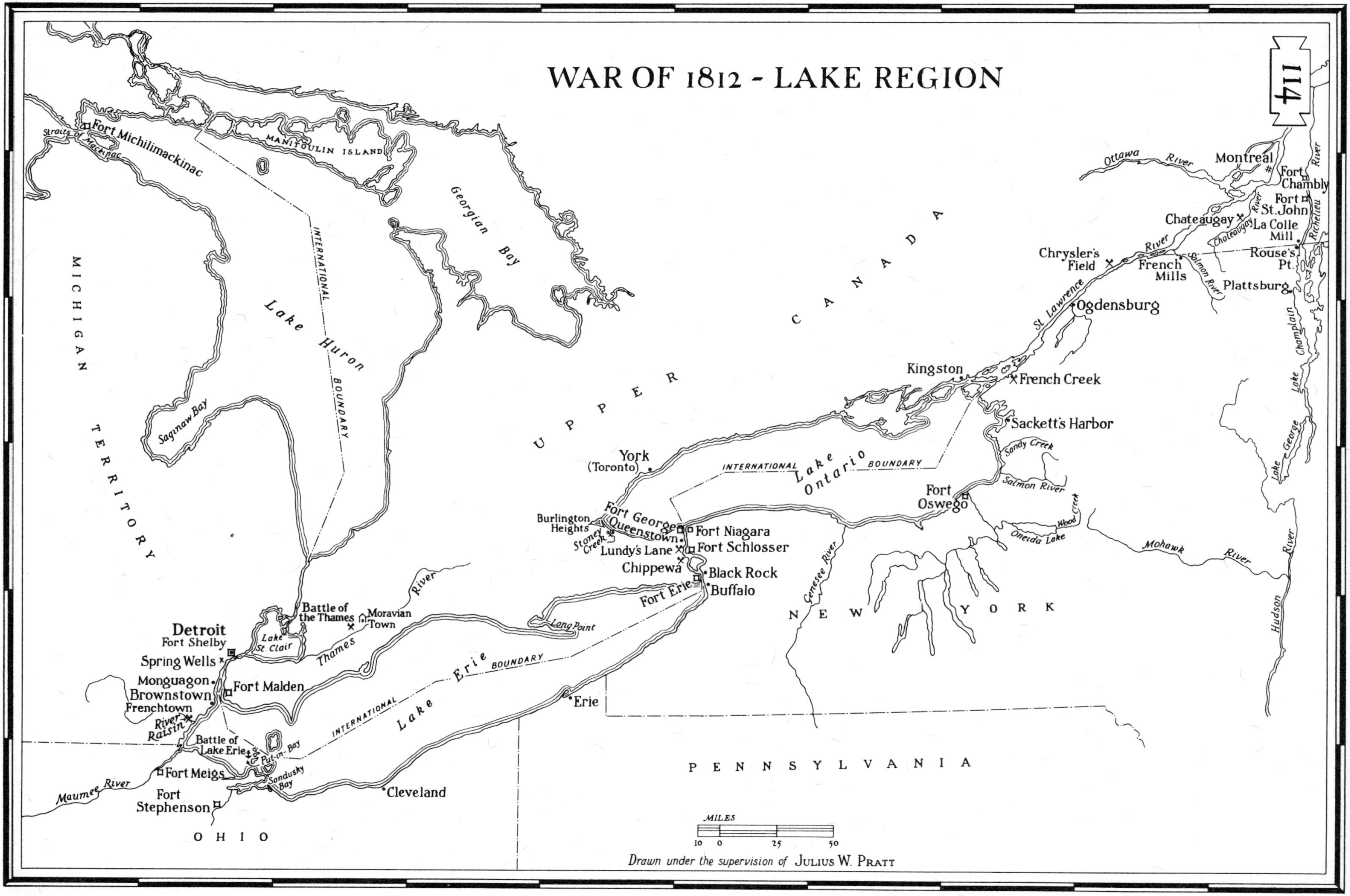
114
WAR OF 1812 - LAKE REGION
Fort Michilimackinac
Straits of Mackinac
MANITOULIN ISLAND
Georgian Bay
INTERNATIONAL BOUNDARY
Lake Huron
Saginaw Bay
MICHIGAN TERRITORY
UPPER CANADA
Ottawa River
Montreal
Fort Chambly
Richelieu River
Fort St. John
Chateaugay
Chateaugay River
La Colle Mill
Rouse's Pt.
Plattsburg
Chrysler's Field
French Mills
Salmon River
St. Lawrence River
Ogdensburg
Lake Champlain
Lake George
Kingston
French Creek
Sackett's Harbor
Sandy Creek
Salmon River
Wood Creek
Oneida Lake
Fort Oswego
Mohawk River
Hudson River
York (Toronto)
Lake Ontario
Burlington Heights
Stoney Creek
Fort George
Queenstown
Lundy's Lane
Chippewa
Fort Niagara
Fort Schlosser
Black Rock
Buffalo
Fort Erie
Genesee River
NEW YORK
Long Point
Battle of the Thames
Moravian Town
Thames River
Detroit
Fort Shelby
Lake St. Clair
Spring Wells
Monguagon
Brownstown
Frenchtown
Fort Malden
River Raisin
Battle of Lake Erie
Put-in-Bay
Sandusky Bay
Lake Erie
Erie
Fort Meigs
Maumee River
Fort Stephenson
Cleveland
OHIO
PENNSYLVANIA
MILES
10 0 25 50
Drawn under the supervision of Julius W. Pratt

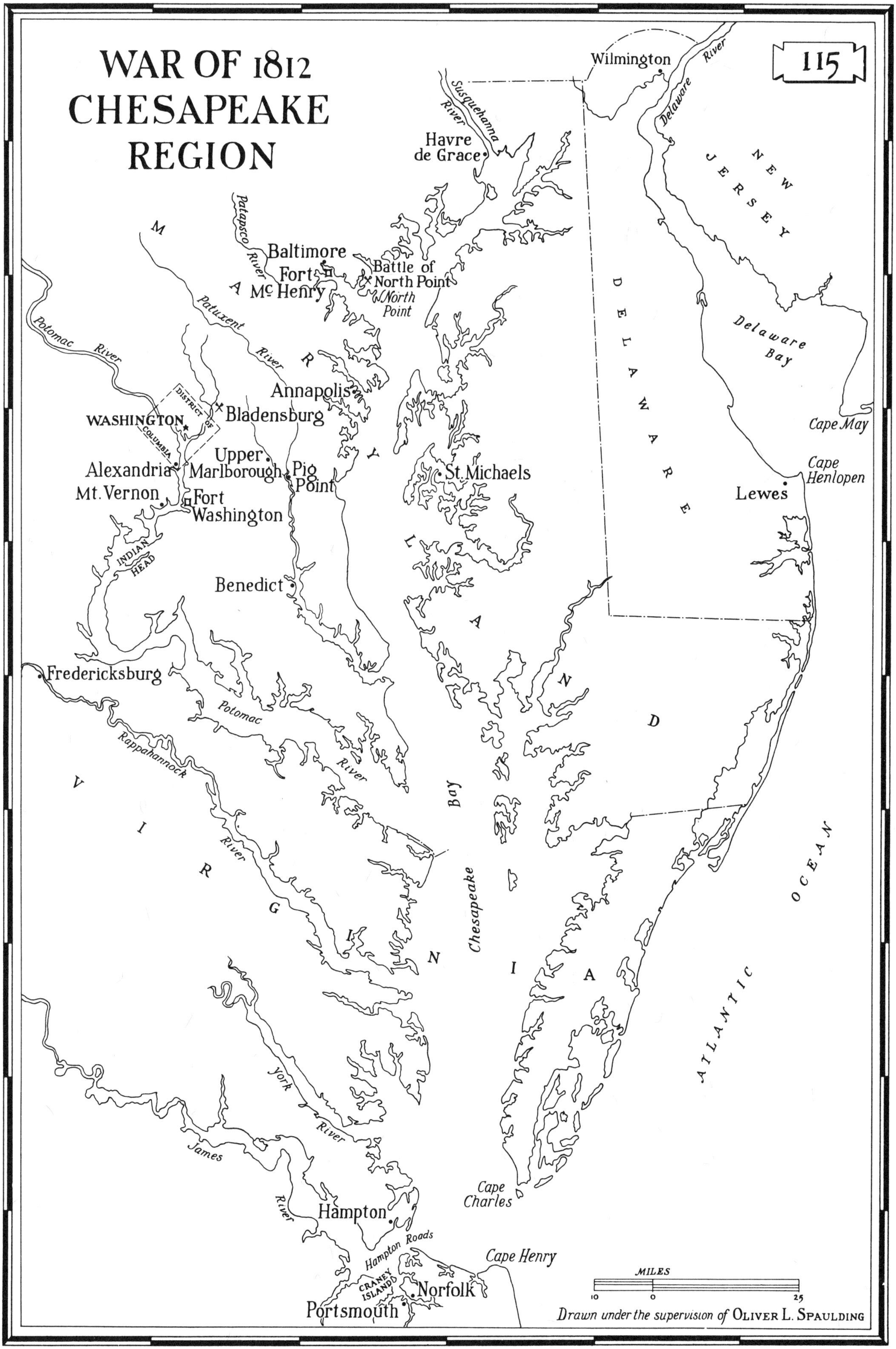
115
WAR OF 1812
CHESAPEAKE
REGION
Wilmington
Delaware River
Susquehanna River
Havre de Grace
NEW JERSEY
Patapsco River
M
Baltimore
Fort McHenry
Battle of North Point
North Point
A
Patuxent River
Potomac River
R
DELAWARE
Delaware Bay
Annapolis
DISTRICT OF COLUMBIA
WASHINGTON
Bladensburg
Upper Marlborough
Pig Point
Alexandria
Mt. Vernon
Fort Washington
St. Michaels
Cape May
Cape Henlopen
Lewes
Y
L
INDIAN HEAD
Benedict
A
N
D
Fredericksburg
Potomac River
Rappahannock River
Bay
Chesapeake
V
I
R
G
I
N
I
A
ATLANTIC OCEAN
York River
James River
Cape Charles
Hampton
Hampton Roads
Cape Henry
CRANEY ISLAND
Norfolk
Portsmouth
MILES
10
0
25
Drawn under the supervision of OLIVER L. SPAULDING

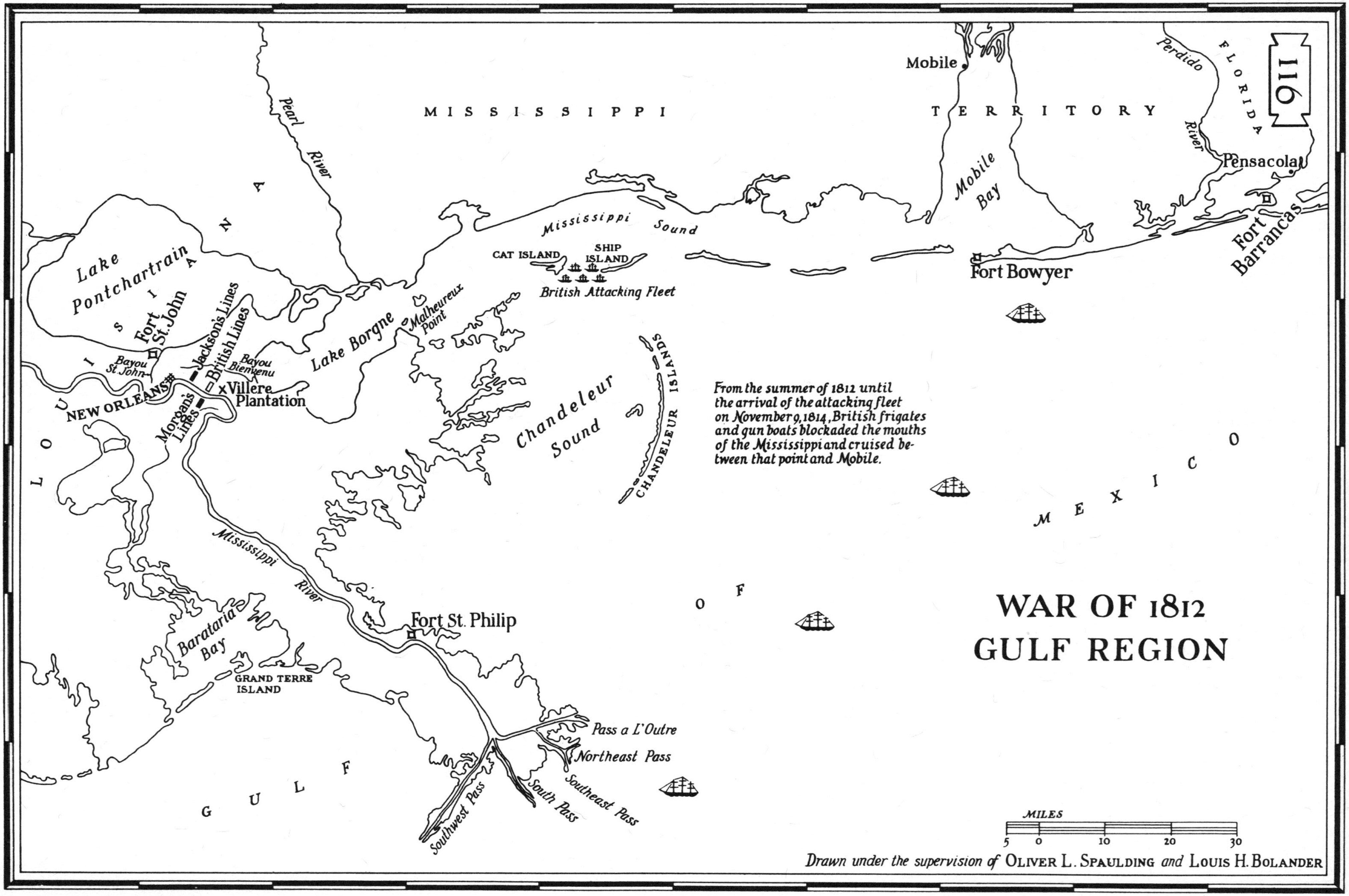
116
WAR OF 1812
GULF REGION
MISSISSIPPI
TERRITORY
FLORIDA
LOUISIANA
GULF OF MEXICO
Mobile
Pensacola
Perdido River
Fort Barrancas
Mobile Bay
Fort Bowyer
Pearl River
Mississippi Sound
CAT ISLAND
SHIP ISLAND
British Attacking Fleet
CHANDELEUR ISLANDS
Chandeleur Sound
Malheureux Point
Lake Borgne
Lake Pontchartrain
Fort St. John
Bayou St. John
NEW ORLEANS
Jackson's Lines
British Lines
Bayou Bienvenu
Villere Plantation
Morgan's Lines
Mississippi River
Fort St. Philip
Barataria Bay
GRAND TERRE ISLAND
Pass a L'Outre
Northeast Pass
Southeast Pass
South Pass
Southwest Pass
From the summer of 1812 until the arrival of the attacking fleet on November 9, 1814, British frigates and gun boats blockaded the mouths of the Mississippi and cruised between that point and Mobile.
MILES
5
0
10
20
30
Drawn under the supervision of Oliver L. Spaulding and Louis H. Bolander

THE BRITISH BLOCKADE ATLANTIC AREA 1813 – 1814

(FOR GULF AREA, SEE PLATE 98)

A state of blockade from New York to Savannah was proclaimed by the British on December 26, 1812, and became increasingly effective during 1813.

A state of blockade on the New England coast was proclaimed in April, 1814, although numerous ships of the line (74 guns), frigates (20 to 50 guns), sloops (18 to 20 guns), and gun boats, were off that coast as early as June, 1813.

A total of fifteen 74's, twenty seven frigates, and many small ships of war appear to have been present on the Atlantic Coast during 1814. The principal 74's were the Bulwark, Poictiers, Ramillies, Dragon, Spencer, Sceptre, Victorious, Valiant, San Domingo and Marlborough.

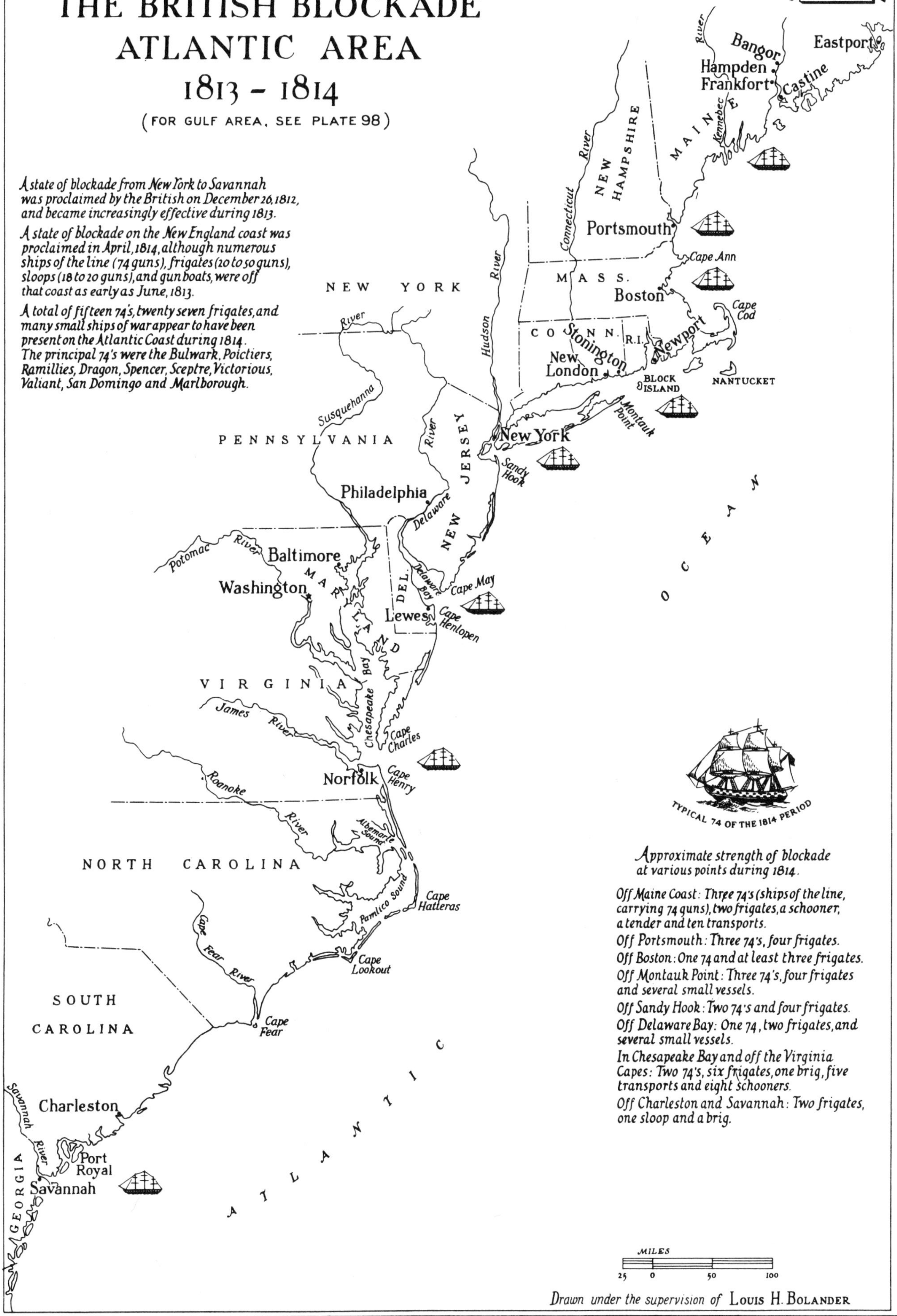

Approximate strength of blockade at various points during 1814.

Off Maine Coast: Three 74's (ships of the line, carrying 74 guns), two frigates, a schooner, a tender and ten transports.

Off Portsmouth: Three 74's, four frigates.

Off Boston: One 74 and at least three frigates.

Off Montauk Point: Three 74's, four frigates and several small vessels.

Off Sandy Hook: Two 74's and four frigates.

Off Delaware Bay: One 74, two frigates, and several small vessels.

In Chesapeake Bay and off the Virginia Capes: Two 74's, six frigates, one brig, five transports and eight schooners.

Off Charleston and Savannah: Two frigates, one sloop and a brig.

Drawn under the supervision of Louis H. Bolander

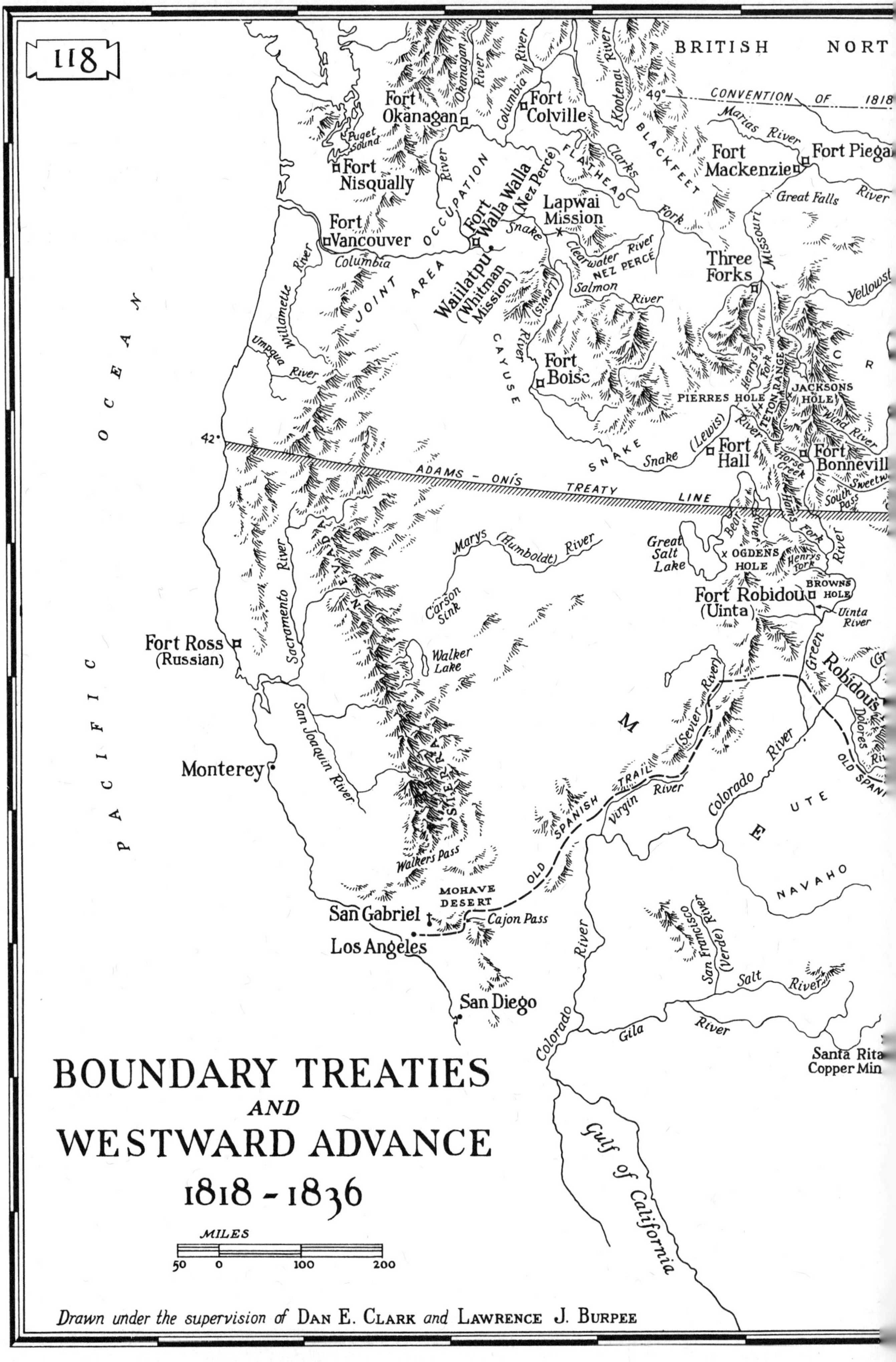

BOUNDARY TREATIES *AND* WESTWARD ADVANCE 1818 - 1836

Drawn under the supervision of Dan E. Clark *and* Lawrence J. Burpee

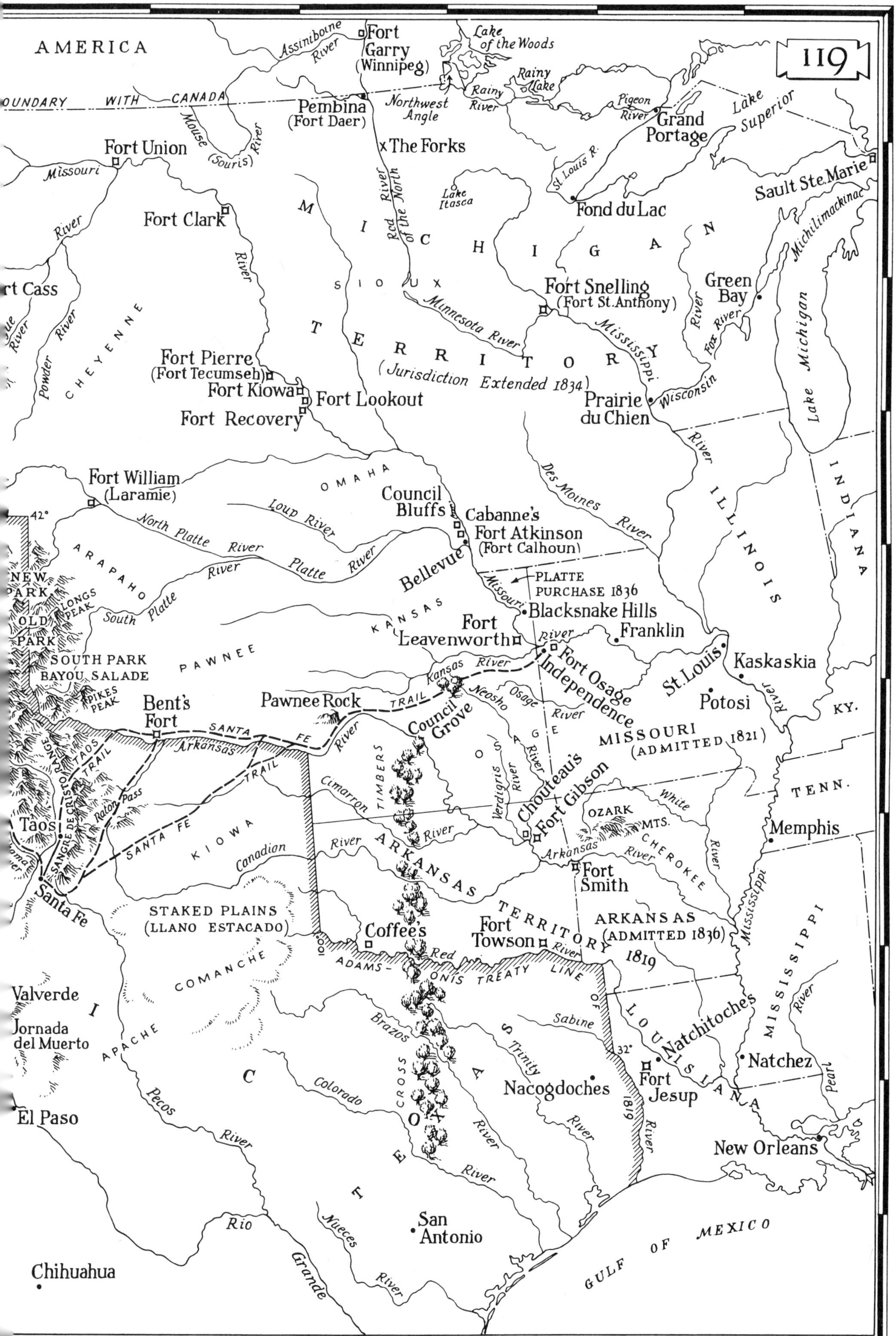
AMERICA
OUNDARY WITH CANADA
Assiniboine River
Fort Garry (Winnipeg)
Lake of the Woods
Rainy Lake
Rainy River
Pembina (Fort Daer)
Northwest Angle
Pigeon River
Grand Portage
Lake Superior
Mouse (Souris) River
Fort Union
Missouri
x The Forks
St. Louis R.
Sault Ste. Marie
Red River of the North
Lake Itasca
Fond du Lac
Fort Clark
River
Michilimackinac
M I C H I G A N
River
rt Cass
S I O U X
Fort Snelling (Fort St. Anthony)
Green Bay
Minnesota River
River
Fox River
C H E Y E N N E
River
Powder River
T E R R I T O R Y
(Jurisdiction Extended 1834)
Mississippi
Lake Michigan
Fort Pierre (Fort Tecumseh)
Fort Kiowa
Fort Lookout
Fort Recovery
Prairie du Chien
Wisconsin
River
I N D I A N A
O M A H A
Fort William (Laramie)
Council Bluffs
Cabanne's
Fort Atkinson (Fort Calhoun)
Loup River
Des Moines River
I L L I N O I S
42°
North Platte River
Platte River
A R A P A H O
River
Bellevue
PLATTE PURCHASE 1836
NEW PARK
LONGS PEAK
OLD PARK
South Platte
Missouri
Blacksnake Hills
K A N S A S
Fort Leavenworth
River
Franklin
SOUTH PARK
BAYOU SALADE
P A W N E E
Kansas River
Fort Osage
Independence
St. Louis
Kaskaskia
PIKES PEAK
Bent's Fort
Pawnee Rock
TRAIL
Neosho
Osage River
Potosi
River
KY.
SANTA FE
Arkansas
Council Grove
River
O S A G E
MISSOURI (ADMITTED 1821)
TAOS TRAIL
SANGRE DE CRISTO RANGE
TRAIL
TIMBERS
Verdigris River
River
Chouteau's
Fort Gibson
White River
TENN.
Cimarron
Raton Pass
Taos
SANTA FE
K I O W A
River
OZARK MTS.
CHEROKEE
Memphis
River
A R K A N S A S
Canadian
Fort Smith
Arkansas River
Santa Fe
STAKED PLAINS (LLANO ESTACADO)
TERRITORY 1819
ARKANSAS (ADMITTED 1836)
Mississippi
Coffee's
Fort Towson
Red River
100°
ADAMS-ONIS TREATY LINE OF 1819
COMANCHE
Valverde
Jornada del Muerto
A P A C H E
Brazos
Sabine
L O U I S I A N A
Natchitoches
M I S S I S S I P P I
River
Trinity
32°
Fort Jesup
Natchez
Pearl
Colorado
CROSS
T E X A S
Nacogdoches
River
River
River
M E X I C O
El Paso
Pecos River
River
New Orleans
River
San Antonio
Rio Grande
Nueces River
GULF OF MEXICO
Chihuahua

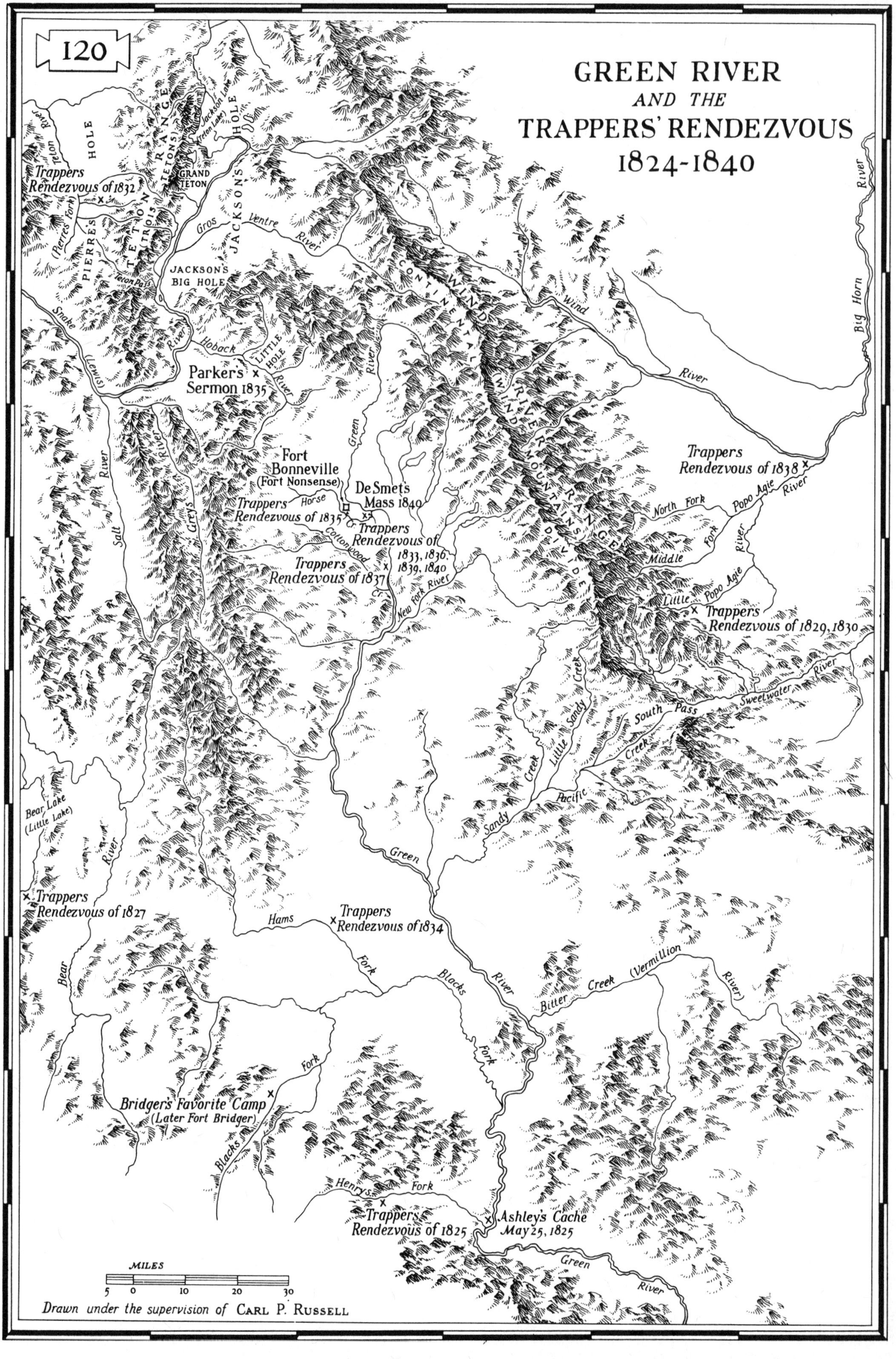
120
GREEN RIVER
AND THE
TRAPPERS' RENDEZVOUS
1824-1840
Trappers Rendezvous of 1832
Teton River
HOLE
PIERRE'S
(Pierre's Fork)
TETON RANGE
(TROIS TETONS)
GRAND TETON
Jackson Lake
(Teton Lake)
JACKSON'S HOLE
Teton Pass
JACKSON'S BIG HOLE
Gros Ventre River
CONTINENTAL DIVIDE
WIND RIVER RANGE
(WIND RIVER MOUNTAINS)
Wind River
Big Horn River
Snake (Lewis) River
Hoback River
LITTLE HOLE
Parker's Sermon 1835
Green River
Fort Bonneville
(Fort Nonsense)
De Smet's Mass 1840
Trappers Rendezvous of 1835
Horse Cr.
Trappers Rendezvous of 1833, 1836, 1839, 1840
Cottonwood Cr.
Trappers Rendezvous of 1837
New Fork River
Trappers Rendezvous of 1838
North Fork
Popo Agie River
Middle Fork
Little Popo Agie
Trappers Rendezvous of 1829, 1830
Salt River
Greys River
Sweetwater River
South Pass
Little Sandy Creek
Sandy Creek
Pacific Creek
Bear Lake
(Little Lake)
Bear River
Trappers Rendezvous of 1827
Hams Fork
Trappers Rendezvous of 1834
Green River
Blacks Fork
Bitter Creek (Vermillion River)
Bridger's Favorite Camp
(Later Fort Bridger)
Blacks Fork
Henrys Fork
Trappers Rendezvous of 1825
Ashley's Cache May 25, 1825
Green River
MILES
5 0 10 20 30
Drawn under the supervision of CARL P. RUSSELL

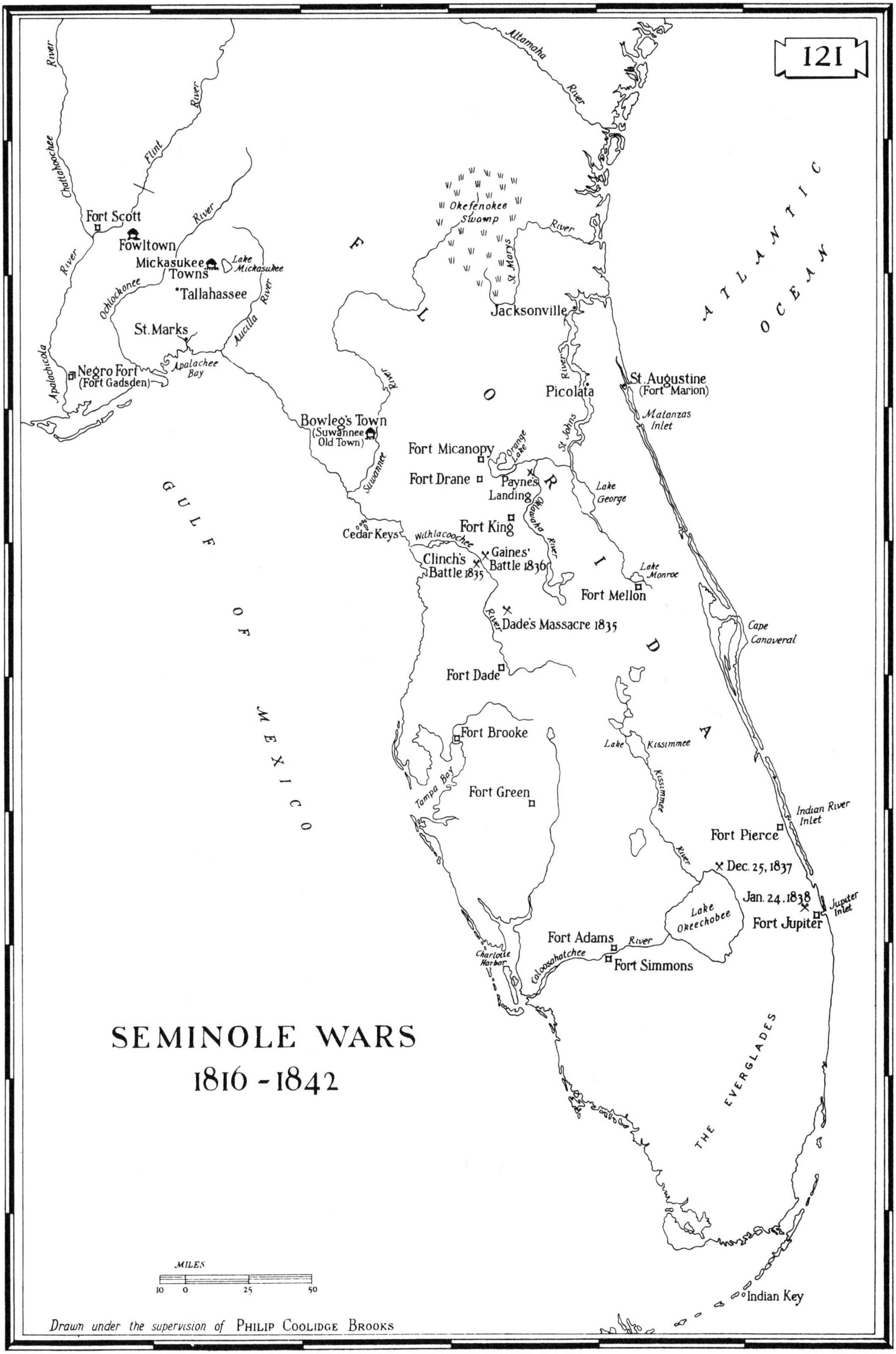
121
SEMINOLE WARS
1816 - 1842
Altamaha River
Chattahoochee River
Flint River
River
Fort Scott
Fowltown
Mickasukee Towns
Lake Mickasukee
Tallahassee
Ochlockonee River
St. Marks
Aucilla River
Apalachee Bay
Apalachicola River
Negro Fort (Fort Gadsden)
Okefenokee Swamp
St. Marys River
Jacksonville
FLORIDA
ATLANTIC OCEAN
GULF OF MEXICO
Suwannee River
Bowleg's Town (Suwannee Old Town)
St. Johns River
Picolata
St. Augustine (Fort Marion)
Matanzas Inlet
Fort Micanopy
Orange Lake
Fort Drane
Paynes Landing
Ocklawaha River
Lake George
Fort King
Cedar Keys
Withlacoochee River
Clinch's Battle 1835
Gaines' Battle 1836
Lake Monroe
Fort Mellon
Dade's Massacre 1835
Cape Canaveral
Fort Dade
Fort Brooke
Tampa Bay
Fort Green
Lake Kissimmee
Kissimmee River
Indian River Inlet
Fort Pierce
Dec. 25, 1837
Jan. 24, 1838
Lake Okeechobee
Jupiter Inlet
Fort Jupiter
Fort Adams
Caloosahatchee River
Fort Simmons
Charlotte Harbor
THE EVERGLADES
Indian Key
MILES
10 0 25 50
Drawn under the supervision of PHILIP COOLIDGE BROOKS

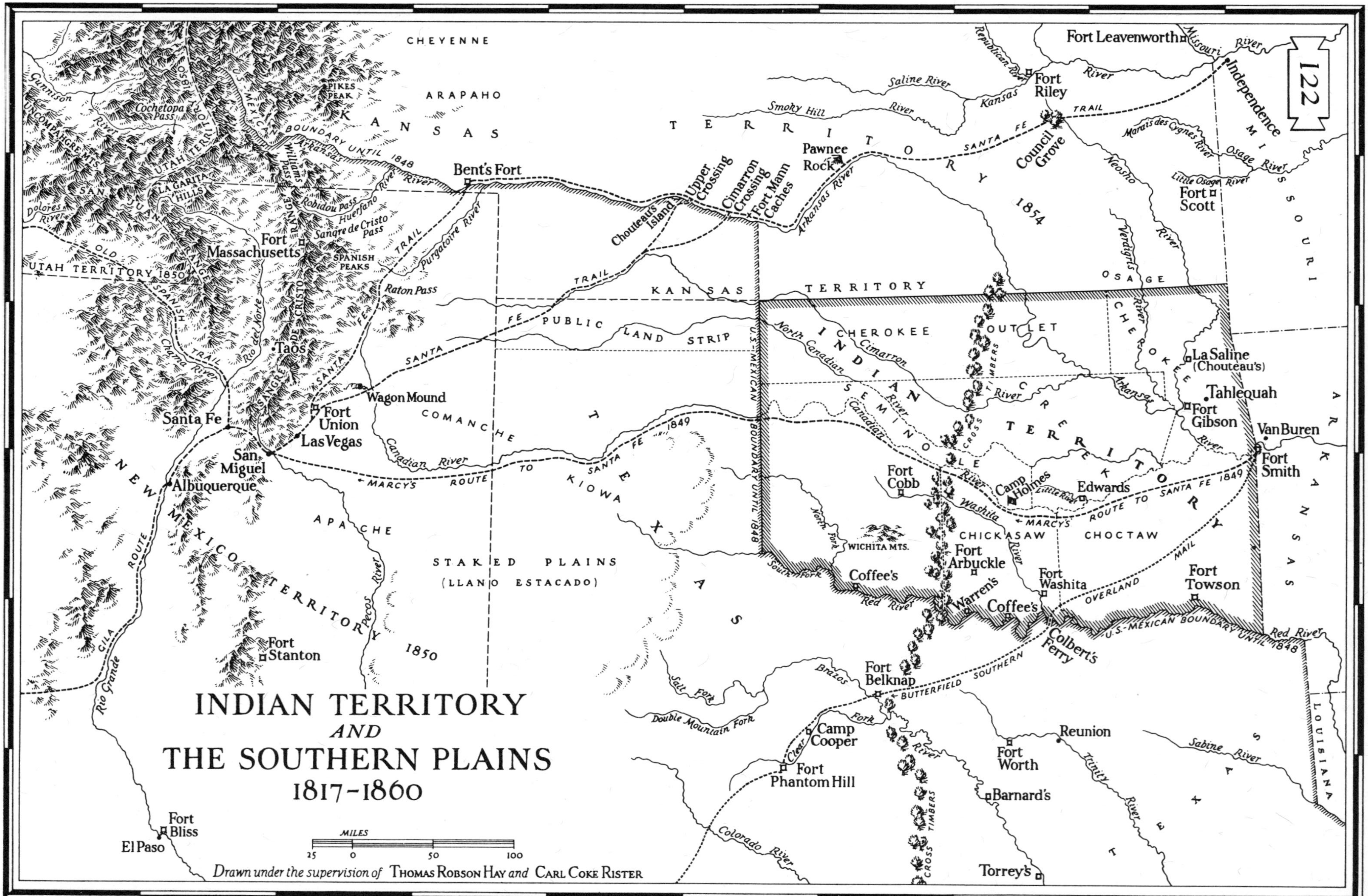

INDIAN TERRITORY *AND* THE SOUTHERN PLAINS 1817-1860

Drawn under the supervision of Thomas Robson Hay *and* Carl Coke Rister

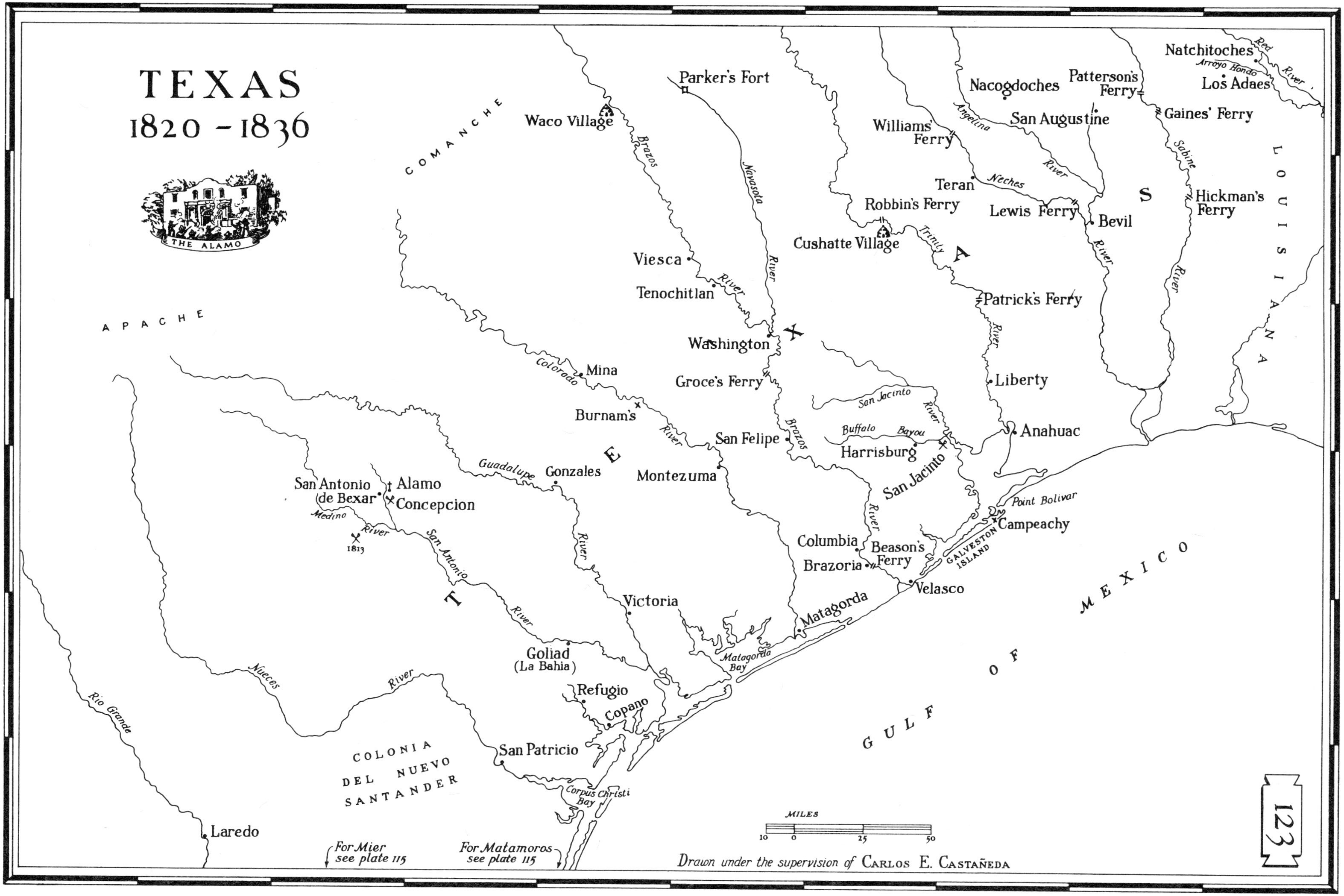
TEXAS
1820 - 1836
THE ALAMO
COMANCHE
APACHE
LOUISIANA
TEXAS
GULF OF MEXICO
COLONIA DEL NUEVO SANTANDER
Natchitoches
Red River
Arroyo Hondo
Los Adaes
Nacogdoches
Patterson's Ferry
San Augustine
Gaines' Ferry
Sabine River
Hickman's Ferry
Williams' Ferry
Angelina River
Teran
Neches
Robbin's Ferry
Lewis Ferry
Bevil
River
Cushatte Village
Trinity River
Patrick's Ferry
Liberty
Anahuac
Parker's Fort
Waco Village
Brazos
Navasota River
Viesca
Tenochitlan
River
Washington
Groce's Ferry
San Felipe
Brazos
San Jacinto River
Buffalo Bayou
Harrisburg
San Jacinto
Mina
Colorado River
Burnam's
Montezuma
Guadalupe River
Gonzales
Victoria
Columbia
Beason's Ferry
Brazoria
Velasco
Point Bolivar
Campeachy
GALVESTON ISLAND
Matagorda
Matagorda Bay
San Antonio de Bexar
Alamo
Concepcion
Medina River
1813
San Antonio River
Goliad (La Bahia)
Refugio
Copano
San Patricio
Corpus Christi Bay
Nueces River
Rio Grande
Laredo
For Mier see plate 115
For Matamoros see plate 115
MILES
10 0 25 50
Drawn under the supervision of Carlos E. Castañeda

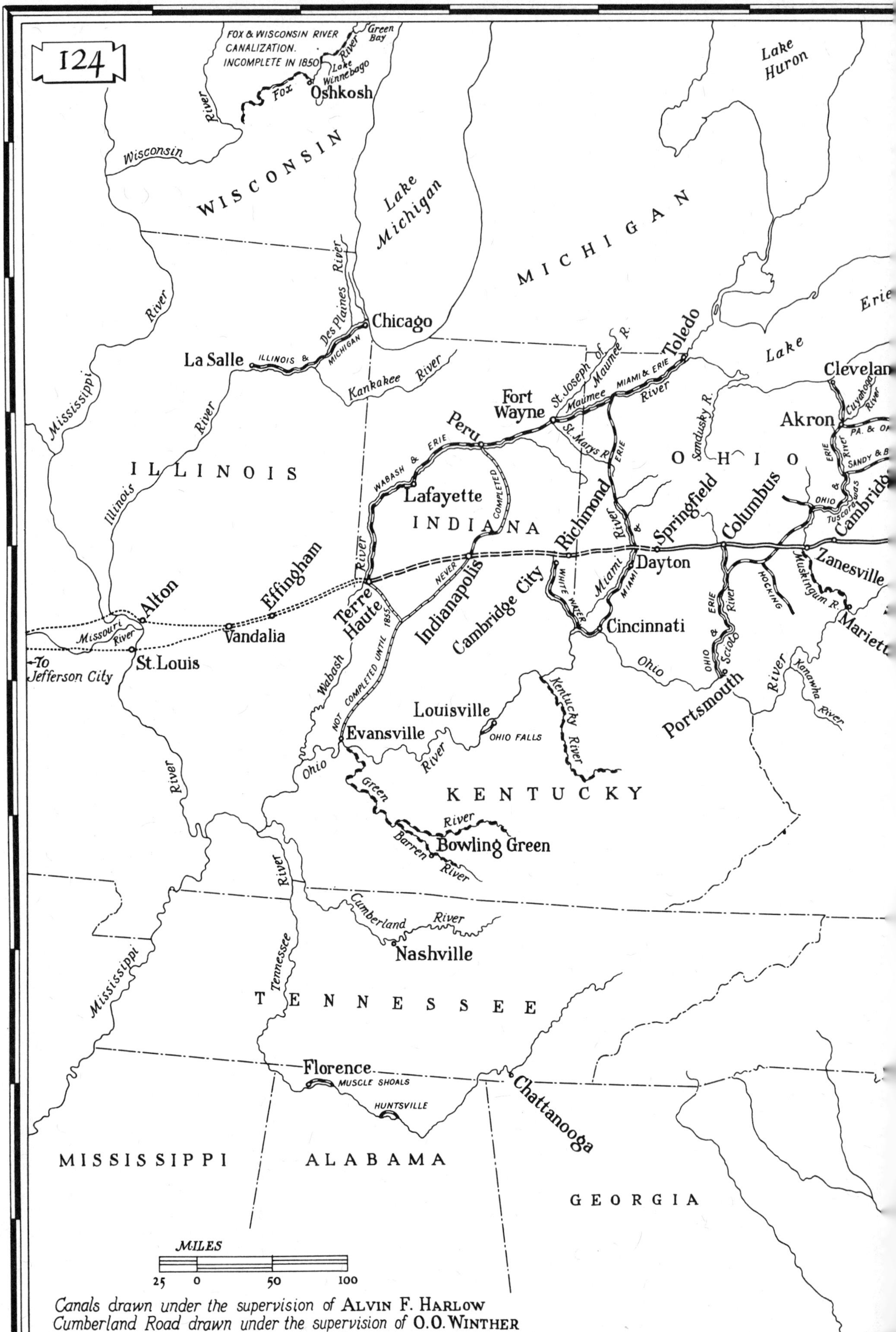

Canals drawn under the supervision of Alvin F. Harlow
Cumberland Road drawn under the supervision of O. O. Winther

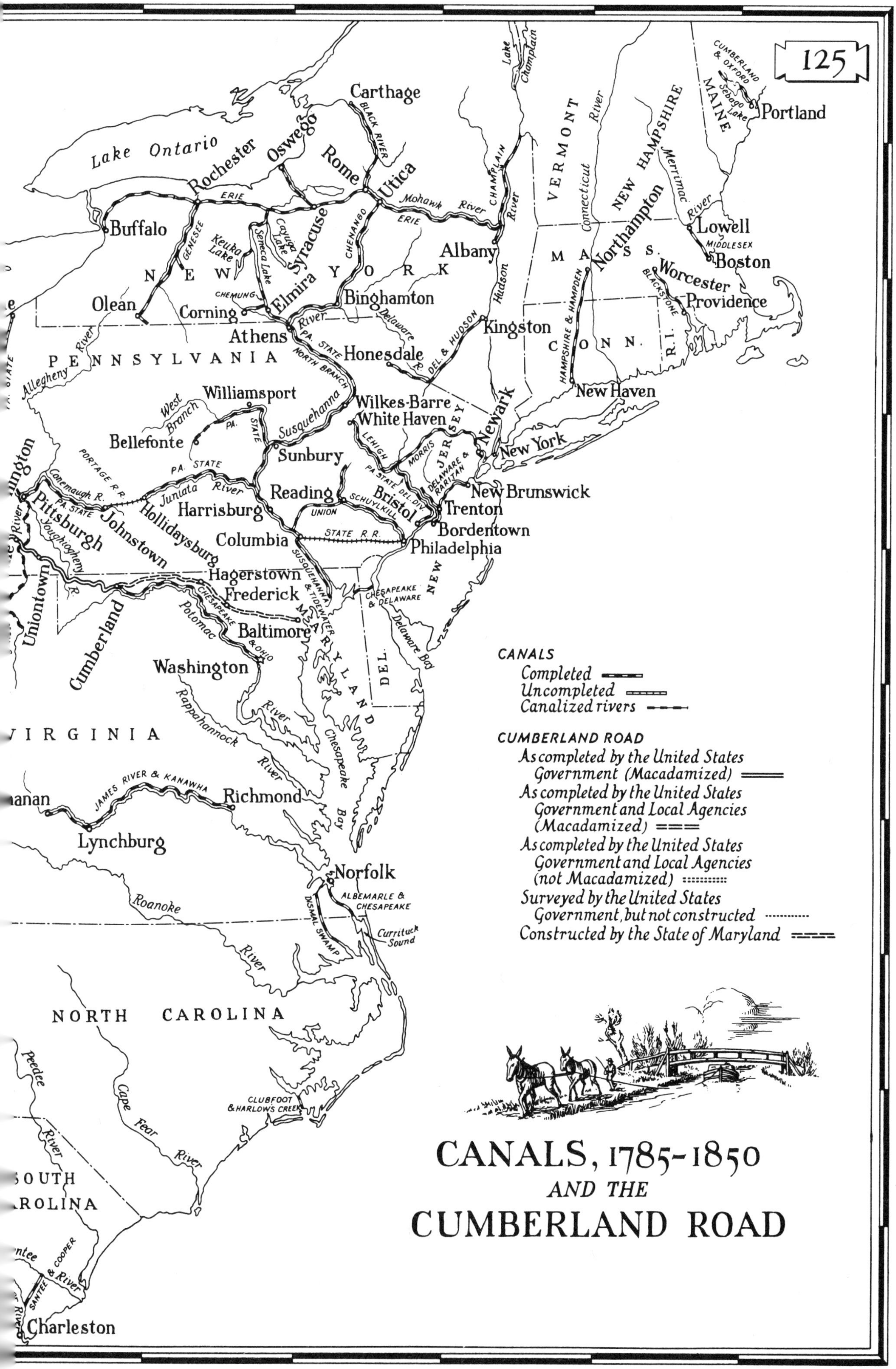
CANALS, 1785-1850
AND THE
CUMBERLAND ROAD
CANALS
Completed
Uncompleted
Canalized rivers
CUMBERLAND ROAD
As completed by the United States Government (Macadamized)
As completed by the United States Government and Local Agencies (Macadamized)
As completed by the United States Government and Local Agencies (not Macadamized)
Surveyed by the United States Government, but not constructed
Constructed by the State of Maryland
Lake Ontario
Lake Champlain
Carthage
BLACK RIVER
Rochester
Oswego
Rome
Utica
Buffalo
ERIE
Mohawk River
CHAMPLAIN
River
VERMONT
Connecticut River
NEW HAMPSHIRE
MAINE
CUMBERLAND & OXFORD
Sebago Lake
Portland
Merrimac River
Lowell
MIDDLESEX
Boston
MASS.
Northampton
Worcester
BLACKSTONE
Providence
R.I.
CONN.
HAMPSHIRE & HAMPDEN
New Haven
GENESEE
Keuka Lake
Seneca Lake
Cayuga Lake
Syracuse
CHENANGO
NEW YORK
Albany
Hudson
Olean
CHEMUNG
Corning
Elmira
Binghamton
Athens
River
Delaware
DEL. & HUDSON
Kingston
PA. STATE
NORTH BRANCH
Honesdale
PENNSYLVANIA
Allegheny River
Williamsport
West Branch
PA. STATE
Susquehanna
Wilkes-Barre
White Haven
LEHIGH
MORRIS
JERSEY
Newark
New York
Bellefonte
Sunbury
PORTAGE R.R.
PA. STATE
Juniata River
Conemaugh R.
Reading
PA. STATE DEL. DIV.
DELAWARE & RARITAN
New Brunswick
Trenton
Bristol
SCHUYLKILL
UNION
Harrisburg
Bordentown
Pittsburgh
Johnstown
Hollidaysburg
Columbia
STATE R.R.
Philadelphia
Youghiogheny R.
Hagerstown
Frederick
SUSQUEHANNA & TIDEWATER
CHESAPEAKE & DELAWARE
NEW
Uniontown
Cumberland
CHESAPEAKE
Potomac
& OHIO
Baltimore
MARYLAND
DEL.
Delaware Bay
Washington
Rappahannock River
River
Chesapeake Bay
VIRGINIA
JAMES RIVER & KANAWHA
Richmond
Lynchburg
Norfolk
ALBEMARLE & CHESAPEAKE
DISMAL SWAMP
Currituck Sound
Roanoke River
NORTH CAROLINA
Peedee River
Cape Fear River
CLUBFOOT & HARLOWS CREEK
SOUTH
SANTEE & COOPER
River
SANTEE
Charleston

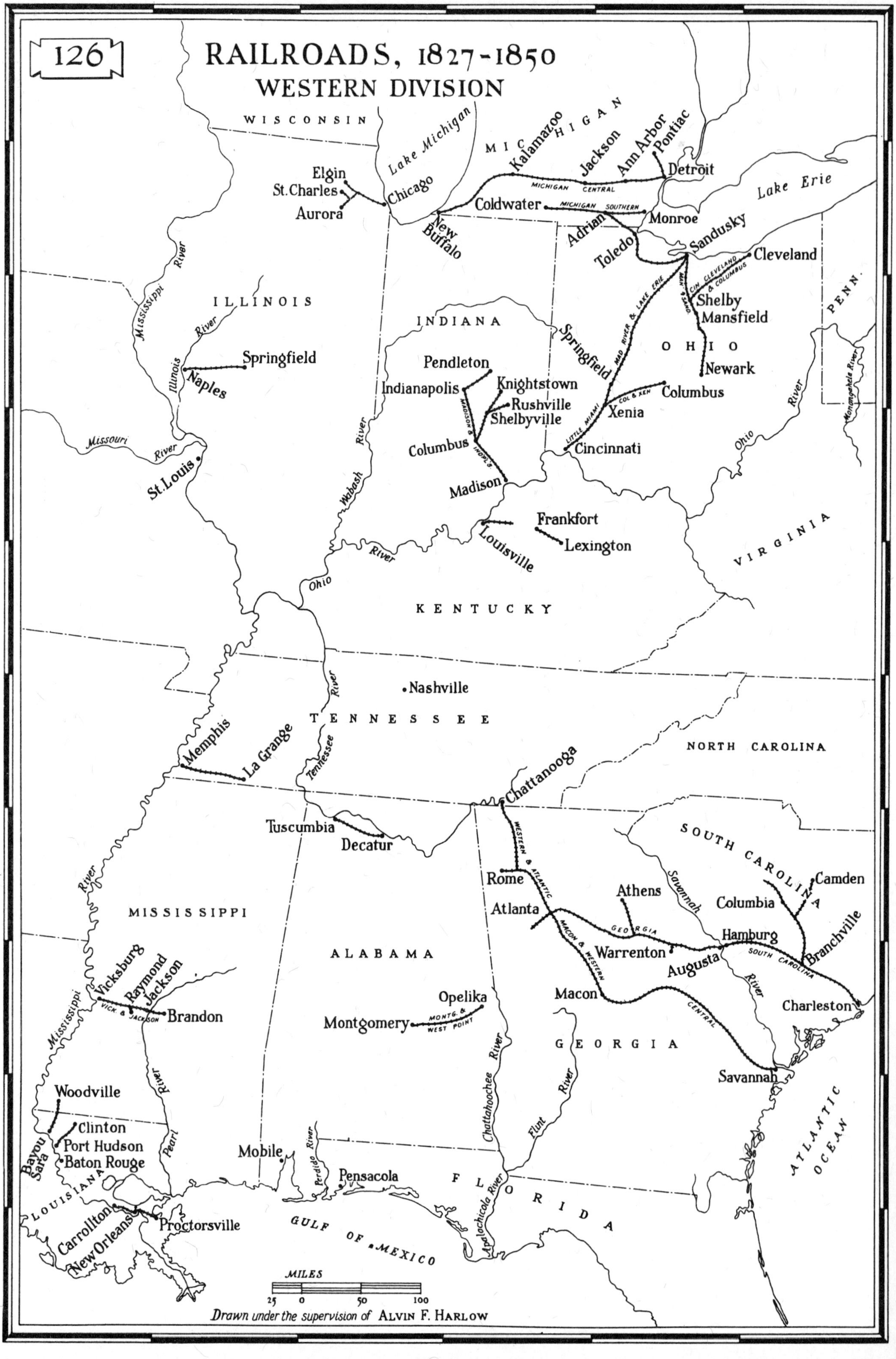
126
RAILROADS, 1827-1850
WESTERN DIVISION
WISCONSIN
MICHIGAN
Lake Michigan
Kalamazoo
Jackson
Ann Arbor
Pontiac
Detroit
Elgin
St. Charles
Aurora
Chicago
MICHIGAN CENTRAL
Coldwater
MICHIGAN SOUTHERN
Monroe
Lake Erie
New Buffalo
Adrian
Toledo
Sandusky
Cleveland
CIN. CLEVELAND & COLUMBUS
MAN. & SAND.
Shelby
Mansfield
PENN.
ILLINOIS
Mississippi River
Illinois River
Springfield
Naples
INDIANA
Springfield
MAD RIVER & LAKE ERIE
OHIO
Newark
Pendleton
Indianapolis
Knightstown
Rushville
Shelbyville
MADISON & INDIANAPOLIS
Columbus
COL & XEN
Columbus
Xenia
LITTLE MIAMI
Cincinnati
Missouri River
St. Louis
Wabash River
Madison
Ohio River
Monongahela River
Frankfort
Lexington
Louisville
VIRGINIA
Ohio River
KENTUCKY
Nashville
Tennessee River
TENNESSEE
NORTH CAROLINA
Memphis
La Grange
Chattanooga
Tuscumbia
Decatur
WESTERN & ATLANTIC
SOUTH CAROLINA
Rome
Athens
Camden
Columbia
Savannah River
Atlanta
GEORGIA
Hamburg
Branchville
MACON & WESTERN
Warrenton
Augusta
SOUTH CAROLINA
MISSISSIPPI
ALABAMA
Vicksburg
Raymond
Jackson
VICK. & JACKSON
Brandon
Opelika
Montgomery
MONTG. & WEST POINT
Macon
CENTRAL
Charleston
GEORGIA
Savannah
Mississippi River
Pearl River
Chattahoochee River
Flint River
Woodville
Clinton
Port Hudson
Bayou Sara
Baton Rouge
Mobile
Perdido River
Pensacola
FLORIDA
Apalachicola River
ATLANTIC OCEAN
LOUISIANA
Carrollton
New Orleans
Proctorsville
GULF OF MEXICO
MILES
25 0 50 100
Drawn under the supervision of ALVIN F. HARLOW

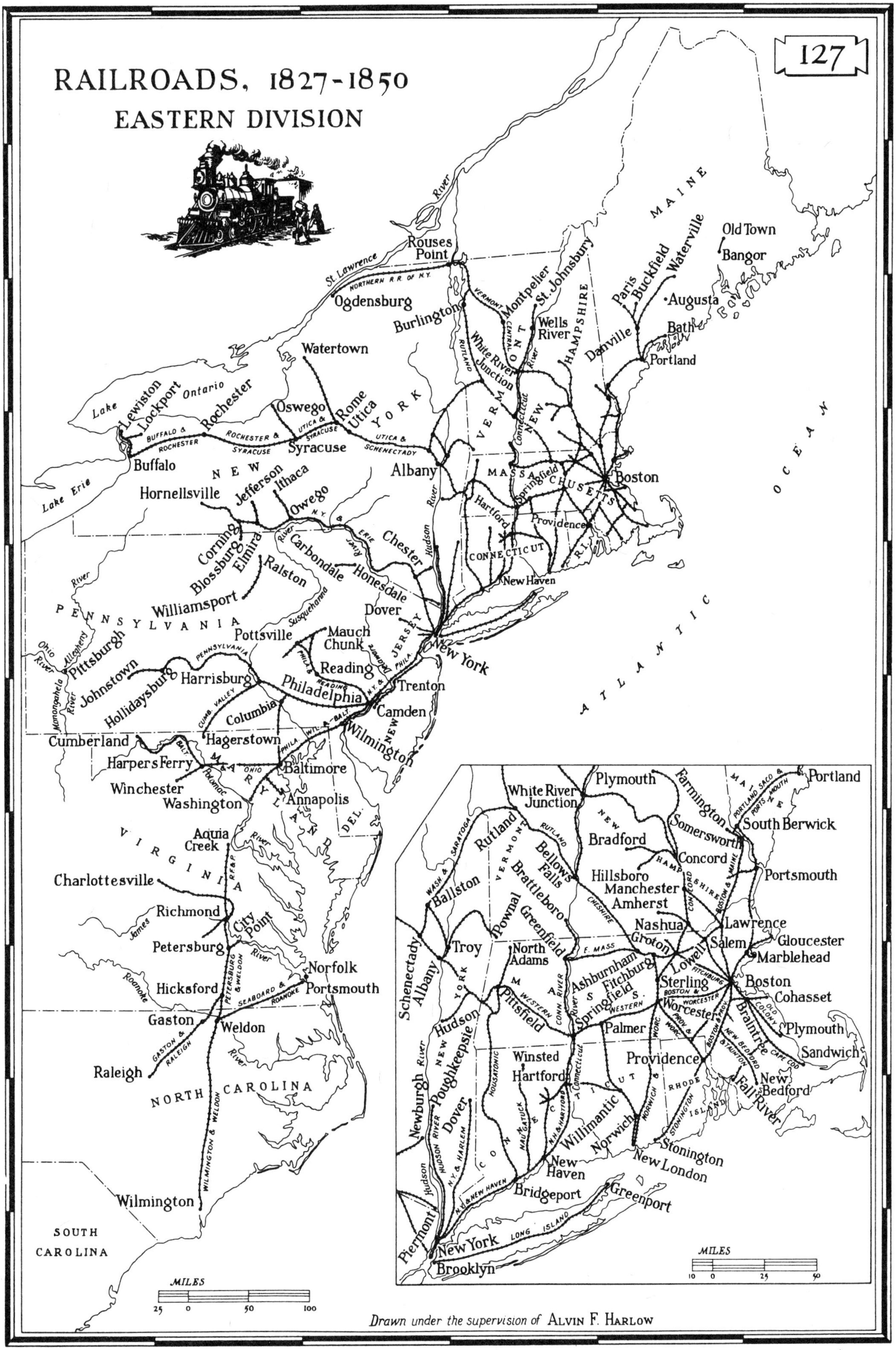
RAILROADS, 1827-1850
EASTERN DIVISION
St. Lawrence
River
Rouses Point
NORTHERN R.R. OF N.Y.
Ogdensburg
Burlington
VERMONT CENTRAL
Montpelier
St. Johnsbury
Wells River
White River Junction
RUTLAND
VERMONT
Connecticut River
NEW HAMPSHIRE
MAINE
Old Town
Bangor
Paris
Buckfield
Waterville
Augusta
Bath
Danville
Portland
Watertown
Lake Ontario
Lewiston
Lockport
Rochester
Oswego
Rome
Utica
NEW YORK
BUFFALO & ROCHESTER
ROCHESTER & SYRACUSE
UTICA & SYRACUSE
UTICA & SCHENECTADY
Syracuse
Buffalo
Lake Erie
Albany
MASSACHUSETTS
Springfield
Boston
Hornellsville
Jefferson
Ithaca
Owego
N.Y. & ERIE
Hartford
Providence
R.I.
CONNECTICUT
New Haven
Hudson River
Chester
Corning
Blossburg
Elmira
Ralston
Carbondale
Honesdale
Lack River
Williamsport
PENNSYLVANIA
Susquehanna
Dover
NEW JERSEY
Pottsville
Mauch Chunk
New York
Ohio River
Allegheny
Pittsburgh
Johnstown
PENNSYLVANIA
Hollidaysburg
Harrisburg
PHILA & READING
Reading
Delaware
PHILA.
N.Y. &
Philadelphia
Trenton
Camden
Monongahela River
CUMB. VALLEY
Columbia
Cumberland
Hagerstown
PHILA. WIL. & BALT.
Wilmington
BALT. & OHIO
Harpers Ferry
MARYLAND
Baltimore
Winchester
Potomac
Washington
Annapolis
DEL.
Aquia Creek
VIRGINIA
RF&P
Charlottesville
Richmond
James
City Point
Petersburg
PETERSBURG & WELDON
River
Norfolk
Portsmouth
Roanoke
Hicksford
SEABOARD & ROANOKE
Gaston
Weldon
GASTON & RALEIGH
Raleigh
NORTH CAROLINA
WILMINGTON & WELDON
Wilmington
SOUTH CAROLINA
ATLANTIC OCEAN
MILES
25 0 50 100
Plymouth
White River Junction
Farmington
Portland
PORTLAND SACO & PORTSMOUTH
MAINE
South Berwick
Rutland
RUTLAND
Bellows Falls
New Bradford
Somersworth
WASH. & SARATOGA
VERMONT
Brattleboro
HAMPSHIRE
Concord
Portsmouth
Ballston
Hillsboro
Manchester
Amherst
CONCORD
BOSTON & MAINE
Pownal
Greenfield
CHESHIRE
Nashua
Lawrence
Schenectady
Troy
North Adams
E. MASS
Groton
Lowell
Salem
Gloucester
Marblehead
Albany
YORK
Ashburnham
Fitchburg
Sterling
FITCHBURG
Boston
Cohasset
MASS.
BOSTON & WORCESTER
WESTERN
Pittsfield
Springfield
Worcester
Braintree
OLD COLONY
Plymouth
Hudson
CONN. RIVER
Palmer
WORC.
PROV. & WORC.
BOSTON & PROV.
NEW BEDFORD & TAUNTON
CAPE COD
Sandwich
NEW
HOUSATONIC
Winsted
Providence
Hartford
Connecticut
RHODE ISLAND
New Bedford
Fall River
Hudson River
Poughkeepsie
NAUGATUCK
NORWICH & WORC.
STONINGTON
Newburgh
HUDSON RIVER
Dover
N.Y. & HARLEM
CONNECTICUT
N.H. & HARTFORD
Willimantic
Norwich
Stonington
New London
New Haven
N.Y. & NEW HAVEN
Bridgeport
Greenport
Hudson
Piermont
New York
LONG ISLAND
Brooklyn
MILES
10 0 25 50
Drawn under the supervision of ALVIN F. HARLOW

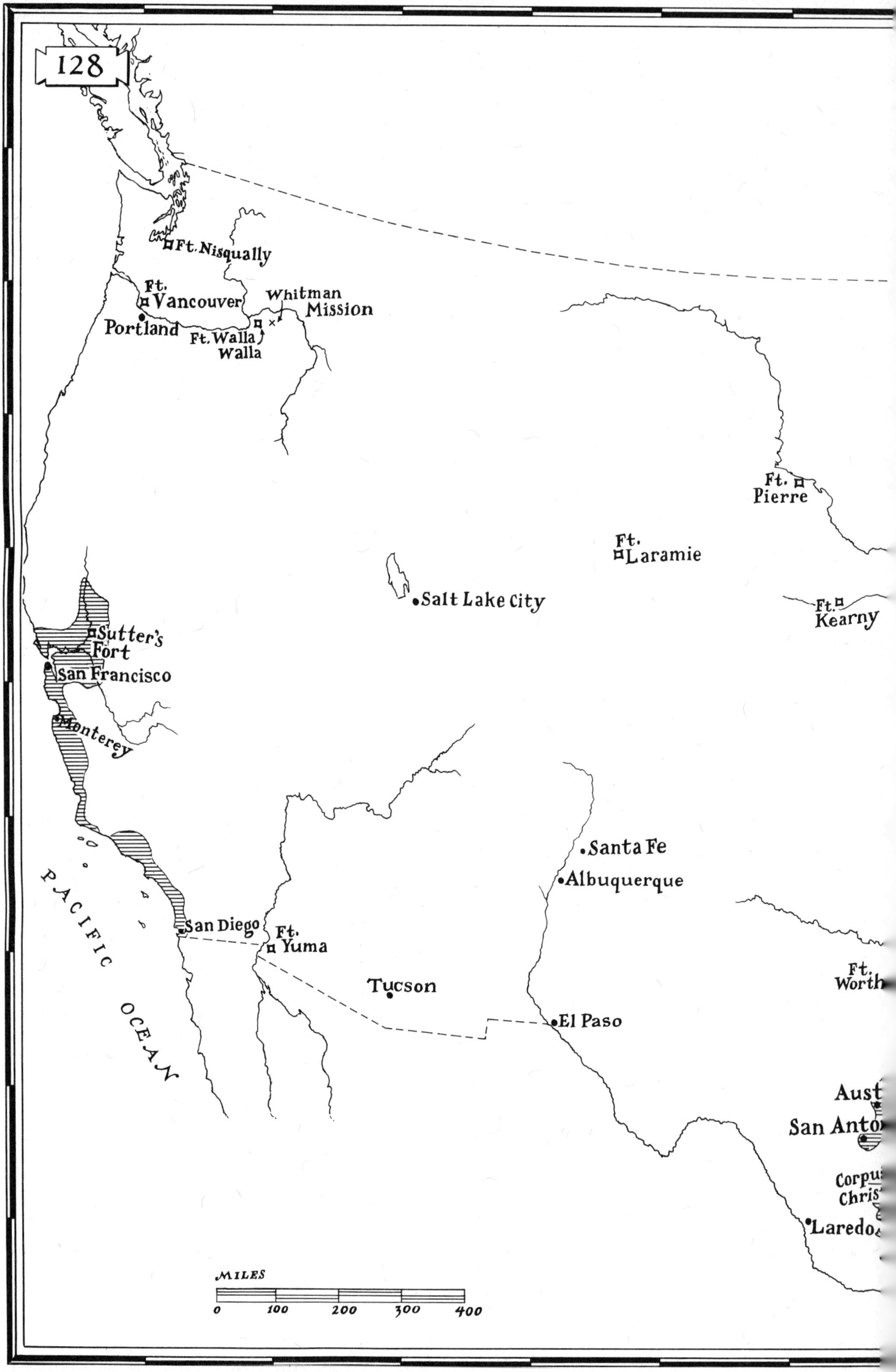
Ft. Nisqually
Ft. Vancouver
Whitman Mission
Portland
Ft. Walla Walla
Ft. Pierre
Ft. Laramie
Salt Lake City
Ft. Kearny
Sutter's Fort
San Francisco
Monterey
Santa Fe
Albuquerque
PACIFIC OCEAN
San Diego
Ft. Yuma
Tucson
El Paso
Ft. Worth
Aust
San Anto
Corpu Chris
Laredo
MILES
0
100
200
300
400

SETTLED AREAS 1850

130
WISCONSIN
MINN.
MILWAUKEE
Racine
(threshers)
IOWA
CHICAGO
(meat packing)
MICHIGAN
DETROIT
Buffalo
(flour)
CLEVELAND
Youngstown
ILLINOIS
OHIO
INDIANA
Steubenville
Wheeling
PITTSBURG
CINCINNATI
(meat packing)
ST. LOUIS
Ironton
Louisville
(cordage)
LEXINGTON
MO.
KENTUCKY
VIRGINIA
ARK.
TENNESSEE
NORTH CARO
MISS.
ALABAMA
GEORGIA
SOUTH CAROLINA
Graniteville

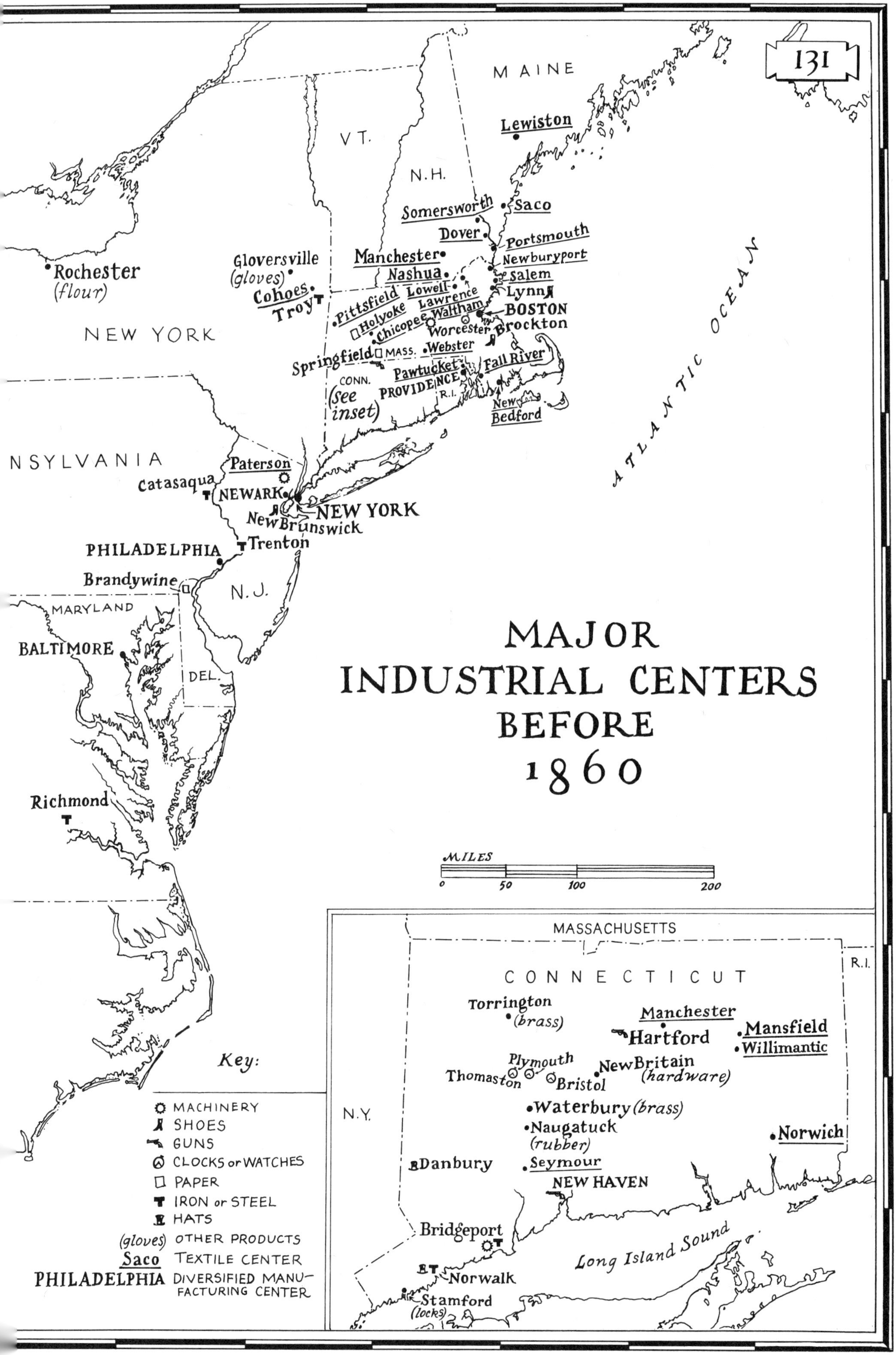
MAJOR INDUSTRIAL CENTERS BEFORE 1860
MAINE
Lewiston
VT.
N.H.
Somersworth
Saco
Dover
Portsmouth
Manchester
Newburyport
Nashua
Salem
Gloversville (gloves)
Cohoes
Troy
Rochester (flour)
Pittsfield
Lowell
Lawrence
Lynn
Holyoke
Waltham
BOSTON
Chicopee
Worcester
Brockton
NEW YORK
Springfield
MASS.
Webster
Pawtucket
Fall River
CONN. (see inset)
PROVIDENCE
R.I.
New Bedford
ATLANTIC OCEAN
NSYLVANIA
Paterson
Catasaqua
NEWARK
NEW YORK
New Brunswick
PHILADELPHIA
Trenton
Brandywine
N.J.
MARYLAND
BALTIMORE
DEL.
Richmond
MILES
0
50
100
200
MASSACHUSETTS
CONNECTICUT
R.I.
Torrington (brass)
Manchester
Hartford
Mansfield
Willimantic
Plymouth
Thomaston
Bristol
New Britain (hardware)
Waterbury (brass)
Naugatuck (rubber)
N.Y.
Norwich
Danbury
Seymour
NEW HAVEN
Bridgeport
Long Island Sound
Norwalk
Stamford (locks)
Key:
MACHINERY
SHOES
GUNS
CLOCKS or WATCHES
PAPER
IRON or STEEL
HATS
(gloves) OTHER PRODUCTS
Saco TEXTILE CENTER
PHILADELPHIA DIVERSIFIED MANUFACTURING CENTER

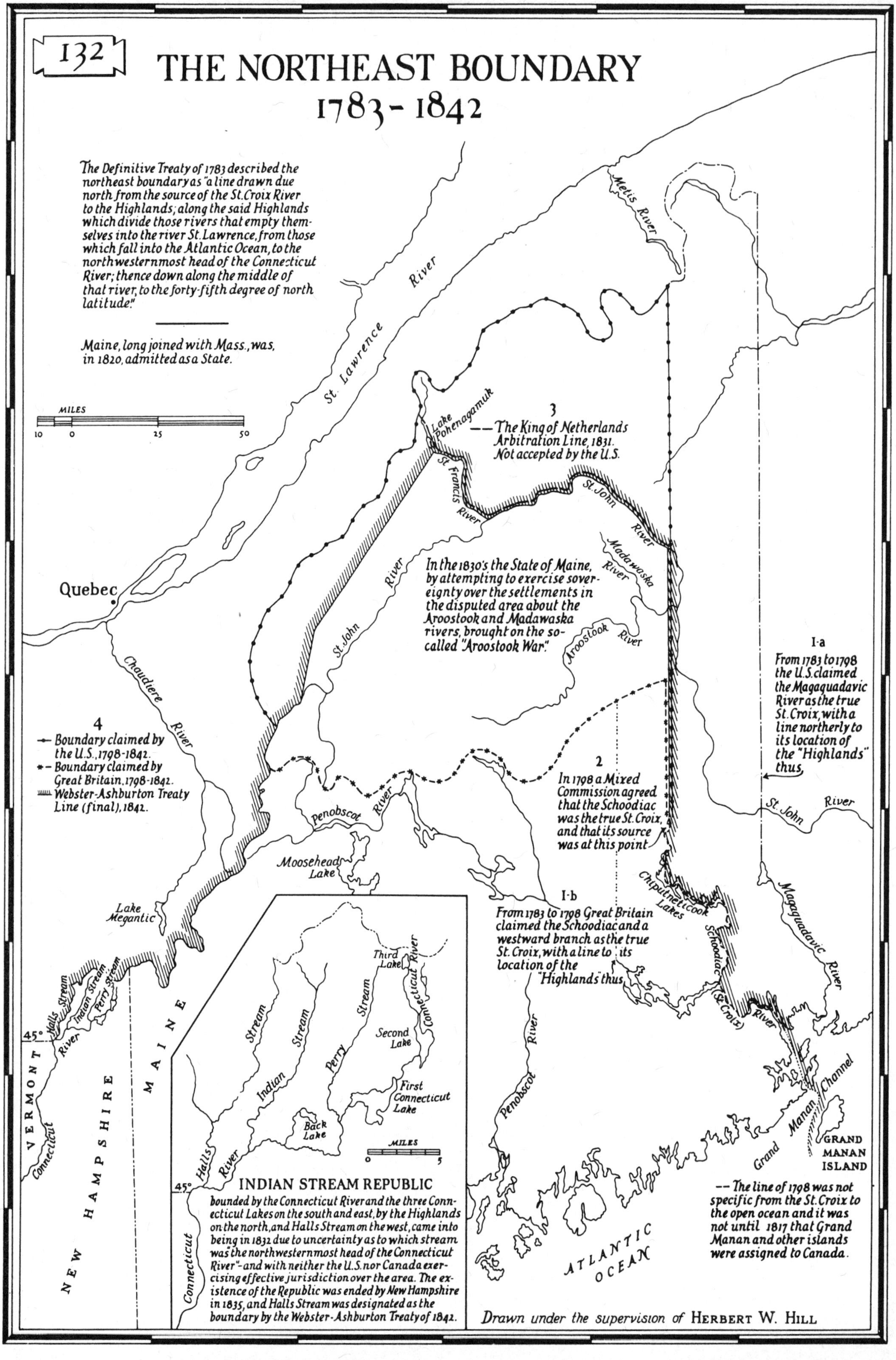
132
THE NORTHEAST BOUNDARY
1783-1842
The Definitive Treaty of 1783 described the northeast boundary as "a line drawn due north from the source of the St. Croix River to the Highlands; along the said Highlands which divide those rivers that empty themselves into the river St. Lawrence, from those which fall into the Atlantic Ocean, to the northwesternmost head of the Connecticut River; thence down along the middle of that river, to the forty-fifth degree of north latitude."
Maine, long joined with Mass., was, in 1820, admitted as a State.
MILES
10 0 25 50
St. Lawrence River
Metis River
Quebec
Lake Pohenagamuk
3
-- The King of Netherlands Arbitration Line, 1831. Not accepted by the U.S.
St. Francis River
St. John River
Madawaska River
In the 1830's the State of Maine, by attempting to exercise sovereignty over the settlements in the disputed area about the Aroostook and Madawaska rivers, brought on the so-called "Aroostook War."
Aroostook River
St. John River
Chaudiere River
4
Boundary claimed by the U.S., 1798-1842.
Boundary claimed by Great Britain, 1798-1842.
Webster-Ashburton Treaty Line (final), 1842.
I-a
From 1783 to 1798 the U.S. claimed the Magaquadavic River as the true St. Croix, with a line northerly to its location of the "Highlands" thus
2
In 1798 a Mixed Commission agreed that the Schoodiac was the true St. Croix, and that its source was at this point
St. John River
Penobscot River
Moosehead Lake
Lake Megantic
I-b
From 1783 to 1798 Great Britain claimed the Schoodiac and a westward branch as the true St. Croix, with a line to its location of the "Highlands" thus
Chiputneticook Lakes
Schoodiac (St. Croix) River
Magaquadavic River
Halls Stream
Indian Stream
Perry Stream
45°
River
VERMONT
Connecticut
NEW HAMPSHIRE
MAINE
Third Lake
Connecticut River
Stream
Stream
Stream
Second Lake
Indian
Perry
First Connecticut Lake
Back Lake
MILES
0 5
Halls River
45°
Connecticut
INDIAN STREAM REPUBLIC
bounded by the Connecticut River and the three Connecticut Lakes on the south and east, by the Highlands on the north, and Halls Stream on the west, came into being in 1832 due to uncertainty as to which stream was "the northwesternmost head of the Connecticut River"- and with neither the U.S. nor Canada exercising effective jurisdiction over the area. The existence of the Republic was ended by New Hampshire in 1835, and Halls Stream was designated as the boundary by the Webster-Ashburton Treaty of 1842.
Penobscot River
Grand Manan Channel
GRAND MANAN ISLAND
-- The line of 1798 was not specific from the St. Croix to the open ocean and it was not until 1817 that Grand Manan and other islands were assigned to Canada.
ATLANTIC OCEAN
Drawn under the supervision of HERBERT W. HILL

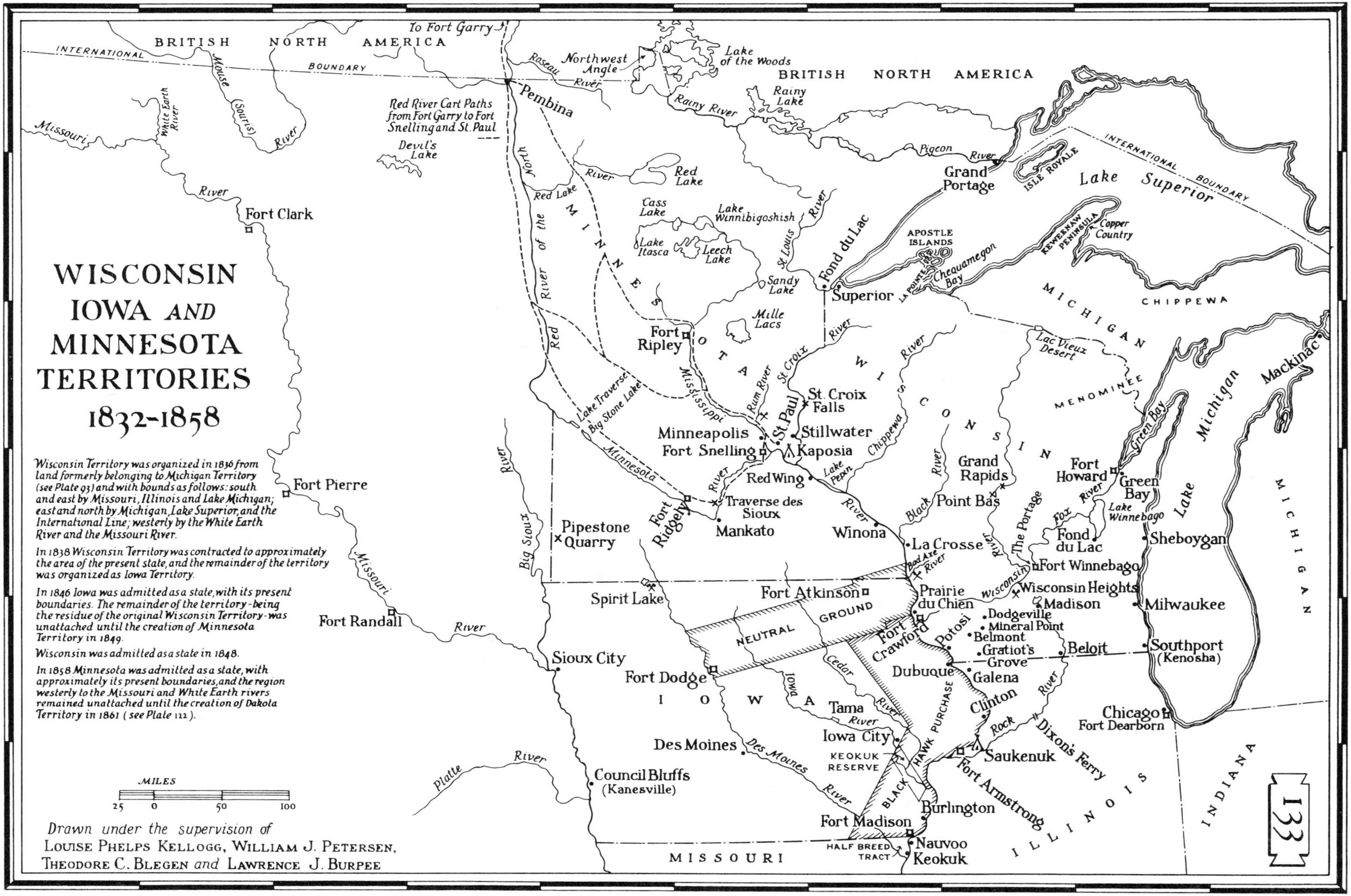

WISCONSIN IOWA AND MINNESOTA TERRITORIES 1832–1858

Wisconsin Territory was organized in 1836 from land formerly belonging to Michigan Territory (see Plate 93) and with bounds as follows: south and east by Missouri, Illinois and Lake Michigan; east and north by Michigan, Lake Superior, and the International Line; westerly by the White Earth River and the Missouri River.

In 1838 Wisconsin Territory was contracted to approximately the area of the present state, and the remainder of the territory was organized as Iowa Territory.

In 1846 Iowa was admitted as a state, with its present boundaries. The remainder of the territory—being the residue of the original Wisconsin Territory—was unattached until the creation of Minnesota Territory in 1849.

Wisconsin was admitted as a state in 1848.

In 1858 Minnesota was admitted as a state, with approximately its present boundaries, and the region westerly to the Missouri and White Earth rivers remained unattached until the creation of Dakota Territory in 1861 (see Plate 112).

Drawn under the supervision of
LOUISE PHELPS KELLOGG, WILLIAM J. PETERSEN, THEODORE C. BLEGEN *and* LAWRENCE J. BURPEE

134
ALASKA
54°40' SOUTHERN RUSSIAN BOUNDARY
QUEEN CHARLOTTE ISLANDS
NEW CALEDONIA
Stuart
54°40'
Queen Charlotte Sound
Fraser River
VANCOUVER ISLAND
Nootka Sound
BRITISH NORT
PACIFIC OCEAN
49°
Strait of Juan de Fuca
Victoria
Puget Sound
Okanagan River
Columbia River
Fort Colville
Clarks Fork
Spokane River
Kootenai River
The definite boundary between th U.S. and Canada was carried thus by the Convention of 1818, the area to the west being under Joint Occupation until divide by the Treaty of 1846.
CONTINENTAL DIVIDE
BLACKFEET
Fort Lewis
Missou
FLATHEAD
Fort Nisqually
New Market
Coeur d'Alene
Cowlitz River
Astoria
Columbia
Fort Vancouver
CASCADES
Fort Walla Walla
Whitman Mission
Snake
Clearwater River
Lapwai Mission
St. Marys
The Dalles
Umatilla R.
BLUE MTS.
Grande Ronde R.
Salmon River
NEZ PERCE
1848
Champoeg
Lee Mission
Willamette River
OREGON TERRITORY
Fort Boise
PIERRES HOLE
JACKSO HOLE
SNAKE
Fort Hall
Snake River
Soda Springs
OREGON TRAIL
Klamath River
NORTHERN MEXICAN BOUNDARY UNTIL 1848
TO CALIFORNIA
OGDENS HOLE
Great Salt Lake
Bear
Fort Bridge
Marys (Humboldt) River
Salt Lake City
Fort Davy Crock
MORMON TRAIL
Sacramento River
Donner Tragedy
UTE
Fort Robidou (Uinta)
Green River
Sutter's Fort
MILES
50 0 100 200
Drawn under the supervision of DAN E. CLARK

THE UNORGANIZED TERRITORY AND OREGON COUNTRY 1836-1848

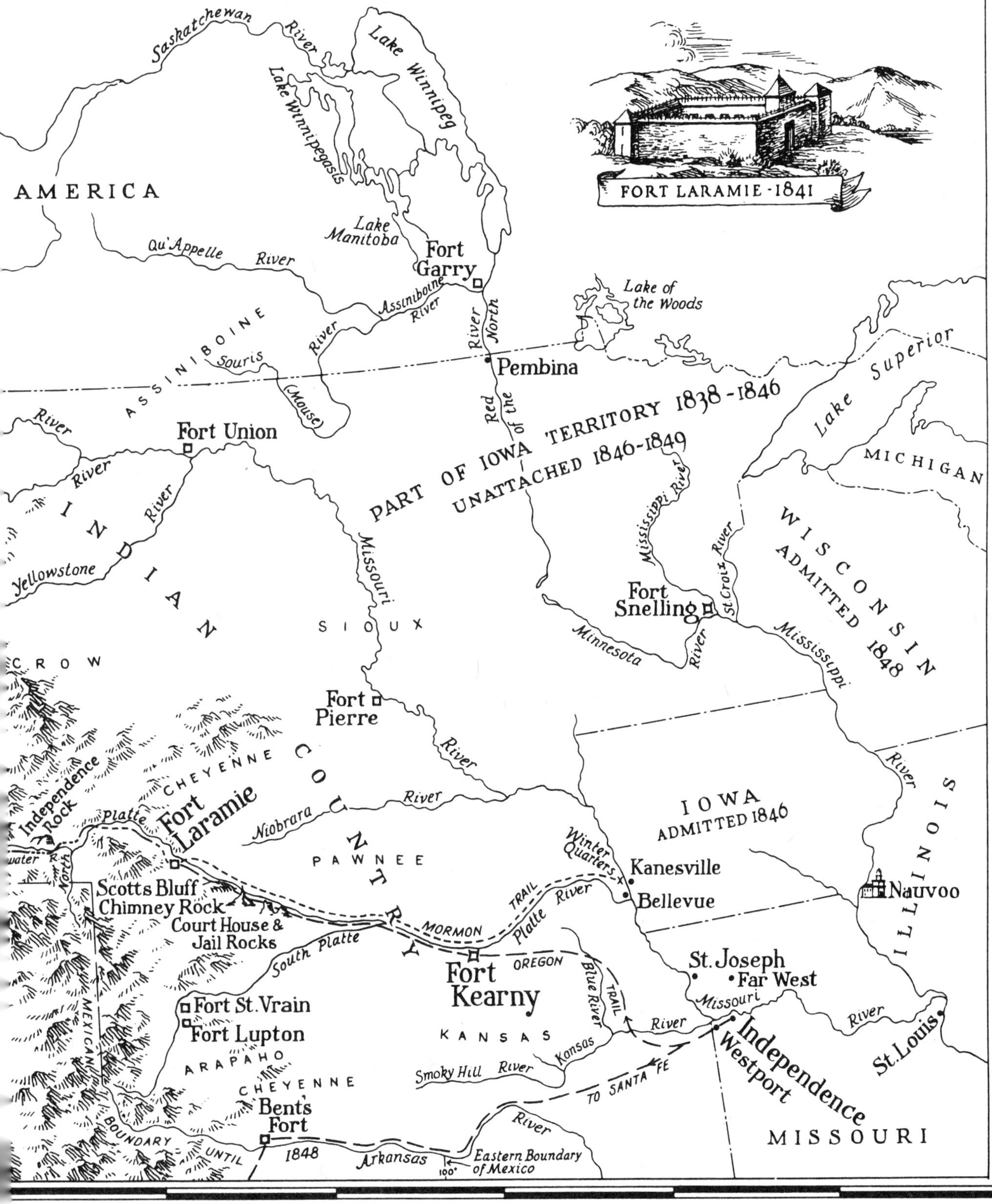

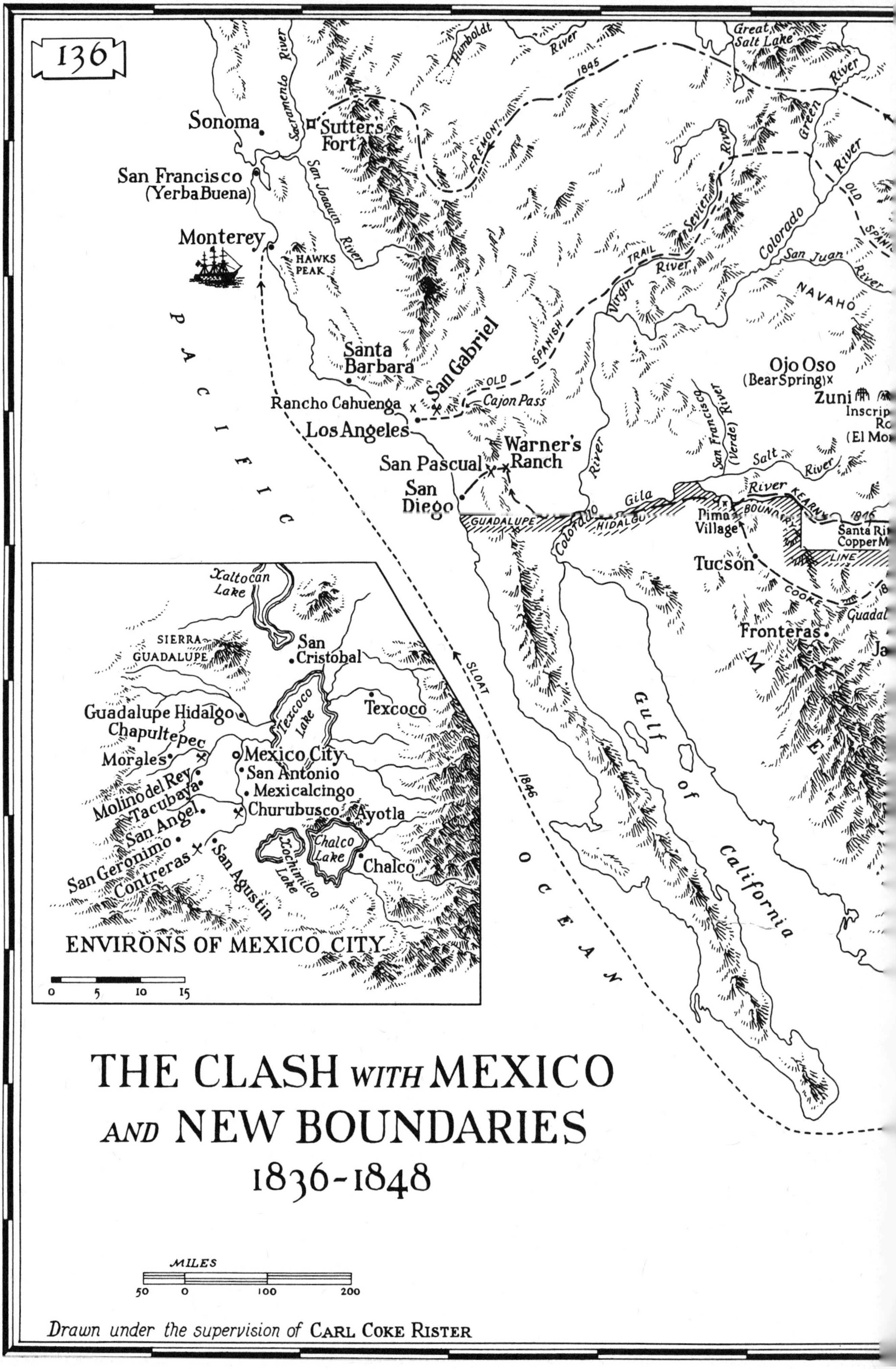
136
THE CLASH WITH MEXICO AND NEW BOUNDARIES
1836-1848
Sonoma
Sutter's Fort
San Francisco
(Yerba Buena)
Monterey
HAWKS PEAK
Sacramento River
San Joaquin River
Humboldt River
Great Salt Lake
1845
FREMONT
Green River
Sevier River
Virgin River
Colorado
San Juan River
NAVAHO
OLD SPANISH TRAIL
Santa Barbara
San Gabriel
Rancho Cahuenga
Cajon Pass
Los Angeles
San Pascual
Warner's Ranch
San Diego
Ojo Oso
(Bear Spring)
Zuni
Colorado River
San Francisco (Verde) River
Salt River
Gila River
KEARNY
GUADALUPE HIDALGO BOUNDARY LINE
Pima Village
Tucson
COOKE
Fronteras
PACIFIC OCEAN
SLOAT
1846
Gulf of California
ENVIRONS OF MEXICO CITY
Xaltocan Lake
SIERRA GUADALUPE
San Cristobal
Guadalupe Hidalgo
Texcoco
Texcoco Lake
Chapultepec
Morales
Mexico City
San Antonio
Molino del Rey
Tacubaya
Mexicalcingo
San Angel
Churubusco
Ayotla
San Geronimo
Contreras
San Agustin
Xochimilco Lake
Chalco Lake
Chalco
0 5 10 15
MILES
50 0 100 200
Drawn under the supervision of CARL COKE RISTER

137
Texas, subsequent to 1836, claimed the Rio Grande (Rio del Norte) and a line due north as its boundary. Mexico claimed the Nueces and a line easterly of the Staked Plains as shown below.
Fort Leavenworth
Missouri River
Kansas River
Westport
KEARNY 1846
Osage River
St. Louis
ILLINOIS
MISSOURI
Bent's Fort
(SANTA FE TRAIL)
Arkansas River
Pueblo
KEARNY 1846
1845
Abiquiu
Taos
Chama
Rio del Norte
Santa Fe
Las Vegas
Cimarron River
Canadian River
BY MEXICO AS CLAIMED
Fort Gibson
Arkansas River
Fort Smith
ARKANSAS
Mississippi River
TENN.
MISSISSIPPI
Albuquerque
Peralta
Socorro
Valverde
Jornada del Muerto
ORGAN MTS.
Brazito
LLANO ESTACADO OR STAKED PLAINS
Red River
TEXAS
ADMITTED 1845
Trinity
Sabine River
Natchitoches
Fort Jesup
LOUISIANA
New Orleans
Pecos River
Brazos River
Torrey's
Colorado River
Nacogdoches
Austin
San Jacinto
GALVESTON ISLAND
TEXAS BOUNDARY
Rio Grande
GUADALUPE
DONIPHAN 1847
Presidio del Norte
BOUNDARY
HIDALGO
Conchos
San Antonio
1846
Brazoria
Victoria
Goliad
Presidio de Rio Grande
Nueces River
Corpus Christi
SCOTT 1846
Chihuahua
Laredo
WOOL
LINE
TAYLOR 1846
Monclova
DONIPHAN
Fort Brown
Mier
Matamoros
1847
Saltillo
TAYLOR 1846-47
Monterrey
Parras
Buena Vista
QUITMAN
Monte Morelos
Salado
1846
Victoria
Cedral
SCOTT 1847
PATTERSON 1847
Mazatlan
Panuco River
San Luis Potosi
Tampico
SCOTT 1847
GULF OF MEXICO
Cerro Gordo
Perote
Mexico City
SCOTT
Jalapa
Vera Cruz
Puebla
Palo Alto
Point Isabel
Resaca de La Palma
Fort Brown
Rio Grande
Gulf of Mexico
Matamoros
PALO ALTO AND RESACA DE LA PALMA
0 5 10

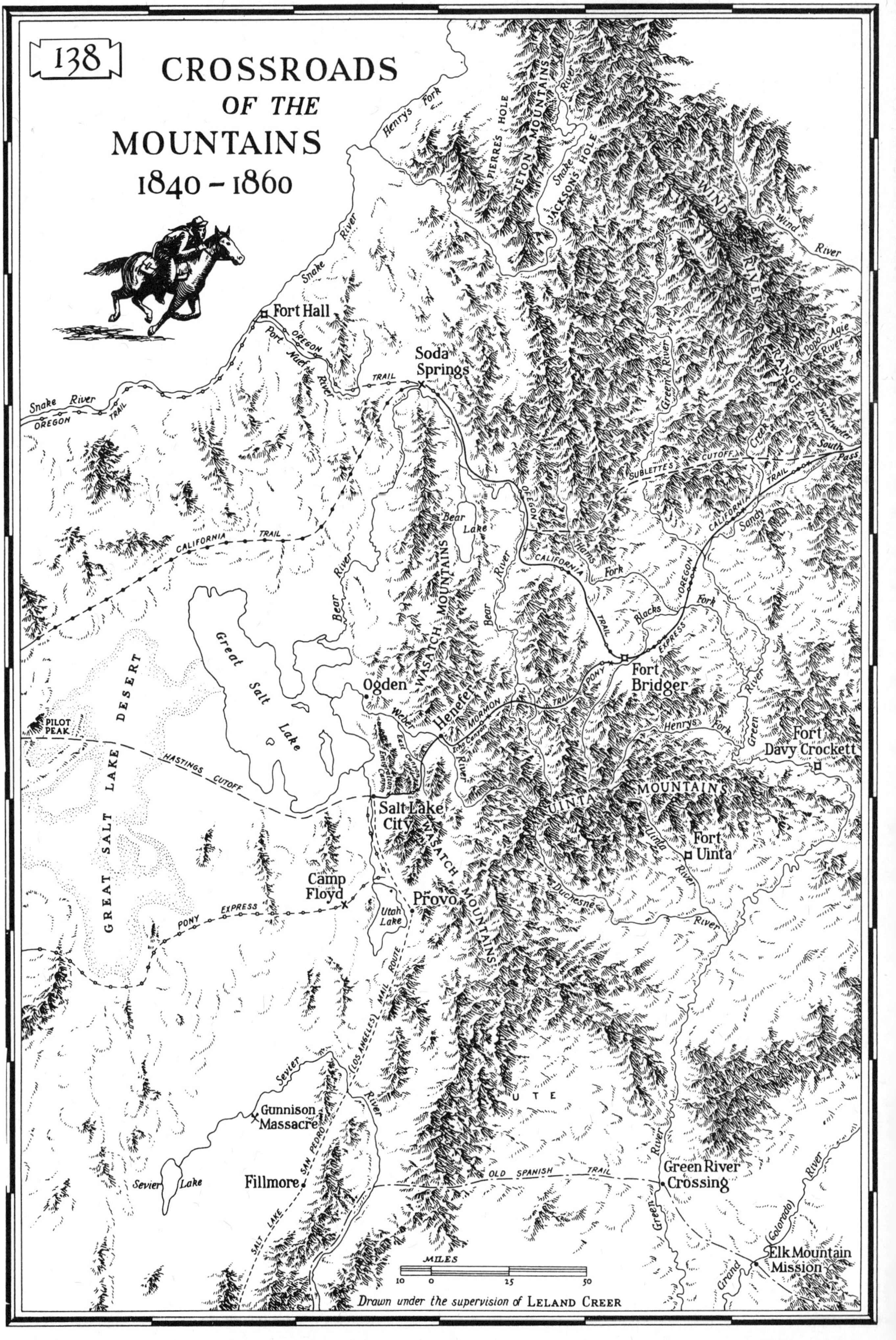
138
CROSSROADS OF THE MOUNTAINS 1840 – 1860
Henrys Fork
PIERRES HOLE
TETON MOUNTAINS
Snake River
JACKSONS HOLE
WIND RIVER RANGE
Wind River
Snake River
Fort Hall
Port Nuef River
OREGON TRAIL
Soda Springs
Snake River
OREGON TRAIL
Green River
Popo Agie River
Sweetwater River
Sandy Creek
South Pass
SUBLETTES CUTOFF
CALIFORNIA TRAIL
OREGON
Bear Lake
Bear River
CALIFORNIA TRAIL
Hams Fork
OREGON
Blacks Fork
Bear River
WASATCH MOUNTAINS
Bear River
TRAIL
PONY EXPRESS
Fort Bridger
Great Salt Lake
GREAT SALT LAKE DESERT
PILOT PEAK
Ogden
Weber
Henefer
MORMON TRAIL
Echo Canyon
Henrys Fork
Green River
Fort Davy Crockett
HASTINGS CUTOFF
East Canyon
Emigration Canyon
Weber River
UINTA MOUNTAINS
Salt Lake City
WASATCH MOUNTAINS
Fort Uinta
Uinta River
Duchesne River
Camp Floyd
PONY EXPRESS
Provo
Utah Lake
MAIL ROUTE
(LOS ANGELES)
UTE
Sevier River
Gunnison Massacre
SAN PEDRO
SALT LAKE
Sevier Lake
Fillmore
OLD SPANISH TRAIL
Green River Crossing
Green River
Green River
(Colorado)
Grand
Elk Mountain Mission
MILES
10 0 25 50
Drawn under the supervision of LELAND CREER

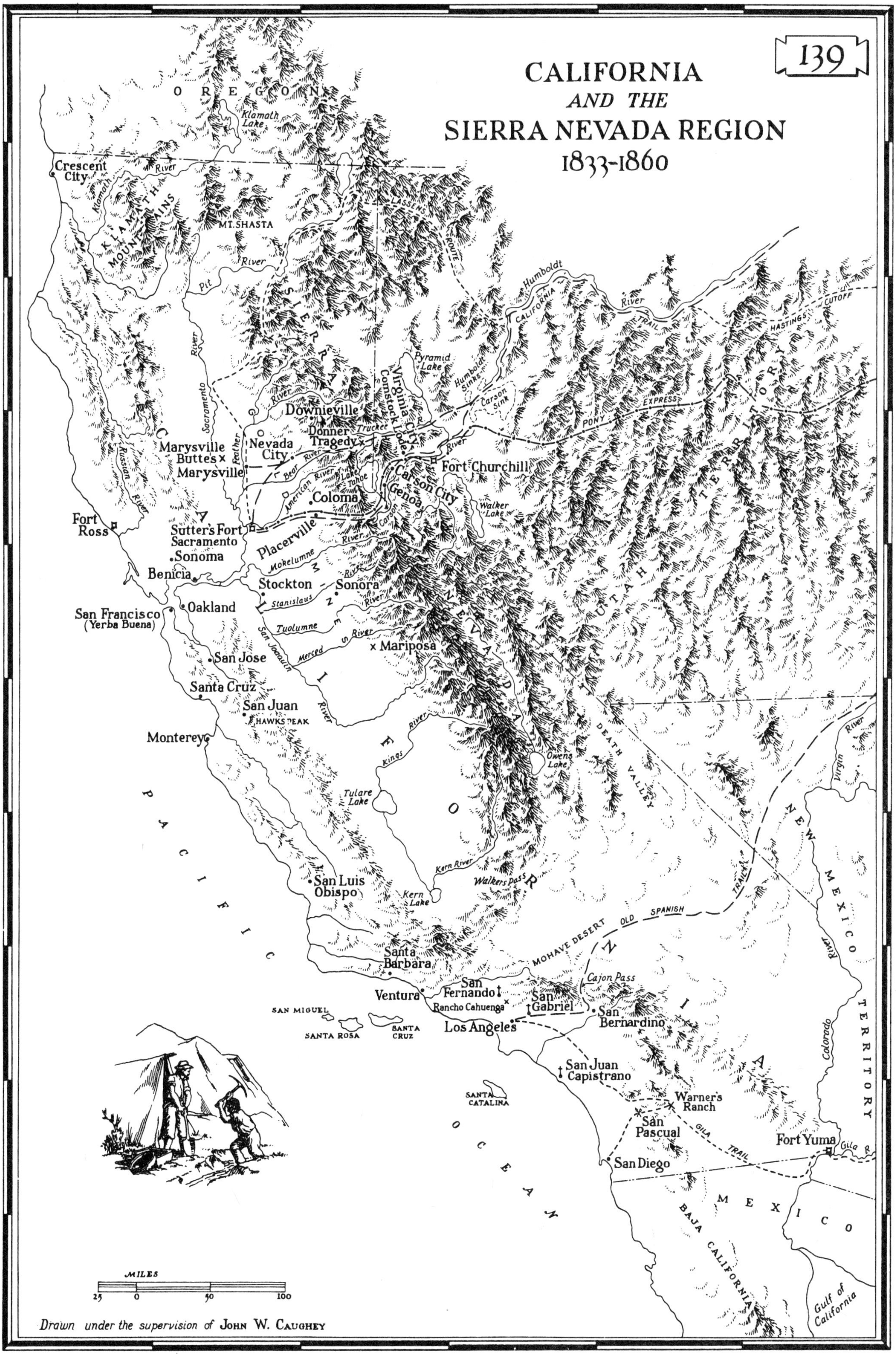
139
CALIFORNIA
AND THE
SIERRA NEVADA REGION
1833-1860
OREGON
Klamath Lake
Crescent City
River
Klamath
KLAMATH MOUNTAINS
MT. SHASTA
LASSENS ROUTE
Pit River
Sacramento River
Feather
Marysville Buttes
Marysville
Nevada City
Downieville
Donner Tragedy
Truckee
Virginia City
Comstock Lode
Pyramid Lake
Humboldt Sinks
Carson Sink
Humboldt River
CALIFORNIA TRAIL
HASTINGS CUTOFF
PONY EXPRESS
Fort Churchill
Carson City
Genoa
Lake Tahoe
Bear River
American River
Coloma
Walker Lake
Fort Ross
Russian River
Sutter's Fort
Sacramento
Placerville
Sonoma
Benicia
Mokelumne River
Stockton
Sonora
Stanislaus River
Tuolumne River
Merced River
San Francisco
(Yerba Buena)
Oakland
San Joaquin River
Mariposa
San Jose
Santa Cruz
San Juan
HAWKS PEAK
Monterey
Kings River
Owens Lake
DEATH VALLEY
UTAH TERRITORY
Virgin River
Tulare Lake
PACIFIC OCEAN
SIERRA NEVADA
CALIFORNIA
NEW MEXICO TERRITORY
Kern River
Walkers Pass
San Luis Obispo
Kern Lake
OLD SPANISH TRAIL
MOHAVE DESERT
Santa Barbara
Cajon Pass
San Fernando
San Gabriel
Ventura
Rancho Cahuenga
SAN MIGUEL
SANTA ROSA
SANTA CRUZ
Los Angeles
San Bernardino
Colorado River
San Juan Capistrano
SANTA CATALINA
Warner's Ranch
San Pascual
GILA TRAIL
Fort Yuma
Gila R.
San Diego
MEXICO
BAJA CALIFORNIA
Gulf of California
MILES
25 0 50 100
Drawn under the supervision of JOHN W. CAUGHEY

WESTWARD ADVANCE 1849-1860

MILES
50 0 100 200 300

Drawn under the supervision of LE ROY R. HAFEN *and* CARL COKE RISTER

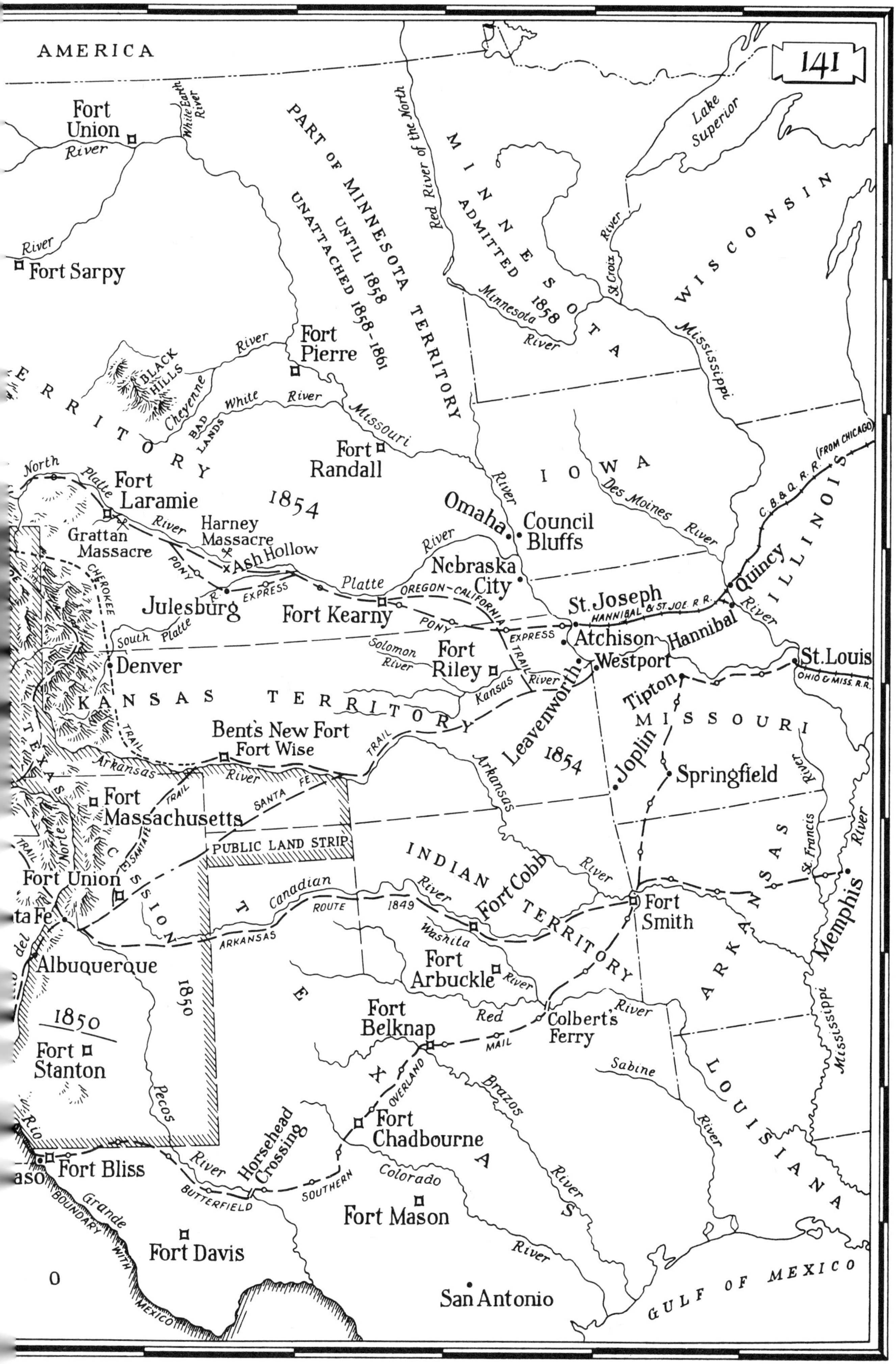
AMERICA
Fort Union
River
White Earth River
Fort Sarpy
Fort Pierre
BLACK HILLS
Cheyenne
BAD LANDS
White River
Missouri
Fort Randall
TERRITORY
1854
North Platte River
Fort Laramie
Grattan Massacre
Harney Massacre
Ash Hollow
PONY EXPRESS
Julesburg
South Platte
Fort Kearny
Platte
OREGON-CALIFORNIA TRAIL
Nebraska City
Omaha
Council Bluffs
PART OF MINNESOTA TERRITORY
UNTIL 1858
UNATTACHED 1858-1861
Red River of the North
MINNESOTA
ADMITTED 1858
Minnesota River
St. Croix River
Lake Superior
WISCONSIN
Mississippi
IOWA
Des Moines River
C.B.&Q. R.R. (FROM CHICAGO)
ILLINOIS
Quincy
St. Joseph
HANNIBAL & ST. JOE R.R.
Hannibal
Atchison
Westport
St. Louis
OHIO & MISS. R.R.
Denver
KANSAS TERRITORY
Solomon River
Fort Riley
Kansas River
Leavenworth
1854
Tipton
MISSOURI
Joplin
Springfield
CHEROKEE TRAIL
Bent's New Fort
Fort Wise
Arkansas River
TEXAS CESSION
Fort Massachusetts
SANTA FE TRAIL
PUBLIC LAND STRIP
Fort Union
Santa Fe
Albuquerque
Rio del Norte
INDIAN TERRITORY
Fort Cobb
Canadian River
ARKANSAS ROUTE 1849
Fort Smith
ARKANSAS
St. Francis River
Memphis
Washita River
Fort Arbuckle
1850
Fort Stanton
Pecos
TEXAS
Fort Belknap
Red River
Colbert's Ferry
MAIL
OVERLAND
Fort Chadbourne
Brazos River
Sabine
River
LOUISIANA
Mississippi
Horsehead Crossing
BUTTERFIELD SOUTHERN
Colorado River
Fort Mason
Fort Bliss
Rio Grande
BOUNDARY WITH MEXICO
Fort Davis
San Antonio
GULF OF MEXICO

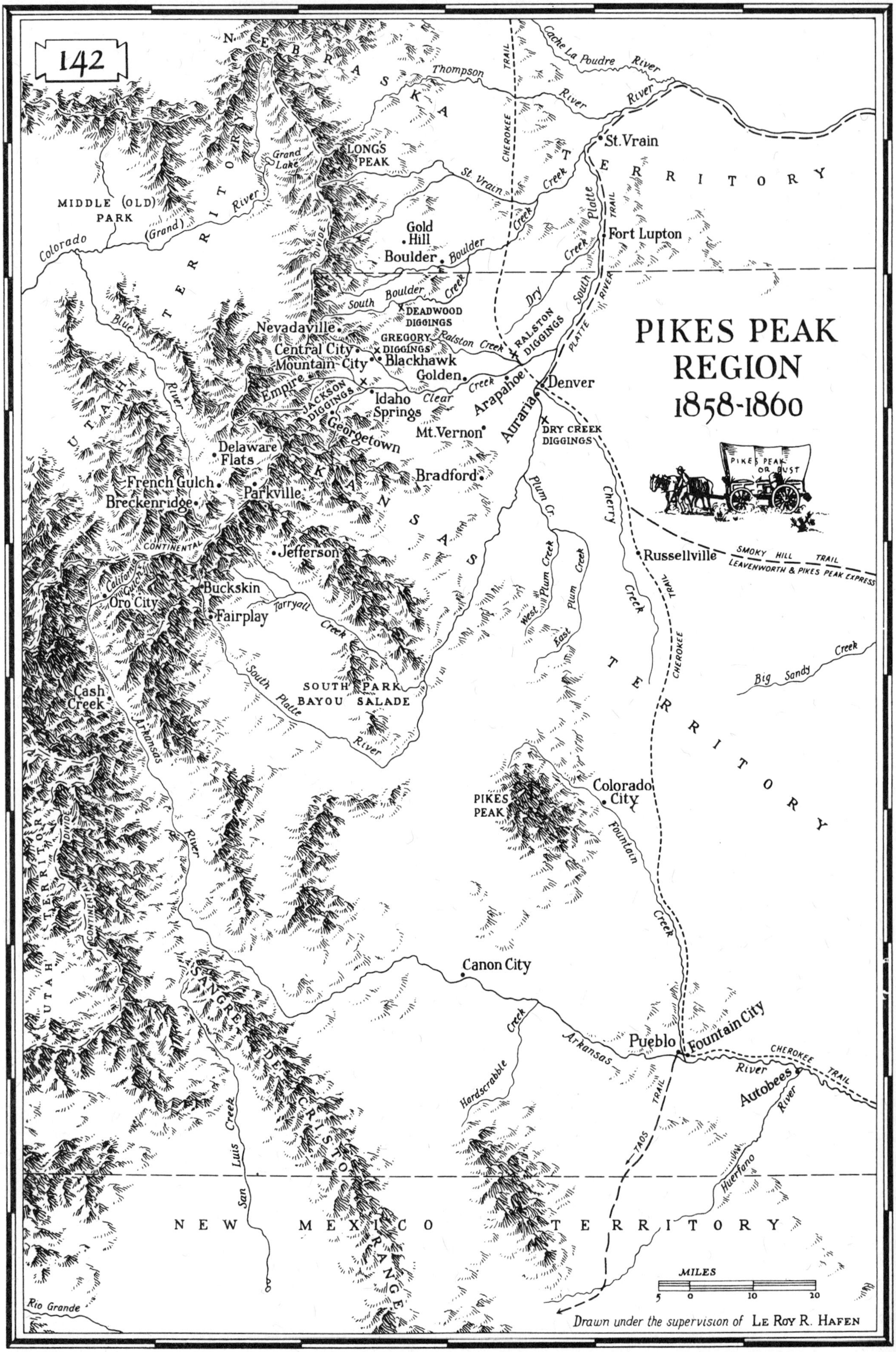
142
PIKES PEAK
REGION
1858-1860
PIKES PEAK OR BUST
NEBRASKA TERRITORY
KANSAS TERRITORY
UTAH TERRITORY
NEW MEXICO TERRITORY
Cache La Poudre River
Thompson River
CHEROKEE TRAIL
St.Vrain
LONG'S PEAK
Grand Lake
MIDDLE (OLD) PARK
Colorado (Grand) River
St. Vrain Creek
Gold Hill
Boulder
Boulder Creek
Fort Lupton
South Platte River
Dry Creek
South Boulder Creek
DEADWOOD DIGGINGS
Nevadaville
GREGORY DIGGINGS
Central City
Mountain City
Blackhawk
Ralston Creek
RALSTON DIGGINGS
Golden
Clear Creek
Denver
Arapahoe
Auraria
Empire
JACKSON DIGGINGS
Idaho Springs
Georgetown
Mt.Vernon
DRY CREEK DIGGINGS
Blue River
Delaware Flats
French Gulch
Parkville
Breckenridge
Bradford
Plum Cr.
Cherry Creek
CONTINENTAL DIVIDE
Jefferson
Russellville
SMOKY HILL TRAIL
LEAVENWORTH & PIKES PEAK EXPRESS
California Gulch
Buckskin
Oro City
Fairplay
Tarryall Creek
West Plum Creek
East Plum Creek
Big Sandy Creek
Cash Creek
SOUTH PARK
BAYOU SALADE
South Platte River
Arkansas River
PIKES PEAK
Colorado City
Fountain Creek
Canon City
SANGRE DE CRISTO RANGE
Hardscrabble Creek
Pueblo
Fountain City
Arkansas River
Autobees
TAOS TRAIL
Huerfano River
San Luis Creek
Rio Grande
MILES
5 0 10 20
Drawn under the supervision of LE ROY R. HAFEN

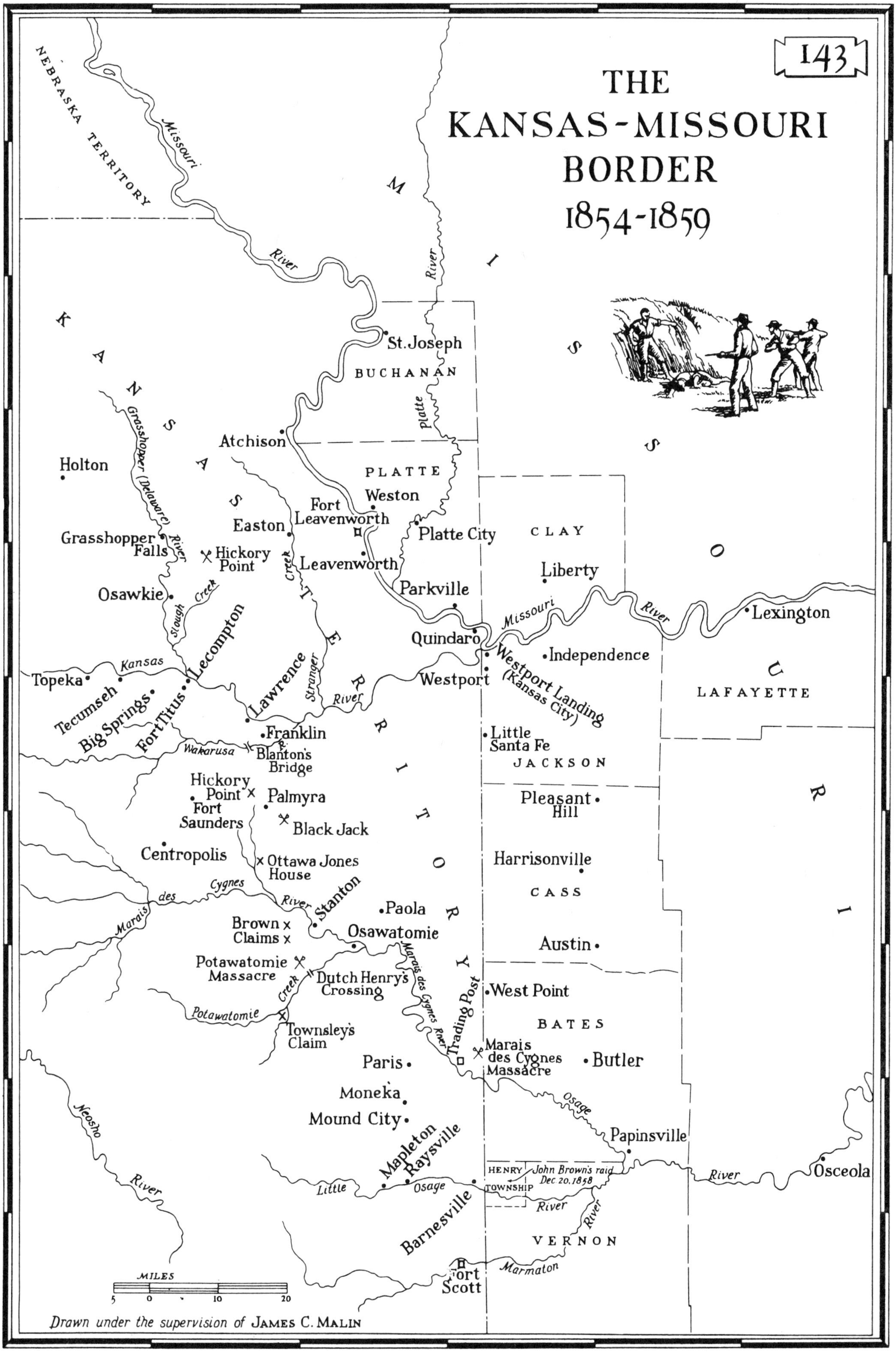
143
THE KANSAS-MISSOURI BORDER 1854-1859
NEBRASKA TERRITORY
KANSAS TERRITORY
MISSOURI
Missouri River
River
Platte
St. Joseph
BUCHANAN
Atchison
PLATTE
Weston
Fort Leavenworth
Platte City
CLAY
Liberty
Holton
Grasshopper (Delaware) River
Grasshopper Falls
Easton
Hickory Point
Leavenworth
Parkville
Osawkie
Slough Creek
Creek
Lecompton
Quindaro
Missouri River
Lexington
Topeka
Kansas
Tecumseh
Big Springs
Fort Titus
Lawrence
Stranger
River
Westport
Westport Landing (Kansas City)
Independence
LAFAYETTE
Franklin
Wakarusa
Blanton's Bridge
Little Santa Fe
JACKSON
Hickory Point
Fort Saunders
Palmyra
Black Jack
Pleasant Hill
Centropolis
Ottawa Jones House
Harrisonville
CASS
Marais des Cygnes River
Stanton
Paola
Brown Claims
Osawatomie
Austin
Potawatomie Massacre
Dutch Henry's Crossing
Marais des Cygnes River
Trading Post
West Point
Potawatomie Creek
Townsley's Claim
BATES
Marais des Cygnes Massacre
Butler
Paris
Moneka
Mound City
Osage
Papinsville
Neosho River
Mapleton
Raysville
Little Osage River
HENRY TOWNSHIP
John Brown's raid Dec 20, 1858
River
Osceola
Barnesville
River
VERNON
Marmaton
Fort Scott
MILES
5 0 10 20
Drawn under the supervision of JAMES C. MALIN

SHAKER BARN, Hancock, Mass.
Lake Superior
MINNESOTA
WISCONSIN
Union Grove 1856
Green Bay 1850
Colony of Equality 1843
Wisconsin Phalanx 1844
Lake Michigan
IOWA
ILLINOIS
Iowa Pioneer Phalanx 1844
Amana Community 1855
Bishop Hill 1846
Canton Phalanx 1845
Moved to region of Great Salt Lake, 1846
Icaria 1860
Nauvoo 1839-46 (Mormons)
Integral Phalanx 1845
Bethel Community 1844
Order of Enoch 1831
KANSAS TERRITORY
MISSOURI
New Harmony 1824
PUBLIC LAND STRIP
NEW MEXICO TERRITORY
INDIAN TERRITORY
Harmony Springs 1860
ARKANSAS
Nashoba 1825
MISSISSIPPI
Icaria 1848
Reunion 1855
Germantown 1836
Grand Ecore 1834
TEXAS
LOUISIANA
Bettina 1847

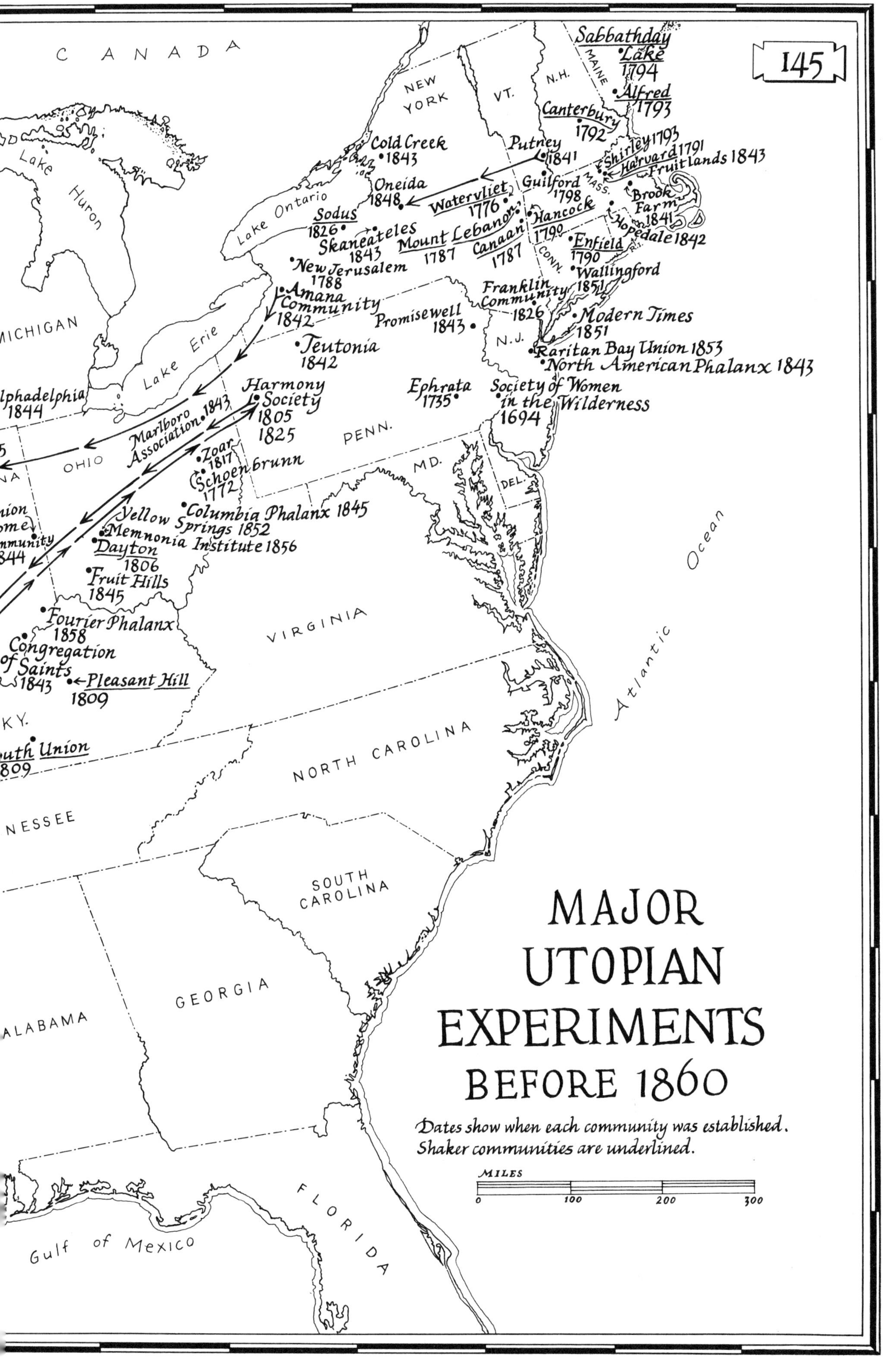
MAJOR UTOPIAN EXPERIMENTS BEFORE 1860
Dates show when each community was established. Shaker communities are underlined.
MILES
0
100
200
300
CANADA
Lake Huron
Lake Ontario
Lake Erie
MICHIGAN
NEW YORK
VT.
N.H.
MAINE
MASS.
CONN.
R.I.
N.J.
PENN.
MD.
DEL.
OHIO
KY.
VIRGINIA
NORTH CAROLINA
SOUTH CAROLINA
GEORGIA
ALABAMA
FLORIDA
NESSEE
Gulf of Mexico
Atlantic Ocean
Sabbathday Lake 1794
Alfred 1793
Canterbury 1792
Putney 1841
Shirley 1793
Harvard 1791
Fruitlands 1843
Guilford 1798
Brook Farm 1841
Hopedale 1842
Cold Creek 1843
Oneida 1848
Watervliet 1776
Sodus 1826
Skaneateles 1843
Mount Lebanon 1787
Canaan 1787
Hancock 1790
Enfield 1790
Wallingford 1851
New Jerusalem 1788
Amana Community 1842
Franklin Community 1826
Modern Times 1851
Promisewell 1843
Teutonia 1842
Raritan Bay Union 1853
North American Phalanx 1843
Harmony Society 1805 1825
Ephrata 1735
Society of Women in the Wilderness 1694
lphadelphia 1844
Marlboro Association 1843
Zoar 1817
Schoenbrunn 1772
Columbia Phalanx 1845
Yellow Springs 1852
Memnonia Institute 1856
Dayton 1806
Fruit Hills 1845
Fourier Phalanx 1858
Congregation of Saints 1843
Pleasant Hill 1809
uth Union 1809

UNIVERSAL MALE SUFFRAGE 1789~1897

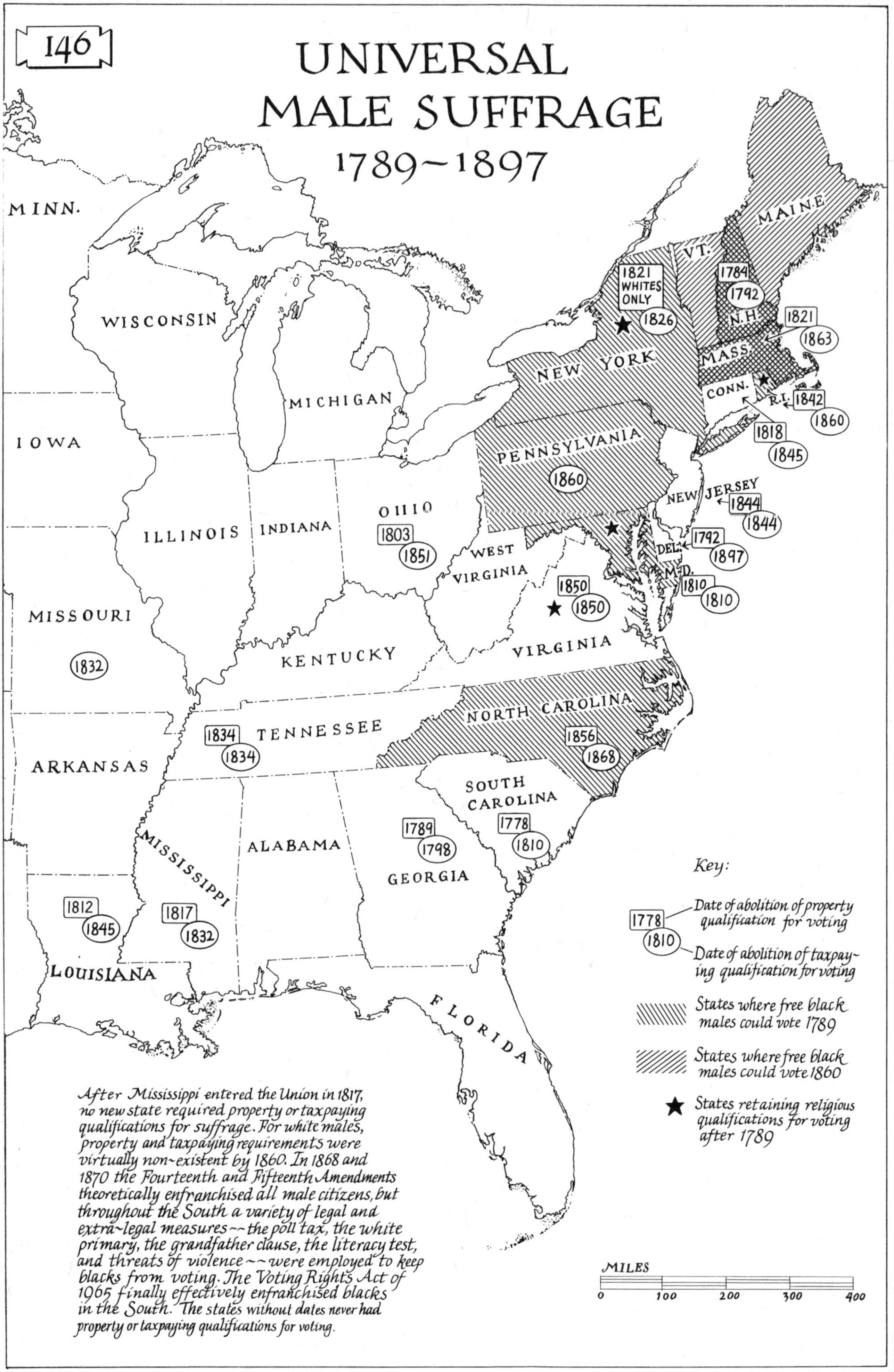

After Mississippi entered the Union in 1817, no new state required property or taxpaying qualifications for suffrage. For white males, property and taxpaying requirements were virtually non-existent by 1860. In 1868 and 1870 the Fourteenth and Fifteenth Amendments theoretically enfranchised all male citizens, but throughout the South a variety of legal and extra-legal measures—the poll tax, the white primary, the grandfather clause, the literacy test, and threats of violence—were employed to keep blacks from voting. The Voting Rights Act of 1965 finally effectively enfranchised blacks in the South. The states without dates never had property or taxpaying qualifications for voting.

VII THE CIVIL WAR AND RECONSTRUCTION

THE UNITED STATES MARCH 4, 1861

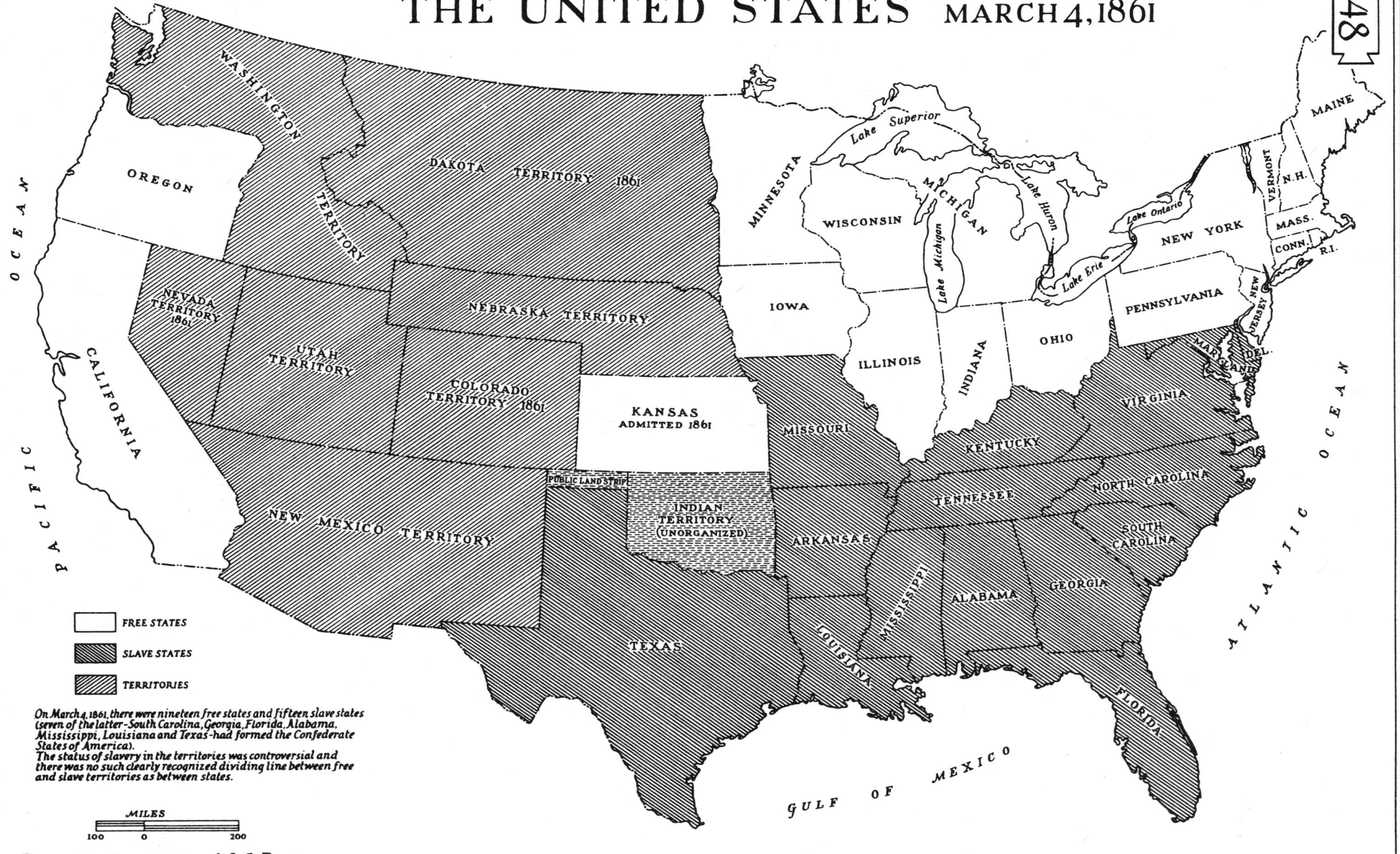

On March 4, 1861, there were nineteen free states and fifteen slave states (seven of the latter–South Carolina, Georgia, Florida, Alabama, Mississippi, Louisiana and Texas–had formed the Confederate States of America).
The status of slavery in the territories was controversial and there was no such clearly recognized dividing line between free and slave territories as between states.

Drawn under the supervision of J. G. RANDALL

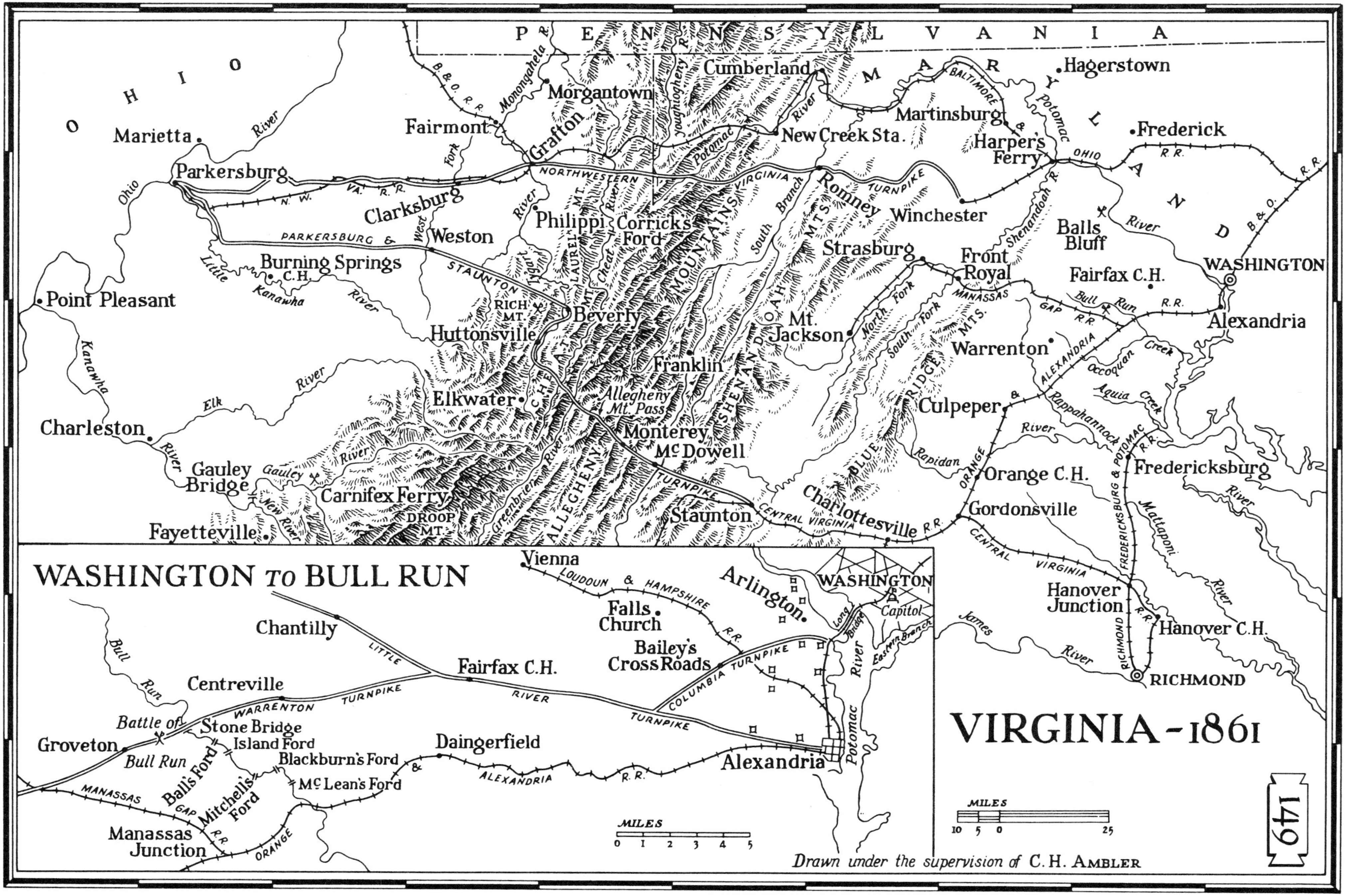
149
VIRGINIA-1861
WASHINGTON TO BULL RUN
Drawn under the supervision of C. H. AMBLER
PENNSYLVANIA
MARYLAND
OHIO
Hagerstown
Cumberland
Morgantown
Fairmont
Grafton
Marietta
Parkersburg
Clarksburg
Weston
Philippi
Corricks Ford
New Creek Sta.
Martinsburg
Harper's Ferry
Frederick
Romney
Winchester
Balls Bluff
WASHINGTON
Alexandria
Fairfax C.H.
Strasburg
Front Royal
Mt. Jackson
Warrenton
Culpeper
Orange C.H.
Gordonsville
Fredericksburg
Hanover Junction
Hanover C.H.
RICHMOND
Charlottesville
Staunton
Franklin
Monterey
Mc Dowell
Allegheny Mt. Pass
Beverly
Huttonsville
RICH MT.
Elkwater
Burning Springs C.H.
Point Pleasant
Charleston
Gauley Bridge
Carnifex Ferry
Fayetteville
DROOP MT.
Vienna
Falls Church
Arlington
Bailey's Cross Roads
Chantilly
Centreville
Fairfax C.H.
Groveton
Battle of Bull Run
Stone Bridge
Island Ford
Blackburn's Ford
Mc Lean's Ford
Ball's Ford
Mitchell's Ford
Manassas Junction
Daingerfield
Alexandria
Capitol
MILES

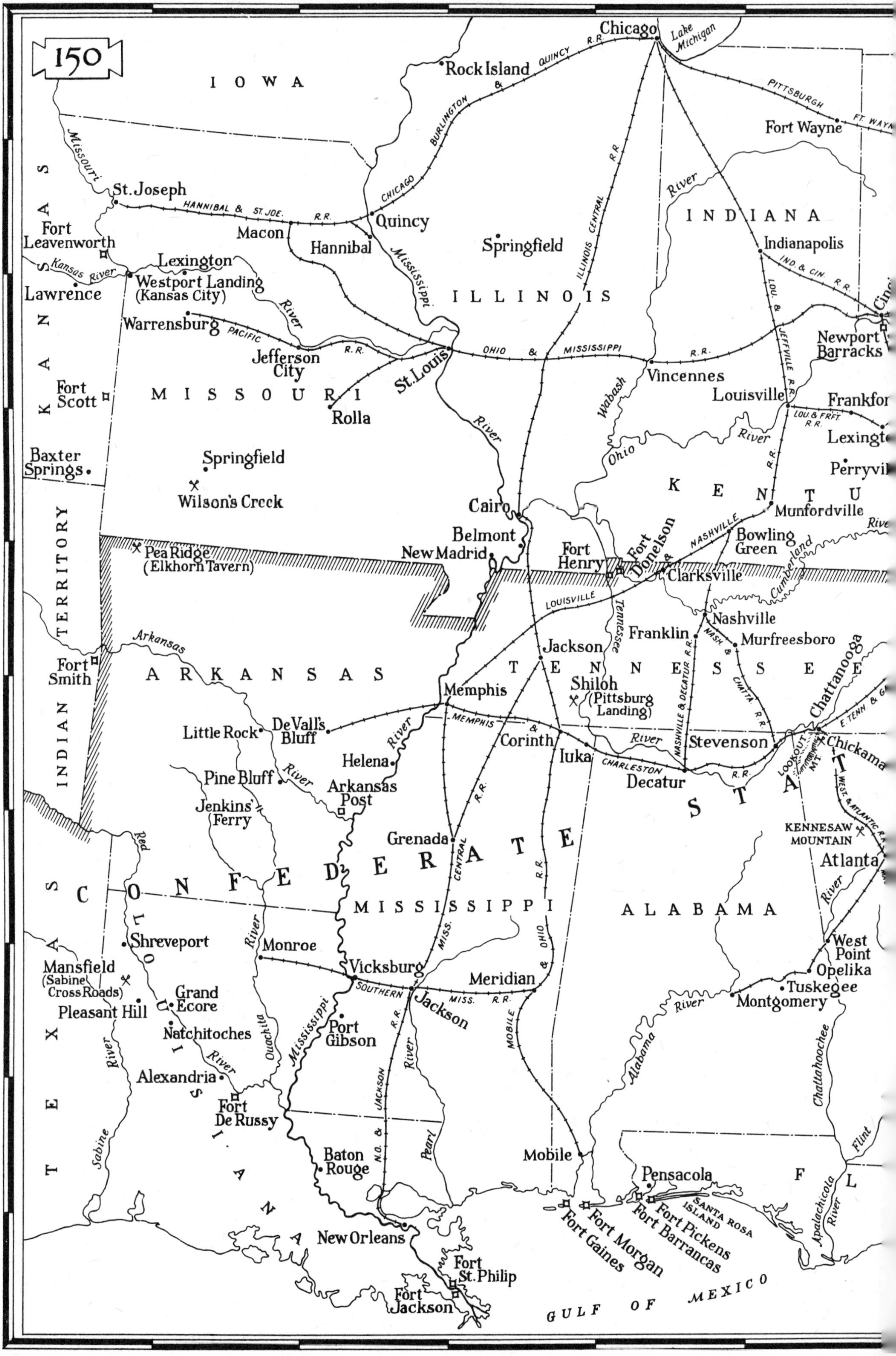
IOWA
Rock Island
Chicago
Lake Michigan
BURLINGTON & QUINCY R.R.
CHICAGO
PITTSBURGH
FT. WAYNE
Fort Wayne
Missouri
St. Joseph
HANNIBAL & ST. JOE. R.R.
Quincy
Macon
Hannibal
Fort Leavenworth
Kansas River
Lexington
Westport Landing (Kansas City)
Lawrence
Springfield
ILLINOIS CENTRAL R.R.
River
INDIANA
Indianapolis
IND. & CIN. R.R.
Mississippi
ILLINOIS
Warrensburg
PACIFIC R.R.
Jefferson City
St. Louis
OHIO & MISSISSIPPI R.R.
Vincennes
LOU. & JEFFVILLE R.R.
Newport Barracks
Louisville
Frankfort
LOU. & FRFT. R.R.
Lexington
Fort Scott
MISSOURI
Rolla
Wabash
River
Ohio
Baxter Springs
Springfield
Wilson's Creek
Perryville
KANSAS
KENTUCKY
Cairo
Munfordville
Belmont
New Madrid
Pea Ridge (Elkhorn Tavern)
Fort Henry
Fort Donelson
NASHVILLE
Bowling Green
Cumberland
River
Clarksville
LOUISVILLE
Tennessee
Nashville
INDIAN TERRITORY
Arkansas
Franklin
NASH. & CHATTA. R.R.
Murfreesboro
Jackson
Fort Smith
ARKANSAS
TENNESSEE
Chattanooga
Memphis
Shiloh (Pittsburg Landing)
NASHVILLE & DECATUR R.R.
E. TENN. & GA.
Little Rock
DeVall's Bluff
MEMPHIS & CHARLESTON R.R.
Corinth
Iuka
Stevenson
Chickamauga
LOOKOUT MT.
Helena
River
Decatur
Pine Bluff
River
Arkansas Post
Jenkins' Ferry
WEST. & ATLANTIC R.R.
KENNESAW MOUNTAIN
Grenada
CENTRAL R.R.
Red
Atlanta
CONFEDERATE STATES
MISSISSIPPI
ALABAMA
River
Shreveport
River
Monroe
MOBILE & OHIO R.R.
West Point
Opelika
Mansfield (Sabine Cross Roads)
Vicksburg
Meridian
Tuskegee
Grand Ecore
SOUTHERN MISS. R.R.
Jackson
Montgomery
Pleasant Hill
Natchitoches
Ouachita
Mississippi
Port Gibson
River
Alabama
Chattahoochee
River
N.O. & JACKSON R.R.
River
Alexandria
Fort De Russy
TEXAS
LOUISIANA
Sabine
Pearl
Flint
Baton Rouge
Mobile
Pensacola
FL
Fort Gaines
Fort Morgan
Fort Barrancas
Fort Pickens
SANTA ROSA ISLAND
Apalachicola River
New Orleans
Fort St. Philip
Fort Jackson
GULF OF MEXICO

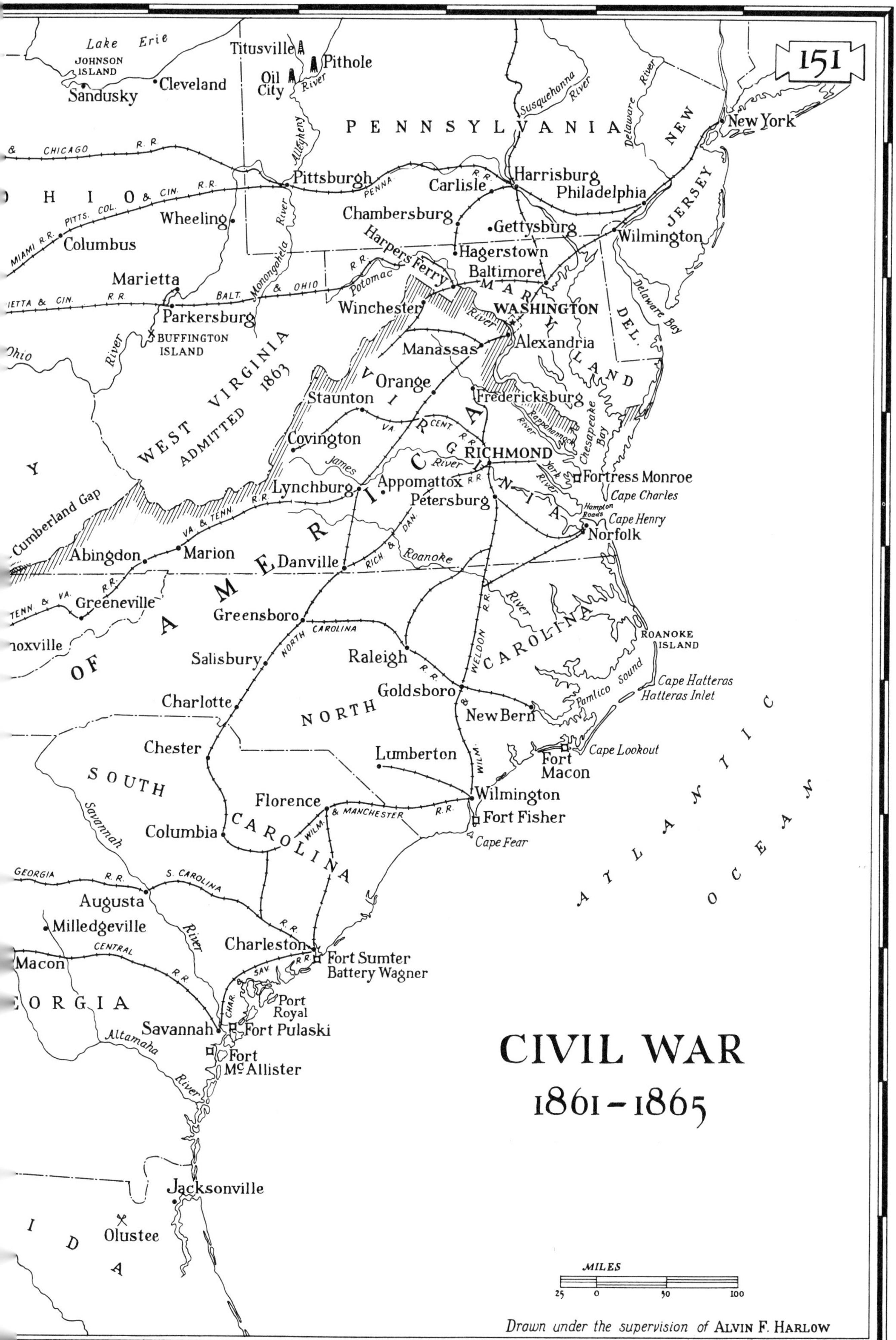
CIVIL WAR
1861–1865
Drawn under the supervision of ALVIN F. HARLOW
MILES
25 0 50 100
Lake Erie
JOHNSON ISLAND
Sandusky
Cleveland
Titusville
Pithole
Oil City
River
Allegheny
PENNSYLVANIA
Susquehanna River
Delaware River
NEW
JERSEY
New York
& CHICAGO R. R.
OHIO
PITTS. COL. & CIN. R.R.
MIAMI R.R.
Columbus
Wheeling
Pittsburgh
PENNA. R.R.
Harrisburg
Carlisle
Philadelphia
Chambersburg
Gettysburg
Wilmington
Harpers Ferry
Hagerstown
Baltimore
Marietta
Monongahela River
BALT. & OHIO R.R.
IETTA & CIN. R.R.
Potomac River
Winchester
WASHINGTON
MARYLAND
DEL.
Delaware Bay
Parkersburg
BUFFINGTON ISLAND
Ohio River
Alexandria
Manassas
WEST VIRGINIA ADMITTED 1863
VIRGINIA
Orange
Staunton
Fredericksburg
Rappahannock River
Chesapeake Bay
VA. CENT. R.R.
Covington
RICHMOND
James River
York River
Fortress Monroe
Cape Charles
Lynchburg
Appomattox
R.R.
Petersburg
Hampton Roads
Cape Henry
Norfolk
Cumberland Gap
VA. & TENN. R.R.
Abingdon
Marion
Danville
RICH. & DAN.
Roanoke River
TENN. & VA. R.R.
Greeneville
Greensboro
NORTH CAROLINA R.R.
WELDON R.R.
ROANOKE ISLAND
noxville
Salisbury
Raleigh
CAROLINA
Y
AMERICA
OF
Goldsboro
Pamlico Sound
Cape Hatteras
Hatteras Inlet
Charlotte
NORTH
New Bern
WILM. &
Chester
Lumberton
Fort Macon
Cape Lookout
SOUTH CAROLINA
Savannah
Florence
WILM. & MANCHESTER R.R.
Wilmington
Fort Fisher
Cape Fear
Columbia
ATLANTIC OCEAN
GEORGIA R.R.
S. CAROLINA R.R.
Augusta
Milledgeville
River
CENTRAL R.R.
Charleston
Fort Sumter
Battery Wagner
Macon
CHAR. & SAV. R.R.
EORGIA
Port Royal
Savannah
Fort Pulaski
Altamaha River
Fort McAllister
Jacksonville
Olustee
IDA

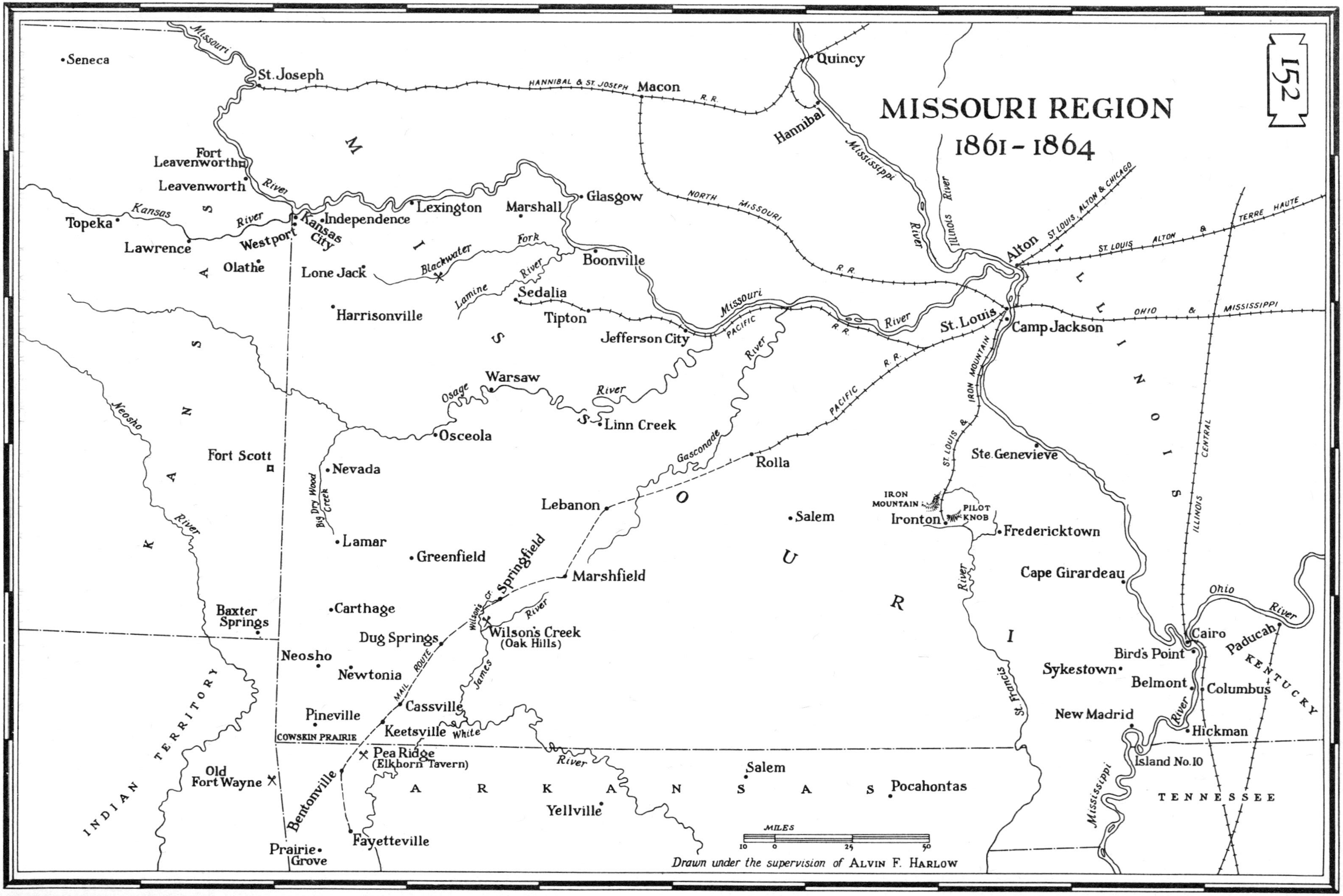
152
MISSOURI REGION
1861 - 1864
Seneca
St. Joseph
Macon
Quincy
Hannibal
Fort Leavenworth
Leavenworth
Topeka
Lawrence
Olathe
Westport
Kansas City
Independence
Lexington
Marshall
Glasgow
Boonville
Lone Jack
Harrisonville
Sedalia
Tipton
Jefferson City
Warsaw
Linn Creek
Osceola
Fort Scott
Nevada
Lamar
Greenfield
Lebanon
Rolla
Salem
Springfield
Marshfield
Wilson's Creek
(Oak Hills)
Carthage
Baxter Springs
Dug Springs
Neosho
Newtonia
Pineville
Cassville
Keetsville
COWSKIN PRAIRIE
Pea Ridge
(Elkhorn Tavern)
Bentonville
Old Fort Wayne
Prairie Grove
Fayetteville
Yellville
Salem
Pocahontas
Alton
St. Louis
Camp Jackson
Ste. Genevieve
IRON MOUNTAIN
Ironton
PILOT KNOB
Fredericktown
Cape Girardeau
Cairo
Bird's Point
Paducah
Sykestown
Belmont
Columbus
New Madrid
Hickman
Island No. 10
MISSOURI
KANSAS
ILLINOIS
ARKANSAS
KENTUCKY
TENNESSEE
INDIAN TERRITORY
Missouri River
Kansas River
Neosho River
Blackwater Fork
Lamine River
Osage River
Big Dry Wood Creek
Gasconade River
Wilson's Cr.
James River
White River
St. Francis River
Mississippi River
Illinois River
Ohio River
HANNIBAL & ST. JOSEPH R.R.
NORTH MISSOURI R.R.
PACIFIC R.R.
ST. LOUIS & IRON MOUNTAIN
ST. LOUIS, ALTON & CHICAGO
ST. LOUIS ALTON & TERRE HAUTE
OHIO & MISSISSIPPI
ILLINOIS CENTRAL
MAIL ROUTE
MILES
10 0 25 50
Drawn under the supervision of ALVIN F. HARLOW

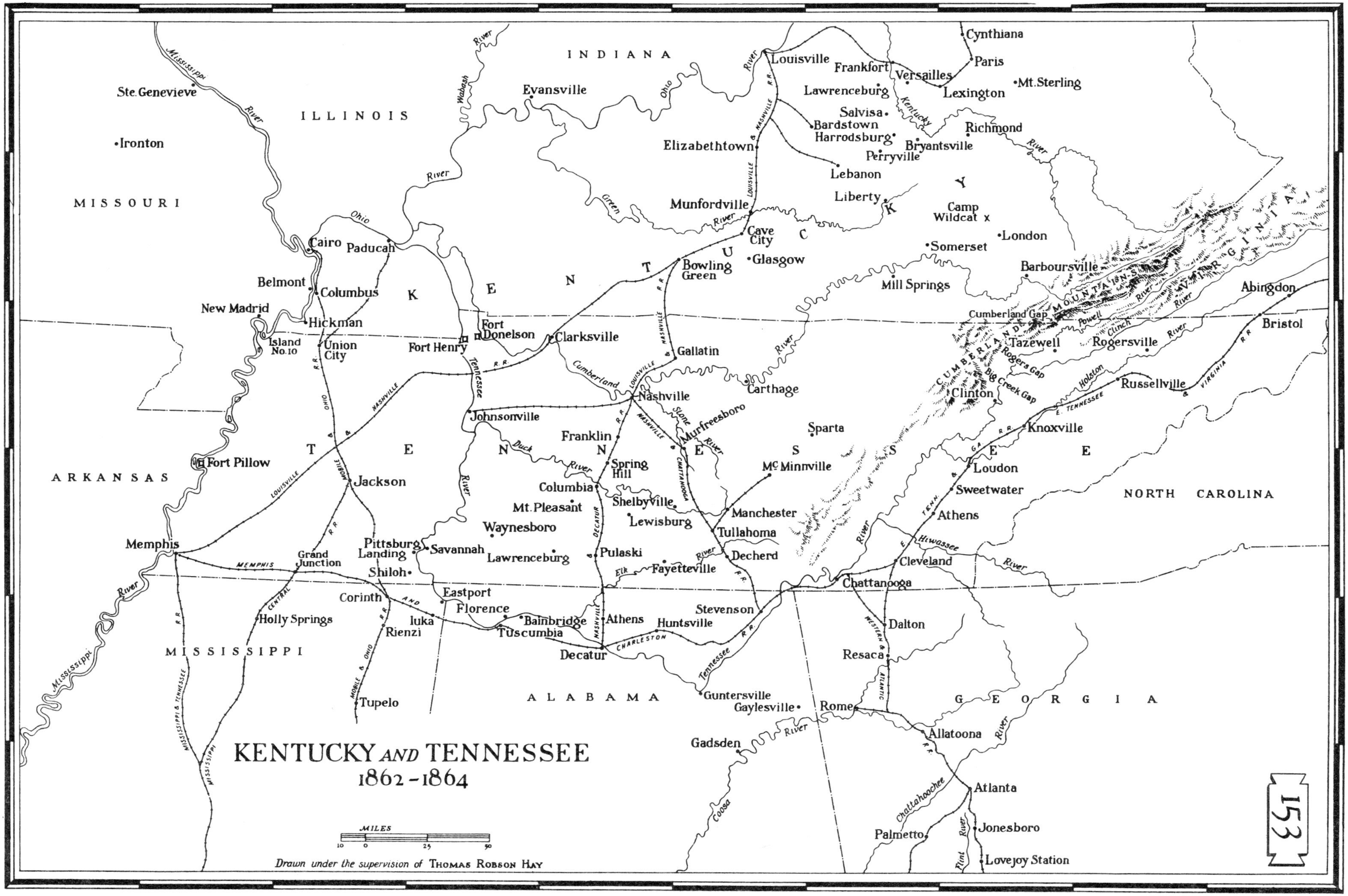
153
KENTUCKY AND TENNESSEE
1862-1864
MILES
10
0
25
50
Drawn under the supervision of Thomas Robson Hay
INDIANA
ILLINOIS
MISSOURI
ARKANSAS
MISSISSIPPI
ALABAMA
GEORGIA
NORTH CAROLINA
VIRGINIA
KENTUCKY
TENNESSEE
CUMBERLAND MOUNTAINS
Ste. Genevieve
Ironton
Evansville
Louisville
Frankfort
Versailles
Cynthiana
Paris
Mt. Sterling
Lexington
Lawrenceburg
Salvisa
Bardstown
Harrodsburg
Bryantsville
Perryville
Richmond
Elizabethtown
Lebanon
Liberty
Camp Wildcat
London
Munfordville
Cave City
Somerset
Glasgow
Bowling Green
Barboursville
Mill Springs
Abingdon
Bristol
Cairo
Paducah
Belmont
Columbus
New Madrid
Hickman
Island No. 10
Union City
Fort Henry
Fort Donelson
Clarksville
Gallatin
Cumberland Gap
Tazewell
Rogersville
Rogers Gap
Big Creek Gap
Clinton
Russellville
Carthage
Nashville
Johnsonville
Murfreesboro
Sparta
Knoxville
Franklin
Fort Pillow
Spring Hill
McMinnville
Loudon
Jackson
Columbia
Sweetwater
Mt. Pleasant
Shelbyville
Manchester
Athens
Waynesboro
Lewisburg
Tullahoma
Memphis
Pittsburg Landing
Savannah
Lawrenceburg
Pulaski
Decherd
Cleveland
Grand Junction
Shiloh
Fayetteville
Chattanooga
Corinth
Eastport
Florence
Stevenson
Holly Springs
Iuka
Bainbridge
Athens
Huntsville
Dalton
Rienzi
Tuscumbia
Decatur
Resaca
Tupelo
Guntersville
Gaylesville
Rome
Allatoona
Gadsden
Atlanta
Palmetto
Jonesboro
Lovejoy Station
Mississippi River
Ohio
Wabash River
River
Green
Kentucky
Cumberland
Tennessee
Duck River
Stone River
Elk River
Powell River
Clinch River
Holston River
Hiwassee River
Coosa
Chattahoochee
Flint River
Louisville & Nashville R.R.
Mobile & Ohio R.R.
Memphis and Charleston
Nashville & Chattanooga
Nashville & Decatur
Mississippi & Tennessee R.R.
Mississippi Central
Western & Atlantic
E. Tennessee & Virginia R.R.
E. Tenn. & Ga. R.R.

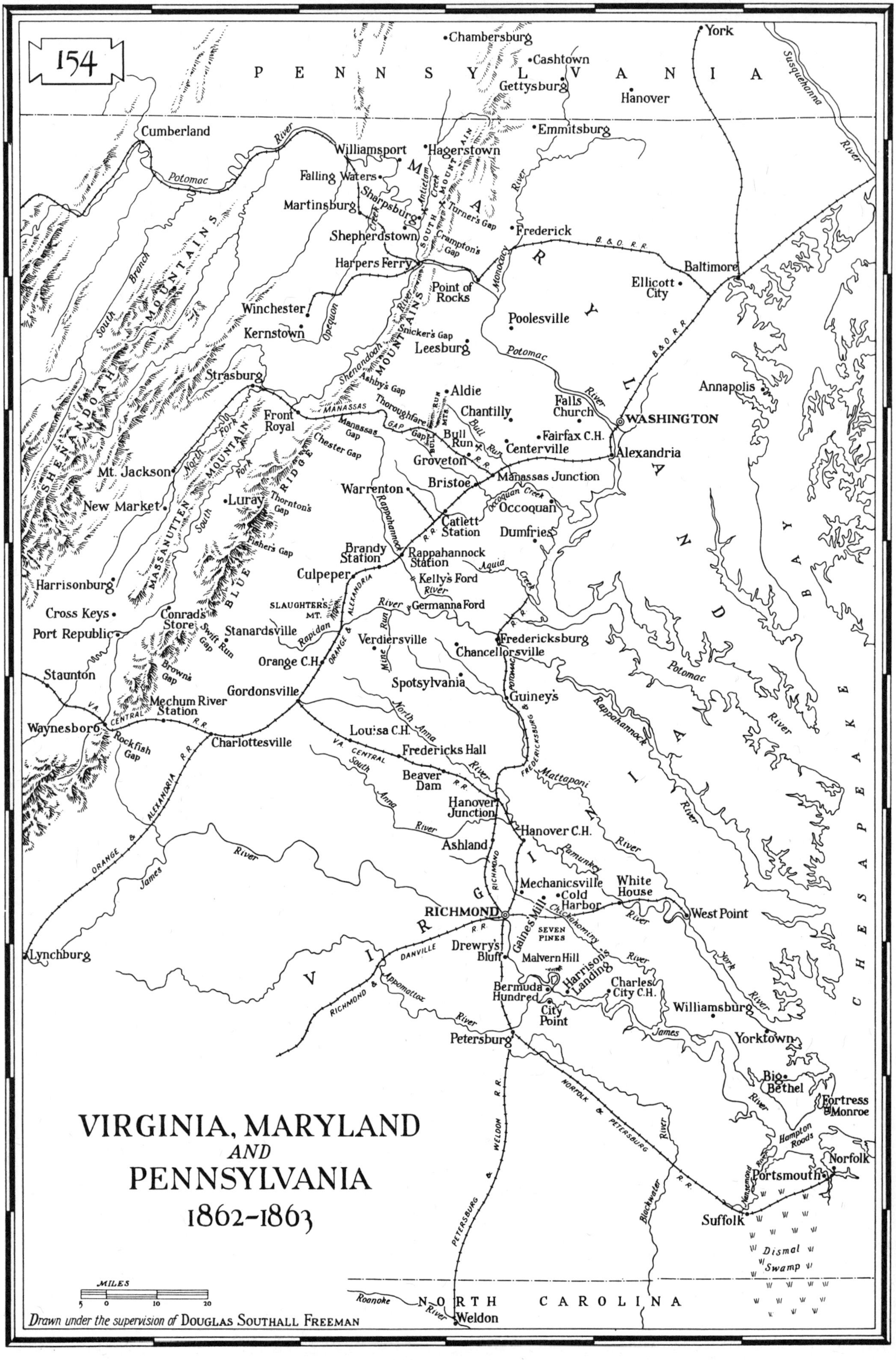
VIRGINIA, MARYLAND
AND
PENNSYLVANIA
1862-1863
PENNSYLVANIA
MARYLAND
VIRGINIA
NORTH CAROLINA
CHESAPEAKE BAY
Chambersburg
Cashtown
Gettysburg
York
Hanover
Emmitsburg
Cumberland
Williamsport
Hagerstown
Falling Waters
Martinsburg
Sharpsburg
Shepherdstown
Turner's Gap
Crampton's Gap
Frederick
Harpers Ferry
Point of Rocks
Baltimore
Ellicott City
Winchester
Kernstown
Poolesville
Snicker's Gap
Leesburg
Strasburg
Ashby's Gap
Aldie
Front Royal
Manassas Gap
Thoroughfare Gap
Chantilly
Falls Church
WASHINGTON
Annapolis
Chester Gap
Bull Run
Fairfax C.H.
Centerville
Alexandria
Mt. Jackson
Groveton
Bristoe
Manassas Junction
Warrenton
New Market
Luray
Thornton's Gap
Occoquan
Catlett Station
Dumfries
Fisher's Gap
Brandy Station
Rappahannock Station
Culpeper
Kelly's Ford
Harrisonburg
Cross Keys
Slaughter's Mt.
Germanna Ford
Conrad's Store
Port Republic
Stanardsville
Swift Run Gap
Verdiersville
Fredericksburg
Chancellorsville
Orange C.H.
Staunton
Brown's Gap
Spotsylvania
Gordonsville
Guiney's
Mechum River Station
Waynesboro
Rockfish Gap
Charlottesville
Louisa C.H.
Fredericks Hall
Beaver Dam
Hanover Junction
Hanover C.H.
Ashland
Mechanicsville
Cold Harbor
White House
West Point
RICHMOND
Gaines's Mill
Seven Pines
Drewry's Bluff
Malvern Hill
Harrison's Landing
Bermuda Hundred
Charles City C.H.
City Point
Williamsburg
Lynchburg
Petersburg
Yorktown
Big Bethel
Fortress Monroe
Hampton Roads
Norfolk
Portsmouth
Suffolk
Dismal Swamp
Weldon
Potomac River
Susquehanna River
Shenandoah River
Rappahannock River
Rapidan River
James River
Appomattox River
York River
Pamunkey River
Chickahominy River
Mattaponi River
North Anna River
South Anna River
Blackwater River
Roanoke River
B. & O. R.R.
Manassas Gap R.R.
Orange & Alexandria R.R.
Va. Central R.R.
Richmond & Danville R.R.
Petersburg & Weldon R.R.
Norfolk & Petersburg R.R.
MILES
5 0 10 20
Drawn under the supervision of DOUGLAS SOUTHALL FREEMAN

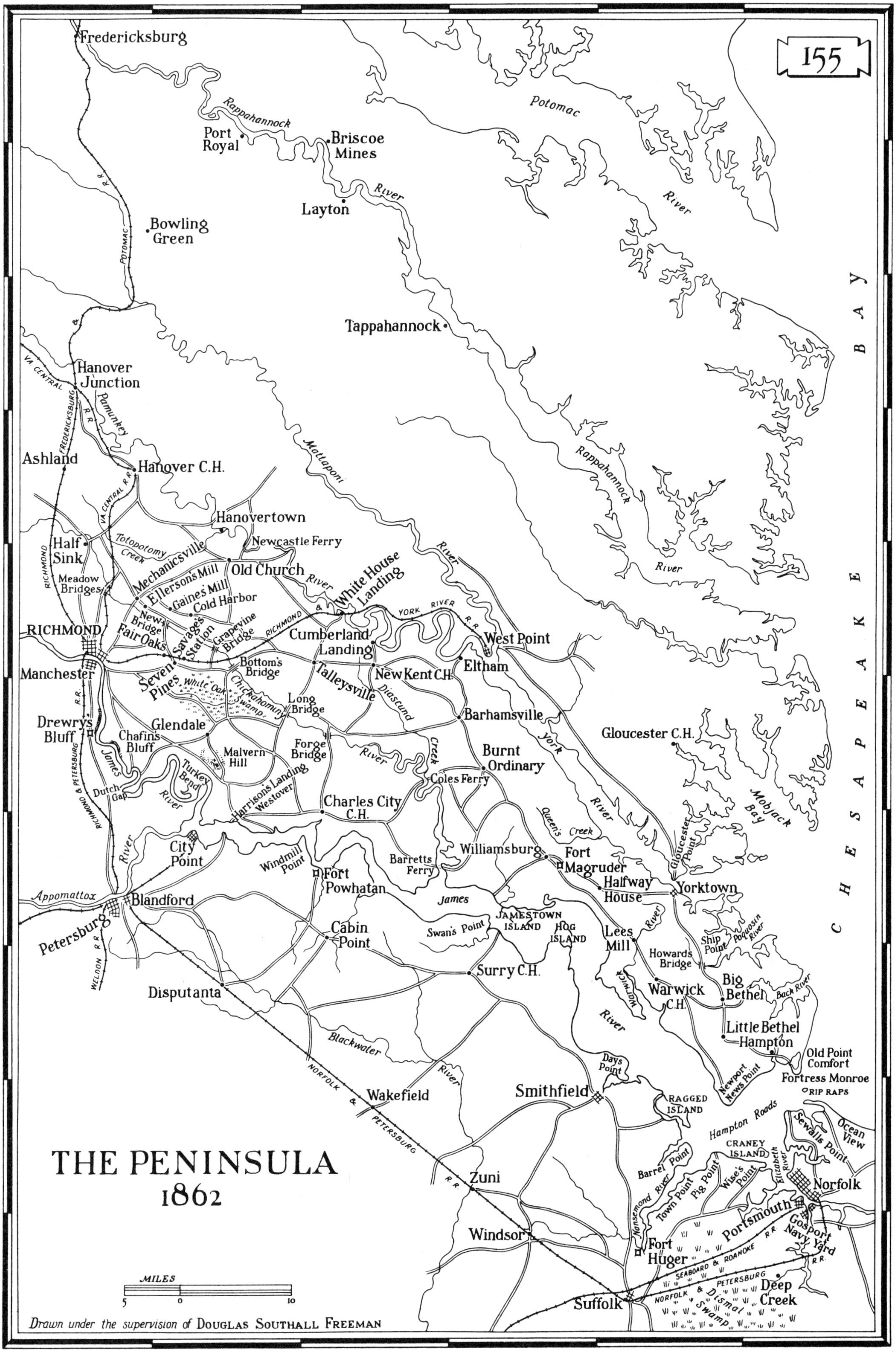
155
THE PENINSULA
1862
MILES
5 0 10
Drawn under the supervision of DOUGLAS SOUTHALL FREEMAN
Fredericksburg
Rappahannock
Port Royal
Briscoe Mines
River
Layton
Potomac
River
Bowling Green
POTOMAC
R.R.
Tappahannock
Hanover Junction
VA CENTRAL
RICHMOND & FREDERICKSBURG R.R.
Pamunkey
Mattaponi
Rappahannock
River
CHESAPEAKE BAY
Ashland
Hanover C.H.
VA CENTRAL R.R.
Hanovertown
Half Sink
Totopotomy Creek
Newcastle Ferry
Mechanicsville
Old Church
Meadow Bridges
Ellerson's Mill
Gaines' Mill
Cold Harbor
River
White House Landing
YORK RIVER R.R.
RICHMOND
New Bridge
Fair Oaks
Savage's Station
Grapevine Bridge
RICHMOND & YORK RIVER
Cumberland Landing
West Point
Manchester
Seven Pines
Bottom's Bridge
Talleysville
New Kent C.H.
Eltham
White Oak Swamp
Chickahominy
Diascund
Long Bridge
Barhamsville
Drewrys Bluff
Chafins Bluff
Glendale
Gloucester C.H.
James
Malvern Hill
Forge Bridge
Creek
Burnt Ordinary
York
River
Turkey Bend
Coles Ferry
Dutch Gap
River
Harrisons Landing
Westover
Charles City C.H.
River
Mobjack Bay
RICHMOND & PETERSBURG
Queen's Creek
Gloucester Point
City Point
Williamsburg
Fort Magruder
River
Windmill Point
Barretts Ferry
Fort Powhatan
Halfway House
Yorktown
Appomattox
Blandford
James
JAMESTOWN ISLAND
HOG ISLAND
Swan's Point
Lees Mill
River
Petersburg
Cabin Point
Ship Point
Poquosin River
WELDON R.R.
Howards Bridge
Surry C.H.
Big Bethel
Warwick River
Warwick C.H.
Back River
Disputanta
River
Little Bethel
Hampton
Blackwater
Old Point Comfort
River
Days Point
Newport News Point
Fortress Monroe
RIP RAPS
NORFOLK & PETERSBURG R.R.
Wakefield
Smithfield
RAGGED ISLAND
Hampton Roads
Ocean View
Sewalls Point
CRANEY ISLAND
Barrel Point
Elizabeth River
Zuni
Pig Point
Wise's Point
Norfolk
Nansemond River
Town Point
Portsmouth
Gosport Navy Yard
Windsor
R.R.
Fort Huger
SEABOARD & ROANOKE
NORFOLK & PETERSBURG
Deep Creek
Suffolk
Dismal Swamp

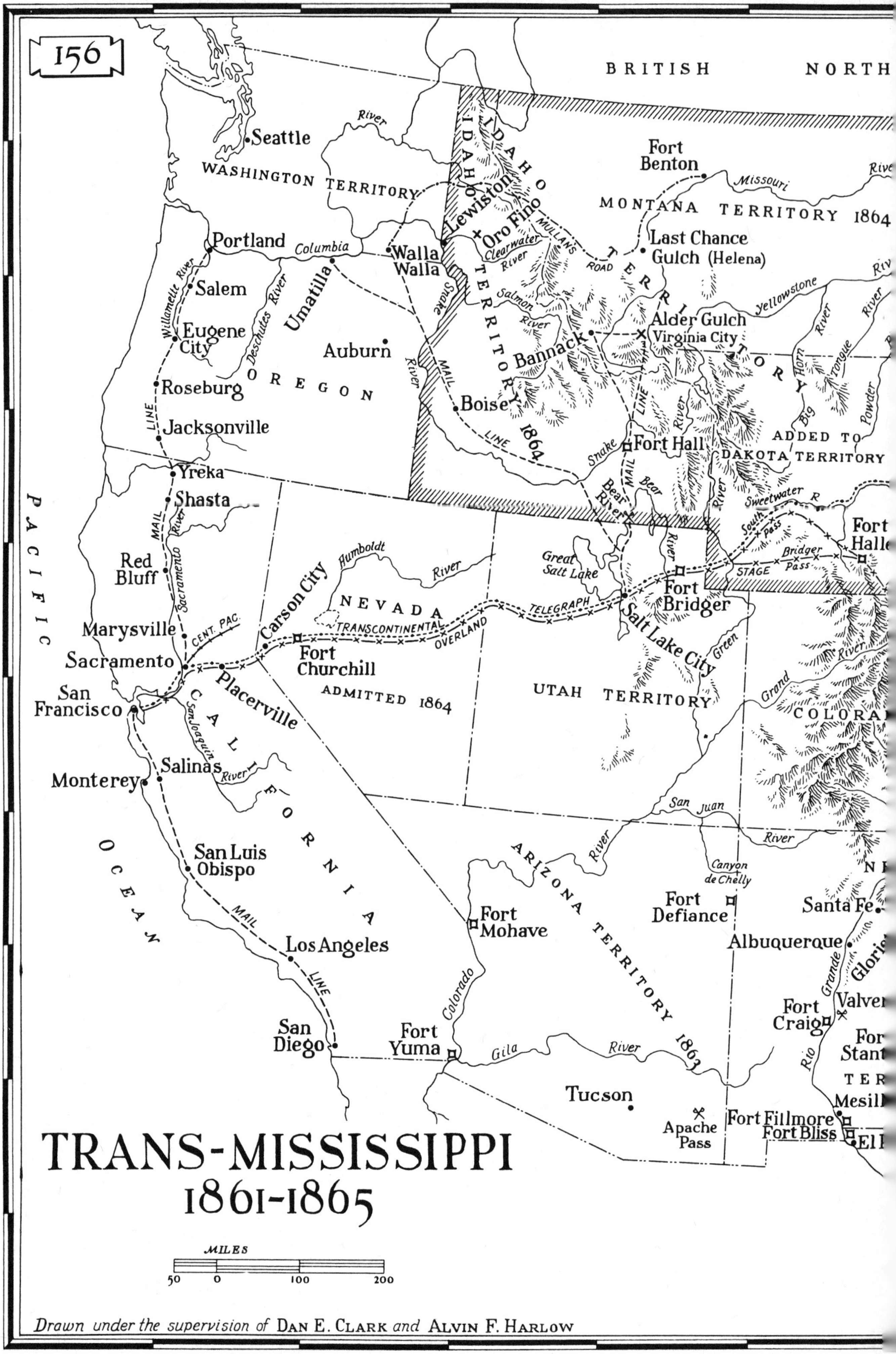
BRITISH NORTH
Seattle
WASHINGTON TERRITORY
River
Fort Benton
Missouri
River
IDAHO
IDAHO TERRITORY
Lewiston
Oro Fino
Clearwater
River
MULLANS ROAD
MONTANA TERRITORY 1864
Last Chance Gulch (Helena)
Portland
Columbia
Walla Walla
Salem
Willamette River
Deschutes River
Umatilla
Snake
Salmon River
Yellowstone
Alder Gulch
Virginia City
Bannack
Eugene City
Auburn
OREGON
River
MAIL
Boise
LINE
1864
TERRITORY
Big Horn River
Tongue River
Powder
Roseburg
LINE
Jacksonville
ADDED TO DAKOTA TERRITORY
Fort Hall
Snake
MAIL
LINE
River
Bear River
Bear
Yreka
Shasta
MAIL
River
Sweetwater R
South Pass
Fort Halleck
Bridger Pass
STAGE
Red Bluff
Sacramento
Humboldt
River
Great Salt Lake
River
Carson City
NEVADA
TRANSCONTINENTAL
OVERLAND
TELEGRAPH
Fort Bridger
Marysville
CENT. PAC.
Fort Churchill
Salt Lake City
Green
Sacramento
Placerville
ADMITTED 1864
UTAH TERRITORY
River
Grand
COLORA
San Francisco
CALIFORNIA
San Joaquin
PACIFIC
Salinas
River
Monterey
San Juan
River
OCEAN
San Luis Obispo
ARIZONA TERRITORY 1863
River
Canyon de Chelly
Fort Defiance
Santa Fe
Fort Mohave
MAIL
Los Angeles
LINE
Albuquerque
Glorieta
Colorado
Rio Grande
Fort Craig
Valverde
San Diego
Fort Yuma
Gila
River
Fort Stanton
Tucson
Apache Pass
Fort Fillmore
Fort Bliss
Mesilla
El Paso
TRANS-MISSISSIPPI
1861-1865
MILES
50 0 100 200
Drawn under the supervision of DAN E. CLARK and ALVIN F. HARLOW

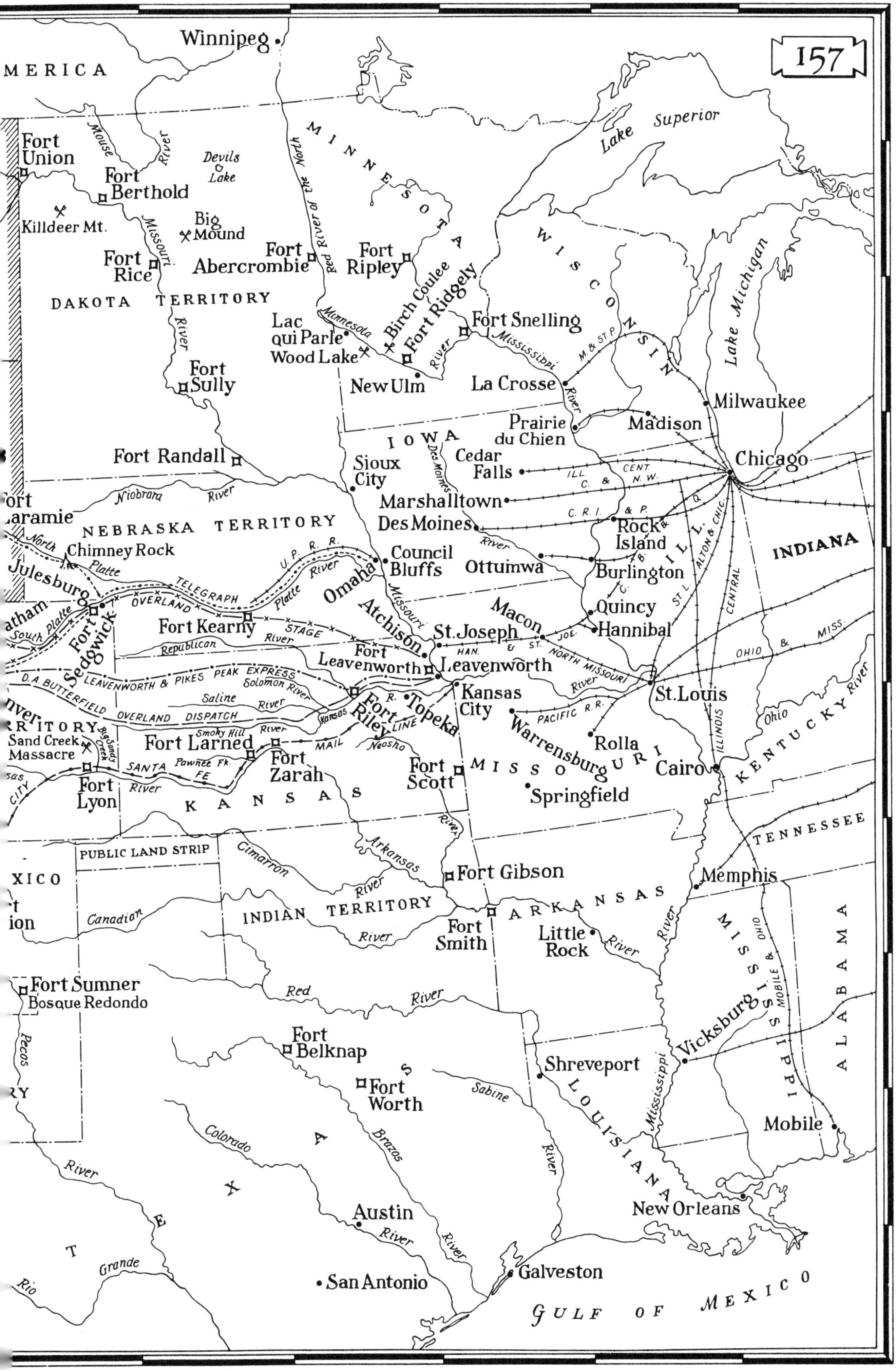

MERICA
Winnipeg
Lake Superior
MINNESOTA
Fort Union
Mouse River
Devils Lake
Red River of the North
Fort Berthold
Killdeer Mt.
Big Mound
Missouri
Fort Abercrombie
Fort Ripley
Fort Rice
WISCONSIN
Lake Michigan
DAKOTA TERRITORY
River
Birch Coulee
Fort Ridgely
Fort Snelling
Lac qui Parle
Minnesota
Wood Lake
River
Mississippi
M. & ST. P.
Fort Sully
New Ulm
La Crosse
Milwaukee
Prairie du Chien
River
Madison
IOWA
Des Moines
Cedar Falls
Chicago
Fort Randall
Sioux City
ILL. CENT.
C. & N. W.
Niobrara River
Fort Laramie
Marshalltown
NEBRASKA TERRITORY
Des Moines
C. R. I. & P.
Rock Island
North Platte
Chimney Rock
U. P. R. R.
Council Bluffs
River
INDIANA
Julesburg
Platte River
Omaha
Ottumwa
C. B. & Q.
Burlington
TELEGRAPH
OVERLAND
Missouri
ILL.
ST. L. ALTON & CHIC.
CENTRAL
South Platte
Fort Sedgwick
Fort Kearny
STAGE
Atchison
Macon
Quincy
Hannibal
St. Joseph
River
HAN. & ST. JOE.
OHIO & MISS.
Republican
Fort Leavenworth
Leavenworth
NORTH MISSOURI
D. A. BUTTERFIELD OVERLAND DISPATCH
LEAVENWORTH & PIKES PEAK EXPRESS
Solomon River
River
St. Louis
Saline River
Kansas City
Kansas R.
Fort Riley
Topeka
PACIFIC R. R.
Ohio
KENTUCKY River
ILLINOIS
RRITORY
Smoky Hill River
Sand Creek Massacre
Big Sandy Creek
Fort Larned
MAIL
LINE
Warrensburg
Rolla
MISSOURI
Neosho
SANTA FE
Pawnee Fk.
Fort Zarah
Fort Scott
Cairo
Springfield
Fort Lyon
River
KANSAS
River
TENNESSEE
PUBLIC LAND STRIP
Cimarron
Arkansas
XICO
Fort Gibson
Memphis
River
INDIAN TERRITORY
ARKANSAS
Canadian
Fort Smith
Little Rock
River
River
River
MISSISSIPPI
MOBILE & OHIO
ALABAMA
Fort Sumner
Bosque Redondo
Red River
Vicksburg
Fort Belknap
Pecos
Fort Worth
Shreveport
Mississippi
Sabine
LOUISIANA
Colorado
Brazos
Mobile
River
TEXAS
River
Austin
New Orleans
River
River
Rio Grande
San Antonio
Galveston
GULF OF MEXICO

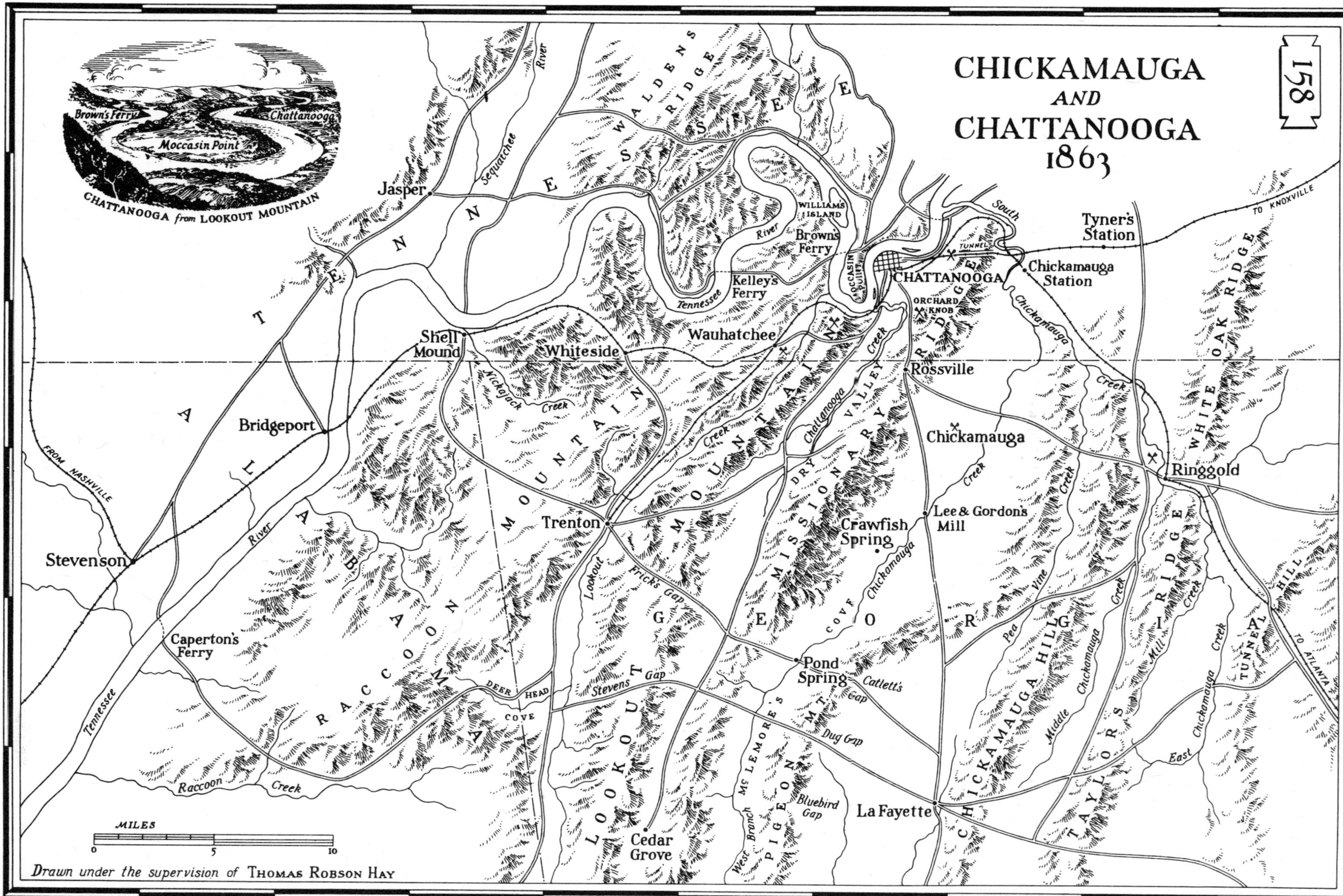
158
CHICKAMAUGA AND CHATTANOOGA 1863
CHATTANOOGA from LOOKOUT MOUNTAIN
Brown's Ferry
Chattanooga
Moccasin Point
TENNESSEE
ALABAMA
GEORGIA
WALDENS RIDGE
RACCOON MOUNTAIN
LOOKOUT MOUNTAIN
MISSIONARY RIDGE
PIGEON MT.
McLEMORE'S COVE
CHICKAMAUGA HILL
TAYLORS RIDGE
WHITE OAK RIDGE
TUNNEL HILL
Jasper
Shell Mound
Whiteside
Wauhatchee
Kelley's Ferry
Browns Ferry
WILLIAMS ISLAND
MOCCASIN POINT
CHATTANOOGA
TUNNEL
ORCHARD KNOB
Chickamauga Station
Tyner's Station
Rossville
Chickamauga
Ringgold
Lee & Gordon's Mill
Crawfish Spring
Bridgeport
Stevenson
Caperton's Ferry
Trenton
Pond Spring
La Fayette
Cedar Grove
Fricks Gap
Stevens Gap
Catlett's Gap
Dug Gap
Bluebird Gap
DEER HEAD COVE
DRY VALLEY
Tennessee River
Sequatchee River
Nickajack Creek
Raccoon Creek
Lookout Creek
Chattanooga Creek
Chickamauga Creek
West Chickamauga
Pea Vine Creek
Middle Chickamauga Creek
Mill Creek
East Chickamauga Creek
West Branch
South
TO KNOXVILLE
TO ATLANTA
FROM NASHVILLE
MILES
0
5
10
Drawn under the supervision of THOMAS ROBSON HAY

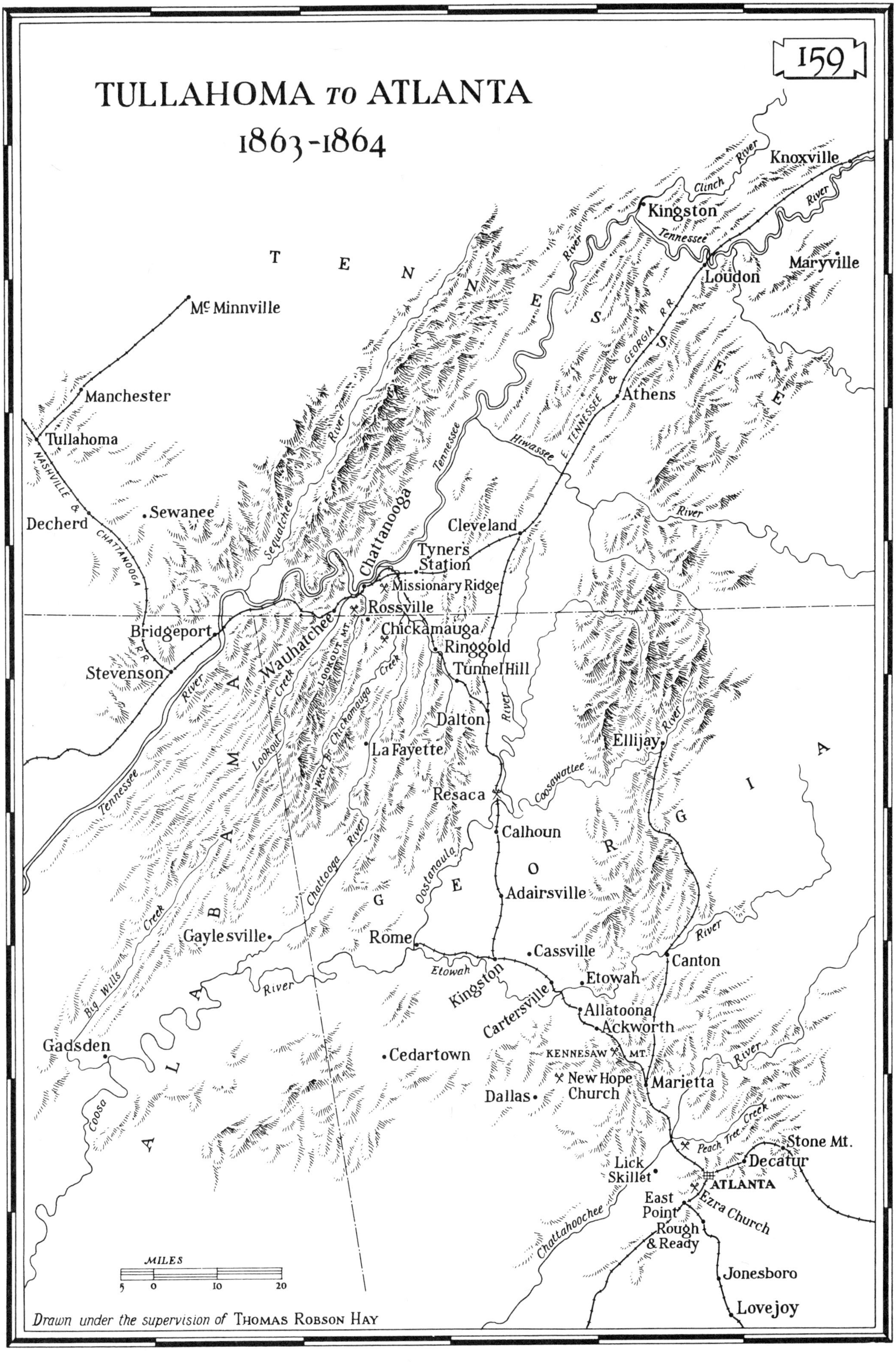
TULLAHOMA TO ATLANTA
1863-1864
T
E
N
N
E
S
S
E
E
Mc Minnville
Manchester
Tullahoma
NASHVILLE & CHATTANOOGA R.R.
Decherd
Sewanee
Bridgeport
Stevenson
Sequatchee River
Tennessee
Chattanooga
Tyners Station
Missionary Ridge
Rossville
Chickamauga
Ringgold
Tunnel Hill
Dalton
Cleveland
Hiwassee
River
Athens
E. TENNESSEE & GEORGIA R.R.
Loudon
Kingston
Clinch River
Knoxville
Maryville
Tennessee
River
Wauhatchee
LOOKOUT MT.
Lookout Creek
West Br. Chickamauga Creek
Chattooga River
La Fayette
Resaca
Coosawattee
Ellijay
Calhoun
Adairsville
Oostanaula
Rome
Etowah River
Kingston
Cassville
Cartersville
Etowah
Allatoona
Ackworth
Canton
KENNESAW MT.
New Hope Church
Marietta
Dallas
Cedartown
Gaylesville
Gadsden
Big Wills Creek
Coosa
Tennessee
River
A
L
A
B
A
M
A
G
E
O
R
G
I
A
Peach Tree Creek
Stone Mt.
Decatur
ATLANTA
Lick Skillet
East Point
Ezra Church
Rough & Ready
Chattahoochee
Jonesboro
Lovejoy
MILES
5 0 10 20
Drawn under the supervision of THOMAS ROBSON HAY

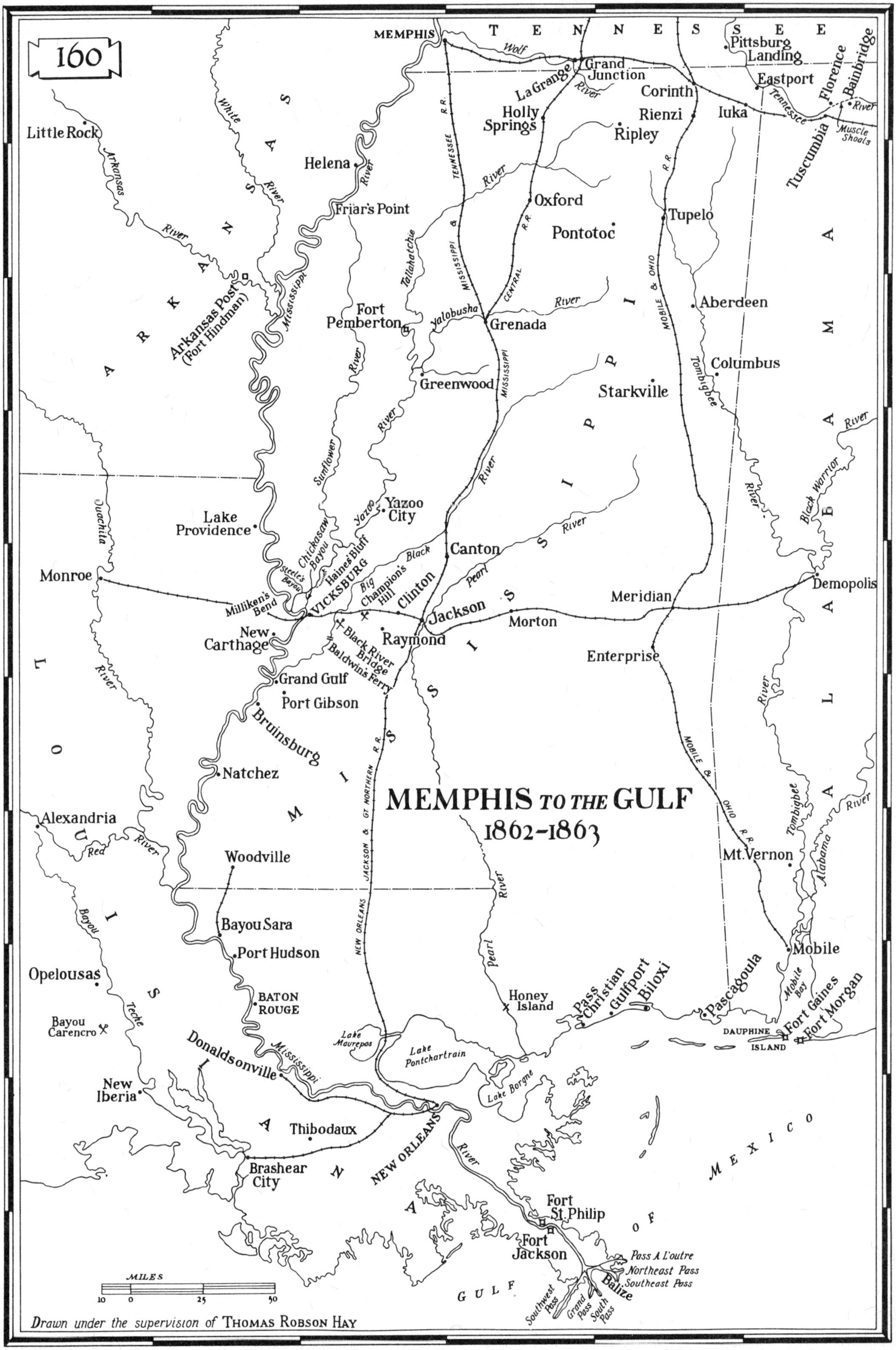
160
MEMPHIS TO THE GULF
1862-1863
TENNESSEE
ARKANSAS
MISSISSIPPI
LOUISIANA
ALABAMA
GULF OF MEXICO
Memphis
Wolf
Grand Junction
La Grange
River
Pittsburg Landing
Eastport
Corinth
Florence
Bainbridge
Tennessee
River
Muscle Shoals
Tuscumbia
Iuka
Rienzi
Ripley
Holly Springs
Little Rock
Arkansas
River
White
River
Helena
Friar's Point
Oxford
Pontotoc
Tupelo
Tallahatchie
River
Mississippi
Arkansas Post (Fort Hindman)
Fort Pemberton
Yalobusha
Grenada
River
Aberdeen
Columbus
Tombigbee
Starkville
Greenwood
Sunflower
River
Yazoo City
Yazoo
Lake Providence
Ouachita
Chickasaw Bayou
Haine's Bluff
Steele's Bayou
Canton
Black
Big Black River Bridge
Champion's Hill
Clinton
Pearl
River
Monroe
Milliken's Bend
VICKSBURG
Jackson
Meridian
Demopolis
Morton
New Carthage
Raymond
Baldwin's Ferry
Enterprise
Black Warrior
River
Grand Gulf
Port Gibson
Bruinsburg
Natchez
Alexandria
Red
River
Woodville
Mt. Vernon
Alabama
Bayou Sara
Port Hudson
Opelousas
Bayou Teche
Bayou Carencro
BATON ROUGE
Honey Island
Pass Christian
Gulfport
Biloxi
Pascagoula
Mobile
Mobile Bay
Fort Gaines
Fort Morgan
DAUPHINE ISLAND
Donaldsonville
Lake Maurepas
Lake Pontchartrain
Lake Borgne
New Iberia
Thibodaux
NEW ORLEANS
Brashear City
Fort St. Philip
Fort Jackson
Pass A L'outre
Northeast Pass
Southeast Pass
Balize
Southwest Pass
Grand Pass
South Pass
TENNESSEE R.R.
MISSISSIPPI & TENNESSEE R.R.
MISSISSIPPI CENTRAL R.R.
MOBILE & OHIO R.R.
NEW ORLEANS JACKSON & GT. NORTHERN R.R.
MILES
10 0 25 50
Drawn under the supervision of THOMAS ROBSON HAY

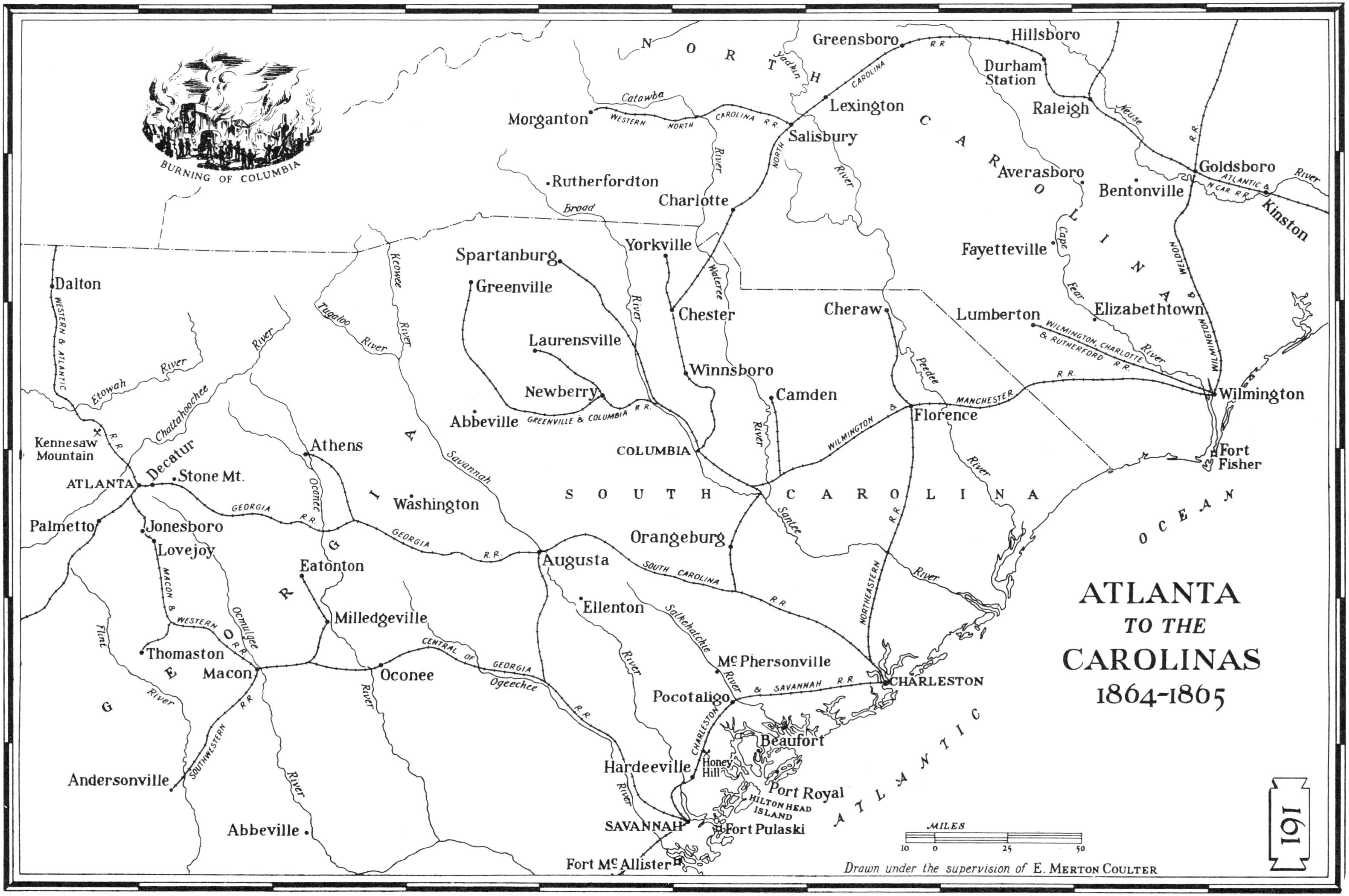
ATLANTA
TO THE
CAROLINAS
1864-1865
161
BURNING OF COLUMBIA
NORTH CAROLINA
SOUTH CAROLINA
GEORGIA
ATLANTIC OCEAN
Greensboro
Hillsboro
Durham Station
Raleigh
Lexington
Salisbury
Morganton
Rutherfordton
Charlotte
Averasboro
Bentonville
Goldsboro
Kinston
Fayetteville
Elizabethtown
Lumberton
Wilmington
Fort Fisher
Yorkville
Spartanburg
Greenville
Chester
Winnsboro
Laurensville
Newberry
Abbeville
Cheraw
Camden
Florence
COLUMBIA
Orangeburg
Dalton
Kennesaw Mountain
ATLANTA
Decatur
Stone Mt.
Palmetto
Jonesboro
Lovejoy
Athens
Washington
Augusta
Eatonton
Milledgeville
Thomaston
Macon
Oconee
Ellenton
McPhersonville
Pocotaligo
CHARLESTON
Beaufort
Honey Hill
Hardeeville
Port Royal
HILTON HEAD ISLAND
SAVANNAH
Fort Pulaski
Fort McAllister
Andersonville
Abbeville
WESTERN & ATLANTIC
WESTERN NORTH CAROLINA R.R.
NORTH CAROLINA R.R.
ATLANTIC & N. CAR. R.R.
WILMINGTON & WELDON R.R.
WILMINGTON, CHARLOTTE & RUTHERFORD R.R.
WILMINGTON & MANCHESTER R.R.
GREENVILLE & COLUMBIA R.R.
GEORGIA R.R.
SOUTH CAROLINA R.R.
NORTHEASTERN R.R.
CHARLESTON & SAVANNAH R.R.
CENTRAL OF GEORGIA R.R.
MACON & WESTERN R.R.
SOUTHWESTERN R.R.
Yadkin River
Neuse River
Catawba River
Broad River
Cape Fear River
Wateree River
Peedee River
Santee River
Keowee River
Tugaloo River
Savannah River
Salkehatchie River
Etowah River
Chattahoochee River
Oconee River
Ocmulgee River
Ogeechee River
Flint River
MILES
10 0 25 50
Drawn under the supervision of E. Merton Coulter

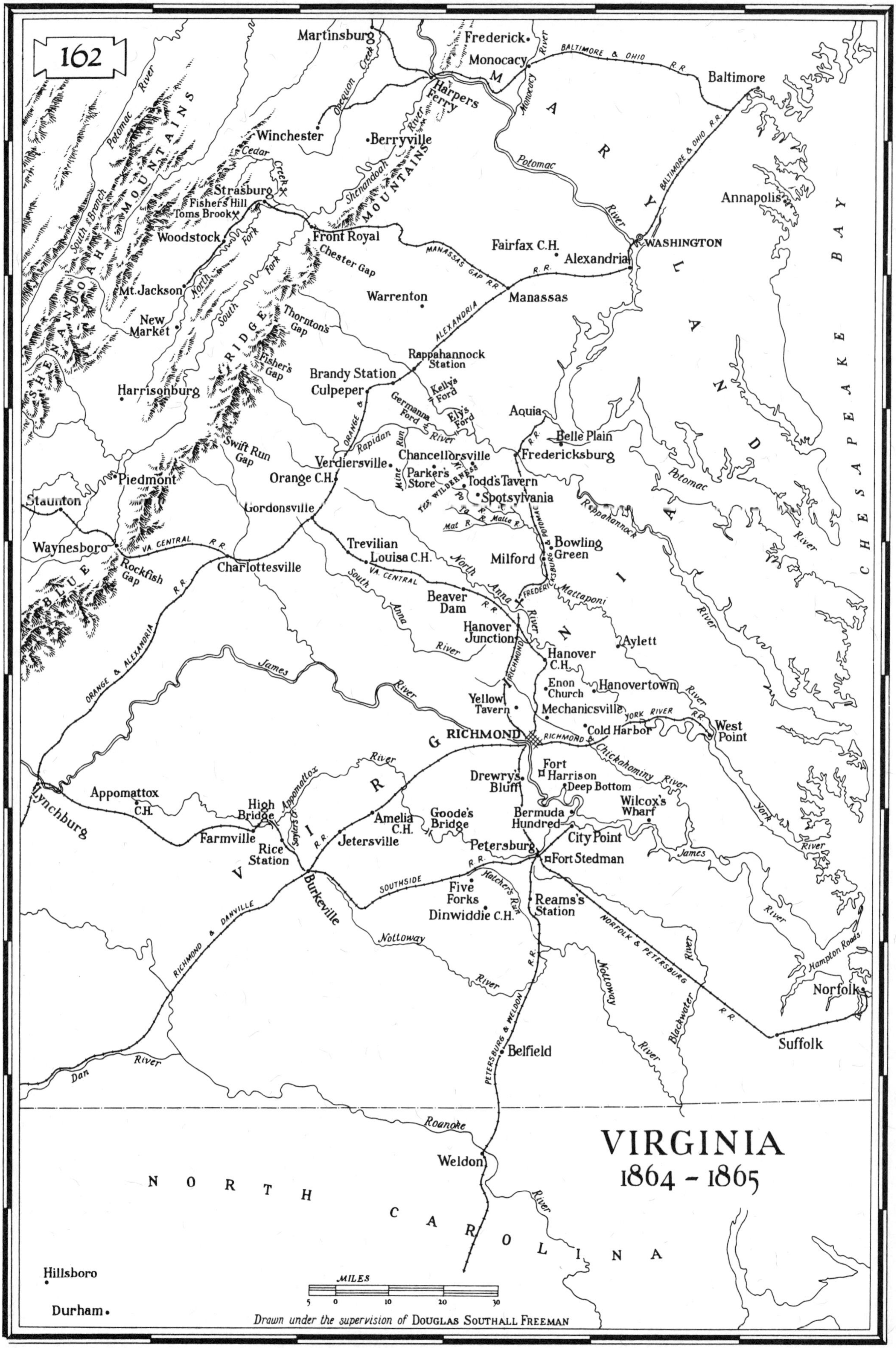
162
Martinsburg
Frederick
Monocacy
Baltimore
Harpers Ferry
Winchester
Berryville
Strasburg
Fishers Hill
Toms Brook
Cedar Creek
Woodstock
Front Royal
Chester Gap
Mt. Jackson
New Market
Thornton's Gap
Fisher's Gap
Harrisonburg
Swift Run Gap
Piedmont
Staunton
Waynesboro
Rockfish Gap
Charlottesville
Gordonsville
Orange C.H.
Verdiersville
Chancellorsville
Parker's Store
The Wilderness
Todd's Tavern
Spotsylvania
Fredericksburg
Belle Plain
Aquia
Annapolis
WASHINGTON
Alexandria
Fairfax C.H.
Manassas
Warrenton
Rappahannock Station
Kelly's Ford
Ely's Ford
Germanna Ford
Brandy Station
Culpeper
Trevilian
Louisa C.H.
Beaver Dam
Milford
Bowling Green
Hanover Junction
Hanover C.H.
Aylett
Enon Church
Hanovertown
Yellow Tavern
Mechanicsville
Cold Harbor
West Point
RICHMOND
Fort Harrison
Drewry's Bluff
Deep Bottom
Bermuda Hundred
Wilcox's Wharf
City Point
Petersburg
Fort Stedman
Five Forks
Dinwiddie C.H.
Reams's Station
Goode's Bridge
Amelia C.H.
Jetersville
High Bridge
Rice Station
Farmville
Burkeville
Appomattox C.H.
Lynchburg
Belfield
Suffolk
Norfolk
Hampton Roads
Weldon
Hillsboro
Durham
MARYLAND
VIRGINIA
NORTH CAROLINA
CHESAPEAKE BAY
SHENANDOAH MOUNTAINS
BLUE RIDGE MOUNTAINS
Potomac River
James River
York River
Rappahannock River
Mattaponi
North Anna River
South Anna River
Appomattox River
Nottoway River
Blackwater River
Chickahominy River
Roanoke River
Dan River
Rapidan River
BALTIMORE & OHIO R.R.
MANASSAS GAP R.R.
ORANGE & ALEXANDRIA R.R.
VA. CENTRAL R.R.
RICHMOND & DANVILLE
SOUTHSIDE R.R.
PETERSBURG & WELDON R.R.
NORFOLK & PETERSBURG R.R.
RICHMOND & YORK RIVER R.R.
MILES
5 0 10 20 30
VIRGINIA
1864 - 1865
Drawn under the supervision of DOUGLAS SOUTHALL FREEMAN

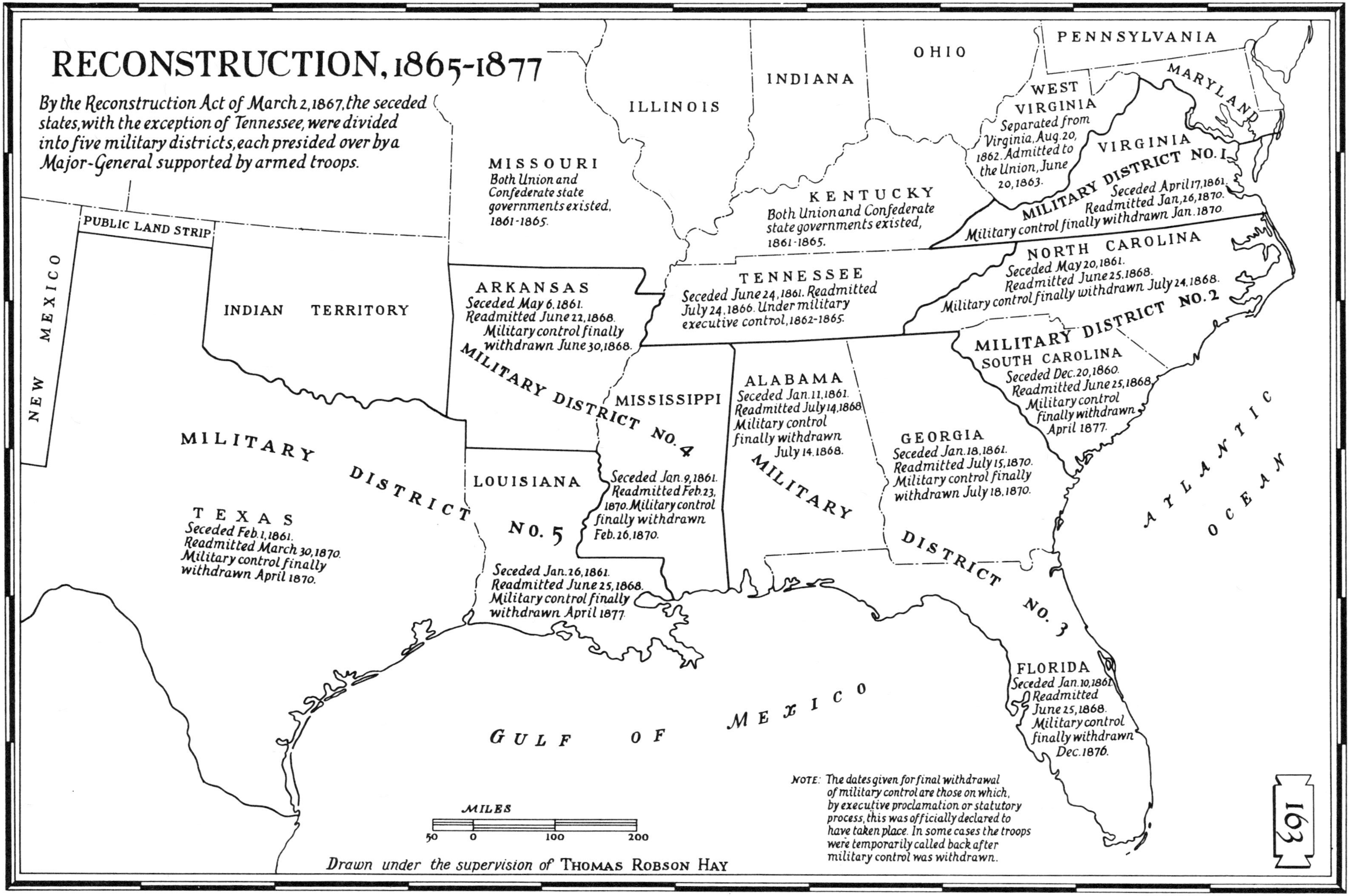
RECONSTRUCTION, 1865-1877
By the Reconstruction Act of March 2, 1867, the seceded states, with the exception of Tennessee, were divided into five military districts, each presided over by a Major-General supported by armed troops.
PENNSYLVANIA
OHIO
INDIANA
ILLINOIS
MARYLAND
WEST VIRGINIA
Separated from Virginia, Aug. 20, 1862. Admitted to the Union, June 20, 1863.
VIRGINIA
MILITARY DISTRICT NO. 1
Seceded April 17, 1861. Readmitted Jan. 26, 1870. Military control finally withdrawn Jan. 1870.
MISSOURI
Both Union and Confederate state governments existed, 1861-1865.
KENTUCKY
Both Union and Confederate state governments existed, 1861-1865.
NORTH CAROLINA
Seceded May 20, 1861. Readmitted June 25, 1868. Military control finally withdrawn July 24, 1868.
MILITARY DISTRICT NO. 2
SOUTH CAROLINA
Seceded Dec. 20, 1860. Readmitted June 25, 1868. Military control finally withdrawn April 1877.
TENNESSEE
Seceded June 24, 1861. Readmitted July 24, 1866. Under military executive control, 1862-1865.
NEW MEXICO
PUBLIC LAND STRIP
INDIAN TERRITORY
ARKANSAS
Seceded May 6, 1861. Readmitted June 22, 1868. Military control finally withdrawn June 30, 1868.
MILITARY DISTRICT NO. 4
MISSISSIPPI
Seceded Jan. 9, 1861. Readmitted Feb. 23, 1870. Military control finally withdrawn Feb. 26, 1870.
ALABAMA
Seceded Jan. 11, 1861. Readmitted July 14, 1868. Military control finally withdrawn July 14, 1868.
GEORGIA
Seceded Jan. 18, 1861. Readmitted July 15, 1870. Military control finally withdrawn July 18, 1870.
MILITARY DISTRICT NO. 3
ATLANTIC OCEAN
MILITARY DISTRICT NO. 5
TEXAS
Seceded Feb. 1, 1861. Readmitted March 30, 1870. Military control finally withdrawn April 1870.
LOUISIANA
Seceded Jan. 26, 1861. Readmitted June 25, 1868. Military control finally withdrawn April 1877.
FLORIDA
Seceded Jan. 10, 1861. Readmitted June 25, 1868. Military control finally withdrawn Dec. 1876.
GULF OF MEXICO
MILES
50 0 100 200
NOTE: The dates given for final withdrawal of military control are those on which, by executive proclamation or statutory process, this was officially declared to have taken place. In some cases the troops were temporarily called back after military control was withdrawn.
Drawn under the supervision of THOMAS ROBSON HAY

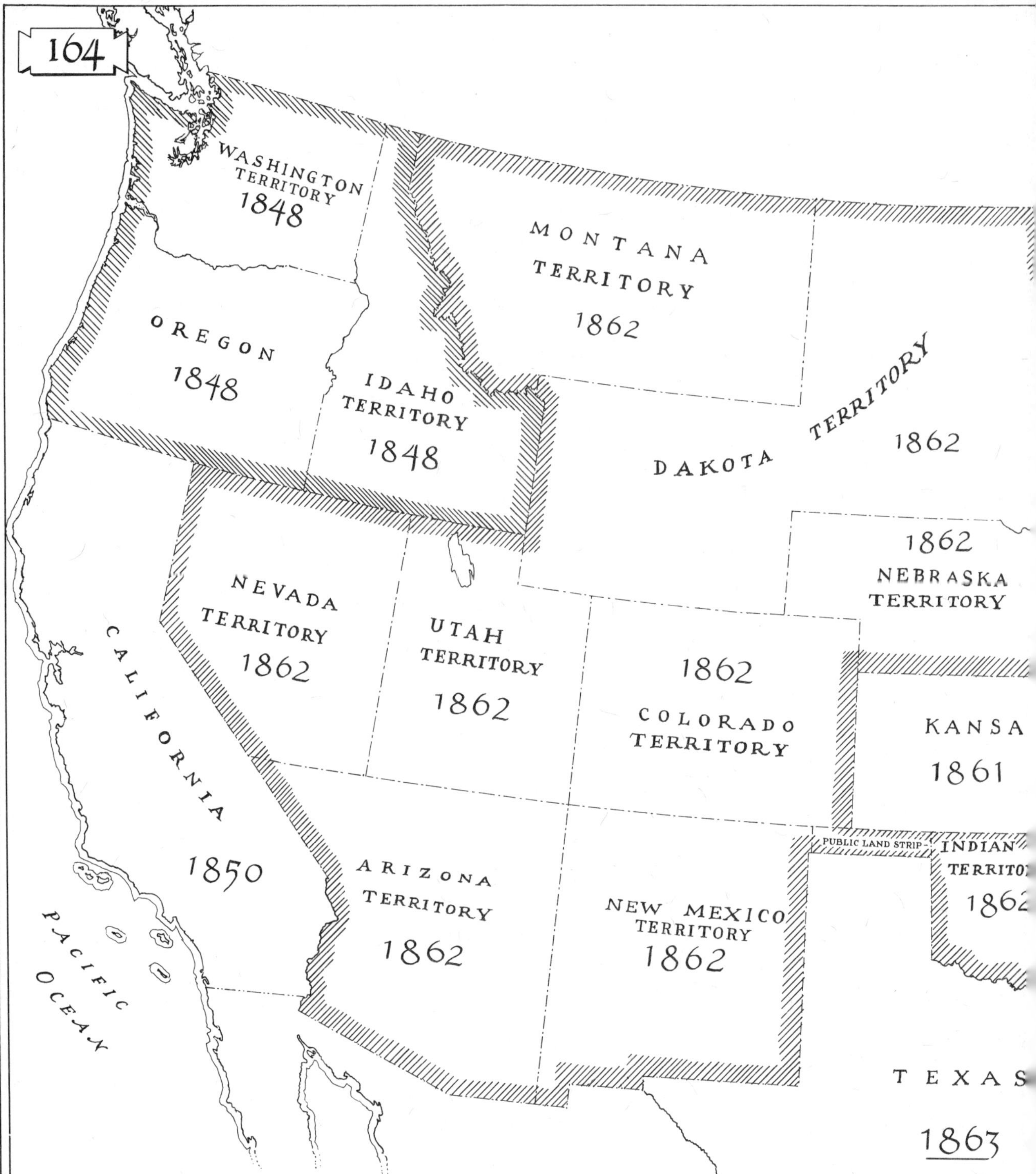

Dates in each state show when slavery was abolished. In states with two dates, abolition was gradual, beginning at the time of the first date and being completed at the time of the second.

Slavery was abolished in all the territories and the District of Columbia in 1862. During the Civil War, Missouri, Tennessee, West Virginia, Maryland and the area of Louisiana occupied by the Union army before 1863 began to emancipate slaves. Lincoln's Emancipation Proclamation freed the slaves in Confederate-held territory in 1863, but freedom didn't actually take effect until Union troops controlled these areas. The Thirteenth Amendment, adopted in 1865, finally abolished slavery throughout the United States.

THE ABOLITION OF SLAVERY 1777~1865

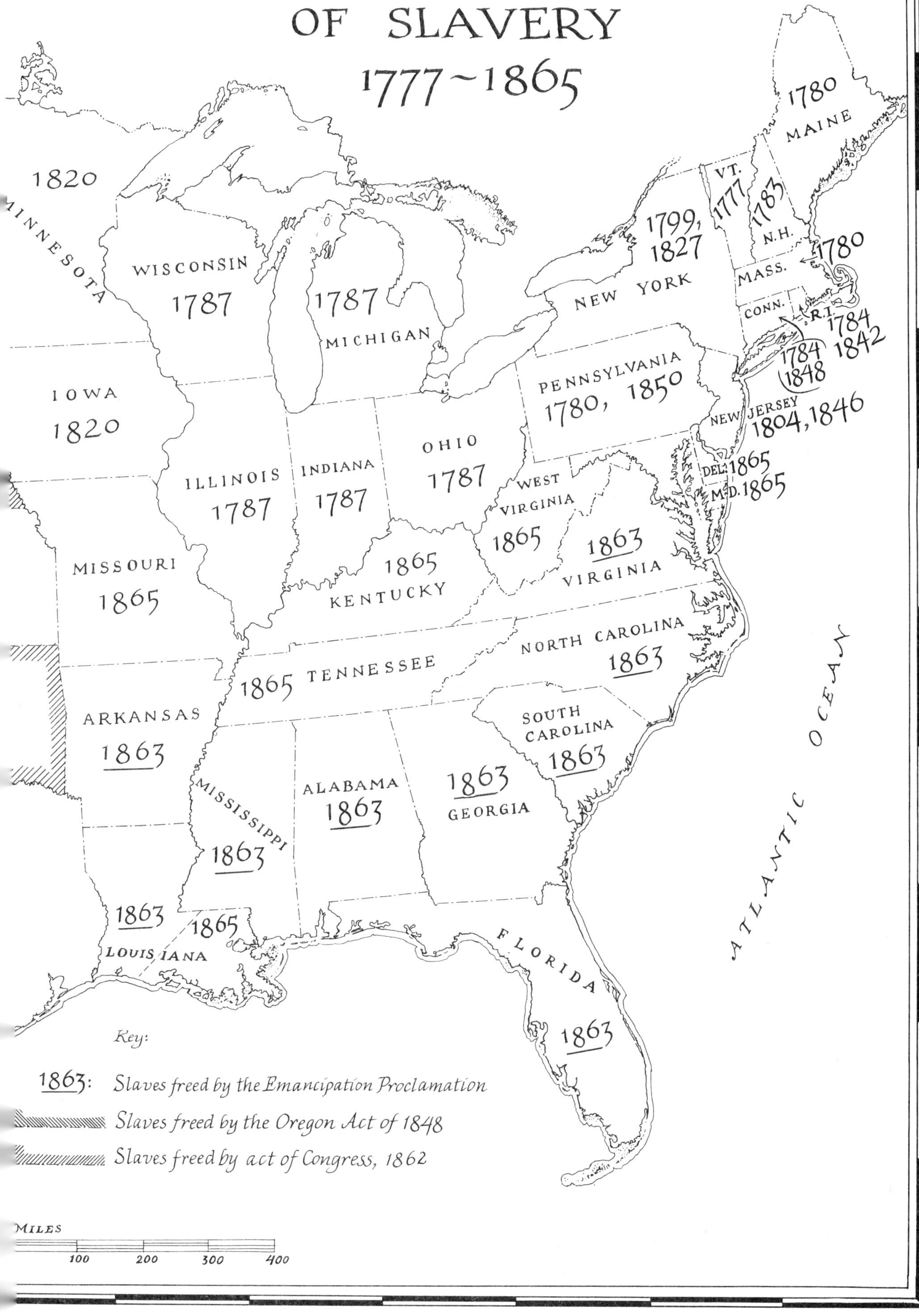

VIII THE END OF THE FRONTIER

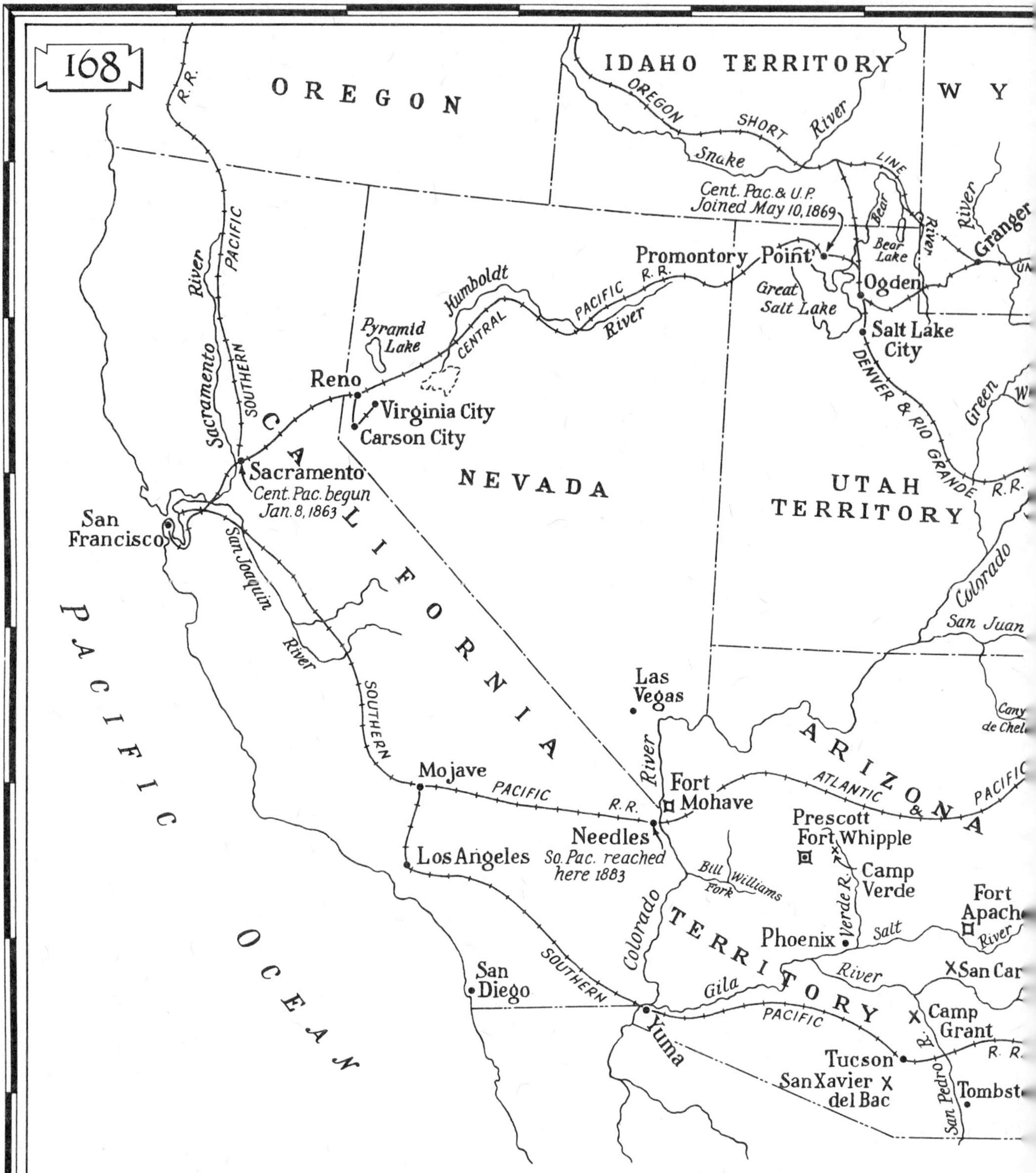

COW COUNTRY, RAILROADS *AND* INDIAN TROUBLES 1865-1885

Drawn under the supervision of ALVIN F. HARLOW *and* CARL COKE RISTER

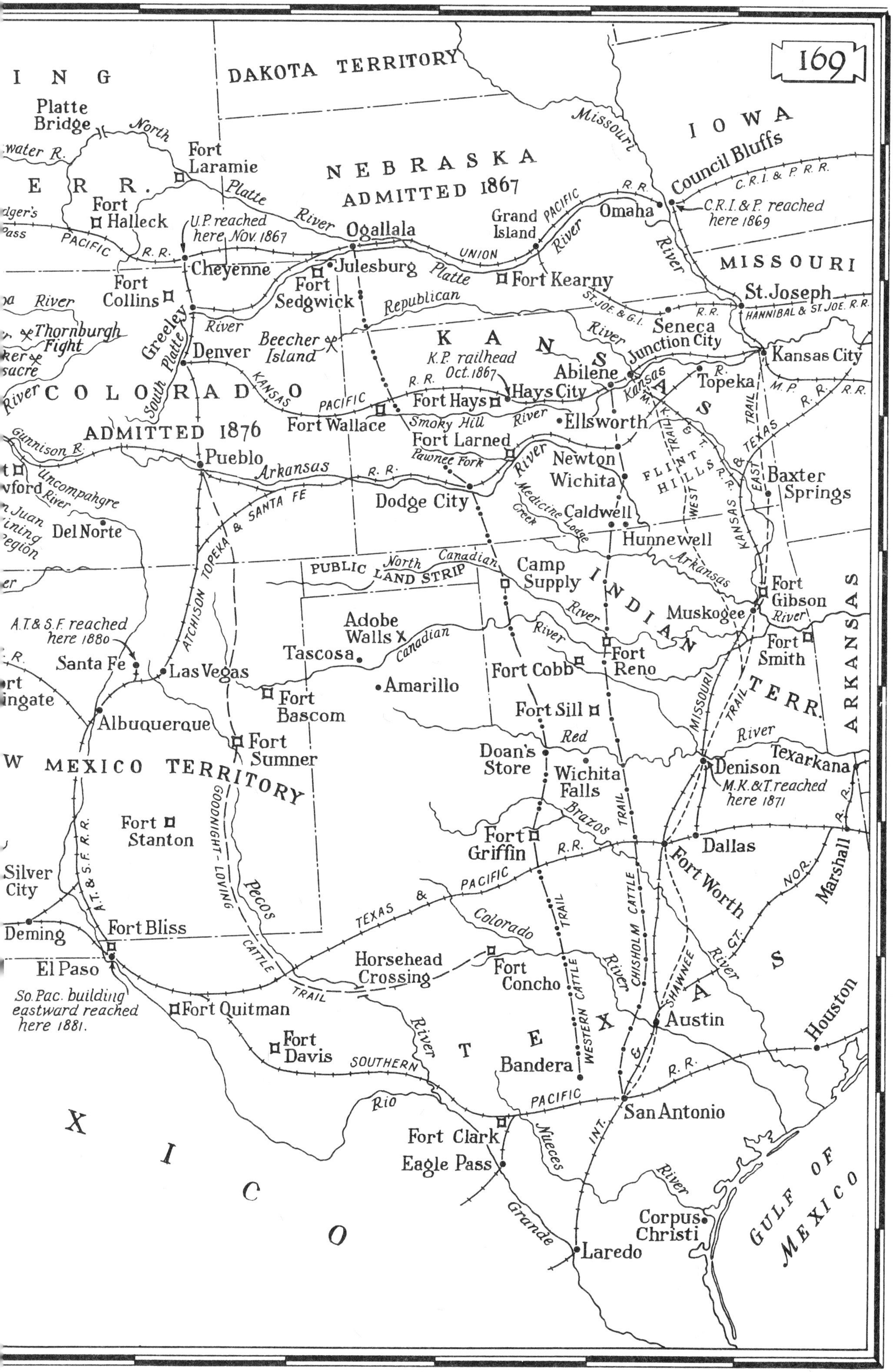
DAKOTA TERRITORY
I N G
Platte Bridge
North
water R.
Fort Laramie
E R R.
Fort Halleck
dger's Pass
PACIFIC R. R.
U.P. reached here Nov. 1867
Cheyenne
Fort Collins
River
Thornburgh Fight
Greeley
South Platte
River
Denver
COLORADO
ADMITTED 1876
Gunnison R.
Uncompahgre River
Del Norte
San Juan Mining Region
Pueblo
Arkansas
NEBRASKA
ADMITTED 1867
Platte River
Ogallala
Julesburg
Fort Sedgwick
Beecher Island
Grand Island
UNION PACIFIC R.R.
Platte
River
Fort Kearny
Omaha
Missouri
River
IOWA
Council Bluffs
C.R.I. & P. R.R.
C.R.I. & P. reached here 1869
MISSOURI
St. Joseph
HANNIBAL & ST. JOE. R.R.
ST. JOE & G.I. R.R.
Seneca
Republican
River
KANSAS
K.P. railhead Oct. 1867
KANSAS PACIFIC R.R.
Fort Wallace
Fort Hays
Hays City
Smoky Hill River
Abilene
Junction City
Kansas
Topeka
Kansas City
M.P. R.R.
Ellsworth
Fort Larned
Pawnee Fork
River
Dodge City
Newton
Wichita
FLINT HILLS
Caldwell
Medicine Lodge Creek
Hunnewell
M.K. & T. R.R.
WEST SHAWNEE TRAIL
KANSAS & TEXAS R.R.
EAST TRAIL
Baxter Springs
ATCHISON TOPEKA & SANTA FE
PUBLIC LAND STRIP
North Canadian
Camp Supply
River
INDIAN TERR.
Arkansas
Fort Gibson
Muskogee
River
Fort Smith
ARKANSAS
A.T. & S.F. reached here 1880
Santa Fe
Las Vegas
Albuquerque
Adobe Walls
Tascosa
Canadian
Amarillo
River
Fort Cobb
Fort Reno
Fort Bascom
Fort Sill
Red
River
MISSOURI TRAIL
Fort Sumner
W MEXICO TERRITORY
Doan's Store
Wichita Falls
Denison
Texarkana
M.K. & T. reached here 1871
Fort Stanton
GOODNIGHT-LOVING CATTLE TRAIL
Pecos
Fort Griffin
Brazos
TRAIL
Dallas
Fort Worth
R.R.
Marshall
INT. & GT. NOR. R.R.
Silver City
A.T. & S.F. R.R.
Deming
Fort Bliss
El Paso
So. Pac. building eastward reached here 1881.
TEXAS & PACIFIC R.R.
Colorado
River
Horsehead Crossing
Fort Concho
WESTERN CATTLE TRAIL
CHISHOLM CATTLE TRAIL
SHAWNEE
River
TEXAS
Austin
Houston
Fort Quitman
Fort Davis
SOUTHERN PACIFIC R.R.
River
Bandera
San Antonio
Rio
Fort Clark
Eagle Pass
Nueces
River
Grande
Laredo
Corpus Christi
GULF OF MEXICO
MEXICO

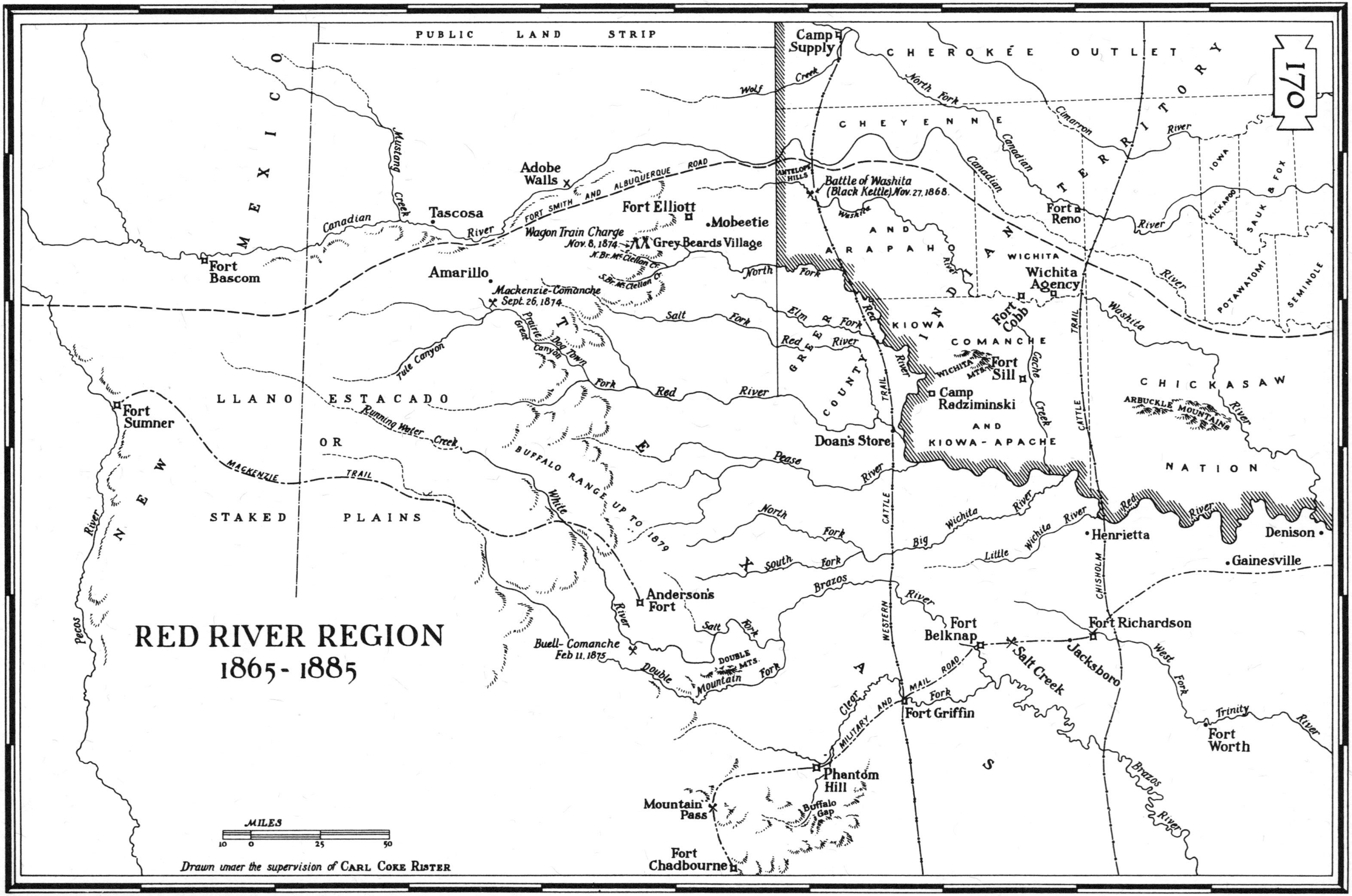
170
RED RIVER REGION
1865-1885
PUBLIC LAND STRIP
CHEROKEE OUTLET
INDIAN TERRITORY
NEW MEXICO
TEXAS
CHEYENNE
AND
ARAPAHO
WICHITA
KIOWA
COMANCHE
AND
KIOWA-APACHE
CHICKASAW
NATION
IOWA
KICKAPOO
SAUK & FOX
POTAWATOMI
SEMINOLE
GREER COUNTY
LLANO ESTACADO
OR
STAKED PLAINS
Camp Supply
Fort Reno
Wichita Agency
Fort Cobb
Fort Sill
Camp Radziminski
Battle of Washita (Black Kettle) Nov. 27, 1868.
ANTELOPE HILLS
Adobe Walls
Tascosa
Fort Elliott
Mobeetie
Wagon Train Charge Nov. 8, 1874.
Grey Beards Village
N. Br. McClellan Cr.
S. Br. McClellan Cr.
Amarillo
Mackenzie-Comanche Sept. 26, 1874.
Fort Bascom
Fort Sumner
Doan's Store
Henrietta
Denison
Gainesville
Fort Richardson
Fort Belknap
Salt Creek
Jacksboro
Fort Griffin
Fort Worth
Phantom Hill
Buffalo Gap
Mountain Pass
Fort Chadbourne
Anderson's Fort
Buell-Comanche Feb 11, 1875
DOUBLE MTS.
BUFFALO RANGE UP TO 1879
FORT SMITH AND ALBUQUERQUE ROAD
MACKENZIE TRAIL
WESTERN CATTLE TRAIL
CHISHOLM CATTLE TRAIL
MILITARY AND MAIL ROAD
ARBUCKLE MOUNTAINS
WICHITA MTS.
Canadian River
Mustang Creek
Wolf Creek
North Fork
Cimarron River
Washita River
North Fork
Red River
Elm Fork
Salt Fork
Tule Canyon
Prairie Dog Town Fork
Great Canyon
Running Water Creek
Pease River
White River
North Fork
South Fork
Big Wichita River
Little Wichita River
Brazos River
Salt Fork
Double Mountain Fork
Clear Fork
Cache Creek
West Fork
Trinity River
Pecos River
MILES
10 0 25 50
Drawn under the supervision of CARL COKE RISTER

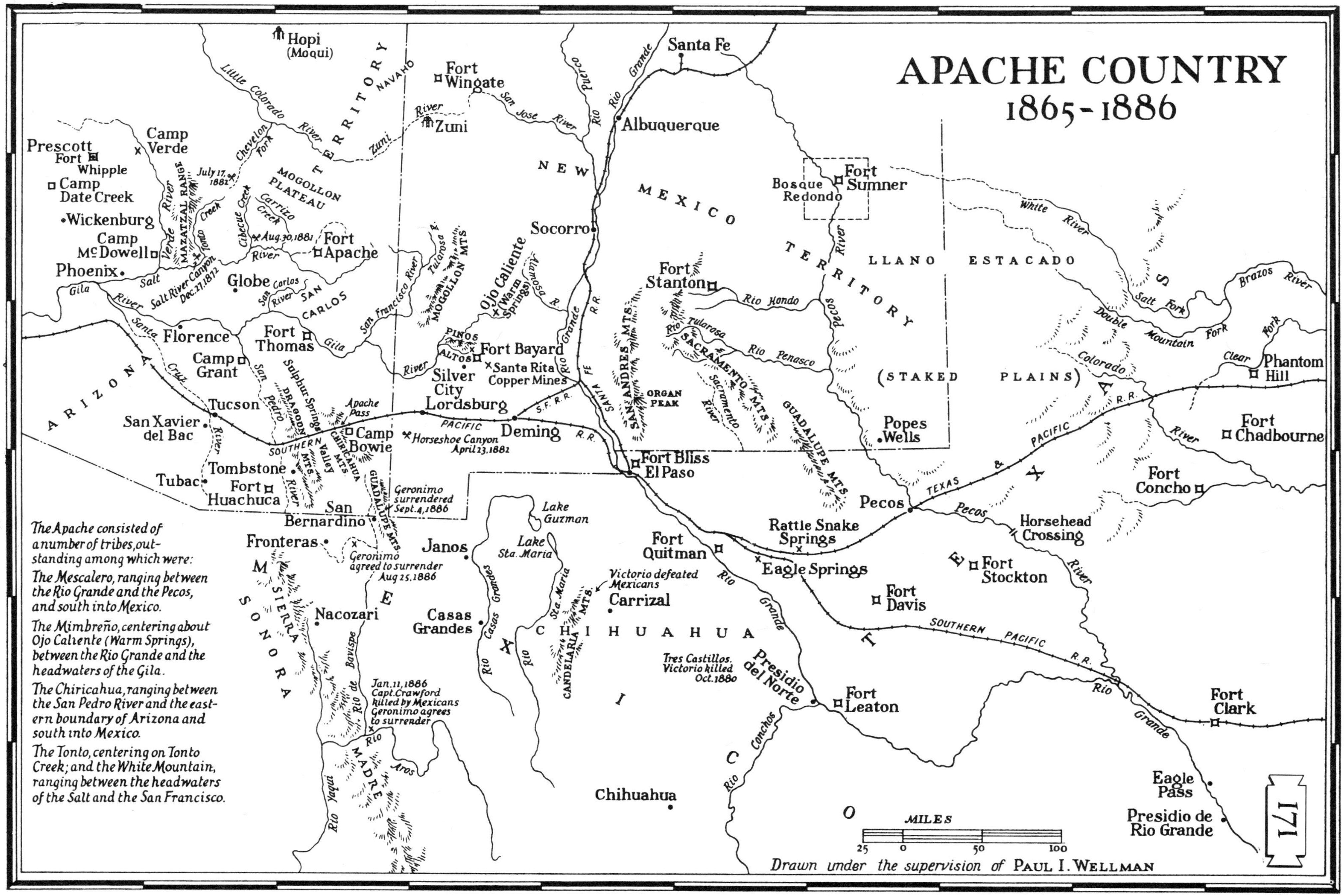
APACHE COUNTRY
1865-1886
171
The Apache consisted of a number of tribes, outstanding among which were:
The Mescalero, ranging between the Rio Grande and the Pecos, and south into Mexico.
The Mimbreño, centering about Ojo Caliente (Warm Springs), between the Rio Grande and the headwaters of the Gila.
The Chiricahua, ranging between the San Pedro River and the eastern boundary of Arizona and south into Mexico.
The Tonto, centering on Tonto Creek; and the White Mountain, ranging between the headwaters of the Salt and the San Francisco.
Drawn under the supervision of PAUL I. WELLMAN
MILES
25
0
50
100
ARIZONA
NAVAHO TERRITORY
NEW MEXICO TERRITORY
TEXAS
MEXICO
SONORA
CHIHUAHUA
LLANO ESTACADO
(STAKED PLAINS)
Hopi (Moqui)
Fort Wingate
Zuni
Santa Fe
Albuquerque
Prescott
Fort Whipple
Camp Verde
Camp Date Creek
Wickenburg
Camp McDowell
Phoenix
Florence
Camp Grant
Tucson
San Xavier del Bac
Tubac
Tombstone
Fort Huachuca
San Bernardino
Fronteras
Nacozari
Globe
Fort Apache
Fort Thomas
Camp Bowie
Apache Pass
Sulphur Springs Valley
Silver City
Lordsburg
Deming
Fort Bayard
Santa Rita Copper Mines
Ojo Caliente (Warm Springs)
Socorro
Fort Stanton
Fort Sumner
Bosque Redondo
Popes Wells
Fort Bliss
El Paso
Fort Quitman
Rattle Snake Springs
Eagle Springs
Pecos
Horsehead Crossing
Fort Stockton
Fort Davis
Fort Leaton
Presidio del Norte
Fort Concho
Fort Chadbourne
Phantom Hill
Fort Clark
Eagle Pass
Presidio de Rio Grande
Janos
Casas Grandes
Carrizal
Chihuahua
Lake Guzman
Lake Sta. Maria
MOGOLLON PLATEAU
MOGOLLON MTS
MAZATZAL RANGE
SAN CARLOS
DRAGOON MTS.
CHIRICAHUA MTS.
GUADALUPE MTS
SAN ANDRES MTS.
ORGAN PEAK
SACRAMENTO MTS.
CANDELARIA MTS.
SIERRA MADRE
PINOS ALTOS
Little Colorado River
Chevelon Fork
Cibecue Creek
Carrizo Creek
Tonto Creek
Verde River
Salt River
Salt River Canyon Dec. 27, 1872
July 17, 1881
Aug. 30, 1881
Gila River
San Carlos River
San Francisco River
Tularosa R.
Alamosa R.
San Jose River
Zuni River
Rio Puerco
Rio Grande
Rio Hondo
Rio Penasco
Rio Tularosa
Sacramento River
Pecos River
White River
Salt Fork
Double Mountain Fork
Brazos River
Clear Fork
Colorado River
Santa Cruz
San Pedro River
Rio de Bavispe
Rio Yaqui
Rio Aros
Rio Casas Grandes
Rio Sta. Maria
Rio Conchos
Horseshoe Canyon April 23, 1882
Geronimo surrendered Sept. 4, 1886
Geronimo agreed to surrender Aug 25, 1886
Jan. 11, 1886 Capt. Crawford killed by Mexicans Geronimo agrees to surrender
Victorio defeated Mexicans
Tres Castillos. Victorio killed Oct. 1880
SOUTHERN PACIFIC R.R.
SANTA FE R.R.
S.F.R.R.
TEXAS & PACIFIC R.R.

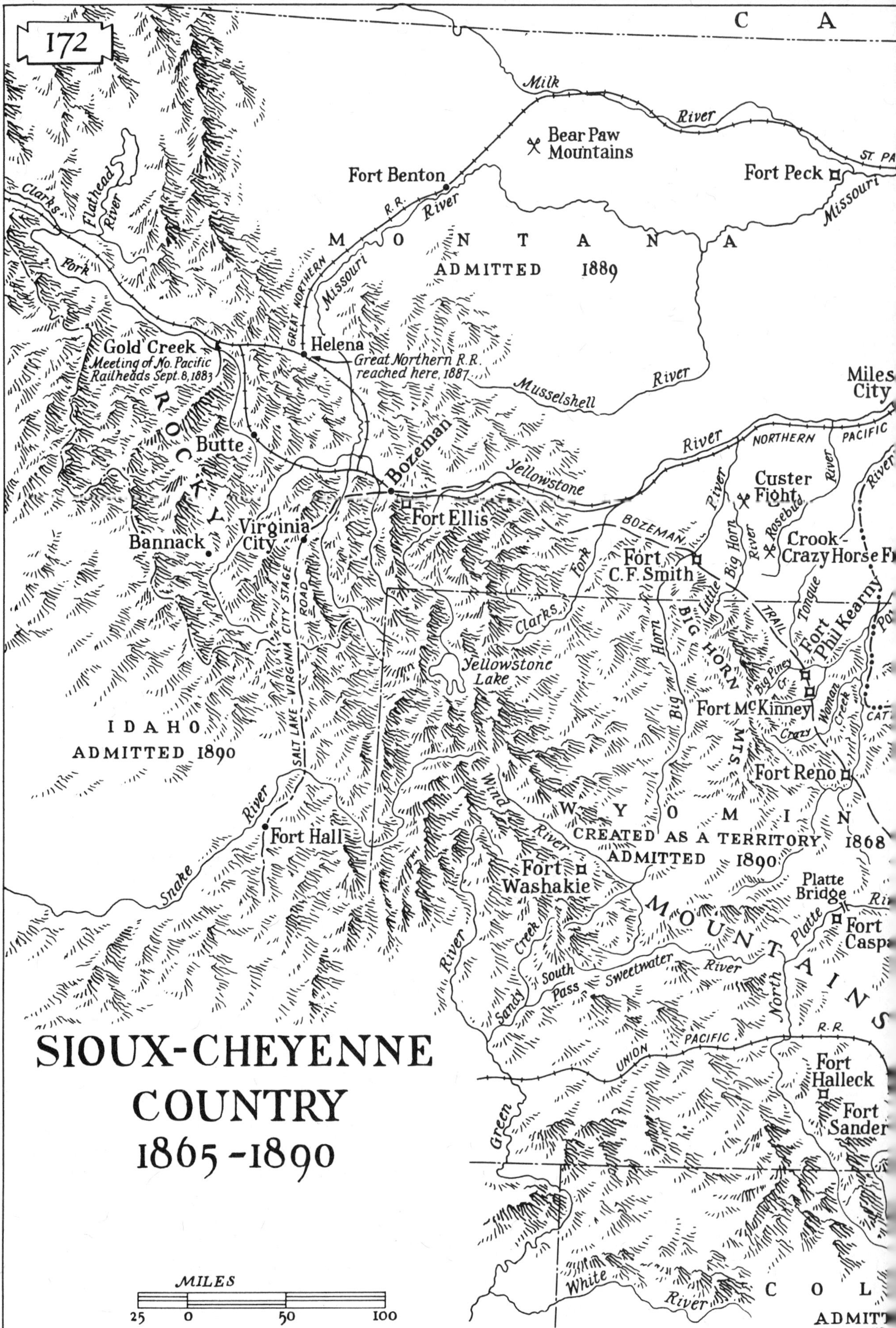

SIOUX-CHEYENNE COUNTRY 1865-1890

Drawn under the supervision of ALVIN F. HARLOW *and* PAUL I. WELLMAN

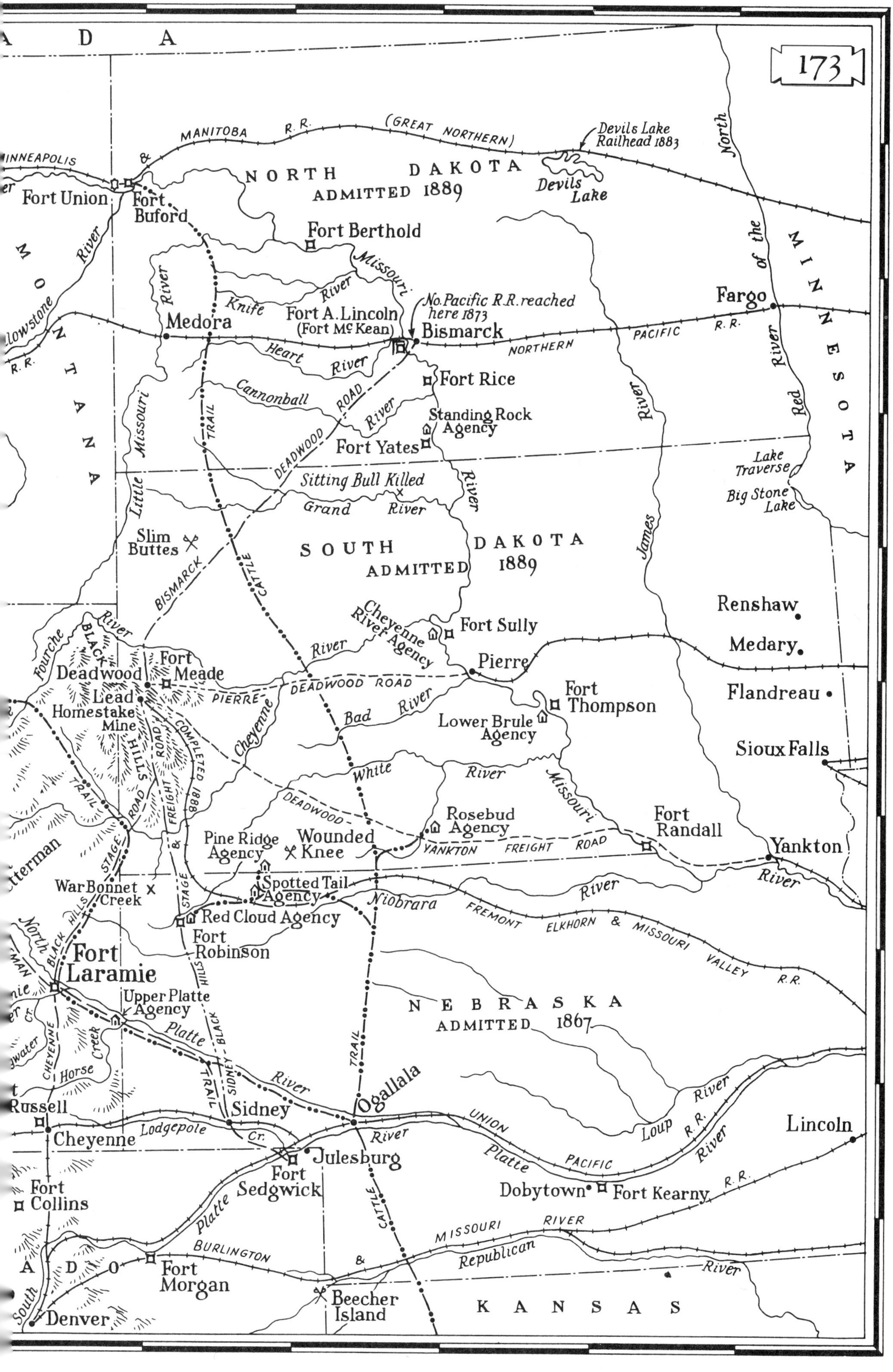

CANADA
MANITOBA R.R. (GREAT NORTHERN)
Devils Lake Railhead 1883
MINNEAPOLIS &
NORTH DAKOTA
ADMITTED 1889
Devils Lake
Fort Union
Fort Buford
Fort Berthold
MONTANA
Yellowstone River
Missouri
Knife River
Fort A. Lincoln (Fort McKean)
No. Pacific R.R. reached here 1873
Bismarck
Medora
Heart River
NORTHERN PACIFIC R.R.
Fargo
Red River of the North
MINNESOTA
Fort Rice
Cannonball River
Standing Rock Agency
Fort Yates
DEADWOOD ROAD
TRAIL
Little Missouri River
River
Lake Traverse
Big Stone Lake
Sitting Bull Killed
Grand River
Slim Buttes
SOUTH DAKOTA
ADMITTED 1889
James River
CATTLE
BISMARCK
Renshaw
Medary
Cheyenne River Agency
Fort Sully
Fourche
BLACK
Deadwood
Fort Meade
Pierre
Flandreau
PIERRE DEADWOOD ROAD
Lead
Homestake Mine
Fort Thompson
Bad River
Lower Brule Agency
Cheyenne
Sioux Falls
HILLS
COMPLETED 1888
FREIGHT
White River
Missouri
TRAIL
DEADWOOD
Fort Randall
Rosebud Agency
Pine Ridge Agency
Wounded Knee
YANKTON FREIGHT ROAD
Yankton
Fetterman
STAGE ROAD
War Bonnet Creek
Spotted Tail Agency
Niobrara River
Red Cloud Agency
FREMONT ELKHORN & MISSOURI VALLEY R.R.
Fort Robinson
North
BLACK HILLS
Fort Laramie
Upper Platte Agency
NEBRASKA
ADMITTED 1867
Platte
Horse Creek
CHEYENNE
SIDNEY
Ogallala
River
Loup River
Fort Russell
Sidney
Cheyenne
Lodgepole Cr.
UNION PACIFIC
Platte River
R.R.
Lincoln
Julesburg
Fort Sedgwick
Dobytown
Fort Kearny
Fort Collins
CATTLE
BURLINGTON & MISSOURI RIVER R.R.
Republican River
Fort Morgan
Beecher Island
South
Denver
KANSAS

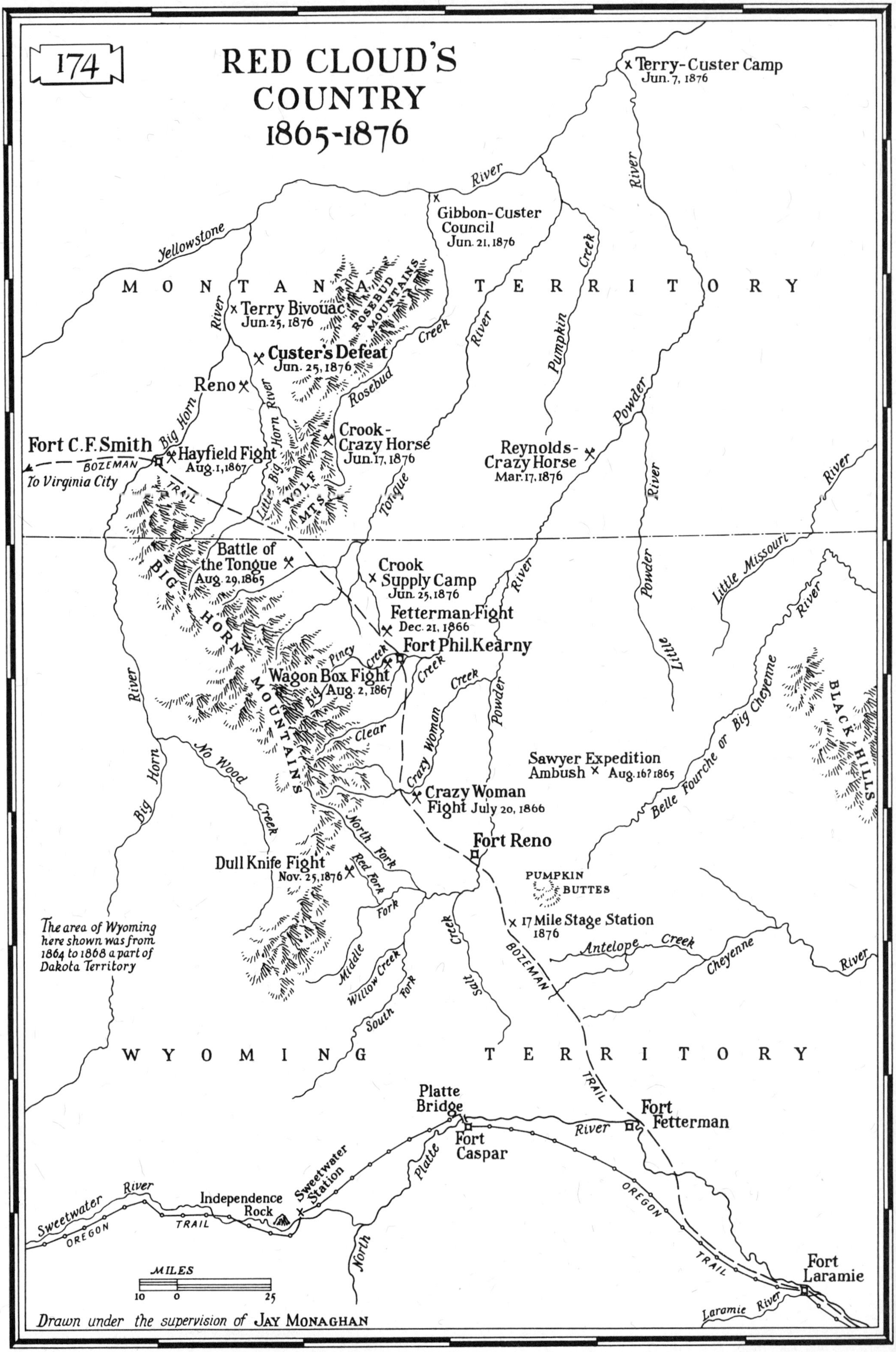

174
RED CLOUD'S COUNTRY 1865-1876
Terry-Custer Camp Jun. 7, 1876
Gibbon-Custer Council Jun. 21, 1876
Yellowstone River
MONTANA TERRITORY
Terry Bivouac Jun. 25, 1876
ROSEBUD MOUNTAINS
Custer's Defeat Jun. 25, 1876
Reno
Rosebud Creek
Pumpkin Creek
Powder River
Big Horn River
Little Big Horn River
Crook-Crazy Horse Jun. 17, 1876
Reynolds-Crazy Horse Mar. 17, 1876
Fort C. F. Smith
Hayfield Fight Aug. 1, 1867
BOZEMAN TRAIL
To Virginia City
WOLF MTS.
Tongue River
Battle of the Tongue Aug. 29, 1865
Crook Supply Camp Jun. 25, 1876
Little Missouri River
Little Powder River
BIG HORN MOUNTAINS
Fetterman Fight Dec. 21, 1866
Fort Phil. Kearny
Piney Creek
Wagon Box Fight Aug. 2, 1867
Big Piney Creek
Clear Creek
Crazy Woman Creek
Belle Fourche or Big Cheyenne River
BLACK HILLS
Sawyer Expedition Ambush Aug. 16? 1865
No Wood Creek
Crazy Woman Fight July 20, 1866
Fort Reno
North Fork
Red Fork
Dull Knife Fight Nov. 25, 1876
PUMPKIN BUTTES
17 Mile Stage Station 1876
Middle Fork
Salt Creek
Antelope Creek
Cheyenne River
The area of Wyoming here shown was from 1864 to 1868 a part of Dakota Territory
Willow Creek
South Fork
BOZEMAN TRAIL
WYOMING TERRITORY
Platte Bridge
Fort Caspar
River
Fort Fetterman
North Platte
Sweetwater Station
Independence Rock
Sweetwater River
OREGON TRAIL
Fort Laramie
Laramie River
MILES
10 0 25
Drawn under the supervision of JAY MONAGHAN

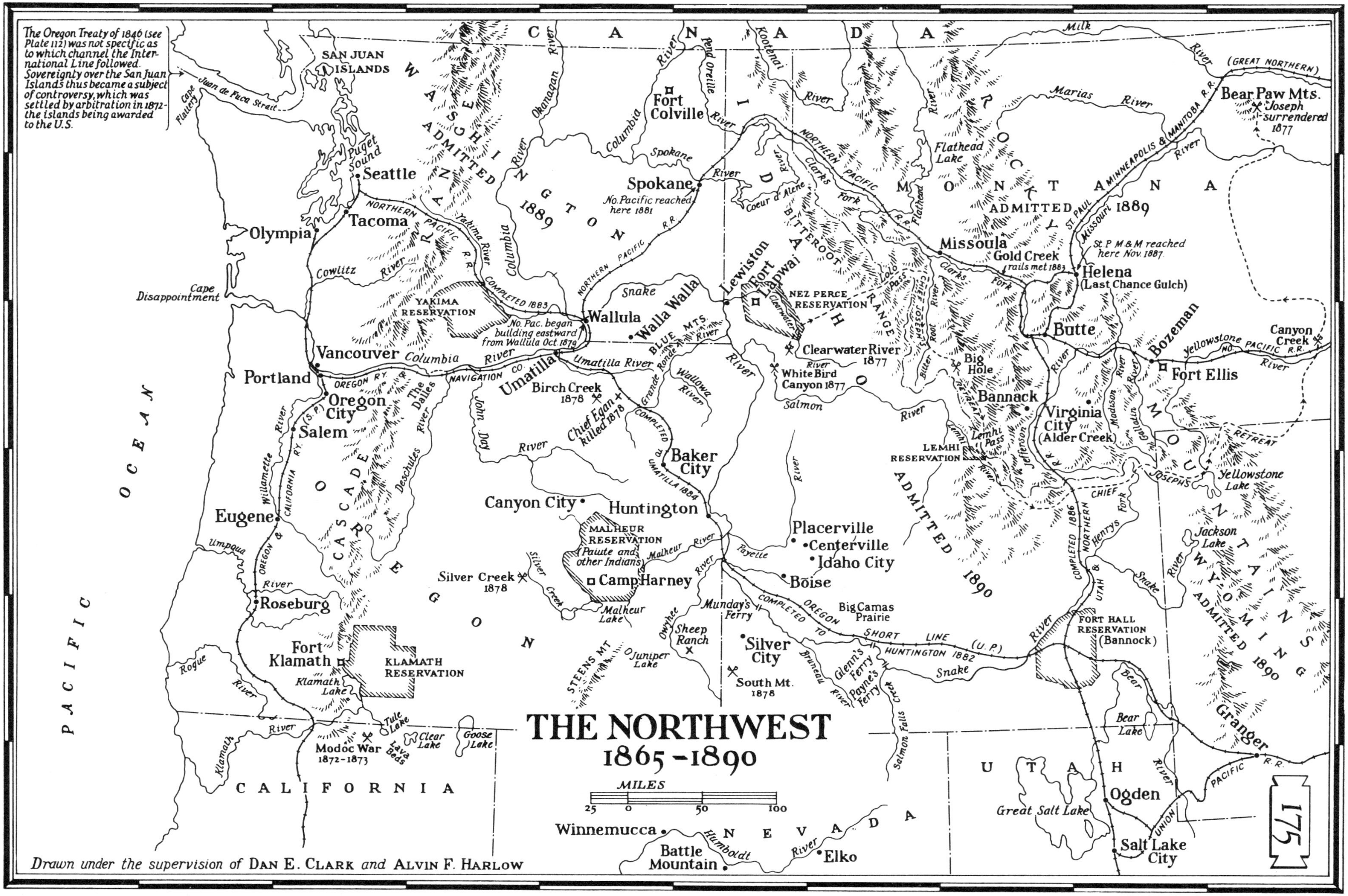
175
THE NORTHWEST
1865–1890
MILES
25 0 50 100
The Oregon Treaty of 1846 (see Plate 112) was not specific as to which channel the International Line followed. Sovereignty over the San Juan Islands thus became a subject of controversy, which was settled by arbitration in 1872–the islands being awarded to the U.S.
SAN JUAN ISLANDS
CANADA
WASHINGTON
ADMITTED 1889
IDAHO
ADMITTED 1890
MONTANA
ADMITTED 1889
WYOMING
ADMITTED 1890
OREGON
CALIFORNIA
NEVADA
UTAH
PACIFIC OCEAN
ROCKY MOUNTAINS
CASCADE RANGE
BITTERROOT RANGE
BLUE MTS.
Seattle
Tacoma
Olympia
Puget Sound
Juan de Fuca Strait
Cape Flattery
Cape Disappointment
Vancouver
Portland
Oregon City
Salem
Eugene
Roseburg
Fort Klamath
KLAMATH RESERVATION
Modoc War 1872–1873
Lava Beds
Tule Lake
Clear Lake
Goose Lake
Klamath Lake
The Dalles
YAKIMA RESERVATION
No. Pac. began building eastward from Wallula Oct. 1879
Wallula
Walla Walla
Umatilla
Birch Creek 1878
Chief Egan killed 1878
Baker City
Canyon City
Huntington
MALHEUR RESERVATION (Paiute and other Indians)
Camp Harney
Malheur Lake
Silver Creek 1878
Juniper Lake
STEENS MT.
Sheep Ranch
Munday's Ferry
Silver City
South Mt. 1878
Glenn's Ferry
Payne's Ferry
Big Camas Prairie
Placerville
Centerville
Idaho City
Boise
Winnemucca
Battle Mountain
Elko
Lewiston
Fort Lapwai
NEZ PERCE RESERVATION
Clearwater River 1877
White Bird Canyon 1877
Lolo Pass
Spokane
No. Pacific reached here 1881
Fort Colville
Missoula
Gold Creek
rails met 1883
Helena (Last Chance Gulch)
St. P. M & M reached here Nov. 1887
Butte
Bozeman
Fort Ellis
Canyon Creek
Bear Paw Mts.
Joseph surrendered 1877
Big Hole
Bannack
Virginia City (Alder Creek)
Lemhi Pass
LEMHI RESERVATION
Yellowstone Lake
Jackson Lake
CHIEF JOSEPH'S RETREAT
FORT HALL RESERVATION (Bannock)
Bear Lake
Great Salt Lake
Ogden
Salt Lake City
Granger
NORTHERN PACIFIC R.R.
COMPLETED 1883
OREGON RY. & NAVIGATION CO.
COMPLETED TO UMATILLA 1884
OREGON & CALIFORNIA RY. (S.P.)
OREGON SHORT LINE (U.P.)
COMPLETED TO HUNTINGTON 1882
UTAH & NORTHERN
COMPLETED 1886
UNION PACIFIC R.R.
ST. PAUL MINNEAPOLIS & MANITOBA R.R.
(GREAT NORTHERN)
Drawn under the supervision of DAN E. CLARK and ALVIN F. HARLOW

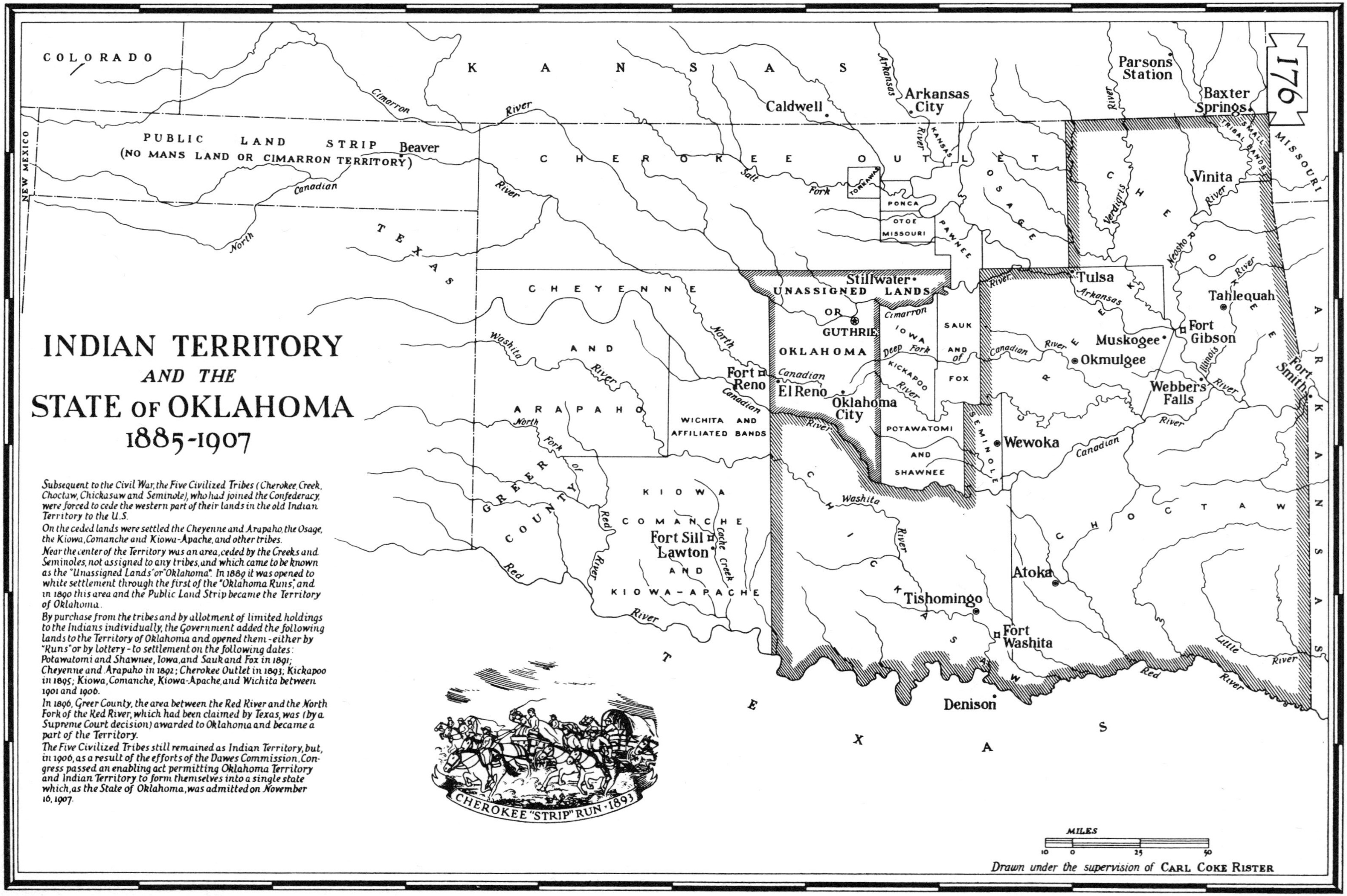

INDIAN TERRITORY
AND THE
STATE OF OKLAHOMA
1885-1907

Subsequent to the Civil War, the Five Civilized Tribes (Cherokee, Creek, Choctaw, Chickasaw and Seminole), who had joined the Confederacy, were forced to cede the western part of their lands in the old Indian Territory to the U.S.

On the ceded lands were settled the Cheyenne and Arapaho, the Osage, the Kiowa, Comanche and Kiowa-Apache, and other tribes.

Near the center of the Territory was an area, ceded by the Creeks and Seminoles, not assigned to any tribes, and which came to be known as the "Unassigned Lands" or "Oklahoma". In 1889 it was opened to white settlement through the first of the "Oklahoma Runs," and in 1890 this area and the Public Land Strip became the Territory of Oklahoma.

By purchase from the tribes and by allotment of limited holdings to the Indians individually, the Government added the following lands to the Territory of Oklahoma and opened them - either by "Runs" or by lottery - to settlement on the following dates: Potawatomi and Shawnee, Iowa, and Sauk and Fox in 1891; Cheyenne and Arapaho in 1892; Cherokee Outlet in 1893; Kickapoo in 1895; Kiowa, Comanche, Kiowa-Apache, and Wichita between 1901 and 1906.

In 1896, Greer County, the area between the Red River and the North Fork of the Red River, which had been claimed by Texas, was (by a Supreme Court decision) awarded to Oklahoma and became a part of the Territory.

The Five Civilized Tribes still remained as Indian Territory, but, in 1906, as a result of the efforts of the Dawes Commission, Congress passed an enabling act permitting Oklahoma Territory and Indian Territory to form themselves into a single state which, as the State of Oklahoma, was admitted on November 16, 1907.

Drawn under the supervision of CARL COKE RISTER

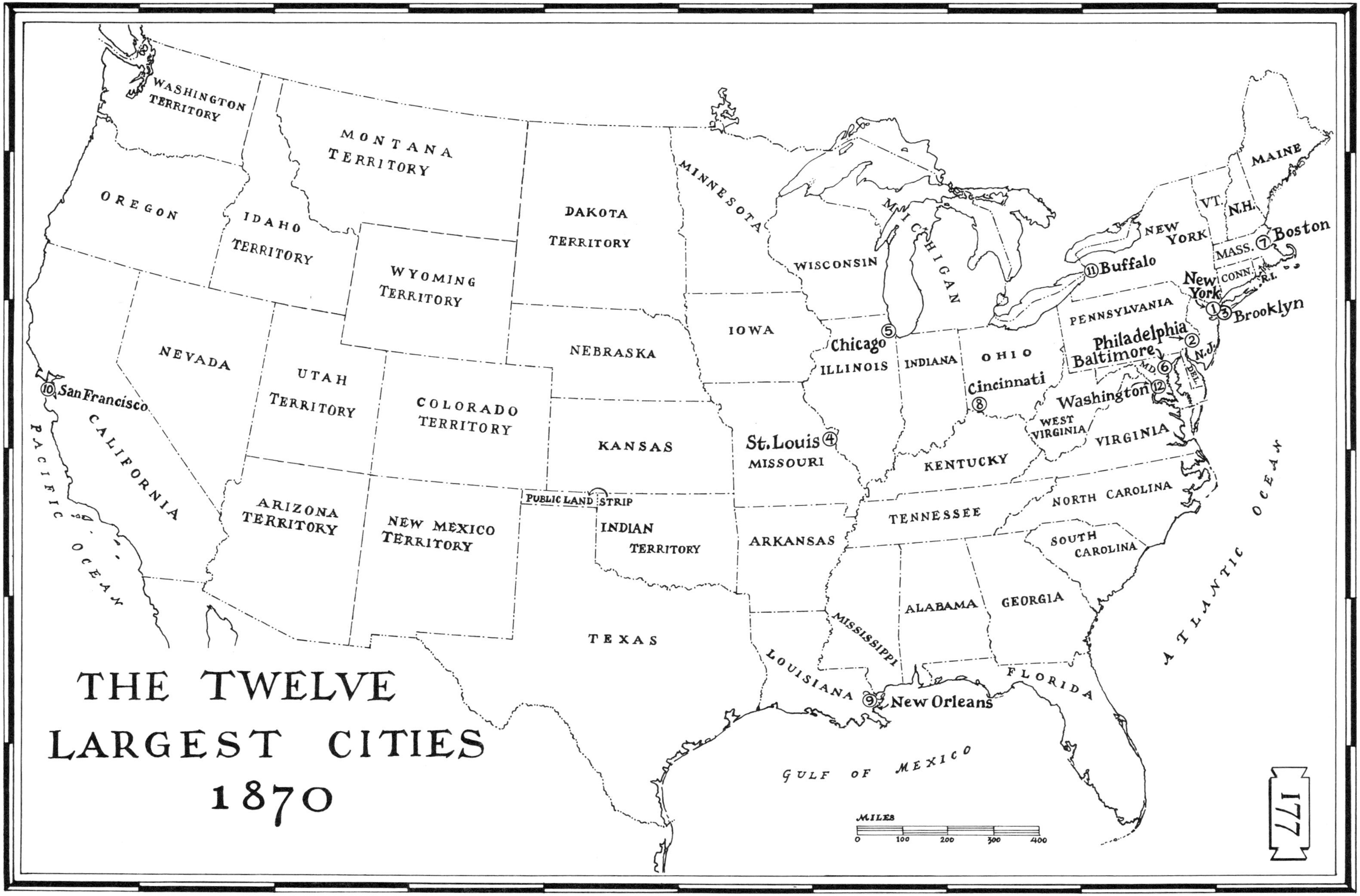
THE TWELVE LARGEST CITIES 1870
177
WASHINGTON TERRITORY
OREGON
CALIFORNIA
NEVADA
IDAHO TERRITORY
MONTANA TERRITORY
WYOMING TERRITORY
UTAH TERRITORY
ARIZONA TERRITORY
COLORADO TERRITORY
NEW MEXICO TERRITORY
DAKOTA TERRITORY
NEBRASKA
KANSAS
PUBLIC LAND STRIP
INDIAN TERRITORY
TEXAS
MINNESOTA
IOWA
MISSOURI
ARKANSAS
LOUISIANA
WISCONSIN
ILLINOIS
MICHIGAN
INDIANA
OHIO
KENTUCKY
TENNESSEE
MISSISSIPPI
ALABAMA
GEORGIA
FLORIDA
SOUTH CAROLINA
NORTH CAROLINA
VIRGINIA
WEST VIRGINIA
MD.
DEL.
PENNSYLVANIA
N.J.
NEW YORK
CONN.
R.I.
MASS.
VT.
N.H.
MAINE
1 New York
2 Philadelphia
3 Brooklyn
4 St. Louis
5 Chicago
6 Baltimore
7 Boston
8 Cincinnati
9 New Orleans
10 San Francisco
11 Buffalo
12 Washington
PACIFIC OCEAN
ATLANTIC OCEAN
GULF OF MEXICO
MILES
0 100 200 300 400

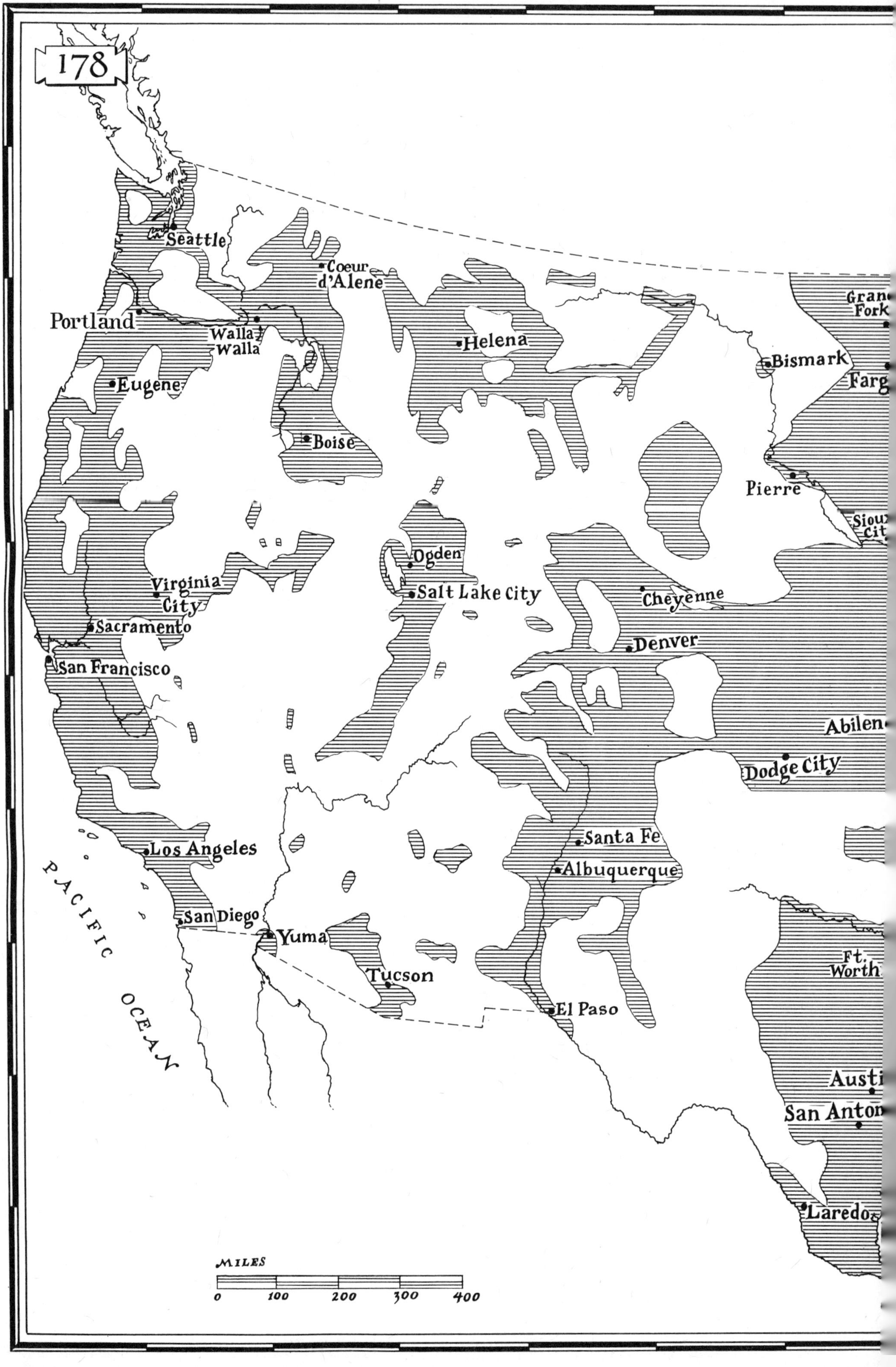
178
Seattle
Coeur d'Alene
Portland
Walla Walla
Helena
Eugene
Boise
Bismark
Pierre
Ogden
Salt Lake City
Virginia City
Sacramento
Cheyenne
Denver
San Francisco
Dodge City
Santa Fe
Los Angeles
Albuquerque
PACIFIC OCEAN
San Diego
Yuma
Tucson
El Paso
MILES
0 100 200 300 400

SETTLED AREAS 1890

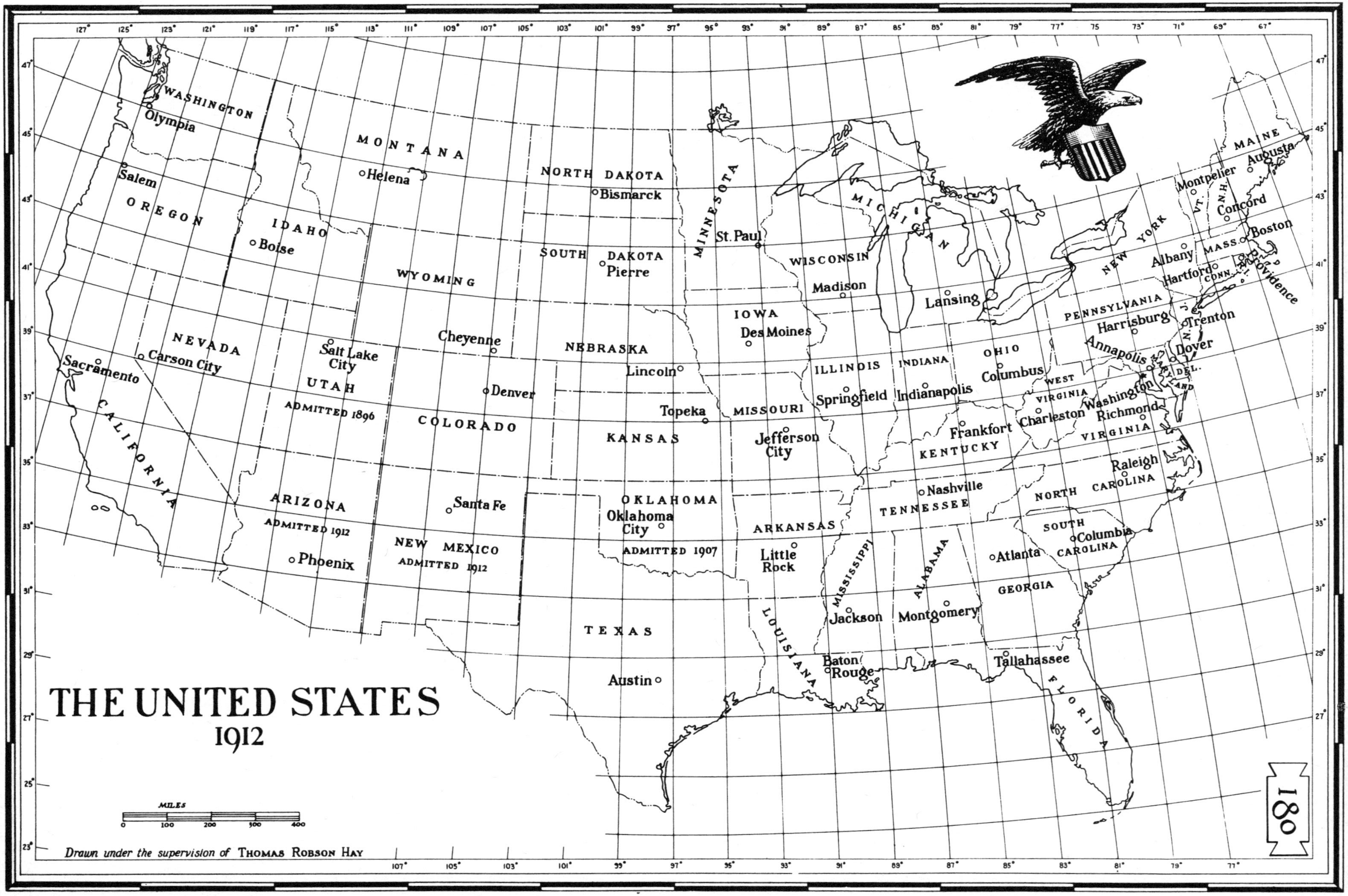

THE UNITED STATES
1912

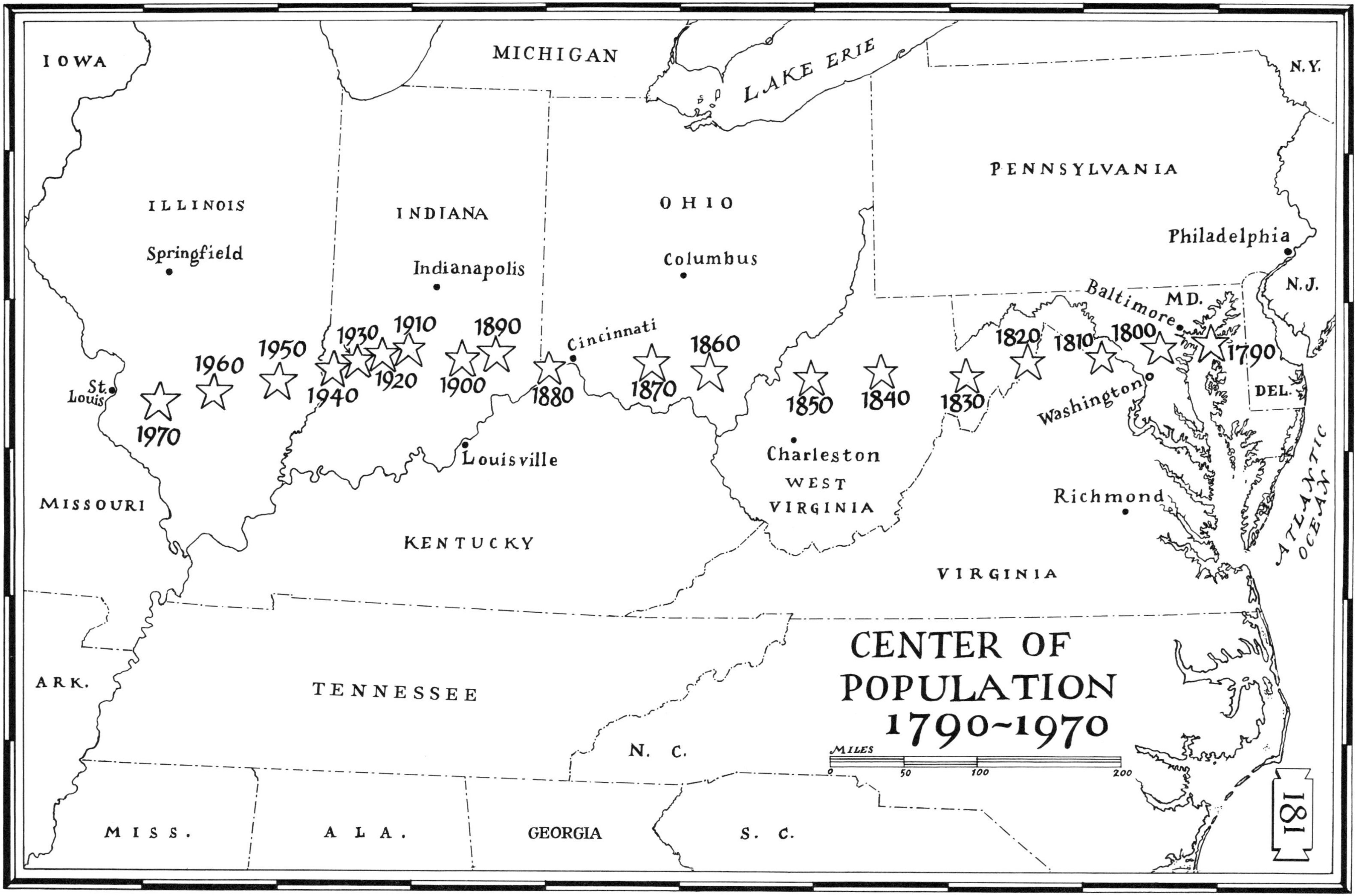
CENTER OF POPULATION 1790~1970
MILES
0
50
100
200
IOWA
MICHIGAN
LAKE ERIE
N.Y.
PENNSYLVANIA
Philadelphia
N.J.
ILLINOIS
INDIANA
OHIO
Springfield
Indianapolis
Columbus
Baltimore
MD.
DEL.
St. Louis
Cincinnati
Louisville
Washington
Charleston
WEST VIRGINIA
Richmond
VIRGINIA
ATLANTIC OCEAN
MISSOURI
KENTUCKY
TENNESSEE
ARK.
N. C.
S. C.
MISS.
ALA.
GEORGIA
1790
1800
1810
1820
1830
1840
1850
1860
1870
1880
1890
1900
1910
1920
1930
1940
1950
1960
1970

IX THE UNITED STATES AS A WORLD POWER, 1898–1977

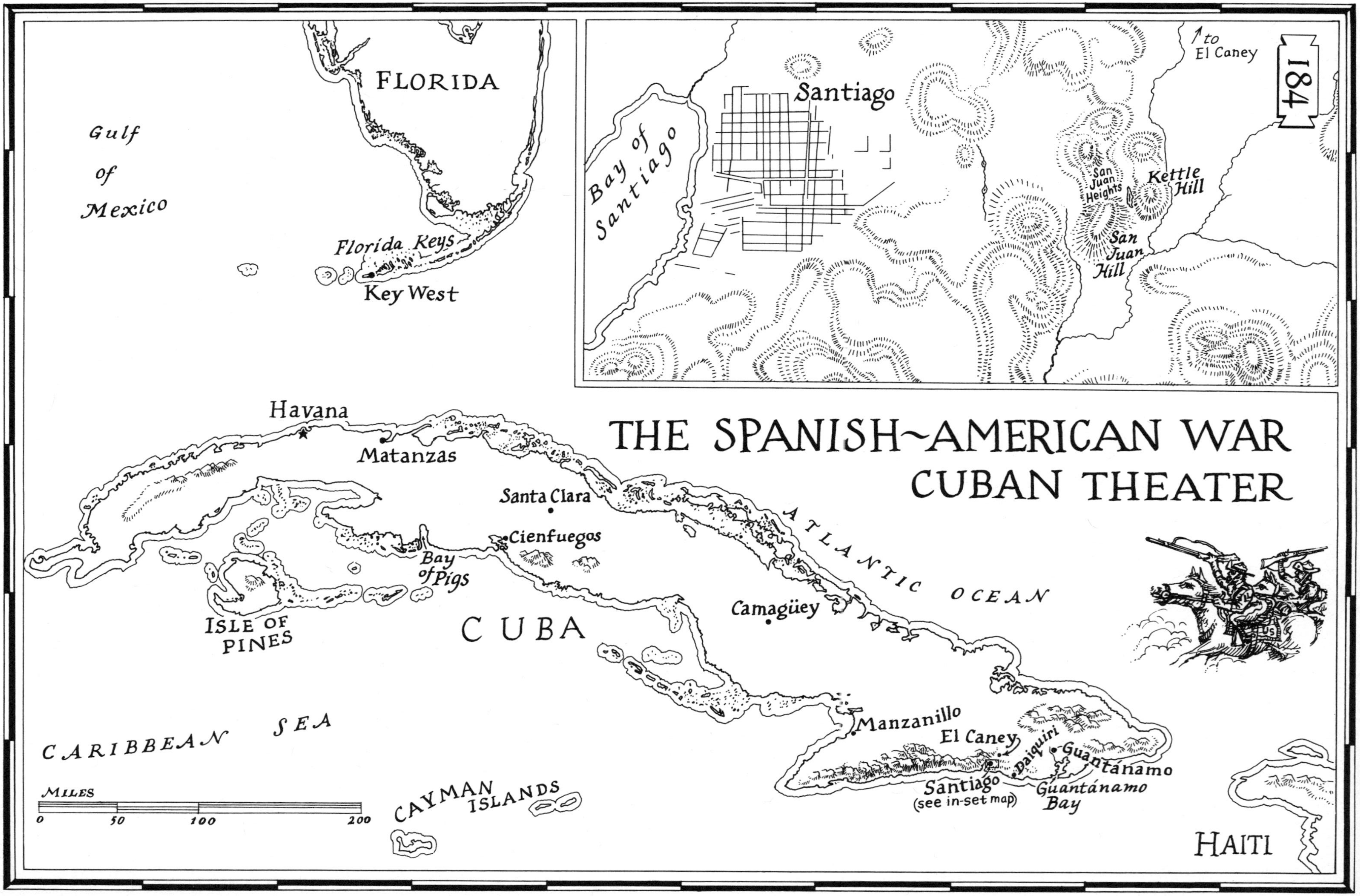
THE SPANISH~AMERICAN WAR
CUBAN THEATER
FLORIDA
Gulf of Mexico
Florida Keys
Key West
Bay of Santiago
Santiago
San Juan Heights
Kettle Hill
San Juan Hill
to El Caney
Havana
Matanzas
Santa Clara
Cienfuegos
Bay of Pigs
ISLE OF PINES
CUBA
Camagüey
ATLANTIC OCEAN
Manzanillo
El Caney
Daiquiri
Guantánamo
Santiago (see in-set map)
Guantánamo Bay
CARIBBEAN SEA
CAYMAN ISLANDS
HAITI
MILES
0
50
100
200

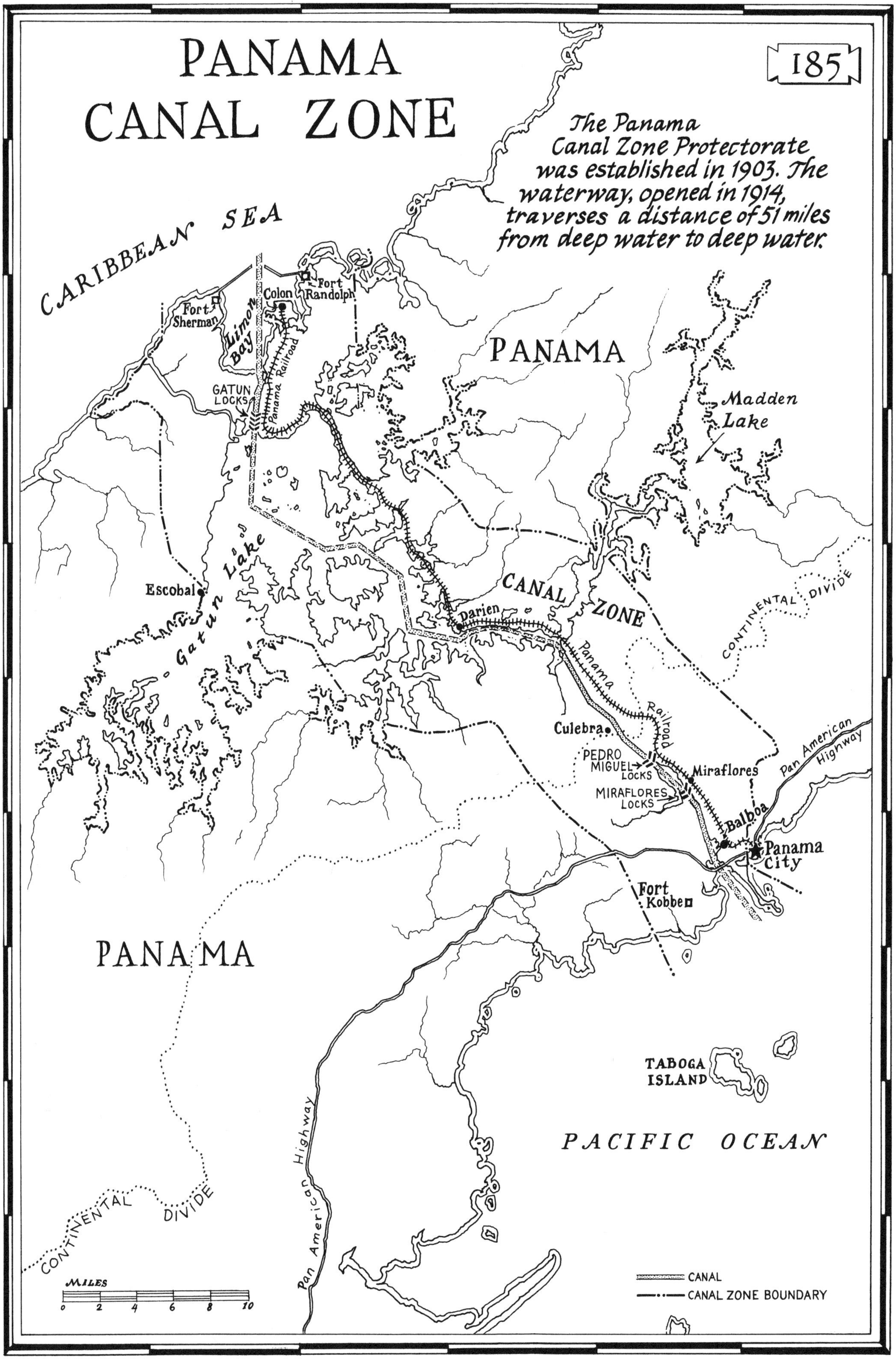
PANAMA
CANAL ZONE
The Panama Canal Zone Protectorate was established in 1903. The waterway, opened in 1914, traverses a distance of 51 miles from deep water to deep water.
CARIBBEAN SEA
Fort Sherman
Limon Bay
Colon
Fort Randolph
Panama Railroad
GATUN LOCKS
PANAMA
Madden Lake
Escobal
Gatun Lake
CANAL ZONE
Darien
CONTINENTAL DIVIDE
Panama Railroad
Culebra
PEDRO MIGUEL LOCKS
MIRAFLORES LOCKS
Miraflores
Pan American Highway
Balboa
Panama City
Fort Kobbe
PANAMA
TABOGA ISLAND
PACIFIC OCEAN
Pan American Highway
CONTINENTAL DIVIDE
MILES
0 2 4 6 8 10
CANAL
CANAL ZONE BOUNDARY

NEW MEXICO
Columbus
Hachita
Fort Bliss
El Paso
UNITED STATES
Carrizal
Madera
Chihuahua
CHIHUAHUA
Parral
Rio Grande
New Orleans
1916-1917 U.S. punitive expedition in Northern Mexico.
MEXICO
Gulf of Mexico
1914 U.S. occupation of Veracruz
Mexico City
Vera Cruz
BRITISH HONDURA
HONDURAS
GUATEMALA
1954 U.S.-supported revolution overthrows government
EL SALVADOR
PACIFIC
OCEAN
Managua
NICARAGUA
1912~1925 U.S. occupation; finances under U.S. control
1926~1933 U.S. occupation
MILES
0
100
200
400

UNITED STATES INTERVENTIONS IN THE CARIBBEAN AND MIDDLE AMERICA 1898–1966

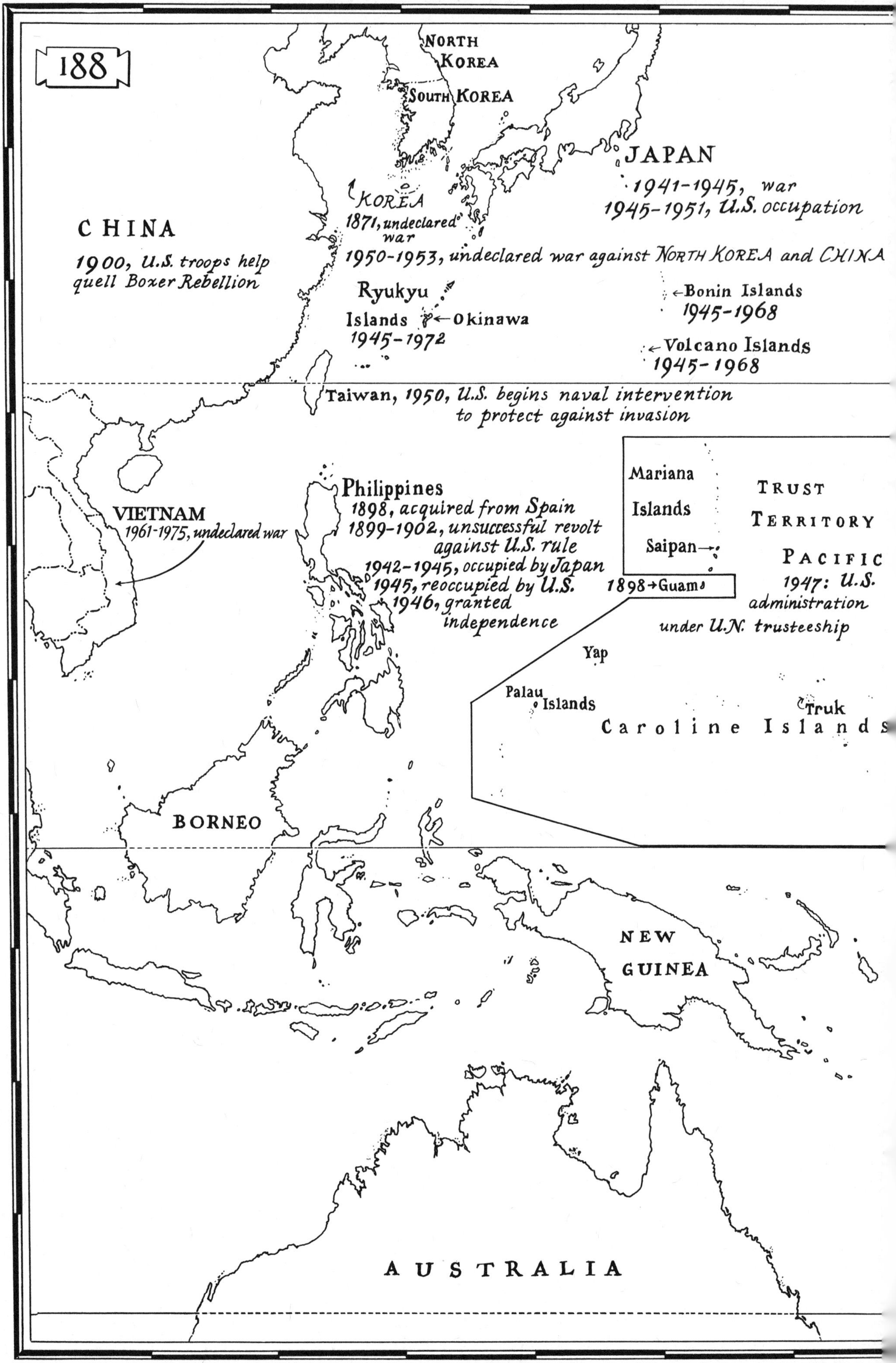
188
NORTH KOREA
SOUTH KOREA
JAPAN
1941-1945, war
1945-1951, U.S. occupation
KOREA
1871, undeclared war
CHINA
1900, U.S. troops help quell Boxer Rebellion
1950-1953, undeclared war against NORTH KOREA and CHINA
Ryukyu Islands
1945-1972
←Okinawa
←Bonin Islands
1945-1968
←Volcano Islands
1945-1968
Taiwan, 1950, U.S. begins naval intervention to protect against invasion
Mariana Islands
Saipan→
1898→Guam
TRUST TERRITORY PACIFIC
1947: U.S. administration under U.N. trusteeship
VIETNAM
1961-1975, undeclared war
Philippines
1898, acquired from Spain
1899-1902, unsuccessful revolt against U.S. rule
1942-1945, occupied by Japan
1945, reoccupied by U.S.
1946, granted independence
Yap
Palau Islands
Truk
Caroline Islands
BORNEO
NEW GUINEA
AUSTRALIA

THE UNITED STATES IN THE PACIFIC
1867 – 1975

Dates indicate the date of U.S. annexation or occupation

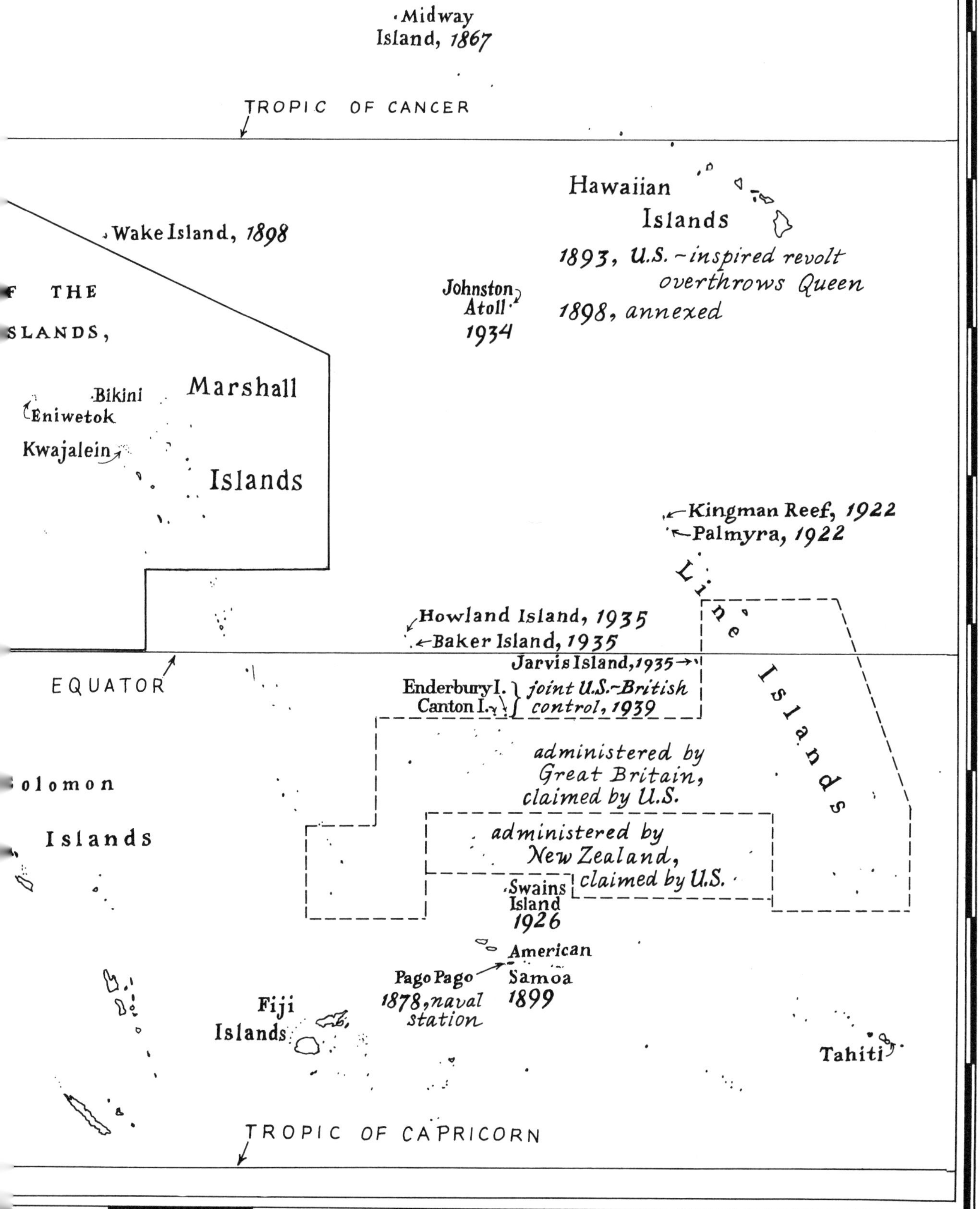

WORLD WAR I
THE WESTERN FRONT, 1917–1918

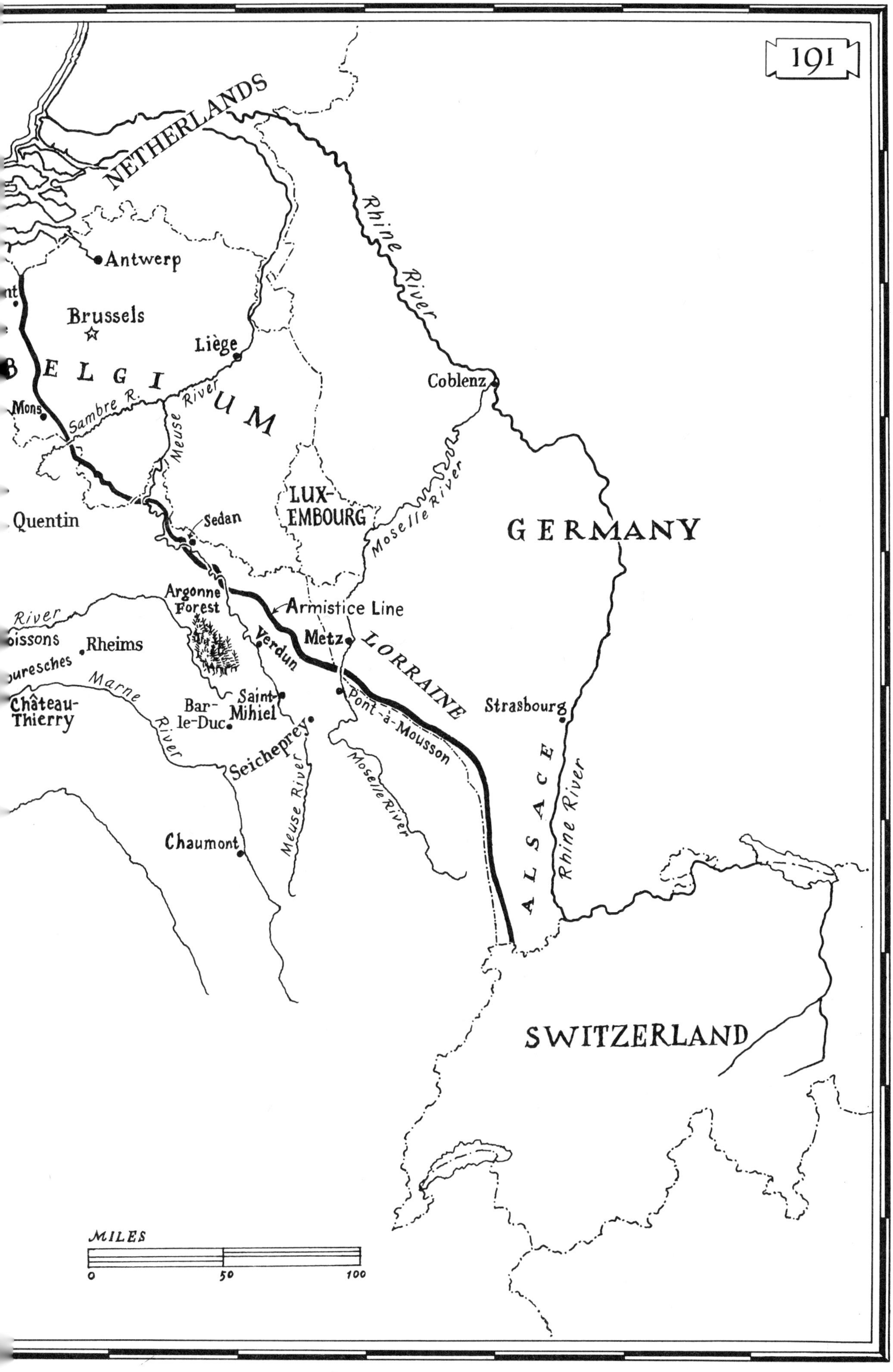
NETHERLANDS
Antwerp
Brussels
Liège
BELGIUM
Mons
Sambre R.
Meuse River
Rhine River
Coblenz
LUX-
EMBOURG
Moselle River
GERMANY
Quentin
Sedan
Argonne
Forest
Armistice Line
River
oissons
Rheims
Verdun
Metz
LORRAINE
ouresches
Marne
Château-
Thierry
Bar-
le-Duc
Saint-
Mihiel
Pont-à-Mousson
Strasbourg
River
Seicheprey
Meuse River
Moselle River
ALSACE
Rhine River
Chaumont
SWITZERLAND
MILES
0
50
100

WORLD WAR II
MEDITERRANEAN THEATER

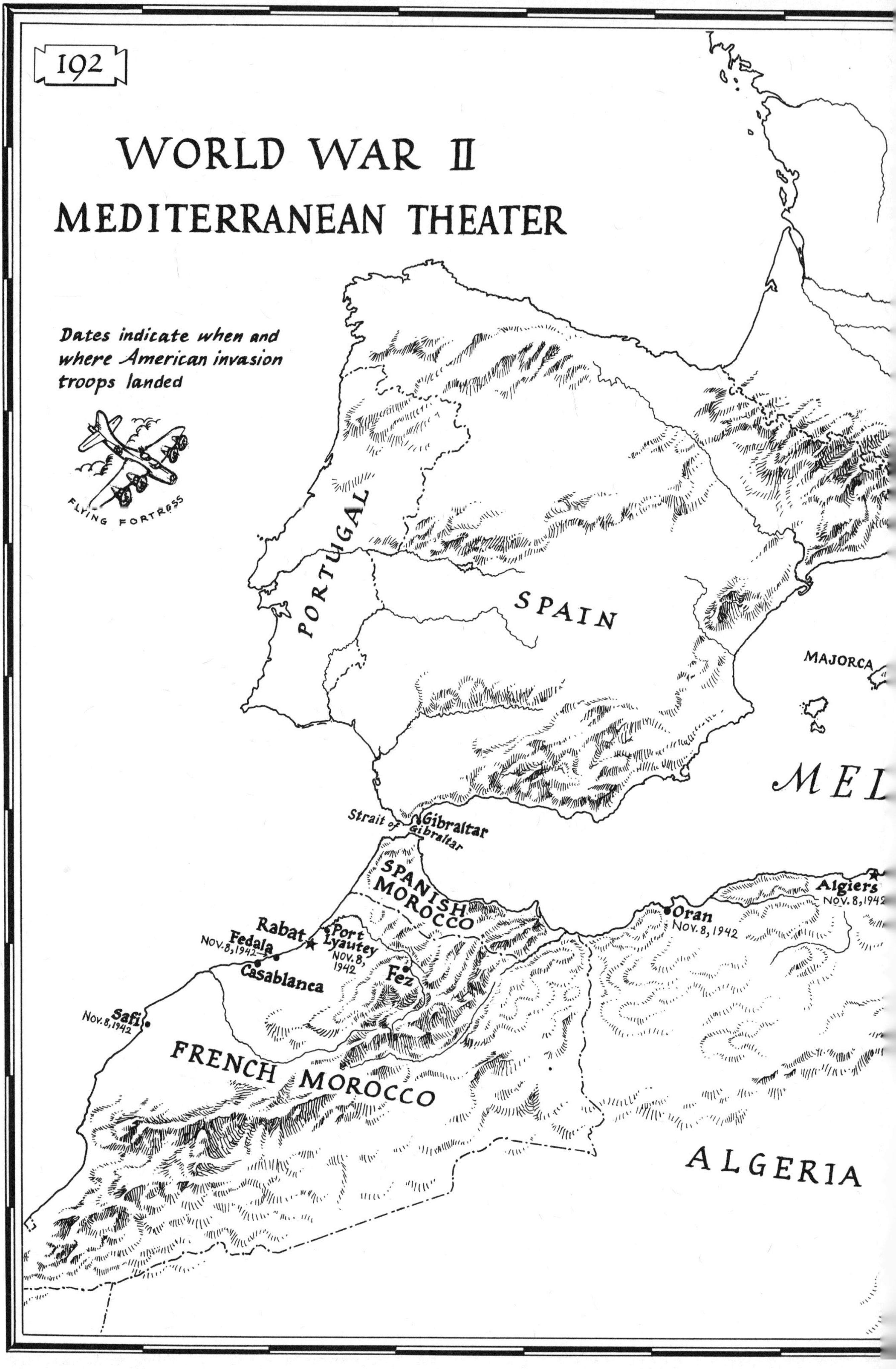

FRANCE
Po River
Ferrara
Bologna
Gothic Line
Marseille
St. Raphael
St. Maxime
St. Tropez
Cavalaire
Cap Negre
Toulon
ALL AUGUST 15, 1944
Pisa
Arno R.
Florence
Ancona
ADRIATIC SEA
ELBA
ITALY
CORSICA
SEPT. 13-30, 1943
Pescara
Gustav Line
Termoli
Rome
Anzio
Nettuno
JAN. 22, 1944
Monte Cassino
Foggia
MINORCA
SARDINIA
Naples
Bari
TYRRHENIAN SEA
Salerno
Amalfi
SEPT. 9, 1943
Paestum
SEPT. 9, 1943
Taranto
MEDITERRANEAN SEA
Palermo
Messina
Marsala
Reggio di Calabria
Strait of Messina
Bougie
Bone
Bizerte
Cape Bon
SICILY
Catania
Licata
JULY 10, 1943
Gela
JULY 10, 1943
Syracuse
Tunis
Scoglitti
JULY 10, 1943
Enfidaville
MALTA
Sbeitla
Kasserine Pass
Gafsa
MEDITERRANEAN SEA
Mareth
TUNISIA
LIBYA
Miles
0
50
100
200

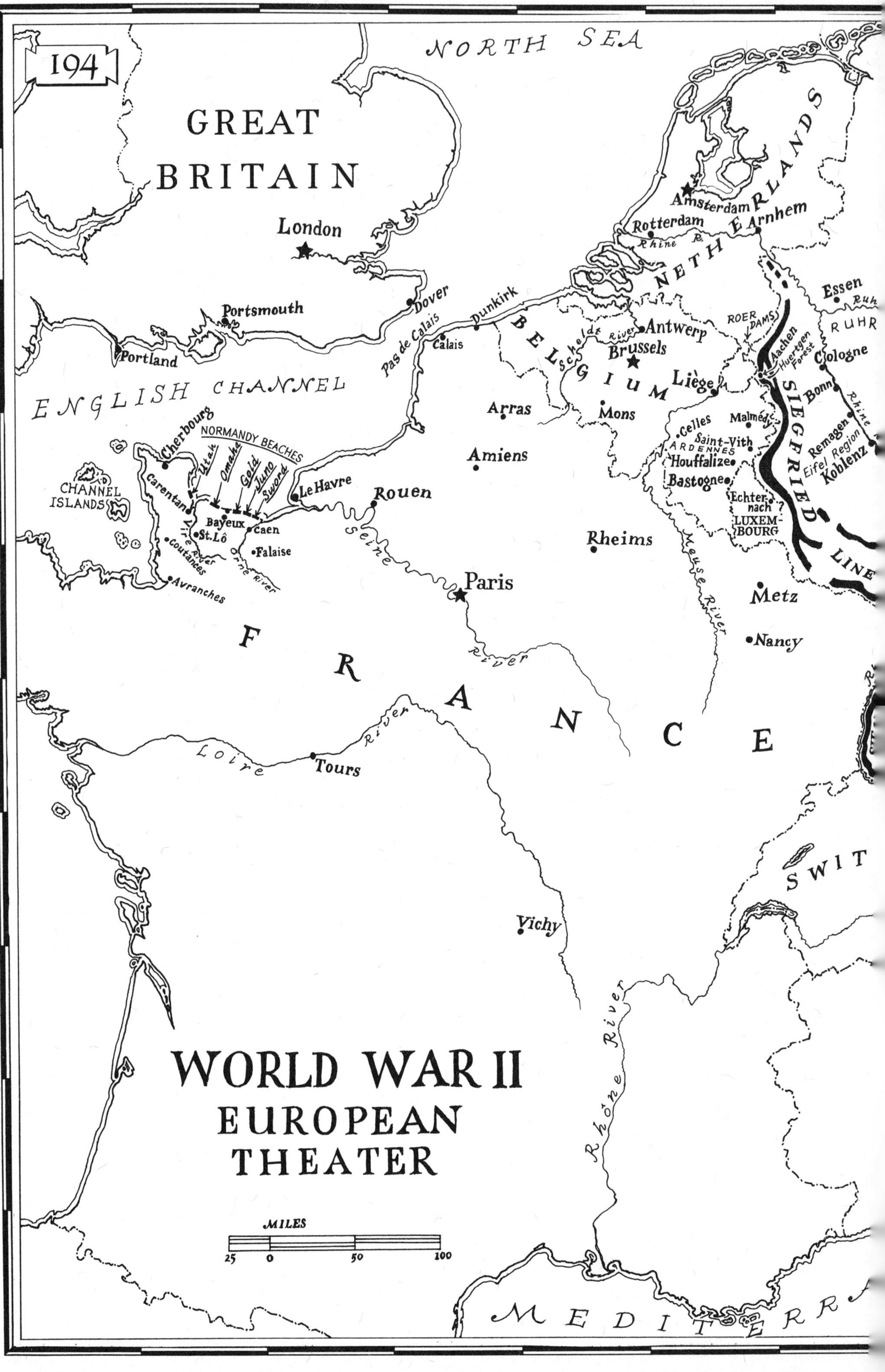

WORLD WAR II
EUROPEAN
THEATER
NORTH SEA
GREAT BRITAIN
London
Dover
Portsmouth
Portland
ENGLISH CHANNEL
Pas de Calais
CHANNEL ISLANDS
Cherbourg
NORMANDY BEACHES
Utah
Omaha
Gold
Juno
Sword
Carentan
Bayeux
St. Lô
Caen
Falaise
Coutances
Avranches
Vire River
Orne River
Le Havre
Rouen
Seine River
Paris
Calais
Dunkirk
Arras
Amiens
Rheims
BELGIUM
Scheldt River
Antwerp
Brussels
Mons
Liège
NETHERLANDS
Amsterdam
Rotterdam
Arnhem
Rhine R.
ROER DAMS
Aachen
Huertgen Forest
Essen
RUHR
Cologne
Bonn
Remagen
Eifel Region
Koblenz
Rhine
SIEGFRIED LINE
Celles
Malmédy
Saint-Vith
ARDENNES
Houffalize
Bastogne
Echternach
LUXEMBOURG
Meuse River
Metz
Nancy
FRANCE
Loire River
Tours
Vichy
Rhône River
SWIT
MEDITERR
MILES
25 0 50 100

Hamburg
U.S. ZONE
Bremen
Elbe River
Bergen-Belsen
Berlin
Potsdam
POLAND
Magdeburg
Lippstadt
Paderborn
GERMANY
Torgau
Mulde River
Leipzig
Dresden
Buchenwald
Frankfurt
Prague
UNITED STATES ZONE OF OCCUPATION
CZECHOSLOVAKIA
Dachau
Munich
Linz
Mauthausen
Vienna
AUSTRIA
BRENNER PASS
HUNGARY
RLAND
ITALY
YUGOSLAVIA
ADRIATIC SEA
EAN SEA

196
U.S.S.R.
SAKHALIN
(U.S.S.R.)
KARAFUTO
(JAPAN)
MANCHURIA
KURIL
Vladivostok
HOKKAIDO
Peking
Tientsin
CHINA
KOREA
JAPAN
Hiroshima
Kobe
Nagoya
Tokyo
Osaka
KYUSHU
Nagasaki
Shanghai
Chungking
Yangtze River
RYUKYU ISLANDS
OKINAWA
IWO JIMA
Ledo
INDIA
LEDO ROAD
BURMA ROAD
Wanting
Kunming
Myitkyina
Lashio
FORMOSA
Hong Kong
BURMA
FRENCH INDO-CHINA
PHILIPPINE SEA
THAILAND
SOUTH CHINA SEA
Lingayen Gulf
LUZON
PHILIPPINES
BATAAN Peninsula
Manila
CORREGIDOR ISLAND
San Bernardino Strait
MARIANAS ISLANDS
SAIPAN
TINIAN
GUAM
SIBUYAN SEA
LEYTE
Tacloban
Leyte Gulf
Surigao Strait
Mekong River
YAP
SULU SEA
MINDANAO
PALAU ISLANDS
CAROLINE
TAWITAWI
TARAKAN
MALAYA
Singapore
MOROTAI
SUMATRA
BORNEO
Balikpapan
Makassar Strait
CELEBES
NEW GUINEA
BISMARC SEA
Nadzab
Lae
Salamaua
NETHERLANDS EAST INDIES
JAVA SEA
BALI
JAVA
Lombok Strait
TIMOR
Port Moresby
Darwin
INDIAN OCEAN
AUSTRALIA

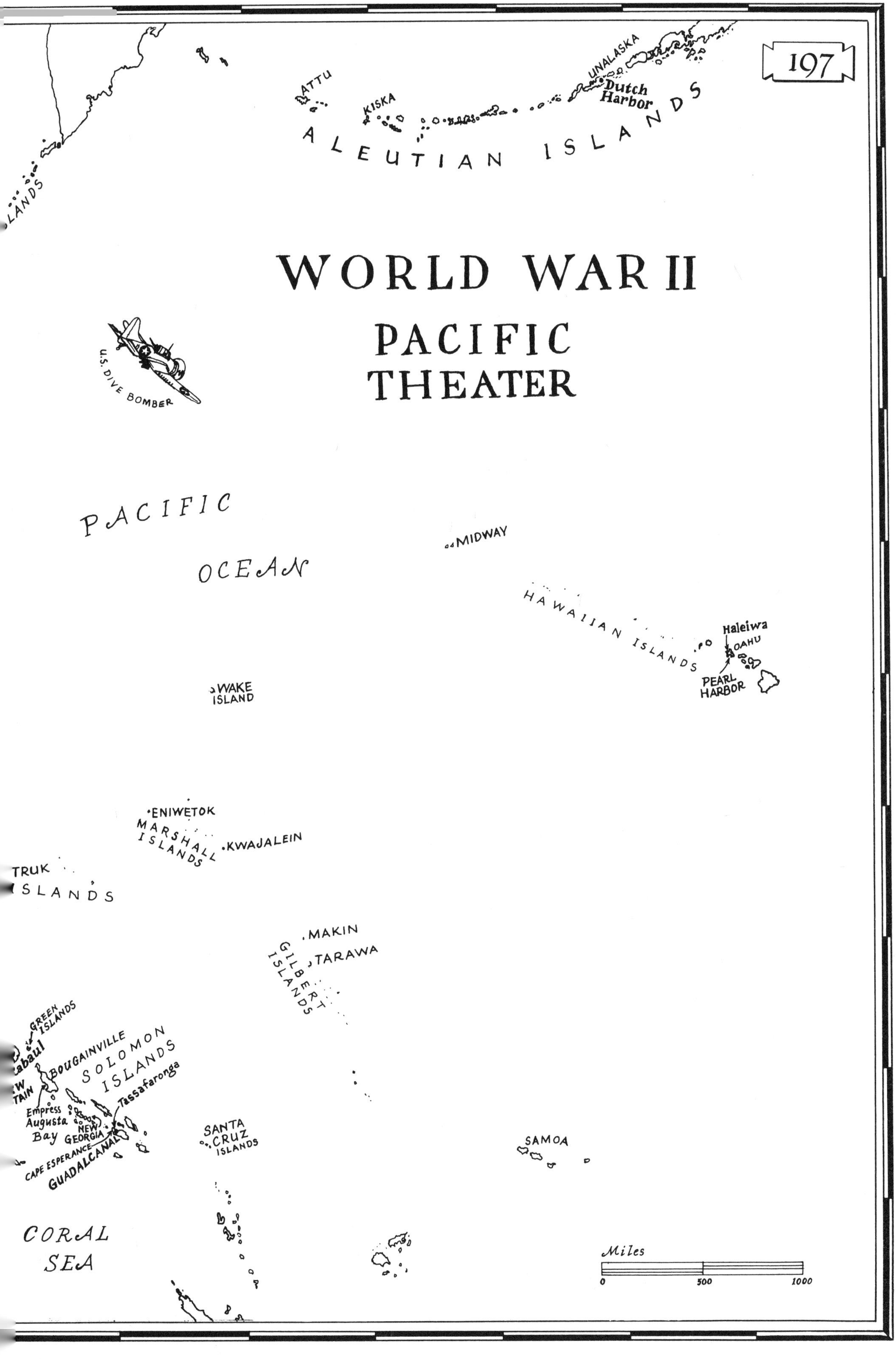
WORLD WAR II
PACIFIC THEATER
ATTU
KISKA
UNALASKA
Dutch Harbor
ALEUTIAN ISLANDS
U.S. DIVE BOMBER
PACIFIC OCEAN
MIDWAY
HAWAIIAN ISLANDS
Haleiwa
OAHU
PEARL HARBOR
WAKE ISLAND
ENIWETOK
MARSHALL ISLANDS
KWAJALEIN
TRUK
ISLANDS
MAKIN
TARAWA
GILBERT ISLANDS
GREEN ISLANDS
BOUGAINVILLE
SOLOMON ISLANDS
Tassafaronga
Empress Augusta Bay
NEW GEORGIA
CAPE ESPERANCE
GUADALCANAL
SANTA CRUZ ISLANDS
SAMOA
CORAL SEA
Miles
0
500
1000

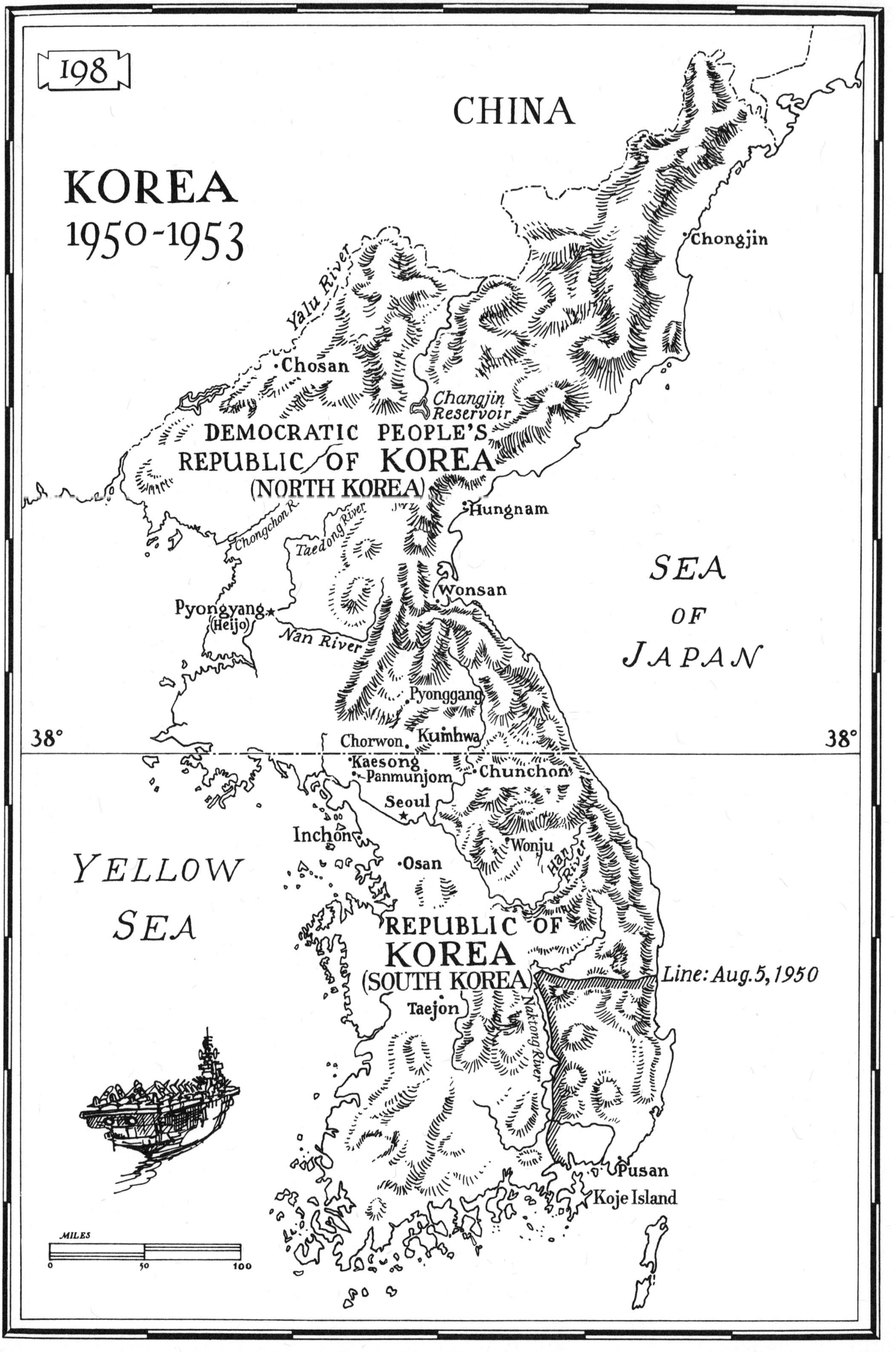
198
CHINA
KOREA
1950-1953
Chongjin
Yalu River
Chosan
Changjin
Reservoir
DEMOCRATIC PEOPLE'S
REPUBLIC OF KOREA
(NORTH KOREA)
Hungnam
Chongchon R.
Taedong River
SEA
OF
JAPAN
Wonsan
Pyongyang
(Heijo)
Nan River
Pyonggang
38°
Chorwon
Kumhwa
38°
Kaesong
Panmunjom
Chunchon
Seoul
Inchon
Wonju
Han River
Osan
YELLOW
SEA
REPUBLIC OF
KOREA
(SOUTH KOREA)
Line: Aug. 5, 1950
Taejon
Naktong River
Pusan
Koje Island
MILES
0
50
100

CHINA
DEMOCRATIC REPUBLIC OF VIETNAM (NORTH VIETNAM)
Hanoi
Dien Bien Phu
Haiphong
GULF OF TONKIN
Mekong River
Mekong R.
Vientiane
Mekong River
LAOS
Udon Thani (Udorn)
HO CHI MINH TRAIL
Demilitarized Zone
17°
Quang Tri
Khe Sanh
Hue
Da Nang
THAILAND
Chu Lai
VAN TUONG PENINSULA
My Lai
Quang Ngai
Ubon Ratchathani
Nakhon Ratchasima (Korat)
Dak To
Kontum
Pleiku
Qui Nhon
IA DRANG VALLEY
CENTRAL HIGHLANDS
Nakhon Phanom
Bangkok
CAMBODIA
REPUBLIC OF VIETNAM (SOUTH VIETNAM)
Nha Trang
CAM RANH BAY
GULF OF SIAM
Mekong River
Phnom Penh
An Loc
Tan Son Hut Air Base
Bien Hoa
Saigon
Sihanoukville
Long Xuyen
MEKONG DELTA
SOUTH CHINA SEA
VIETNAM 1961-1975
Phuoc Long
Miles
0 50 100
Air Force bases in Thailand

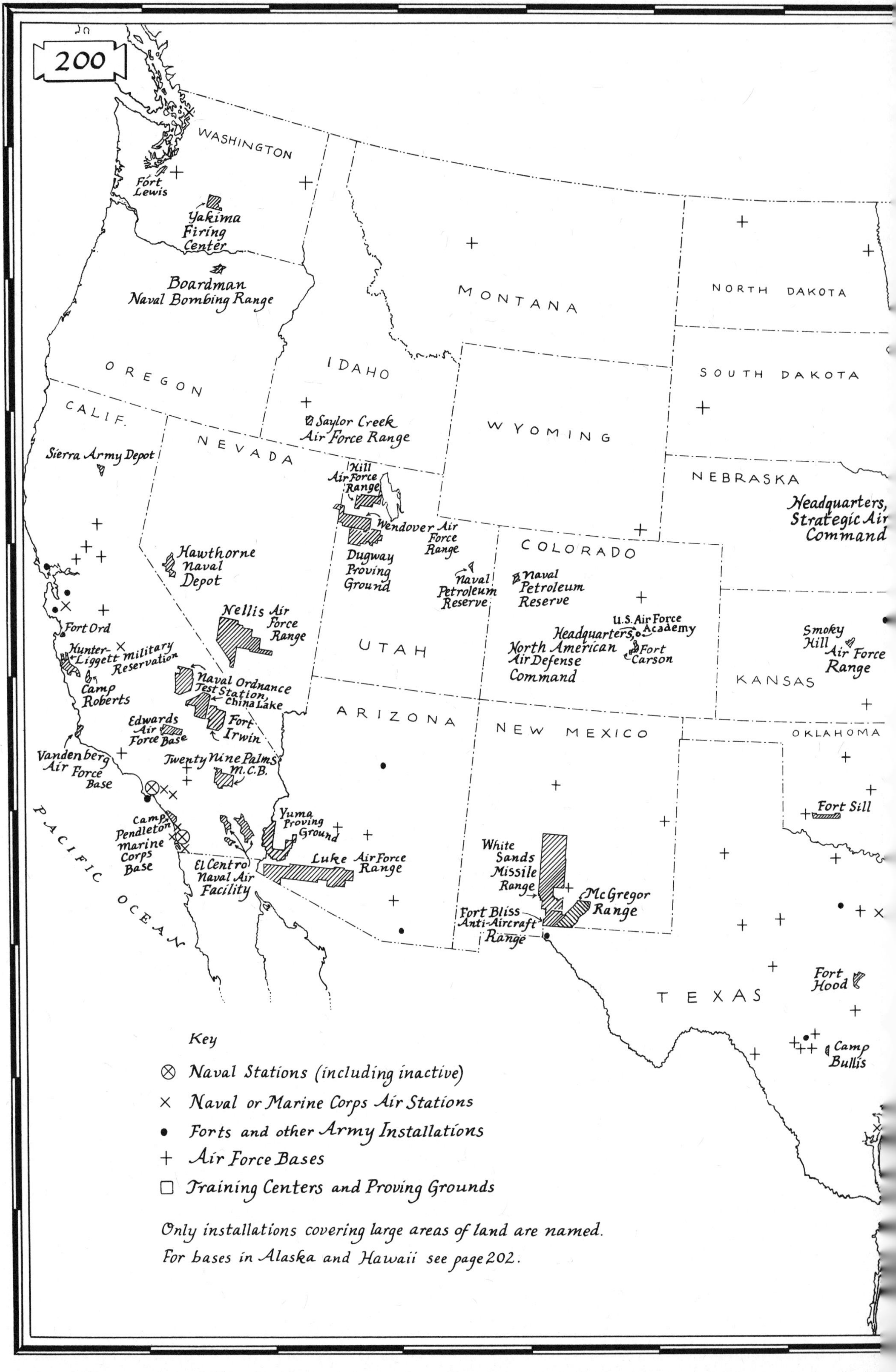
WASHINGTON
Fort Lewis
Yakima Firing Center
Boardman Naval Bombing Range
OREGON
MONTANA
NORTH DAKOTA
SOUTH DAKOTA
IDAHO
Saylor Creek Air Force Range
WYOMING
CALIF.
NEVADA
Sierra Army Depot
Hill Air Force Range
Wendover Air Force Range
NEBRASKA
Headquarters, Strategic Air Command
Hawthorne Naval Depot
Dugway Proving Ground
Naval Petroleum Reserve
COLORADO
Naval Petroleum Reserve
U.S. Air Force Academy
Headquarters, North American Air Defense Command
Fort Carson
Nellis Air Force Range
UTAH
Smoky Hill Air Force Range
KANSAS
Fort Ord
Hunter-Liggett Military Reservation
Camp Roberts
Naval Ordnance Test Station, China Lake
Fort Irwin
Edwards Air Force Base
ARIZONA
NEW MEXICO
OKLAHOMA
Vandenberg Air Force Base
Twenty Nine Palms M.C.B.
Fort Sill
PACIFIC OCEAN
Camp Pendleton Marine Corps Base
Yuma Proving Ground
El Centro Naval Air Facility
Luke Air Force Range
White Sands Missile Range
McGregor Range
Fort Bliss Anti-Aircraft Range
TEXAS
Fort Hood
Camp Bullis
Key
Naval Stations (including inactive)
Naval or Marine Corps Air Stations
Forts and other Army Installations
Air Force Bases
Training Centers and Proving Grounds
Only installations covering large areas of land are named.
For bases in Alaska and Hawaii see page 202.

MAJOR MILITARY BASES IN THE CONTINENTAL UNITED STATES, 1976

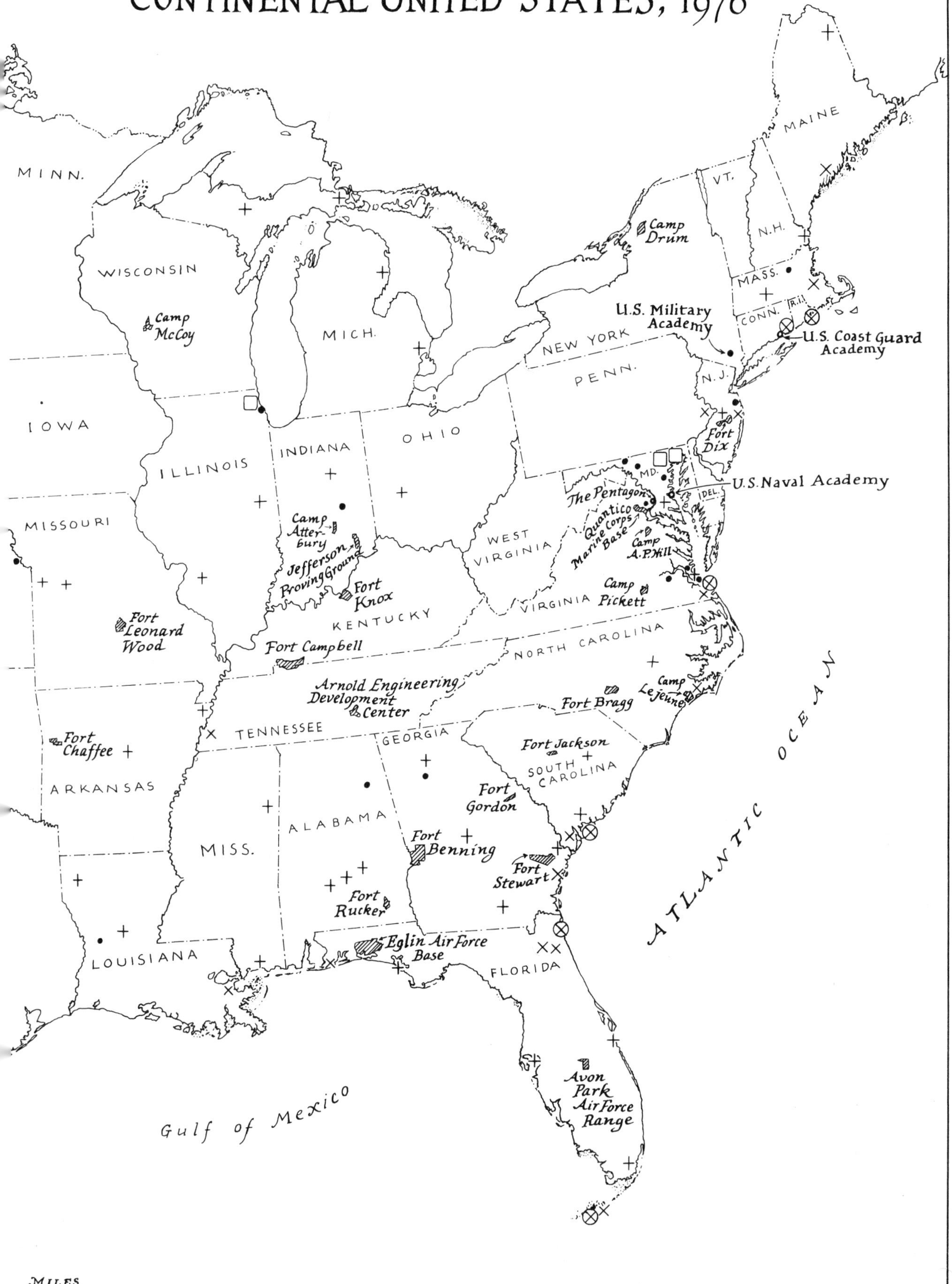

MAJOR AMERICAN MILITARY INSTALLATIONS ABROAD, 1977

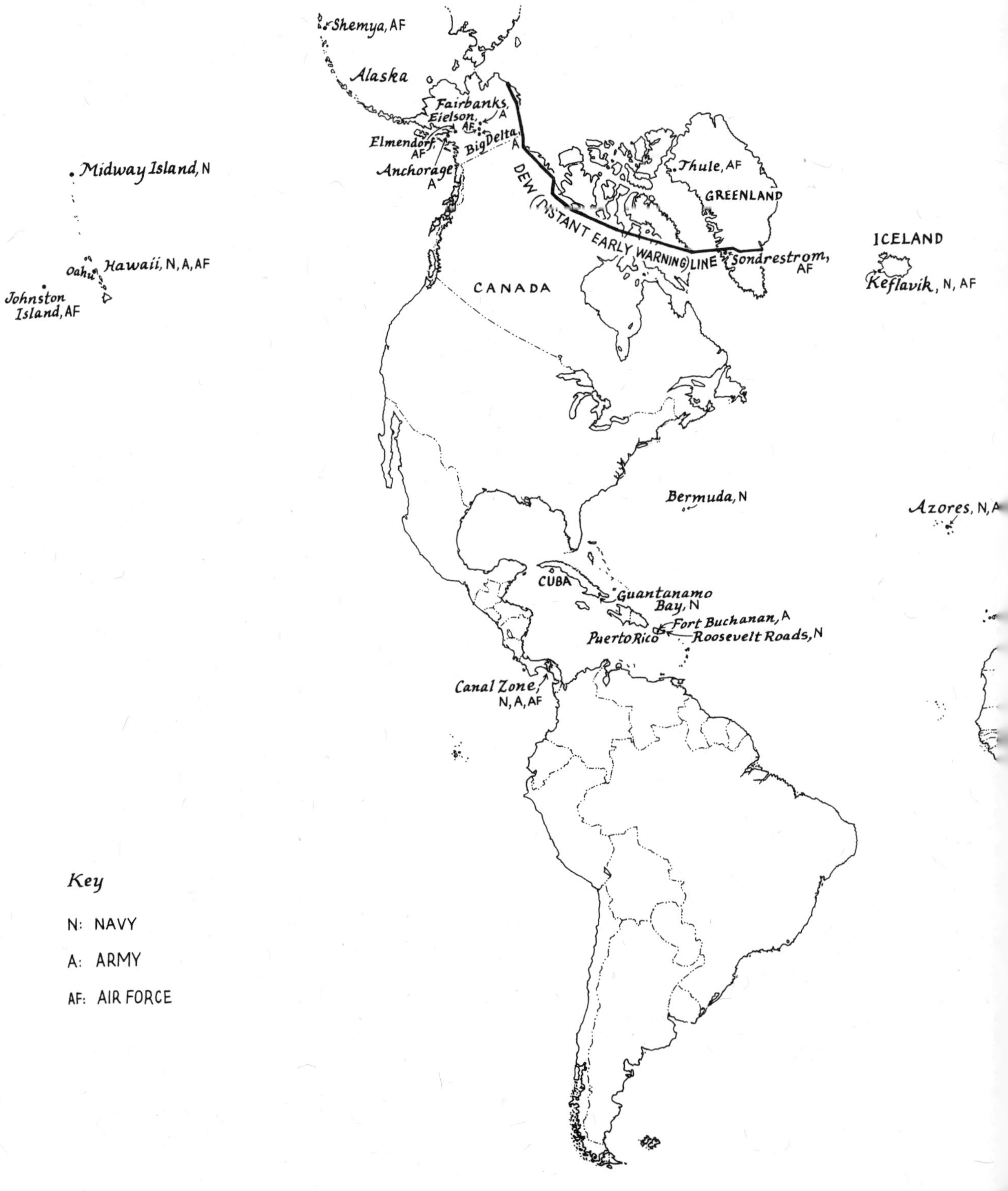

Machrihanish, N
UNITED KINGDOM
Upper Heyford, AF
Sculthorpe AF
Alconbury, AF
Lakenheath AF
Mildenhall N, AF
Bentwaters AF
London, N
FEDERAL REPUBLIC OF GERMANY
Berlin, A
BELGIUM
Brussels, NATO Headquarters
Frankfurt, A
Wiesbaden AF
Hanau, A
Hahn, AF
Rhein Main, AF
Mannheim, A
Heidelberg, A
Bitburg, AF
Spangdahlem, AF
Sembach, AF
Ramstein, AF
Zweibrucken, AF
Berchtesgaden, A
MILES
100
200
300

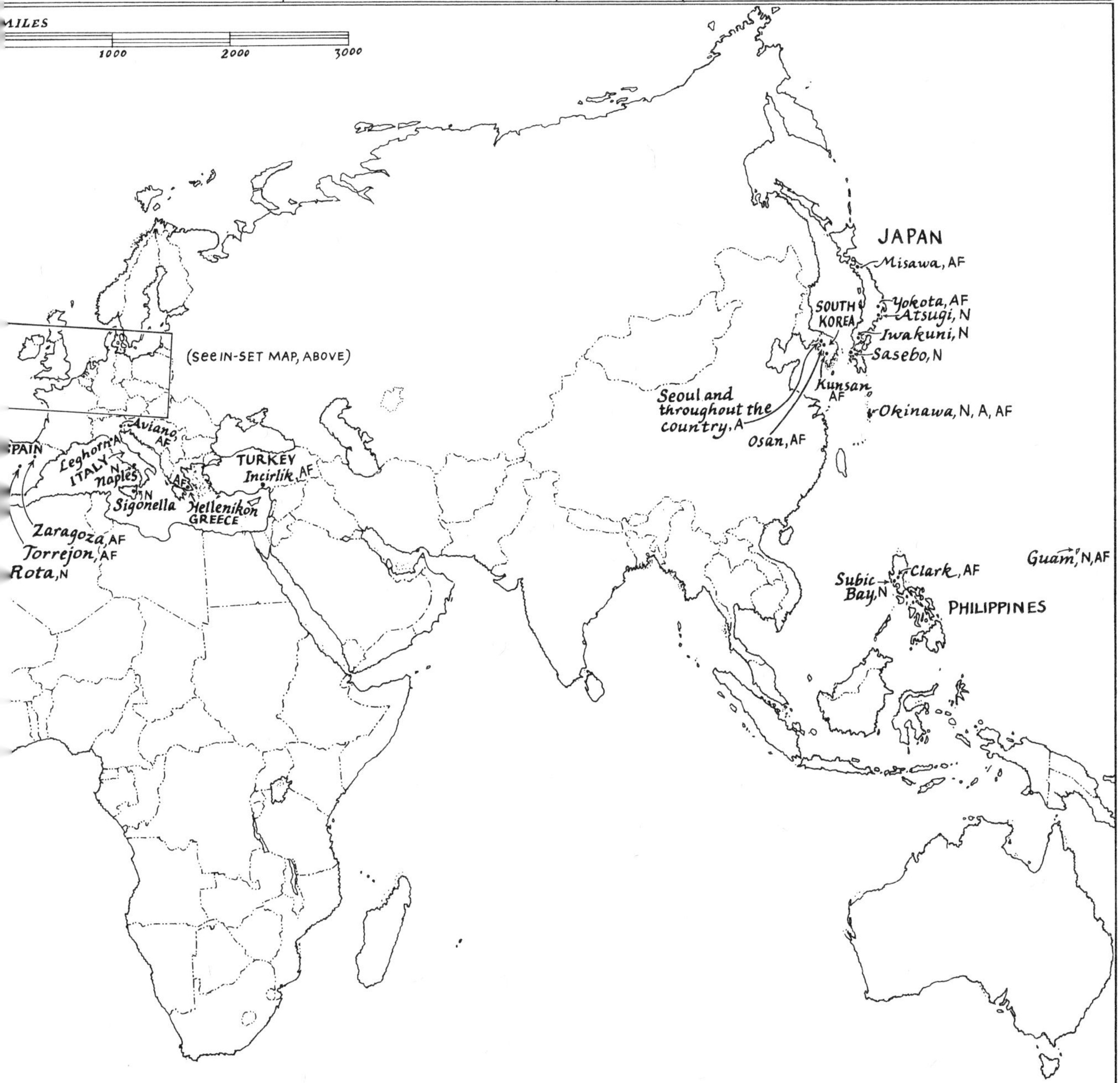
MILES
1000
2000
3000
(SEE IN-SET MAP, ABOVE)
JAPAN
Misawa, AF
Yokota, AF
Atsugi, N
Iwakuni, N
Sasebo, N
SOUTH KOREA
Kunsan AF
Seoul and throughout the country, A
Osan, AF
Okinawa, N, A, AF
SPAIN
Aviano AF
Leghorn, A
ITALY
Naples N
AF
N
Sigonella
Hellenikon
GREECE
TURKEY
Incirlik, AF
Zaragoza, AF
Torrejon, AF
Rota, N
Guam, N, AF
Subic Bay, N
Clark, AF
PHILIPPINES

X SOCIAL AND ECONOMIC DEVELOPMENTS

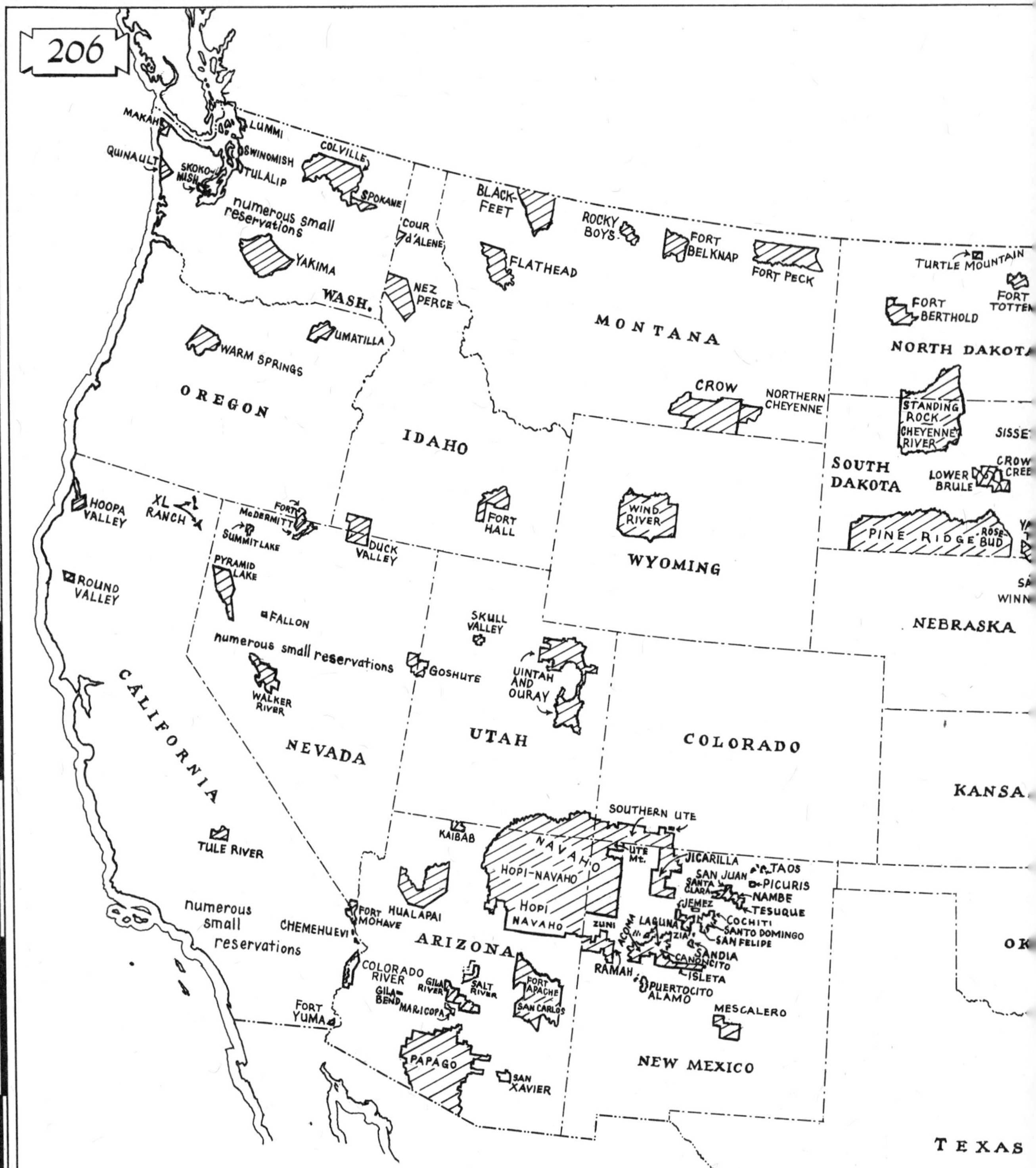

MAJOR INDIAN RESERVATIONS *IN THE* CONTINENTAL U.S. 1976

RED LAKE
NETT LAKE
DEER CREEK
GRAND PORTAGE
LEECH LAKE
WHITE EARTH
FOND du LAC
L'ANSE
BAD RIVER
LAC du FLAMBEAU
LAC COURT OREILLES
STOCKBRIDGE
ONEIDA
MICHIGAN
MINNESOTA
WISCONSIN
IOWA
OMAHA
ILLINOIS
INDIANA
OHIO
SAC AND FOX
KICKAPOO
POTAWATOMI
MISSOURI
KENTUCKY
OSAGE
OMA
TENNESSEE
ARKANSAS
CHOCTAW
MISSISSIPPI
ALABAMA
GEORGIA
LOUISIANA
FLORIDA
MAINE
SAINT REGIS
VT.
N.H.
NEW YORK
ONONDAGA
TUSCARORA
TONAWANDA
CATTARAUGUS
OIL SPRINGS
ALLEGANY
MASS.
CONN.
R.I.
PENNSYLVANIA
N.J.
MD.
DEL.
WEST VIRGINIA
VIRGINIA
NORTH CAROLINA
CHEROKEE
SOUTH CAROLINA
BRIGHTON
BIG CYPRESS
HOLLYWOOD
MICCOSUKEE
MILES
0
100
200
300
400

SOURCES OF IMMIGRATION

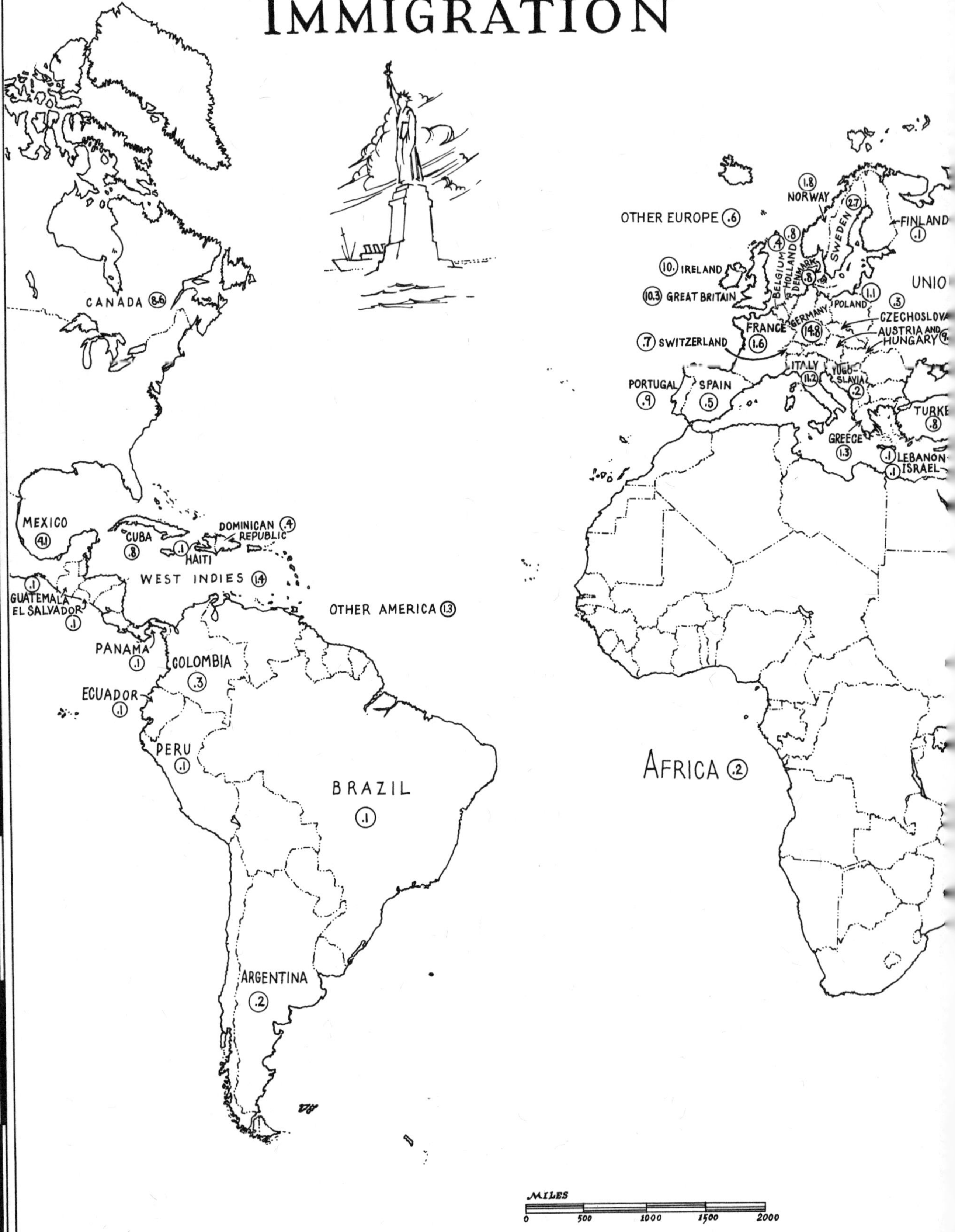

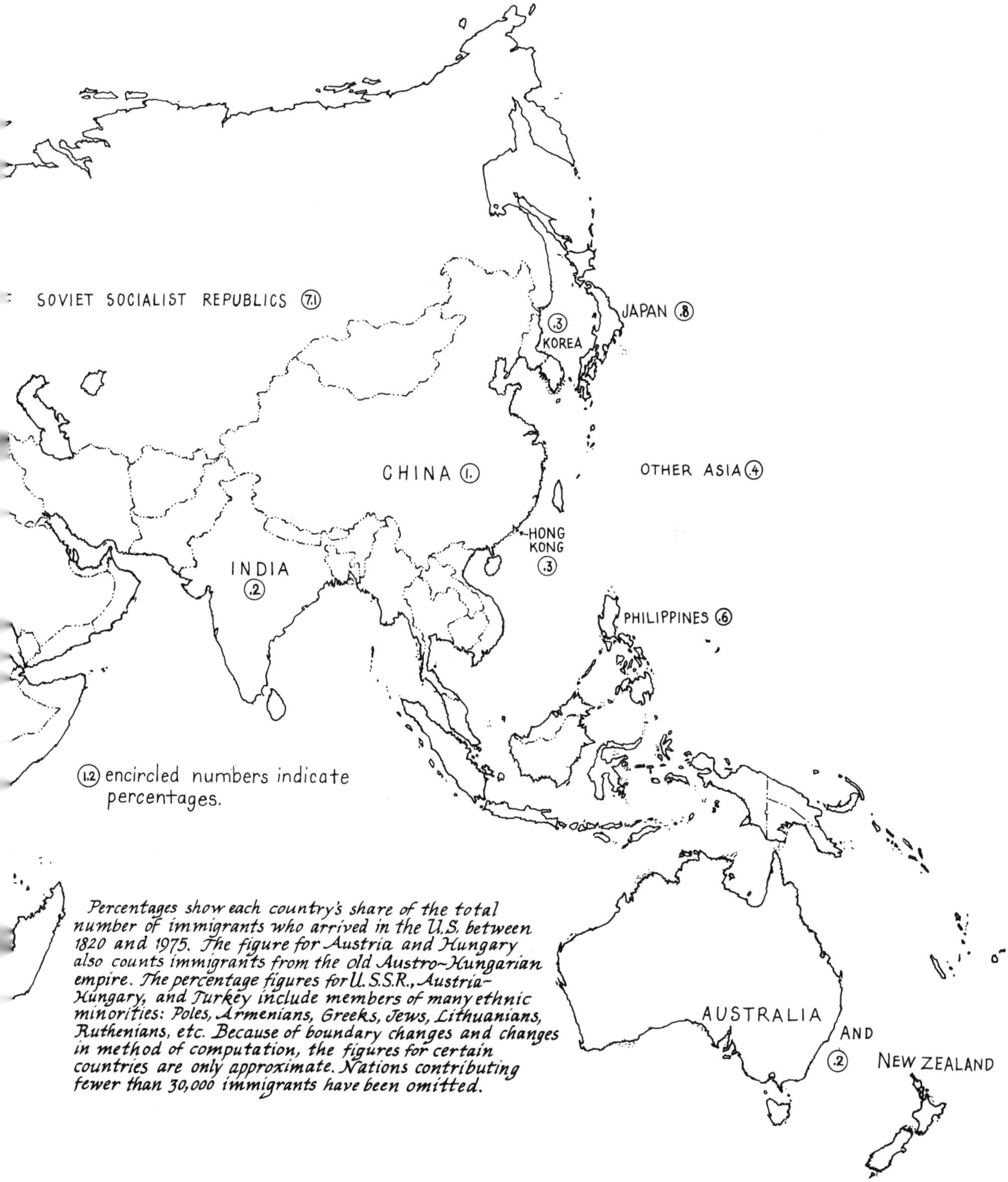

Percentages show each country's share of the total number of immigrants who arrived in the U.S. between 1820 and 1975. The figure for Austria and Hungary also counts immigrants from the old Austro-Hungarian empire. The percentage figures for U.S.S.R., Austria-Hungary, and Turkey include members of many ethnic minorities: Poles, Armenians, Greeks, Jews, Lithuanians, Ruthenians, etc. Because of boundary changes and changes in method of computation, the figures for certain countries are only approximate. Nations contributing fewer than 30,000 immigrants have been omitted.

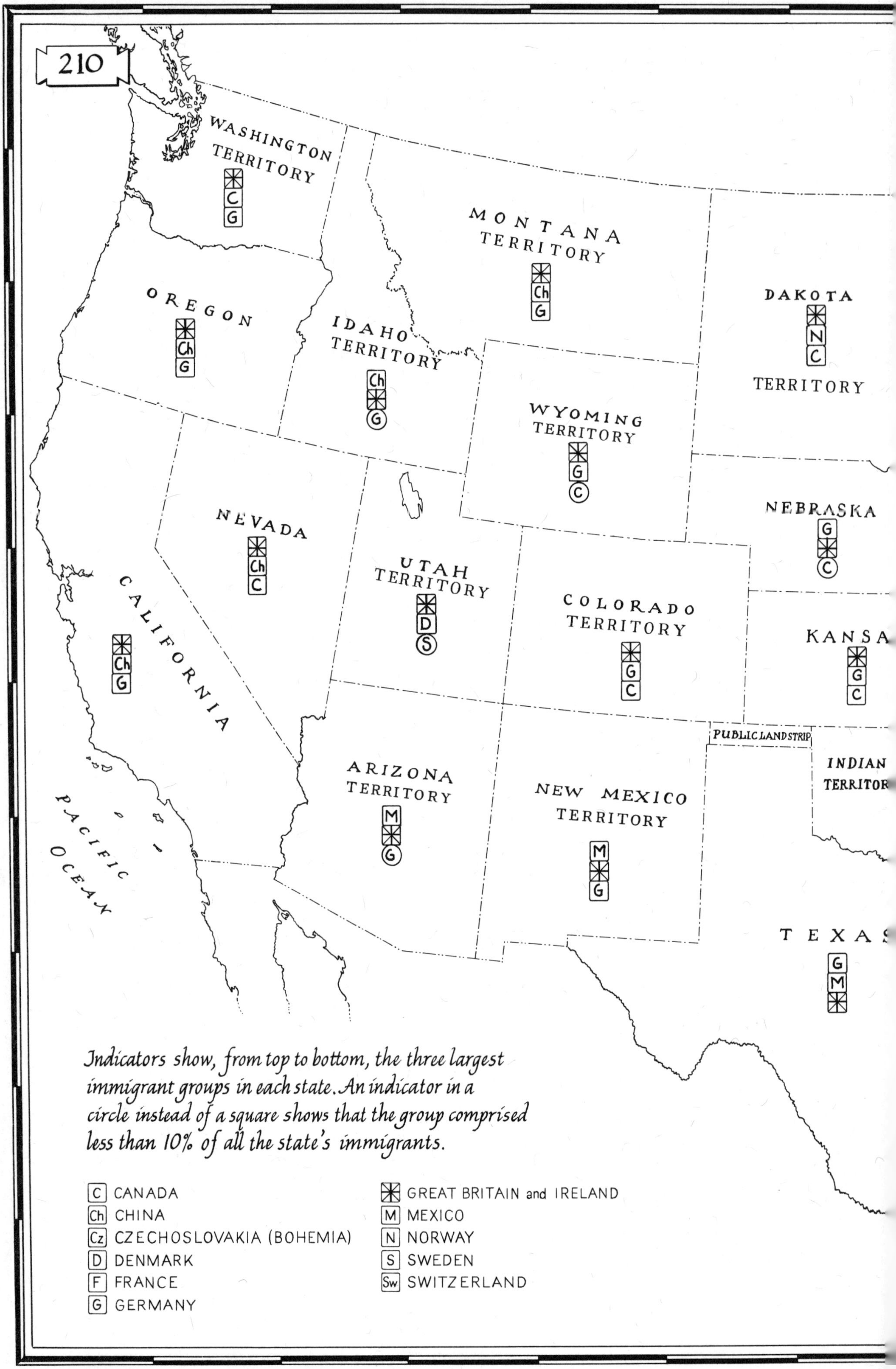
WASHINGTON TERRITORY
MONTANA TERRITORY
DAKOTA TERRITORY
OREGON
IDAHO TERRITORY
WYOMING TERRITORY
NEBRASKA
NEVADA
UTAH TERRITORY
COLORADO TERRITORY
KANSA
CALIFORNIA
PUBLIC LAND STRIP
INDIAN TERRITOR
ARIZONA TERRITORY
NEW MEXICO TERRITORY
PACIFIC OCEAN
TEXAS
C
Ch
G
N
D
S
M
Indicators show, from top to bottom, the three largest immigrant groups in each state. An indicator in a circle instead of a square shows that the group comprised less than 10% of all the state's immigrants.
C CANADA
Ch CHINA
Cz CZECHOSLOVAKIA (BOHEMIA)
D DENMARK
F FRANCE
G GERMANY
GREAT BRITAIN and IRELAND
M MEXICO
N NORWAY
S SWEDEN
Sw SWITZERLAND

SOURCES OF IMMIGRATION 1870

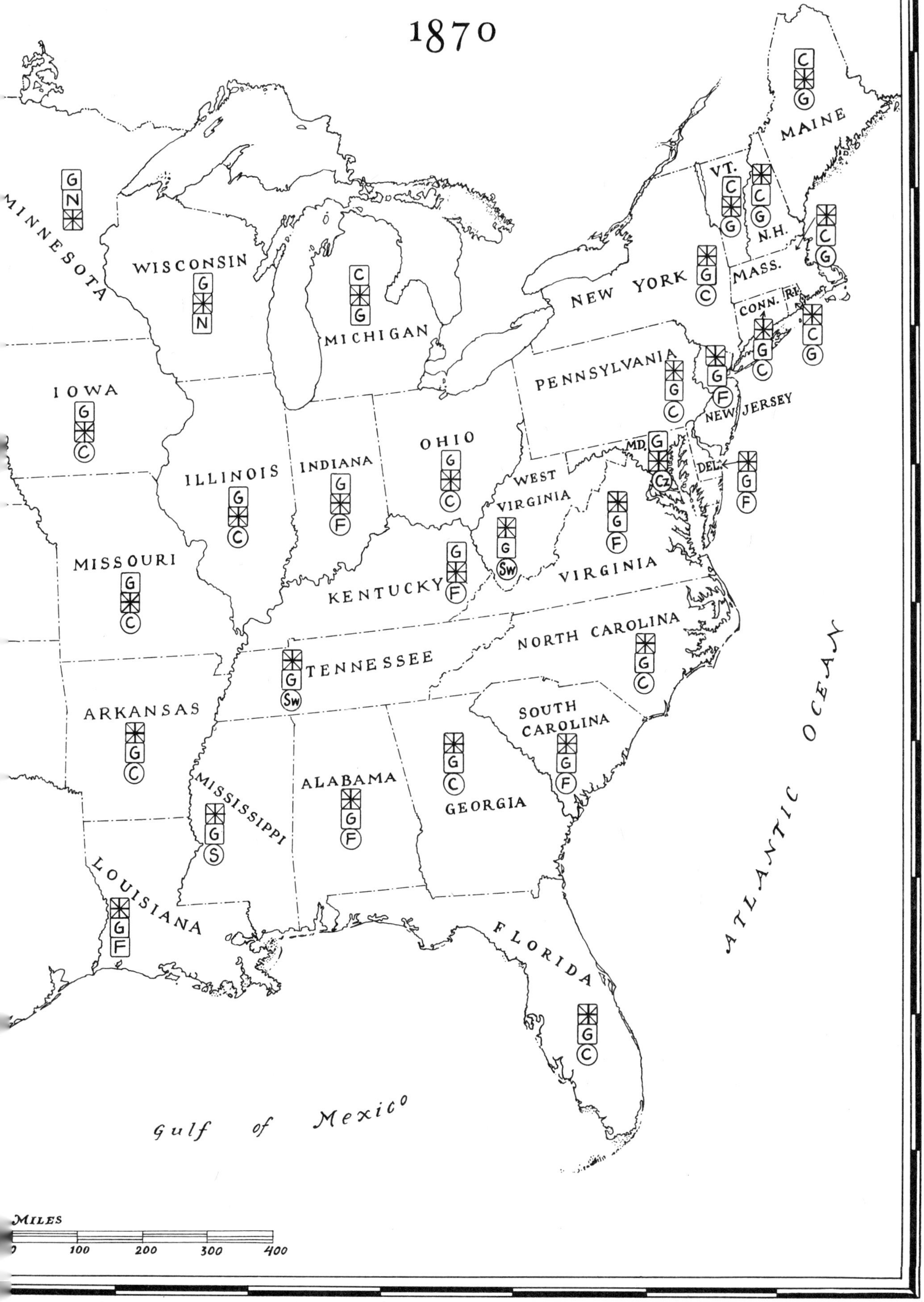

THE FOREIGN BORN 1870

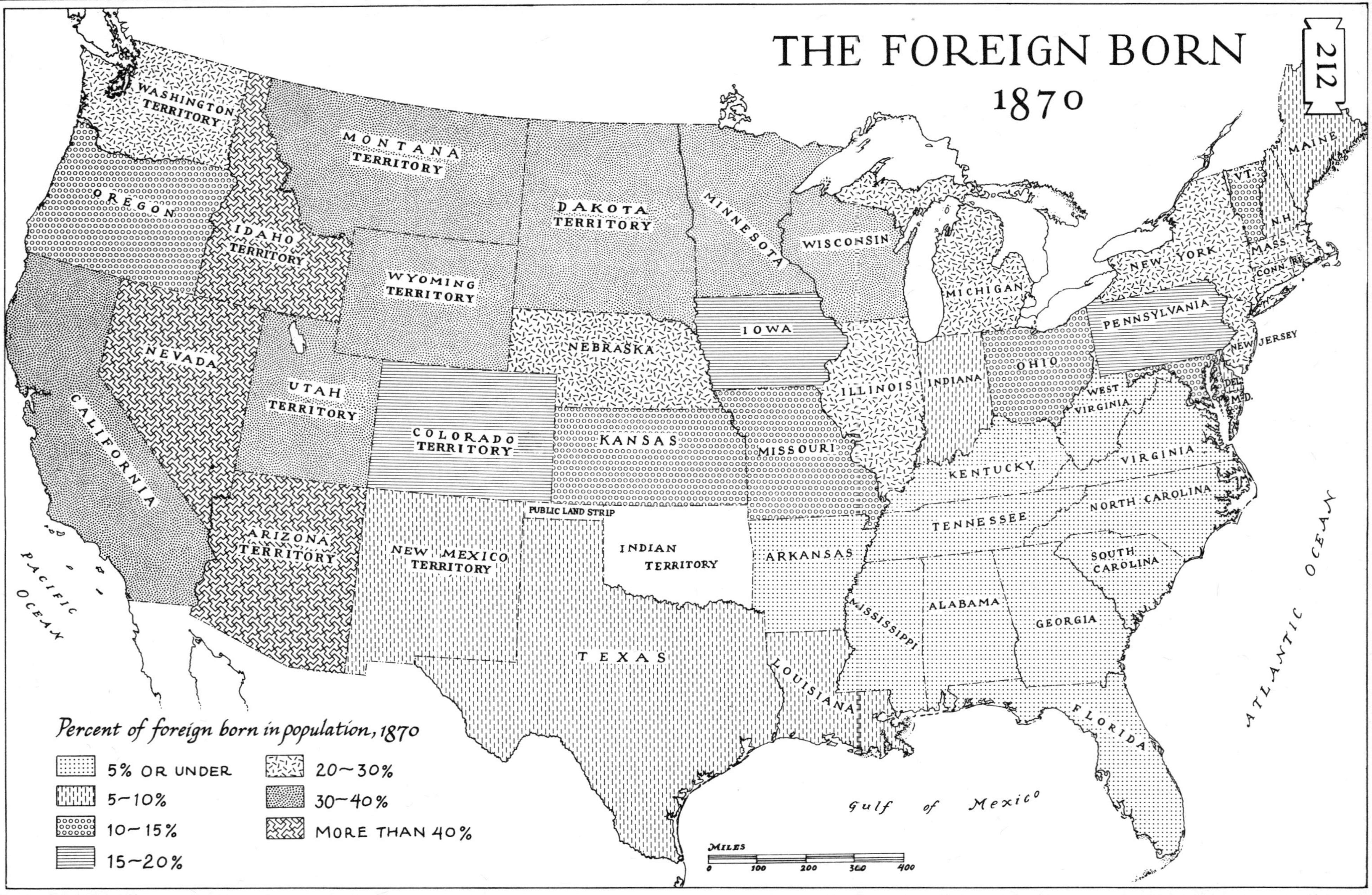

THE FOREIGN BORN 1920

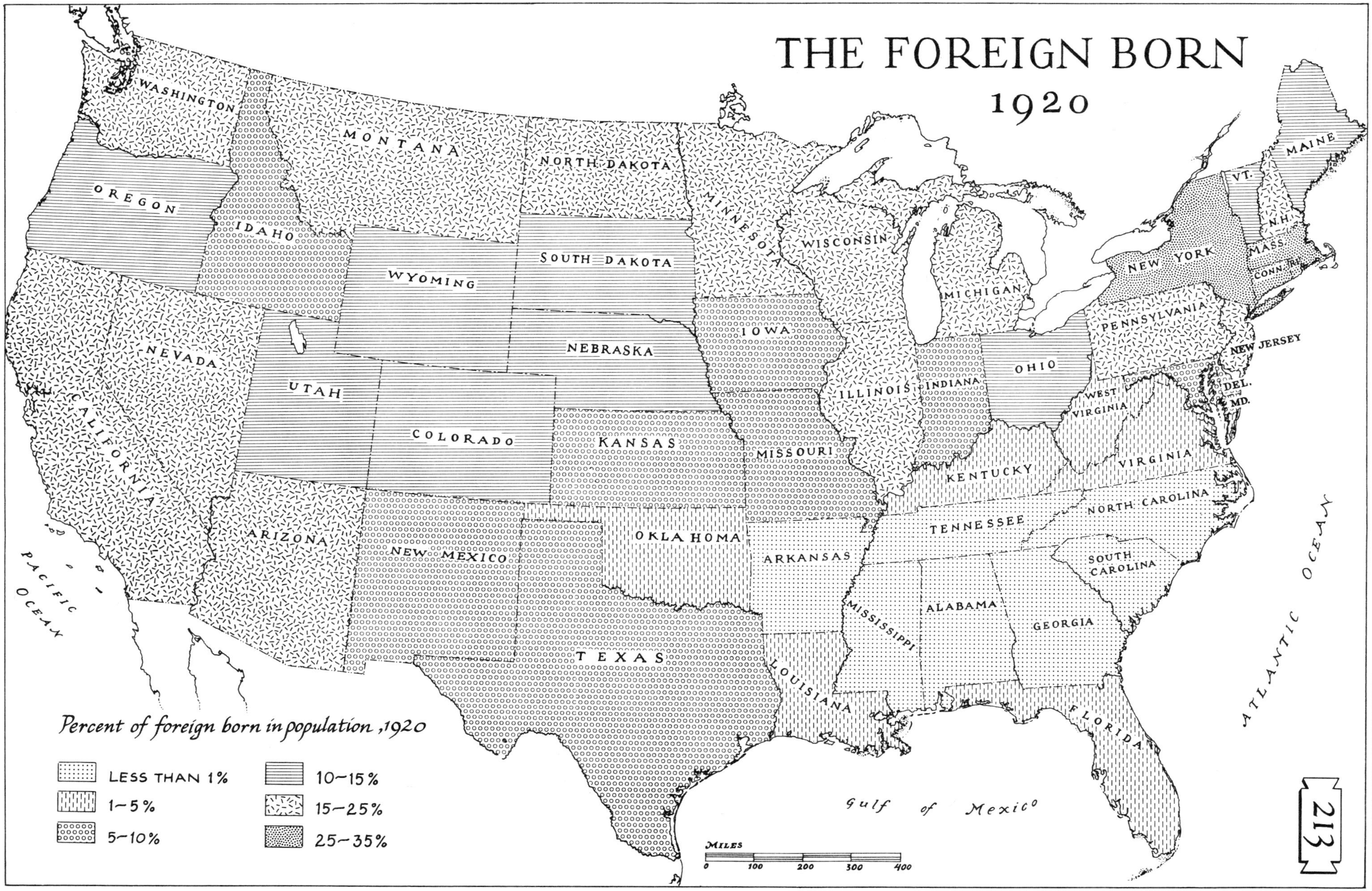

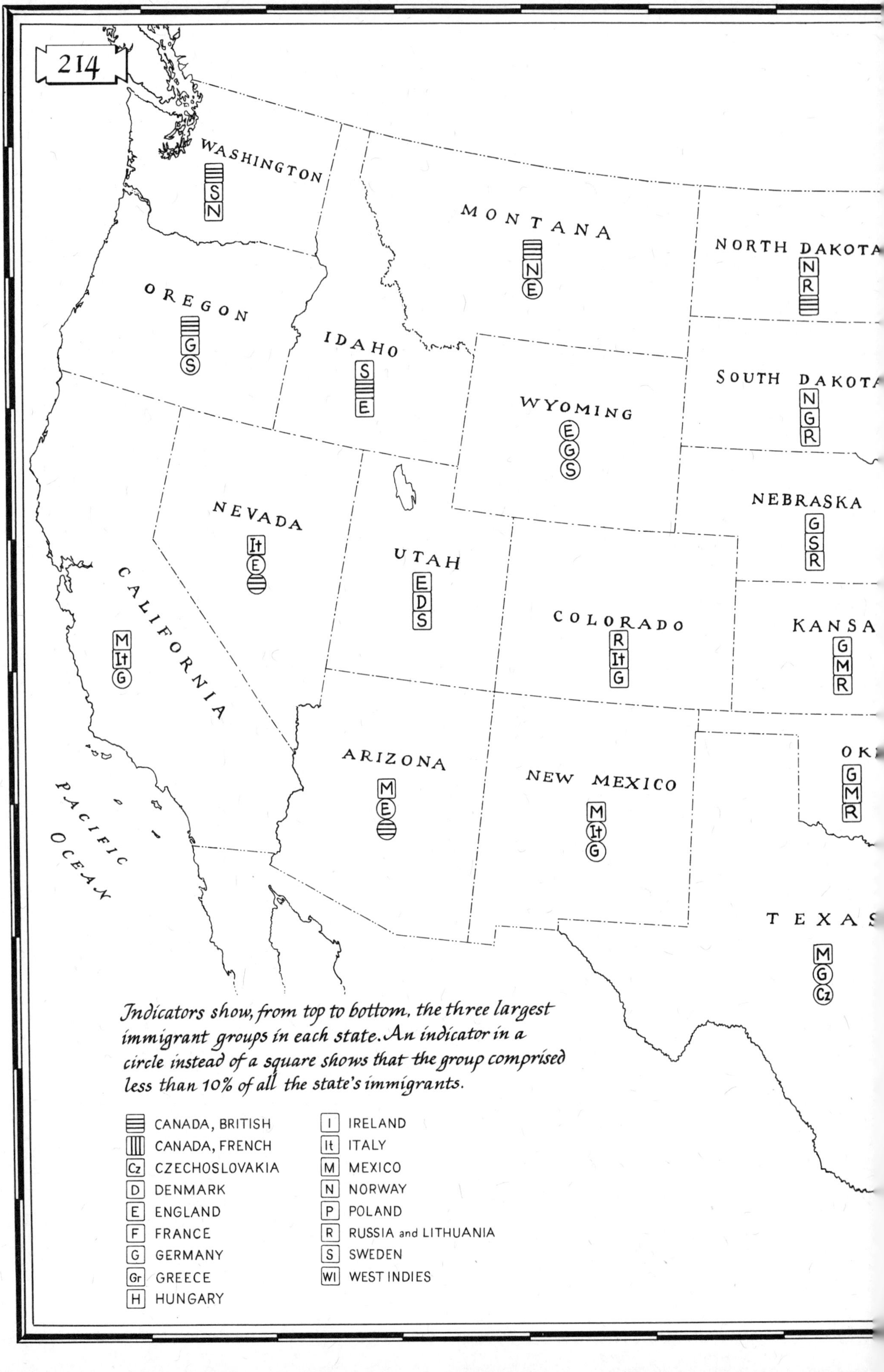

Indicators show, from top to bottom, the three largest immigrant groups in each state. An indicator in a circle instead of a square shows that the group comprised less than 10% of all the state's immigrants.

SOURCES OF IMMIGRATION 1920

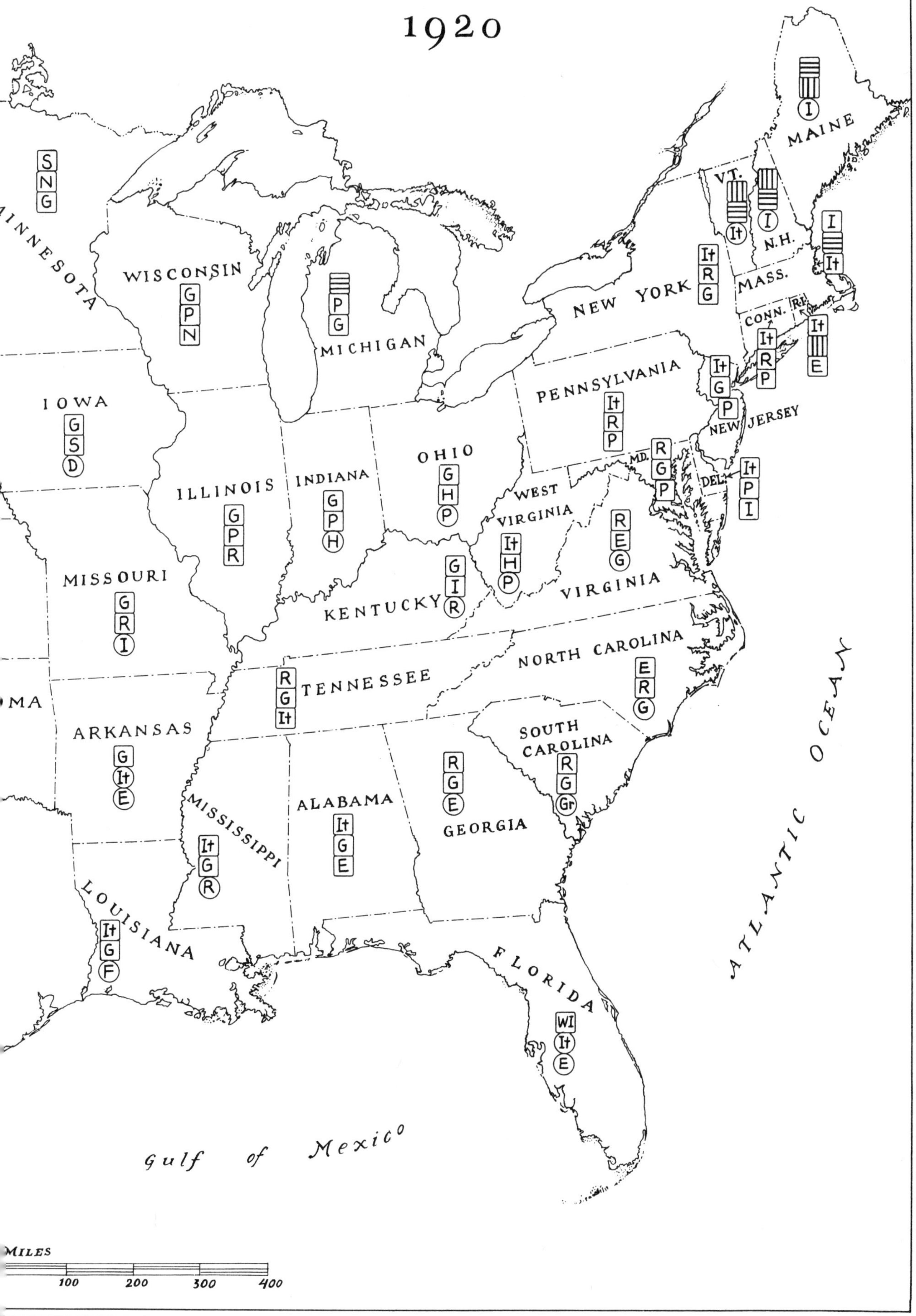

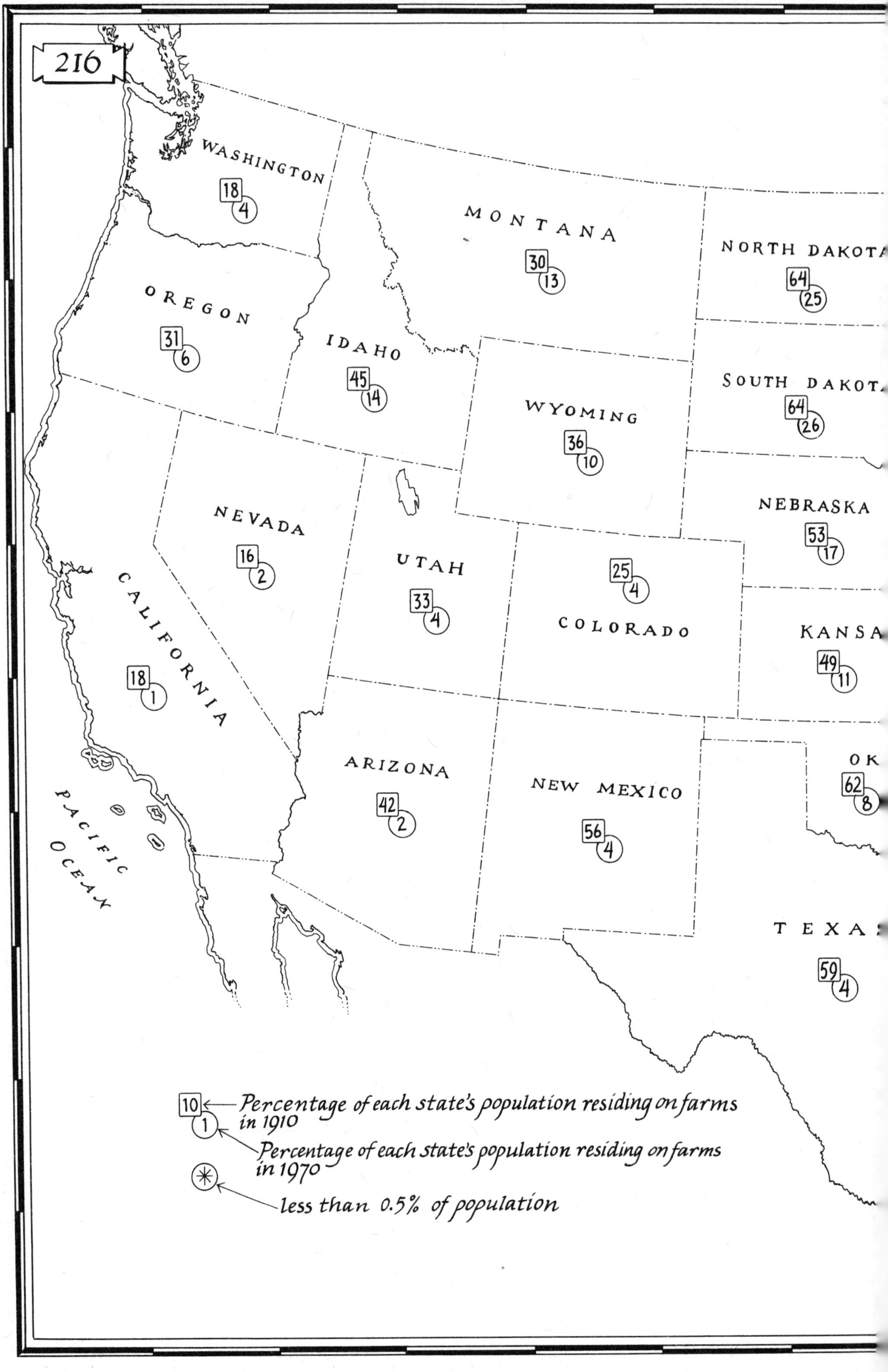
WASHINGTON 18 4
OREGON 31 6
CALIFORNIA 18 1
NEVADA 16 2
IDAHO 45 14
MONTANA 30 13
WYOMING 36 10
UTAH 33 4
COLORADO 25 4
ARIZONA 42 2
NEW MEXICO 56 4
NORTH DAKOTA 64 25
SOUTH DAKOTA 64 26
NEBRASKA 53 17
KANSA 49 11
OK 62 8
TEXAS 59 4
PACIFIC OCEAN
10 Percentage of each state's population residing on farms in 1910
1 Percentage of each state's population residing on farms in 1970
* less than 0.5% of population

FARM POPULATION 1910~1970

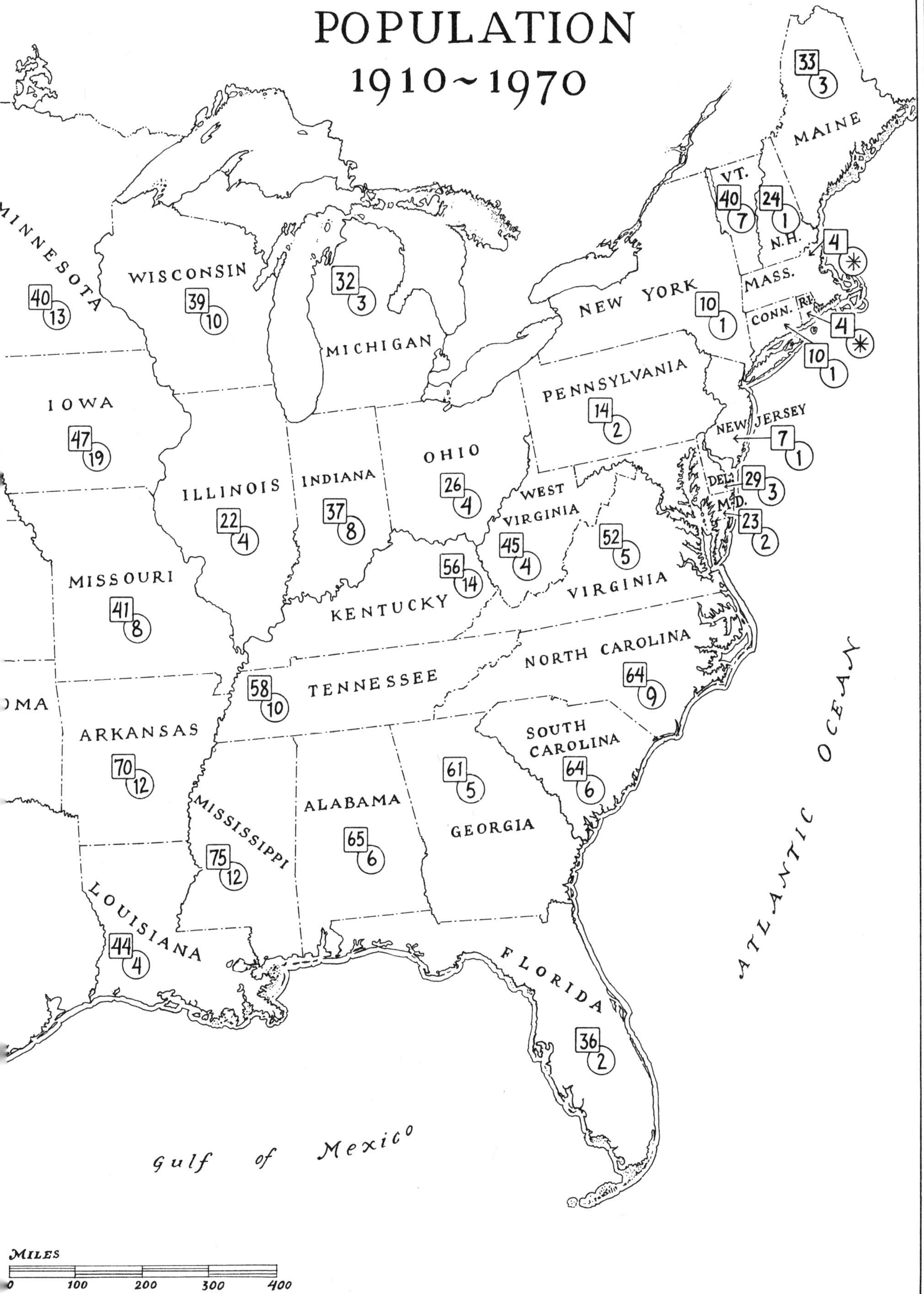

218
BLACK MIGRATION 1890~1970
In 1890, 20% of the black population was urban.
In 1970, 81% of the black population was urban.
① rank among the twelve cities with the largest black population, 1890
[2] rank among the twelve cities with the largest black population, 1970
✳ black population exceeded 40% in 1890
In the cities underlined, the black population exceeded 40% in 1970.
WASHINGTON
OREGON
CALIFORNIA
NEVADA
IDAHO
MONTANA
WYOMING
UTAH
ARIZONA
COLORADO
NEW MEXICO
NORTH DAKOTA
SOUTH DAKOTA
NEBRASKA
KANSAS
OKLAHOMA
TEXAS
MINNESOTA
IOWA
MISSOURI
ARKANSAS
LOUISIANA
WISCONSIN
ILLINOIS
MICHIGAN
INDIANA
OHIO
KENTUCKY
TENNESSEE
MISSISSIPPI
ALABAMA
GEORGIA
FLORIDA
SOUTH CAROLINA
NORTH CAROLINA
VIRGINIA
WEST VIRGINIA
PENNSYLVANIA
NEW YORK
MD.
DEL.
N.J.
CONN.
R.I.
MASS.
VT.
N.H.
MAINE
⑩ San Francisco
[6] Los Angeles
[8] Houston
③ [10] New Orleans
St. Louis ⑫ [12]
[2] Chicago
Detroit [3]
[9] Cleveland
⑨ Louisville
⑦ Nashville
⑧ ✳ Memphis
Atlanta ⑪ ✳ [11]
✳ ⑥ Charleston
Richmond ⑤
Washington ① [5]
Baltimore ② [7]
Philadelphia ④ [4]
[1] New York
PACIFIC OCEAN
ATLANTIC OCEAN
Gulf of Mexico
MILES
0
100
200
300
400

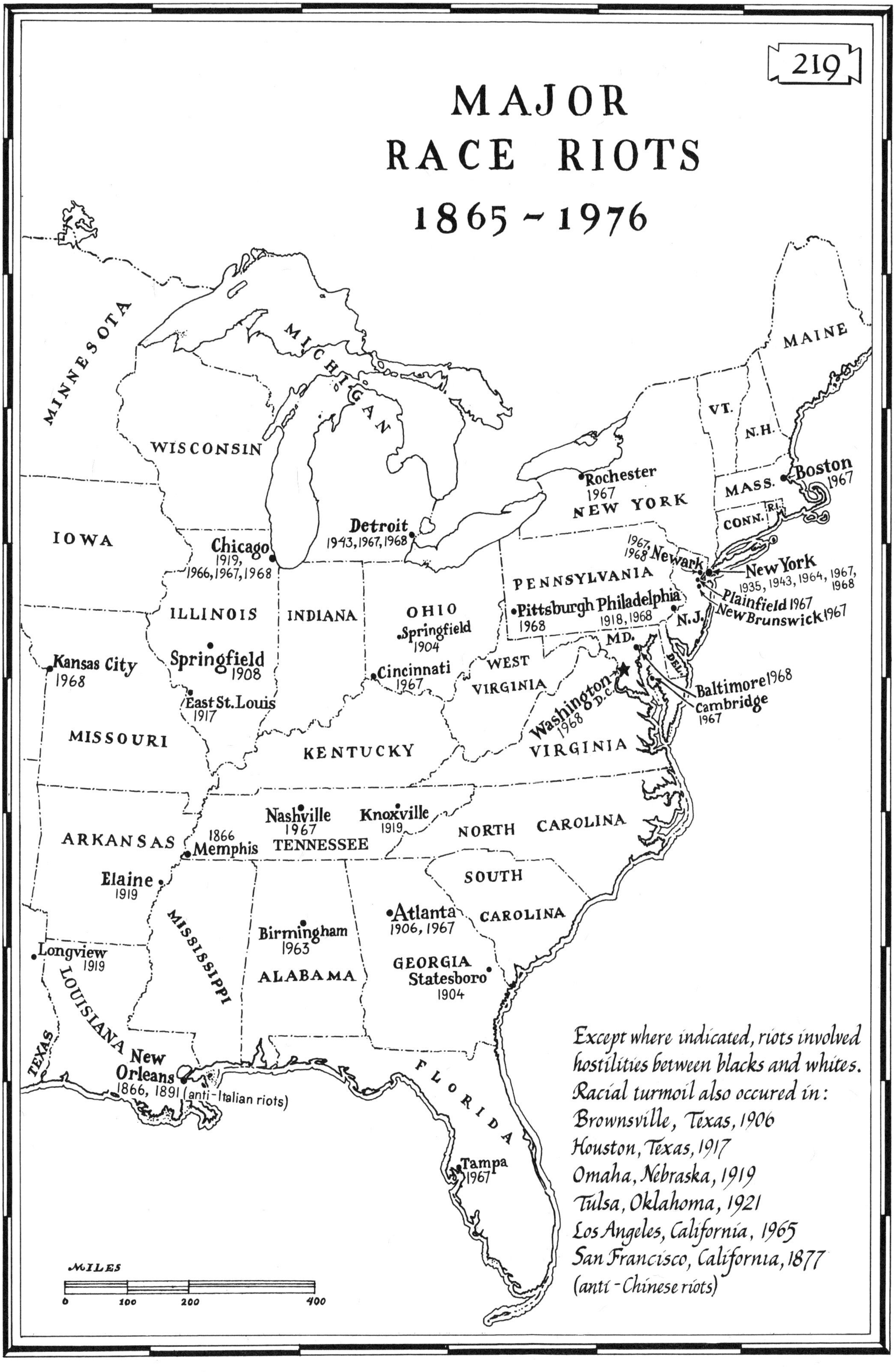
MAJOR
RACE RIOTS
1865 ~ 1976
MINNESOTA
WISCONSIN
MICHIGAN
MAINE
VT.
N.H.
MASS.
CONN.
R.I.
NEW YORK
IOWA
ILLINOIS
INDIANA
OHIO
PENNSYLVANIA
N.J.
MD.
DEL.
WEST VIRGINIA
VIRGINIA
MISSOURI
KENTUCKY
TENNESSEE
NORTH CAROLINA
SOUTH CAROLINA
ARKANSAS
MISSISSIPPI
ALABAMA
GEORGIA
LOUISIANA
TEXAS
FLORIDA
Rochester 1967
Boston 1967
Detroit 1943, 1967, 1968
Chicago 1919, 1966, 1967, 1968
1967, 1968 Newark
New York 1935, 1943, 1964, 1967, 1968
Plainfield 1967
New Brunswick 1967
Pittsburgh 1968
Philadelphia 1918, 1968
Springfield 1904
Kansas City 1968
Springfield 1908
Cincinnati 1967
East St. Louis 1917
Washington D.C. 1968
Baltimore 1968
Cambridge 1967
Nashville 1967
Knoxville 1919
1866 Memphis
Elaine 1919
Atlanta 1906, 1967
Birmingham 1963
Statesboro 1904
Longview 1919
New Orleans 1866, 1891 (anti-Italian riots)
Tampa 1967
Except where indicated, riots involved hostilities between blacks and whites.
Racial turmoil also occured in:
Brownsville, Texas, 1906
Houston, Texas, 1917
Omaha, Nebraska, 1919
Tulsa, Oklahoma, 1921
Los Angeles, California, 1965
San Francisco, California, 1877 (anti-Chinese riots)
MILES
0
100
200
400

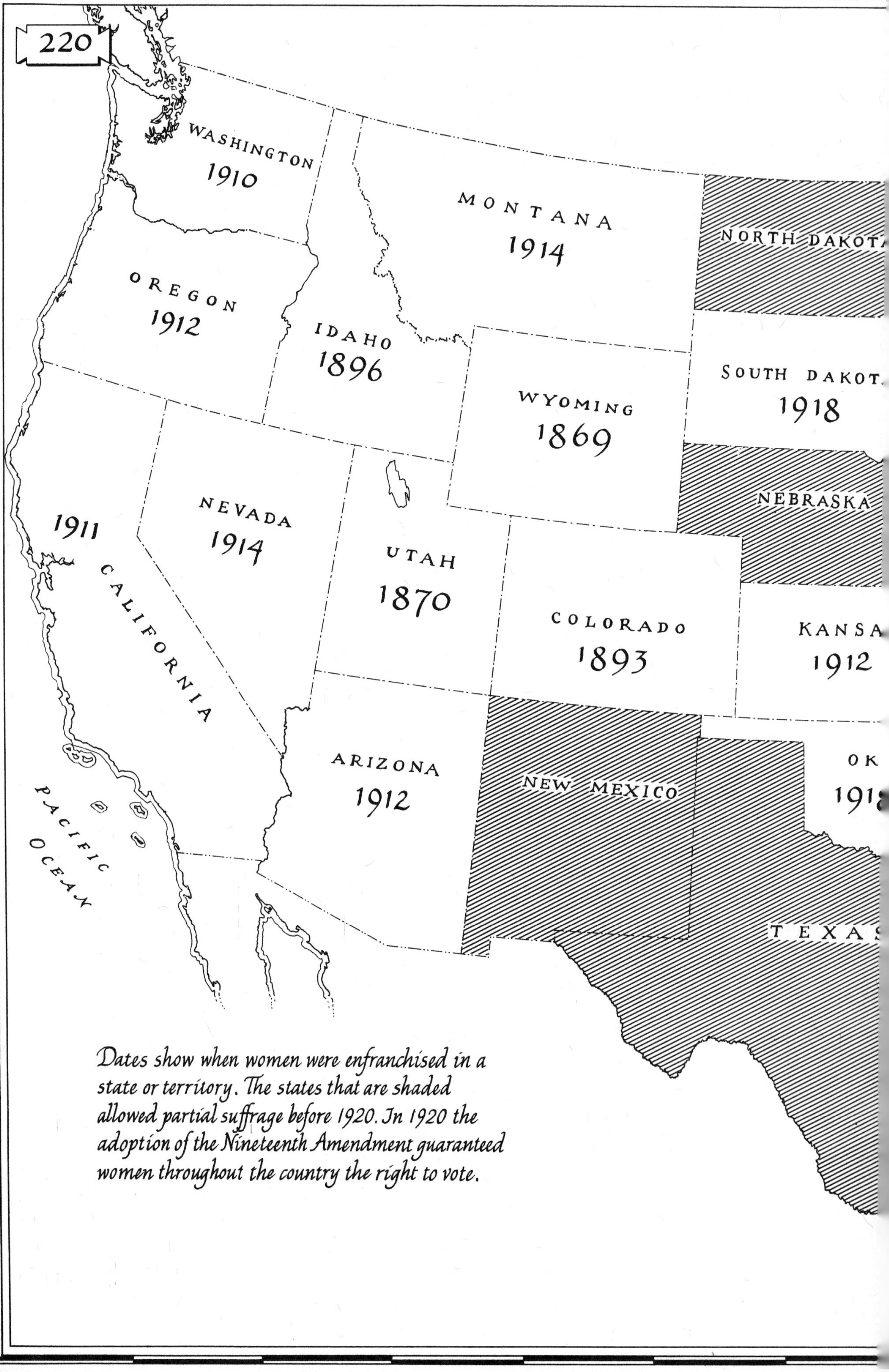

Dates show when women were enfranchised in a state or territory. The states that are shaded allowed partial suffrage before 1920. In 1920 the adoption of the Nineteenth Amendment guaranteed women throughout the country the right to vote.

WOMAN'S SUFFRAGE 1869~1920

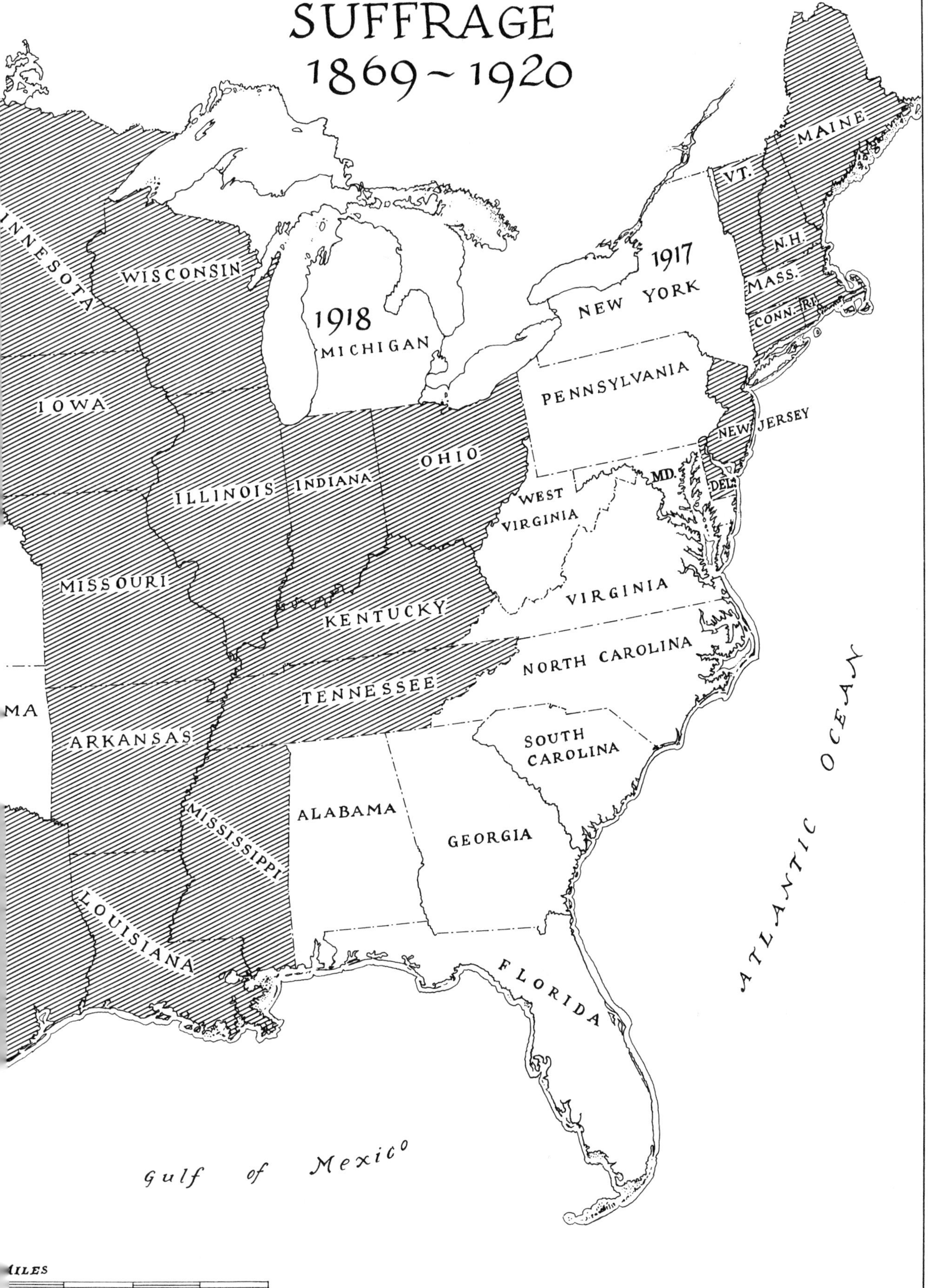

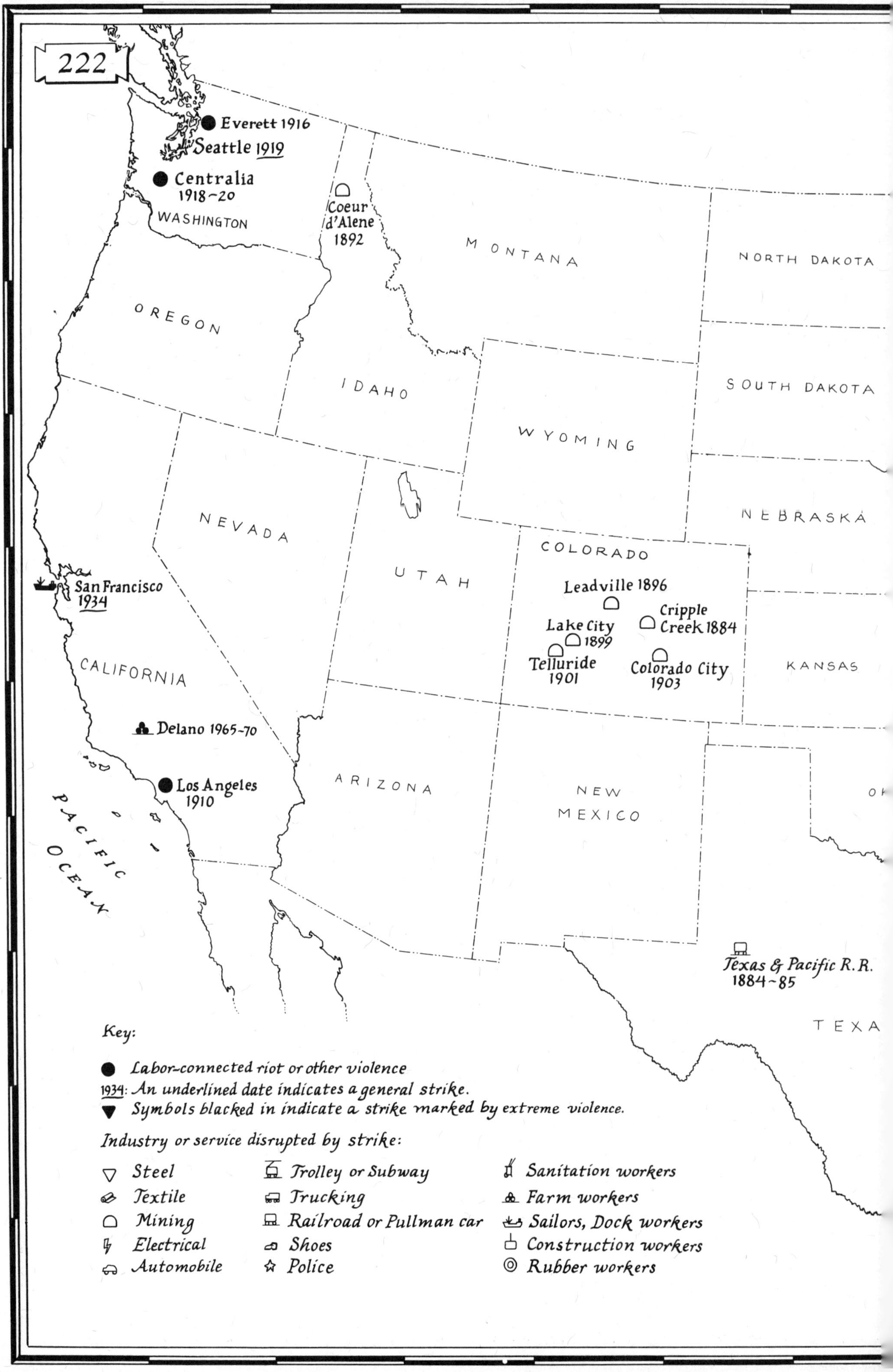
Everett 1916
Seattle 1919
Centralia
1918–20
WASHINGTON
Coeur d'Alene
1892
MONTANA
NORTH DAKOTA
OREGON
IDAHO
SOUTH DAKOTA
WYOMING
NEBRASKA
NEVADA
UTAH
COLORADO
Leadville 1896
Cripple Creek 1884
Lake City 1899
Telluride 1901
Colorado City 1903
KANSAS
San Francisco 1934
CALIFORNIA
Delano 1965–70
Los Angeles 1910
ARIZONA
NEW MEXICO
PACIFIC OCEAN
Texas & Pacific R.R.
1884–85
TEXA
Key:
Labor-connected riot or other violence
1934: An underlined date indicates a general strike.
Symbols blacked in indicate a strike marked by extreme violence.
Industry or service disrupted by strike:
Steel
Textile
Mining
Electrical
Automobile
Trolley or Subway
Trucking
Railroad or Pullman car
Shoes
Police
Sanitation workers
Farm workers
Sailors, Dock workers
Construction workers
Rubber workers

LABOR STRIFE 1803–1970

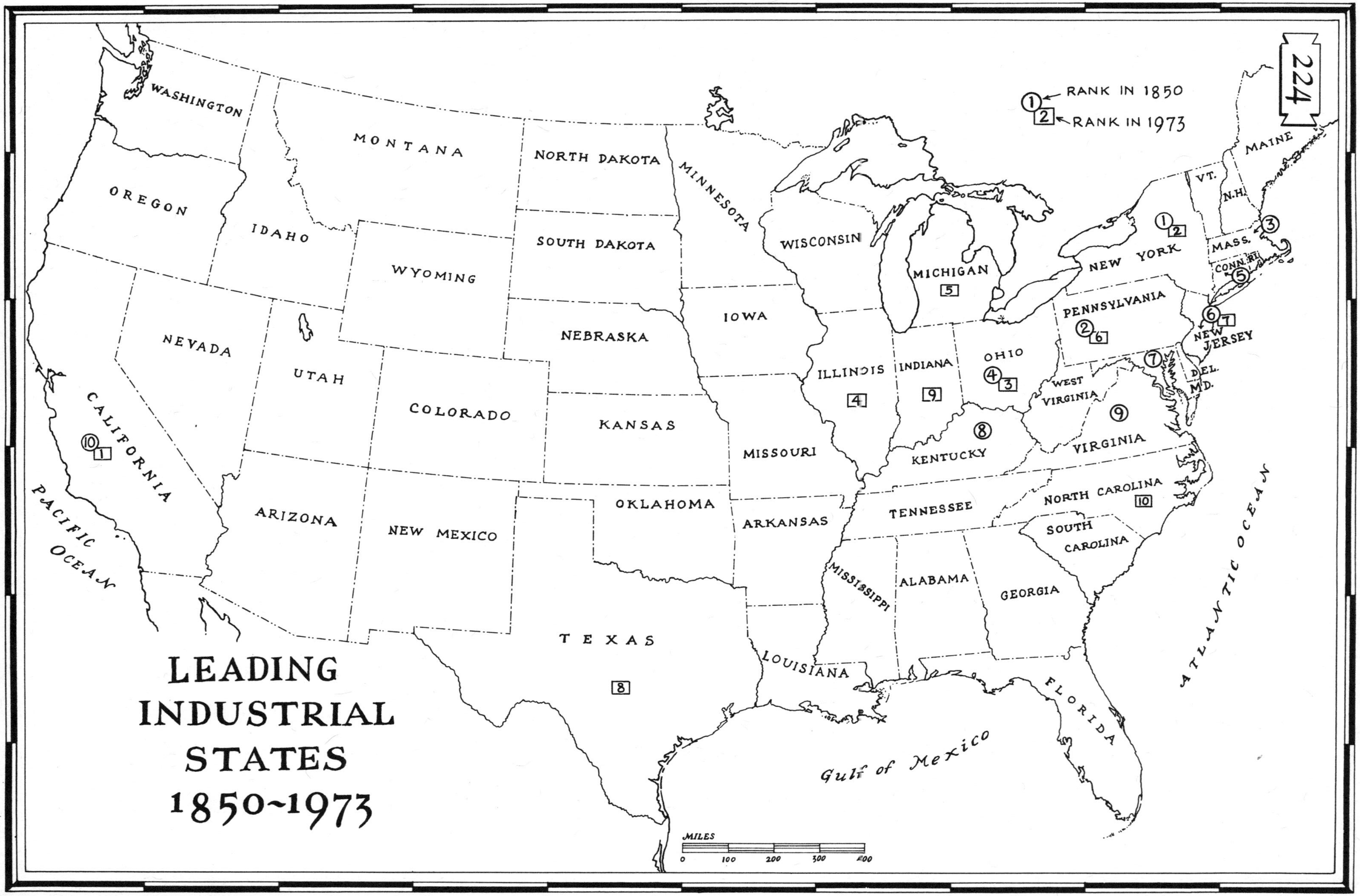
224
LEADING INDUSTRIAL STATES 1850-1973
RANK IN 1850
RANK IN 1973
WASHINGTON
OREGON
CALIFORNIA
NEVADA
IDAHO
MONTANA
WYOMING
UTAH
ARIZONA
COLORADO
NEW MEXICO
NORTH DAKOTA
SOUTH DAKOTA
NEBRASKA
KANSAS
OKLAHOMA
TEXAS
MINNESOTA
IOWA
MISSOURI
ARKANSAS
LOUISIANA
WISCONSIN
ILLINOIS
MICHIGAN
INDIANA
OHIO
KENTUCKY
TENNESSEE
MISSISSIPPI
ALABAMA
GEORGIA
FLORIDA
SOUTH CAROLINA
NORTH CAROLINA
VIRGINIA
WEST VIRGINIA
PENNSYLVANIA
NEW YORK
NEW JERSEY
DEL.
MD.
CONN.
R.I.
MASS.
VT.
N.H.
MAINE
PACIFIC OCEAN
ATLANTIC OCEAN
Gulf of Mexico
MILES
0 100 200 300 400

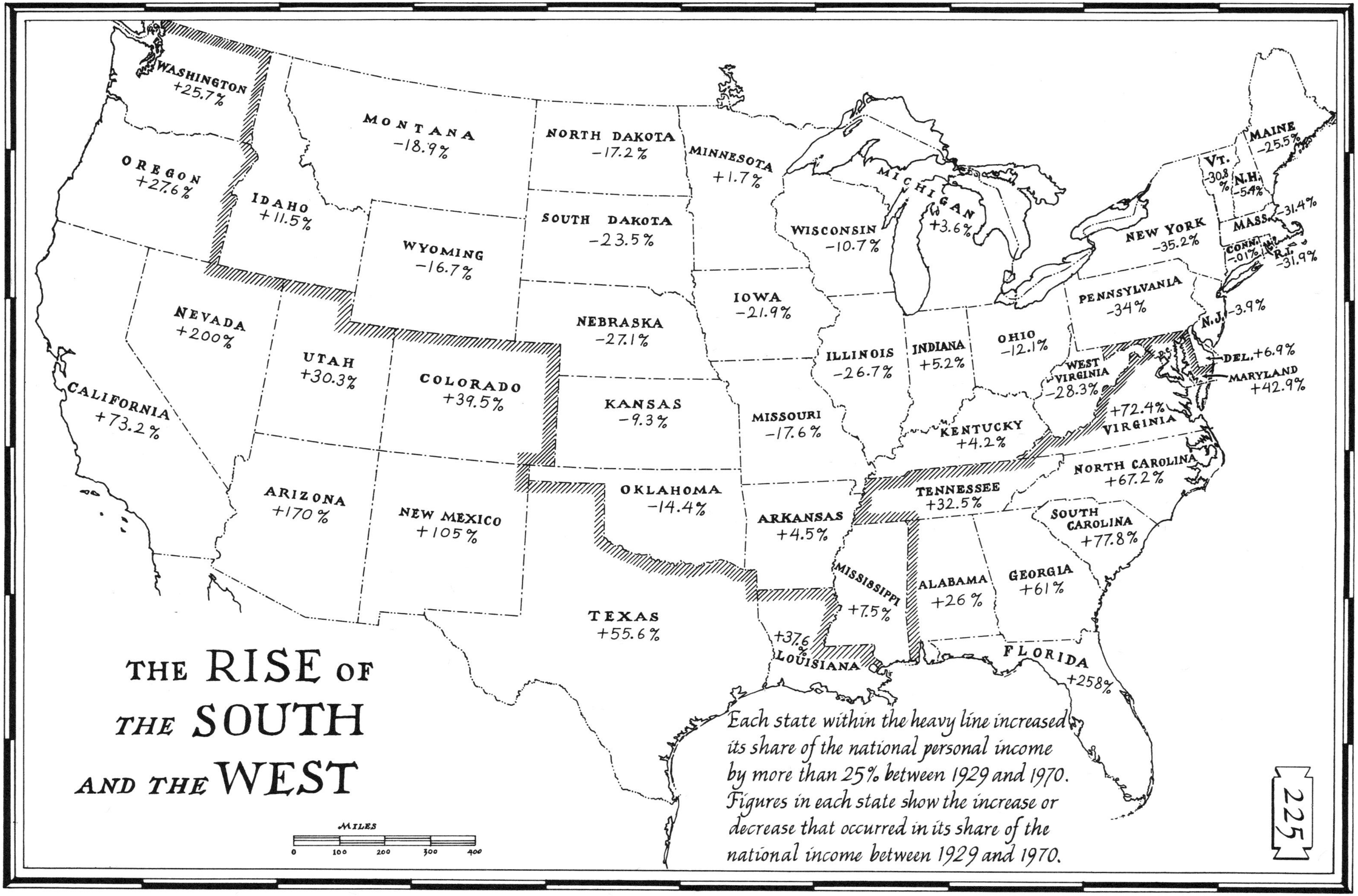
THE RISE OF THE SOUTH AND THE WEST
WASHINGTON +25.7%
OREGON +27.6%
CALIFORNIA +73.2%
IDAHO +11.5%
NEVADA +200%
MONTANA -18.9%
WYOMING -16.7%
UTAH +30.3%
ARIZONA +170%
COLORADO +39.5%
NEW MEXICO +105%
NORTH DAKOTA -17.2%
SOUTH DAKOTA -23.5%
NEBRASKA -27.1%
KANSAS -9.3%
OKLAHOMA -14.4%
TEXAS +55.6%
MINNESOTA +1.7%
IOWA -21.9%
MISSOURI -17.6%
ARKANSAS +4.5%
LOUISIANA +37.6%
WISCONSIN -10.7%
ILLINOIS -26.7%
MICHIGAN +3.6%
INDIANA +5.2%
OHIO -12.1%
KENTUCKY +4.2%
TENNESSEE +32.5%
MISSISSIPPI +7.5%
ALABAMA +26%
GEORGIA +61%
FLORIDA +258%
SOUTH CAROLINA +77.8%
NORTH CAROLINA +67.2%
VIRGINIA +72.4%
WEST VIRGINIA -28.3%
PENNSYLVANIA -34%
NEW YORK -35.2%
N.J. -3.9%
DEL. +6.9%
MARYLAND +42.9%
VT. -30.8%
N.H. -5.4%
MAINE -25.5%
MASS. -31.4%
CONN. -.01%
R.I. -31.9%
MILES
0
100
200
300
400
Each state within the heavy line increased its share of the national personal income by more than 25% between 1929 and 1970. Figures in each state show the increase or decrease that occurred in its share of the national income between 1929 and 1970.

226
OREGON
CALIFORNIA
1900-1976
MAJOR IRRIGATED AREAS
OIL FIELDS
NEVADA
Redwood National Park
TULE LAKE RESERVOIR
Lassen Volcanic National Park
North Fork
Middle Fork
South Fork
Reno
LAKE TAHOE
Sacramento
San Francisco
Berkeley
Oakland
HETCH HETCHY RESERVOIR
Yosemite National Park
San Jose
CALIFORNIA AQUEDUCT
SAN JOAQUIN VALLEY
Kings Canyon Nat'l Park
Sequoia Nat'l Park
Fresno
Coalinga
DEATH VALLEY
Las Vegas
Hoover Dam
SEARLES LAKE (DRY SALT)
LAKE MOJAVE
Davis Dam
Bakersfield
LOS ANGELES AQUEDUCT
Mojave
Boron
Needles
SAN ANDREAS FAULT
MOJAVE DESERT
Santa Barbara
Mount Wilson
Pasadena
Hollywood
Los Angeles
LAKE HAVASU
Santa Monica
Watts
Whittier
Anaheim
Riverside
COLORADO RIVER AQUEDUCT
Parker Dam
Wilmington
Long Beach
Huntington Beach
Santa Ana
San Clemente
Mount Palomar
PACIFIC OCEAN
IMPERIAL VALLEY
Imperial Dam
San Diego
MEXICO
MILES
25 0 50 100

ARIZ.
NEW MEXICO
OKLAHOMA
ARKANSAS
LOUISIANA
MISS.
TEXAS
MEXICO
GULF OF MEXICO
Amarillo
Lubbock
Wichita Falls
Denison
Texarkana
Red River
Dallas
Irving
Fort Worth
Arlington
Garland
Mesquite
Tyler
Sabine River
Corsicana
Trinity River
Sweetwater
Abilene
Big Spring
Odessa
Brazos River
Waco
Colorado River
Sam Rayburn Reservoir
Fort Hood Military Reservation
LBJ Ranch
Fredericksburg
Johnson City
Austin
San Marcos
San Antonio
Pasadena
Houston
Beaumont
Port Arthur
Spindle Top
Galveston Bay
Galveston
Texas City
U.S. Manned Spacecraft Center
El Paso
Guadalupe Mountains National Park
Pecos River
Rio Grande River
Big Bend National Park
Del Rio
Nueces River
Lake Corpus Christi
Corpus Christi
Corpus Christi Bay
Padre Island National Seashore
Laredo
Brownsville
TEXAS 1900~1976
MILES
0 50 100 200 300

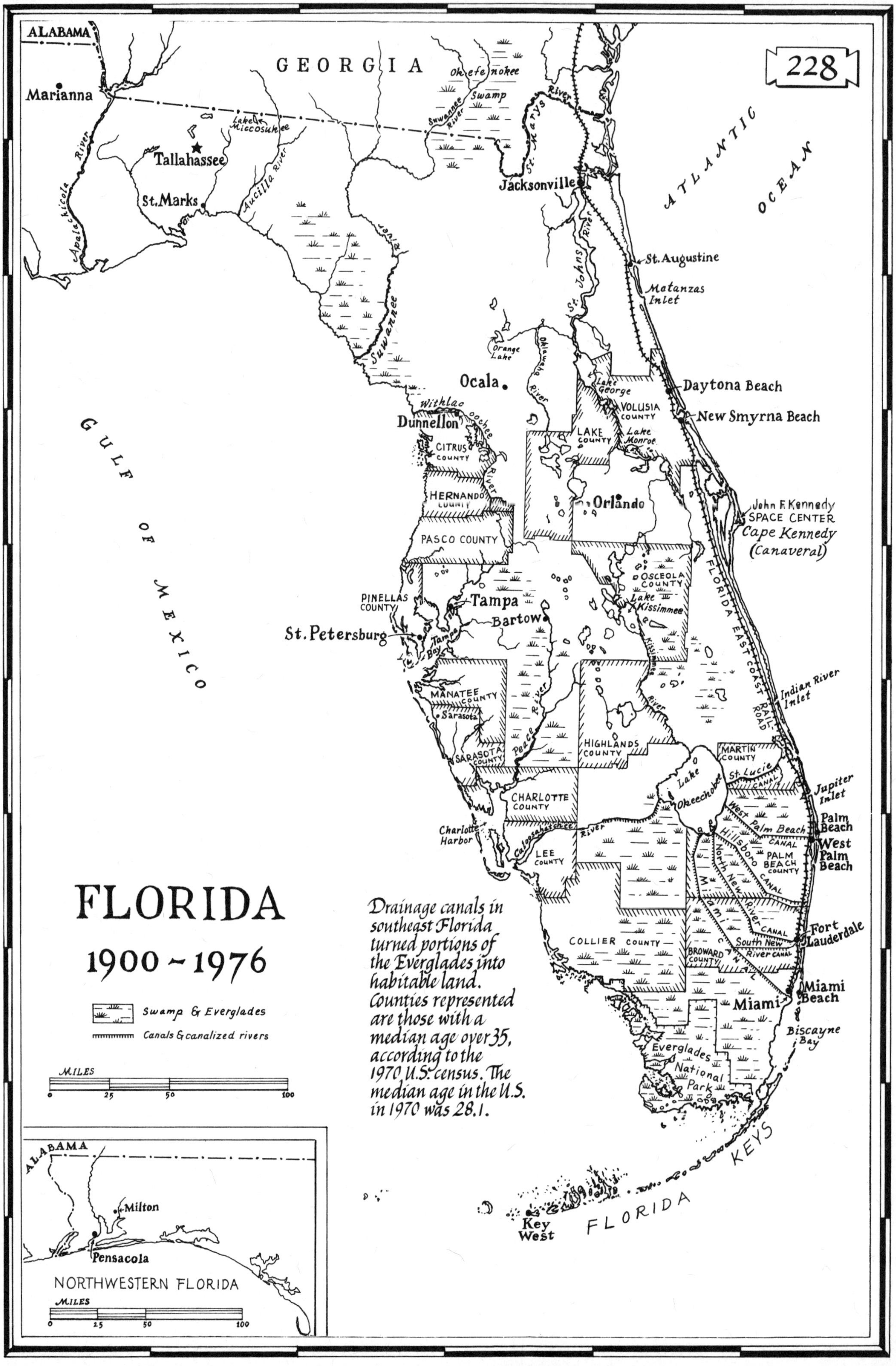

FLORIDA

1900 ~ 1976

Drainage canals in southeast Florida turned portions of the Everglades into habitable land. Counties represented are those with a median age over 35, according to the 1970 U.S. census. The median age in the U.S. in 1970 was 28.1.

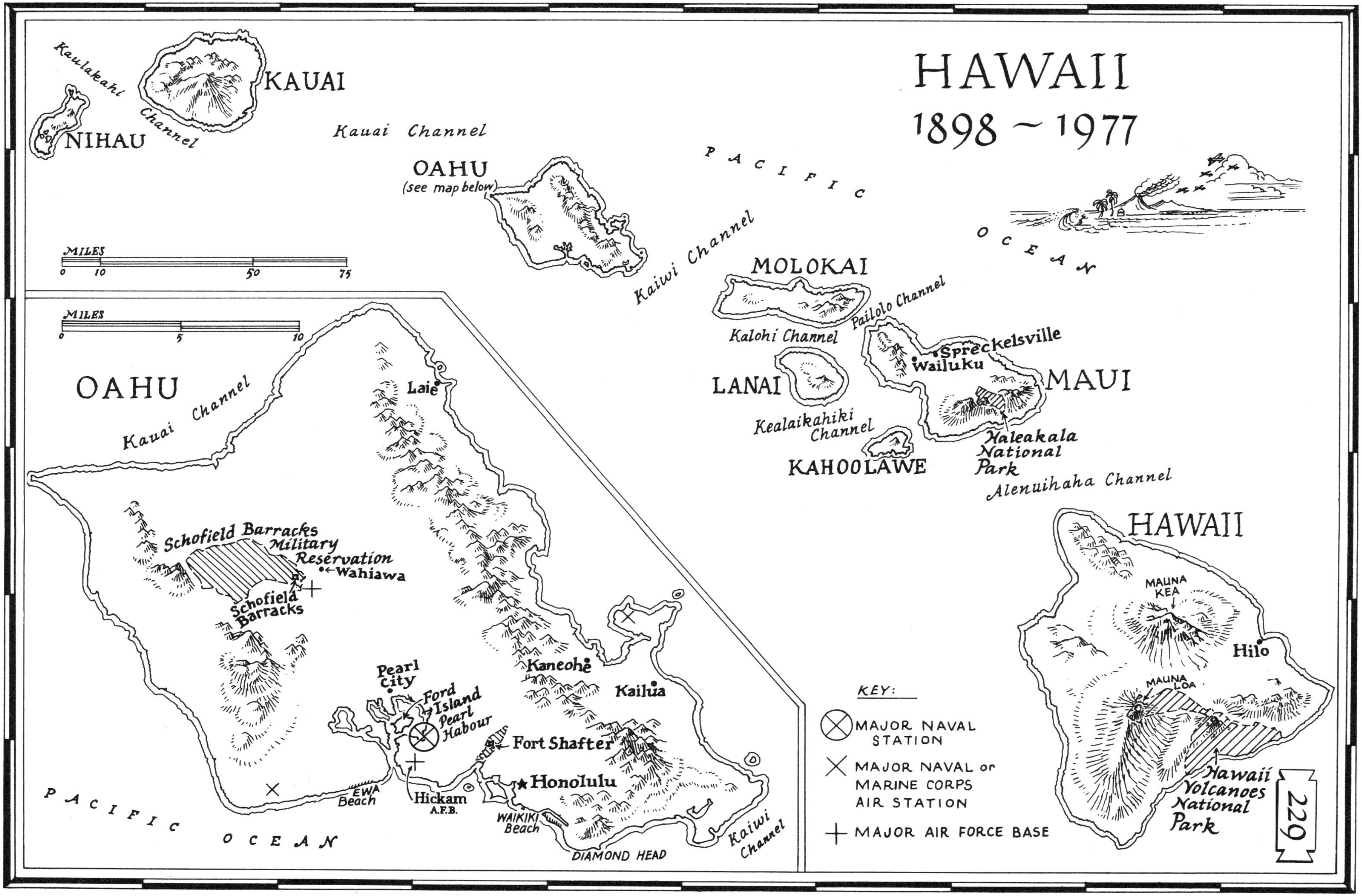
HAWAII
1898 ~ 1977
KAUAI
NIHAU
Kaulakahi Channel
Kauai Channel
OAHU
(see map below)
PACIFIC OCEAN
Kaiwi Channel
MOLOKAI
Pailolo Channel
Kalohi Channel
LANAI
Spreckelsville
Wailuku
MAUI
Kealaikahiki Channel
KAHOOLAWE
Haleakala National Park
Alenuihaha Channel
HAWAII
MAUNA KEA
MAUNA LOA
Hilo
Hawaii Volcanoes National Park
MILES
0 10 50 75
MILES
0 5 10
OAHU
Kauai Channel
Laie
Schofield Barracks Military Reservation
Wahiawa
Schofield Barracks
Pearl City
Ford Island
Pearl Habour
Kaneohe
Kailua
Fort Shafter
Honolulu
Hickam A.F.B.
EWA Beach
WAIKIKI Beach
DIAMOND HEAD
Kaiwi Channel
PACIFIC OCEAN
KEY:
MAJOR NAVAL STATION
MAJOR NAVAL or MARINE CORPS AIR STATION
MAJOR AIR FORCE BASE

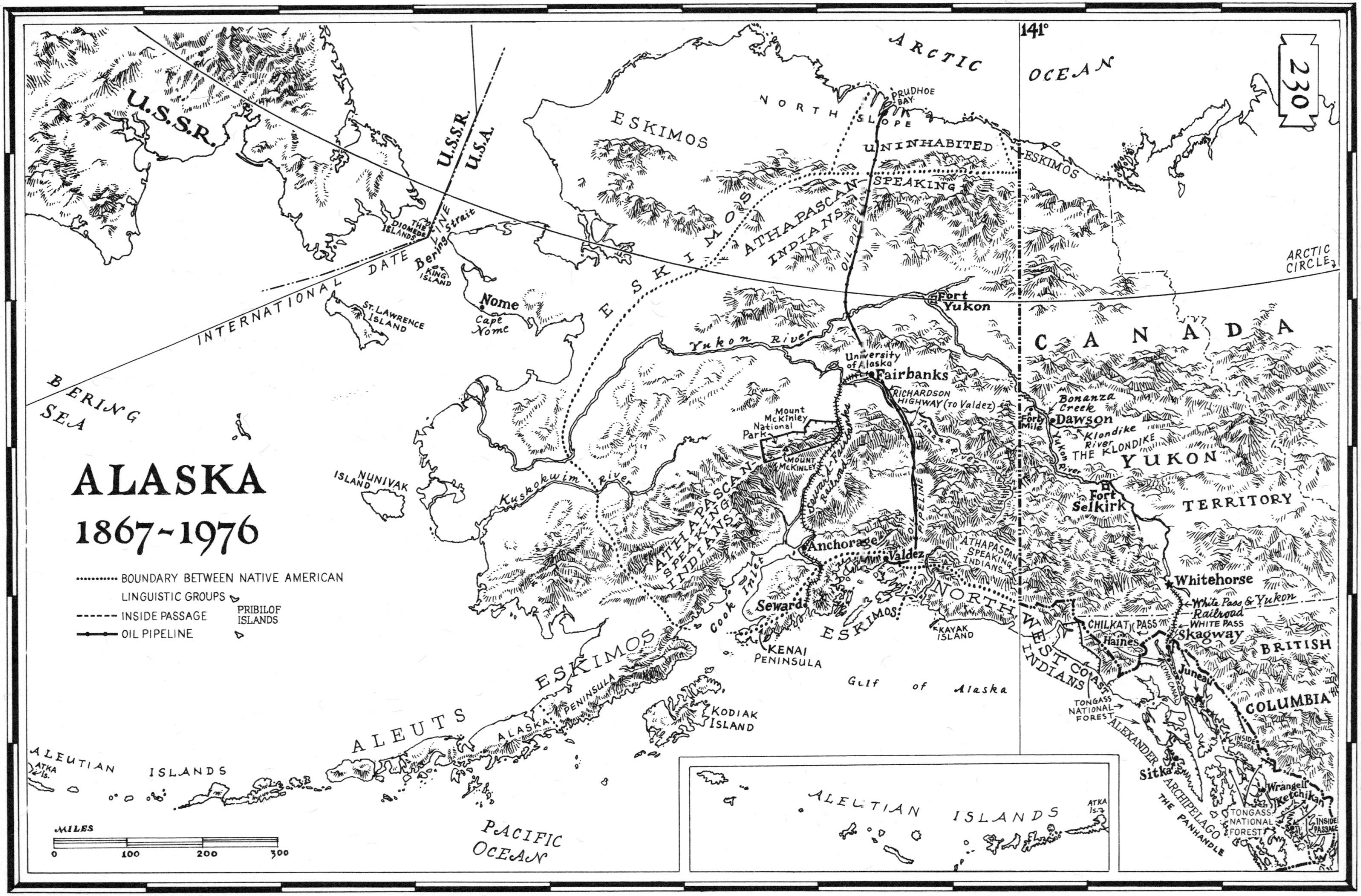
230
ALASKA
1867-1976
BOUNDARY BETWEEN NATIVE AMERICAN LINGUISTIC GROUPS
INSIDE PASSAGE
OIL PIPELINE
PRIBILOF ISLANDS
U.S.S.R.
U.S.A.
ARCTIC OCEAN
BERING SEA
PACIFIC OCEAN
INTERNATIONAL DATE LINE
ARCTIC CIRCLE
141°
CANADA
YUKON TERRITORY
BRITISH COLUMBIA
NORTH SLOPE
PRUDHOE BAY
ESKIMOS
UNINHABITED
ATHAPASCAN SPEAKING INDIANS
OIL PIPELINE
THE DIOMEDE ISLANDS
Bering Strait
KING ISLAND
ST. LAWRENCE ISLAND
Nome
Cape Nome
Yukon River
Fort Yukon
University of Alaska
Fairbanks
RICHARDSON HIGHWAY (TO Valdez)
Tanana River
Mount McKinley National Park
MOUNT McKINLEY
Seward-Fairbanks Railroad
NUNIVAK ISLAND
Kuskokwim River
Anchorage
Valdez
Seward
Cook Inlet
KENAI PENINSULA
KAYAK ISLAND
Gulf of Alaska
KODIAK ISLAND
ALASKA PENINSULA
ALEUTS
ALEUTIAN ISLANDS
ATKA Is.
NORTHWEST COAST INDIANS
Forty Mile
Bonanza Creek
Dawson
Klondike River
THE KLONDIKE
Yukon River
Fort Selkirk
Whitehorse
White Pass & Yukon Railroad
WHITE PASS
Skagway
CHILKAT PASS
Haines
LYNN CANAL
Juneau
TONGASS NATIONAL FOREST
ALEXANDER ARCHIPELAGO
THE PANHANDLE
Sitka
INSIDE PASSAGE
Wrangell
Ketchikan
MILES
0
100
200
300

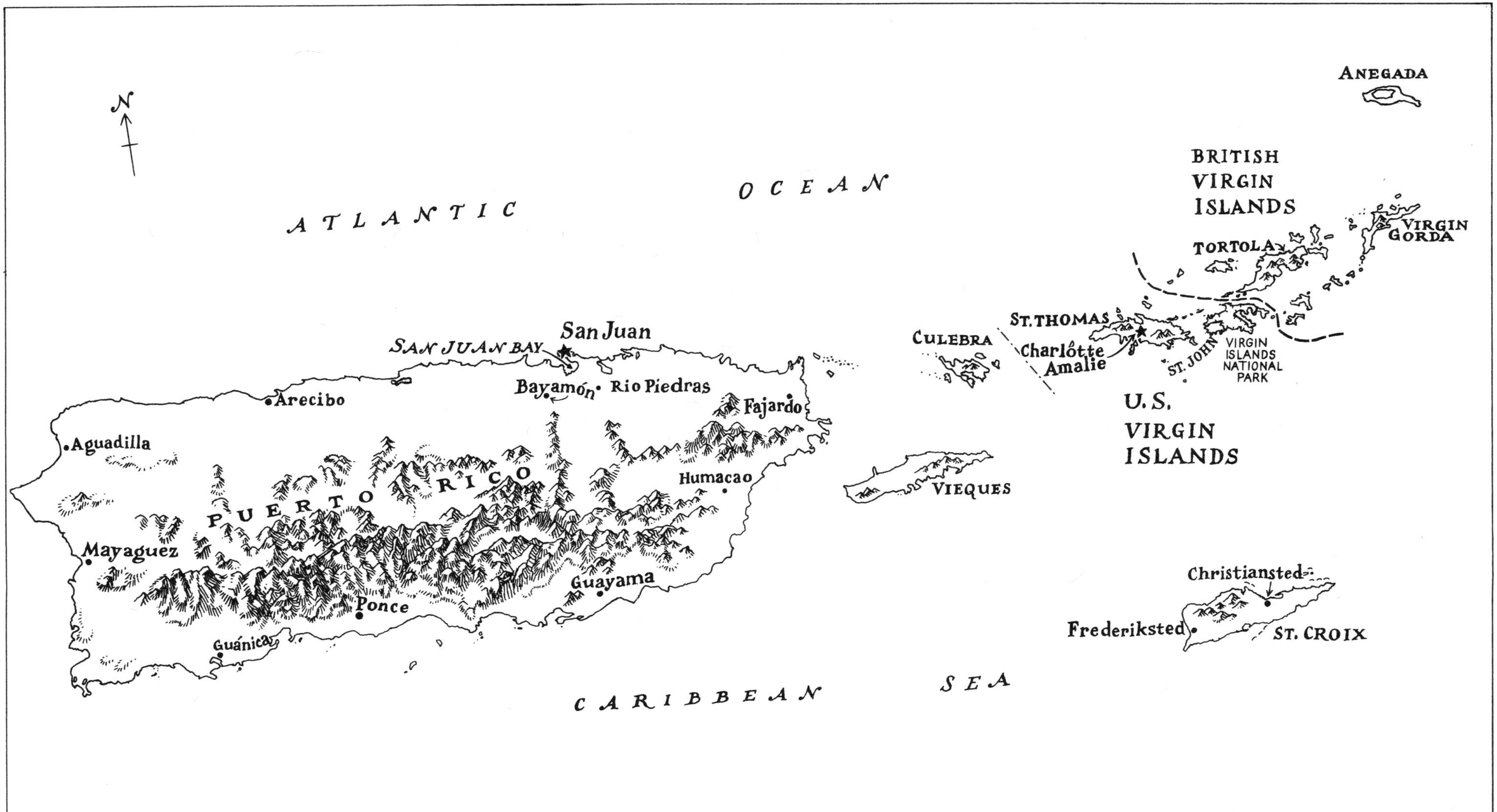

PUERTO RICO AND THE UNITED STATES VIRGIN ISLANDS

The date of each park's establishment is indicated beneath its name. Other national parks appear on plates 229 (Hawaii Volcanoes National Park and Haleakala National Park), 230 (Mt. McKinley National Park) and 231 (Virgin Islands National Park).

NATIONAL PARKS 1872–1976

COMMERCIALLY NAVIGABLE WATERWAYS, 1976
CAN
WASH.
ORE.
IDAHO
MONT.
N. DAK
S. DAK
WYO.
NEB.
NEV.
UTAH
COLO.
KAN.
CALIF.
ARIZ.
N. MEX.
OKLA
TEXAS
PACIFIC OCEAN
Seattle
Tacoma
Columbia River
Snake
Lewiston
Snake River
Portland
Salem
Albany
Willamette R.
Sacramento R.
Sacramento
Stockton
San Francisco
San Joaquin River
Los Angeles
San Diego
Rio Grande
Corpus Chri
Brov vi
MILES
0
100
200
300
400

A D A
LAKE SUPERIOR
Duluth
Sault Ste. Marie
LAKE MICHIGAN
LAKE HURON
LAKE ONTARIO
LAKE ERIE
WIS.
MICH.
Minneapolis
Green Bay
Appleton
Milwaukee
Saginaw
Detroit
Chicago
Toledo
Cleveland
Toronto
Buffalo
Oswego
Syracuse
Albany
St. Lawrence River
N.Y.
VT.
N.H.
MAINE
MASS.
CONN.
R.I.
Penobscot R.
Kennebec R.
Bangor
Belfast
Bath
Augusta
Portsmouth
Boston
Providence
New London
Connecticut R.
Hudson R.
New York
Delaware R.
PA.
N.J.
DEL.
MD.
Pittsburgh
Philadelphia
Baltimore
Washington D.C.
Allegheny River
Potomac R.
IOWA
Sioux City
Missouri River
Mississippi River
Illinois River
ILL.
IND.
OHIO
Cincinnati
Ohio River
W. VA.
Charleston
Kanawha River
Rappahannock R.
Richmond
James River
York River
Norfolk
Elizabeth City
VA.
Roanoke River
Kansas City
St. Louis
MO.
KY.
Louisville
Kentucky R.
Bowling Green
Cumberland R.
Nashville
Knoxville
Tennessee R.
TENN.
N.C.
Cape Fear R.
Fayetteville
Wilmington
S.C.
Tulsa
Muskogee
Arkansas River
ARK.
Little Rock
Memphis
MISS.
Tombigbee River
Black Warrior R.
Birmingham
Selma
Alabama R.
ALA.
Chattahoochee River
Columbus
GA.
Augusta
Savannah R.
Savannah
Charleston
Camden
Ouachita River
Pearl River
Baton Rouge
Atchafalaya R.
LA.
Beaumont
Houston
Victoria
New Orleans
Mobile
Apalachicola R.
Jacksonville
St. Johns River
St. Marks
FLA.
Tampa
Caloosahatchee River
Miami
ATLANTIC OCEAN
Gulf of Mexico
Navigable waterway

236
Seattle
Spokane
WASHINGTON
Portland
MONTANA
NORTH DAKOTA
Bismarck
Billings
IDAHO
Eugene
OREGON
Boise
SOUTH DAKOTA
WYOMING
Reno
NEVADA
Salt Lake City
Cheyenne
NEBRASKA
San Francisco
Sacramento
Oakland
San Jose
UTAH
Denver
COLORADO
KANSAS
Fresno
CALIFORNIA
Wichita
Los Angeles
Pasadena
ARIZONA
Albuquerque
Oklahoma City
San Diego
Phoenix
NEW MEXICO
Fort Worth
El Paso
TEXAS
MILES
50 0 100 200 300 400

RAILROAD PASSENGER LINES 1977

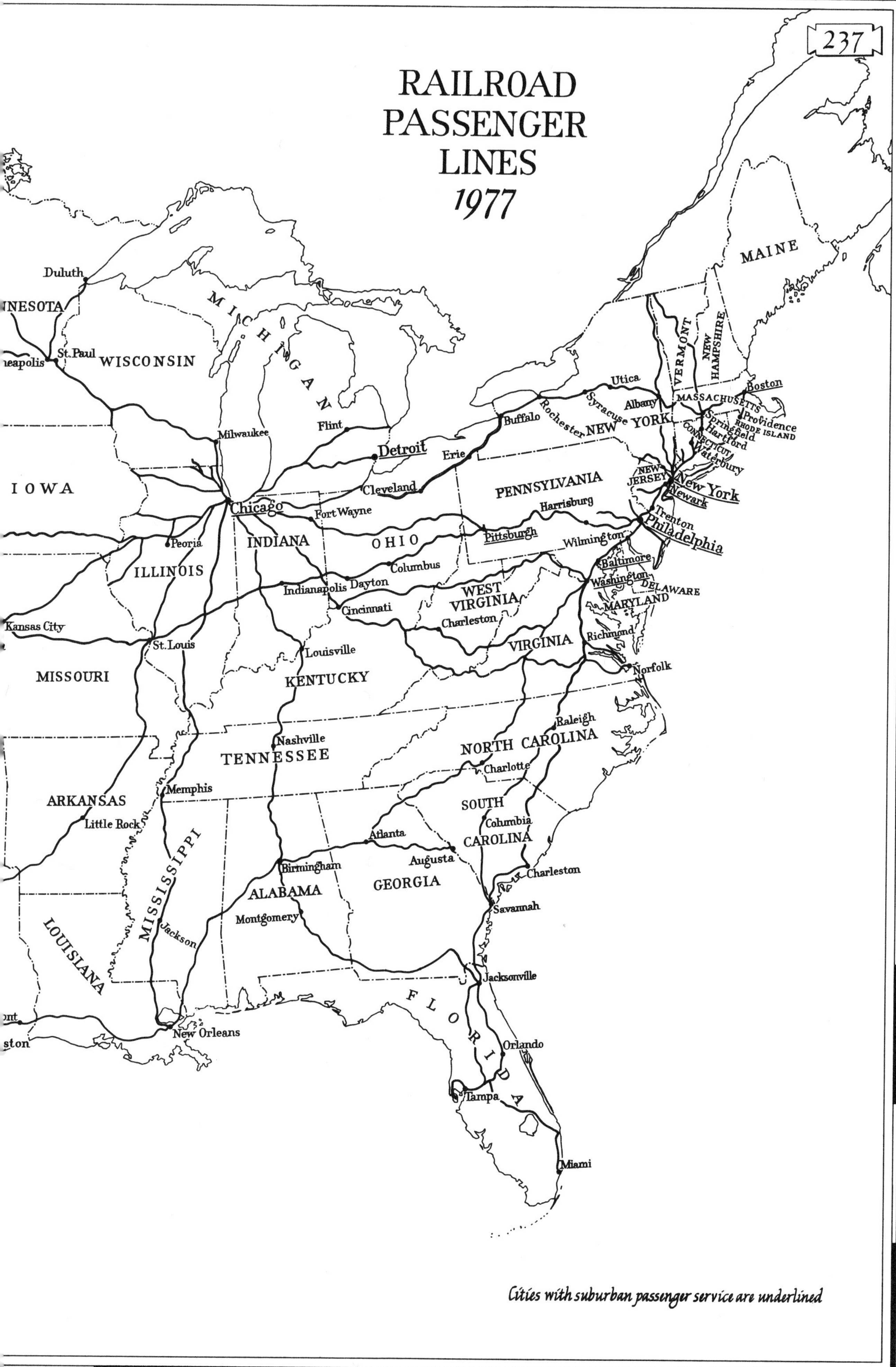

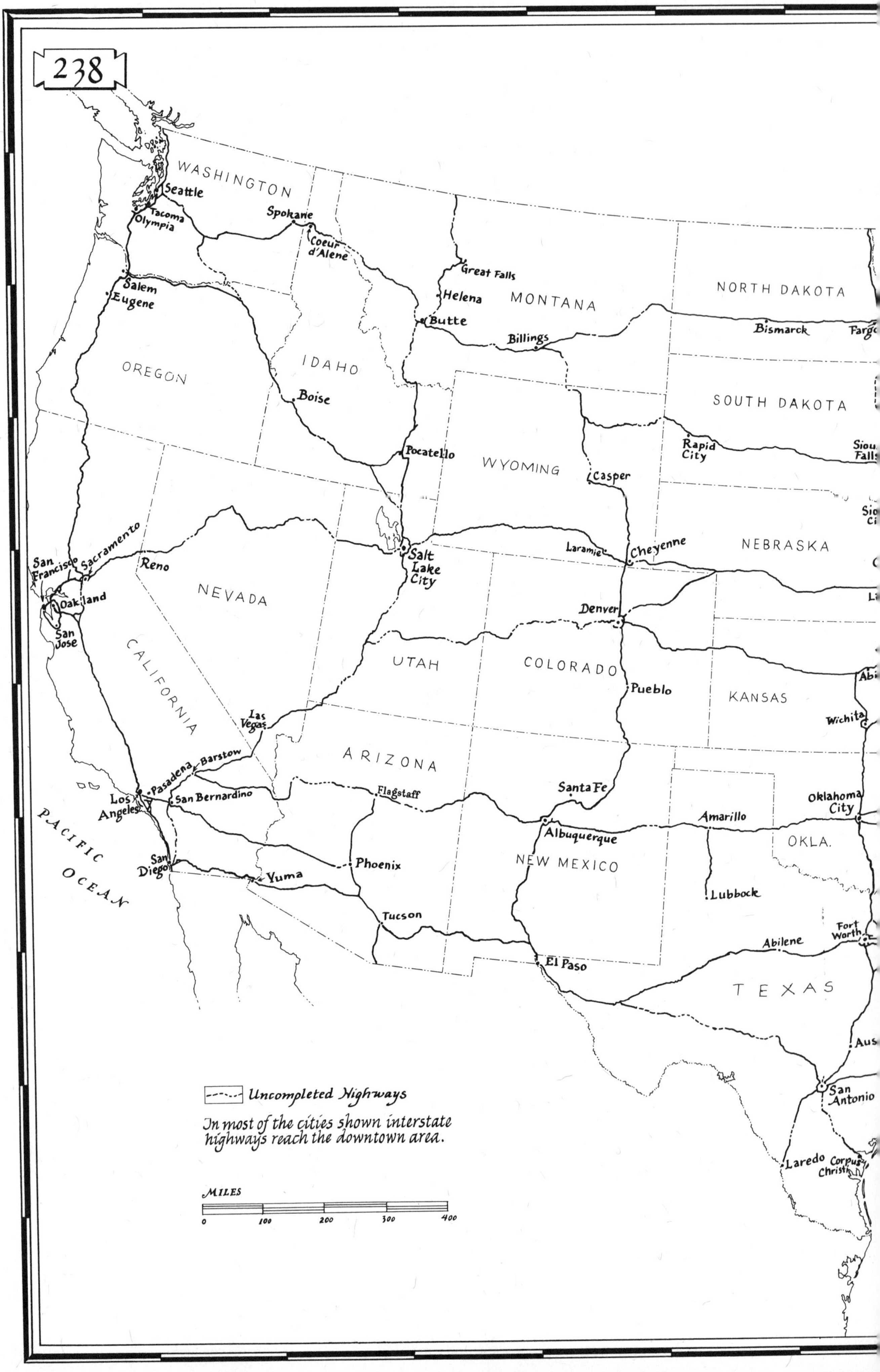
WASHINGTON
Seattle
Tacoma
Olympia
Spokane
Coeur d'Alene
Salem
Eugene
OREGON
IDAHO
Boise
Pocatello
Great Falls
Helena
Butte
MONTANA
Billings
NORTH DAKOTA
Bismarck
Fargo
SOUTH DAKOTA
Rapid City
WYOMING
Casper
Laramie
Cheyenne
NEBRASKA
San Francisco
Sacramento
Reno
Oakland
San Jose
NEVADA
Salt Lake City
Denver
UTAH
COLORADO
Pueblo
KANSAS
Wichita
CALIFORNIA
Las Vegas
Barstow
Pasadena
Los Angeles
San Bernardino
ARIZONA
Flagstaff
Santa Fe
Oklahoma City
Amarillo
Albuquerque
OKLA.
NEW MEXICO
San Diego
Yuma
Phoenix
Lubbock
Tucson
El Paso
Abilene
Fort Worth
TEXAS
PACIFIC OCEAN
San Antonio
Laredo
Corpus Christi
Uncompleted Highways
In most of the cities shown interstate highways reach the downtown area.
MILES
0
100
200
300
400

INTERSTATE HIGHWAY SYSTEM 1977

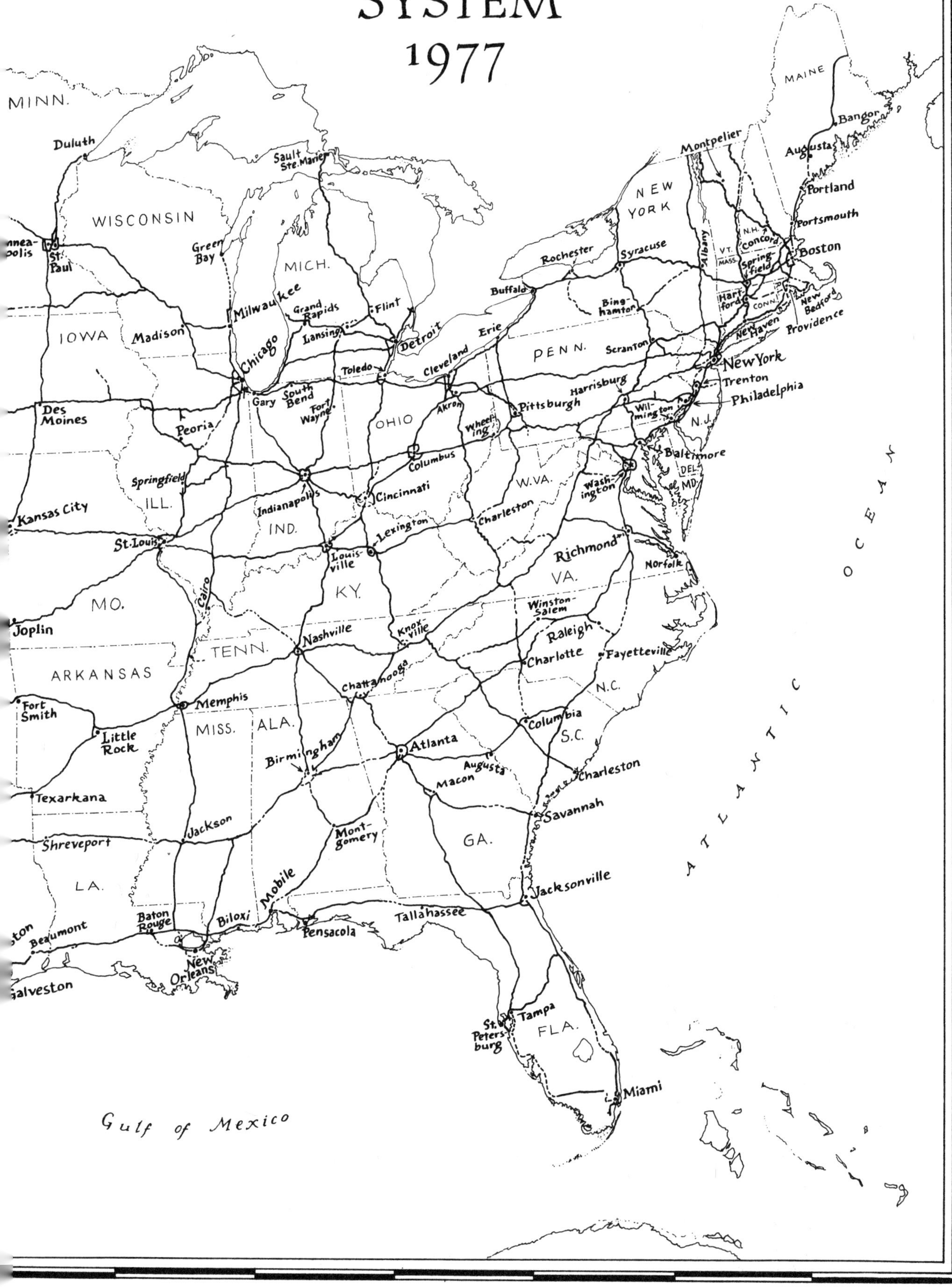

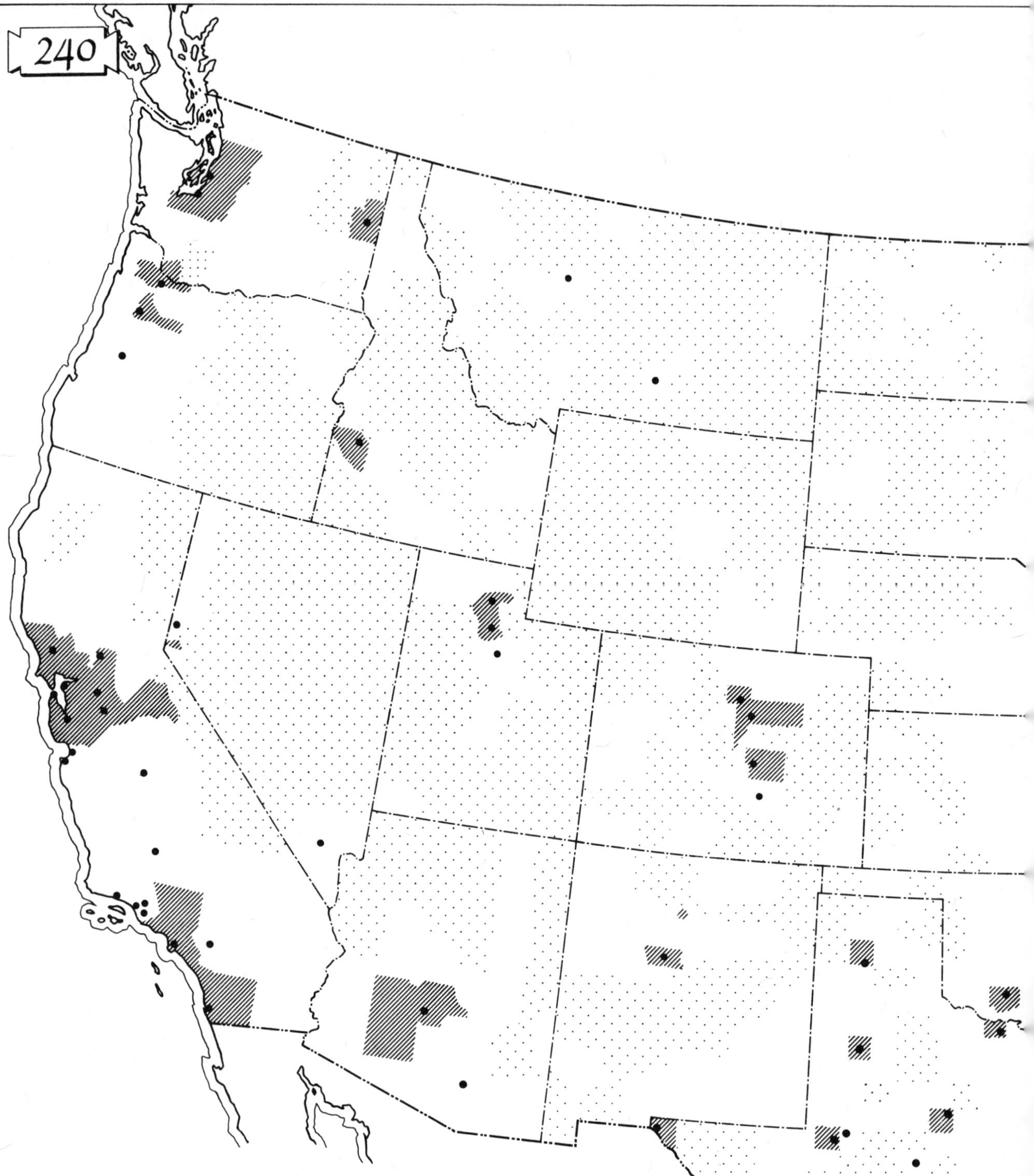

Fewer than five people per square mile

More than one hundred people per square mile

Urbanized areas (as defined by the Bureau of the Census)

Because this map is based on information gathered on a county-by-county basis in the 1970 census, there may be slight distortions caused by the unusual size of certain counties. Particularly in the Southwest, where some counties are very large, a few fairly sizable areas seem more thickly populated than they actually are. Despite this, the map provides a fair picture of the country's most sparsely populated and most thickly populated regions.

POPULATION DENSITY
IN THE
CONTINENTAL U.S.,
1970

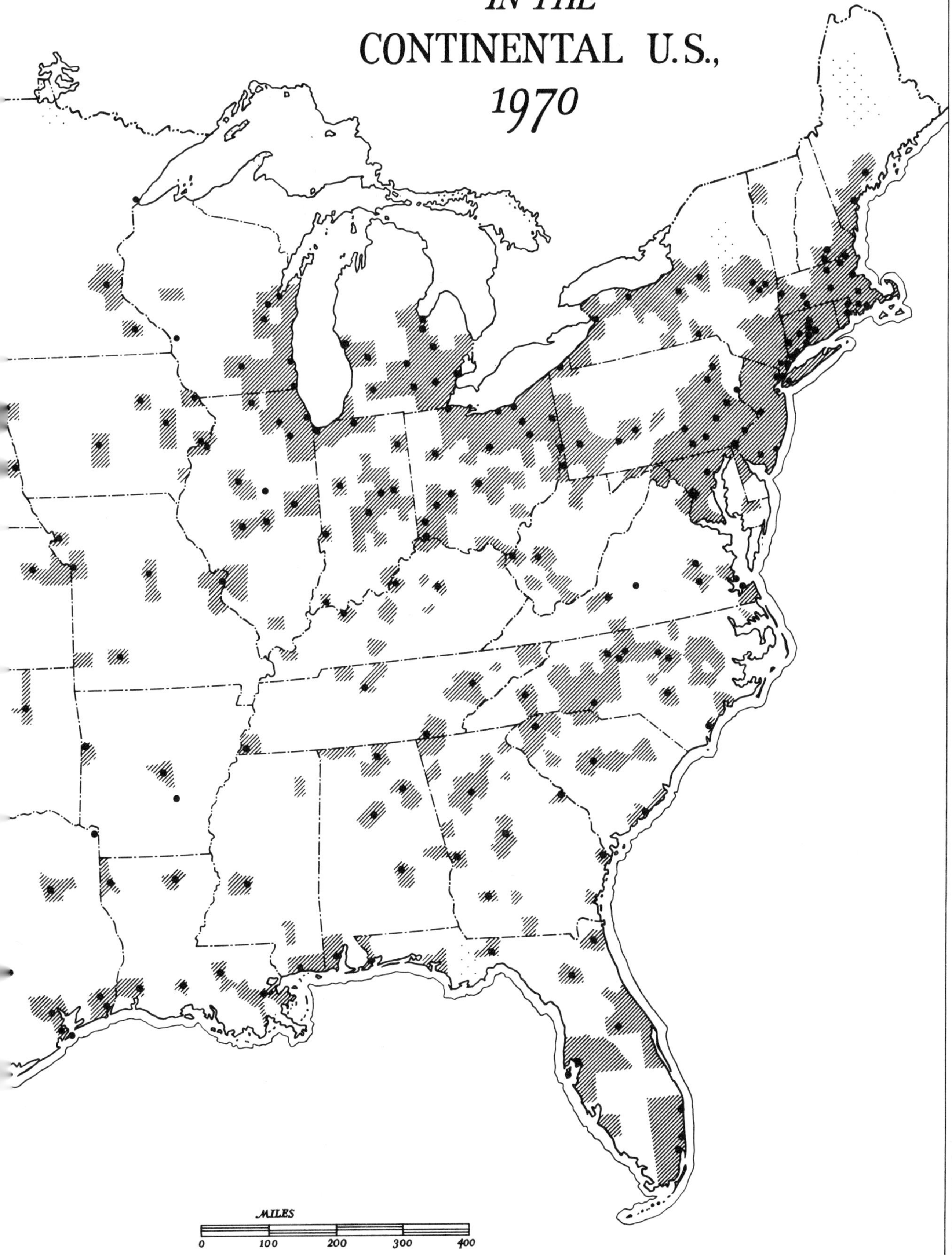

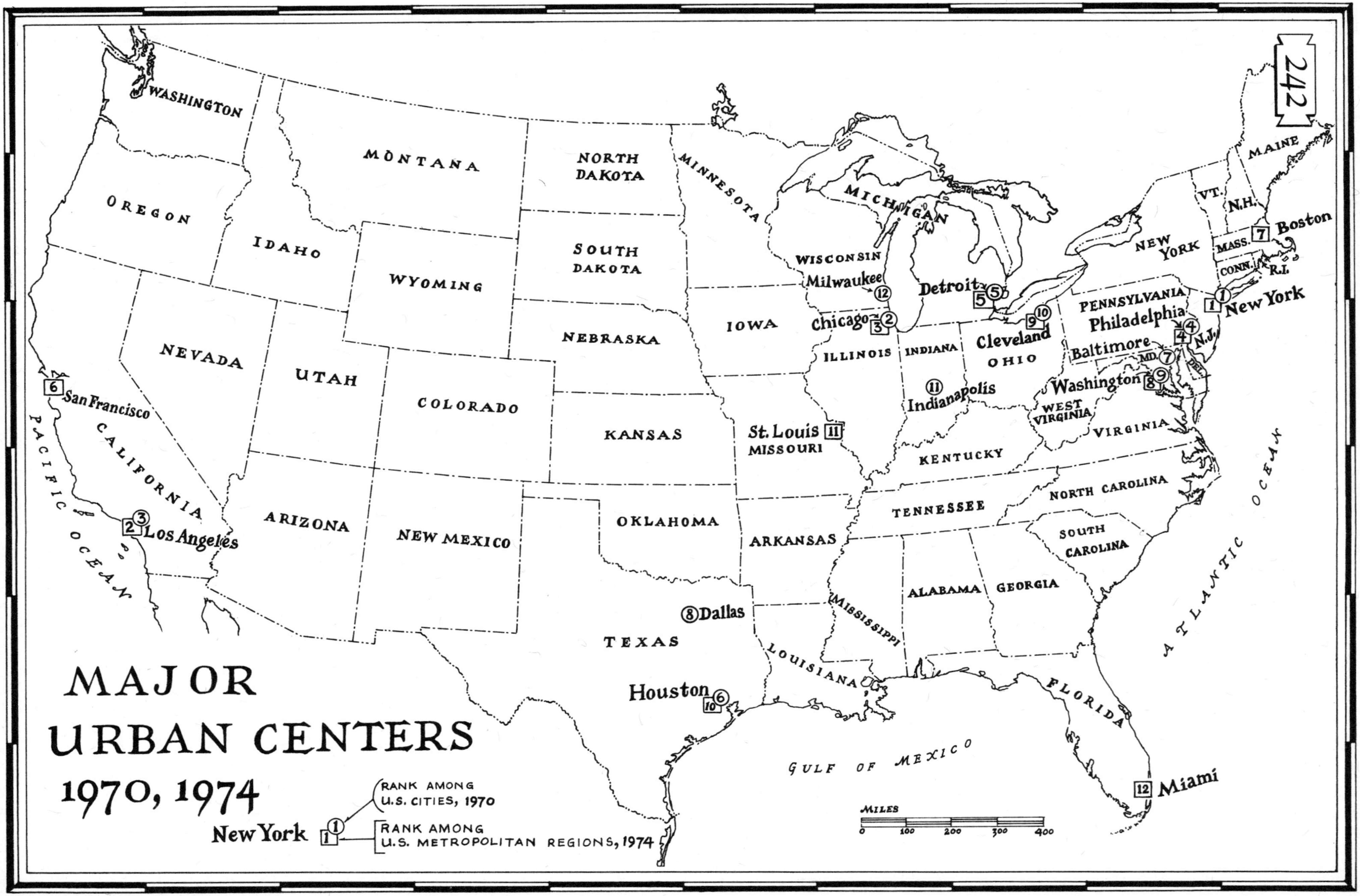
242
MAJOR
URBAN CENTERS
1970, 1974
New York
RANK AMONG
U.S. CITIES, 1970
RANK AMONG
U.S. METROPOLITAN REGIONS, 1974
MILES
0 100 200 300 400
WASHINGTON
OREGON
CALIFORNIA
NEVADA
IDAHO
MONTANA
WYOMING
UTAH
ARIZONA
COLORADO
NEW MEXICO
NORTH DAKOTA
SOUTH DAKOTA
NEBRASKA
KANSAS
OKLAHOMA
TEXAS
MINNESOTA
IOWA
MISSOURI
ARKANSAS
LOUISIANA
WISCONSIN
ILLINOIS
MICHIGAN
INDIANA
OHIO
KENTUCKY
TENNESSEE
MISSISSIPPI
ALABAMA
GEORGIA
FLORIDA
SOUTH CAROLINA
NORTH CAROLINA
VIRGINIA
WEST VIRGINIA
MD.
DEL.
PENNSYLVANIA
N.J.
NEW YORK
CONN.
R.I.
MASS.
VT.
N.H.
MAINE
PACIFIC OCEAN
GULF OF MEXICO
ATLANTIC OCEAN
6 San Francisco
3 2 Los Angeles
8 Dallas
Houston 6 10
St. Louis 11
Milwaukee 12
Chicago 2 3
Detroit 5 5
Cleveland 9 10
Indianapolis 11
Philadelphia 4 4
Baltimore 7
Washington 8 9
1 1 New York
7 Boston
12 Miami

INDEX

This Index is designed to serve two main purposes. First, it enables the user of the *Atlas* to turn, quickly and definitely, to the map or maps on which a given location is shown.

Second, it serves as a cross reference, enabling the user of the work to follow, from map to map, the development of areas in succeeding periods of our history. Thus, the advance of the frontier may be visualized; or the evolution of a Territory, in its changing extents, may be followed through to the final creation of the State; or the migrations and removals of the various Indian tribes may be traced.

In the indexing of historical locations some inconsistencies are inevitable. An Indian village of the time of DeSoto can scarcely be listed as being in a present-day state. On the other hand, Harpers Ferry was important historically long before the existence of the state of West Virginia; Vincennes was a French frontier post sixty years before the Territory of Indiana was formed; yet, for the purposes of an index, it would be confusing to identify these places other than in their present states. Again, as between towns which have had a continuing existence and those which have disappeared or which are not direct descendants of existing towns of the same name, a distinction in the form of listing is desirable—although the basis for decision is often very slight indeed.

Also, there is the matter of spellings, accents and possessives. No uniformity existed, nor is it the province of an atlas of American history to establish uniformity, but rather, in each case, to follow the form most used over the greatest period of time, and, where distinct variations occur, to list those variations with a reference to the form used.

Thus, without departing too greatly from consistency, the editors, in compiling the following Index, have endeavored to so list each location that it may be readily found in the Index—from which the user will turn to the proper map, where the status of the place, during the period of the map, will be amply evident.